Mesolithic Europe

This book focuses on the archaeology of the hunter-gatherer societies that inhabited Europe in the millennia between the Last Ice Age and the spread of agriculture, between ten thousand and five thousand years ago. Traditionally viewed as a period of cultural stagnation, new data now demonstrates that this was a period of radical change and innovation. This was the period that witnessed the colonisation of extensive new territory at high latitudes and high altitudes following postglacial climatic change, the development of seafaring, and the synthesis of the technological, economic, and social capabilities that underpinned the later development of agricultural and urban societies. Providing a pan-European overview, *Mesolithic Europe* includes up-to-date regional syntheses written by experts in each region as well as a diversity of theoretical perspectives.

Geoff Bailey is Anniversary Professor of Archaeology in the Department of Archaeology at the University of York. He has published widely on a variety of topics in prehistory, including a major monograph on *Klithi: Paleolithic Settlement and Quaternary Landscapes in Northwest Greece*. He is a Fellow of the Society of Antiquaries and a Member of the Institute of Field Archaeologists.

Penny Spikins is Lecturer in Prehistory in the Department of Archaeology, University of York. She has published on a broad range of topics in prehistoric archaeology, directed the West Yorkshire Mesolithic Project and the Searching for Submerged Sites Project in Northern England, and has carried out research in Argentina.

Mesolithic Europe

Edited by

Geoff Bailey
University of York

Penny Spikins
University of York

CAMBRIDGE
UNIVERSITY PRESS

CAMBRIDGE UNIVERSITY PRESS
Cambridge, New York, Melbourne, Madrid, Cape Town,
Singapore, São Paulo, Delhi, Tokyo, Mexico City

Cambridge University Press
The Edinburgh Building, Cambridge CB2 8RU, UK

Published in the United States of America by Cambridge University Press, New York

www.cambridge.org
Information on this title: www.cambridge.org/9780521855037

First published 2008
Reprinted 2009
First paperback edition 2010
Reprinted 2010

A catalogue record for this publication is available from the British Library

Library of Congress Cataloguing in Publication Data

Mesolithic Europe / edited by Geoff Bailey, Penny Spikins.
p. cm.
Includes bibliographical references and index.
ISBN 978-0-521-85503-7 (hardback)
1. Mesolithic period – Europe. 2. Prehistoric peoples – Europe. 3. Hunting and gathering societies –
Europe. 4. Agriculture, Prehistoric – Europe. 5. Europe – Antiquities. I. Bailey, G. N. II. Spikins, Penny.
III. Title.
GN774.2.AIM46   2008
936–dc22   2007007409

ISBN 978-0-521-85503-7 Hardback
ISBN 978-0-521-14797-2 Paperback

Contents

Figures and Tables

Figures

Tables

Preface and Acknowledgments

In this volume, we bring together a series of regional syntheses of the Mesolithic in different parts of Europe, intended to be of interest and benefit both to specialists and to those with a more general interest in archaeology. Mesolithic archaeology has witnessed an acceleration of activity in recent years, with many new projects, more communication across old geographical and political barriers, and calls for archaeologists to examine the Mesolithic on its own terms, rather than as an inconvenient rung in some ladder of human progress. Accounts of the Mesolithic are typically absorbed into general syntheses of prehistory, submerged in works unified by wider-ranging theoretical or methodological themes, fragmented in publications of individual site-based or regional field projects, or combined in the proceedings of specialist conferences. Here, our aim is to provide an up-to-date overview of the current state of knowledge about the Mesolithic period, a demonstration of the richness and diversity of the material now available and the various approaches to its study, and a source for those who wish to delve more deeply into the literature.

Our brief to our contributors was to provide an interpretive synthesis of their region, varying the emphasis according to the available material and drawing on broad categories of information: the history of research and the definition of the Mesolithic, environment and geography, chronology, technology and subsistence, settlement and social organisation, and art and ritual. We also encouraged them to range both backwards and forwards in time to consider the nature of the boundaries that traditionally mark the beginning and the end of the Mesolithic, including the transition to agriculture.

We are, of course, acutely aware of the arbitrary nature of our selections and the boundaries they imply, and the inevitable unevenness of coverage. In a continent notable for a history of political fragmentation reinforced by barriers of geography, language, nationality, and cultural tradition, total coverage, let alone uniformity of approach, was hardly to be expected. Archaeologically, the field of enquiry has been further complicated, and indeed enriched, by different intellectual traditions, by the historical dominance of the French and the Danes, by Anglophone traditions of method and theory, and most recently by regional synthesis and diversification.

We could have devoted a single chapter to every nation-state within the geographical boundaries of Europe. But that would have produced far too large and uneven a volume, and it is questionable how far modern political boundaries are helpful or relevant in assessing the prehistoric record, although we acknowledge the influence of modern political history on intellectual traditions of investigation and interpretation. Our selection of chapters is necessarily a compromise between what we would have liked to include and what was realistically possible. Some chapters range widely across geographical and political boundaries, others focus more sharply on areas delimited by modern political borders. Some areas achieve disproportionate attention because of the long histories of study, the abundance of material, or the impact of distinctive types of new evidence or new ideas.

Others may seem underrepresented or referred to only tangentially in relation to adjacent areas. If nothing else, the volume of material presented here should leave little doubt about the substantial nature of the Mesolithic record, its potential to illuminate new dimensions of human variability, and the prospect of a truly comparative picture ranging from the Atlantic coast of Ireland to the Urals, and from the sub-Arctic to the Aegean.

The regional chapters are organised in broadly geographical order. Chapter 2 provides a wide-ranging geographical and thematic overview, focussed on the Baltic, followed in Chapter 3 by a review of Norway, where new investigations have produced a substantial and distinctive body of new material, and in Chapter 4 by a discussion of the classic material of southern Scandinavia. Subsequent chapters move from west to east across the middle zone of Europe, from the British Isles, via the Low Countries, France, and the Rhine and Danube drainages, to the vast territory comprising Belarus, Russia, and the Ukraine, and thence to the south, to the Iberian Peninsula and the Mediterranean coast.

In our editorial contributions, our opening chapter provides an introduction to the field of study, to the issues raised in subsequent chapters, and to some of the ideas that are beginning to influence a new generation of interpretation. Our final chapter provides an overview of the Mesolithic period as a whole and an indication of new directions for future research. The editorial chapters are single-authored, reflecting both the dominant input of each editor and the differences of perspective and approach among the editors and contributors. They are, nevertheless, also the result of joint effort and discussion and in their totality reflect a body of ideas to which we both subscribe, and a jointly held belief that the Mesolithic record offers an unparalleled opportunity to explore the relationship between the very large scale and the very small, between millennial and pan-continental trends and the actions of social groups and individuals.

Not the least of the problems of dealing with a period often regarded as transitional is that it also marks a zone of overlap between different conventions for expressing dates as either 'before the present' or 'before Christ'. The position has become more confused in recent years by the refinement and widespread adoption of calibration curves and by a host of different abbreviations – BP, BCE, bp, bc, cal BP, cal BC, kyr, ka, rcybp. Tree-ring counting provides the most accurate conversion of radiocarbon years to annual solar years and then only back to 8329 cal BC, or to 9908 cal BC with a degree of uncertainty. The calibration curve can be extended further back in time, in principle across the full fifty-thousand-year time range of radiocarbon, using uranium series dating of coral terraces and annual growth increments in varved lake-sediments and speleothems (Van der Plicht 2004). In general, calibration suggests a broadly progressive divergence of radiocarbon and solar chronologies, the former providing underestimates amounting to as much as two thousand years or more, a degree of divergence that affects the time ranges dealt with in this volume. One might argue that such divergence is of no consequence unless one is comparing radiocarbon dates with dates derived from historical records, but the intervals of time measured by radiocarbon dates may differ from their calendar equivalent by a significant amount. Within the Mesolithic period, 500 radiocarbon years may refer to as little as 280 calendar years or as much as 580 calendar years, depending on the particular part of the calibration curve, differences that are potentially significant for archaeological interpretation.

It would be a mistake to suppose that calibration has introduced more accurate radiocarbon dates. The convention for expressing calibrated dates as range within two standard deviations is a healthy reminder that a single radiocarbon date actually represents a probability distribution covering quite a long span of time. Moreover, different calibration schemes are currently in use and under continuous revision, producing somewhat different albeit minor calibrations. The problem of plateaux in the production of radioactive carbon in the upper atmosphere is an irreducible problem, resulting in periods within which the same radiocarbon date may refer to a wide range of calendar dates, and several of these plateaux occur in the Mesolithic period. To these uncertainties, one should add the problems of correcting for the marine reservoir effect, other potential sources of contamination from a variety of sources, inter-laboratory variations, large standard deviations especially for radiocarbon assays undertaken at an earlier stage in the development of the method, uncertainties of stratigraphic association, and the fact that a great deal of archaeological material has not been radiocarbon dated and that much will probably remain undateable.

In Europe, specialists who study Neolithic and later periods have long used the 'BC' convention, whereas those studying Palaeolithic and Mesolithic periods have preferred the 'BP' convention. That difference tends to reinforce a boundary between Mesolithic and Neolithic that is obstructive rather than helpful to interpretation. Hence, the current convention is to express the original radiocarbon date in radiocarbon years BP (before the present, that is, before AD 1950) with a margin of error at one standard deviation, and to express the calibrated version in years BC (cal BC) as a range that encompasses the 95.4 percent probability range of two standard deviations. This convention may be confusing for those used to BP chronologies and of doubtful relevance in other parts of the world beyond Europe and the Near East. It is, nevertheless, the currently preferred convention in European prehistory, and we use that convention here. Appendix 1 provides a correspondence table for uncalibrated radiocarbon years and calibrated years BC, at one-hundred-year intervals between 2,500 and 13,000 BP.

All of this suggests that although we now have very many more radiocarbon dates than before, there are some respects in which we actually know less about chronology, or at any rate rather more about the extent of our ignorance. When we first planned this volume, we intended to ask all our contributors to provide a list of radiocarbon dates for their region. That directive has proved more difficult to implement than we had supposed. Many authors pointed out the uncertainties associated with the dates in their region and the need for critical use of the resulting material. In consequence some authors have produced quite selective lists, and one or two others more generalised dating schemes. It is significant that some of the longest lists are in those regions where Accelerator Mass Spectrometry dating has been widely applied, typically in collaboration with the Oxford Radiocarbon Accelerator Unit, producing dates on individual artefacts or other items, which circumvent some of the uncertainties of radiocarbon dating.

The idea for this book originated in 1999 following a suggestion from Graeme Barker for a volume that would be part of a series on European prehistory to be published by Leicester University Press, and a first group of chapters were drafted in 2001 and 2002. With changes in the publishing world, Cambridge University Press took over the project in 2003 and encouraged us to expand the regional coverage and our editorial input with additional chapters. Some chapters have thus been in gestation for considerably longer than others, but all authors have had the opportunity to update their reviews in the light of more recent findings.

We thank our contributors for their patience; Jessica Kemp for assistance in preparing the illustrations; Robert Hedges of the Oxford Radiocarbon Accelerator Unit for advice on radiocarbon dating; Jeremy Boulton, Head of the School of Historical Studies, University of Newcastle upon Tyne, for funding assistance with the preparation of the book; and Simon Whitmore of Cambridge University Press for encouraging the project through to completion. We also acknowledge financial support from the AHRC through grant B/RG/AN1717/APN14658 and from the Leverhulme Trust through its Major Research Fellowship scheme.

We would like to thank Cambridge University Press for permission to reproduce Figures 5.2, 5.4, 5.5, and 5.8; The Prehistoric Society for permission to reproduce Figure 5.3; The Society of Antiquaries of Scotland for permission to reproduce Figure 5.6; Oxford University Press for permission to reproduce Figure 5.7; Ashschehoug Publications for permission to reproduce Figures 4.3, 4.4, and 4.5, and Table 4.1; C. Christiansen (National Museum of Denmark) for permission to reproduce Figure 4.2; and Acta Archaeologica for permission to reproduce Figure 4.8.

Preface to the Paperback Edition

We have taken the opportunity to correct errors, to update references, and to add new information that has become available since the hardback edition.

Geoff Bailey
Penny Spikins
Department of Archaeology
University of York
December 2009

Contributors

Geoff Bailey
Anniversary Professor of Archaeology
Department of Archaeology
University of York
The King's Manor, York
YO1 7EP, UK
email: gb502@york.ac.uk

Recent publication:
Bailey, G. N. 2004. The wider significance of submerged archaeological sites and their relevance to world prehistory. In N. C. Flemming (ed.), *Submarine Prehistoric Archaeology of the North Sea: Research Priorities and Collaboration with Industry*, London: CBA Research Report 141, pp. 3–10.

Hein Bjartmann Bjerck
Associate Professor of Archaeology
Museum of Natural History and Archaeology
The Norwegian University of Science and Technology
Postal address:
Vitenskapsmuseet
NTNU
NO-7491 Trondheim, Norway
email: hein.bjerck@vm.ntnu.no

Recent publication:
Bjerck, H. B. 2000. Stone Age settlement on Svalbard? A re-evaluation of previous finds and results of a recent field survey. *Polar Record* 36 (197): 97–122.

Hans Peter Blankholm
Professor of Archaeology
Institute for Archaeology
University of Tromsø, Norway
Postal address:
Institutt for arkeologi, SV-Fak
Universitetet i Tromsø

Contributors

N-9037 Tromsø, Norway
email: Hanspb@sv.uit.no

Recent publication:
Blankholm, H. P. 2004. Earliest Mesolithic Site in Northern Norway? A reassessment of Sarnes B4. *Arctic Anthropology* 41(1): 41–57.

Clive Bonsall
School of History, Classics, and Archaeology
University of Edinburgh
Old High School
Infirmary Street
Edinburgh, EH1 1LT
Scotland, UK
email: c.bonsall@ed.ac.uk

Recent publication:
Bonsall, C., Macklin, M. G., Payton, R. W., and A. Boroneanţ. 2002. Climate, floods and river gods: Environmental change and the Meso–Neolithic transition in south-east Europe. *Before Farming: The Archaeology of Old World Hunter-Gatherers* 3–4(2): 1–15.

Pavel Dolukhanov[†]
Emeritus Professor of East European Archaeology
School of Historical Studies,
University of Newcastle upon Tyne
NE1 7RU, UK
email: pavel.dolukhanov@ncl.ac.uk

Recent publication:
Dolukhanov, P., Shukurov, A., Gronenborn, D., Timofeev, V., Zaitseva, G., and D. Sokoloff. 2005. The chronology of Neolithic dispersal in Central and Eastern Europe. *Journal of Archaeological Science* 32: 1442–58.

Michael A. Jochim
Professor of Archaeology
Department of Anthropology
University of California, Santa Barbara
Santa Barbara, CA 93106, USA
email: jochim@anth.ucsb.edu

Recent publication:
Jochim, M. 2000. The origins of agriculture in south-central Europe. In T. D. Price (ed.), *Europe's First Farmers*. Cambridge, UK: Cambridge University Press, pp. 183–96.

Mark Pluciennik
Senior Lecturer in Archaeology
School of Archaeology and Ancient History

University of Leicester
LE1 7RH, UK
email: mzpl@le.ac.uk

Recent publication:
Pluciennik, M. 2004. The meaning of "hunter-gatherers" and modes of subsistence: A comparative historical perspective. In A. Barnard (ed.), *Hunter-gatherers in History, Archaeology and Anthropology*. Oxford: Berg, pp. 17–29.

Penny Spikins
Lecturer in Prehistory
Department of Archaeology
University of York
The King's Manor, York
YO1 7EP, UK
email: ps508@york.ac.uk

Recent publication:
Spikins, P. A. 2003. *Prehistoric People of the Pennines: Reconstructing the Lifestyles of Hunter-Gatherers on Marsden Moor*. Leeds: English Heritage and West Yorkshire Archaeology Service Publications.

Lawrence Guy Straus
Distinguished Professor of Anthropology
Department of Anthropology
University of New Mexico
Albuquerque, NM 87131-1086, USA
email: lstraus@unm.edu

Recent publication:
Straus, L. G. (ed.) 2005. *Armageddon or Entente? The Demise of the European Neandertals in Isotope Stage 3*. Oxford: Quaternary International/Elsevier.

Jiří A. Svoboda
Institute of Archaeology
Academy of Sciences of the Czech Republic
Královopolská 147, 612 00 Brno
Czech Republic
email: svoboda@iabrno.cz

Recent publication:
Svoboda, J., van der Plicht, J., and V. Kuželka. 2002. Upper Palaeolithic and Mesolithic human fossils from Moravia and Bohemia (Czech Republic): Some new C14 dates. *Antiquity* 76: 957–62.

Chris Tolan-Smith
Formerly Senior Lecturer in Archaeology

Contributors

School of Historical Studies
University of Newcastle upon Tyne
NE1 7RU, UK

Recent publication:
Tolan-Smith, C. 2003. The social context of landscape learning and the Lateglacial-Early Postglacial recolonization of the British Isles. In J. Steele and M. Rockman (eds.), *The Colonization of Unfamiliar Landscapes: The Archaeology of Adaptation*. London: Routledge.

Nicolas Valdeyron
Maitre de Conference
Département Histoire de l'art et archéologie
Université Toulouse-Le Mirail
5 allées Antonio Machado
31058 Toulouse
Cedex 9, France
email: valdeyro@univ-tlse2.fr

Recent publication:
Valdeyron, N. 2000. Géographie culturelle du Mésolithique récent/final dans le Sud-Ouest de la France. In M. Leduc, N. Valdeyron, and J. Vaquer (eds.), *Sociétés et Espaces*. Toulouse: Actes des IIIèmes Rencontres Méridionales de Préhistoire Récente, 1998, pp. 23–34.

Leo Verhart
National Museum of Antiquities, Leiden
Post-box 11114
2301 EC, Leiden
Netherlands
email: l.verhart@rmo.nl

Recent publication:
Verhart, L. B. M. 2003. Mesolithic economic and social change in the southern Netherlands. In L. Larsson, H. Kindgren, K. Knutsson, D. Loeffler, and A. Akerlund (eds.), *Mesolithic on the Move*. Oxford: Oxbow, pp. 442–50.

Marek Zvelebil
Professor of Archaeology
Department of Archaeology and Prehistory
University of Sheffield
Northgate House
West Street, Sheffield
S1 4ET, UK
email: m.zvelebil@sheffield.ac.uk

Recent publication:
Zvelebil, M. 2005. Homo habitus: Agency, structure and the transformation of tradition in the constitution of TRB foraging-farming communities in the North European plain (ca. 4500–2000 BC). *Documenta Praehistorica* 32: 87–101.

Chapter 1

Mesolithic Europe: Glimpses of Another World

Penny Spikins*

Introduction

Mesolithic Europe holds a special place in our imagination. Perhaps more than any other region and period, it is unique in conjuring up a strange sense of both 'otherness' and familiarity. The people who lived here were in many ways fundamentally different from ourselves. As hunters and gatherers, their experience, worldview, and knowledge could not be further from ours. In our imagination, we can conjure up images of how these people might have looked or felt, but even some of the most basic elements of their existence or perception, something far more knowable in later periods, are things of which we know little. The physical world in which they lived is somehow more tangible but, like its people, familiar and yet fundamentally distinct from our own experience. This was a place with landscapes that were vast and, to our minds, untamed, familiar to our experience at a local scale, yet at the same time extending over seemingly immense territories with swathes of dark forests, mountains, and relentlessly rising seas.

Bounded by the Ural Mountains in the East, the Atlantic Ocean in the North, and the Mediterranean in the South, Europe covers an area of over 10 million square kilometers (Figure 1.1). It houses some of the most varied and distinctive landscapes within any comparable-sized region anywhere in the world, landscapes ranging from Mediterranean woodlands to Artic Tundra and across 40 degrees of latitude. In this volume, we pass by the Aegean islands of the eastern Mediterranean to the shores of northern Scandinavia and northern Russia, across the mountainous backbone of Europe, the intricate network of lake basins around the Alpine fringe and in the north and east the vast windswept plain that extends almost unbroken from lowland Britain to the Siberian border interrupted only by great river systems such as the Rhine, the Danube, the Dniepr, and the Don, and across offshore islands and archipelagos in the Mediterranean and the Atlantic.

* Department of Archaeology, University of York, UK.

Mesolithic people carry a real significance for many. In some regions, the Mesolithic holds a special importance as the time of first settlement, of hardy and intrepid colonisers who carry a symbolic presence for the region. About a third of the European land mass and much of its higher mountain slopes and offshore islands was occupied by human settlement during the Postglacial for the first time in human experience. In other regions, the Mesolithic might appear to be the phase of human history within which the first signs of 'settling' of society into increasingly familiar environments and habits can be found, with enduring ties between people and place. For all, however, the Mesolithic carries a sense of fascination.

Alongside the 'otherness' of Mesolithic Europe, knowledge and understanding brings a sense of rational or even perhaps 'scientific' familiarity. The very notion of 'Mesolithic Europe' as a definable period and region with boundaries of some kind makes us feel that this world is knowable, almost manageable. We can define and analyse its limits, and the ways in which environments change. We can reconstruct how people made and used flint tools, follow them genetically, reconstruct and understand what they ate and how they moved around. In the different spheres of environment, subsistence, settlement and society, we can come to an understanding of the Mesolithic world. By building up our knowledge in this way, the 'other world' of Mesolithic Europe is made familiar. In some senses, we can even 'know' the world of Mesolithic people in a depth that they themselves could not perceive or understand. We can see how societies, activities, resources, and settlement systems changed not only over generations but also millennia. We can 'understand' or at least approach the mechanisms creating change, something far beyond the perceptions of Mesolithic people themselves.

This opening chapter gives an introduction to this world, to some of the history of concepts of the Mesolithic, issues, directions and ideas that draw together research on the period, and suggests further complementary frameworks. Each chapter of the volume paints a picture of environments, people, and changes in each different region. The narratives of the Mesolithic in each region, each grounded in their own historical and research trajectory, reveal different insights about the period. Finally, the concluding chapter brings together a comparative overview in a broad summary of the leading features of the Mesolithic and emergent areas of new and future research.

The 'Story' of the Mesolithic

Human origins and prehistory inevitably form a 'story' of the past (Stoczkowski 2002, Joyce et al. 2002), with powerful metaphors for who we are today. Different dialogues and narratives compete for our acceptance, and it is perhaps in the Mesolithic period more than any other that different frames of reference, or perhaps lenses through which we see the archaeological evidence, come most into play. These different understandings are more than just 'theoretical standpoints' but, rather, perceptions and viewpoints that colour and define not only our interpretations but also our sense of what 'the Mesolithic' is, or what it might have meant to have experienced life in those times. Different stories of the Mesolithic and its place in history both merge and conflict to create our current understanding.

Some long-standing stories permeate our sense of what the Mesolithic might mean, how it might be interpreted or what is 'allowed'. One of the deep-seated concepts of the Mesolithic is as a time of cultural stagnation – passive societies in which little changed and social relationships were uncontested. The most likely root for such ideas lies in a long-standing view of Mesolithic societies as being dominated by their environment. In fact, we only need to look back to the earlier decades of the twentieth century to understand how Mesolithic societies may have been disenfranchised

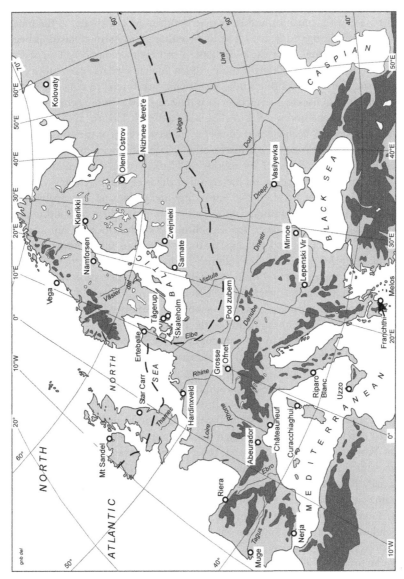

Figure 1.1. Map of Europe showing major topographic features and key sites. The dashed line shows the maximum extent of the continental ice sheet during the Last Glacial (© G. Bailey).

from discussions of social and cultural changes. The prevailing view of the Mesolithic at this time was that memorably expressed by Gordon Childe, who viewed Mesolithic societies, sometimes with undisguised contempt, as impoverished descendants of the Palaeolithic, gripped by 'a state of helpless barbarism' (Childe 1925: 1) and contributing nothing to later European civilisation. Sir Mortimer Wheeler wrote in a similar vein about the inhabitants of Mesolithic Star Carr (Tolan-Smith this volume) – and in the same year as the final publication of the Star Carr excavations by Grahame Clark (1954) – as 'as squalid a huddle of march-ridden food gatherers as the imagination could well encompass' (Wheeler 1954: 231). For these authors, European civilisation began with the spread of Neolithic societies from the Near East, a process that supposedly erased the preceding hunter-gatherers of Europe (Zvelebil 1996c). Even Grahame Clark, excavator of Star Carr and pioneer and champion of Mesolithic studies in Britain, was forced to concede with evident reluctance in 1952 that the archaeological evidence for the coastal Mesolithic peoples of Northwest Europe hardly contradicted the notion of 'a low level of culture' (Clark 1952: 63).

The concept of passivity has been echoed equally in understandings of the cultural relationship between the Mesolithic and the Neolithic as in that of the relationship with the environment. Even from the start of the first use of the label 'Mesolithic' in Clark's (1932: 5) definition of the period as 'between the close of the Pleistocene and the arrival of the Neolithic' (Rowley-Conwy 1996), the period appears to be caught between two apparently inexorable and inescapable events, the first environmental and the second cultural. In the south of Europe where Mesolithic occupation followed that of the Palaeolithic, the term 'Epipalaeolithic' (a continuation or culmination of the Palaeolithic) has been widely used and still appears today (cf. Straus this volume, Valdeyron this volume, Pluciennik this volume, Bonsall this volume). In the north, however, the term Mesolithic highlighted the apparent dynamism and distinctiveness of societies that succeeded in expanding into new areas. Further north again (Bjerck this volume), the terms Older and Younger Stone Age are more commonly used. In each region, we can see how the narratives of the origin of Mesolithic societies influenced understanding of the nature of the period itself.

There have been various challenges to the concept of Mesolithic peoples as rather impoverished communities. In the 1980s, there was a radical transformation when the material record of certain coastal Mesolithic societies, particularly those on the coastlines of Northwest Europe, was interpreted as indicating large socially complex communities living in permanent villages. Drawing on ethnographic analogies with societies of the Northwest Coast of North America, these communities, with material evidence typically associated with later periods, such as specialist task groups, food storage, social ranking, cemeteries, and high levels of population density on a par with early farming societies (Rowley-Conwy 1983, Renouf 1984), were seen as sufficiently densely populated and organised to resist the invasion of farming communities. 'Complex' Mesolithic communities were seen as socially powerful rather than stagnant. Unsurprisingly, the concept of rising social complexity became an appealing characteristic of the whole period and the Mesolithic-Neolithic transition a new source of stimulus for Mesolithic studies (Zvelebil 1986c, Price 2001). The origins of the Neolithic were extended into the Mesolithic and discussions focussed on progressive intensification or diversification of resources, and a move towards agriculture.

Extrapolating the origins of social complexity to certain contexts in Mesolithic Europe marked a powerful departure from ideas of small, marginalised groups apparently 'going nowhere'. However, subtle but pervasive parts of the narrative remained intact. 'Complexity' was built on dense, productive coastal resources that were available all year. 'Complex' societies were still inexorably and rather passively built on seasonal resources and subsistence relationships, with concerns about their logistic organisation taking primacy over social interpretations. This meant that the 'story' of the Mesolithic was still one in which society and social change were determined by environments.

Ironically, discussions of social changes in complex societies rather contributed to the relegation of many of the societies of Mesolithic Europe as ever more 'passive', as societies outside of maritime locations became rather 'left out in the cold' of discussions of social changes. The lack of dense resources, and the self-fulfilling and apparently uncontested arrival of the Neolithic, in some ways further disenfranchised 'simple' Mesolithic hunter-gatherers.

Challenges to ways of interpreting the Mesolithic have come from various sources. A long history of research from the time of Grahame Clark and beyond (1932, 1975, 1980), three decades of international meetings (Kozlowski 1973, Gramsch 1981, Bonsall 1989, Vermeersch and Van Peer 1990, Larsson et al. 2003), and new approaches and overviews (Mellars 1978, Zvelebil 1986c, Price 1987, Conneller 2000, Young 2000a, Bevan and Moore 2003, Milner and Woodman 2005, Conneller and Warren 2006) provide healthy disagreements over issues and approaches. New approaches to themes with a deeply entrenched traditional stance such as subsistence (Milner 2006), and technology (Warren 2006), are being developed, many of which move beyond environmental determinism and readdress interpretations to incorporate views of experience and perceptions. Even the narrative of increasing complexity has gradually become deconstructed (Bonsall this volume). A gradual intensification of resources and a move towards agriculture has also been seen as being rather simplistic, with archaeological evidence for a decline in social complexity suggesting that a progression towards complexity is far from inevitable (Rowley-Conwy 2001).

Approaches to the Mesolithic continue to be contested. However, as valuable as new perspectives and vigorous debate may be, we might pause to wonder if the large scale narrative has really changed. We have overviews of the Palaeolithic, usually as part of a global synthesis, for example, Gamble (1986, 1993, 1999) or of the Neolithic and later, for example, Bradley (1984), Whittle (1985, 1996), Hodder (1990) and Thomas (1991), but, with the exception of Mithen (2003), little attempt to pull together any large scale understanding for the Mesolithic. The evidence, particularly for so-called simple societies, often dominated by surface lithic scatters, might be that which is at fault, falling almost naturally into a passive extension of artefacts from environments and perhaps too meagre to address any large scale social questions of interest. Nonetheless, Conneller and Warren (2006) argue that it is not the material remains of Mesolithic societies that are to blame for the limitations of interpretations but, rather, the need for new approaches and understanding. Without confronting the narrative of rather passive societies, the questions asked in the Mesolithic can, on the one hand, become overly practical, related to the technicalities of subsistence and settlement or, on the other hand, reach out to incorporate perceptions and experience that often end up drawing on what Strassburg (2003: 543) has called 'banal phenomenological truisms'. Young (2000b: 1) concluded that the discipline was still 'waiting for the great leap forwards'. A long-standing story of Mesolithic hunter-gatherers so immersed in their environments and nature, both ecologically and ideologically, as to be almost socially inert seems to retain a strong hold on our imaginations.

Mesolithic Europe – A Complex Tapestry

Could we rewrite a narrative of the Mesolithic, to write a 'social story' of the period? 'Mesolithic Europe' encompasses over five thousand years across a vast territory, that is over two hundred generations of very different people living in dynamic and changing environments. It might seem reasonable to resist any attempt to pigeonhole such diverse societies into some broad plan. In fact, Kozlowski (2003: xxi) goes so far as to conclude that the range of societies and environments is so great that there is no shared attribute (apart from chronology) that can reliably define the entire Mesolithic formation. Any attempt to draw together such varied societies, to seek comfort from some unproblematic perspective, a great (and simple) leap, may of itself be flawed. Mesolithic communities were diverse and varied, perhaps there is no more to say than that these are the only terms on which we can study them.

Diversity and variability are certainly a key theme in this volume. The contributions illustrate a 'tapestry' of Mesolithic Europe, which is complex and varied with remarkably different societies falling under the blanket term of 'Holocene hunter-gatherers'. Societies as diverse as specialised maritime seal hunters, small groups in varied woodland environments, elaborately symbolic settlements such as the Iron Gates of the Danube, early colonisers of barren landscapes, all occupy their place in 'the Mesolithic'. Each local society has its own distinctive feel. This diversity is increasingly being recognised even at the end of the period and into the Neolithic. Patterns of population replacement, coexistence or assimilation show regional and local differences across Europe (Gkiasta et al. 2003, Perrin 2003, Bentley et al. 2003). The pattern of dietary changes, although contentious (Milner et al. 2004), also appears to be regionally and locally varied (Lidén et al. 2004). Similar patterns of differing regional trajectories also affected the transition to the Neolithic in other areas of the world, such as China (Li Lui 2004). The material evidence for Mesolithic Europe reminds us of a complex, multicoloured tapestry.

Like a tapestry, however, there are discernible patterns in this evidence, and threads link different societies as we view Mesolithic Europe as a whole. There is more to the material evidence of Mesolithic Europe than simply wide-ranging diversity. As humans, we naturally seek stories and metaphors to understand patterns around us. However much we might welcome complexity and diversity, without finding other means to interpret large-scale patterns, we are left with our old narratives to structure understanding.

A Structure behind Diversity?

Making sense of the tapestry of Mesolithic Europe is a challenge. We would be mistaken to deride or dismiss ecological and environmental models. Even when environments are stable, hunter-gatherer communities are strongly influenced in their lifestyles and movements by their environments and the rhythm of the seasons, and Holocene environments in contrast were complex and constantly varying. In some cases, the dynamics of Holocene environments would have had immediate and far-reaching effects on local hunter-gatherer groups. Mesolithic Europe was a world in which there were towering glaciers, cataclysmic floods, tsunamis, and rising and falling seas. There is evidence for various sudden and cataclysmic events, which would have left a trail of effects on human societies. Dolukhanov (this volume) describes interpretations of a cataclysmic 'Flood' of the Black Sea at around 6100 cal BC, which would have rapidly inundated more than 100,000 m² of land with its Mesolithic inhabitants, and allegedly accelerated the dispersal of early Neolithic farming into Europe. At around the same time, the Storegga tsunami off the coast of Norway would have been equally devastating and may have caused cataclysmic effects on coastal populations, with 10 m high waves potentially devastating boats, equipment, and food supplies. Moreover, because this happened in autumn, there would have been little time for survivors to prepare for the harsh winter. In the Baltic region, there were fundamental changes to the freshwater Ancylus Lake, which became linked to the ocean through the straits of Øresund, Storebælt, and Lillebælt (Bjerck this volume).

We can scarcely imagine the ideological effect on local populations of these drastic changes. Of course, less dramatic changes also would have had perceptible effects and such dynamism and unpredictability in their surrounding landscape would have been a major influence on how many groups understood their world. Bjerck (this volume) describes a drop in sea level of about 3 m per century in parts of Norway such that the configuration of the coastline would have changed, altered fishing and hunting grounds, and potentially blocked sea passages. Periodic transgressions of about 1 m are recorded at Vedbæk in Eastern Zealand (Blankholm this volume). Within many people's lifetimes, there would have been noticeable changes in their surroundings, whether subtle or more significant in their effects. Population movements must have been common, and changing environments and landscapes must have influenced understandings and beliefs about the world.

The influence of environment is perhaps most complex at the regional and local scale. Holocene environments were uniquely structured and differentiated, and in many cases remarkably different from those today despite broadly similar climatic conditions. Where dry scrub is common in much of the modern Mediterranean, Pluciennik (this volume) describes a mosaic of forest communities in southern France, southern Spain, and central Italy during the Mesolithic. Macchia, evergreen forests, and deciduous forests with lime and elm, would have been common, with alder-dominated forests along river and stream margins, as well as pine forest and heath interspersed with coastal and estuarine salt marshes and lagoons. Landscapes in regions such as the British Isles (Tolan-Smith this volume) would have been different from today's, with lowlands dominated early on by forests of pine, birch, and hazel, and later by oak, elm, and lime. Landscapes and vegetation would have been much more patchy and diverse than those with which we are familiar today. The dynamics of vegetation competition and replacement following Postglacial warming mean that conditions also would have been in flux throughout the period, with stable climax communities only becoming established in many regions after several thousand years. Mesolithic communities were intimately connected to their environment, and the complex dynamic of replacement of pine and birch by oak, hazel, and lime in regions such as Britain and Germany had clearly defined influences on large mammal communities and thus on hunting practices (Spikins 1999, Spikins 2000, Jochim and Tolan-Smith this volume).

The most obvious area of environmental influence on Mesolithic societies is that of colonisations. Large-scale patterns of change in environments and resources undoubtedly influenced both new colonisations and population movements within inhabited Europe. Concepts of early pioneers, hardy explorers of previously unused terrain and a 'shifting up' and gradual infilling pervade discussions of all the regions, from new occupation of previously unoccupied landscapes in Scandinavia (Bjerck this volume), Scotland (Finlayson 1998, Hardy and Whickham-Jones 2002, Tolan-Smith this volume), islands such as Ireland (Tolan-Smith this volume), Corsica (Valdeyron this volume, Pluciennik this volume), and Sardinia (Pluciennick this volume), to expansion to high altitudes in the mountains of central Europe (Svoboda this volume). The motivations and processes behind colonisation and how this relates to changing environments and landscapes can be surprisingly elusive, however. In areas such as Ireland (Tolan-Smith this volume) or Corsica (Valdeyron this volume), colonisation reflects a complex relationship between environmental opportunity and human motivation, ingenuity and desire for exploration. Ethnographic evidence can provide further insight. Tolan-Smith (this volume) suggests several different stages in population expansion in the British Isles, from initial colonisation of new regions to consolidation and infilling and further expansion following climatic changes. We might even begin to imagine the different social contexts of settlement with emphases on 'exploration' or 'tradition'.

There is more to colonisation than simply a response to environmental changes, however. Bjerck illustrates the role of technological innovation in colonisation, the risk associated with pioneering settlement of Arctic landscapes and the technological component of specialised maritime occupation and its development. He attributes the delay in colonisation of the extreme north to the delay in developing specialised methods of marine exploitation, in particular the technological capacity for safe movement using sea craft that could be righted if submerged – particularly important in extremely cold seas. Without these innovations, Bjerck (this volume) describes northern coastal environments as 'inaccessible as the moon'.

Environmental change also will have influenced population migration in occupied areas. Although the concept of migrations is unfashionable, large-scale changes in technology, in artefact types and distributions, and how these relate to environments and regions, have fascinated archaeologists studying the Mesolithic from its first recognition. Across all regions, we can document the movement of certain artefacts, such as Star Carr and Deepcar assemblage types in early Mesolithic Britain (Tolan-Smith this volume) or scalene or Montclus triangles in Late Mesolithic France (Valdeyron this volume). To some extent, shifts of groups with changing environments or changing subsistence practices can be seen as influencing movements and change in artefact styles (see Tolan-Smith this volume, Jochim this volume). Microlithisation, the gradual reduction in size of microliths, a pattern common to Mesolithic Europe, also can be seen in terms of changing woodland types and changing technologies for medium and large game hunting. However, changes in artefact styles have other, more predominantly social explanations. Pluciennik (this volume) also suggests that microliths performed other functions, such as plant food processing, and microlithisation might have other explanations. Innovation, the spread of ideas, and the negotiation of stylistic identities between groups linked across areas of landscape are also key features of Mesolithic Europe. In some areas, there *is* a relationship between changes in lithic technology and changes in game resources, as in the British Isles (Tolan-Smith this volume), or the Upper Danube and Upper Rhine (Jochim this volume). In other areas such as southwest France (Pluciennik this volume), there is no consistent pattern, suggesting that relationships between groups and the spread of knowledge were important influences.

Other types of changes in artefacts also suggest a story of social changes, which remains to be uncovered. Increasing *regionalisation* of patterns of artefacts, both in terms of distinctive styles and increasingly regional networks of raw material procurement, require explanation. Increasing regionalisation can in part be explained by a fragmentation of increasingly complex and dense woodland environments throughout the Mesolithic (Spikins 1999, Spikins 2000). Other explanations include an increasing intensification of subsistence. However, in many areas, arguments for increasing territoriality (Gendel 1984, 1987) seen in stylistic or assemblage distinctions in artefacts such as stone axes in west Norway (Bjerck this volume), distinctive types of microlith styles in different regions of Denmark (Blankholm this volume) or other elements of material culture such as rock art traditions, have proved more supportable than a focus on intensification *per se* (Arias 2004). The social context of regionalisation is, nevertheless, difficult to address, given the complex relationship between what might be seen as defined 'territories' and ethnicity (Bergsvik 2003). Insight has been gained from considering the spread of techniques of manufacture rather than by focusing on final form, for example, the spread of blade techniques and changes in platform preparation in Norway (Bjerck this volume, see also Warren 2006).

A particularly interesting argument for a relationship between environment and society lies in the apparent connection between social complexity and maritime and lakeside environments (Mithen 1994). Similarities appear in societies in which there are rich maritime or lakeside resources from the far north to the Mediterranean. In the far northern latitudes, where for four months of the year the sun does not set, the icy cold but resource-rich northern sea was the focus of settlement for maritime hunter-gatherers such as those at Vega in northern Norway. Here we see settlements with pit houses, with people using elaborate seagoing vessels in their specialised focus on marine foods, probably associated with seal hunting (Bjerck 1995, Bjerck this volume). Further south, other structured settlements echo the theme of marine or lakeside focus. At Tågerup in Sweden, large houses were constructed in a 'village' at the confluence of two rivers, with permanent structures such as jetties and moorings for boats (Zvelebil this volume). Coastal and lakeside regions also provide evocative glimpses of societies for whom the sea and water played an important economic and symbolic role. We see richly symbolic pendants of amber and animal teeth, wooden artefacts such as bows, decorated paddles, canoes, and leisters in evidence from submerged sites in the Baltic (Blankholm this volume). Rock art sites such as Nämforsen in Sweden offer fascinating glimpses of symbolism associated with images of elk, boats, fish, and birds that show commonalities with the cosmological system of the modern Khanty, and appear to mark an important locus for ritual, aggregation and exchange (Zvelebil this volume). Riverine resources also appear to have been particularly influential in the development of settlements such as Lepenski Vir and Vlasac in the Iron Gates (Bonsall this volume). Here, in relative isolation from the rest of Europe, we see an apparently 'sacred' site at Lepenski Vir, comprising houses with plastered floors, carved figurines, and neonates interned under the floors.

The distinctive difference between these societies and those in inland areas is a common theme running through the volume. In interior regions, typified by often-dense Holocene woodland, the evidence for occupation can be scarce, and for ritual or symbolic life scarcer still. We see similar elusive evidence with scattered sites and interpretations of woodland hunting in Germany (Jochim this volume), France (Valdeyron this volume), and Britain (Tolan-Smith this volume), and in the distinctive woodland areas of the Mediterranean such as Greece (Pluciennik this volume). Postdepositional processes undoubtedly play a role in influencing the patchiness of the hinterland record, but it is difficult to escape the conclusion that such wooded environments were in general less resource-rich and populations more mobile and organisationally 'simpler'. Zvelebil suggests that these inland areas are typified by simple forager groups exemplifying Ingold's 'forager mode of production' (Ingold 1988, Zvelebil 1998). Distinctively different societies occupied many lakeside and marine locations and exhibited status differentiation and distinctions along dimensions of age and sex. Nonetheless, the relationship between environment, landscape, and society in Mesolithic Europe is far from clear-cut. Each region, or even local area, has a distinctive mark, which reflects a subtle and individual engagement between resources, settlement, and belief, and that is also negotiated through and affected by connections between groups at a larger scale.

The interpretation of apparently different degrees of social organisation in societies across the whole region and the extent to which this relates to environments is challenging. Traditionally, social differences are seen as being driven by differences in settlement/mobility patterns. Drawing on ethnography, the contrast between so-called delayed return and immediate return hunter-gatherers (Woodburn 1980) has been seen as the structuring principle explaining difference in Mesolithic society. In Woodburn's model, 'immediate return' groups make frequent moves of their main residential base, foraging on a daily basis to collect local food sources. Mobility of this kind has been seen as a classic hallmark of small-scale egalitarian societies in which resources are unpredictable and sparse, who might tend to show a kinship structure based on exogamy and wide-ranging alliance networks (Tolan-Smith this volume). 'Delayed return' hunter-gatherers, by contrast, appear to be associated with predictable resource-rich environments where collecting food resources can be organised using task groups, who forage away from the main residential base. These are the 'logistic foragers' in Binford's terms (1980), in which through organised exploitation the returns on collection are 'delayed'. The latter kind of movement involves planning and organisation, and typically use of complex technology such as fish traps and boats.

Applying these models appears to 'make sense' of much of the material evidence for Mesolithic Europe. Several regions provide good examples of logistically organised societies that have been seen as examples of 'complexity'. Specialised maritime exploitation patterns as in Scandinavia provide one example, with certain clear-cut cases of organised procurement, such as specialised hunting sites for swans or whales in Denmark (Blankholm this volume). Societies in the Baltic show evidence for marking out of social distinctions and illustrate many instances of different social groups in burial (Zvelebil this volume). However, the association of resources and settlement with other changes, such as social stratification, intensification, the rise of sedentism, and the appearance of cemeteries, is not altogether clear-cut. In northern Scandinavia, evidence suggests that a suite of social changes occurred throughout the Mesolithic – a longer-lasting occupation of sites, the appearance of more distinct regional groupings, a widening range of species in subsistence, and an intensification in the use of symbols (Bjerck this volume). The progressive development of social organisation and the relationship between characteristics of social organisation and environments is increasingly being questioned in other regions. In southern Scandinavia, the concept of a progressive increase in sedentism, the rise of complexity, and the appearance of cemeteries is not borne out by close inspection of the material record (Blankholm this volume), although variety of grave goods at Skateholm and association of blade knives with some male burials at Bøggebaken does suggest increased social diversity and the rise of leadership and competition for power. For the Iron Gates, despite earlier interpretations, Bonsall (this volume) finds sedentism unlikely, and although some suggestions of high-status burial exist, social distinctions are hard to define. Across Mesolithic Europe, the relationship among 'delayed return' economies, 'complexity' discernible in evidence of increased sedentism, exchange relationships, and defined stratification in burial is often unclear.

The arguments for relating use of resources and settlement pattern to apparent social changes are not as straightforward as they might appear. Certainly, the concept of clear modes of settlement can be seen to be rather simplistic. Almost all hunter-gatherers use both immediate and delayed return strategies at various times (Kelly 1995, Spikins 1999, 2000) with a fluid transition between 'mapping onto' food resources and the organisation of specialist task groups. As Jochim (1991) illustrates, seasonal rounds in ethnographic societies are rarely clearly defined, with variation from year to year being the norm. Differences within regions are also marked in ethnographic cases (Spikins 1999, Spikins 2000). In recent years, there also has been an increasing recognition of the fluidity of social changes. Rowley-Conwy notes that the appearance of what we might call 'complexity' is a fluid process, which can be reversed (Rowley-Conwy 2001). The relationship between subsistence changes and ideological changes also has become an area of much debate that remains to be resolved for the Mesolithic-Neolithic transition (Rowley-Conwy 2004). A gradual rise of complexity through intensification of exploitation patterns and increasing organisation of people and time has become a hard principle to sustain, and there seems to be far more to the picture of different societies than variability in resource exploitation.

Of course, the 'missing pieces' of the tapestry of evidence in Mesolithic Europe compound the difficulties of distinguishing modes of society related to immediate or delayed return settlement systems, and even more so of identifying or beginning to understand any transition between them. As many have argued (Coles 1998, Bailey 2004, Bailey and Milner 2002, Fleming 2004), the missing evidence from submerged prehistoric coasts may be crucial, as almost all our evidence of early Mesolithic coastal societies has been submerged by rising seas and much Late Mesolithic evidence as well. It is precisely the coastal locations where the most 'organised' societies tend to exist. For Britain, tantalising glimpses of supposedly emergent complexity occur in early Mesolithic coastal settings, such as evidence for structures, which might have been occupied for an extended period, at Howick (Tolan-Smith this volume, Waddington et al. 2003) or glimpses of symbolism and exchange in the elaborate bead production at Nab Head in South Wales (Tolan-Smith this volume). The 'missing pieces' of the tapestry not only frustrate interpretations but may even bias them towards certain types of sites. Blankholm (this volume) notes that discussions of southern Scandinavian social complexity frequently compare late Mesolithic coastal sites with early Mesolithic interior sites (with early Mesolithic coastal sites being underwater at depths that are largely inaccessible), creating a biased picture and artificially suggesting the appearance of more 'complex' societies over time.

Cosmology and Belief

Although evidence for changes in social relationships can be biased and often ambiguous, this is even more true of cosmology and belief. Many researchers close interpretations of the period with suggestions about settlement systems or possibly social structure, leaving ideology and beliefs as a kind of 'Pandora's Box' best left untouched. In fact, beliefs and cosmology traditionally have been seen as a separate sphere from the day-to-day activities of subsistence and social relationships in the Mesolithic. However, new perspectives and analogies with recent hunter-gatherers increasingly place cosmology and belief at the heart of our understanding not only of how hunter-gatherers see the world but also what they actually do (Zvelebil and Fewster 2001, Jordan 2003a, Grøn and Kuznetsov 2003, Lodoen 2003, Nordquist 2003, Chatterton 2006, Jordan 2006, Zvelebil this volume).

The most direct access to beliefs for most periods comes from burial evidence. However, if we want to elucidate some clear pattern in the burial evidence from Mesolithic Europe, we are likely to be disappointed. It is perhaps in this material evidence where we see the most intriguing and evocative record of diversity and unpredictability. There appear to be few if any broad structuring principles that hold together approaches to treatment of the dead (Schulting 1998), making it difficult to see a common thread.

The most famous burials are the large collections of graves in Scandinavia, the Baltic, and the Iron Gates sites, and it is here that we see evidence for a consistent pattern in social differentiation, if not the means by which this is displayed. In the north, Olenii Ostrov, dating to the mid-seventh millennium cal BC, on a small island within Lake Onega in Karelia, probably held more than three hundred interments (Zvelebil this volume). Here there is a mix of individual and collective burials with certain graves marked out differently, particularly shaft graves that have been interpreted as those of shamans. Gravestones, small cairns, or stone linings also marked some interments. The implications of differentiation in grave goods and burial type are contested, but it is possible to suggest three specialised ranks expressing band membership: age, sex, and personal wealth. Similar complex differentiations are seen in the famous burial complexes of around eighty-five graves at Skateholm (I and II) in southern Sweden, which include cremations, interment in a sitting position, double graves containing both women and men with children, rich child graves, and dog burials. Once again, certain individuals are specifically marked out with timber structures built over two graves at Skateholm I, whereas Skateholm II had a mortuary house. Skateholm has been interpreted as a territorial marker of a unilineal descent group claiming rights to resources through ancestors (Zvelebil this volume). About three hundred individuals were interred with various grave goods at Muge in Portugal (Straus this volume) and large numbers of graves – over one hundred at Vlasac – are also found in the Iron Gates sites with a variety of burial rituals (Bonsall this volume).

Taken as a whole, there is considerable diversity in burial practice and the structure of burial sites across Europe. Body positions at Lepenski Vir, Padina, and Schela Cladovei are widely varying, with special treatment of the skulls in some cases. Some burials were lacking the skull, and cutmarks at Schela Cladovei suggest that the burials were revisited and the skulls removed after the flesh had decayed (Bonsall this volume). Communal graves dug in earth-cut pits are seen at the burial complex of Téviec and Hoëdic (Valdeyron this volume). Whether any of these large burial complexes can rightly be called 'cemeteries' is contentious (Blankholm this volume), as there seems in most cases to be little differentiation between settlement and burial place, the concept of cemetery being perhaps something inspired more by our modern concepts of treatment of the dead (Conneller 2006). The Vedbaek complex in Zealand, for example, consists of burials interred in settlements that dotted the ancient coastline of the Vedbaek fjord (Blankholm this volume).

Other burial practices reflect different identities and intentions. 'Founding statements' in northern Sicily consist of burials dug into archaeologically sterile layers at the beginning of a sequence of lengthy deposition (Pluciennik this volume). These might share some parallels with the burial of neonates under floors at Lepenski Vir. Unusual rites also abound, such as the so-called skull cult of Eastern France, Baden-Württemberg, and Bavaria. At Ofnet Cave, Bavaria, two shallow pits contain skulls, jaws, and vertebrae. Bludgeon wounds on most of the skulls appear to be the cause of death, which could be described as a 'Mesolithic massacre' (see Jochim this volume). At Agnis Charente, there are human bones from eight individuals in domestic refuse, with butchery marks characteristic of disarticulation and defleshing, probably indicating cannibalism (Valdeyron this volume). The evidence for violence in many of the burial complexes and elsewhere (Vencl 1999, Thorpe 2000, Blankholm this volume, Jochim this volume, Bonsall this volume) contests the image of passive, purely giving and sharing societies in the Mesolithic as put forward by Bradley (1998) and Tilley (1996) on the basis of Bird-David's (1990, 1992a) account of hunter-gatherer society.

The role of violence in society is complex, however, and it is important to remember that there may be differences between different hunting and gathering societies in Mesolithic Europe that are as fundamental or even more so than those between the Mesolithic and the Neolithic. Formal burials in so-called cemeteries, Mesolithic 'massacres', or burials with clear evidence for violence almost certainly reflect a particular element of society or practice. However, we have little idea how common structured burial was, and it seems likely that elaborate burial was rare. In Mesolithic Europe as a whole, common burial practice might have been disarticulation, with the occasional finds of human bones in middens or other areas of settlement often attracting much less archaeological attention than would a formal burial (Conneller 2006). Understanding the disarticulation and dismemberment of human bones, for example, in cases such as the Oronsay shell middens, demands an understanding of similar practices in ethnographically known societies, in particular concepts of individuality and commonality (Conneller 2006).

Other evidence for beliefs and cosmology from art or personal ornamentation (Bjerck this volume, Verhardt this volume, Zvelebil this volume) complements evidence from burials, with equal complexity. Taken as a whole, the evidence from across Europe for environment, settlement, society, and belief forms a complex multicoloured tapestry. Threads and patterns exist but can often be hard to discern and, where they appear, demand more subtle explanation than many of our current narratives supply.

Other Approaches to Interpreting Social Change

The issues are complex; however, there is a real sense of important social distinctions identified in all the contributions to the volume. Available resources, resource use, and mobility clearly play an important role in marking the differences between distinct societies. Nevertheless, we are left feeling that there must be more to the picture of societies and social relationships in the Mesolithic. Our deep-seated narratives easily apportion social change, competition, and social dynamics to certain very specific societies and contexts, leaving most in an uncontested and passive relationship with each other and with their environments. Rethinking the apparent link between environments and social structure demands a much better understanding of social relationships in Mesolithic societies, one that goes beyond the structure of settlement patterns.

There may be several different routes to a better understanding of people and relationships in the Mesolithic. Discussions in anthropology contribute important concepts such as identity and relatedness (Bird-David et al. 1999, Fowler 2004, Conneller and Warren 2006, Jordan 2006, Milner and Woodman 2005) and relationships between material culture and society (Finlay 2003, 2006, Warren 2006). The call to understand emotion in archaeology (Tarlow 2000, Gosden 2004) might provide another framework.

One route explored here is to draw on discussions within the social psychology of hunter-gatherers (see also Spikins 2008). Although social psychological rather than anthropological discussions of ethnographic populations are limited, this perspective provides a useful interpretative framework of structured relationships between people. Certain concepts have particular relevance, of which mechanisms of *deference* between people in hunter-gatherer societies may be notably useful (Heinrich and Gil-White 2001). Deference can perhaps be thought of as a means of showing respect or acknowledgment of social standing and so mechanisms of deference exist in all societies (even the social environment of school playgrounds). Such mechanisms and understandings structure relationships and the gestures and attitudes of individuals towards each other. As such, deference is not simply about behaviour but also about emotions and common understandings.

Heinrich and Gil-White (2001) illustrate how social relationships and deference in egalitarian hunter-gatherer societies are largely mediated through what can be termed 'prestige'. They describe prestige as associated with people who have particular valued skills, such as at flint-knapping or story-telling, and as such it is a quality that comes from showing excellence in valued areas. Relationships mediated through prestige allow certain people *influence* through emulation or copying of their abilities. However, prestige does not confer any ability to dictate or sanction behaviour, that is, prestige may be associated with influence but not *power*. Prestige is achieved through 'nonagonistic' stances and actions (i.e., nonviolent, nonintimidating, and nonaggressive). Someone with prestige is listened to, that is, their opinions are heavily weighed. They are not 'obeyed,' and by implication these individuals are not feared and do not have 'power over' others. Individuals with prestige attract others towards them who will tend to copy their behaviour, publicly praise them, seek eye contact, and direct their posture towards the prestigious individual.

In contrast to prestige, status relationships mediated through *social dominance tactics* involve those who are socially dominant taking an aggressive stance and attempting to dictate behaviour. Deference in reaction to this behaviour takes the form of avoidance of eye contact and deferent body posture. The experienced emotion of deferring to someone dominant is markedly different – associated with fear rather than inspiration. The emphasis is on controlling the behaviour of others rather than inspiring or influencing them. The distinct types of relationship are not mutually exclusive, although the acceptability of either varies markedly. Heinrich and Gil-White (2001) describe both tactics in school children in playground negotiations of social dynamics. Crucially, each means of relating to others appears to draw on different deep-seated psychological and emotional responses. Most of us can easily imagine how it would feel to be inspired by someone we respect or controlled by someone we fear.

The maintenance of prestige rather than social dominance is important in egalitarian hunter-gatherer societies (Erdal and Whiten 1996, Heinrich and Gil-White 2001, see also Heinrich et al. 2001). Social relationships mediated through prestige are constantly contested. Influence through prestige involves listening to the prestigious person with respect, and, as Erdal and Whiten (1996: 145) note, 'there is nothing permanent about respect'. Thus, prestige is very fluid, and maintaining or achieving prestige is a process of constant social negotiation. Crucially, people who are prestigious are prevented from assigning authority or power to themselves in various ways amongst ethnographically documented hunter-gatherers. Amongst the Semai, if someone seeks to assert their authority, it is generally accepted that others will cease to 'hear' them. As Dentan (1979, cited in Heinrich and Gil-White 2001) notes, individuals with prestige amongst the Semai use rhetorical techniques such as self-deprecation to assure listeners that they are not trying to compel compliance. Counterdominance tactics operating in egalitarian societies to maintain prestige-based social relationships are known to be widespread (Erdal and Whiten 1996). Turnbull (1965: 181), for example, notes that for the Mbuti, 'Individual authority is unthinkable'. For the Netsilik, 'Where there are named roles, the leaders, whose leadership role is taken by the 'inhumataq' or 'thinker', are not 'obeyed' but rather 'listened to' (Riches 1982: 74, in Erdal and Whiten 1996). Erdal and Whiten also illustrate how ridicule is used to prevent leaders from being dominant. Numerous ethnographic illustrations can be found. Lee notes, for example, that 'The !Kung are a fiercely egalitarian people . . . cutting down to size the arrogant and boastful' (Lee 1979: 244). Turnbull (1965: 183, in Erdal and Whiten 1996) notes for the Mbuti that 'Some men, because of exceptional hunting skill, may come to resent it when their views are disrespected, but if they try to force these views they are very promptly subjected to ridicule'. Likewise, amongst the Selk'nam, any boastful individual would be derided, humility being seen as an important principle to teach children (Bridges 1948). Situations illustrating the way prestige 'works' are widespread in ethnographies of hunter-gatherer societies.

Whereas prestigious individuals are prevented from asserting their own authority, the transition to a type of social dominance might occur when authority is invested in them by others in a particular context. A good example of the potentially transitory nature of emerging social dominance can be found in ethnographic accounts of the Yamana (Yahgan) of Tierra of Fuego. The Yamana were largely maritime hunter-gatherers, occupying the southern part of the islands of Tierra del Fuego, and were recorded most notably by Gusinde during the 1920s (Gusinde 1986). The mobility and social relationships of the Yamana are typical of small-scale egalitarian hunter-gatherers, with no clear marking-out of status and a very mobile lifestyle with little opportunity for material accumulation. Of particular interest in terms of the acceptance of social dominance within a normally prestige based society is the Yamana ceremony called the Chiexaus. The Chiexaus is one of the most important ceremonies, an extended event taking about two months during which young men and women were initiated into society. A large specially constructed oval hut was built and various complex performances took place in which different members of the group wear specific dress and body paint imitating spirits. The ceremonies had a 'director', nominally in charge of the organisation of the events (although taking wishes of the participants into account). Other individuals, such as the Winefkema, who represented a predatory seabird, also had specific authority. In the case of the Winefkama, he would have authority (and helpers) to forcibly escort the initiates to the hut. Boys who resisted would be caught with a large strap, or in the case of girls a skin thrown over her head, and dragged to the hut. A clearly disobedient initiate might be tied to the entrance and left without food or water for half a day or more (Chapman 1987). This relationship might appear to be a clear example of social dominance – the initiates, normally part of a society in which influence comes only through respect and inspiration, are afraid of Winefkama who has the power to control them. However, the authority invested in the director or the Winefkema was transitory and such rights were negotiated in a sensitive and complex way, and often, although not always, accorded to shamans (Gusinde 1986). In all cases, these individuals were felt to be trusted by the wider group, who temporarily accorded such privileges so that the ceremony could be organised. Whether a Chiexaus took place was context-dependent and also negotiated according to the willingness of the group to accord such privileges. Similar contexts might have arisen at different times and places within the Mesolithic, sometimes very fluid and at other times more sustained. Rather than passively uncontested social roles, we can imagine that competition for prestige and transitory cases of social dominance coloured social relationships.

Identifying prestige relationships or status defined through social dominance in the archaeological record presents a challenge. Naturally, ethnographic evidence may provide the main source for suggestions as to how material culture may reflect societies governed by prestige. Ironically, however, we are faced with the paradox that in prestige-based egalitarian hunter-gatherer societies, the bases for prestige, such as skills, are rarely 'marked out' through material culture – to do so would be to assert authority, contrary to the ethic of self-derogation. So predominantly prestige-based societies may be associated with an *absence* of material 'marking-out' of specific skills in life, and perhaps also in death.

To make identifying prestige even more challenging, the relationship between prestige and personhood is also clearly multifaceted. Prestige is only one element of identity. Elements of a constantly negotiated personal identity that may be marked out in both life and death may not be connected with prestige relationships. Attractiveness, for example, although associated with 'desirability', need not be seen as prestigious (Heinrich and Gil-White 2001), that is, attractive individuals are not necessarily 'listened to'. Thus, Shostak (1981) notes that, amongst the !Kung, all women are considered attractive, and use personal ornamentation to mark out attractiveness, whereas individual skills, although valued, are not marked materially (Lee 1979). A marking-out of identity through personal ornamentation, such as the beads known from Nab Head in Wales (Tolan-Smith this volume) or items of adornment from the Danube and Upper Rhine (Jochim this volume), might equally be related to attractiveness or other social distinctions rather than ones based on prestige. Bonsall (this volume) notes that items of adornment present in burials in the Iron Gates are not necessarily related to status distinctions. Although it is difficult to base conclusions on negative evidence, it is tempting to conclude that a relative paucity of any material evidence of any marking out of *skills* in life or death in most areas of Mesolithic Europe might in this light echo the maintenance of prestige-based social dynamics.

Social dominance tactics may be easier to identify materially. Contributions to this volume call to mind several themes that also might appear to relate to social dominance relationships. Evidence for violent deaths might, certainly on first reading, illustrate social dominance tactics, for example. However, such evidence of death is ambiguous, as aggressive tactics (or outbursts of jealousy) may be the result of occasional episodes of social dominance rather than evidence of societies in which social dominance is either temporarily or permanently the accepted basis of social relationships and 'normal' codes of conduct.

Sustained marking-out of skills and social distinctions appears to have been relatively rare in Mesolithic Europe, but instances in which some kind of socially dominant authority has arisen nonetheless exist. In some cases, this dominance appears to have some permanence. The shaft graves of supposed shamans at Olenii Ostrov (Zvelebil this volume), or individuals buried with flint knives at Bøggebaken (Blankholm this volume), certainly appear to draw on a continuing basis for social status and authority defined through certain skills. Likewise, sculptures of waterbirds, elk, beaver, bear, and snake in burials at the Zvejnieki, Kreichi, and Sope cemeteries in the East Baltic (amongst other instances in Mesolithic Europe) appear to be related to more permanent status distinctions (Zvelebil this volume). Such sustained and widespread 'marking-out' of skills or authority provides suggestive evidence for the acceptability of social dominance and a radical departure from prestige based social relationships in these societies. In other cases, we might interpret a more transitory and fluid social dominance, such as in the burial contexts in the Iron Gates (Bonsall this volume). Taking an analogy with the Yamana Chiexaus, the acceptance of social dominance might conceivably largely emerge in a ritual context. The antler frontlets apparently constructed to be worn as head gear recovered from the early Mesolithic site at Star Carr could from this perspective be marking out the wearer as a transitory figure of socially dominant authority, perhaps as part of a ritually constituted context. We can easily imagine how material culture might be drawn on to symbolise (and make acceptable) the transitory nature of ritual dominance. Headgear such as antler frontlets that are visibly put on and removed could operate much like the costume and headgear of Winefkama to transform the 'normal' codes of prestige relationships. In a different context, the organisation forming part of the construction of large structures (such as at Howick, Waddington et al. 2003) at various times and places in Mesolithic Europe might be more explained through temporary, perhaps ritually situated, socially dominant authorities than a more permanent level of social organisation.

Elusive though they may appear, we are left with a real sense of significant changes in social dynamics and the emotional context of social relationships taking place at various time and places in the Mesolithic. Perhaps those people who buried their dead within demarcated graves had fundamentally different constructions of meaning, social dynamics, and means of social competition from those who conveyed the social meaning of individuals in death by disarticulation and disposal of the corpse within settlements. Only by beginning to wrestle with complex issues of deference, prestige, and emotion will we begin to understand these issues. 'Prestige' adds a dimension to understanding social and ideological differences and perhaps an opportunity for teasing apart the types of social changes occurring in Mesolithic Europe, without necessarily assuming that these are merely a by-product of differences in resource procurement. The concept of prestige-based societies and their transformation into ones based on social dominance raises many issues for understanding the archaeological record. Marked differences in social practices, even down to the level of gestures and accepted means of rhetorical speech and the emotional context of relationships, may well have separated societies. We might even pause to consider if societies in which practices of self-derogation or the role of ridicule were 'understood' would feel 'uncomfortable' to those used to marked patterns of social dominance. Prestige is only one concept that can contribute to a more socially situated concept of Mesolithic societies. Others, such as a better understanding of the social and emotional context of technology and artefact production and use (Finlay 2003, Warren 2006), might contribute to some of these issues.

Conclusion

Evocative and tantalising glimpses of the world of Mesolithic peoples, such as the wooden statuette from Willemstad (Verhart this volume and cover illustration) might be rare, but the aspirations and motivations of people in the Mesolithic are emerging as a new focus in current discussions. Past, somewhat passive, narratives of Mesolithic societies, coupled with an expectation of finding dramatic material evidence of social changes, can easily blind us to the subtleties of social change in the Mesolithic. Considerations of the subtle deference techniques and emotions in the social relationships within hunter-gatherers suggest that a dynamic sphere of contested social relationships existed in Mesolithic societies. Nonetheless, glimpses of Mesolithic lives appear and can be drawn out from the material record whether we choose to focus on emotions, perception, social relationships, activities, technology, subsistence, or settlement structure. The various perspectives derived from considerations of resources and economy, ideology, and society make the tapestry of Mesolithic Europe all the richer, as each of the chapters in the volume make their own contribution to writing new and more dynamic narratives of the period.

Acknowledgments

I would like to thank Steve Roskams, Geoff Bailey, Nicky Milner, Martin Carver, Terry O'Connor, Ivan Briz, and Wendy Romer for their valuable comments and suggestions on earlier drafts of this chapter and Steve, Terry, and Ivan in particular for their tolerance of in-depth discussions of prestige. I also would like to thank Niel Sharples and Julian Thomas for comments on the potentially transitory nature of social dominance, and the invaluable support of Leverhulme grant SAS/30212 for research into southern Patagonian hunter-gatherers. Last, but not least, I would like to thank Geoff Bailey for his enduring patience and enthusiasm during the completion of the volume.

Chapter 2

Innovating Hunter-Gatherers: The Mesolithic in the Baltic

Marek Zvelebil*

Introduction

There was no other region in Europe where Mesolithic settlement was as fully represented and where hunter-gatherer communities continued to flourish until so recently as Northern Europe. Atlantic Scandinavia and the basin of the Baltic Sea, with their network of marine coastlines and freshwater lakes and rivers, provided fertile territory for hunting, fishing, and gathering. It is impossible to do justice here to the full story of the development and transformation of hunting-gathering communities who utilised this landscape in the past twelve thousand years. Instead, I shall focus on some pivotal themes, outlining the main features and principal events in the region and summarising recent advances in research. It is of course difficult in such a wide-ranging review to avoid overgeneralisation at the expense of detailed variation and historical contingency, and for additional detail and critique the reader is advised to consult the regional studies referenced later in this chapter.

There is an extensive literature on the Mesolithic of the Baltic region extending well back into the nineteenth century. In fact, the concept itself owes its origin to Scandinavian archaeology (Westropp 1872, Zvelebil 1986a, Rowley-Conwy 1996). In English, two classic accounts illustrate the level of knowledge attained by the 1970s: Grahame Clark's *Earlier Stone Age Settlement of Scandinavia* in 1976, and an edited volume by Paul Mellars, *The Early Postglacial Settlement of Northern Europe* in 1978. Against these benchmarks, an English reader can compare the progress made since then by reference to specialised edited volumes (Bonsall 1989, Mithen 1990, Vermeersch and Van Peer 1990, Fischer 1995a, Larsson 1996, Zvelebil et al. 1998a, Larsson et al. 2003, Fischer and Kristiansen 2002, Dolukhanov, Sarson, and Shukurov 2009, McCartan et al. 2009) and journal overviews (Nygaard 1989, Larsson 1990b, Zvelebil and Dolukhanov 1991, Knutsson, 2004, Lovis et al. 2006). Regional overviews covering the Mesolithic are written mostly in local languages (e.g., Zalizniak 1989, Baudou 1992, Larsson and Olsson 1997, Zhilin 2001, Sulgustowska 2005,

* Department of Archaeology and Prehistory, University of Sheffield, UK.

Kriiska and Tvauri 2007), although some are written in English (Dolukhanov 1979, Malinowski 1986, Bogucki 1988, Halén 1994, Åkerlund 1996, Zalizniak 1997, Fischer and Kristiansen 2002, Samuelson and Ytterberg 2003, Andersson et al. 2004, Larsson 2005).

Environmental Background

The Baltic basin is a lowland region of rivers, lakes, and marshes, the landscape of which has been shaped by processes of deglaciation, isostatic uplift, and eustatic changes in sea level. In the centre of the area lies the Baltic Sea with the two large gulfs of Finland and Bothnia, the major islands of Bronholm, Öland, Åland, Gotland, and Saarema, and numerous smaller islands. Today, the area is shared by Sweden, Poland, the East Baltic countries – Lithuania, Latvia, and Estonia – Russia and Finland (Figures 2.1, 2.2).

During the late Pleistocene, this area was mostly buried under the Scandinavian glacier. As the ice melted with deglaciation, the sea first flooded the low-lying areas in peninsular Scandinavia, Latvia, Estonia, and Finland; but isostatic rebound of the landmass freed of ice followed, resulting in an overall emergence of the land over time. Only along the southern shores of the Baltic and in parts of southern Scandinavia the eustatic rise in sea level outpaced isostatic rebound and land dry during the late Palaeolithic was flooded by the sea in the early part of the Holocene. These processes resulted in unstable and changing shorelines throughout the region. The stages of development in the Baltic Sea basin are marked by five different environments: the Late Glacial Ice Dammed Lake (until about 10,000 BP), the Yoldia Sea (10,000–9400 BP), the Ancylus fresh/brackish water lake (9400–8000 BP), the transgressive Littorina Sea (8000–4500 BP) and the current Baltic (Limaea) sea (Clark 1976, Siiriäinen 1974, Eronen 1975, Morner 1979, Björck 1995, Matiskainen 1996, Hyvärinen 2000, Kriisska 2003, Rankama 2003, Sulgustowska 2003, Riede 2009 for broader discussion, see also Strauss et al. 1996, Larsson et al. 2003, Gamble et al. 2005, McCartan et al. 2009).

The beginning of the Postglacial was marked by a rapid rise in temperature by 5 to 6 degrees C to a July mean of approximately 15 degrees C (Blankholm and Dolukhanov this volume). Climatic amelioration peaked during the Climatic Optimum of the Atlantic period (c. 8000–5000 BP), when July mean temperatures reached twenty-one degrees C. The introduction of farming, marking the conventional end of the Mesolithic period, began around 5000 BP, just as the temperatures began to decline to current mean July levels of sixteen degrees C.

Climatic changes facilitated changes in the biome, particularly in more northerly regions. In outline, the forest succession and the associated faunal changes were marked by the predominance of birch and pine in the Preboreal period (10,300–9500/9300 BP), pine and hazel in the Boreal (9500/9300–8000/7500 BP), mixed oak forest of elm, oak, lime, and beech in the Atlantic (8000–5000/4500 BP), and a more mixed broadleaved-conifer forest in the cooler, more arid Subboreal period (c. 5000/4500–2500 BP). The last was marked by the disappearance of elm, reduction in the presence of warm-loving species and in their contraction southwards, in the development of raised bogs over previously more productive wetlands, and in the colonisation of many eastern parts of the circum-Baltic area by spruce forests (Berglund 1969, Clark 1975, Dolukhanov 1979, 1998a, Jonsson 1995, Sandgren 2000, Rankama 2003).

In terms of terrestrial food resources, these changes meant a shift from more open, reindeer inhabited landscapes of the Late Glacial/Early Postglacial, to boreal fauna dominated by elk, beaver, bear, and fur-bearing game. During the Atlantic, the more temperate fauna of broadleaved woodlands included wild pig, red and roe deer, wild cattle, and, in the eastern Baltic, wild horse, in addition

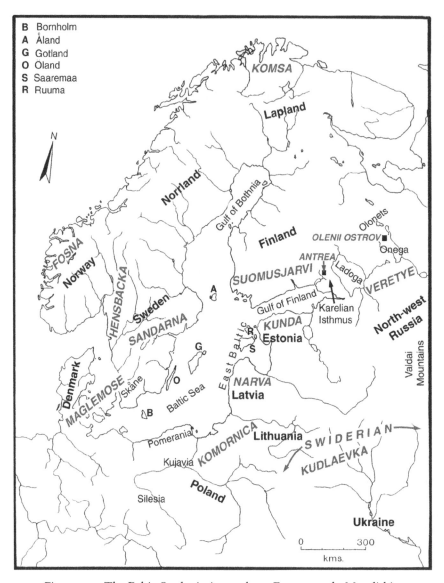

B Bornholm
A Åland
G Gotland
O Öland
S Saaremaa
R Ruuma

Figure 2.1. The Baltic Sea basin in northern Europe: early Mesolithic.

to elk and fur game. In northern parts of the Baltic Sea basin (Norrland, Finland, Karelia) boreal woodland prevailed throughout and boreal fauna remained dominant. For aquatic resources, the main trends were the gradual colonisation of developing aquatic environments by an increasingly broader range of marine and anadromous fish and different species of seal, and fluctuations in resources such as shellfish or anadromous fish in response to changing water temperature and salinity during different stages in the development of the Baltic Sea basin (Forsten and Alhonen 1975, Rowley-Conwy 1983, 2001, Lepiksaar 1986, Fischer 1995a, Lõugas 1997, Hyvärinen 2000). In aggregate, these developments indicate an increasingly rich and varied resource environment

B Bornholm
A Åland
G Gotland
O Öland
S Saaremaa
R Ruuma

Figure 2.2. The Baltic Sea basin in northern Europe: late Mesolithic.

peaking in the Atlantic and early Subboreal period, covering the period from about 8000 to 4000 BP (Paaver 1965, Zvelebil 1981, 1985, Sandgren 2000, Dolukhanov this volume).

Located mostly between 55 degrees and 70 degrees North, circum-Baltic Europe is marked by strong seasonal regimes, with the type and quantity of resources varying from season to season. Much of this variation is a result of the migratory nature of many aquatic food resources, such as waterfowl, eel, salmon, and some seals. The pattern of migrations means that some species are available in abundance for a brief period of the year, principally in the spring and autumn. Between these peaks in potential food supply, people had to rely on less mobile and often more dispersed food resources.

The distribution of food resources also varied from region to region. The presence of the Gulf Stream substantially increased the productivity of the coastal regions along the North Atlantic seaboard. Inland resources concentrated in lacustrine, riverine, or estuarine habitats created by the process of deglaciation and changes in the sea (Somme 1968, Dolukhanov 1979, Zvelebil 1981, Siiriäinen 1981, 1982, Rowley-Conwy 1983, Nuñez 1997). In contrast, the interior regions without many shoreline habitats – mostly moraine uplands, glacial outwash plains, and river basins covered by gravel, sand, and clay – were relatively poor in natural resources.

Thus, Postglacial conditions in northern Europe were marked by an uneven distribution of resources both over the seasons and in space. For hunter-gatherer societies, the implications were twofold: on the one hand, seasonal and longer-term fluctuations increased survival risks in that people had to find their regular food supply from fluctuating resources; on the other hand, effective exploitation of seasonally concentrated food resources could generate a food surplus and raise the population capacity of the area.

The Colonisation of Northern Europe

Colonisation and settlement of northern Europe is one of the key events in the history of hunter-gatherer communities of the region. During the Last Glacial Maximum (c. 22,000–18,000 BP), the whole region was covered by the Scandinavian glacier. By 18,000–16,000 BP, improved climatic conditions were causing ice sheets to melt and exposing new land for colonisation by plants, animals, and humans. It took some four thousand years for the retreating ice to reach the southern margin of peninsular Scandinavia, where it lingered for a further two thousand years (Larssen 1996, Matiskainen 1996, Nuñez 1997, Dolukhanov 1998a). It was at this time that human groups from surrounding regions began to penetrate the ice-free margins of Fennoscandia, their routes highly dependent on water and ice barriers in their path (Figure 2.3). This process of colonisation was gradual and time-transgressive, laying foundations for major patterns in the cultural diversity of northern Europe during the Mesolithic.

The people who were settling the ice-free margins of Fennoscandia between 12,500 and 9500 BP can be divided into two broad cultural traditions (Matiskainen 1996, Nuñez 1997, Wiik 2002a, 2002b, Dolukhanov 1998a), in the west and the east, respectively (Figure 2.3).

Communities of the western tradition, derived ultimately from the Magdalenian culture, penetrated southern Scandinavia by 12,500 BP at the latest (Burdkiewicz 1986, 1996, Fischer 1991, B. Eriksen 1996, Bratlund 1996, Housley et al. 1997, Eriksen and Bratlund 2002, Gamble et al. 2005) and used it as a staging post for further expansion into Scania and central Sweden, as well as moving along the ice-free corridor along the Norwegian coast towards the north. They reached Norway's northernmost Atlantic coast between 10,300 and 9600 BP, and went on to settle parts of Lapland from there (Knutsson 1993, Björck 1995, Larssen 1996, Thommessen 1996, Matiskainen 1996, Nuñez 1997, Bjerck this volume). The northern part of Sweden (Norrland) was settled between 10,600 and 9400 BP, shortly after deglaciation and probably from the Trondheim area of coastal Norway by the bearers of the Komsa culture (Knutsson 1993, Forsberg 1996). Originally reindeer hunters, these communities turned increasingly to fishing and sea hunting as they colonised the ice-free margins of peninsular Scandinavia (Clark 1976, Schmitt 1995, Jonsson 1995, Petersen and Johansen 1996, Bjerck 1995, Bjerck this volume, Kindgren 1996, Åkerlund 1996; but see Fischer 1996, who argues for a strong maritime orientation in the late Palaeolithic as well). The material culture of these people was characterised by various tanged point assemblages, flake axes, unifacial bi- or unipolar cores, 'Lyngby' reindeer antler axes and microburins; from 9500 to

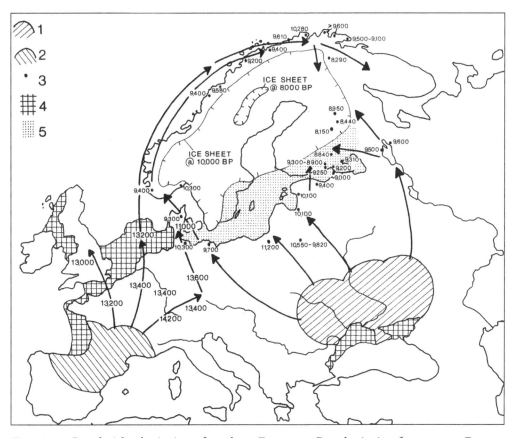

Figure 2.3. Postglacial colonisation of northern Europe. 1. Recolonisation from eastern Europe. 2. Recolonisation from southwest Europe. 3. First regional settlement. 4. Late Glacial coastlines. 5. Yoldia Sea.

9000 BP, microblade technology, conical microblade cores, 'handle cores' and Sandarna and other core axes took over. The chipped stone industry was augmented by the development of ground stone and semipolished axes, antler and bone harpoons, leisters, and fishhooks. Various regional names are given to this early Mesolithic cultural tradition, including Hensbacka in Sweden, Fosna in southern Norway, and Komsa in northern Norway and Finnmark (Nygaard 1989, Fischer 1991, 1996, Bjerck 1995, Bjerck this volume, Schmitt 1995, Forsberg 1996, Larsson et al. 2003, Rankama 2003).

Communities of the eastern tradition occupied the southern (Swiderian culture, Kozlowski 1989) and eastern (tanged point cultures, Zhilin 1996) areas to the south of the ice margin in eastern Poland, Byelorussia, and northwest Russia at the end of the last glaciation. In central Europe, they came into contact with people of the Magdalenian tradition expanding from the west (Oliva 2005, Poltowicz 2006). From these areas, people penetrated at first the East Baltic (Rimantiené 1971, Kozlowski 1989, Martin 1995, Dolukhanov 1998b, Zhilin 1996, Zagorska 1999, Kriiska 2003, Sulgustowska 2003), and the Karelian Isthmus by about 9500 BP, then went on to colonise Finland, reaching the coast of the Bothian Gulf, as it then was, between 8500 and 7500 BP (Figure 2.3), Clark 1975, Matiskainen 1996, Nuñez 1997, Dolukhanov 1998b, Sulgustowska,

23

2003, Rankama 2004, Takala 2005). In a process analogous to developments in the west, the end of the Swiderian culture 9500–9000 BP marks the transition from an open-country reindeer-hunting culture to more broad-based communities exploiting resources of forest, lake, and sea. One of the earliest fishing nets anywhere, produced by people of this tradition, was found at Antrea on the Karelian Isthmus and dated to 9300–9200 BP (Clark 1975, Matiskainen 1996). Regional variants of this early Mesolithic cultural tradition include the Komornica culture in northeast Poland, Kudlaevka in Belorussia, Narva in Latvia, Kunda in Estonia, Veretye in northwest Russia, and Suomusjärvi in Finland. Swiderian artefacts included double-platformed cores, tanged points, Lyngby-type antler axes, and single-barbed harpoons; in post-Swiderian times, there was a trend towards microlithisation, the development of a ground and polished axe element and an antler point industry, the appearance of bone pin-shaped points (Clark's type 16, Clark 1936) and of slotted bone points, an increase in backed pieces and microretouched bladelets, and the gradual disappearance of tanged points (Jaanits 1966, Kozlowski 1989, Martin 1995, Matiskainen 1996, Schild 1996, Sulgustowska 1996, 1998, Zhilin 1996).

In considering radiocarbon evidence for recolonisation of northern Europe, Housley et al. (1997: 50) have noted that 'the accent of research must now be on the process rather than the event which produced the newest old Europeans . . . .' But there are relatively few studies of this major colonisation process and of the consequent culture change as a whole. Housley et al. (1997) make a useful distinction between the pioneer and residential phases of the recolonisation process, the first marked by temporary and seasonal exploration of the new territory from bases further south, the second by the establishment of permanent residential settlements in the new regions (Gamble et al. 2005). The time lag between the two phases on the North European plain was about four hundred to six hundred years (Gamble et al. 2005). According to this scenario, then, the southern Baltic region (northern Germany, northern Poland and Denmark) experienced the pioneer phase between 13,200 BP and 12,400 BP, after which the residential phase began. The shift from the pioneer to the residential phase was made possible by the increase in diversity of food resources, marked here by the addition of horse and bovids (and later elk too; Fischer 1991) to a reindeer-dominated community, 'which made a seasonal round possible within rather than between regions' (Housley et al. 1997: 46, but see also Blockley et al. 2000).

The colonisation process must have produced specific social situations with specific archaeological signatures. Social aspects of the process would have included small population densities, rapid population growth, population dispersal, and rapid culture change. These social conditions seem to be reflected in settlement patterns, technology, and the use of raw material (Fischer 1991, Housley et al. 1997: 49, table 4, Riede 2009). Housley et al. note that the pioneer phase is marked by the exploitation of a single species, usually reindeer, small size of sites, temporary settlement marked by open-air hearths and tents, paucity of symbolic expression, and the presence of predominantly male burials in informal locations such as caves. The residential phase marks the establishment of larger, more permanent settlements, greater resource diversity, multiseasonal occupation, increase in symbolic behaviour, and the development of formal burial areas including both sexes. In lithic technology, the pioneer phase was marked by simplicity and by opportunist use of raw materials. Fischer (1991) notes that the first people in southern Scandinavia had only three types of retouched tools, and the blade technology was simpler in terms of technical refinement than during other periods, the detachment of blades being carried out by hard hammer and direct percussion. The unifacial cores of this period also reflect the simplicity of the technology. This highly wasteful method of blade production can be explained as a response to the abundance of flint in the recently deglaciated areas of southern Scandinavia (Fischer 1991) and more generally along the southern rim of the Baltic Sea.

The pioneer situation marked by abundant resources and rapid population dispersal is also reflected in the areas to the north and east, although in different ways. Here, the colonisation process seems to have been even more rapid than on the North European Plain, with people utilising landscapes very close to the ice margin (Forsberg 1996). The speed of colonisation was so rapid as to be virtually simultaneous in radiocarbon years along the entire coast of Norway (Bjerck 1995, Bjerck this volume, Forsberg 1996), whereas in the east the distance between the East Baltic coast and northern Finland was covered in less than one thousand years (Figure 2.3, Matiskainen 1996, Nuñez 1997, Rankama). This was not merely because of improved climatic conditions in the early Holocene: the development of a technologically complex and effective use of aquatic resources (sea mammals, fish and water birds) also allowed the Early Postglacial hunter-fishers to break through ecological barriers posed by large bodies of water (marshes, lakes, seas, and rivers) and turn them to their advantage as transport routes and as sources of food.

Describing the first settlement of peninsular Scandinavia, Bjerck (1995: 140) notes that 'The Fosna culture represents the true pioneer settlement in Norway.' Along with the cognate Hensbacka groups in western Sweden, and Komsa communities in northern Norway, these people are credited with developing technologies for the effective exploitation of marine and other aquatic resources, an 'arctic marine economy' (Bjerck 1995: 141, Bjerck this volume; see also Schmitt 1995), even though they also hunted reindeer in the interior. Only seafaring boats could make such a rapid expansion possible along the mountainous coastline of western Scandinavia. It is possible to trace the routes adopted and cultural changes associated with this process of colonisation in some regions. To begin with, intraregional similarities in cultural repertoire are 'almost total' (Fischer 1996: 166) in the earliest phase of the colonisation, as, for example, among Ahrensburg, Fosna, and Hensbacka culture groups in South Scandinavia, West Sweden, and south Norway. The routes and direction of settlement are often marked by the use of imported technology and lithic materials. For example, exotic grey flint artefacts of the earliest inland settlements of northern Sweden were brought from the Trondelag area of coastal Norway (Forsberg 1996). In the later 'residential' phase, similarities in artefact style and technology gradually diminished, and in northern regions of Scandinavia, flint was gradually replaced by local materials such as quartz, quartzite, and slate (Fischer 1996, Forsberg 1996).

In the East Baltic, northwest Russia and Finland the colonisation process is marked by similar developments, although they have not been comprehensively investigated so far. Even so, the presence of 'ephemeral' and temporary settlements, transfer of exotic raw materials, interregional similarities in lithic technology within the broader tanged-point and later the Mesolithic Kunda/Suomusjärvi tradition are all key features of the colonisation process (Kozlowski 1989, Matiskainen 1996, Kriiska 2003, Sulgustowska 2003, Kriiska and Tvauri 2007). They show that similar processes of human colonisation and settlement were at play in both eastern and western parts of the Baltic basin. The more specific social and cultural changes associated with these processes are a subject that merits further rigorous investigation.

Genetic and Linguistic Patterns

Archaeological evidence of similarities in material culture is not in itself a reliable guide to human migration patterns, and much new genetic and linguistic research has been carried out recently to cast new light on the provenance of the colonising populations. Most interpretations converge on the 'dual centre' model, referring to Franco-Iberia in the west and the modern Ukraine as centres of relatively high population density in the late Palaeolithic and the main sources for subsequent dispersal (Dolukhanov 1979, 1998b, Nuñez 1987, Otte 1990, Matiskainen 1996). Thus, according to one point of view, the western colonisation route may reflect the dispersal of non-Indo-European populations, whose nearest surviving relatives are the Basques, the eastern route with Uralic and Proto-Finnic speakers (e.g., Dolukhanov 1998b, 2000, Wiik 1997, 1999, 2000, 2002a, 2002b, Balanovsky 2009, Dolukhanov, Sarson, and Shukhurov 2009).

Genetic evidence, in the main, includes mitochondrial, Y-chromosomal, and classical marker evidence derived from modern populations. Recently, it has become possible to extract mtDNA (passed intergenerationally in the maternal line only) from individuals dated to the Mesolithic and early Neolithic (Haak et al. 2005, 2008, Bramanti et al. 2009). The emerging picture emphasizes the existence of three genetically distinct populations: Mesolithic communities with clear genetic links to the earlier Palaeolithic populations, Neolithic populations showing a genetic contribution of 15–30 percent from incoming farming groups from the Near East/Anatolia, and a present population genetic profile of Europe, that, on the whole, was principally constituted by the late glacial and early postglacial recolonizations from the Franco-Cantabrian region of southwest Europe and from the north Pontic region of modern Ukraine (Richards et al. 1996, 1998, Gamble et al. 2006, Kracmarova et al. 2006, Zvelebil and Pettit 2006). The modern composition of the European gene pool, then, appears to reflect mainly the early colonising movements rather than any other demographic event in prehistory (Torroni et al. 1998, 1149). According to Richards et al. (1996, 1998), around 85 percent of European mitochondrial sequences probably originated in the Upper Palaeolithic of Europe (see also Tambets et al. 2000, Villems et al. 2002, Gamble et al. 2005, 2006, Soares et al. 2009).

The Baltic region, lying between these two geographical centres, could have been colonised initially from the west and the east, no doubt with subsequent contact and mixing of population. A number of linguists and archaeologists regard the Ukrainian centre as the original homeland of people ancestral to Finno-Ugric speakers, who moved into Finland from eastern Europe in the initial process of colonisation (Matiskainen 1996, Nuñez 1997, Wiik 1997, 1999, 2000, 2002a, 2002b, for broader discussion see Dolukhanov, Sarson, and Shukhurov 2009). Other evidence suggests a strong western connection. A key haplotype in the mitochondrial DNA, which is passed on in the female line only, is haplotype V. This shows the highest modern concentration in northern Iberia and southwest France and among the Saami populations in northern Finland, suggesting a 'major late Palaeolithic population expansion from south-western to north-eastern Europe' (Torroni et al. 1998, 1137). This could be via the Scandinavian Atlantic coast into northern Finland and Karelia (Figure 2.3), and is supported archaeologically by the presence in northern Finland of technological traits of western tradition, such as handle cores (see Knutsson 1993, Forsberg 1996, Matiskainen 1996). Others have questioned the reliability of haplogroup V as a marker of late Palaeolithic migration and suggested instead that its frequency may rather reflect genetic drift in small and isolated populations (Izagirre and de la Rua 1999). Nevertheless, the western dispersal route is reinforced further by the distribution of haplotype 15 on the Y-chromosome (passed in the male line only) (Gamble et al. 2005). Other genetic markers suggest a mixed ancestry for Saami and Finnish populations, strongly differentiated along gender lines, suggesting a record of incremental palimpsest of long-term, small-scale gene exchanges, with genes in the male line representing circum-Uralic and circumpolar migrations of small groups of males of Uralic provenance joining, over time, resident females whose ancestry goes back to the original settlement of northern Europe (for further discussion, see Niskanen 1998, Tambets et al. 2000, Künnap 2000, Villems 1998, 2002, Villems et al. 2000, Gamble et al. 2005, 2006).

Alone, neither archaeological nor genetic evidence can shed much light on the linguistic identity or ethnicity of the colonising populations, although when combined together, some suggestions can be made. It is generally assumed that the western populations were either pre-Indo-European (with Basques being the surviving isolate), or proto-Indo-European, setting the stage for north-central Europe as the homeland of Indo-Europeans. Populations moving from the eastern centre in the Ukraine and the Urals are sometimes associated with the Uralic, or Proto-Finnic speakers (see Julku 1997, 2002, Nuñez 1997, Dolukhanov 1998b, Wiik 2000, 2002, Künnap 2000 for recent summaries). This is intriguing. If the original populations in the Upper Palaeolithic of Western Europe were non-Indo-European, and those in Eastern Europe were Uralic-speaking, then this implies that the entire Mesolithic population in the eastern part of Europe was also Uralic/Finno-Ugric speaking at this time. Large sections of this population in northern Europe would have to adopt Indo-European speech subsequently from Indo-European farming groups penetrating Central Europe from the Near East and the East Mediterranean as suggested by Renfrew (1987), and modified for temperate and northern Europe (Zvelebil 1995a, Wiik 1997, 1999, 2000, 2002a, 2002b). All these hypotheses, however, remain speculative until a carefully considered combination of archaeological, genetic, and linguistic data is brought to bear on them in a methodologically sophisticated assessment.

Later Developments

From the initial colonisation episode, we can trace the development and florescence of Mesolithic, hunter-gatherer communities over the following eight thousand years. It is generally agreed that these communities were characterised by technological, economic, and social complexity, effective use of resources, greater sedentism and relatively high population densities, more so than in other parts of Europe (Paludan-Muller 1978, Price 1985, 1987, Rowley-Conwy 1983, 1999, but see also Rowley-Conwy 2001, Zvelebil and Rowley-Conwy 1986, Renouf 1988, L. Larsson 1990b, Andersen 1995, Fischer 1995a, Zvelebil 1997, Janik 1998, Karsten and Knarrström 2001, Larsson et al. 2003, McCartan et al. 2009, Blankholm this volume). The evidence for such forms of complexity, for the operational structure of these logistic, residentially more permanent hunter-gatherers, as well as the chronology of these developments, comes mostly from coastal southern Scandinavia. This has led to some suggestions that this area represented an exception even within the broader region of southern Scandinavia, that such complexity is overemphasised by excessive focus on the coastal settlement of the later Mesolithic, disregarding the evidence of earlier sub-merged coastlines and settlement patterns inland, or that 'complexity' is too vague a term, and one with social-evolutionary overtones, to be of any use (Rowley-Conwy 1999, 2001, Warren 2005a). Although this may be partly true, a closer look reveals that enduring patterns of residential permanence and socioeconomic complexity were displayed regionally throughout the Baltic.

Using southern Scandinavia as a frame of reference, the chronology of the Mesolithic can be broadly divided into the Early and Late Mesolithic (Table 2.1). The transformation of the early Mesolithic Maglemose culture to late Mesolithic Kongemose and Ertebølle cultures marks the division in southern Scandinavia at c. 8000 BP. Cultural groups cognate with the Maglemose operated in the eastern parts of the Baltic (Komornice in northwest Poland, Neman in northeast Poland, Neman, Narva, and Kunda in East Baltic, Sandarna in southern Sweden, and Suomusjärvi in Finland). Salient features of the technological equipment include a developed bone and antler industry, core and flake axes, and microblade/microlith technology, which decreased in use from west to east, where the older tanged point technology prevailed within traditions such as the Kunda in Estonia (Table 2.1).

Table 2.1. Regional chronologies

BP	12,000	11,000	10,000	9000	8000	7000	6000	5000	4000	3000	2000
Cal BC	11,900	10,970	9530	8250	6940	5910	4890	3780	3580	1250	0
DENMARK											
Ahrensburg		Δ									
Maglemose			Δ								
Early Kongemose					Δ						
Late Kongemose						Δ					
Early Ertebølle						Δ					
Late Ertebølle							Δ				
Middle Ertebølle							Δ				
Funnel Beaker/ Neolithic								Δ			
Battle Axe – M Neolithic – L								Δ			
Bronze Age									Δ		
Iron Age									Δ		
Vedbæk								○			
S SWEDEN											
Skateholm								○			
Kams						○					
Tågerup					○						
N SWEDEN											
Namforsen									○		
NORTH POLAND/ SOUTH BALTIC											
Komornica			Δ								
Chojnice-Pienki						Δ					
Early Neo/TRB						Δ					
Jasnislawice							○				
Dudka						○					
Narva						Δ					
Kunda			Δ								
Kretuonas									○		
Abora									○		
Zvejnieki							○				
Sārnate						○					
Duokalnis						○					
Žemaitiške							○		○		
Šventoji									○		
NORTH RUSSIA											
Olenii Ostrov					●						
Antrea			○								
FINLAND											
Suomusjärvi			Δ								
Kierikki									○		
Hartikka											

For correspondence between uncalibrated and calibrated dates, see Appendix.

Δ Start dates for cultures
○ Sites with a dating range
● Cluster date for Olenii Ostrov

28

The beginning of the late Mesolithic at about 8000 BP is marked by the introduction of broader rhombic and trapezoidal microliths, a shift from microblade to core and blade technology and a number of regionally specific new items (Table 2.1). At a later stage, marking the beginning of the Ertebølle culture in Denmark and Scania at c. 6500 BP, transverse arrowheads, trimmed core axes, and T-shaped antler axes appear. Regional groupings include Kongemose and Ertebølle in Scania, late Suomusjärvi (Litorina Suomusjärvi, Matiskainen 1989) in Finland, Chojnice-Pienki in northwest Poland, Janislawice in northeast Poland, late Neman, Narva, and Kunda in the East Baltic, and Lihult in southern Sweden.

The introduction of ceramics into this cultural context marks the beginning of another phase in the prehistory of hunter-gatherers in northern Europe (Zvelebil 1986a: 171, fig. 4). It is becoming increasingly clear that ceramics were first introduced into the area from the east at an earlier date than previously thought, possibly originating in China, where they are now dated to the Late Palaeolithic (Zhao and Wu 2000, Jordan and Zvelebil 2009). Either the Volga-Ural interfluve, where the earliest ceramics are now dated to c. 9000 BP, or the Upper Volga Basin (with earliest dates at 7300 BP) may have served as source areas for the East Baltic, where the first pottery appears by 6500 BP (Rimantiené 1980, Cyrek et al. 1986, Kempisty 1986, Timofeev 1987, 1996, 1998b, Nuñez 1990, Dolukhanov et al. 2009, Jordan and Zvelebil 2009, Dolukhanov this volume).

In southern Scandinavia, ceramic-using hunter-gatherers are still regarded as Ertebølle and 'Mesolithic' (as little else has changed in cultural repertoire), but in Finland, Suomusjärvi is succeeded by Combed Ware 'Neolithic', whereas in the East Baltic the addition of ceramics to the existing cultural assemblages ushers in the 'Forest Neolithic'. In keeping with long-established tradition in Russian and Soviet research terminology, the term Neolithic is used here solely in its technological sense (i.e., the introduction of ceramics) rather than in an economic one (i.e., introduction of agro-pastoral farming). The pottery-using communities of northern Europe continued to manage their indigenous undomesticated resources through hunting, fishing, and gathering, with the addition of locally developed practices of resource management that may have led to taming but not full (i.e., biological) domestication of some resources (see later). In this sense, the 'Combed Ware Neolithic' and 'Forest Neolithic' cultures of eastern and northeast Europe are comparable to the better-known Ertebølle and related culture units of southern Scandinavia, north Germany and the Netherlands (e.g., Kooijmans 1993, Kooijmans 2001, Raemakers 1999, Blankholm this volume, Verhart this volume). The introduction into this cultural context of imported domestic plants and animals – cattle, sheep, goat, pig, horse, pulses, and cereals – occurred very gradually from the south, mostly during the last 5000 years (Table 2.1).

Mesolithic Society: Subsistence and Land Use

Economic and Technological Strategies

In northern circum–Baltic Europe, characteristically variable spatial and seasonal distribution of natural resources elicited a *dual* technological and economic response, comprising strategies of *diversification* and *specialisation* (Torrence 1983, Zvelebil 1985, 1986a, 1986b, 1997, Vierra 1992; see also Jochim this volume). Economic diversification consisted of encounter foraging of a wide range of resources. This practice is reflected in the faunal evidence by the 'broad spectrum' of food remains characteristic of the Mesolithic since the early Maglemosian period in southern Scandinavia and equivalents elsewhere.

Economic specialisation consisted of interception of seasonally aggregated migratory resources, especially sea mammals, seal in particular, anadromous fish; waterfowl, fur-bearing animals, and reindeer in the north. This activity was often carried out from seasonal aggregation sites or specialised exploitation camps, where the majority of faunal remains belong to a single species, as, for example, waterfowl at Narva-Riigikula (Gurina 1966), fish at Dudica, northeast Poland (Gumiński 1998, Gumiński and Michniewicz 2003 or Tlokono, northeast Poland (Schild et al. 2003), seals at Konnu, Kopu, Loona, and Naakamäe in Estonia (Paaver 1965, Zvelebil 1989, Jaanits 1995), and Alträsket in Sweden (Halén 1994). Economic specialisation also has been recorded in Denmark (Rowley-Conwy 1983, Rowley-Conwy 1999, Andersen 1995, 2009, Blankholm this volume), in eastern Sweden (e.g., Welinder 1975, 1977, 1981a), southwest Sweden (Wigforss 1995) and in coastal Finland (Forsten 1972, Zvelebil 1978, 1981, Siiriäinen 1981, Siiriäinen 1982, Matiskainen 1989).

Recent analyses of dietary patterns using isotopic nitrogen and carbon in human bone show that in many coastal areas people tended to specialise in marine resources from the early Mesolithic onwards (the earliest samples date to 9100 BP) – for example, in Denmark (Tauber 1981, Tauber 1983, Price 1989, Blankholm this volume), Skåne (Karsten and Knarrström 2001), southwest Sweden (Nordquist 1995, 192–3), Åland (Nuñez and Liden 1997), Gotland (Lindqvist and Possnert 1999, Rowley-Conwy 1999), Estonia (Lõugas et al. 1995), Latvia (Eriksson 2003), and Lithuania (Antanaitis 2001, Antanaitis and Ogrinc 2000). Those individuals living (and dying) inland, depended largely on terrestrial resources – in Skåne (Karsten and Knarrström 2001), southwest Sweden (Nordquist 1995), the East Baltic (Lõugas et al. 1995, Zagorska and Lõugas 2000: 230, Antanaitis 2001, Eriksson 2003, Eriksson et al. 2003), but often including large amounts of fish (Lõugas et al. 1995, Antanaitis 2001) – a dietary pattern common in inland northern and eastern Europe (Meiklejohn and Zvelebil 1991, Lillie 1997). The coastal-inland dietary differentiation becomes more marked with time (Lõugas et al. 1995, Antanaitis 2001, but see also Milner et al. 2004). If this preliminary pattern is supported by more comprehensive analysis, then we have a remarkable pattern of two different dietary traditions emerging in coastal and inland areas between 8000 and 4000 BP.

Duality of economic practice was linked to differences in technology. The diversified strategy was served by multicomponent, maintainable tools consisting of bone or antler shafts – probably curated in advance of use – and versatile microliths, which formed the expedient components that could easily be replaced. The microliths, then, can be seen at least partly as the archaeological signature of a technology developed to meet the demands of a generalised use of resources under *resource-stress*. The microlithic component tends to dominate on sites interpreted as hunting stands or kill sites, where hunting of a wide range of (usually terrestrial) game went on and hunting weapons had to be re-tooled rapidly as the situation demanded (e.g., Wigforss 1995: 203).

Economic specialisation, on the other hand, was served by highly efficient, specialised tools, curated in advance of use and designed with some redundancy to ensure reliability and maximum efficiency in the exploitation of seasonal resources under *time-stress* (Bleed 1986; see also Jochim this volume). Capture facilities such as fish weirs, dams, nets, and traps, as well as antler and bone tool types such as harpoons, serrated points, fish hooks, and bird darts, serve as archaeological signatures of this technology. Such technology was most commonly employed in connection with fishing, fowling, marine hunting, and plant gathering, activities occurring mostly in lowlands, wetlands, and along the shores of rivers, lakes, and the sea coast (e.g., Andersen 1995, 2009, Wigforss 1995: 203, Rowley-Conwy 1999, Larsson et al. 2003, McCartan et al. 2009).

While hunter-gatherer communities appear to have employed both strategies concurrently from the onset of the Mesolithic, specialised strategies increased in relation to diversified ones as time went on: a feature evident in the faunal record from c. 8000 BP in the west and from c. 7000 BP in the East Baltic, and reflected, probably, in the relative decline of microlithic technology towards the end of the Mesolithic.

Resource Exploitation and Husbandry

Within such a system of economic organisation defined by the practice of hunting, fishing, and gathering, subsistence strategies may have developed that included elements of resource management or husbandry, and that together produced an alternative to the agro-pastoral farming characteristic of the Neolithic. In northern and temperate Europe, there are indications that such an integrated system operated to varying degrees in some regions and that it was based to a large extent on the intensive use of aquatic resources, plant foods, and wild pig.

There is little doubt that fishing, fowling, and specialised hunting of sea mammals formed an important element of the economy among the late Mesolithic and Neolithic communities in many coastal zones of Northern Europe (Clark 1952, Mellars 1978, Rowley-Conwy 1983, 1999, Zvelebil 1986c, Matiskainen 1989, Andersen 1995). The distribution of fish weirs, fish traps, and nets in the Baltic Sea basin shows that the employment of delayed-capture facilities was a common practice, at least in the late Mesolithic, although fish nets had already been in use since the early Mesolithic (Clark 1975, Gramsch 1981, Burov 1989, Gramsch and Kloss 1989, Andersen 1995: 63, Pedersen 1995, Rowley-Conwy 1999). The fishing/sea hunting tool kits also included equipment for more individual hunting by fishhook, fish spear (leister), and harpoon. Remains of boats and paddles are common on sites with good preservation of organic materials (e.g., Clark 1975, Burov 1989, Gramsch and Kloss 1989: 322, Fischer 1995a). The development of specialised fishing, sealing, and fowling finds confirmation in faunal remains from a number of sites in Scandinavia and Eastern Europe (Paaver 1965, Forsten 1972, Forsten and Blomquist 1974, Forsten and Alhonen 1975, Welinder 1975, 1977, 1981a, Dolukhanov 1979, Siiriäinen 1981, Zvelebil 1981, 1985, Jonsson 1982, 1995, Rowley-Conwy 1983, Enghoff 1995, Lõugas 1997, Antanaitis 2001), pointing to the existence of a logistic system of resource procurement in the circum-Baltic zone (Rowley-Conwy and Zvelebil 1989, Rowley-Conwy 1999). Specialised exploitation of seal and other coastal resources increases in the late Mesolithic (after 8000 BP) and among ceramic-using hunter-gatherers. This is evident from faunal data, site locations (Welinder 1975, 1977, 1981a, Zvelebil 1981, Andersen 2009) and human dietary analyses (see earlier). Indeed, some workers have suggested that the adoption of ceramics facilitated in a major way the processing and storage of seal oil and so encouraged specialisation and trade (Siiriäinen 1981, 1982, Edgren 1982, Nuñez 1987, 1990, 1997, Matiskainen 1989, Jordan and Zvelebil 2009).

Recovery of plant remains depends on the seasonality of site occupation, preservation conditions, method of retrieval and sampling, and method of processing. Despite the biases against finding evidence for plant use introduced by these factors, the body of information on the use of wild plants in Mesolithic Europe is steadily growing (Clarke 1976, Zvelebil 1994, Antanaitis 2001).

Hazelnuts, water chestnuts, berries, roots, tubers, and leafy plants formed an important element in the diet and in food procurement strategies (Clarke 1976, Zvelebil 1994; for regional studies, see Vankina 1970, Rimantiené 1971, 1979, 1992, Gramsch and Kloss 1989, Wigforrs 1995, Loze 1998, Antanaitis et al. 2000, Antanaitis 2001). Moreover, in some areas such as southern and middle Sweden (Welinder 1989, Berglund 1991, Larsson et al. 1992, Larsson 2001), southern Finland (Vuorela 1972, 1976, 1998), Poland (Nowak 2001, Zvelebil et al. 1998a, Gumiński and Mickniewicz 2003), Lithuania (Antanaitis et al. 2000, Antanaitis 2001) and eastern Latvia (Loze and Yakubovkaya 1982, Loze 1998), palynological evidence for burning and clearance phases is too extensive to be explained by acts of nature alone. A good case can be made for deliberate forest clearance and the maintenance of more open landscapes by late Mesolithic groups as part of a strategy to increase the productivity of nut and fruit trees, shrubs, wetland plants, and possibly native grasses (Bogucki 1988, Zvelebil 1994, 1998, Nowak 2001, Loze 1998).

Artefact evidence points to a widespread distribution of soil-working tools (hoes and antler mattocks) especially in lowland zones, which, together with the presence of reaping and grinding equipment, supports the argument for the existence of a specialised plant processing tool kit for digging, reaping, and plant processing (Rimantiené 1971, 1979, 1992, Zvelebil 1994, Loze 1998).

The variation in size of 'wild' pig bones in north temperate Europe has led to suggestions of local domestication (Jonsson 1986, Lindquist and Possnert unpublished manuscript). In the circum-Baltic region, this evidence is coeval with the increased reliance on pig as the main food resource, with selection for juvenile pigs, the introduction of pigs to islands such as Bronholm, Gotland, Saaremaa, and Ruuhaa, where they had to be transported across the sea by humans, and the increased residential permanence of the sites where pig bones are abundant. One possible explanation for these patterns is that pigs, initially attracted to human settlement as scavengers, came to be fed on surplus food waste arising from seasonal abundance of fish and seal and so regarded as 'storage on the hoof'. As I have argued elsewhere (Zvelebil 1995b), they may have been tamed and even though initially such pigs were not fully biologically domesticated but, rather, tamed in a behavioural sense, with feeding and restriction on movement leading to their greater predictability and productivity as a food resource, recent biomolecular evidence suggests that in some regions local domestication of pigs did take place. Larson et al. (2005) and Albarella et al. (2005, 2006) have shown that there were three local centres of pig domestication in Europe, one of which was located in temperate Central Europe, including the south Baltic area. If tamed and subjected to some form of herding or restriction of movement, this could have led to an increased rate of morphological change in the population (Zvelebil 1995b; but see Rowley-Conwy 1995, 2001, Dobney et al. 2004).

Settlement Patterns

As in southern Scandinavia (Paludan-Muller 1978, Rowley-Conwy 1983, Rowley-Conwy and Zvelebil 1989, Blankholm this volume), the practical use of the landscape includes several different settlement patterns (for regional studies, see, for example, Dolukhavov 1979, Loze 1979, Zvelebil 1981, Zvelebil 1987, Malinowski 1986, Renouf 1988, Baudou 1992, Larsson et al. 1992, 2003, Fischer 1995a, Girininkas 1998, Zvelebil et al. 1998a, Antanaitis 2001, Ramqvist 2002, McCartan et al. 2009). In broad terms, however, it is possible to distinguish two forms of spatial organisation throughout the Baltic region: a coastal pattern and an inland one (Figure 2.4). In coastal and lacustrine areas, the organisation of settlement involved the main village, and satellite camps for seasonal harvesting of resources exploited from the main settlement, together with transhumance to specialised exploitation sites and seasonal aggregation sites for trading, exchange, and ritual activities.

Tågerup, for example, represents one of the largest Stone Age settlements in Sweden. Situated on a sandy knoll at the confluence of two large streams close to the coastline, the site represents a classic location for a hunting-gathering village (Dolukhanov 1979, Zvelebil 1981, 1987, Andersen 1995, Fischer 1995a, Karsten and Knarrström 2001). Occupied from 8000 to 6500 BP (6800–5400 cal BC), the site is marked by a complex conglomeration of wooden stakes and poles, some serving as jetties and moorings for boats, remains of dwellings and of other structures such as thirteen fish

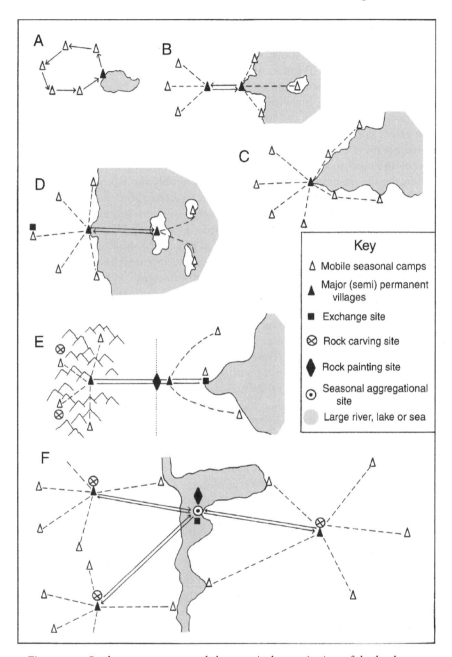

Figure 2.4. Settlement patterns and the practical organisation of the landscape.

baskets and a larger V-shaped fish trap. The largest house, dated to the middle of the Ertebølle culture, was about 15 m long and 6 m wide, with stone paving and postholes marking the house walls. Discarded or deposited artefacts include antler axes, arrow shafts, axe handles, antler blanks and partly made tools, burned tar torches, tooth pendants, wild boar tusks, needles, bone points, stone artefacts, and more than two tonnes of flint. About 100 m east of the settlement, a group

33

of five graves was excavated, the layout of which suggests this was a part of a larger cemetery extending beyond the limits of the excavation (Karsten and Knarrström 2001).

Kierikki, in northern Finland, is one among many so-called pit-house settlements in Finland (Matiskainen and Jussila 1984, Pesonen 1995, Karjailnen 1996, 1999, Raihala 1996, Nuñez and Uino 1998, Nuñez and Okkonen 1999), similar to those in northern Norway (Gjessing 1944, 1975, Simonsen 1975, Renouf 1988, Engelstad 1989) and Norrland (Halén 1994). In the Kierikki area alone, more than three hundred house floors have been found (Lehtienen pers. comm.), suggesting a dense settlement along the lower reaches of the Li River in an estuarine environment. The area had been in use between c. 4800 and 3800 BP (3600 and 2200 cal BC). At Kierikki, remains of thirty semisubterranean houses in a village-like arrangement were investigated. People almost certainly lived here during the six-month winter period, and probably throughout the year (Nuñez and Okkonen 1999). They engaged in long-distance trade, represented by a variety of exotic materials: amber, copper, flint, and greenstone and a new pottery form, characterised by large vessels, some over 100 litres in volume, made of asbestos-tempered clay and probably used in the production of seal oil. From about 5000 BP, stone cairns and large rectangular stone structures up to 50 m by 30 m, formed by stone embankments up to 1.5 m in height, appear at these settlements, suggesting ritual or an assembly place and an advanced level of organisational complexity. It seems that here, then, we are dealing with fairly sedentary hunter-gatherer communities involved in long-distance trade using the northern European marine coastal routes and extensive river network, reinforced by seal hunting and production of seal oil as a locally produced trading commodity.

Sārnate, located along the Baltic coast of Latvia, is representative of settlement along the East Baltic coast in the late Mesolithic and 'Forest Neolithic', c. 7000–4000 BP (Zvelebil 1987). Settlements are organised into a main settlement with satellite sites used for seasonal sealing and fishing, and other specialised camps. Similar estuarine locations are found in favourable coastal areas in Estonia: the Narva sites (Gurina 1956, 1966, Kriiska and Tvauri 2007, Kriiska 2009) and the Šventoji sites in Lithuania (Rimantiené 1979, Rimantiené 1992a, Rimantiené 1992b, Rimantiené 1998). Sārnate has been dated to the first half of the fifth millennium BP. The settlement consisted of log-constructed wooden houses, some with internal divisions and storage niches, with evidence of occupation in all seasons (Vankina 1970). The economy was entirely based on hunting (especially seal), fishing, and gathering. Large-scale processing of waterchestnut (*Trapa natans*) is evident from the presence of specialised toolkits (pounders, mallets), shell heaps, and storage deposits inside dwellings (Vankina 1970, Zvelebil 1987).

Abora is a settlement along the shores of lake Lubana in eastern Latvia, dated between 5200 and 3800 BP (Loze 1979, 1988, 1998). Similar hunting and gathering villages have been found along lakeshores in northeast Poland (Malinowski 1986, Timofeev 1990, 1998a, Larsson et al. 2003, McCartan et al. 2009), Lithuania, and northern Byelorussia (Miklyayev 1969, Dolukhanov 1979, 1986, Rimantiené 1979, 1992a, 1992b, 1998, Girininkas 1990, Antanaitis 2001, Dolukhanov, Lavento, and German 2009), elsewhere in Latvia (Zagorski 1987, Zagorska and Zagorskis 1989), Estonia (Jaanits 1959, 1970, 1975, 1984, Kriiska and Tvauri 2007, Kriiska 2009), and northwest Russia (Innostrantsev 1882, Dolukhanov 1979, Dolukhanov 1998b, Oshibkina 1982, 1989, Dolukhanov and Miklyayev 1986, Dolukhanov, Season, and Shukurov 2009, Dolukhanov, Lavento, and German 2009). As a rule, the cultural layers are associated with the most productive phase in the development of these lakeshore environments, marked by eutrophic fen or grassy peat deposits (Dolukhanov 1979, Zvelebil 1987). Like Abora, these settlements are characterised by substantial, elaborate wooden dwellings, often built on posts or wooden piles, with ridged roofs and overhanging eaves. Internally, the dwellings were subdivided into rooms, or single-roomed with add-on sheds, with bark floors and stone-lined or boxed-in hearths.

The size of dwellings ranged from 30 to 50 m². Large concentrations of material were found within the buildings, indicating fishing, hunting, and plant gathering, and possibly some form of cultivation. There is a difference of opinion over the extent of agro-pastoral farming (e.g., Loze 1998 contra Zvelebil 1987, Daugnora and Girininkas 1995, Dolukhanov 1998b, Antanaitis 2001), but the bones of domesticates are usually less than 5 percent and never more than 15 percent (Dolukhanov 1979, 1998b, Loze 1979, Zvelebil 1981, 1987, Dolukhanov and Miklyaev 1986), and only a single grain of barley and some cereal pollen (attributed to barley) suggest a possibility of agriculture. By contrast, large quantities of water chestnuts, hazelnuts, abundant seeds of hemp, hemp pollen, pollen indicators of clearance and ruderals indicating open landscape suggest plant husbandry focussed on native plants. Other evidence suggests processing of hemp and nettle fibres for making clothes and cordage (Rimantiené 1992a, 1992b, 1998, Loze 1998).

These patterns of settlement and land-use indicate a degree of sedentism and organisational complexity not normally associated with hunter-gatherer communities. This is particularly true of coastal societies. A degree of sedentism does not, of course, mean that everyone returned every evening to the main village all year around: this is not the case even in our own society. But the indicators of residential permanence suggesting year-round human presence at some of these major settlements, and the solid, permanent nature of the house structures, does suggest the existence of permanent, continuously inhabited, centrally placed villages.

In contrast to coastal and lacustrine regions, the upland interior did not present early opportunities for residential permanence. The inland pattern was marked by greater residential mobility, greater reliance on terrestrial resources, and more direct, rather than logistic procurement strategies (Figure 2.4). Seasonally occupied base camps were located by shores of smaller lakes and watercourses. From there, people moved in a seasonal pattern to temporary habitation sites and specialised exploitation camps within larger annual territories (L. Larsson 1975, 1978a, 1990, Zvelebil 1981, Forsberg 1985, Baudou 1992, Tilley 1993, Bergman 1995 [in Ramqvist 2002], M. Larsson and Molin 2000, Ramqvist 2002, Larsson et al. 2003, Anderson and Wigforss 2004, McCartan et al. 2009). Seasonal aggregation sites, which were associated both with more sedentary coastal and more mobile settlement patterns, played an especially important role within the inland organisation of landscape as the main location for the coming together of different communities for trade, exchange, social activities, and courting, and for the performance of rituals. In order to support large gatherings, such places were often placed in good fishing locations by rapids or at river narrows connecting larger lakes, for example, at Nämforsen in Norrland (see later), or at the Harjavalta rapids on the Kokemäenjoki River, or along the Tampere straits linking Nasijärvi and Pyhäjärvi, both in southwest Finland (Salo 1972, Paavola and Hartikainen 1973, Zvelebil 1981).

Long-distance contacts, circulation of exotic prestige items and of sought-after raw materials, as well as channels for the dispersal of innovations, were all maintained through trade and exchange (Ahlback 2003, Zvelebil 2006, in press). In northern Europe, the use of skis and sledges in winter and of boats in the summer months facilitated such contacts (Clark 1953, 1975, Burov 1989, Fischer 1995a). The ritual associations of such means of transport are shown by elk-headed carvings tipping ski runners found in northwest Russia and elsewhere (Burov 1989) and by carvings of elk placed on the sterns of boats (Tilley 1993, Lindquist 1994, Nuñez 1995). Examples of regional and interregional trade linking vast distances are too numerous to describe here (see Figure 2.5); they include circulation of flint and ochre in Poland (Sulgustowska 1990, 2005, 2006), green Olonets slate and flint from Karelia across Finland, northwest Russia and the eastern Baltic, amber from the East Baltic coast and flint from the Valdai mountains distributed throughout the East Baltic and Finland (Vankina 1970, Loze 1998, Zhilin 2003, Zvelebil 2006), flint and amber from southern to northern Scandinavia, pumice from northern Norway to other regions in Scandinavia, seal oil and other products from coastal regions of the Baltic and the central Baltic islands (Saaremaa, Gotland, Öland, Åland) to northern Poland and other parts of northern Europe, and raw material for axes and adzes throughout the region (Zvelebil 1996a, 1998, 2000a, 2006, Bengtsson 2003, Bergsvick and Olsen 2003, Carlsson 2003, Fischer 2003a), as well as the importation of metal artefacts, polished stone axes, and other items from outside of Northern Europe (Loze 1998).

Time Trends

It is important to note that settlement and resource use varied from region to region and changed over time. It is difficult, for an area so large as the Baltic, to capture in summary major patterns of change. Overall, the general trend was towards greater regional and territorial definition. This is evident from a gradual shift from flint, of superior quality and often imported, to local lithic sources later in the Mesolithic (e.g., M. Larsson and Molin 2000), in the development of regional stylistic variation in stone and bone tools, and later in ceramics (e.g., Vang Petersen 1984, Stillborg and Bergenstrahle 2000), and in territorial appropriation marked in the landscape and within settlements by burials, cemeteries, rock carvings and paintings, and other marks of enculturation (e.g., Loze 1998, Zvelebil 1997, 2003b, 2003c, Rowley-Conwy 1998, 1999, Larsson et al. 2003, McCartan et al. 2009).

Patterns of contact and trade changed alongside these developments. In the early Mesolithic, the impression is one of a more direct procurement of resources, linked perhaps to greater general mobility, and of a generalised, intermittent, and locationally diverse long-distance trade and exchange. In the later Mesolithic, trading patterns became more streamlined, enduring and regular, suggesting more formalised contact and greater control over traded items by specialist individuals. At the same time, the number of source locations of traded items for any one region appears to decline.

In terms of subsistence, the composition of exploited species reflects the regional climatic regimes and broader environmental changes. In the Early Postglacial period and continuing later in the far north (northern Sweden, northern Finland, and Lapland), reindeer was the principal hunted species. In regions where boreal conifer forests and wetlands were dominant (southern Finland, Middle Sweden, and Estonia) elk, beaver, and other fur animals were the main game. In the south and East Baltic (southwest and southeast Sweden, Skåne, northern Poland, Lithuania, and Latvia), areas marked by mixed broadleaved-coniferous forests, wild pig, red deer, roe deer, and wild cattle joined elk and fur game as principal resources. This broader range of terrestrial resources, linked to the temperate forest biome, extended further north during the climatic optimum, covering Middle Sweden, coastal Norrland, southern Finland, the Karelian Isthmus, and Estonia, all areas that have reverted to predominantly boreal forest cover since then (Clark 1975, Dolukhanov this volume).

In coastal and lacustrine areas, there was a tendency towards greater permanence of settlement, logistic procurement, and specialisation on aquatic resources − seal, fish, and waterfowl. This development is in evidence in the west and the East Baltic after about 8000 BP and 7000 BP, respectively, probably marking a genuine shift in resource use (Zvelebil 1985, 1987, K. Jaanits 1995, Rowley-Conwy 1999, but see Blankholm this volume).

There is nothing inevitable about a course towards increased cultural complexity and greater control over resources. Such developments occurred in coastal and some inland lacustrine regions of circum-Baltic Europe, but in other areas, for example across the north European Plain or inland within peninsular Scandinavia, the more residentially mobile pattern of life continued throughout, although space does not permit more detailed description here of regional variation. There is

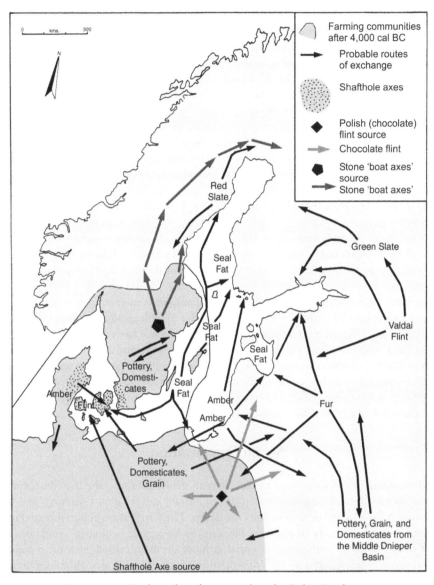

Figure 2.5. Trade and exchange within the Baltic Sea basin.

no evidence in the Baltic area for episodes of increased mobility and greater use of terrestrial resources in the late Mesolithic observed by some in southern Scandinavia (e.g., Larsson 1990b, 1996, Rowley-Conwy 2001, Blankholm this volume), although there is evidence in some areas such as southwest Finland for the disappearance of settlement and probably depopulation just prior to the area receiving farming settlement. This is probably an effect of the 'agricultural frontier', the proximity of farmers interfering with hunter-gatherer activities to such an extent that the boundary zone was vacated by the latter in order to maintain the effectiveness of their foraging strategies (Moore 1985, Zvelebil 1986c, 1996b).

More controversially, in some regions, the greater use of marine mammals, fish and waterfowl, appears to be coeval with specialised exploitation – or management – of biologically undomesticated pigs, and increasingly sophisticated use of plant resources (Zvelebil 1994, 1998, see also Rowley-Conwy 1995, 2001, Larsson et al. 2005, Albarella et al. 2006). The latter includes the development of an integrated tool kit for woodland clearance and forest manipulation, for harvesting and perhaps planting roots, tubers, nuts, and other plant food, and for processing grains and nuts. Forest clearance by controlled burning, coppicing, and pollarding, and the maintenance of open meadowland conditions, are all strategies of landscape manipulation documented palynologically and sedimentologically in a number of regions: southern Sweden (Goransson 1986, Berglund 1991, Larsson 2001), Poland (Nowak 2001), southern Finland (Vuorela 1976, 1998), East Baltic and northern Russia (Loze and Yakubovskaya 1984, Dolukhanov 1986, Loze 1998, Antanaitis 2001).

Although in the west Baltic (southern Sweden, northwest Poland), the transition to farming occurred in the context of the TRB culture from c. 5300 BP, in the East Baltic, agro-pastoral domesticates – goat, sheep, cattle, and domesticated pig – began to join the existing resource base from the middle of the fifth millennium BP. The very small number – usually less than 5 percent of the total bone assemblage – suggests, the acquisition by trade at least initially, rather than the adoption of agro-pastoral husbandry, and a prestige or ritual rather than economic role for these new resources.

In aggregate, such evidence suggests the existence of management strategies in the Mesolithic, which may have formed the basis for the local husbandry of biologically undomesticated plants and animals, while at the same time remaining a part of an existence based principally on hunting and gathering. Such 'forest farming' systems varied from region to region, and involved varying degrees of resource control. Within this framework, the existence of local plant and animal management or husbandry practices can be seen as a crucial development foreshadowing the changes attendant on the introduction of agro-pastoral farming, on the one hand, and providing a viable alternative to it, on the other (Zvelebil 1986c, 1995b, 1998, Lõugas et al. 1995).

Social Organisation

Our understanding of social structure and ideology in the Mesolithic – the late Mesolithic in particular – is based principally on the evidence from burials, and from rock-carvings and sculpted, 'ritual' artefacts found alone or among domestic debris. The distribution of burial areas (Figure 2.6) reflects not only the intensity of research, but also the favourable ecological conditions of these areas for hunter-gatherer settlement: all burial grounds occur in coastal areas or in major lacustrine or riverine zones, marked by the concentration of aquatic resources. Burial grounds as such may have acted as territorial markers, indicating increased sedentism, territoriality and claims to ownership of land and resources (Petersen 1984, Larsson 1989, 1993, Rowley-Conwy 1998, 1999, Larsson et al. 2003, McCartan et al. 2009).

Burial Evidence

Between them, the burial grounds cover the entire Mesolithic period, from c. 10,000 BP to the end of the fifth millennium BP. Some are cemeteries, that is interments grouped in burial grounds marked exclusively for ritual and burial, others are isolated burials or interments within or underneath houses or within settlements (e.g., Jochim this volume, Dolukhanov this volume, Blankholm this volume, and references cited later in this chapter). Some long-used locations, such

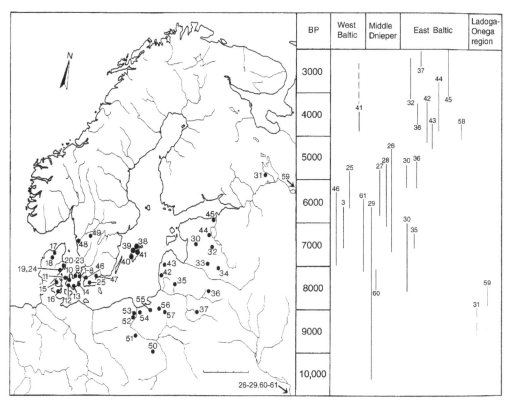

Figure 2.6. Burial grounds: their distribution and duration. 1. Nivågaard. 2. Vœnget Nord. 3. Vedbœk Boldbaner. 4. Henriksholm-Bøgebakken. 5. Gøngeshusvej. 6. Maglemosegaard. 7. Stationsvej 19. 8. Bloksberg. 9. Melby. 10. Dragsholm. 11. Serejø. 12. Korsør. 13. Holemegaard V. 14. Strøby Egede. 15. Tybrind Vig. 16. Møllegabet II. 17. Brovst. 18. Ertebølle. 19. Vœnge Sø. 20. Holmegård. 21. Fannerup. 22. Nederst. 23. Koed. 24. Norsminde. 25. Skateholm. 26. Derievka. 27. Nikolskoya. 28. Yasionovatke. 29. Vasil'evka. 30. Zvejnieki. 31. Olenni Ostrov. 32. Tamula. 33. L. Lubāna. 34. Krieči. 35. Duonkalnis. 36. Kretuonas. 37. Turlojiške. 38. Ire. 39 Visby. 40. Ajvide. 41. Västerbjers. 42. Šventoji. 43. Sārnate. 44. Akali. 45. Narva-Riigiküla. 46. Tågerup. 47. Barum. 48. Uleberg. 49. Almeö. 50. Janislawice. 51. Lojewo. 52. Żurawki. 53. Smolag. 54. Prabuty. 55. Brajnieki. 56. Giżycko-Pierkunowo. 57. Woźna-Wies. 58. Abora. 59. Popovo. 60. Marievka. 61. Osipovka.

as Zvejnieki in Latvia, saw the burial practice change from a cemetery practice in the Mesolithic to a deliberate burial within the settlement among the ceramic-using hunter-gatherers of the so-called Forest Neolithic (c. 6000–4000 BP).

Located on a small island within lake Onega in Karelia, Olenii Ostrov (or Oleneostrovski Mogilnik, Deer Island Cemetery), probably held more than three hundred interments, of which about half have been excavated (Gurina 1966). Dated to the mid-eighth millennium BP (Price and Jacobs 1990, Zaitseva et al. 1997), the cemetery revealed the existence of at least seven social dimensions, expressing band membership, age, sex, personal wealth, and three specialised ranks: namely, ritual specialists or shamans, buried in a standing or reclining posture, individuals interred with effigy figures (clan identity office holders?), and males buried with bone points only (members

39

of a hunting moiety) (O'Shea and Zvelebil 1985: 19–20, Zvelebil 1993a, but see Jacobs 1995, Janik 2005). In summary, we seem to be dealing with a descent-based society organised into sequential hierarchies (Aldenderfer 1993), which are linked to ritual (i.e., shamans, effigy holders, possibly bone-point holders), but that operate independently of one another and that are divorced from ranking defined by wealth. Although the ritual roles could be inherited (i.e., child/juvenile effigy holders), the wealth could not: it tended to decline in old age. In another context, O'Shea (1996) has suggested that such patterned decline in status goods with age may reflect intergenerational circulation of symbolic artefacts as age and gender-related social roles were passed from one age group to another. Both men and women could acquire a high-status position, although men tended to acquire higher rank more often than women. Sex-specific variation in the grave goods and the age and sex associations in collective burials suggest that we may be dealing with a patrilineal or dual-descent social structure.

Olenii Ostrov is only one among several burial grounds in the north and circum-Baltic Europe displaying similar variation. In the East Baltic, major concentrations of burials have been found at Zvejnieki, Kreichi, and Sope cemeteries, and within settlements at Narva-Riikiküla I (Gurina 1956, 1966), Valma, Kvapani, Tamula, Abora 1, Spiginas, Kretuonas, and Duonkalnis (Jaanits 1957, 1959, 1984, Zagorskis 1987, Girininkas 1990, Loze 1995, Antanaitis 1999, Zagorska 2001). With 315 excavated burials, Zvejnieki is the largest among these (Zagorskis 1987, 2004, Zagorska 2000, 2001, 2009, Eriksson 2003, Eriksson et al. 2003, Larsson and Zagorska 2006, Larsson 2009). The cemetery at Zvejnieki was used over a 4000-year period, between c. 8200 and 4200 BP. Mortuary practice changed from the early period (8200–7300 BP) to the later (7300–4200 BP), when amber objects replaced tooth pendants as the most common grave goods and principal symbols of value. In the later period, too, burials are strongly associated with settlements – shown at Zvejnieki by black cultural soil transported from the adjacent settlement and deposited as the grave fill (Zagorskis 1987, 2004, Antanaitis 1998, Zagorska 2000a, 2000b, 2001). Despite these and other changes, we find throughout this period the same use of the wild-animal symbolism as at Olenii Ostrov, as well as differences in social status similar to those at Olenii Ostrov. Individual and collective burials may indicate the presence of corporate groups (Tainter 1976, Goldstein 1981: 57, Jelsma 2000: 44). Gravestones, small cairns or stone lining marked some interments (Zagorska 2000, 2001, 2009) – features that are notably present also in other parts of eastern and northern Europe (Edgren 1966, Miettinen 1990, 1992, Larsson 1993, Nielsen and Brinch Petersen 1993, Loze 1995, Antanaitis 1999).

The end phase of the Zvejnieki cemetery is contemporary with burials at Abora, (c. 4500–3800 BP), where sixty-one interments were placed in the central part of a residential hunter-gatherer settlement (Loze 1979). Single, dual, and collective burials, perforated tooth pendants, and sculptures of water birds, elk, beaver, bear, and snake, attest to the same range of burial practices and symbolism seen already at Zvejnieki and Olenii Ostrov. The absence of pottery in the burials is striking, as the Abora community belongs with ceramic-using hunter-gatherers. So the same symbolism and the same ideology appear to have lasted in the East Baltic until the mid-fourth millennium BP (Zvelebil 1993a, 1997, Antanaitis 1998).

Burial practice in the western Baltic shows both differences and similarities with the East Baltic. Even though the number of burials dated to the Mesolithic has increased significantly in recent years (Nielsen and Brinch Petersen 1993, Meiklejohn et al. 1998, 2000, Stutz 2003, Larsson 2001, 2005), the main concentrations are at Skateholm in southern Sweden and Vedbaek-Bøgebakken in Zealand (Denmark), both dated to the Early and Middle Ertebølle period, c. 6500–5800 BP (see Blankholm this volume). Although the two burial complexes at Skateholm (I and II) are true cemeteries, the Vedbaek complex consists of burials interred in settlements that dotted the ancient coastline of the Vedbaek fjord (Clark and Neeley 1987, Larsson 1989, 1990a, 1990b, 1993, 2005).

At Skateholm, two cemeteries, both located on islands and containing some eighty-five graves, were excavated by Lars Larsson (1988, 1989, 1990, 1993 with refs, 2004, 2005). In brief, it is again possible to distinguish three wealth or status ranks, with younger females and older males receiving the richest grave goods (Larsson 1989). Burials include cremations, interment in sitting position, double graves containing both women and men with children, rich child graves, and dog burials. Timber structures were built over two graves at Skateholm I, and Skateholm II had a mortuary house. With their exceptional grave goods and burial ritual (dog sacrifice in SII-8, headdress covering a young man SII-15), the sitting burials can be linked to the shaft graves at Olenii Ostrov, and the rich child graves again suggest some inherited social position.

In an effort to understand the division of labour, Constandse-Westerman and Newell (1989) have investigated markers of stress such as limb lateralisation and joint degeneration caused by physical labour at Skateholm I and II. They conclude that higher-ranking females show consistently less lateralisation than those in poorer graves, whereas the males show the opposite pattern: stronger lateralisation in higher ranked individuals. Ethnographically, such a status-related pattern is consistent with the distribution of work-related stress in socially stratified societies. Moreover, the results suggest that women at Skateholm gained their status through means other than physical work: through personal achievement, perhaps as child-bearers (cf. Tilley 1996: 61), through descent (suggesting a matrilineal society) or perhaps by association with high-ranking males.

At Vedbaek, the grave goods divide the burials again into three groups, and again, as at Olenii Ostrov and Skateholm, there are rich juvenile graves, whereas some of the oldest individuals are buried without any personal equipment (Albrethsen and Brinch Petersen 1976, Larsson 1990a; but see Blankholm this volume).

As a cemetery – a formal burial area – Skateholm has been interpreted as a territorial marker of a unilineal descent group claiming rights to resources through ancestors (Larsson 1993, Rowley-Conwy 1998, 1999). The internal groupings within Skateholm I may suggest discrete lineages, and the notion of territoriality receives further support in the distribution of functionally analogous artefact types such as axes, outlining discrete territories (Petersen 1984, Larsson 1989, Rowley-Conwy 1998).

In anthropological and ethnographic terms, then, many of the late Mesolithic communities in the coastal areas of the Baltic Sea would qualify as 'delayed-return' foragers (Woodburn 1982, 1988), whose social structure was, if anything, more hierarchically ranked than was the case among the delayed-return foragers in the ethnographic record. Status distinctions along the major, horizontal social dimensions of age, sex, and achieved status are discernible in general (Clark and Neeley 1987: 125), whereas evidence for vertical differentiation occurs at Skateholm, Zvejnieki, and Olenii Ostrov, as discussed earlier, as well as at other cemeteries along the Atlantic façade in Denmark, France, and Portugal (Clark and Neeley 1987: 125–6).

The degree of social differentiation attributed to Mesolithic communities here is based on the assumption that mortuary treatment reflects the social position of an individual within society, symbolised in an intelligible way by a set of acknowledged social identities (Goodenough 1965, O'Shea 1984, 1996, 1998: 109). Not all agree with this. Although some researchers accept the view of a Mesolithic society as socially complex in coastal parts of Europe (O'Shea and Zvelebil 1985, Price 1987, Clark and Neeley 1987, Newell and Constandse-Westermann 1988, Neeley and Clark 1990, Zvelebil 1995a, more tentatively Larsson 1993, Nielsen and Brinch Petersen 1993: 78–9), others see Mesolithic communities as essentially egalitarian (e.g., Meiklejohn et al. 2000: 231, 234, Price 2000: 269, Blankholm this volume). Yet others regard the mortuary record of the prehistoric period as so affected by regional variation and so transformed by ritual practice and ideology as to be virtually unintelligible as a guide to social positions in normative terms (Ucko 1969, Hodder 1980, Chapman and Randsborg 1981, Durkheim 1995). Only more sophisticated treatment of the mortuary deposits and their interpretation can produce some resolution to these different readings of the archaeological record (e.g., O'Shea 1996, Jelsma 2000, Nilsson Stutz 2003, 2009).

In my view, the broader, interregional scale reveals a degree of variation in social structure that corresponds to the complexity of economic organisation. Although there is evidence for social differentiation in the economically more complex areas, such as coastal southern Sweden and the East Baltic, or the great lakes of northern Russia, where Olenii Ostrov is located (Figure 2.6), in the surrounding interior regions, our present state of knowledge supports the notion of mobile, organisationally simple, and socially undifferentiated hunter-gatherers. This evidence may be speculatively linked to egalitarian hunter-gatherers of the ethnohistorical past, and to Ingold's 'forager mode of production' (Ingold 1988, Zvelebil 1998).

The Role of Ideology

Ideology – the overarching belief system – must have been fundamental in specifying the nature of social relations among hunter-gatherers and in encoding subsistence strategies with social meaning (Boas 1940, Ingold 1986, 1988, Woodburn 1988, Bird-David 1990, 1992b, Durkheim 1995 [1912]). Yet, relatively little effort has been expended in trying to comprehend the belief system of Mesolithic hunter-gatherers in Europe. Partly, this is because of the conviction that such research would be an idle exercise in unscientific imagination, and that little or nothing can be concluded about the prehistoric beliefs with certainty. Partly this scepticism is based on the lack of artefacts with obvious symbolic content in many parts of Mesolithic Europe. In this respect, circum-Baltic Europe represents an exception: ritual landscapes and symbolic artefacts are very clearly in evidence within the region.

Northern hunter-gatherer and reindeer herding communities in northeast Europe and western Siberia can serve as a source of analogy for the earlier belief systems of prehistoric communities in circum-Baltic Europe. In the first instance, such use of ethnographic analogy is valid because we are dealing with a direct historical analogy: at least some of the societies in question are historically linked and they operated in similar ecological and economic conditions (e.g., Dalton 1981, Hultkrantz 1985, 1996, Tilley 1991, Pentikäinen 1996, Zvelebil and Jordan 1999, Bowie 2000, Jordan 2001, 2006, Zvelebil and Fewster 2001).

Additionally, the validity of such analogies is considerably strengthened if we perceive the historical continuity and change between the hunter-gatherer societies in northern Europe/western Siberia in terms of structure and agency (Levi-Strauss 1968, Bourdieu 1977, Giddens 1984, Layton 1985, 1991, Barrett 1994). At the broadest level, material culture and social structure are both organised according to distinctive principles of a still wider, cognitive order. There can be little doubt that the elaboration of material culture in foraging societies is an indication of elaboration in social relations, objectified and symbolised through things (Tilley 1991: 152, Chapman 1993: 109, Barrett 1994). Elaboration in grave goods, burial rites, organisation of the landscape and in symbolic aspects of material culture, then, should reflect elaboration of social relations, structured according to some wider, cognitive order, or conceptual structure.

Material culture derives its meaning by reference to the natural and supernatural worlds. If these worlds share the same practical and ideological structures, it follows that the meaning of material culture in its historical context – prehistoric or ethnohistorical – is encoded with respect to the same sources. It can be argued that prehistoric and ethnohistorical hunter-gatherer communities in the northern Eurasian zone shared broadly similar temporal, practical and cosmological structures (Zvelebil 1997, 2002, Zvelebil and Jordan 1999). The conception of time within this context acted to perpetuate the structural framework, the reinterpretation or alteration of which was slow to occur (Zvelebil 1993a, Zvelebil and Jordan 1999). Changes that varied from region to region, however, clearly did take place at different rates in historical time.

Structuring Principles

Hunter-gatherer communities in the temperate and boreal zones of Eurasia organised their lives according to basic elements of a structural framework that promoted cultural and ideological continuity. These were the societies of *longue durée* (cf. Braudel 1958). Such structures included environmental variables, seasonal food procurement regimes, and cosmological beliefs. They provided a structural framework that was interpreted and reinterpreted through the agency of individuals, communities, and outside groups linked by contact and exchange. The social practice of doing things and passing knowledge from one individual to another involved deliberate decisions and manipulation and replication of tasks, in the course of which changes were introduced into social practice. The new knowledge and skills were incorporated into the existing tradition in relationship to existing rules. Ideology, as an overarching system of beliefs mediated through ritual practice, provided the supervisory context within which this process was conceptually played out.

Elements of the structural components of the boreal forager belief system can be abstracted from Siberian and northeast European ethnohistorical data (Karjalainen 1922, Hultkrantz 1965, 1996, Hóppal 1984, 1986, Kulemzin 1984, Eliade 1989, Ingold 1986, Balzer 1990, Dioszegi and Hóppal 1996, Pentikäinen 1996, 1998, Bowie 2000, Jordan 2001), and focus on the following key themes:

(1) The Three-Tier World. A three-tier universe of the upper (sky) world, the middle (earth) world and the underworld (underground) (Golovnev 1984, Kulemzin 1984: 171–2), which correspond to air, land, and water, respectively. These layers are linked by a 'cosmic pillar' (Ingold 1986, Pentikäinen 1996, 1998) or 'cosmic river' (Anisimov 1963), symbolised in the shaman's turu or a tree, often placed in the centre of the shaman's tent. The three-tier world is also perceived as existing on a horizontal plane where the underworld equates with the cold north and the upper world with the south (possibly tracing its roots from the Upper Palaeolithic) (Kulemzin 1984: 171–2). The souls of the dead travel down the river to the underworld and burials in dugout canoes are typical for western Siberia at least as far back as AD 700 (Semenova 1998). Reflecting this cosmology, holy sites, where the local guardian spirit lives, are always located upstream from the settlement (Martynova 1995: 97), whereas graveyards are located downstream of the settlement (Kulemzin 1994: 370, Jordan 2001).

(2) The Supernatural World. Every part of the surrounding world is seen as being inhabited by supernatural beings or 'spirits' (Karjalainen 1922, Eliade 1964, 1989, 1996, Pentikäinen et al. 1998, Kulemzin and Lukina 1977), which are seen as being good and bad, anthropomorphic and zoomorphic. The power and influence of the supernatural being varies.

(3) Nature, Reciprocity, and the Spirit World. Nature is perceived as the 'giving environment', marked by the unity of the natural and cultural domain and indifference towards distinguishing the two as separate categories (e.g., Edsman 1965, Ingold 1986, 1996), and by reciprocal relations of sacrifice, and gift exchange between different elements within the natural-cultural domain. Relationships of exchange and reciprocity with the 'giving earth'

occur through communication with supernatural spirits whose power and/or sphere of influence is varied. Proper conduct and relations with them ensure health, welfare, and hunting success (Edsman 1965, Kulemzin and Lukina 1992: 97), whereas a failure to meet obligations may bring misfortune. Communication with the spirit world is facilitated through sacrifice and gift-giving.

(4) Reciprocity and the Animal World. This revolves around concepts of exchange and reciprocity with the animal world and attempts to ensure the 'revival' of hunted animals. This involves the appropriate treatment of their remains (bones) following killing and consumption in order to maintain hunting success (Edsman 1965, Kulemzin 1984: 82–103) and to avoid punishment in the form of illness sent down by their spirit protectors. The spirit protectors of the animals (often local guardian spirits) also must be afforded suitable treatment where necessary (Karjalainen 1922: 72–3, Edsman 1965).

(5) Conception of Souls. Human and animal persons normally possess a physical self and several souls. According to Chernetsov (1963) and Balzer (1980), among the Khanty each person possesses four main souls, which include the 'reincarnation or breath soul', the 'material or shadow soul', and the 'illness soul', which travels to the underworld after death (see also Jordan 2001). According to other authors (Ingold 1986), it is the division of humans and animals into the physical self, the body soul, and the free soul, which presents the most significant categories. Human beings and those animals who are masters of their animal charges, such as the bear, possess all three substances. Wild animals normally possess physical self and the body soul (their collective 'free soul' residing in the animal master), whereas 'the spirit of the domestic animal is the soul of man, controlling the animal from without' (Ingold 1986: 255). Dualism between a free soul and body soul is held to be embedded in the practice of shamanism (Hultkrantz 1984).

(6) The Role of the Shaman. Pentikäinen states, 'shamanism is rather a world-view system than a religion' (Pentikäinen et al. 1998, 61), 'an ideological premise' (Hultkrantz 1996) or 'grammar of mind', articulating the beliefs outlined earlier. Shaman is a religious leader of the community, whose principal role is to act as mediator between the three worlds in a three-level universe by practising techniques of ecstasy (shaman), aided by his or her ritual equipment and spirit helpers. Ritual equipment almost always includes a drum or other musical instruments, dress, bag, horned mask, and models of animal spirit helpers (Hultkrantz 1990, Pentikäinen et al. 1998). Most prominent spirit helpers take the shape of water birds (as swimmers and flyers they can lead the shaman to all three worlds), the bear (as the master of other animal beings and a celestial being), and the elk or deer (celestial beings too as guides to and in the heavens). A shaman 'shares in the mentality of animals' (Eliade 1989).

Within this cognitive framework based on ethnographies of Eurasian hunter-gatherers, elk, bear, and water birds play clearly defined roles as guardians of other animals and as 'messenger animals': channels of communication with other, nonterrestrial worlds. Amongst the Khanty, for example, the 'heavenly elk' is seen as being a symbol of wealth and general prosperity (Kulemzin 1984: 87) as well as being linked to, and protected by, the upper world spirits (Pentikäinen 1996: 174). Among other groups, elk plays a central role in the myths of revival and regeneration, as well as a role in the mediation between the world of spirits and of humans. The bear plays an analogous but somewhat different role as the chief guardian of wild animals and a mediator between animal beings and human beings. Water birds are perceived as the messengers between the other world and the earth, guarding the entrance to the lower world, and acting as guides to the 'sea of the deceased' in some myths (Lönnrot 1963), to the 'burial beyond the water' in others (Aleksenko 1967, Balzer 1980,

Table 2.2. Enculturation through ritual: hunter-gatherer landscapes (after Zvelebil and Jordan 1999)

---

(1) All routine areas are also ritual areas.
(2) In some locales, ritual has distinct expression: there are some areas dedicated to ritual alone.
(3) Activities at these locales represent communication and symbolic exchange with the worlds of the dead and the supernatural, some of whom are ancestors.
(4) These include household, ancestral, cosmological, legendary, and ceremonial locations.
(5) Ritual areas also include landscapes of the dead: burial locations and cemeteries.
(6) Activity at these holy sites involves the creation and deposition of material culture in a structured symbolic context.

Ingold 1986). As a result, shamans can identify themselves with 'messenger animals' by wearing cloaks and headgear during their sessions (Eliade 1989, Pentikäinen et al. 1998, Jelsma 2000).

Material Expressions of Ritual and Symbolism

We have to beware of mapping the ethnography of modern hunter-gatherers onto the past without careful scrutiny of the archaeological evidence. So how far is the ethnographically derived belief system outlined here reflected in the archaeological record?

In the hunter-gatherer prehistory of northern Europe, the symbolism of rock-carving sites, of carved objects, and of burial ritual clearly relates to this system of beliefs. Material representations include sculpted terminals of wooden household utensils, such as spoon-bowls and ladles, zoomorphic axes and mace heads, rock carvings, and zoomorphic ornamentation on pottery. Elk, bear, and water birds are the most common designs.

The symbolism of these objects makes sense within the cosmological framework of Eurasian shamanism. The duration of this tradition appears extremely long and encompasses, in conventional terms, the Mesolithic of the whole area, the Neolithic (i.e., pottery-using hunter-gatherers) of eastern Europe and Siberia, the Bronze and Iron Ages of northeast Europe and Siberia, and the historic period in Siberia and along the northern margins of Europe. Throughout this period, people in these regions appear to have maintained their identity as hunter-gatherer communities, irrespective of various degrees of herding and tentative cultivation, and adhered to the cosmological system to which I refer as Eurasian shamanism. The contexts in which these symbolic artefacts occur cannot be easily categorised but perhaps can be best comprehended as part of an encultured landscape, organised into ritual and habitual (practical) zones according to general structuring principles (Table 2.2, Zvelebil 1997, 2003a, Zvelebil and Jordan 1999, for further elaboration, see Jordan 2001, Goldhahn 2002, Nash and Chippindale 2002, Bergsvick 2009, Lindgren 2009).

Within this spatial and symbolic context, the meaning of ritual sites can be comprehended by reference to this ideology. For example, the ritual distinction between land and water and the association of water birds with the dead finds expression in rock carvings, petroglyphs, and burial deposits. In some cases, the burial of the dead 'beyond the water' is reflected in the common location of burial grounds on islands or promontories. Island locations are, for example, Olenii Ostrov, Karelia, Skateholm 1 and 2, Sweden, Duokalnis and Spiginas in Lithuania; peninsular locations are Zvejnieki and Abora, Latvia). Water birds are commonly found in burials as bone remains, sculpted objects or carved images; the interment of a child on a swan's wing at Vedbaek (Nielsen and Brinch Petersen 1993) is especially loaded with symbolism.

Marek Zvelebil

Ritual Locations and Rock Art

Rock carving and rock painting sites of northern Europe represent perhaps the best record of cosmology and ideology of northern hunter-gatherers in Europe (Hultkrantz 1986, 1989, Coles 1991, Lindqvist 1994). Painted and/or engraved at several hundred such locations, there are thousands of images representing principally anthropomorphic figures, cervids, boats, sea mammals, bears, water birds, fish, reptiles (snakes and lizards), tracks or foot prints, weapons and hunting-fishing gear, and abstract designs (Ravdonikas 1936, Hällström 1960, Bakka 1975 Taavitsainen 1978, Malmer 1981, Helskog 1985, Ramqvist et al. 1985, Tilley 1991, Baudou 1993, Lindqvist 1994, Nuñez 1995, Nash 2002, Sognnes 2002, for a summary of interregional differences, see Ramqvist 2002). The youngest of such rock-carvings can be dated on geological grounds to c. AD 500 (Nuñez 1995 with references).

One of the largest among these is Nämforsen in Swedish Norland, situated on the river Ångerman along the last rapids before the river enters the sea at the junction of the interior uplands and the coastal plain. It is a major rock-carving site, dated very broadly to between 5500–3500 BP. About 1,750 petroglyphs were carved into the smooth rocky surface of three islands in the centre of the river (Hallström 1960, Malmer 1975, 1981, Tilley 1991, Baudou 1992, 1993, Sognnes 2002).

The rock carvings at Nämforsen depict elks, boats, people, fish, birds, shoe/foot imprints, and tools, arranged into compositions that are remarkably lacking in hierarchical structure. The meaning of the rock carvings at Nämforsen is interpreted in several ways: as sympathetic magic designed to ensure hunting success, as totemic representations, as a 'tribal encyclopaedia' – a record of social knowledge – as a 'visual statement of myths, cosmic categories and associations held to structure both the supernatural world and human existence' (Tilley 1991: 145), as a ritual confrontation between different interest groups within the community, or as a symbol of power and control by male elders over others. The function of the site is variously identified as a major ritual centre (Baudou 1977), or a seasonal aggregation centre and a centre for exchange with farmer traders from the south (Hallström 1960, Malmer 1975, Tilley 1991).

At the same time, there are clear parallels between the cosmological system of northern hunter-gatherers and the landscape and the images of Nämforsen. These include the importance of rivers in the cosmological system, their centrality in territorial identification, and their links with specific clans or communities (Tilley 1991, Martynova 1995, Wiget and Balalaeva 1997, Zvelebil 1997, Jordan 2001). The specific location of the Nämforsen carvings can be read in terms of the liminality of the location and of the passage of the souls to the 'sea of the deceased'. Images of boats at Nämforsen have no paddles, possibly an image of death, of groups of people on their last journey to the world beyond the water, the underworld, guided, in some depictions, by a ritual specialist (the shaman) recognisable by the elk-headed terminal or turu held upright in his/her hand. Carvings themselves, their composition as well as their overall organisation, provide additional insights by reference to the same belief system (Tilley 1991, Zvelebil 1997, 2002, Zvelebil and Jordan 1999).

Nämforsen is centrally located in relation to some 600 Stone Age sites within the Ångerman river system, and about 60 to 70 km from the next rock carving/painting site. At the rock carving site itself, seasonal occupation during the summer half of the year is suggested by the presence of bones of pike, salmon, seal, water birds, and beaver – typically a spring/summer prey – whereas elk, usually hunted during the winter, is absent (Zvelebil 1981, Fosberg 1985). One of the largest known settlements is located near Nämforsen itself, and was intermittently occupied from 5000 BP to the Iron Age, with the most intensive occupation dating to the late Stone Age (c. 4500–4000 BP), marked by the presence of asbestos-tempered pottery (Malmer 1975, 1981), although the settlement, apparently, has not been fully excavated (Broadbent pers. comm. 1998).

46

Ramqvist (2002) noted the differences in location, size and subject of images between Nämforsen, on the one hand, and rock painting sites in the surrounding landscape of Norrland, on the other. He suggested that Nämforsen was an intracommunal 'tribal' location serving as a major summer aggregation site for the hunter-gatherer communities in central Norrland, each of which in turn was based on 'larger lake systems occurring within the larger river system' and each of which had a rock-painting location as their central ritual location (idem.: 155). This, to my mind, is a plausible description of a settlement hierarchy in the north European inland regions whereby several communities, each with their own territory and a ritual (rock-painting) site, came together during the summer months at Nämforsen as their regional ritual and aggregation centre (see Figure 2.4).

In summary, Nämforsen played the role of a central ritual, aggregation and exchange site of hunter-gatherer social groups, each associated with and symbolically relating to a major river system (Forsberg 1985, Tilley 1991, Ramqvist 2002). The symbolism at Nämforsen can be comprehended by reference to the northern hunter-gatherer cosmology. The landscape analogies to the ethnographically known situation of west Siberian groups (such as Kets, Mansi, Khanty) are also clear, and a similar pattern has also been historically documented for north Scandinavian Saami groups (Manker 1963, Nuñez 1995, Zvelebil and Jordan 1999).

Zoomorphic Artefacts and Animal Symbolism

In addition to such ritual locations, we find items of material culture in burial contexts, 'domestic' contexts, or 'lost', often deposited in bogs and wet places, perhaps as votive artefacts, which were carved, sculpted, or otherwise altered to instil symbolic and ritual meaning. Again, such artefacts were widespread in the circumpolar Stone Age and later hunter-gatherer societies and refer to 'messenger animals', capable of communicating with nonterrestrial worlds. They include bear and elk-headed effigies (also known as terminals because they are sometimes depicted in rock art mounted on poles), and other objects carved with the representation of these animals (Carpelan 1975, Nuñez 1995, Lindquist 1994: 65, fig. 3.8, Ahlback 2003, Lødøen 2009, Mansrud 2009). They also include representations of waterfowl – swan and duck, in particular – snakes, beavers, and human beings (Figure 2.7). In her survey of ritual representations on artefacts in the East Baltic, Antanaitis noted that zoomorphic objects outnumber anthropomorphic ones in the Neolithic, but when treated together, anthropomorphic figurines represent 31 percent of the total, waterfowl 22 percent, unidentified animal, but including bear or boar, 15 percent, elk/deer 9 percent and snake 8 percent, respectively (1998: 62, see also Eliade 1989: 158–65).

For the traditional societies of the boreal zone, birds, more specifically water birds, played a role not only in guiding the dead to the underworld but also in myths of world creation and regeneration (Eliade 1989, Antanaitis 1998, Lonnröt 1963). Given this multidimensional symbolism related to the migratory life cycle of water birds, marked by regeneration (spring), and death (autumn), it is hardly surprising that zoomorphic artefacts such as duck-headed ladles (Figure 2.7) are commonly found in archaeological contexts ranging from the Narva culture in the East Baltic (6000–4500 BP) to the Ust-Poluy culture on the lower Ob River in western Siberia (2500–2300 BP).

Elk and bear-headed terminals (Figure 2.7), which are depicted carried around on sticks or poles both at Nämforsen and also in the rock carvings on the shores of Lake Onega, where Olenii Ostrov is located (Gurina 1956, Savvateyev 1973, Maula 1990)) find a direct parallel in the shaman's turu, a ritual rod used to mediate between the natural and supernatural worlds. Carvings of elk also may have had a broader significance as a means of coming to terms with the outside world. After killing and consumption of an elk, appropriate treatment of the carcass ensured the revival of the animal and continued success for the hunter (Kulemzin 1984: 86). If elk hides were being traded out of the area, then they were being symbolically lost downstream – away from the local area in which the elk could 'revive'. Carving an elk would restore the items lost. Similarly, on the Vas Yugan, white stones were carved into elk shapes to bring luck in the hunt. Vas Yugan Khanty also produce hammers in the shape of an elk's head, which are used to make fish weirs. The symbolic referent here is the general association among well-being, replenishment, and the elk (Kulemzin 1984: 87). Carved wooden or lead images of game animals (including elk and water birds) are 'sacrificed' or given to the local spirits thought to reside at certain holy locations in the landscape (Karjalainen 1922: 70–3, Kulemzin and Lukina 1977: 131–2). The animals portrayed are thought to be under the protection of the spirit, and so donating these gifts will maintain hunting success.

The bear was treated as an animal of veneration honoured with special treatment in the ethnohistorical and prehistoric past: one to be addressed with circumspection only on special ritual occasions. After a successful bear hunt, the Maly Yugan Khanty carve an image of the bear on adjacent trees at a special location beside the pathway leading home so that the deity Torum will gaze from the Upper World and see the bear has been killed and not waste time looking for it. In Lapland as well as in western Siberia, the sending back of bear to the bear country involved 'singing hunters walking in procession with the bear soup' (Edsman 1965: 186), part of which was poured into a river as a votive offering, representing the essence of messenger animals returned to the 'cosmic river' (Aleksenko 1967, Resketov 1972). Similar elaborate bear rituals among the Ainu are described by Ohnuki-Tierney (1974). Such veneration is reflected, for example, in the modern Slavic, Finnic, Ob-Ugrian, and Germanic languages, where there is no direct name for a bear: it is either referred to a 'honey-eater' or 'honey-paw' (i.e., *medved* in Russian or Czech, also in Finnish, see Ingold 1986: 258) or 'the brown one' (i.e., *björn* in Scandinavian Germanic), or 'the grandfather in a fur coat' among the Khanty (Jordan, 2001). In Lapland, we find ritually buried bear skulls and other bear graves, which were accorded elaborate treatment (Edsman 1965, Zachrisson and Igegren 1974). Sculpted bear axes, bear-headed terminals, and images of bear in rock art are a recurrent feature of the symbolic repertoire of northern hunter-gatherers. It is important to note that the presence of such artefacts also served to ritualise habitual spaces often perceived by archaeologists as secular, profane, or practical (Zvelebil and Jordan 1999).

There are other aspects of similarity in ritual and symbolism between ethnohistorically attested northern hunter-gatherers and the prehistoric record of hunter-gatherer communities in northern and circum-Baltic Europe. Although too numerous to describe here, they include the choice of teeth of specific animals as pendants, the burial of the deceased on antlers, burial of dogs as memorials to their human masters, and ritual treatment of animal bones in keeping with beliefs in reciprocity, resurrection of animals, and regeneration of resources (Zvelebil 1985, 1992, 1997, 2002 with references, Oshibkina 1989, Jordan 2001, Edsman 1965, Zachrisson and Igegren 1974, 1985, Bradley 1997, 1998, Larsson 1990a, Nielsen and Brinch Petersen 1993).

Shamans

Finally, can we identify the presence of shamans in the prehistoric record of northern and circum–Baltic Europe? Both rock art and burial evidence contain a range of symbols, which in ethnographic contexts would be clearly identified with shamans.

In rock art, we find petroglyphs of anthropomorphic figures with horns and masks, for example, from the shores of Lake Onega in Karelia. There are also numerous petroglyphs of individuals

Figure 2.7. Elk, bird, and bear images in the material culture of circum-Baltic hunter-gatherers. Approximate scale 1:4.5.

wielding elk-headed terminals, for example, from Nämforsen (Tilley 1991), and other places (Lindquist 1994, Nuñez 1995). This corresponds to numerous finds of the actual artefacts: elk-headed stone carved sculptures, mace-heads, and terminals carved from wood (Carpelan 1975, 1979, Nuñez 1995, Zvelebil 1997). The symbolic referent for both these symbols is the shamans' 'turu' or tree of life, symbolizing the ability to undertake a journey between the different world, aided by reptiles and horned animals. A number of petroglyphs show anthropomorphic figures with drums or other musical instruments, for example, examples from Skavberget, Tromsø, in Norway. There are also symbols of the sun or sun discs, horned creatures, and x-ray depictions, more broadly corresponding to shamanistic rituals and to motifs on shamans' personal gear, drums especially (Autio 1995, Nuñez 1995, Manker 1968, Luho 1976, Helskog 1985). Bearing in mind ethnographic descriptions of 'shaman' ecstatic states and the artefacts used in the process, these depictions correspond to shamans performing rituals (for further discussion, see Hultkrantz 1986, 1989, 1990, Pentikainen 1998, Eliade 1989, Price 2001, Helskog 1985, Devlet 2001, Hayden 2003, Hernek 2009).

The location of the rock carvings themselves are not randomly chosen but are often associated with significant natural features in the landscape (Nuñez 1995, Jordan 2001, Bradley 2000), denoting the existence of holy places where shamanistic rituals were performed and enculturated materially by offerings such as antlers or by the carving of images. Saami *seids*, or *bugady* in eastern Siberia serve as ethnographic analogues (Nuñez 1995, Okladnikov 1970, 1974, 1977). They usually include rocks by the lakeside, grottoes, caves, hollow trees, sacred groves of cedar trees, cliffs by lakes, and earlier rock carvings (for further discussion of 'natural places', see Bradley 2000: 3–17).

In burial evidence, we find interments that are significantly different from standard practice and that in terms of grave architecture, treatment of the body and grave goods relate to shamanistic roles and symbols (Larsson 2005: 378–83). For example, four shaft graves at Olenii Ostrov containing four individuals – two males, one female, one juvenile – in a seated or reclining position, can be comprehended as shamans' graves: first, their western orientation (while everyone else was facing east) can be explained as facing the entrance to the lower world, the domain of spirit ancestors of the shamans and of the rulers of the underworld (Anisimov 1963, Zvelebil 1997). The recovery of beaver mandibles from one of these graves reinforces the argument, as mandibles of beaver form part of the shaman's attire among some Siberian groups, in reference to beavers' perceived medicinal and ritual qualities (Gurina 1956, Eidlitz 1969, O'Shea and Zvelebil 1985). Beaver incisors, a category of pendants normally associated with females at Olenii Ostrov, are found in the shaft graves with male and female individuals, and this is also significant, as the shaman's role as a spiritual mediator with the underworld represented both men and women; consequently, his or her robe retained symbols of both genders (Anisimov 1963, Czaplicka 1914, Sokolova 1989, Schmidt 2000, Holliman 2001).

There are other locations containing exceptional burials, which can arguably be attributed to shamans. These include an exceptionally rich burial of a thirty-year-old man buried in a seated position from Janislawice in Poland, dated to 6580 BP (Sulgostowska 1990, Chmielewska 1954, Tomaszewski 1988), a double burial from Duonkalnis in Lithuania, dated to c. 7000 BP (Antanaitis 1999, Butrimas et al. 1995), and a triple burial (burial 19) from Vedbæk-Bogebakken apparently of a male individual with a female range of goods (specimen 19c), a female killed by a bone point (19a) and a child (Meiklejohn et al. 2000). Holliman (2001) and Schmidt (2000) have drawn attention to the transsexual, or 'third gender' role of shamans in North American and Siberian societies, the latter particularly among the Chukchi, which could be regarded as an elaboration of the more general notion of shamans representing both male and female genders. As at Olenii Ostrov, then, female grave goods interred with a male person might indicate the office of a shaman.

At Skateholm II a burial of a young man in a seated position and equipped with an elaborate head-dress (SII-15), can be linked to the shaft graves at Olenii Ostrov and to shamanism for the same reasons (Schmidt 2000, see also Nash 2001, Pugsley 2005 for broader discussion). As Newell and Constandse-Westerman (1989: 165) note regarding this burial: 'Culturally it fits with neither the males nor the females. Both the composition and the quantity of grave accoutrements set this person very much apart from the rest of the samples'. There are other burials at Skateholm II as well as Skateholm 1 placed in a sitting position. Both the burial grounds have been dated to c. 6500–6000 BP (Larsson 1989, 1993, 2005: 386). As Larsson notes, this practice 'is based on a deep-rooted tradition': at Kams on Gotland, two burials, dated to c. 8100 BP, also were placed in a sitting position (Larsson 1989: 217).

At Zvejnieki, both earlier (8200–5300 BP) and later (5300–4200 BP) phases contained extraordinary burials attributed to ritual specialists or shamans (Zagorska 2000a: 81, 92, 2000b: 238, 241, 2001: 123). In the earlier period, a large number of some 2400 animal tooth pendants were arranged into headdresses buried with the deceased. These burials belonged to nine males, eight adolescents, two females, and two adults of indeterminate sex, representing about 7 percent of all the burials, or about a quarter of those with pendants. Ornamental headgear decoration has been found only at two other places, Olenii Ostrov in Karelia and Donkalnis in Lithuania (Gurina 1956, Antanaitis

1999, Zagorska and Lõugas 2000: 240, see also Jelsma 2000: 152 for a North American example). Amber pendants, rings, beads, and sculptures replaced tooth pendants in the later, Pit-Comb Ware ceramic phase. In four cases, mortuary masks of red or blue clay covered the faces of the dead (three male, one adolescent) with amber rings pressed into the eye sockets (Zagorska 2001). Similar finds were made at Hartikka and Pispa in southern Finland (Miettinen 1992) and at Tudozero, northern Russia (Ivaniščev 1992, 1996). Both headgear and masks form an essential part of the shaman's ritual equipment, and ethnographically, we know of shamans buried with their gear (i.e., Devlet 2001, Pentikainen et al. 1998). These artefacts complement the more specific symbolism of finds representing 'messenger animals' such as bear, beaver, elk, snakes, and water birds (Zagorska 2000a, 2000b, 2001).

Let us now return to the evidence for social differentiation in some Mesolithic contexts. It would appear that burial practice and the overarching cosmology attributed here to the Mesolithic hunter-gatherers are in contradiction. Although the burials demonstrate some degree of social differentiation and ranking based on achieved, perhaps even inherited, social status and wealth, the cosmological structure was founded on principles of sharing, circulation, and redistribution of goods based on a fundamental perception of nature as a 'giving environment' that dictates proper relationships between humans, and between humans and animals.

The social (and economic) organisation of the societies in question, embedded within a practical and cognitive structural framework, would change through the operation of dynamic factors resulting from 'agency'. By agency, I refer to historically situated negotiations for power, control, or the attainment of goals between different segments of society, played out at different scales of organisation, starting with individuals, and then moving on to households, kinship groups, communities, and larger units. The use and meaning of symbols would change as a part of this process of negotiation, but within an ideological frame of reference that constrained changes in such manipulations. Inter-community contact, through the exchange of symbolically significant artefacts, helped to maintain the shared cognitive tradition and Mesolithic worldview (Ahlback 2003, Terberger 2003, Zvelebil 2006, 2009, in press). Although such agency modified the use of symbols, the hunter-gatherer ideological structure itself did not change until the corpus of symbols associated with hunter-gatherer societies was replaced by those associated with Neolithic farming, or with later, post-Neolithic ideologies: that is, not until about 5000 BP in southern Scandinavia, c. 3500–3000 BP in Finland and the East Baltic, c. AD 500 in Karelia (Nuñez 1995, Sarvas and Taavitsainen 1976, Taavitsainen and Kinnunen 1979, Carpelan 1975), and not even until modern times, for example, AD 1500–1800 among some groups such as the Kets in Western Siberia (Aleksenko 1967, Resketov 1972, Jordan 2001).

Within this broadly egalitarian framework, people acted to challenge its fundamental ideological principles. Increasingly, the ideology of sharing, although adhered to nominally, did not reflect social practice in the late Mesolithic. The tension between ideological prescription and practice increased with technological innovation, increase in territoriality and, later, contact with farming societies. Territoriality and delayed-return technologies imply labour investment in land and resources, restriction of access to resources, and encourage resource ownership. Consequently, the appropriation of resources appears no longer a matter of ritually sanctioned, collective exchange between humans and animals but a product of individual human labour.

It is the organisation of labour that is crucial here. In this respect, descent-based social structures, controlled by elders through alliance and exchange, created the structural conditions for social dependency (Bender 1978, 1985, Tilley 1991, Peterson 1993). This may have been achieved through competitive gift-giving and feasting (Hayden 1990, 2003), or the control of sexual reproduction and of ritual knowledge (Tilley 1991), and may have led to the concentration of social power in the hands of a restricted number of individuals. Ritual specialists were in the best position to assume the control of lineages on the basis of their moral authority (Aldenderfer 1993, Hayden 2003), and in doing so, to enhance their power base by creating a 'simultaneous' hierarchy rather than a 'sequential' hierarchy, that is a hierarchy whereby several prestige positions and social ranks are invested in a single person (Johnson 1982).

Such authority may have been enhanced in situations of increasing contact and confrontation. Jordan (2003b: 93) notes that, within the context of Khanty shamanism, 'The shamans constitute the only agents empowered with the ability to enact change, awarding them sole responsibility for ensuring the community's security within a dangerous and hostile world', whereas Wallis (2002: 225) draws attention to the essentially liminal and transformational qualities of shamanism, endowed with the potential for 'dismantling all fixed notions of identity' (Taussig 1987: 57 quoted in Wallis 2001: 225). It seems clear, then, that within northern hunter-gatherer societies, shamans, as moral guardians with power to validate ideological shifts in social relations and social structure, provided powerful agents of change. It is not surprising then that the role of shamans historically appears to have increased in importance with time as contact-related tensions built up (Pentikäinen 1998).

Transition to Farming – Resistance and Transformation

As we know, hunter-gatherer communities in the circum-Baltic zone adopted agro-pastoral farming at different rates. In the west Baltic, this process lasted 100–300 years, whereas further east the introduction of imported domestic plants and animals – cattle, sheep, goat, pig, horse, pulses, and cereals – occurred very gradually over a period of 5000 years, from c. 5000–500 BP (Table 2.1, Figure 2.8).

Farming was introduced from Central Europe between 6400–6000 BP into northern Poland and Germany by enclave-forming, isolated settlements of the LBK and derivative traditions (SBK, Lengyel). Following this episode, the first extensive farming communities in northern Poland and Germany, Denmark, southern Norway, and southern and middle Sweden belong to the TRB culture and date from c. 5700 BP on the north European Plain and from c. 5200 BP (4000 cal BC) in southern Scandinavia (Midgley 1992, Bogucki 1996, 1998, 2000, Price 2000, Nowak 2001, Fischer and Kristiansen 2002, Larsson et al. 2003, McCartan et al. 2009, Blankholm this volume). In certain regions of Poland, such as Silesia, Kashubia, Mazovia, and Masuria, hunter-gatherer communities survived into the Bronze Age, c. 3500 BP (Bagnienvski 1986, Cyrek et al. 1986, Kobusziewicz and Kabaciński 1998). In more eastern regions of the Baltic, the agricultural transition unfolded between 4500 and 2500 BP (Zvelebil 1981, 1987, 1993b, Daugnora and Girninkas 1995, Antanaitis et al. 2000, Antanaitis 2001, Kriiska 2003, Lang 2007). In parts of Lithuania hunter-gatherers continued until c. 2500 BP (Daugnora and Girninkas 1995, Antanaitis 2001). In southern Finland, farming was gradually adopted between 3500 and 2000 BP (Zvelebil 1981, Vuorela 1976, 1998, Meinander 1984, Vuorela and Lempiainen 1988, Taavitsainen 1998). In Swedish Norrland, and in northern and eastern Finland, the transition only ended with the Medieval period after the domestication of reindeer by the Saami and the development of swidden farming among the Karelians (Mulk and Bayliss-Smith 1999, Taavitsainen et al. 1998). In this sense, there is no break between the Mesolithic hunter-gatherer communities of the Early Postglacial period and the later prehistoric and early historical hunters within this region. Rather than viewing these later hunter-gatherers as Stone Age survivals, however, we should regard them as communities who have successfully responded to the historical necessity of living in an increasingly farming world by developing the trading potential of hunter-gatherer existence: they became commercial hunter-gatherers.

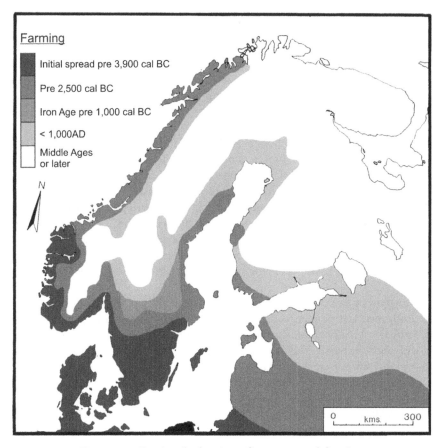

Figure 2.8. Regional adoption of agro-pastoral farming.

Forager-Farmer Contacts

Although practical reasons and broader socioideological motivations for the adoption of farming no doubt varied from region to region (e.g., Dennell 1983, Zvelebil 1986c, Hodder 1990, Harris 1996, Thorpe 1996, Price 2000), contact and exchange between foraging and farming communities was bound to play a key role as a vehicle for the adoption of farming. The nature of such exchange within the conditions of the agricultural frontier has been much discussed in recent years (Alexander 1978, Dennell 1983, 1992, Green and Perlman 1985, Zvelebil 1986c, 1996b, 2000a, 2002, 2004a, 2005, Zvelebil and Dolukhanov 1991, Zvelebil et al. 1998a, Zvelebil and Lillie 2000, Barker 2006). It is clear that there is extensive archaeological evidence for trade and contact between the first farming communities of the north European plain (and later, southern Scandinavia) and hunter-gatherer settlements to the north and east (but see Blankholm this volume). Settlements of each community were often located close to one another, as in Kujavia (Malinowski 1986, Bogucki 1988, Bogucki and Grygiel 1993, Zvelebil 1998, 2005, Nowak 2001), or were sometimes separated by relatively unexploited 'no-man's lands' as in southern Finland (Zvelebil 1981). Exchanges occurred in a patterned, structured way. Characteristically, raw materials and products of hunting and gathering such as furs, honey, and seal fat were exchanged by hunter-gatherers for finished products such as

53

axes, ceramics, and ornaments (Vankina 1970, Andersen 1975, 1987, Schwabedissen 1981, Siiriäinen 1981, 1982, Zvelebil 1985, 1996b, 2000a, 2006, Solberg 1989, Nuñez 1990, Price and Gebauer 1992, Timofeev 1998a, Zvelebil et al. 1998, Nuñez and Okkonen 1999, Rowley-Conwy 1999, Fischer 2002). In some areas, such as Scania and the East Baltic, grain and domestic animals also may have been exchanged (Dolukhanov 1979, Jennbert 1984, Zvelebil 1985, Zvelebil and Dolukhanov 1991). Such exchanges would pass, as Sherratt (1982: 23) has suggested with particular reference to cattle 'as transactions between acephalous groups linked by alliances and as symbols of competitive prestige'.

Forager-farmer contacts also may have been developed in terms of patron–client relationships, where foragers acted as providers of services or as rented herders of livestock for farming communities (Fewster 1994, 2001). Typically, foragers derived economic benefits from livestock or its products, whereas farmers were able to extend the grazing area and increase the size of their herds through renting out to client foragers. The close and enduring proximity of early Neolithic settlements and foraging communities on the north European Plain in Poland, and the subsequent pattern of emergence there of the 'secondary' Neolithic TRB, Corded Ware and Globular Amphorae groups lends considerable support to such a scenario. Such patterns of contact and exchange would have had social, economic, and demographic consequences for hunter-gatherer communities.

In many regions of the circum-Baltic in the later Mesolithic, differences in social status are apparent. Both men and women could achieve high status, but social standing did not seem to accrue with age. At Skateholm, Zvejnieki, and Olenii Ostrov we have young individuals, even children, with elaborate burials, suggesting some degree of social ascription, that is, inherited status. Although regional differences exist, and more nuanced approaches are needed in the interpretation of mortuary remains (e.g., Nilsson Stutz 2003), overall, such social differentiation would appear to contradict the normative egalitarian ideology of sharing, and thus to provide a basis for promoting social change. Additional social tensions may have resulted from relations with farming communities and the incorporation of hunter-gatherer societies into broader exchange networks. The impact of the agricultural frontier would have been felt in many aspects of hunter-gatherer social life: particularly if relations assumed a competitive, rather than cooperative character. Farming goods and products, such as polished stone axes, ceramics, or cattle contained a component of added value, arising from their exotic origin and prestigious – perhaps subversive – ideological associations. Unless reinterpreted in the context of hunter-gatherer ideology, such exchange goods were bound to promote a more permanent establishment of social elites.

At the same time, the presence of agricultural communities in regions neighboring hunter-gatherer settlement may have engendered disruption of hunter-gatherer patterns of resource use, for example, by the opportunistic use of hunter-gatherer territories by farmers. As Moore (1985) has shown, this would cause serious interference with planning and information exchange among hunter-gatherers essential for an effective exploitation of their wild resources. Disruption also might have been caused by the direct procurement of raw materials and wild foods by farmers establishing their own 'hunting lands' in hunter-gatherer territories. Both of these processes are recorded in the Baltic region from historically and ethnographically attested encounters between hunting and farming populations (e.g., Hvarfner 1965, Taavitsainen et al. 1998, Mulk and Bayliss-Smith 1999). The late Bronze Age site of Otterböte in the Åland Islands, which may have been a seal-hunting outpost of Lusatian farmers from northern Poland, provides a convincing prehistoric antecedent (Gustavsson 1997). Such predatory relations were bound to result in declining resources and ecological damage to the hunter-gatherer environment.

The demographic consequences of greater population growth among farmers as opposed to foragers have been much highlighted as an explanation for farming dispersals (e.g., Ammermann and Cavalli-Sforza 1984, Renfrew 1987, Renfrew and Boyle 2000), although in my opinion such demographic differences have been exaggerated (Zvelebil 1986a, 2000a, 2003b). This must have been especially true for coastal and riverine zones in circum–Baltic Europe, where, as we have seen, dietary focus on the consumption of marine and freshwater resources was fairly common. Recent research indicates that consumption of n-3 fatty acids, found in marine fish, shellfish, and other marine food resources as well as in oily freshwater fish, increases human reproductive potential. A study by Olsen and Secher (2002) of pregnant Danish women shows that those who regularly consumed fish rich in n-3 fatty acids had a significantly reduced rate of preterm delivery (1.9 percent as opposed to 7.1 percent for those who did not eat fish), whereas the birth weight was significantly higher among the fish-eaters. The importance of fat in hunter-gatherer diets is well known, and the easy access to fish and marine fat by women in hunter-gatherer communities, would have had major reproductive implications (Speth 1990, Moss 1993, Zvelebil 2000b, 2003a, 2003b).

However, a major and potentially disruptive effect for hunter-gatherer communities may have been the departure of women, through marriage or other means, to farming settlements, thereby generating an excess of women among farmers (hypergyny) and a shortage among hunter-gatherers (hypogyny). This is an ideologically conditioned practice, occurring in situations in which women perceive existence in farming communities as being of greater advantage to themselves and their children than a hunting and gathering existence. Although first noticed in ethnographic contexts, there is now some prehistoric evidence for hypogyny-generating population transfers in the context of the first farming LBK culture in southwest Germany. Biochemical trace element analysis of bone remains from early LBK sites in Germany has revealed that males in these communities found as partners exogenous females from surrounding regions that were still inhabited by hunter-gatherers. Intermarriage of LBK farmers with indigenous women would explain some ancient DNA patterns in these populations (Price et al. 2001, Bentley et al. 2002, Haak et al. 2005). In response to these tensions, we can perhaps identify in the archaeological record examples of both transformation and resistance.

Strategies of Transformation

Within the circum-Baltic zone, it was only in southern Sweden (M. Larsson 1987, Solberg 1989, L. Larsson 1990, Rowley-Conwy 1999) that the adoption of farming was relatively rapid and resembled that of Denmark. Elsewhere, we can observe a much more gradual transformation, marked by the development of societies who successfully combined hunting and gathering with elements of farming:, and in so doing, created communities that do not fit easily our prevailing categories; they remain suspended between our conventional notions of hunter-gatherers and farmers.

One of the most striking features of the conditions prevailing on the north European Plain in Poland is the long coexistence of farming and hunting-gathering communities, coexistence that lasted for more than 2500 years between 6400 and 3700 BP (Malinowski 1986, Zvelebil et al. 1998a, 1998b, Nowak 2001). In some areas, such as Kujavia or Pomerania, hunter-gatherers and farmers of both the TRB and the Danubian tradition lived side by side only a few kilometres apart. Despite the coarse spatial and temporal resolution of the evidence available today, such patterning suggests a very gradual incorporation of foraging communities with those of farmers after an extended history of contact, occurring within an established and effective social framework, and marked archaeologically by trade and exchange (Nowak 2001). Within such a framework, hunter-gatherers would play the role of suppliers of specialized goods and services, and act perhaps as herders in client-patron relationships. Intermarriage between the two communities would have contributed to the breakdown of the early farming (LBK and Lengyel) social and ideological structure, witnessed, for example, in the final stage of the Brzesc Kujawski settlement in Kujavia (Bogucki and Grygiel 1993, Bogucki 1995, 1996, 1998) and the subsequent development of a new foraging-farming community, identified archaeologically as TRB (Midgley 1992, Nowak 2001, Zvelebil 2005). This process would have been accomplished across as number of generations, as communities replicated and combined the cultural traditions of their foraging and farming predecessors in an act of cultural (and genetic) integration and innovation. Later, during the fifth millennium BP, similar developments arose from contacts between TRB farming farmers and Pit- and Comb-ware using hunter-gatherers in central and eastern Poland, leading to the constitution of two new cultural traditions: the Globular Amphorae and Corded Ware (for archaeological correlates of this process, see Malinowski 1986, Zvelebil et al. 1998a, Nowak 2001).

In the eastern Baltic, the picture is again somewhat different. Instead of generations of separate coexistence and cultural exchange, we can identify the slow and staggered adoption of cultural traits and innovations, traditionally associated with the 'Forest Neolithic' by communities of indigenous hunter-gatherers. The use of ceramics was adopted first, between 6500 and 6000 BP (see Dolukhanov 1979, 1986, Timofeev 1987, 1998b, Zvelebil and Dolukhanov 1991, Jordan and Zvelebil 2009, Dolukhanov this volume). Elements of agro-pastoral farming were adopted at a very slow rate over the following three thousand years, and it was a process marked by remarkable regional variation over relatively short distances. For example, in Latvia and Lithuania, between 5500 and 3500 BP there were enduring hunting and gathering communities such as Kretuonas and Zemaitiške around Lake Kretuonas (Girininkas 1990, 1998, Daugnora and Girininkas 1996, Antanaitis 2001), who incorporated some degree of farming, such as Šventoji (Rimantienė 1979, 1992a, 1992b, 1998), coastal settlements specializing in seal hunting such as Sārnate (Vankina 1970, Zvelebil 1987), and communities focussed on the intensive exploitation and management of native plant foods and vegetal resources, such as Abora, Lagazha and Zvidze around Lake Lubans (Loze 1979, 1998, Loze and Yakubovkaya 1984, Loze et al. 1984). This was a society based principally on hunting and gathering for subsistence, yet making some occasional use of domesticates and possibly cultigens from about 4500 BP. The presence of domesticates in such low numbers can be explained as a result of wide-ranging trading networks, operating within the context of the Corded Ware/Boat Axe culture (Dolukhanov 1979, Zvelebil 1993b), and their limited use continuing until the end of the fourth millennium BP fits well with the notion of a ritual and symbolic, rather than economic, significance (Hayden 1990). The decisive shift to an agro-pastoral economy occurred only in the Late Bronze Age, between 3100 and 2500 BP (Zvelebil 1985, 1987, 1998, Daugnora and Girininkas 1996, Janik 1998, Antanaitis et al. 2000, Antanaitis 2001). The picture emerging here, then, is one of acquisition of Neolithic technology by hunter-gatherers and selective adoption of elements of the agro-pastoral economy to fit local conditions for some 3000 years before the full and final adoption of farming (see also Knutsson et al. 2003 for northern Sweden).

We can identify similar, regionally variable patterns for the adoption of agro-pastoral farming in Finland (Vuorela 1975, 1998, Zvelebil 1978, 1981, Siiriäinen 1981, 1982, Taavitsainen et al. 1998, etc.) Norway (Nygaard 1989, Prescott 1995, 1996, Rowley-Conwy 1999), and central and northern Sweden (Welinder 1979, 1981a, Holm 1992, Åkerlund 1996, Welinder et al. 1998, Knutsson et al. 2003, McCartan 2009). These transitions unfold between the end of the Neolithic and the Medieval period, that is, between c. 4000 BP and AD 1500, which, for reasons of space, cannot be detailed here. It is worth noting, however, that cultural horizons such as the Pitted Ware culture in Sweden indicate a return to hunting and gathering after a limited period of farming – in these regions, the farming experiment appears, at least temporarily, to have failed (Welinder 1975, 1981a, 1998, Åkerlund 1996, Zvelebil 1996b, Rowley-Conwy 1999, Lindqvist and Possnert 1994).

Strategies of Resistance

Several people have noted the incompatibility of foraging and farming both as an economic practice (Zvelebil and Rowley-Conwy 1984, 1986) and as a social and symbolic tradition. Chapman (1993), for example, argues that products that symbolised farming were excluded from Lepenski Vir (see Bonsall this volume). Tilley (1991) describes how the fishing and hunting communities at Nämforsen accommodated their economy to the demands of an exchange system controlled by farmers, and how they restructured their symbolic system in the process. In both cases, however, farming appears to have been rejected symbolically and in practice. The subsequent cultural simplification, evident during the final phases of hunter-gatherer settlement in some parts of southern Scandinavia (Blankholm this volume), as well as in inland southwest and central Finland, or in parts of Sweden just before the adoption of farming, suggests a process of prehistoric 'encapsulation', whereby hunter-gatherer communities are marginalised and impoverished by encroaching farming settlement (Woodburn 1982, 1988).

Overlapping chronologically with this, we can identify another 'strategy of resistance', as northern hunter-gatherers became increasingly drawn into the 'world system' of trading relations in the more recent past (Budil 2001). This was perhaps the most effective hunter-gatherer survival strategy, based on the commercialisation of hunting-gathering economic practices in a world increasingly dominated by farming societies. The beginnings of this process can be identified already in the late Mesolithic of northern and circum-Baltic Europe (e.g., Zvelebil 1996b, 1998, 2000a, 2002, Fischer 2002). The adoption of ceramics by hunting and gathering communities from about 6600 BP is held by many to have aided in a major way the production of seal grease and oil, some of it for exchange (Nuñez 1990 with references, Nuñez and Okkonen 1999). Patterned discard of bone remains of fur-bearing animals at specialised kill-sites suggests trade in fur in the East Baltic from the mid-6th millennium BP (Zvelebil 1985, 1993b, Timofeev 1998a), and trade in amber, flint, green, and red slate by circum-Baltic hunter-gatherer communities is also documented (Vankina 1970, Loze 1980, Zvelebil 1996a, 1998, 2006, Timofeev 1998a, Nuñez and Okkonen 1999). In aggregate, the participation of hunting and gathering communities of the Baltic in trade and exchange with farming settlements in southern Scandinavia and central and eastern Europe resulted in or at least contributed to the florescence of residentially permanent, trading settlements such as Kierikki in northern Finland in the fifth and fourth millennium BP (Nuñez and Okkonen 1999), to the persistence of, or return to, a hunter-gatherer existence in central Baltic within the cultural context of the Pitted Ware culture, c. 4500–3800 BP (Welinder 1975, 1977, 1981a, Åkerlund 1996, Zvelebil 1996b, fig 18.3, Nuñez and Liden 1997, Rowley-Conwy 1999, Lindquist and Possnert 1994), and to the continued existence of hunting and gathering communities in eastern and northern Finland and Karelia during later prehistory and into the Medieval period (c. 3200 BP–AD 1600) (Taavitsainen et al. 1998, Hvarfner 1965). The domestication of reindeer, the incorporation of reindeer herding within existing strategies of hunting and fishing, and trade in the products of reindeer husbandry further reinforced the viability of hunter-gatherer social and economic traditions, and contributed to their continuation into modern times (Hvarfner 1965, Igegren 1985, Aikio 1989, Mulk and Bayliss-Smith 1999, Zachrisson 1994).

Marek Zvelebil

If we need to identify an end to the communities that remained essentially hunting and gathering in terms of subsistence and social life, the key transition appears to have been social and symbolic rather than economic (Zvelebil 1993a, 1993b, 1998, 2003a). This is marked by the abandonment of symbols and rituals associated with the traditional hunter-gatherer cosmology, described earlier, which had survived first intact and then in a more fragmented form beyond the introduction of farming. Their replacement by other forms of symbolic expression associated with agro-pastoral existence began in the Late Neolithic in the south Baltic, and continued slowly across the East Baltic in the Bronze Age, then in Finland and other regions of northeast Europe in the Iron Age and the early Medieval period. As first historical sources show, the hunter-gatherer system of beliefs and symbols still operated in early modern times in northern Finland and Karelia (Shefferus 1673, Hvarfner 1965).

Conclusion

Our current perception of the Mesolithic masks important variation in the organisation of Post-glacial hunter-gatherer communities, and obscures continuity between the Mesolithic and the Neolithic. In some – mostly interior – regions of northern Europe, we are probably dealing with egalitarian, territorial yet residentially mobile hunter-gatherers, albeit this impression is certain to be exaggerated by more recent postdepositional processes that have acted to remove the more central riverine core areas of hunter-gatherer settlement, and to destroy maritime elements of the archaeological record. In the interior regions of Europe, then, our archaeological record is impov-erished compared to coastal areas (Zvelebil 1998). In some – mostly coastal – regions of northern and circum-Baltic Europe, hunter-gatherer communities were fully or partly sedentary, socially differentiated, and managed their resources in logistically organised seasonal schedules, exercising a degree of control which offered an effective alternative to agro-pastoral husbandry. These organ-isational features foreshadowed those of the Neolithic and suggest a continuity of economic and social practices between the two periods.

Among such hunter-gatherer communities, the overarching belief system or cosmological frame-work must have played an important role in promoting or proscribing social and economic change. Based on the continuity of symbols and on ritual and symbolic similarities between ethnohistori-cally known and prehistoric hunter-gatherers in northern Eurasia, the cosmological framework of the Mesolithic hunter-gatherers in northern and temperate Europe was based on egalitarian prin-ciples, communal ownership of resources and the convention of sharing, inherent in the perception of nature as a 'giving' environment. Such ideology gradually came into conflict with social reality in the late Mesolithic. This was brought about by the development of delayed-return technologies, an increase in social competition, social differentiation, and, later, contact with farming commu-nities. The resolution of this conflict differed from region to region. Arguably, we can identify two responses. One is ideological approbation, marked by the abandonment of hunter-gatherer symbols linked to an egalitarian ideology of sharing, by symbolic and ritual transformation, and by the full adoption of farming. The second is ideological censure, marked by the continuation of the old 'egalitarian' symbols, by nominal adherence to the ideology of sharing, and by continued reliance on hunting and gathering. In practical terms, such ideological resistance led to frontier adjustments and innovations, marked by the development of hunting, fishing, and sealing for trade, by the domestication of reindeer for transport and husbandry, and by the inclusion of swidden farming into existing schedules of wild resource management and land use. In this sense, the existence of hunting and gathering populations in many parts of the circum–Baltic region never ended, but through innovation and transformation continues to the present day.

Acknowledgments

I would like to thank the Leverhulme trust for grant F/00 118/AP, which enabled me to carry out research that contributed to the preparation of this chapter.

Chapter 3

Norwegian Mesolithic Trends:
A Review

Hein Bjartmann Bjerck*

Introduction

This chapter presents an overview of the Mesolithic societies of Atlantic Scandinavia, with particular reference to environmental variation, technocomplexes, and chronological and spatial trends in technology, economy, and social developments. The current discussion is also set within the context of the research history on the Norwegian Mesolithic over the past one hundred years and especially within the changing theoretical perspectives of recent decades, which have witnessed a formidable increase in levels of knowledge. The sheer volume of data, the variety and number of theoretical perspectives, interpretations, publications, and actors – everything related to Norwegian Mesolithic research – seems to be accelerating, and fully half of the works cited in this chapter are later than 1992.

We no longer live in the world that older established researchers remember, when one knew all the other active researchers, could cite radiocarbon dates by heart and quickly summarise key sites and relevant literature. Then, one sought to advance Mesolithic research secure in the positivistic belief that the many fragments of archaeological data would one day come together to create a representation of a true past, and that one's own contribution however small was helping to build something 'bigger' as part of a wider scientific community with a common purpose.

An important factor in this development has been a multiplicity of theoretical perspectives that continually challenge the established boundaries of what can be known about the past. This would hardly have been possible without the postprocessual opposition to the strict scientific ideals of the logical-positivistic New Archaeology. However, archaeology has increasingly evolved into a game in which poorly defined and fragmentary data are used to advance new theoretical perspectives, and hypothesis testing and graphical presentation of measured parameters are replaced by colourful 'might-have-beens' based on data carefully selected for the occasion. The divide

* The Norwegian University of Science and Technology, Trondheim, Norway.

between observation and assumption is being erased, key facts must be extracted from subordinate clauses, and important skills such as accurate presentation of archaeological data, concise definitions, and statistical evaluation are falling out of fashion. Today, underlying attitudes and movements that even the author may not be aware of are often given more attention than the intended message. Previously, notions of 'truth' and 'falsity' were an important force in archaeological discussion. As they have weakened, so, too, paradoxically, has the readiness to engage in scholarly debate. This is an awkward and perhaps worrying contrast to the individual projects of archaeological field research, which are more exciting than ever. Cultural history and empirical data have intrinsic values, and should not be reduced to mere *vehicles* for elegant demonstrations of the latest theoretical perspective. Nevertheless, working on this review has left me with optimism for the future of Norwegian Mesolithic research.

A Century of Mesolithic Research

Traditional Archaeology

A hundred years ago, hardly anything of what we today associate with the Mesolithic existed. The 'Early Stone Age' was simply the absence of ceramics, agriculture and polished tools. In Norway, the dissolution of the union with Sweden in 1905 formed a focus for anything that could contribute to the national identity. Stone Age research highlighted the nation's solid cultural-historical foundations with prehistoric roots in a hunter population long before farming, pots and polishing (E. Eriksen 1996, Tansem 1998).

A. M. Hansen (1904) was one of the first to focus on specifically Norwegian Mesolithic material, notably the semipolished stone axes found in considerable numbers around Oslo fjord that became a lead-type of the '*Nøstvet Culture*' (Brøgger 1905). A few years later, A. Nummedal discovered clusters of flint artefacts along the coast off Kristiansund, Northwest Norway. These were deemed to be older than the Nøstvet finds (Rygh 1911, Nummedal 1912), and eventually labelled as the *Fosna* (Nummedal 1924). These large, coarse artefacts resembled Mesolithic/Late Palaeolithic finds from the continent. In 1925, Nummedal discovered artefacts in Finnmark with certain typological similarities to the Fosna material, and named the *Komsa* after the site where this material was first recovered (Nummedal 1927, Bøe and Nummedal 1936).

The following fifty years of Mesolithic research in Norway operated within the framework of Nøstvet, Fosna, and Komsa technocomplexes. The research-profile was securely anchored within what we today would call 'traditional archaeology,' focusing on the mapping of sites, collection building, and typological definitions that formed the basis for discussions of dating and origins (e.g., Brøgger 1909, Shetelig 1922, Nummedal 1922, 1924, Bjørn 1928, 1930, 1931, Gjessing 1945, Freundt 1949). However, the limited understanding of lithic technology resulted in typologies that were often based on mere morphological similarities. This resulted in several time-consuming misinterpretations (Waraas 2001: 22). Some scholars related Fosna to the Danish *Ertebølle*, with reference to the marked flake-axe element (e.g., Rygh 1913). But claims for the presence of transverse points, also an Ertebølle lead-type (ibid.), were later rejected when the artefacts turned out to be blade fragments with the shape of a transverse point but not its technological features (Bjørn 1930: 14).

Although it was agreed that Nøstvet was the youngest of these three traditions, the relationship between Fosna and Komsa was unclear and the subject of much debate (e.g., Nummedal 1927, Bjørn 1928, 1930, Gjessing 1937, 1945, Freundt 1949, and later research history in Hauglid 1993,

Tansem 1998, Waraas 2001). Bjørn (1928, 1930) saw the coarse character of the material as evidence of primitiveness and therefore of great antiquity. In this light, Fosna was interpreted as a development of Komsa, in its turn assumed to be rooted in Eastern Palaeolithic communities. However, lack of parallels for Fosna/Komsa in their 'natural' areas of origins on the continent remained a problem. At an early stage, Nummedal (1924) introduced discoveries from the North Sea into the debate on origins, but this received little attention until reintroduced by Odner (1966) many years later.

In hindsight, it might seem as if Mesolithic research before the 1960s contributed rather limited insight into Mesolithic societies. Although neither theory nor method were explicitly focussed, one can find elegant examples of hypothesis testing (Nummedal 1933), excavations of complex contexts with organic remains (Bøe 1934, Lund 1951) and dwelling sites (Gjessing 1943), and syntheses full of insights into environmental adaptation and social factors (e.g., Shetelig 1922, Brøgger 1925, Gjessing 1943, 1945). In addition, site-registration in various regions of the country, combined with continued collection building and the systematic definition of artefact-types and culture groups, formed a solid base for the new methods and research focus of the 1960s and onwards.

New Archaeology/Processual Archaeology

The new research focus and scientific perspectives of Anglo-American archaeology during the 1960s greatly influenced Norwegian Mesolithic research. So, too, did developments beyond the confines of narrow academic discourse. The threatening signs of global population growth, industry and agriculture, overexploitation, and their effect on global ecosystems, were as clear in Norway as elsewhere, and highlighted interactions between human societies and their ecological habitats in archaeological investigations. The introduction of radiocarbon dating implied an important synergy between archaeology and the natural sciences. A common timescale, liberated from the earlier archaeological methods of dating, created an opening for interdisciplinary research focused on the interaction between people and environment. This wider context is important for understanding the trend towards a more scientific archaeology, emphasizing quantitative analysis, objectivity, and a hypothetico-deductive approach. Cultural heritage legislation in Norway and the accelerating speed and scale of construction and development projects throughout the 1960s led to several large-scale archaeological investigations. These projects provided an important focus for interdisciplinary studies (e.g., A. B. Johansen 1973). Initially, projects related to large scale hydroelectric dam projects in mountain and forest regions gave insights into areas where little had previously been known. Later, in the 1980s, the discovery of large oil and gas reserves in the North Sea gave impetus to large-scale construction projects. These were mainly in the coastal zone where there was a high concentration of Stone Age sites. Improvements in infrastructure (mainly roads, tunnels, bridges) also resulted in comprehensive archaeological investigations.

All in all this led to a formidable professionalisation of all aspects of archaeological investigation, from project organisation to excavation, documentation and analytical methods. Systematic excavations using reference-grids, a scientific approach to stratigraphical information, water sieving of deposits, and the gathering of environmental samples all became standard in large archaeological investigations.

Within academic discourse, new trends in research focus following the integration of archaeology and anthropology in Anglo-American research are easily traced in Norwegian Mesolithic scholarship. Increasingly, anthropology became popular in the combination of disciplines in formal education at university level, and Stone Age research was exposed to many sources of inspiration that focused on general laws in cultural processes, economic structures, ecology and cultural adaptation (e.g., Barth 1956, Kleivan 1962). An early example of this trend is Odner's work on the adaptive strategies of the Komsa Culture at Varanger (1966). Many more followed (e.g., Mikkelsen 1971, 1975a, 1975b, 1976, 1978, Rolfsen 1972, Indrelid 1973, 1978, Gjessing 1975, Simonsen 1975a, 1975b, Welinder 1981b, Lindblom 1982). A. B. Johansen's works from this period (1970, 1971, 1973, 1975, 1978) also reflect these perspectives, and illustrate the new focus on a stringent scientific methodology. Helskog, Indrelid, and Mikkelsen's *Morphologic Classification of Flaked Stone Artefacts* (1976) introduced a national set of 'objective' definitions that marked a break with the traditional type-terminology and formed the basis for the current classification-system in Norway.

Towards the end of the 1950s, *The National Laboratory for ^{14}C Dating* was established in Trondheim (Nydal and Westin 1979). The scientific significance of the new dating methods is obvious in studies from the 1970s and onwards (Hagen 1979), with a series of works presenting absolute dated chronological frameworks (e.g., Indrelid 1975, Mikkelsen 1975a, Møllenhus 1977, Bjørgo 1981, Bjerck 1986, Nygaard 1989, 1990). Radiometric dating made it possible to work beyond the typological-chronological structures based on southern Scandinavian material, and opened up studies of artefact-groups in raw materials, such as quartz, quartzite, and basaltic rock, that are important and specific categories in the North Scandinavian Mesolithic (e.g., A. B. Johansen 1971). These works also illustrate the shift from qualitative to quantitative approaches.

Radiometric dating resulted in a similar boom in the natural sciences. The detailed understanding and dating of Postglacial shoreline displacement was of huge importance for Mesolithic studies. A detailed empirical base for the dating of relative sea levels was established for most coastal areas (e.g., Donner et al. 1977, Sørensen 1979, Hafsten 1983, Lie et al. 1983, Kaland 1984, Møller 1989, Anundsen 1985, Kjemperud 1986, Svendsen and Mangerud 1987). The later development of models of sea level change that allowed interpolation of shoreline positions made this information more accessible to archaeologists (e.g., Møller 1989). Archaeological data also contributed to palaeoenvironmental studies, for example, studies of culture layers associated with beach sediments (Indrelid 1973c, Bjerck 1982, Bostwick Bjerck and A. B. Olsen 1983: 15, Kleppe 1985, Møller 1987, Møller 2003, Bondevik 2003).

Postprocessual Archaeology

Indicative of the movement towards critical, postprocessual perspectives towards the mid-1980s was the well-meant 'off-the-record' mocking of Helskog's (1984) analysis of the large collections of dwellings at Varanger. Were these well-run villages as Simonsen (1979) had indicated? Helskog's thorough analysis using the New Archaeology's finely tuned tools and a logical-positivistic, minimalist perspective, where 'lesser and younger' was always more likely than 'greater and older,' seemed to indicate that this was significantly exaggerated. It was difficult to produce scientific evidence that more than one or two dwellings had been occupied at the same time. But could Helskog even be sure that the *whole* house had been in use at the same time?

The new orientation of theory and research focus is evident from the mid-1980s. Many of the new approaches were first introduced and implemented via the international oriented archaeologists at the University of Tromsø. An early example relating to Mesolithic research is Sandmo's (1986) work on Preboreal material from Troms, in which choices of raw material are interpreted as intentional markers of social identity.

Hein Bjartmann Bjerck

The new orientation is particularly visible in rock-art research. Up until the end of the 1960s, research had proceeded along traditional lines with the systematic documentation of sites and figures, comparative studies of motifs, and questions related to dating and origins (e.g., Gjessing 1932, Bøe 1932, Engelstad 1934, Hallström 1938, Simonsen 1958). Tellingly, rock-art studies were not highly profiled within Processual Archaeology. Rock art was apparently not a particularly attractive category for scientific discourse in the 1960s and 1970s. It was difficult to measure, impossible to evaluate and marginalised within the troublesome subsystems of religion, ideology, ritual, and symbolism. The few studies that do exist from this period are attempts to create order within the data with respect to terminology and chronology (e.g., Hagen 1969, Bakka 1973, 1975), and the term 'petroglyph' was coined in preference to 'rock-carvings' by O. S. Johansen (1972). Others attempted to examine rock art in the context of more fashionable themes such as economy and ecology (e.g., Mikkelsen 1976, 1986). However it is interesting to note that Anders Hagen's (1976) popular book, *Rock Art*, touches on a far broader range of possible interpretations, probably because of a more liberated position outside the scientific sphere.

Of course, it was precisely this ambiguity that attracted more postprocessually oriented researchers. One example is Hesjedal's (1994) research on *Rock Art in North Norway*. Using structuralist/textual theory he constructed an elegant analysis of sites and motifs and presented an interpretation that highlighted cultural and social issues. This marked a radical break with earlier interpretations that circled around the costs and benefits of ecofunctionalistic hunting rituals. Typically, Hesjedal closes his work by pointing out that the proposed interpretation is not necessarily correct – his aim had been to demonstrate that alternative theoretical perspectives could lead to new interpretations with a commensurable internal logic based on the same material.

This break with the Processual paradigm paved the way for extensive use of rock art as empirical data within most research themes in Postprocessual Archaeology: social aspects, the use of symbols, gender-issues, ethnicity, phenomenology and critical research history (e.g., Helskog 1987, 1995, 1999, Hood 1988, Sognnes 1994, 1995, 1998, 2002, Helskog and B. Olsen 1995, Grønnesby 1998, Mandt 1998, Fuglestvedt 2001, 2003, Haukalid 1999, Ramstad 2000a, Lødøen 2003, 2009).

From the late 1980s, one can discern a clear shift of focus away from *economy* and chronology (processes, continuity, change) to *social* and *spatial* issues, both on a micro and a macro level. A relevant example is A. B. Olsen and Alsaker's (1984) documentation of the long-term utilisation of the stone quarries at Hespriholmen and Stakaneset. The spatial distribution of axes from these quarries was related to 'social territories' in an analysis where lithic raw materials were treated as group markers within Mesolithic societies. This perspective has been developed in a series of studies on the geographical distribution of the Mesolithic material (e.g., Sandmo 1986, Gjerland 1990a, Sjurseike 1994, Bergsvik 2003b, Grydeland 2000, 2005, Bergsvik and A. B. Olsen 2003, Berg 2003). Similar spatial studies also have been carried out on groups of artefacts and on combinations of raw material and artefact groups (Gjerland 1988, Glørstad 2002, Nyland 2002, Skår 2003, Skjelstad 2003, Lødøen 1995, 1998, Bergsvik 2004, Gundersen 2009).

Research on settlements has largely followed the same direction. At an intra-site level, a series of studies focused on structures and distribution patterns pinpointing activity patterns and social organisation (e.g., Schaller 1984, Skar and Coulson 1986, Schanche 1988, K. Johansen 1990, Nærøy 1995, Nærøy 2000, Bang-Andersen 2003a, 2003b). In addition, one finds a series of works analysing settlement systems at the intersite level, with definitions of site types and interrelated systems of sites linked to topographical features and resources, and debates on the structuring of space and activities in relation to subsistence and social structures (Indrelid 1973b, Bjerck 1989, 1990, Bergsvik 1991, 1995, Barlindhaug 1996, Boaz 1998, Havas 1999, Grydeland 2000). Research in this field opened up discussions of developments towards sedentism in maritime foraging communities, and created a notion of greater diversity in relation to subsistence patterns, social organisation, and ethnicity (Engelstad 1984, 1990, Renouf 1984, 1989, Warren 1994, Bergsvik 2001a, 2001b). Regional distribution patterns in material culture are increasingly related to interactions within and between a larger diversity of Mesolithic groups (Fuglestvedt 1999b, Bergsvik and A. B. Olsen 2003, Bergsvik 2003b, 2004, Gundersen 2009).

The Natural Setting

The Scandinavian natural environment has been subject to dramatic variations throughout the Pleistocene. The Postglacial landscape, with its skerries, fjords, sediments, and elevated shorelines is to a large extent the result of glaciation. It is important to understand the history of such a landscape to be able to interpret archaeological remains, but whereas the chronology of such developments is a common focus of study, the enormous geographical variations are less emphasised, despite their imperative significance throughout prehistory.

The Glacial Sequence

During the last ice age (the Weichselian, 115,000–10,000 BP), glaciers covered most of Scandinavia. There are indications of significant climatic fluctuations during the Weichselian and several ice-free warm phases have been detected (Larsen et al. 1987, Lauritzen 1993, Anundsen 1996, Valen et al. 1996).

Here is the Baltic ice shield reached its maximum around 22,000 BP (Andersen and Borns 1997: 54). From about 13,000 BP, a marked climatic improvement and subsequent retreat of ice margins took place (Bølling interstadial). During much of this late glacial period, long stretches of the Norwegian coast were ice free, and a rich and varied arctic flora and fauna is documented (e.g., Lie 1986, 1990, Larsen et al. 1987, A. B. Johansen and Undås 1992). Including the Allerød, this late glacial warm phase lasted about two thousand years. The cold phase of the Younger Dryas (11,000–10,000 BP) represents the end of the Weichselian. Many of the most noticeable ice-margin moraines originate from glacial advances in this period. Even during the Younger Dryas there were large ice-free areas along the Norwegian coast (Andersen et al. 1995) (Figure 3.1), but there is no certain evidence of human settlement in this rich arctic biotope before the very end of this period.

Significant climatic improvement at around 10,000 BP led to a rapid melting of the ice cap and subsequent changes in fauna and flora. The glacial retreat is a complex series of events, with large ice-dammed lakes and swollen melt rivers, catastrophic breaches, and flooding (e.g., Longva and Thoresen 1991, Andersen and Borns 1997: 86). There are indications that large areas of the high-mountain plateaus were ice free already in the early part of the Preboreal period, if not earlier (Garnes and Bergersen 1980), and that reindeer quickly established themselves in these areas (e.g., Bang-Andersen 2003a).

Compared to the knowledge of glacial sequences on land, the large environmental transformations in the Atlantic Sea are less well understood. Obviously, the Oceanic polar front, at present near Svalbard, was situated further south, that is, off the Norwegian coast (Kellogg 1976, Hald and Aspeli 1997, Andersen and Borns 1997: 43). The present system of currents, in which the Gulf Stream passes along the whole Norwegian coast, was probably established during the Preboreal.

This development must have had a dramatic impact on marine life. The marine biotopes in early Preboreal times must have been similar to Svalbard today (Theisen and Brude 1998): drifting pack ice and frozen fjords, large populations of ringed seal (*Pusa hispida*), harp seal (*Phoca groenlandica*), bearded seal (*Erignathus barbatus*), and polar bear (*Ursus maritimus*) (Blystad et al. 1983), and abundant colonies of varied species of maritime birds (Auk/Guillemot families). Most of the fish species found today belong to a marine biotope to the south of the polar front and were not present. If the environmental parallel to Svalbard is valid, it is reasonable to expect that the small but abundant polar cod (*Boreogadus saida*) was dominant. This is an important food source for many seal species but hardly a decisive resource for humans.

Postglacial Climate, Flora, and Fauna

The dramatic rise in temperature in the Early Postglacial caused a transformation of the natural environment from arctic vegetation with an arctic fauna to a woodland landscape with subarctic/boreal fauna in the early Boreal. Open birch forests with crowberry and eventually heather gradually gave way to the boreal forests of pine and hazel. In the Atlantic period, dense forests of temperate deciduous trees developed. Elm, alder, and lime dominated, and the tree line in the mountains was higher than today (Gjærevoll 1992). With the exception of a few species such as wild boar (*Sus scrofa*) and great auk (*Alca impennis*), the present-day fauna and biotopes are most likely representative of the Postglacial fauna. Nothing in the sparse empirical data (subfossil faunal remains, archaeological finds, and rock art depictions) contradicts this (Indrelid 1978: 155, Lie 1988, 1989, Hufthammer 1992, Valen et al. 1996). However, the extensive geographical variations in climate, flora and fauna are such that the Scandinavian landscape is best understood as a complex mosaic of many different biotopes (see later). It is likely that today's important marine species such as pollack (*Pollachius virens*), Atlantic cod (*Gadus morhua*), herring (*Clupea harengus*), grey seal (*Halichoerus grypus*), harbour seal (*Phoca vitulina*), and common porpoise (*Phocoena phocoena*), established themselves in the wake of the Oceanic polar front as it gradually moved northwards.

Relative Sea Level

During the Pleistocene, large parts of the oceans were bound up in the ice sheets, and global sea level fluctuated according to the dynamics of the ice cover (*glacio-eustasy*) (Coe et al. 2003: 43, 101, Andersen and Borns 1997: 140). At 17,000 BP, the sea level was as much as 120 m lower than today (Fairbanks 1989). In step with the accelerating Late Glacial/Early Postglacial melting of the ice sheets, the sea level rose. The final deglaciation of Northern Europe between 10,000 and 9000 BP led to a marked rise in sea levels. This created a domino effect including large-scale calving of ice-masses in today's Hudson Bay, which accelerated the deglaciation. The marked Holocene transgression maximum (Tapes, c. 9000–6000 BP) represents the rapid final melting of the ice cover on the North American continent, the largest of the Pleistocene ice sheets (Flint 1971: 78).

The Pleistocene bodies of ice were of enormous weight, which led to a depression of the earth's crust, in the Baltic by as much as 300 m. The crustal rebound during and after deglaciation (*isostasy*) eventually waned and stabilised. In areas with the heaviest glacial depression (e.g., Bothnia Bay), traces of these forces are still measurable after ten thousand years. The early deglaciation in the Baltic, and the subsequent rapid isostatic uplift, resulted in elevated shorelines of late glacial age in

Figure 3.1. Younger Dryas (11,000–10,000 BP) marginal moraines in Fennoscandia, illustrating the maximum extent of the Baltic ice shield in the Late Glacial period (redrawn after Andersen 2000: 112).

many parts of coastal Scandinavia. To my knowledge, these are among the very oldest preserved Quaternary shorelines in the world, and the scientific and cultural-historical data gathered from these raised shorelines is of global significance.

Relative sea level is a product of the combination of eustasy and isostasy. This dynamic explains the large geographical variation in shoreline displacement (Figure 3.2). The minor isostatic uplift in Southern Scandinavia means that a majority of Mesolithic beaches are found below present sea level (Fischer 1995b, 2001). In large parts of coastal Norway, the isostatic uplift is likewise limited and the Holocene transgression is marked. In areas with considerable isostatic uplift and a late glacial marine limit of 100–200 m a.s.l., this transgression had little impact (e.g., Hafsten 1983, Svendsen and Mangerud 1987, Møller 1989). The rate of Early Postglacial shoreline displacement exceeded 3 m per one hundred years in parts of Norway, and must have been noticeable to Mesolithic people. Fishing/hunting grounds and natural harbours changed and pathways of movement were blocked. However, in a few days' journey, one would reach areas where the opposite was the case, and local traditions would tell that the sea was rising, not retreating. Whether this was the subject of as much debate to Mesolithic people as to present-day scientists, we do not know. But these regional variations in relative sea-level change are likely to have had an impact on Mesolithic worldviews.

Shoreline Displacement and the Archaeological Record

In areas with substantial isostatic rebound, the elevated shorelines provide chronological control for the archaeological record, and the possibility of shoreline dating has been an important asset in Scandinavian archaeological research. The method has been tested by radiocarbon dating, and proved to be useful, especially in dating archaeological remains from the coast (Kleppe 1985, Møller 1987).

However, the large geographical variation in relative shoreline displacement has led to a series of problems resulting from differential representation of the archaeological record. Sites that were situated close to the shore in areas with minor isostatic rebound (and subsequent marked transgression) have been flooded and eroded or covered by beach deposits (Figure 3.2, Nummedal 1933, Bjerck 1986). This may explain the absence of Early Mesolithic sites on some parts of the coast. However, one cannot rule out the possibility that observed differences in the number of sites (e.g., abundant sites in Rogaland and Northwest Norway) reflect true variations in Mesolithic activity levels.

The chronological division between *Fosna* and *Nøstvet technocomplexes* became clearer as Post-glacial shoreline displacement was better understood in the 1980s, and it became clear that the Holocene transgression posed a problem of differential representation of Middle Mesolithic evidence. In areas with minor isostatic uplift, sites on shorelines from the period 9000–7500 BP (8000–6500 cal BC) would have been flooded by the transgression, and hence eroded or covered by beach deposits. In time, archaeological material from this period was brought to light, and continuity in material culture between the two traditions became clear (Bjerck 1983, 1986).

The Storegga Tsunami

The catastrophic finale to the glacial modification of Scandinavia was a series of submarine slides from the continental shelf off the coast of Norway. Loose sediments that had accumulated along the margins of the Baltic ice shield slid down into deep-sea areas. The most famous is the Storegga slide off the coast of Norwest Norway. It is said to be the world's largest documented submarine slide with a rear slide-face of 300 km and with sediments transported up to 800 km out onto the seafloor. The slide was seemingly a sudden event that took place c. 7300 BP (Bondevik et al. 1997, Bondevik 2003), generating a disastrous tsunami that must have had catastrophic consequences for coastal populations at the time. The calculated 10 m high waves must have wreaked havoc on dwellings, boats, riggings, equipment, and food supplies. Remains of fish in tsunami sediments suggest the catastrophe happened sometime during the autumn, leaving people little time to 're-prepare' for the harsh winter. The tsunami affected the whole Norwegian Sea (Harbitz 1992), and is documented in both Scotland and the Faeroe Islands (Dawson et al. 1988, Dawson and Smith 2000). However, apart from the suggested tsunami deposits at Dysjvika, northwest of Ålesund (Bondevik 2003), the impact of the tsunami on Norwegian archaeological sites is not documented.

Spatial Variation

The Scandinavian landscape is unique in a European context but has clear parallels with other glaciated areas, for example, North America and Patagonia. These areas share geomorphological characteristics created by glacial erosion and deposition during the various ice ages of the

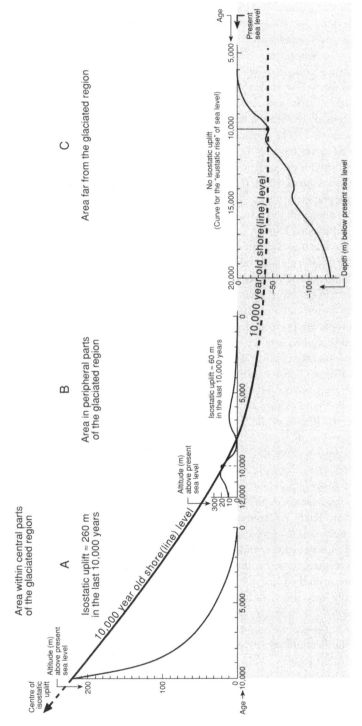

Figure 3.2. Shoreline displacement graphs (A, B, C) and a reconstructed ten-thousand-year-old shoreline along a profile from central areas of Fennoscandia (high isostatic uplift) to areas outside the glaciated area (no istostatic uplift). **A**: Shore displacement graph from the Oslo region; **B**: Southwest Norway (with a marked Holocene transgression); **C**: North Sea basin, illustrating global eustatic changes (after Andersen and Borns 1997: figs. 3–51A).

Pleistocene. The geographical diversity in Scandinavia is considerable both in relation to land-scape, biotopes, climate, and seasonal variations.

The special strandflat along the whole of the Norwegian coast is a product of a complex dynamic between frost weathering, ice movements, and wave action across fluctuating sea levels throughout the various ice ages of the Pleistocene. The formation comprises a low-lying hinterland with an adjoining shallow coastal zone, roughly within 50–100 m of present sea level (Nansen 1922, Nansen 1928, Klemsdal 1982, Coe et al. 2003). A zone more than 100 km wide of islands, inlets, and skerries with a maze of straits and currents, and bays and headlands, characterise this coastal topography. In more exposed areas on the outer coast, the strandflat ends in sheer rock faces, with shorelines carved into solid rock. The characteristic deep fjords represent ice drainage channels that cut up to 200 km into the mainland.

These dramatic geomorphologic variations hardly need any other reference than a good map. However, for comparative reasons, characteristics of the Scandinavian *fjord/skerry coastal landscape* may be expressed in geographical terms. The contact zone between land and sea is a particularly productive biotope, containing vast areas of shallow water with strong tidal currents that mix seawater of different temperature, salinity, and nutritional content. A numerical representation of the relationship between coastline and shoreline therefore provides a measure of marine productivity. The length of the Norwegian shoreline including islands and fjords is as much as 83,280 km (http://statbank.ssb.no/statistikkbanken/), that is, about twice the earth's equatorial diameter. Along the 2700 km length of the Norwegian coastline, there is on average about 30 km of shoreline per 1 km coastline. The corresponding value for Continental Europe is probably less than a tenth of this, and marine biotopes are probably likewise less productive. This rich marine environment must have been of decisive significance for Mesolithic subsistence patterns.

Environmental overviews often focus on processes, generalising successive stages along a time axis. However, considering a region as varied as Scandinavia this is often more misleading than informative. When referring to the Holocene climatic optimum with deciduous forests (with implicit reference to the country's capital), one also must remember that North Scandinavia at the same time was (and is) 'Preboreal' (cf. Gjærevoll 1992, Hesjedal et al. 1996: 21). Scandinavia extends as far as 71 degrees North, with many climate-zones and biotopes, from arctic to temperate ecological zones with a great biodiversity.

Detailed environmental data from the Mesolithic are scant. However, there is likely to have been a similar range of geographical and climatic variation as today. The graphs extracted from recent meteorological observations depict an interesting picture of the climatic consequences of this geographical diversity. There are major differences in temperature and precipitation between north and south, and between coast and inland (Figure 3.3). It is also important to note that regional variations are far greater in the winter than in the summer. An important fact with special relevance to the archaeological record is the increased seasonal differences from south to north. During the four summer months there are no nights, and in mid winter merely a few hours of bluish twilight. Naturally, this affects the occurrence, diversity, amounts and concentrations of natural resources. However, the northern climate is favourable for storage of air-dried and frozen food, providing a means of counteracting seasonal differences in resource availability. This is also likely to affect a series of other cultural activities, logistical strategies, social organisation, notions of wealth and status – not to mention symbolic and practical ideas. Snow and ice are not merely cold things, but also building material, fresh water, and a wide and even surface covering the summer's rivers, lakes, and fjords. The frozen landscapes entail different means of transportation and lines of communications, and the different seasons close or open connections between places, people, and

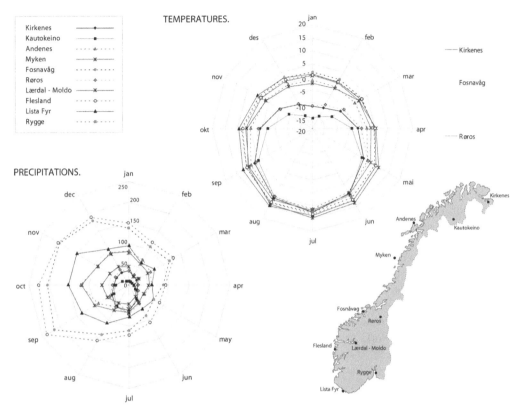

Figure 3.3. Annual variations in precipitation and temperatures in different regions of Norway. The diagrams illustrate substantial regional variations from north to south/coast to inland. Note the more pronounced climatic differences during fall/winter. The diagrams are based on normals (averages) from 1961 to 1990, Norwegian Meteorological Institute, listed in http://met.no/observasjoner/index.html.

societies. An understanding of regional variations in climate is a precondition for understanding cultural, economic, and social diversity.

A rather small part of Norway is true lowland, only 16 percent of the landmass is below 160 m a.s.l. In total, 40 percent of the landmass (306,253 km² + 17,505 km² freshwater) is elevated more than 600 m a.s.l. The large variation in relief implies significant climatic and biological differences within short distances. In many places, the distance between the shoreline and the mountain plateaux is less than a day's journey (walking and climbing). The coastal areas of West Sweden, East Norway, and Trøndelag border on large areas of forest, but are quite a distance from mountain plateaux. In West Norway, the fjords cut deeply into the hinterland and make it possible to rationalise transport by way of boats, and the distance to highland areas is often short but steep). In Nordland and Troms, there are few mountain plateaux; following steep slopes up from the coast, one crosses into highland areas that slope down to the Swedish forests. In Finnmark, the fjords cut their way right into the lower-lying hinterland. The arctic climate means that in low-lying areas close to the coast, one finds biotopes that are similar to those on the mountain plateaux of South Norway. The coastal landscape varies from south to north. In the north, the islands are larger, fjords and sounds are wider, and generally the landscape is rougher. Nevertheless, the innumerable fjords and channels along the coast constitute a network of safe and rapid transport routes connecting large and varied areas on land.

Spatial environmental diversity is also reflected in regional variations in the amount, combination, distribution, concentrations and stability of the flora and fauna: bird migration routes and nesting places, schools of herring and mackerel, cod, salmon, and pollack, concentrated niches for whale and seal, shellfish, forest and highland, edible plants, plants that are easily stored, frost- and fly-free areas for the drying of meat and fish, to mention but a few.

Technocomplexes, Traditions, and Chronozones

In traditional preradiocarbon research, chronological control was achieved by defining groups of archaeological material (cultures, traditions, phases, *technocomplexes*), and establishing their relative dating. *Technocomplexes* were linked to geographical areas, more often current national or administrative areas than culture-historically significant regions (e.g., Fosna and Hensbacka in Norway and Sweden respectively). These archaeologically defined units were necessary stepping stones in the construction of absolute chronology, constructed by intricate cross references between key sites and correlations with geological and botanical data in supraregional structures with some reference to calendar years (e.g., Freundt 1949).

Chronological frameworks in the natural sciences were traditionally based on the same principles. In Scandinavia, the Blytt-Sernander scheme, which referred to Postglacial climate and floral changes, was employed (*Preboreal*, *Boreal*, etc.). One of the problems with chronological units defined on the basis of specific environmental events is that of their regional validity, especially within areas of great environmental diversity such as northern Europe. The introduction of radiometric dating brought this complication to the fore, and the Blytt-Sernander climate zones were redefined as *chronozones*, that is, segments of time in radiocarbon years. This redefinition was the product of wide discussion at Pan-Scandinavian level and resulted in a major article that has since been a key reference (Mangerud et al. 1974). Later research based on Greenland ice-cores has further detailed the complexity of this issue. The problems with time transgressive climatic development have highlighted the need for a new structure. However the solution can hardly be to redefine a concise and well-established time reference (Eriksen 2002).

A similar approach has been proposed for the Norwegian Mesolithic (Bjerck 1986, Bjerck et al. 1987), but unfortunately without the backing of a Pan-Scandinavian agreement. The Mesolithic is here defined as a chronozone 10,000–5000 BP, with a further subdivision into the periods Early, Middle, and Late at 9000 BP and 7000 BP. The reasoning is that such a system is better equipped to describe gradual changes, more open to new data, and above all simplifies and clarifies the presentation of regional variations in the archaeological record. A neutral time reference also avoids cementing together certain combinations of characteristics in archaeological data that are not necessarily synchronous (ibid.).

Archaeological developments in recent years have further convinced me of the usefulness of this proposal. New sites and analyses have added important details to our understanding of chronological changes but entail a constant need to move the time boundaries between archaeological entities. Regional differentiation also has become clearer and has led to a similar need to create new phases with their own terminology, relating to smaller and smaller regions.

As a base for the interpretation of cultural history, these new data are of vital importance. However, the use of archaeological units as a basic chronological reference hampers the understanding of the culture-historical multiplicity that is increasingly evident. In order to defend these phases and traditions, one is forced to overemphasize internal similarities in different groups of material, and likewise exaggerate the differences between them. Unintentionally, this contributes to an image of stability broken by rapid changes that at best is a distortion. These constructions also entail both a camouflaging and an exaggeration of regional variation that is unfortunate. And again, this creates a confusing picture that limits the understanding of supraregional trends. It is as if geographers were constantly to adjust the UTM-grid in relation to ever-changing river courses or political-administrative borders.

Without it being made explicit, one can read between the lines an ambition to create an all embracing chronological framework incorporating both time boundaries and supraregional trends in the archaeological record, but without a clear presentation of regional variability. This confusion reaches a peak in the proposal to redefine unspecified parts of the Fosna complex as a part of the continental Ahrensburgian. The reasoning behind this is partly that Fosna is an old-fashioned archaeological construction tainted by nationalistic undertones (Fuglestvedt 1999a: 198). It is indeed decidedly more modern to label this group as Ahrensburgian, but would it be any less political? The Pan-European perspective is a centrepiece of contemporary political and social debate and a mantra in the struggle for research funding. And what are the benefits to archaeological understanding? As the Ahrensburgian technocomplex itself is not without cultural relations to other bordering traditions, the benefit would be limited to having moved the problem to a larger regional sphere. Wouldn't it be more constructive and informative instead to examine in depth the *character* of common traditions around the Skagerrak basin within the Early Mesolithic chronozone?

One of the few trends we can be certain of in future archaeological research is an increased level of detail in the archaeological material. A chronological framework that allows for this variation is essential. The calibrated curve for radiocarbon dates now extends throughout the whole Mesolithic period. It provides a neutral chronological structure that permits a tidy ordering and clear presentation of archaeological data and interpretation, so that research can focus on the culture-historical content instead of artificially imposed boundaries. It also allows a truer picture of time spans and duration, as it is now clear that units of five hundred calendar years within the Mesolithic vary from 280 to 580 radiocarbon years (Table 3.1).

In the following, the term *Mesolithic* refers to chronozones defined in calibrated dates BC, compared with uncalibrated dates BP (Table 3.1). The division between the *Early, Middle,* and *Late Mesolithic chronozone (EMC, MMC, LMC)* is largely in line with mainstream chronology, and the precision levels in existing data are too low for this to cause serious difficulties. A '*c*' is added to the chronozone term to avoid confusion. Each period is further divided into periods of five hundred calendar years (*EM1, EM2,* etc.) to make the system more operational. *LM5* therefore defines the period 4000–4500 cal BC, where I have chosen to set the focus more on *culture-historical trends* in this time period rather than discussing the problem of *delimiting* such entities as the Late Microblade tradition (Bjerck 1986), Late Mesolithic *technocomplex* (Bergsvik 2002), Early Stone Age Phase III/Late Stone Age Period I (B. Olsen 1994, Hesjedal et al. 1996: 186), Phase 4 Late flint-point using groups (Mikkelsen 1975a), Transverse points phase (Jaksland 2001a), or the Kjeøy phase (Glørstad 2004).

Several recent studies present detailed regional chronological frameworks and cultural-historical trends. These studies are often based on larger excavations or dissertations, and are normally found in reports or theses that are not widely distributed, and usually in Norwegian. The following description is a synthesis of the most important studies with ^{14}C based chronological frameworks for *East Norway* (Mikkelsen 1975a, 1978, Lindblom 1982, Ballin 1995, 1998, 1999, Ballin and Jensen 1995, Jaksland 2001a, Glørstad 2004, Berg 2003), *West and Central Norway* (Indrelid 1975,

Table 3.1. Mesolithic chronozones

Chronozone		Age Range Cal BC		Duration (calibrated)	Age Range uncal. BP		Duration (uncalibrated)
EMC	EM1	9500	9000	500	10020	9590	430
Early Mesolithic	EM2	9000	8500	500	9590	9270	320
Chronozone	EM3	8500	8000	500	9270	8900	370
Total EMC				1500			1120
MMC	MM1	8000	7500	500	8900	8400	500
Middle	MM2	7500	7000	500	8400	7970	430
Mesolithic Chronozone	MM3	7000	6500	500	7970	7690	280
Total MMC				1500			1210
LMC	LM1	6500	6000	500	7690	7110	580
Late	LM2	6000	5500	500	7110	6560	550
Mesolithic Chronozone	LM3	5500	5000	500	6560	6090	470
	LM4	5000	4500	500	6090	5680	410
	LM5	4500	4000	500	5680	5230	450
Total LMC				2500			2460
Total MC				5500			4790

Radiocarbon dates are supplied by S. Gulliksen, Dept. of Archaeometry (National Laboratory for ^{14}C Dating), NTNU, Trondheim. Based on IntCal04 (Reimer et al. 2004).

1978, Bjørgo 1981, A. B. Olsen 1981, 1992, Bjerck 1986, Nærøy 1988, Nærøy 1999, Kutchera and Waraas 2000, Waraas 2001, Bang-Andersen 2003a, Bergsvik 2002) and *North Norway* (Simonsen 1975a, Helskog 1980b, Schanche 1988, Woodman 1993, 1999, Hauglid 1993, B. Olsen 1994, Hesjedal et al. 1996, Myklevoll 1998).

The Early Mesolithic Chronozone 9500–8000 cal BC (10,020–8900 BP)

EMC includes the *Fosna* technocomplex (Indrelid 1975, 1978, Bjerck 1986, A. B. Olsen 1992, Nærøy 1999), the earliest parts of *Komsa* (Woodman 1993: *Komsa Phase*; B. Olsen 1994: *Phase I*), and *Phase 1* in East Norway (Mikkelsen 1975a, Jaksland 2001a). Fosna is almost identical with the West Swedish *Hensbacka* and both these traditions display clear commonalities with the *Ahrensburgian*, which in its turn is understood as a forerunner to the Preboreal *technocomplexes* in Scandinavia (Fischer 1996).

This tradition includes a series of chronologically significant formal tools (Figure 3.4a): flake adzes (often with secondary edge blows), tanged points (especially single-edged points), lanceolate microliths (apparently associated with EM2–3), and burins (blades/flakes, burin blows on breaks). Significant technological features include the macrolithic character (despite the dominance of smaller debitage) and a broad spectrum of blades (heterogeneous, irregular, broad) produced on one-sided cores (one or two platforms) with acute striking angles. It has been suggested that the blades are produced by a hard, direct percussion technique (Waraas 2001: 103, Fuglestvedt 1999a: 189, 2007). The microburin technique is present, both in the production of tanged points and

Table 3.2. Key Mesolithic sites in Norway, showing sites that are prominent in the literature and current discussions (see Figure 3.8 for locations)

Site No.	Site Name	County	EMC	MMC	LMC	Loc	Reference
0	Akseløya, Svalbard	Svalbard					Bjerck 2000
1	Seilmerket, Kirkenes	Finnm	x			C	Bøe and Nummedal 1936, Woodman 1993
2	Varangerbotten, Varanger	Finnm	xX D	xxX D	xxx D	C	Simonsen 1961, Odner 1966, Engelstad 1989, Woodman 1993, Grydeland 2000, 2005.
3	Mortensnes, Varanger	Finnm	xx D	xX D	xxX D	C	Schanche 1988
4	Sarnes, Magerøya (FATIMA)	Finnm	x	X		C	Thommesen 1996, Blankholm 2004
5	Melkøya, Hammerfest	Finnm	x		xxX D	C	Hesjedal and Niemi (eds.) 2003, Ramstad et al. 2005
6	Slettnes, Sørøya	Finnm	xX	xX D	xxX D	C	Hesjedal et al. 1996
7	Tollevik, Alta	Finnm	xx		xx	C	Nummedal 1927, Bøe and Nummedal 1936, Gjessing 1945, Woodman 1993
8	Simavik, Ringvassøy	Troms	X			C	Sandmo 1986
9	Almenningen, Rostavatnet	Troms			XX	M	Blankholm 2004
10	Målsnes, Målselv	Troms	x			C	Blankholm 2004, 2008
11	Fure, Steigen	Nordland	x			C	Bjerck 1991, Hauglid 1993
12	Saltstraumen, Bodø	Nordland	xX			C	Hauglid 1993
13	Træna	Nordland		x D	x D	C	Gjessing 1943
14	Gressvatnet, Rana	Nordland			xX	M	Gaustad 1969, Alterskjær 1985, Holm 1985
15	Vega	Nordland	xX D	XXX D	x D	C	Alterskjær 1985, Pettersen 1982, Bjerck 1989, 1990
16	Uransbrekka, Flatanger	N-Trøndelag	xx			C	K. Johansen 1990
17	Foldsjøen, Malvik	S-Trøndelag		x	X	F	Skar 1989
18	Storlidalen	S-Trøndelag	x			M	Callanan 2007
19	Ålbusætra	S-Trøndelag		X		M	Gustafson 1988

(continued)

75

Table 3.2. (*continued*)

Site No.	Site Name	County	EMC	MMC	LMC	Loc	Reference
20	Leksa, Agdenes	S-Trøndelag			X D	C	Pettersen 1999, Pettersen pers. comm.
21	Tjeldbergodden	S-Trøndelag	x		Xx	C	Berglund (ed.) 2001, A.B. Johansen pers. comm.
22	Straumsvik, Aure	Møre & R			X	C	Auset n.d.
23	Kristiansund	Møre & R	xxx			C	Møllenhus 1977
24	Stavneset, Averøy	Møre & R	X			C	Åstveit 2005
25	Draget, Molde	Møre & R	x			C	Nummedal 1937
26	Nyhamna/Ormen Lange, Aukra	Møre & R	XX D	X	XXX D	C	Bjerck et al. 2008
27	Baraldsnes, Haram	Møre & R	X	X		C	Waraas 2005
28	Korsvika/Trollvika, Midsund	Møre & R	xx	x	x	C	Møllenhus 1977
29	Dysjvika, Fjørtofta	Møre & R		X		C	Indrelid 1973c, Bjerck 1983, Bondevik 2003
30	Stølen, Longva	Møre & R			X	C	Bjerck 1982
31	Breheimen, Stryn	Sogn & Fj			X	M	Randers 1986
32	Nyset Stegge	Sogn & Fj		X	XX	M	Bjørgo et al. 1992
33	Lærdalsfjellene	Sogn & Fj		X	XX	M	Johansen, A. B. 1970, 1978
34	Skatestraumen, Bremanger	Sogn & Fj			XXX D	C	Bergsvik 2002b
35	Vingen, Bremanger	Sogn & Fj			X D	C	Lødøen 2003
36	Båtevik II, Flora	Sogn & Fj		X		C	Olsen 1981, Bjerck 1983, 1986, Ballin 1995
37	Botnaneset, Flora	Sogn & Fj	x		X	C	Bostwick Bjerck and Olsen 1983
38	Stakaneset, Flora	Sogn & Fj		Xxx	XXX	C	Olsen 1981, Olsen and Alsaker 1984
39	Kotedalen, Radøy	Hordaland	X	X	XXX	C	Olsen 1992, Hjelle et al. 1992
40	Kollsnes, Øygarden	Hordaland	xx	x	xX	C	Nærøy 1994, 2000
41	Toftøy, Øygarden	Hordaland	x			C	Bjerck 1983, 1986
42	Vindenes, Sotra	Hordaland	x		X	C	Ågotnes 1981
43	Flatøy	Hordaland			XXX	C	Bjørgo 1981, Simpson 1992
44	Skipshelleren	Hordaland			XH	C	Bøe 1934, Indrelid 1978, Sellevoll and Skar 1999
45	Hardangervidda	Hordaland		X	XXX D	M	Hagen 1963a, Indrelid 1973a, 1973b, 1977, 1994

Site No.	Site Name	County	EMC	MMC	LMC	Loc	Reference
46	Austvik Brandasund	Hordaland	xx		xx	C	Kristoffersen 1990
47	Litla Skiftesvika, Bømlo	Hordaland	x	x		C	Waraas 2001
48	Hespriholmen Bømlo	Hordaland		xxx	xxx	C	Alsaker 1982, Olsen and Alsaker 1984
49	Tjernagel, Sveio	Hordaland	xx	x	xx	C	Bjerck 1985
50	Bleivik, Haugesund	Rogaland		H		C	Sellevoll and Skar 1999
51	Breivikklubben	Rogaland	x			C	Kutchera and Waraas 2000, Waraas 2001
52	Galta, Rennesøy	Rogaland	xx			C	Prøsch-Danielsen and Høgestøl 1995, Fuglestvedt 2007
53	Fløyrli, Forsand	Rogaland	XX D			M	Bang Andersen 2003a, 2003b
54	Myrvatnet, Gjesdal	Rogaland	XX D			M	Bang Andersen 1988, 2003a, 2003b
55	Håvik, Karmøy	Rogaland			xx	C	Nygaard 1974
56	Vistehula	Rogaland		X	X	C	Brøgger 1908, Lund 1951, Mikkelsen 1971, Indrelid 1978
57	Sunde, Stavanger	Rogaland			X	C	Braathen 1985
58	Hundvåg, Stavanger	Rogaland	xx			C	Hemdorff 2001, Juhl 2001, Dugstad 2007
59	Lego, Klepp	Rogaland		x		C	Mikkelsen 1971
60	Botne II, Strand	Rogaland			X	C	Glørstad 1999
61	Lundevågen, Lista	V-Agder		xX	XX	C	Ballin and Jensen 1995
62	Hummerholmen, Søgne	V-Agder		H		C	Sellevoll and Skar 1999
63	Torsrød, Brunlanes	Vestfold			X	C	Østmo 1976
64	Frebergsvik	Vestfold			x	C	Mikkelsen 1975b
65	Skavli, Borre	Vestfold			X	C	Glørstad 1998b
66	Svinesund	Østfold			Xxx D	C	Gløstad (ed.) 2004
67	Tørkop	Østfold				C	Mikkelsen et al. 2001
68	Høgnipen	Østfold	x			C	E. Johansen 1964, Skar and Coulson 1986
69	Vestby	Akershus			xx	C	Berg 1995, 1999
70	Årungen, Ås and Frogn	Akershus		X	X	C	Berg 1997, 1999
71	Drøbaksundet	Østfold			Xx	C	Ballin 1998
72	Stunner	Akershus	x			C	Gustafson 1999, Fuglestvedt 1999
73	Vinterbro	Akershus		xx	X	C	Jaksland 2001a
74	Skoklefald	Akershus			X	C	Jaksland 2001b
75	Etna-Dokka	Oppland		X	XX	F	Boaz 1998, 1999
76	Svevollen	Hedem			X D	F	Fuglestvedt 1992, 1995
77	Rødsmoen	Hedem		x	X D	F	Boaz 1997, 1998

(continued)

Table 3.2. (*continued*)

Site No.	Site Name	County	EMC	MMC	LMC	Loc	Reference
78	Flendalen	Hedem			x	F	Sjurseike 1994
79	Alvdal Vestfjell	Hedem			X	F	Fretheim 2002
80	Falningssjøen, Tynset	Hedem			XX	M	Gustafson 1988
81	Innerdalen	Hedem			X	F	Gustafson 1987, 1988, 1990

The table shows major development projects and subsequent archaeological investigations demanded by Norwegian Cultural Heritage Legislation. The names of these sites are highlighted in gray. Sites dated by radiocarbon are marked in bold with a capital **X**, sites dated by shoreline or typological dating are marked with a small **x** and are subdivided by period – Early, Middle, or Late Mesolithic Chronozone (see Table 3.1). Sites with important organic remains are marked by a white letter in a black cell, with documented dwelling structures by **D**, and with human remains by **H**. For location: C = Coast; F = Forest; and M = Mountain.

lanceolate microliths. Recent research suggests a chronological change in the projectile material (Waraas 2001: 78, Bang-Andersen 2003a); however, a broader analysis is needed to bring clarify this. The macrolithic character is to a certain extent seen in connection with the production of flake axes. The presence of EMC flake adzes is peculiar to Scandinavia and marks a break with the Ahrensburgian.

Scrapers produced on both blades and flakes are usual, but not chronologically significant. In addition a large number of informal tools appear (i.e., primary flakes/blades with use-wear). Besides differences in lithic raw materials and their associated technologies, one finds few indications of regional differentiation.

Shoreline dates indicate that the group of polished rock art in northern Nordland may date to EM2/MM1. The group includes elk, reindeer, bear, whale, and seal in monumental naturalistic style (Figure 3.5, Gjessing 1932, Hesjedal 1994, Sognnes 2003).

The Middle Mesolithic Chronozone: 8000–6500 cal BC (8900–7690 BP)

MMC/LMC encompasses the traditional South Norwegian technocomplex *Nøstvet* (Indrelid 1975, Indrelid 1978, Mikkelsen 1975a). Mikkelsen (ibid.) was the first to propose a subdivision of this material that was then defined as *Phase 2* (MM2), preceding classical Nøstvet (*Phase 3*). In West and Central Norway, a similar phase was labelled as the *Early Microblade Tradition* (Bjerck 1986) (Figure 3.4b). In Finnmark, MMC includes the *Sælneshøgda Phase* (Woodman 1993) or *Phase II* (B. Olsen 1994).

The material from this period is more subject to regional variation. Chronologically significant tools are adzes of basaltic rock, and polished and pecked *chubby adzes* (*trinnøks*), seemingly introduced in MM1 (Figure 3.6). Blade production is a fundamental technological element and very common. The blades are regular and homogeneous, and are produced from multifacial cores (conical, normally one striking platform) with a striking angle of 80 to 90 degrees, producing both *blades* and *microblades*. This orientation in blade production seems to have its roots in EM3. In Finnmark, blade technique is abandoned in MM2 at about 7000 cal BC. Borers/engravers (blades/flakes) are

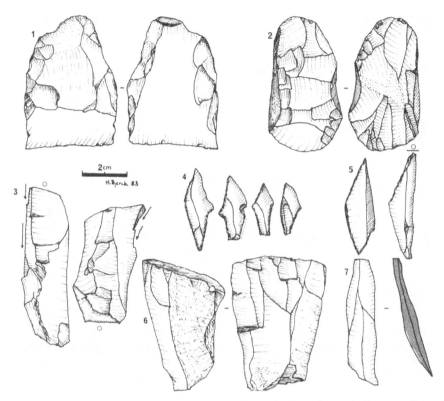

Figure 3.4a. Key artefacts in the Norwegian Mesolithic (after Bjerck 1986). Fosna tradition (Early
Mesolithic Chronozone). 1: Flake adze; 2: Core Adze (Lerberg adze); 3: Burins, 4: Single edged
points; 5: Microliths; 6: Unifacial blade core; 7: Irregular blade with acute flaking angle.

common. *Microliths* appear on some sites, and seem to be more abundant in Southeastern Norway
(Ballin 1995, Ballin and Jensen 1995, Mikkelsen et al. 1999, Jaksland 2001a). Usually, blades are
modified by breaks rather than retouch. Primary flakes with use-wear indicate a far wider repertoire
of tools, probably various forms of *composite tools* that are only rarely preserved (A. B. Olsen 1992,
Mikkelsen 1971, 1975b).

From West Norway, two stone-quarries are known, Hespriholmen (greenstone) and Stakaneset
(diabase). Shoreline dates show considerable activity in both quarries in MM1 (A. B. Olsen and
Alsaker 1984, Bergsvik and A. B. Olsen 2003).

Shoreline dates indicate a continuation of the polished rock art tradition in North Norway in
MM1–2.

The Late Mesolithic Chronozone: 6500–4000 cal BC (7690–5230 BP)

In East Norway, the first part of LMC incorporates the technocomplexes of *Phase 3* – the *classical
Nøstvet* (Mikkelsen 1975a, Indrelid 1978, Glørstad 1998a), in West and Central Norway the *Late*

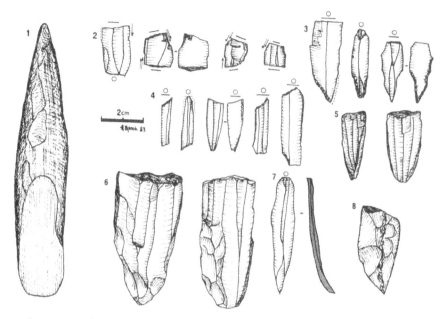

Figure 3.4b. Key artefacts in the Norwegian Mesolithic (after Bjerck 1986). Early Microblade tradition (Middle Mesolithic Chronozone). 1: Polished chubby adze, 2: Small; narrow edged burins of blade fragments; 3: Borers/engravers; 4: Microliths; 5: Multifacial microblade cores; 6: Multifacial blade cores; 7: Regular blade with straight flaking angle; 8: Microblade core preform.

Microblade Tradition (Bjerck 1986), the *Late Mesolithic* (A. B. Olsen 1992, Bergsvik 2002), and in North Norway (i.e., Finnmark) *Phase III* (B. Olsen 1994, Hesjedal et al. 1996).

LM4–5 is more complicated, with technocomplexes bordering the Early Neolithic traditions. In East Norway, this material is defined as *Phase 4: Late flint-point using groups* (Mikkelsen 1975a). It is also referred to as the *transverse point Phase* (Jaksland 2001a) or the *Kjeøy Phase* (Glørstad 2004). In West Norway, the boundary between the Mesolithic and Neolithic traditions has been set to c. 4000 cal BC (i.e., 5200 BP, Alsaker 1982, Nærøy 1988, Nærøy 1994, A. B. Olsen 1992, Bergsvik 2002). In Finnmark, changes in material culture in LM4 are documented (B. Olsen 1994: 52, Hesjedal et al. 1996: 187), and the boundary between Early and Late Stone Age is moved back to 5000 cal BC (ibid.: 190). This means that the whole of *Period I* (5000–4000 cal BC) of the Late Stone Age in Finnmark is placed in a time period that elsewhere in Norway is labelled as Mesolithic (LM4/LM5).

Regional differentiation in material culture accelerates from LM1 to LM5, as is indicated by the complex listing earlier. In a supraregional perspective, the observed chronological boundaries seem increasingly time-transgressive. However, the empirical basis for phase boundaries is not always well founded. Slightly older or younger sites would probably produce different internal divisions, depending on their location. But it seems beyond doubt that the somewhat chaotic panorama in LM3–5 is an expression of important social developments. Obviously, the focus on chronological divisions obscures insight into cultural processes and illustrates the problems related to technocomplexes as a basic time reference.

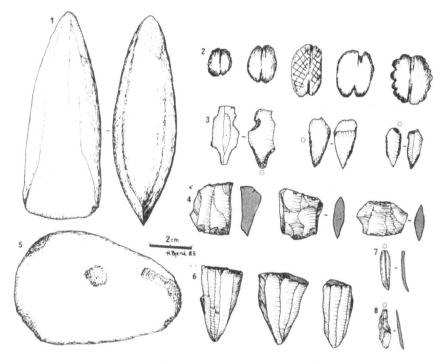

Figure 3.4c. Key artefacts in the Norwegian Mesolithic (after Bjerck 1986). Late Microblade tradition/Nøstvet (Late Mesolithic Chronozone). 1: Polished chubby adze; 2: Soapstone 'coffe bean' sinkers; 3: Borers/engravers; 4: Bipolar cores; 5: Hammer stone/anvil stone; 6: Multifacial microblade cores; 7: Microblade from platform core; 8: 'Microblade' from bipolar core.

Classic lead artefacts for LMC are a continuation of the *chubby adzes*, associated *grinding slabs*, and the *microblade technique* (Figure 3.4c). In East Norway the classic *Nøstvet adzes* appear from LM1 to LM4. The chubby adze-tradition in West Norway is abandoned in LM5, but there seems to be a gradual transition to the *Vespestad adzes* that are introduced in LMC5. In West Norway, *polished knives of sandstone slabs* (*platekniver*) and small '*coffee bean*' *sinkers* of soapstone are chronologically significant, the latter often decorated with geometric line engravings. Occasional borers/engravers appear, but not in the numbers characteristic for the MMC. Neither tanged points nor microliths are known. *Transverse points* also seem to be generally present throughout North Scandinavia in LM4 and LM5.

Extensive production of highly uniform microblades (<8 mm) indicates a specialised blade production and a continued development of composite tools. The microblades are produced from platform cores (handle/conical cores) with a striking angle around 80 to 90 degrees.

Above all, the lithic material is dominated by the extensive use of *bipolar technique*, often with associated hammer stones and anvil stones used in the reduction process (Figure 3.4c). This tradition is probably connected to the widespread use of composite tools. There are few formal tools – the finds are dominated by amounts of small debitage in a wide variety of lithic raw materials: flint, chert, mylonite, quartz, quartz crystal, various quartzite, jasper, or generally whatever stone

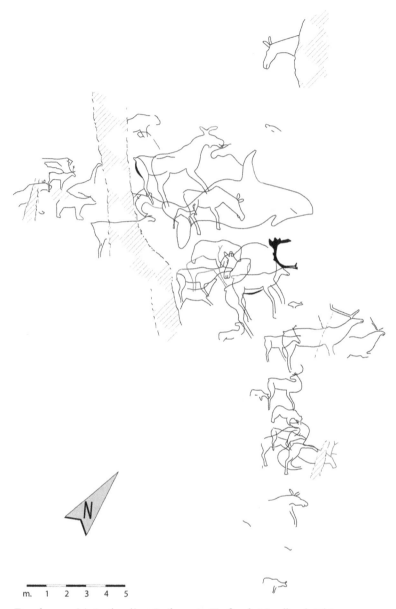

Figure 3.5. Dyreberget (*Animal rock*) at Leiknes in Tysfjord, Nordland. This represents the oldest, reliably dated, open-air rock art tradition in Europe, shoreline dated to c. 9000 BP (8000 cal BC). The polished lines show monumental, life size, naturalistic reindeer, elk, killer whale, and bears. Redrawn after Gjessing 1932, including new details and weathering (Bjerck 1994), marked in grey lines.

Figure 3.6. Chubby adzes. From left: Polished thin-butted chubby adze. Length 24.5 cm (after Alsaker 1987: fig. 102). Pecked chubby adze. Length 22.2 cm (after Gjessing 1920: fig. 77).

type that could be reduced to some controllable degree. The presence of primary flakes with varying types of retouch and visible use-wear again serves as a reminder that this group contains many nonformal tools. The intensification in the production and use of pointed/sharp primary flakes may imply an increased use of bone and wood. The lack of insight into the composite tool tradition hampers analyses of chronological and regional variation.

The Late Stone Age Period I in Varanger (LM4/LM5) is defined by the introduction of *Säräisniemi type 1* comb ceramics and in the rest of Finnmark by the introduction of bifacial retouched projectiles with acute bases. In West Norway, the transition between the Mesolithic and Neolithic is marked by the transition from the chubby adze-tradition to Vespestad adzes. The microblade technique is abandoned, and blade technique based on cylindrical cores is introduced. The cylindrical blade technology is associated with tanged points (i.e., pitted ware complex). This tradition is concurrent with the extensive quarrying of *ryholite* at the peak of the Siggjo Mountain at Bømlo, Southwest Norway (Alsaker 1987). In East Norway, the period 5800–5000 BP is defined as a separate technocomplex with a marked decrease in the use of stone axes and transverse arrowheads.

Shoreline dates indicate intensification in the production of *rock art* in the later parts of LMC, a tradition continued into the Neolithic period. The group of motifs labelled as hunting rock art mainly comprises stylistic presentations of red deer, elk, reindeer, whales, occasional bears, seals, birds (geese), and fish (halibut, salmon). Human beings are present, on rare occasions in boats, on skis (Figure 3.7), or in sexual acts. There are marked stylistic differences in the rock art traditions in different regions, both in contour lines and internal body fills (Bøe 1932, Gjessing

1932, 1936, Hagen 1969, 1976, Mikkelsen 1976, 1986, Helskog 1985, 1987, 1999, Hesjedal 1994, Ramstad 2000, Lødøen 2003, 2009, Mandt and Lødøen 2005). An exceptional wooden artefact from Oppdal, Central Norway (radiocarbon-dated to LM1) has decorations in the form of line patterns (Gustafson 1986). This is also the case of the cross-shaped soapstone clubs dated to MM2–SM1 (Glørstad 2002, Skår 2003).

Colonisation and the Emergence of Specialised Maritime Adaptations

The final deglaciation of Scandinavia occurred around 10,000 BP, but large parts of the West coast were ice-free throughout the entire late-glacial period, in any case from 13,000 BP. Before about 10,000 BP/9500 cal BC there are no definite traces of human activity. There are, of course, sporadic indications – single artefacts believed to be of Late Glacial age (e.g., Rolfsen 1972: 148, Fuglestvedt 1989: 39), and the much debated faunal remains dated to the Ålesund (c. 30,000 BP) and Bølling interstadials (12,000 BP) in the Sjong cave, and from the Bølling deposits at Blomvåg (Lie 1986, 1989, 1990, Larsen et al. 1987: 285, Indrelid 1989: 27, A. B. Johansen and Undås 1992), but this lack of hard evidence contrasts sharply with the wealth of traces of human activity from the period just *after* 10,000 BP/9500 cal BC (Bjerck 1994, 1995, 2009, Pettersen 1999: 164, Woodman 1999, Bang-Andersen 2003a: 10).

In summary, the Preboreal Fosna technocomplex constitutes the pioneer settlement of Norway. It seems the entire Norwegian coastline, from Oslo Fjord to Varanger, was colonised in the course of EM1, that is, earlier than 9,500 BP/9000 cal BC (Bjerck 1994: 138). Archaeologically speaking, this seems to be a very short time. Nonetheless, the Finnish kayaker Petri travelled the 5,000 km of Scandinavian coastline from Bottenviken to Varanger in seventy-one days (Bengtson 2003).

The earliest part of the North-European Postglacial period is characterised by marked similarities in material culture (technology, tool tradition, and choice of raw material). Recent research points to strong affinities between the Fosna technocomplex, the Swedish Hensbacka (Kindgren 1996, Nordqvist 1995, 1999, Schmitt 1999), Ahrensburg (Fischer 1996, Eriksen 2002: 34, Kutchera 1999, Fuglestvedt 1999a, 2001, 2003, Waraas 2001), and Danish finds of Preboreal age (Fischer 1982, 1996).

The late-glacial hunter groups of the North European plains seem to have had a mobile settlement pattern with large fauna, particularly reindeer, as the important resource base. That hunter groups followed reindeer herds towards the north, as the Baltic ice shield melted, has been a common explanation of the earliest motivation for colonising Scandinavia (e.g., Rolfsen 1972: 146, A. B. Johansen and Undås 1992: 16, Fuglestvedt 2001, 2003). Preboreal sites, most likely related to seasonal reindeer hunting, are documented in the high mountain areas of South Norway (Gustafson 1988, Bang-Andersen 2003a). Still, an overwhelming majority of sites are found in the outer-lying areas of the Norwegian fiord/skerry coastal landscape. Obviously, marine resources were a significant factor in the subsistence pattern of the Fosna tradition (Bjerck 1994, Pettersen 1999, Bang-Andersen 2003a, Svendsen 2007). Although remains of boats are unknown, we need not doubt the existence of a well-developed boat technology, which is an important prerequisite for a marine-oriented lifestyle, since it is impossible otherwise to travel in this landscape – or move among the Preboreal settlements (Bjerck et al. 2008: 566ff). This picture is very similar to the distribution of the Preboreal sites in the coastal landscapes of Sweden (Kindgren 1995, 1996, 1999: 58, Larsson 1996, Schmitt et al. 2006, 2009, Wikell and Pettersson 2009).

A crucial archaeological problem is that of the origin of the maritime lifestyle in the Fosna/Hensbacka traditions. Reading between the lines of the archaeological literature, we get the

Figure 3.7. Mesolithic skier, a reminder of the changing lines of communication in the Fennoscandian winter landscape. Recently discovered rock carving at Bøla, Snåsa, Nord-Trøndelag, probably from LMC (tracing by K. Sognnes; Sognnes 2001, 2005). Scale: 0–50 cm.

impression that the enormous subsistence potential of the sea has been important for settlement and way of life since the dawn of human existence. However, our understanding of the roots of *specialised, marine adaptations* is as yet limited, in Europe as elsewhere. The reason for this is the dramatic changes in global eustasy during and immediately after the last ice age. The coastal areas of the glacial period are today situated at sea depths that are relatively inaccessible for archaeological research (e.g., Nummedal 1924, Orquera and Piana 1987, Erlandson 1994, Fischer 1995b, 2001, Fischer and Schou Hansen 2005, Borrero 1996, Borrero and McEwan 1997, Faught 2004, Bell and Renouf 2004).

Of special relevance to this discussion is the Scandinavian *fiord/skerry coastal landscape*. In addition to the rich marine resources, this landscape encompasses large areas with protected waters that ensure safe conditions for seafaring, and ample numbers of natural harbours that secure the connection between land and sea. The rich resources and lower risk factor of this coastal landscape offer advantages that are not found on open coastlines elsewhere.

With all of these environmental advantages one would expect that humans established themselves in the Scandinavian fiord/skerry coastal landscape immediately after it had been freed from the ice caps, but current data do not support this. If the development of specialised maritime adaptations goes far back and occurred in the now submerged coastal regions along the North-European plains as Fischer (1996: 171) claims, why did colonisation first occur 3000 to 4000 years after the emergence of the advantageous Norwegian coastal landscape? There is a definite possibility that the arctic marine lifestyle is a Mesolithic development that occurred parallel with, and as an integrated part of the colonisation of Scandinavian coastal areas (Bjerck 1995, 2009). The circumstances of the colonisation of Ireland seem to be similar (Woodman 2003) and also may be related to this process.

The development of a marine oriented lifestyle is a complicated cultural process that must not be underestimated, a question of motivation, technology and organization. Seal hunting may have played an important role in this development (Bjerck 1995, 2009, Schmitt 1995, Schmitt et al. 2006, Kindgren 1996). Presumably there were large populations of various seal species in the arctic waters of Northern Europe. Seal has many characteristics that were probably of interest to people specialised in the hunting of large fauna. It is a mammal with fat, meat, skin, blood, bone, and teeth. It can be hunted on beaches and, often, in large numbers. For people in this arctic landscape, this mammal's large fat reserves must have been an important resource both as food, fuel, and in the production and maintenance of tools and equipment (e.g., Eidlitz 1969), and the easy killing of seals basking on land must have been a temptation that was hard to resist. Seal can also be hunted on sea ice during winter and spring, that is, without a fully developed maritime adaptation. But if this activity is integrated as an important part of the subsistence strategy, a problem quickly arises. Seals tend to avoid kill-sites and continually move to new areas. Hence the need for more reliable supplies of seal may have been an important motivation towards open-sea hunting and a powerful impulse towards a specialised maritime adaptation.

The numbers of seals, reliable hunting sites, and sheltered seas that make sea hunting safer are more favourable along the Scandinavian coastline. The Swedish Skagerak coast is a meeting point between the continental plains and the fjord/skerry coastal landscape, and this may have been an important area for the development of hunting at sea using seaworthy vessels.

There is no reason to believe that people in the Late Glacial had any less clearly defined notions about the relationship between land and sea than modern people. This barrier has powerful onto-logical connotations and the development towards hunting at sea must have been much more than merely a technical and practical challenge. This may have been a threshold that the Late Glacial hunters lacked the motivation to cross. Without seaworthy vessels and an established maritime subsistence pattern, the fjord/skerry coastline is inaccessible. However, this cultural process may have taken place rapidly, in the course of a generation or two. This would have led to the opening up of the vast and favourable Scandinavian coast. Such a development seems to be in accordance with both the absence of archaeological remains from the Late Glacial period, as well as with the rapid colonisation in the Early Postglacial.

Technology and Raw Materials

As with the Hensbacka and the Ahrensburgian, the Fosna technocomplex is based mainly on flint. Flint does not occur in bedrock in North Scandinavia, but is found in glacial deposits. Seemingly, the flint nodules from South Scandinavia have been transported by ice and icebergs, with quantities decreasing northwards (Berg Hansen 1999). This may explain the widespread use of other rock types for tool production in North Norway already from the EMC. Presumably, this entailed technological adaptations. One example may be the widespread use of the bipolar technique in Troms and Finnmark (e.g., Sandmo 1986: 131, Schanche 1988: 104, Hesjedal et al. 1996: 163). Another is the disc cores (Woodman 1993, Hesjedal et al. 1996: 164), which seem linked to the production of flakes with good cutting edges. Other nonflint lithic raw materials are also known from EMC contexts in South Norway, for example, quartz crystal. This material is often reduced by bipolar technique, but formal tools or modified flakes are rare. Material from a series of EMi sites at Saltstraumen in Nordland is illustrative. Primary flakes of quartzite and quartz crystal dominate, with only few indications of secondary modification or use wear. However, the debitage (here as elsewhere) encompasses amounts of flakes with qualitative equivalents (points, edges) to formal tools in the Fosna tradition (Hauglid 1993). The nearby site of Fure at Steigen contained both disc-formed cores of quartzite and the Fosna tradition tanged-points in the same material (Bjerck 1991), and illustrate technological adaptations to local lithic materials, as well as the cultural affiliation to the Fosna technocomplex.

The use of other raw materials with 'flint-like' characteristics increases throughout the Mesolithic and varies greatly by region. In coastal areas of South Norway, the use of flint dominates. However, West Norway is characterised by increased use of local lithic material from MMC to LMC. A similar tendency is even more pronounced in the interior mountains and woodlands, for example, Holm 1985, 1991, Boaz 1997, 1999a, 1999b). Most of the lithics were probably extracted from glacial deposits, but clearly defined stone quarries are also documented both of quartzite (A. B. Johansen 1970, 1978) and jasper (Sjurseike 1994) with a widespread distribution of artefacts. Lithic variations on LMC sites indicate that there are many other, as yet undetected, quarry sites.

It is tempting to view the limited availability of flint as a shortage of lithic material, and an important catalyst towards both the microblade and bipolar techniques, which maximise the exploitation of what is available. However, the broad variation in lithic material documented on LMC sites indicates a wealth of available and suitable lithic materials. Archaeological research tends to overemphasise flint artefacts, where both technological indicators and use wear are easier to interpret. When other lithic materials are described as 'flint-supplements' (e.g., Jaksland 2001a: 37), there lurks in the background an assumption of an inferior material for both Mesolithic people and archaeologists. Continued research on the technological, social, and phenomenological aspects of the use of a broad spectrum of lithic materials has great potential to produce new insights into Mesolithic societies (e.g., Hood 1988, Gjerland 1990a, K. Johansen 1990, Holm 1994, Knutsson 1998, Bergsvik 1999, 2002b: 275, Simpson 1999, Larsson 2003, Lindgren 2003, 2004, Eigeleand 2006).

The Production and Use of Blades

The changes in the production and use of blades constitute a clear continuum throughout the Mesolithic (Bjerck 1983, 1986, Ballin 1995, 1999). Broadly speaking this development is common for the whole of Scandinavia, but with distinct regional variations.

The blade material of the EMC is characterised as heterogeneous, small and large, but normally broad with irregular sides and crests. Blades are produced from characteristic one-sided cores, with an acute angle (70–80 degrees) between platform and flaking surface. The heterogeneous blade material reflects a wide variety of uses for blades – for projectiles, knives, scrapers, and burins – all tools that are often based on blades and modified by retouch techniques. The irregularity of the blades is therefore not an indication of a lack of mastery, but more likely a careful adaptation to the varied use of blades of different sizes and forms (Callanan 2007).

There are clear indications of a gradual change in flake production from EM3, which results in a more specialised blade production in MM1 (Bjerck 1986). One-sided cores are replaced by many-sided conical cores with a flaking angle close to 90 degrees. This development may encompass a change from an indirect striking technique to a pressure technique (Bergsvik 2002: 287). However, this has not been closely studied. In MMC, it seems as if production starts with large cores that are gradually reduced in length by reduction/platform preparation. The small conical cores that dominate the core material must be viewed as the final stage. The fact that the cores were once considerably larger can best be seen in the blade material itself and in larger platform flakes and core-side flakes. This is an important difference from the LMC handle cores, where the retreating flaking surface has the same length throughout the whole production sequence.

Blade-production develops in the direction of narrower blades with more regular sides and crests, with increased homogeneity in size and form. Parallel with this, it appears as if the number of modified blades decreases. Microliths appear, but are less common than in Southern Scandinavia. The material is dominated by large numbers of blade fragments, indicating intentional modification by truncation techniques. Especially common are blade fragments with use wear on the edge

87

adjacent to the truncated corner, probably for use as knives (e.g., Bjerck 1990: 28). Some blade fragments have had small burin spalls removed, and are probably burins with particularly small burin edges.

This tendency seems to be linked to fundamental changes in tool traditions associated with an accelerating development of composite tools and an increased standardisation of hafted tools with replaceable cutting edges. This in turn would stimulate a standardisation of blade production and is probably the cause of the changes documented in blade production (Bjerck 1986, 1985). However, as organic materials are not usually preserved, a clear understanding of this tool tradition is lacking. Composite tools, especially flint-edged projectiles are documented in Southern Scandinavia, and are in certain lucky circumstances found in Norway (Mikkelsen 1971, 1975b: 80, Matland 1990, A. B. Olsen 1992: 175). This trend seems to be a common development in the Mesolithic communities in Norway until around 7000 cal BC. At this time, blade production from platform cores is abandoned in Finnmark (ref. B. Olsen 1994: 33, Hesjedal et al. 1996: 185, Grydeland 2005).

The tradition of *composite tools* seems to be developed further in LMC, where the technique becomes more specialised towards the classic microblade technique, with extremely uniform and narrow blades produced from small platform cores (conical cores/handle cores). Parallel with this, one can trace a further reduction in the number of identifiable blade tools. The retouching of microblades is not usual, but numbers of fragments are found, indicating modification by truncation. This tendency indicates a further refinement of a broad spectrum of composite tools.

It is likely that the noticeable rise in the numbers of bipolar cores throughout the Mesolithic is linked with the same development. The bipolar technique is present in the EMC and increasingly widespread during MMC/LMC. A similar trend is documented in both North Norway (Hesjedal et al. 1996: 186) and North Sweden (Callahan 1987). This method, which entails crushing the lithic material against a hard surface, can produce large amounts of razor-sharp points and edges. One can then select suitable flakes to be placed in hafts and handles, often without further modification. This technique maximises utilisation of the lithic material; even very small flakes can be modified to a series of points and edges (Fossum 2009). Bipolar flaking may be applied to a wide range of lithic material, meaning increased flexibility in its use. This may have been an important factor in the accelerating use of bipolar flaking throughout the Mesolithic.

Ethnographic and archaeological material comprising organic remains shows an almost unlimited variety of composite tools – cutting-edges in knives, points in projectiles, perforators, planes, scrapers, harpoons, and fishing hooks. It is worth remembering that composite tools incorporate more than just hunting equipment. One example of this is 'graters' – hundreds of pointed primary flakes, mounted on wooden bases and used in the processing of leaves, roots and seeds (e.g., Clarke 1976). In a context without organic remains, tools like this would appear as a concentration of flakes of various forms that would be impossible to sort out from normal debitage without elaborate microscopic analysis of use wear. As the bipolar technique produces large quantities of debitage, the identification and study of these tools is next to impossible.

The introduction of a cylindrical blade technique in LM5 (and Early Neolithic) in South Norway seems to mark a rupture in the bipolar core tradition. Besides the production of longer, more powerful edges, this technique seems to be directed towards the production of high-backed blades with pointed distal ends that form the basis for the Neolithic tanged points (A. B. Olsen 1992: 93, Nærøy 1993, Jaksland 2001a: 37, Bergsvik 2002: 292, Glørstad 2004: 37). At the same time, the use of bipolar cores seems to wane. The communities north of Stad (Norway's West Cape) did not take up the cylindrical blade technique, and here the use of bipolar technique seems to continue unabated (Skjelstad 2003: 126, Bergsvik 2003a).

The lithic material outlines a development towards a broadening and refinement of composite stone tools throughout MMC and LMC, with the production of edges and points increasingly by way of bipolar reduction and crushing on an anvil. The extent of this technique indicates that it must have been a fundamental element in the LMC, but archaeological insight into the intention and use of this technique is limited. And there may be further complications. It is not unusual for bipolar cores to bear signs of lateral modification that open the possibility that the core itself has functioned as an edge-piece in a chisel-like tool and that the crushed edges are the result of strong mechanical stress (woodwork?). Deeper insights into this elusive but important technique are important for our future understanding of Mesolithic tool traditions.

Landscapes, Sites, and Adaptation

With few exceptions, sites are open-air settlements, and appear as larger or smaller concentrations of lithic artefacts. Open-air shell middens are next to unknown (although shells are part of cultural deposits in rock shelters). Organic remains are often heavily decomposed, and identifiable remains are normally limited to charcoal and in favourable circumstances (in the LMC) to fragments of burnt bone. Organic material that may give information on subsistence is usually only preserved in rockshelters (Indrelid 1978, Mikkelsen 1978, Bjerck 2007). Unfortunately, rockshelters were not used as dwellings unless they were situated precisely where they were needed in relation to resources and transport routes. However, this does not mean that we are shut off from insights into the Mesolithic economy. The interaction between site location (that we must assume is related to subsistence) and the character of the surrounding landscape (that is related to varied biotopes) contains a wealth of information. The raised shorelines present a series of topographical situations, with repeated regularities in choice of site location and site-layout. The landscape is the interface between hunter and prey. Because we possess knowledge of landscape and related biotopes, the location of sites has great research potential to illuminate Mesolithic economies.

The sites display a wide range in land use that probably reflects varying subsistence patterns throughout time and space (Figure 3.8). It seems natural to suppose that the biodiversity and differences in landscape have favoured a development towards a broad spectrum of subsistence patterns. Even within small, homogeneous biotopes in Denmark, both social territories (Petersen 1984) and subsistence diversity (Fischer 2003b) have been documented (see also Blankholm this volume). The great environmental diversity of North Scandinavia implies an even broader spectrum of natural possibilities and limitations and considerable variation in subsistence patterns.

At a macrolevel, there are clear concentrations of Mesolithic sites in coastal areas, from outlying small islets to fjord mouths along the mainland (Figure 3.8). The distribution of sites is a reflection of a varied subsistence pattern connected to marine biotopes (e.g., Odner 1964, Møllenhus 1977, Lindblom 1982, Bjerck 1983, A. B. Olsen and Alsaker 1984, Svendsen 2007, Gundersen 2009). At a microlevel, the clear association of sites with natural harbours that offer a secure interface between sea and land further reflects a marine orientation (e.g., Bjerck 1989, Bergsvik 1991, 1994, 1995, Barlindhaug 1996). This is a recurring characteristic for the Mesolithic along the whole Norwegian coast. However significant numbers of high-mountain sites have also been discovered (Bøe 1942, Hagen and Martens 1961, Hagen 1963a, Simonsen 1963, 1986, Gaustad 1969, A. B. Johansen 1970, 1978, Indrelid 1973a, 1973b, 1977, 1994, Helskog 1980a, Gustafson 1988, Holm 1985, Bjørgo et al. 1992, Havas 1999, Fretheim 2002, Bang-Andersen 2003a, Rankamaa 2003). Mesolithic finds from forest areas were practically unknown (e.g., Bjørn 1934, Hagen 1946) until focussed investigations in these areas in recent years (e.g., Gustafson 1990, Boaz 1997, 1998, 1999a,

1999b, Fuglestvedt 1992, 1995, Sjurseike 1994, Fretheim 2009), suggesting that we can expect many more sites here.

Svalbard seems to be among the very few areas Holocene hunter-gatherers never settled (Bjerck 2000). Although this environment is comparable to the habitat of Inuit groups of Northern Greenland, large stretches of Arctic Ocean probably prevented the colonisation of this area.

EMC Landscapes and Sites

The density of sites in the skerry landscape throughout the whole EMC is a strong indication that marine resources were fundamental in the subsistence-pattern. It is not unusual for sites to lie on small islands towards the open ocean. The main concentrations seem to lie in the skerry belt outside fjord mouths (e.g., Bjerck 1995: 139). The sites are often surprisingly exposed to extremes of weather, but at the same time these areas are highly productive marine biotopes. With the exception of coastal stretches heavily influenced by the Holocene transgression, sites from the EMC cover all areas of the coast from Kattegat to Varanger. The skerry coastline disappears just east of Fiskerhalvøya and with it the presence of EMC sites (cf. Figure 3.1). The location of the sites indicates that these people had developed seaworthy vessels, which in the tree-less Preboreal landscape must have been hide boats.

Sites are especially abundant along the coast of Northwest Norway, and it is not unlikely that this rich coastal region with its associated accessible high-mountain areas has served as the focus for particularly widespread activity. Sites also have been discovered on the highlands of Trollheimen that probably represent reindeer hunting activities (Gustafson 1988, Svendsen 2007). This picture is similar to Rogaland, with many sites in coastal areas, and pronounced evidence of highland reindeer hunting in EM1–2 (Figure 3.9, Bang-Andersen 2003a). Recently, a site in North Finland was discovered 60 km from the coast of Varangerfjord, which is dated to EMC on its typological characteristics. The site is interpreted as evidence of hunting expeditions by coastal groups (Rankamaa and Kankaanpää 2004). EMC sites have at the moment not been found in lower lying forest areas (Boaz 1999b), but this may be a problem of site visibility. The distribution of EMC sites in relation to landscape and biotopes is strikingly parallel to West Sweden (e.g., Kindgren 1995, 1996) and seems to support the idea of a Scandinavian tradition in EMC.

EMC sites are usually small, 10–50 m², with less than 2000 artefacts, rarely more than 10,000 (Nærøy 1995, 2000: 182). With the exception of charcoal on some sites, organic material is not preserved. Clearly defined fireplaces are a rarity. There are several cases where a combination of sites together covers an area of up to several hundred m², for example, the Galta site (Prøsch-Danielsen and Høgestøl 1995), with significantly higher numbers of artefacts. However, it is uncertain if these are a distinctive type of large settlement or simply the accumulation and overlapping of many smaller sites at repeatedly visited points in the landscape (Nærøy 2000: 183, Bang-Andersen 2003a, Dugstad 2007). The recently excavated Nyhamna site 48 (EM2) may be an example of the latter (Figure 3.10), probably representing repeated use of the site by a smaller number of groups. Small excavation units and fine water sieving (2 mm) provide a detailed picture of defined artefact clusters. A less-detailed excavation would produce a record of a large site, likely to be interpreted as a larger, coherent settlement consisting of many smaller social units (Bjerck et al. 2008: 217ff).

In conclusion, a clear-cut differentiation between EMC sites has not been documented. Nevertheless, this we can presume that the social composition varied, and that the sites represent a broad range of different activities.

Figure 3.8. Mesolithic key sites in Norway (see Table 3.2 for details). Rock art sites are not included. Dotted lines show coastal areas with marked Holocene transgression, and subsequent under representation of the archaeological record from EMC and MMC (illustration by T. Gil).

EMC Dwellings

At the Fløyrli sites in Rogaland (EM1–2), at least seven clearly defined tent rings have been documented. The structures consist of largely coherent rings of large stones that encircle inner floors measuring between 4–10 m², with centrally placed fireplaces (Bang-Andersen 2003a, 2003b) (Figure 3.9). Similar structures have been observed on EMC sites at Mohalsen, Vega (pers. observation) and at Mortensnes (Schanche 1988: 57). Clearly defined patterns in artefact distribution may

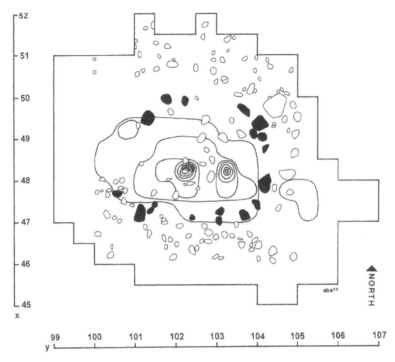

Figure 3.9. EM2 Tent ring with central fireplace (radiocarbon dated to 9360 ± 80 and 9400 ± 70 BP) and artefact distribution, site Fløyrlivatn 7. At Fløyrli and Myrvatnet (Figure 3.8: Nos. 53 and 54), 17 similar sites have been excavated. The twenty-six radiocarbon dates from fireplaces are all within EM1–2. These sites represent the earliest evidence from reindeer hunting in the mountain plateaus in Scandinavia (after Bang Andersen 2003a, fig. 8).

indicate that similar dwelling-structures may have been usual (e.g., Nærøy 2000, Kutchera and Waraas 2000, Thuestad 2005, Bjerck et al. 2008: 559ff, Åstveit 2009).

MMC Landscapes and Sites

The Holocene transgression means that the MM is badly represented in many coastal areas and it is hard to generalise about settlement patterns. MM sites seem to be closely associated with the outer coast, and there is reason to believe that marine resources had a central role in economic strategies.

Radiometric dates are available from high-mountain sites from MM1 (A. B. Johansen 1978: 299, Gustafson 1988: 57), MM2–3 (Indrelid 1994: 145, Bjørgo et al. 1992: 82, 99). One important change in MMC, however, is activity in forest areas, especially in East Norway, where a series of sites from MM3 have been discovered (Boaz 1998: 98). Seemingly, these sites are connected to seasonal hunting of large forest mammals, primarily elk. This activity is particularly noticeable in MM3–LM1 and seems to dwindle rapidly after 6000 cal BC (Boaz 1999b: 140). This is also documented in Central Norway (e.g., Gustafson 1988, Skar 1989). The finds contain a pronounced flint element that may indicate that these groups had their base in coastal areas. Similar finds are also documented

Figure 3.10. EM2 Location 48, Nyhamna, Aukra (Figure 3.8: No. 26), with thirteen defined radiocarbon-dated fireplaces. Well-preserved fireplaces and sharply defined artefact scatters show the contours of at least twelve activity units within a site-area of some 500 m², containing approximately 70,000 artefacts. Alignments of stones in association with several fireplaces are probably remnants of tent rings. The site probably represents repeated visits from small family-based social units (photo: H. Bjerck 2004).

in Northern Fennoscandia both in MM1 and MM2 (Jussila and Mattiskainen 2003, Rankamaa 2003, Bergman et al. 2004).

The rather scanty archaeological record from MM can hardly sustain general interpretations of detailed site patterns. Vega in Nordland offers however an exciting exception, with a series of sites that seem to constitute a network of functionally differentiated sites (Bjerck 1989, 1990). In MM2, Vega was a collection of three large islands some 20 km from the mainland. The rapid shore displacement gives some chronological control of sites and landscape. The area must have been rich in resources and had attracted people already in EM2. The islands are exposed to the open sea in all directions, and people were largely dependent on the few usable landing sites that existed, that is, topographical features that offered natural harbours. A strategic survey of natural harbours along an elevated shoreline on the 60 m a.s.l. contour line (dated to MM2) resulted in the discovery of twelve different sites, believed to be members of an interrelated structure of sites (Figure 3.11). The finds indicate clear differences in site-types. *Åsgarden 1*, located by the best natural harbour in the islands stands out as by far the largest site, probably a residential base (Figure 3.12). However, perhaps of greater interest is the series of smaller stations (less than 50 m² and five hundred artefacts), spread over the majority of the islands. On some of these sites, single pit house foundations are documented. The distribution of artefacts is confined to the houses. The artefact assemblages suggest qualitative differences. The hunting stations contain a high number of tools (30–70 percent formal tools, that is, blades and flakes with visible use wear), whilst the

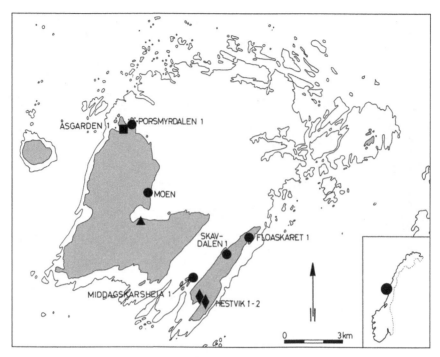

Figure 3.11. MM2 sites mapped along an elevated shoreline (60 m a.s.l.) at Vega, Northern Norway (Figure 3.8: No. 15). Size, artefact amounts, and artefact assemblages and locations demonstrate different types of sites, of which the residential base Åsgarden (square symbol) and the series of boat stations (circles) are the most prominent. Two camps (diamonds) are believed to be short time residential sites. A more casual stop (triangle) is probably not part of the organised system of sites. The rapid shoreline displacement suggests that the sites represent a period of two hundred to three hundred years (after Bjerck 1990, fig. 4).

corresponding ratio for the residential base at Åsgarden is 13 percent. The variation in tools is also different. Hunting stations are associated with a narrow range of tools (knives and scrapers) that may represent on-site use of tools in initial procurement activities and basic tool maintenance. The tool composition at Åsgarden displays a much broader range of activities, reflecting also the production and maintenance of a wide range of equipment and tools. Excavations of dwelling-structures at Åsgarden 1 and the station *Middagsskarheia* 1 (Figure 3.12) confirm impressions from the survey, and the radiocarbon dates strengthen the interpretation of a contemporaneous and coherent network of sites. The solid dwelling structures at several of the stations represent labour investment appropriate to important strategic sites of repeated use, and not the remains of haphazard activities that the limited number of finds might otherwise suggest. The model was further tested by surveys and excavations along a lower shoreline (50 m a.s.l., i.e., LM1), which revealed a similar network of site types.

The network of sites located close to safe landing-sites encircles open sea areas where hunting took place and must have made this activity both safer and more effective in this rough environment. It does not seem unreasonable to presume that similar sites existed elsewhere along the Scandinavian coast.

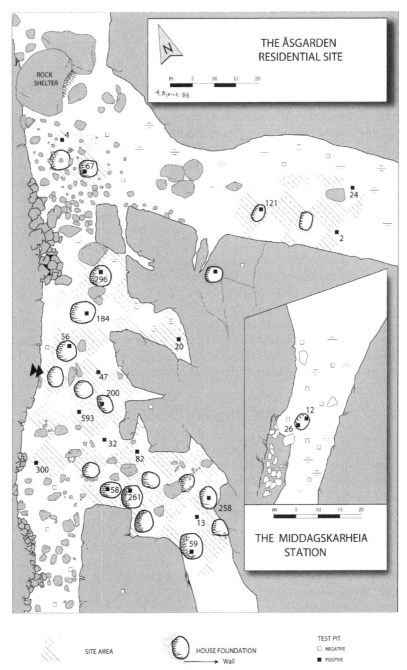

Figure 3.12. Two examples of sites belonging to the network of sites at Vega, c. 7500 cal BC. The Åsgar-den site is about 2300 m², containing an estimate (test-pits) of 280,000 artefacts and 20 visible house-pits, and is likely to represent a coherent, large residential base. The house foundation marked with a double arrow has been excavated and radiocarbon dated to 8330 ± 90 BP (7570–7140 cal BC). The Mid-dagskarheia station is also excavated and radiocarbon dated to 8490 ± 130 BP (7950–7150 cal BC). The station is a single pit house (13 m²), with artefacts confined to the floor area of the house (7 m²). The two houses are similar in size and construction, but the artefact assemblages are different. The Åsgarden house contains about 3500 artefacts and a low tool ratio (9 percent blades, formal tools, flakes with use wear), the Middagskarheia station about 100 artefacts and a tool ratio of 68 percent (after Bjerck 1990, including seven newly mapped house foundations at Åsgarden [pers. observation 2005], redrawn by T. Gil).

MMC Dwellings

Unlike the EMC structures, MMC dwelling structures seem to be solid semi-subterranean houses (Figure 3.14, Gjessing 1943, Simonsen 1961, 1975, Schanche 1988: 72, Engelstad 1989, B. Olsen 1994: 38, 1997: 185, Hesjedal et al. 1996: 61, Pettersen 1999). The two excavated house foundations from Vega (Figure 3.12) are illustrative. The round foundations (3–4 m in diameter) were dug down approximately 0.5 m, and a floor of approximately 10 m² was cleared, with a centrally placed fireplace. In the house at Middagskarheia 1, half of the floor was covered with larger stones, which may have served as a foundation for a sleeping platform. No traces of posts were uncovered, but marked wall-mounds suggest that stone or turf were included in the superstructure. There is no clear trace of an entrance. The houses were often built into coarse beach sediments, where the drainage is good. The sunken floors must have facilitated the construction of a superstructure able to withstand the rough conditions, securely based in the solid wall-mound (Bjerck 1989: 81, 1990). These houses are well built and permanent constructions, and indicate a more stable settlement pattern. Similar houses radiocarbon dated to MM1 have been excavated at Mortensnes in Varanger (Schanche 1988: 74, 7650–7500 cal BC) and Slettnes IVA tuft F45 (Hesjedal et al. 1996: 64, 7680–7500, 8200–7860 cal BC).

MMC dwellings are yet not documented in South Norway. This absence may be related to different construction methods here, lacking the eye-catching sunken floors and therefore more elusive in the archaeological record. Variations in dwelling constructions may be linked to the wide geographical variation in climate and available building materials.

MMC Organic Remains

There is scarcely any organic material that can be related to the MMC. An exciting new element is carbonised hazelnut shells, an indication of an orientation towards a more plant-based diet (Mikkelsen 1975a: 32, 1978). It has been claimed that the hazel appears 'unnaturally' early in coastal areas in the Postglacial floral succession, which may indicate human utilisation of this resource (Kaland and Krzyvinski 1978). Nuts are easy to gather in large quantities, highly nutritious and easy to store. Nuts may have been an important food supply in the winter. The extensive use of hazelnuts may mark widespread use of other plant material that is difficult to trace.

The Viste cave, Layer I, is a fortunate exception, with a relatively large osteological assemblage dated to MM3 (Brøgger 1908, Lund 1951, Indrelid 1978). Because the cave is on the coast, it is surprising that forest mammals dominate (70 percent), with wild boar (57 percent) and elk (8 percent) as the best represented species. The share of marine mammals (seal) is only 10 percent. However, the material represents a broad-spectrum adaptation. All in all, 70 different species are represented (22 *Mammalia*, 37 *Aves*, 11 *Pisces*). The composition of species indicates occupation primarily during the summer months, with some use in autumn/winter (Indrelid 1978: 163).

The exceptional Tørkop site in Østfold, a coastal site dated to MM1, has yielded an interesting assemblage of burnt bone fragments – fifteen hundred fragments from reliable contexts. This also seems to be a seasonal site (autumn/winter), dominated by terrestrial mammals (75 percent) and birds (24 percent), a few fish bones, and a total absence of marine mammals. Beaver (*Castor fiber*) and wild boar seem to be the most prominent species (Mikkelsen et al. 1999).

Figure 3.13. Mesolithic house foundation from Mohalsen, Vega, with shoreline dates suggesting a MM1 age. The wall consists of alignments of two to three layers of large cobbles, suggesting that these are permanent houses built for repeated/long-lasting occupation. The diameter of the structure is approximately 3.5 m (photo: H. Bjerck 2005).

MMC Human Remains

The oldest known human remains in Norway are found at Søgne (Figure 3.8). The find includes at least two and perhaps as many as five individuals, all adult females (Sellevold and Skar 1999). The site lies below present sea level and has been interpreted as graves related to a submerged dwelling site. Incorporating the correction for the marine component (–three hundred years), four radiocarbon dates are within MM2 (7490–7375, 7445–7270, 7435–7210, and 7260–7018 cal BC). The latest date (6665–6527 cal BC), suggests that one of the individuals is five hundred to seven hundred years younger than the rest. The $\delta^{13}C$ values from the three oldest and the latest samples are −13.4 percent, indicating a diet comprising 86 percent marine protein and a clear maritime-oriented life style (ibid.: 10). Parts of an adult female skeleton found at Bleivik in Rogaland are dated to the MM2/3 transition (7031–6743 cal BC). As the $\delta^{13}C$ value is unknown, the date is not corrected for the marine component (ibid.: 8). Because the site was below sea level at that time, this is most likely the result of a drowning accident.

LMC Landscapes and Sites

The majority of LMC sites are situated in the skerry/fjord costal landscape. The sites are concentrated in areas with rich and stable marine resources, for example, tidal currents and fjord mouths

(Bergsvik 2001a). LMC encompasses a large number of sites, and numerous larger sites are found. Many of the sites from West Norway have thick cultural deposits, especially from LM3–5, indicating a greater permanence in settlement patterns than earlier (A. B. Olsen 1992: 235, Bergsvik 2001b). The cultural deposits are sandy organic layers with quantities of charcoal, fire-cracked rocks and heavily decomposed bone material. Similar sites are documented in North Norway, both numerous house structures (e.g., Karlebotten, LM1, Engelstad 1989) as well as middens (LM4, Schanche 1988: 78).

It should be emphasised that the LMC represents a period of twenty-five hundred years, significantly longer than the EMC or MMC. In addition the period coincides with the Holocene transgression-maximum and a two-thousand-year period of stable sea level. Sites with thick cultural deposits are most common in West Norway where the transgression maximum was most stable. In East Norway, where the crustal uplift was significant and the transgression is absent, sites with extensive cultural deposits are rare (e.g., Glørstad 2004). Both these factors distort the archaeological record of the period. Despite this, the picture remains one of greater settlement stability.

LMC is associated with distinct changes in the use of inland areas. Sites display broader and more intensive activities of both mountain- and forest-areas. Numerous sites with quantities of fire-cracked rock, some with substantial pit-houses (radiocarbon-dated to LM1–5) have been documented in the forests of East Norway. The sites are interpreted as occupation sites used during the winter months (Fuglestvedt 1995, Boaz 1999b: 145). The occurrence of flint bears witness to connections with coastal areas (Boaz 1999b: 136), but the lithic assemblages are dominated by local raw material found in glacial deposits, as well as lithics from documented quarries, for example, quartzite (A. B. Johansen 1970, 1978) and jasper (Sjurseike 1994). The sites are related to hunting groups with specialised subsistence patterns based on year-round occupation of forest areas (Boaz 1999b: 147). There is substantial activity in the innermost forests, beyond the likely range of seasonal hunting expeditions from coastal areas. It is likely that both production and consumption took place in the interior.

A similar picture of an intensified use of inner forest and high-mountain areas is portrayed by finds from other areas, in Central Norway (Gustafson 1987, Gustafson 1988, Gustafson 1990, Fretheim 2002), in Finnmark (B. Olsen 1994: 38) and not least in the North Swedish forests (Baudou 2003, Forsberg 2003, Knutsson et al. 1999, Knutsson 2003).

LMC Dwellings

From North Norway there are many examples of a continuation of the pit-house tradition (e.g., Schanche 1988, Bjerck 1989: 101, Engelstad 1989, Hesjedal and Niemi 2003, Ramstad et al. 2005). In LMC, evidence of houses is also found in South Norway, postholes, shallow depressions, cleared floors, earthen floors, especially on the larger sites from LM1–3. From Svinesund, house foundations from LM4–5 are documented on the sites Berget 1 (Jaksland 2002: 66) and Torpum 13 (Jaksland 2003: 264). The dwellings appear as circular cleared, levelled floors measuring 15–17 m², surrounded by diffuse walls. The floor was not dug down into the ground and postholes are not observed.

At Skatestraumen, remains of houses were observed in the form of a series of postholes and cleared floors corresponding with artefact concentrations, without any sunken floors or visible wall mounds (e.g., Loc. 17, Havnen (LM3–4), Bergsvik 2002: 184, 305). At Nyhamna, Aukra, a series of complex structures relating to various types of dwellings is dated within the period

LM2–5, with postholes, clearings, ditches, depressions, fireplaces and kerbing (e.g., Localities 30, 50, 67, and 68). The house sites appeared as faint depressions surrounded by broad, low walls, and floor areas of around 12–16m². The finds from Nyhamna offer detailed insights into complex structures. Foundation posts were placed both centrally and towards the wall. A series of ditches for drainage, wall foundations and air channels was uncovered. Some of the foundations represent a series of houses that were built, rebuilt and maintained almost on the same spot. The main structure is usually obvious, whilst details are far more complex (Åstveit 2008a, 2009).

The excavated remains of pit-houses in forest areas of East Norway are dated to LM2–5, and appear as pronounced pits up to 0.7 m deep, with a circumference of 5–8 m. The remains of wooden constructions, platforms along the walls, a bark floor underlain by pine branches, and postholes are documented. The sites are associated with middens containing quantities of fire-cracked stones and are interpreted as winter dwellings (Boaz 1999b: 144). These sites resemble the somewhat younger sites (LM5) from the Swedish forests, also with pit-houses and middens with fire-cracked stones (Lundberg 1997: 136).

During recent excavations in Norway, the approach has been to expose large coherent spaces (Ramstad 2003, Glørstad 2004, Bjerck et al. 2008). The preliminary results seem to indicate that we can expect a greater wealth of detail concerning Mesolithic dwellings in the near future, which will contribute to the understanding of the various traditions in house size, function, and construction techniques.

LMC Organic Material

The cultural layers on many LMC sites are probably the remains of thick deposits of decomposed organic material. Except for minor deposits in rockshelters, shell middens are largely unknown. Large accumulations of shell tend to be self-conserving, and would probably have been preserved if the use of shellfish was as comprehensive as in southern Scandinavia. Seemingly the wealth of nearby, reliable fish-resources has stabilised the use of residential bases.

The cultural deposits contain amounts of charcoal, but beyond their use as dating-material there has been little research on this material. Throughout the whole LMC, carbonised hazelnut shells are abundant in the cultural layers of South Norway, indicating that nuts have been an important part of the diet. The carbonized organic remains probably have a considerable research potential, and species classification and distribution analyses could provide important information about activity patterns on dwelling sites.

Bone material occurs at some sites, but normally consists of badly preserved, burnt fragments that are difficult to classify. However, these deposits probably contain chemical traces of great information value (cf. Bakkevig 1980, Linderholm 2003, Rønne 2004) yet to be explored. One example is the concentrations of *Vivianite* in culture layers at Locality 30 at Nyhamna, Aukra. Vivianite ($Fe_3P_2O_8 \cdot H_2O$) is a golden-white material that resembles decomposed bone when excavated but develops a striking blue colour on being exposed to air. Vivianite is the product of quantities of decomposed organic material that together with other structures forms interesting patterns on the site (Åstveit 2008b). By developing further analytical tools, investigation of such materials could provide new information and should be a priority for the future.

The few sites that do reveal information on the species represented in refuse layers present a varied picture. The large culture layer at Kotedalen, West Norway, represents a series of occupational phases through the Neolithic and Mesolithic periods. From four phases radiocarbon dated to LM1–2, a large and varied bone assemblage has been collected (forty-two thousand fragments) (Hufthammer

1992, A. B. Olsen 1992). The material contains a broad spectrum of *Aves* (six species) but is dominated by *Mammalia* (twenty species) and *Pisces* (sixteen species). The material that could be classified includes cod (*Gadidae*), pollack and coalfish (*Pollachius sp.*), seal (*Phocidae*), and otter (*Lutra lutra*) in significant numbers. Quantities of carbonised hazelnut shell also were present. In and around the strong tidal currents adjacent to the site there are rich, varied and stable sources of these species, as well as a broad array of others. A closer examination of the composition of species indicates that the site was not in use through the whole year. Material from the LM1–2 periods can hardly represent anything other than a long-lasting and intensive occupation, but with a distinct seasonal character that contrasts with the Neolithic phases at the same site (A. B. Olsen 1992, Hufthammer 1992, Warren 1994, Bergsvik 2001b). A similar situation has been documented at Skatestraumen, despite the far more limited bone material (Bergsvik 2002: 304, Senneset and Hufthammer 2002).

Excavations at Skipshelleren in the inner-fjord region of Hordaland resulted in one and hundred seventy-five thousand bone fragments, the majority from Neolithic and Mesolithic layers. The Mesolithic sequence (LM3–5) also contained exceptional quantities of mussel (*Mytilus edulis*) and common periwinkle (*Littorina littorea*) (Bøe 1934, Indrelid 1978: 159). Unfortunately, the Mesolithic component in this material is difficult to differentiate without a thorough reanalysis. However, the number of lithic artefacts was limited to seven hundred, in contrast to twenty-eight thousand from the four phases at Kotedalen. Thus, Skipshelleren is an illustration of the vast quantities of organic components that probably once existed at the badly preserved open-air sites (Bjørgo 1981: 136).

Another example is the midden at Mortensnes, Varanger (LM4). This produced five thousand bone fragments of which less than two thousand could be classified. The group *Mammalia* (318 fragments) is dominated by seal (*Phocidae*), with a smaller number of whale (*Cetacea*), beaver (*Castor fiber*) and dog (*Canidae*). *Aves* (504 fragments) include at least thirteen species, of which kittiwake (*Rissa tridactyla*) and other sea birds dominate. The *Pisces* group (4,368 fragments) contains eight species, dominated by cod (*Gadus morhua*). The midden also contained large quantities of a cyprinid bivalve and common periwinkle (Schanche 1988: 78). The organic assemblage indicates a specialised marine adaptation based on a broad range of species during spring/summer, with a striking absence of reindeer or elk that must have been available as prey in the area (ibid.: 158).

The two sites at Frebergsvik in the Oslo fjord (LM3) also seem to represent specialised marine hunting. *Mammalia* (725 fragments) is dominated by porpoise (*Phocaena phocaena*) with representation of seal, otter, fox, and dog. *Aves* (forty-one) are mainly of the Auk family, *Pisces* (three) are surprisingly sparse (Mikkelsen 1975b, Indrelid 1978: 163). This contrasts with the recently discovered Skoklefald site (LM2), which is dominated by fish (mainly herring) and abundant shells (oysters, periwinkle, and mussel) (Jaksland 2001b). A midden with abundant burnt bones (12,862) is also reported at a LM3–5 coastal site at Saugbruks in Østfold. This assemblage is totally dominated by mammals. Among the 1 percent of burnt bone fragments that it was possible to identify, wild boar (*Sus scrofa*), otter (*Lutra lutra*) and red deer (*Cervus elaphus*) are present (Mikkelsen et al. 1999: 47).

Middens with considerable quantities of fire-cracked rock and burnt bones have been documented in the forest areas of East Norway (LM1–5). As is to be expected, beaver (*Castor fiber*), and elk (*Alces alces*) are the dominant species (Boaz 1999b: 144). An interesting site with radiocarbon dated faunal remains in an interior area is Langesjøen Location 1039 at Hardangervidda, which interestingly enough contained bones from trout (*Salmo trutta*) of Mesolithic age (LM4, Indrelid 1978: 164).

LMC Human Remains

Except for a few finger bones from a single adult individual from Skipshelleren (LM4), neither graves nor human remains from the LMC have been found (Sellevold and Skar 1999). The total absence of human remains from these sites may indicate that the LMC societies in Norway practised a different form of burial than that documented in Southern Scandinavia.

Regional Differentiation . . . and Ethnic Groups?

Throughout the Norwegian Mesolithic, one can trace an increasing regional differentiation in the archaeological record. Within the EMC, similarities more than differences dominate, and differences are probably related to different raw materials and their resultant technological adaptations. More fundamental technological elements, for example, the production and use of blades and the production of formal tools, share clear similarities. This common lithic tradition is evident until about 7000 cal BC, when the blade technique appears to be abandoned in Finnmark. As the use of blades is a fundamental element in the EMC tool tradition, there is reason to emphasise this development. Another feature distinctive to North Norway is the tradition associated with naturalistic, polished rock art in MM1–2, a tradition that seems to be confined to the Salten/Ofoten area in Nordland.

A series of distinctive traits is also discernible in the MMC material of South Norway. The characteristic cross-shaped/star-shaped clubs are related to the period MM2–LM1 (Glørstad 2002, Bergsvik and A. B. Olsen 2003: 400, Skår 2003). Cross-shaped clubs are distributed throughout the costal areas of South Norway, with a concentration on the Southwest coast. Star-shaped clubs have only been found within Southwest Norway.

The chubby adze tradition reveals an even clearer regional differentiation. This can be traced back to MM1, with comprehensive activity in the greenstone and diabase quarries at Stakaneset and Hespriholmen (Figure 3.8, Nos. 38 and 48). It is probably of importance that this tool group appears in combination with the emergence of the boreal forests. The chubby adzes represent heavy edge tools well suited for woodworking, made in tough, basaltic rocks able to withstand substantial mechanical stress. Thus, the emergence and the impact of this tradition may represent increased use of wood in tools, utensils, vessels and dwellings.

The fact that 50–60 percent of the known Mesolithic stone adzes in West Norway can be traced to the Hespriholmen and Stakaneset quarries, demonstrates their central role to Mesolithic communities (A. B. Olsen and Alsaker 1984: 89, Bergsvik and A. B. Olsen 2003: 398). Adzes from the two sources have distinctive distribution areas with their boundary just south of the Sognefjord. The main distribution area for Stakaneset diabase adzes stretches north to the Trondheimsfjord. Further north, only a few adzes of Stakaneset diabase are found. In North Norway, the chubby adze tradition seems to be less pronounced (Helskog 1980b: 45, Myklevoll 1998). In addition, technological and typological differences have been documented in the adzes from the two quarries (Gjerland 1988, Bergsvik and A. B. Olsen 2003: 399). In the coastal areas east from Lista (Norway's South Cape), one can trace a separate adze tradition centred in MM2 (Boaz 1999b: 141), in which pecked chubby adzes of a variety of basaltic rocks dominate (Ballin 1999: 206–8). The characteristic Nøstvet adzes, rough-outs with edge polish, appear in LM1 in the same area (Berg 1997: 43, 2003: 285, Jaksland 2001a: 36). The chubby adze tradition of East Norway has clear parallels with the LMC West Swedish material (Sandarna/Lihult) (Nordqvist 1999). Quarries for materials that can be linked to the production of adzes have not been documented in either East or North Norway.

This is reflected in the adzes, which represent a broad range of rock types (Berg 1999), probably extracted from glacial sediments.

Bergsvik and A. B. Olsen (2003: 402) interpret the distribution of the adzes as the result of direct access to the quarries within each of the two areas, and suggest that the distinct borders in the distribution patterns depict the contours of at least four social territories in Atlantic Scandinavia: North Norway (outside the diabase area), Northwest Norway (Stakaneset adzes), Southwest Norway (Hespriholmen adzes), and East Norway with pecked adzes and eventually Nøstvet axes. It is worth remembering that this is a general picture of developments throughout MMC and LMC, that is, a period of some four thousand years (representing 130 generations), and that this social development probably encompasses important dynamics. For the time being, the chubby adze chronology is coarse grained, and the details of the developmental characteristics associated with the emergence of these territories are unknown.

However, studies of a broader range of archaeological material from West Norway reveal a more detailed picture of increasing regional diversity from the MMC to the LMC (Skjelstad 2003). Nuances can be traced in the use of various lithic materials, in technological variation (extent of bipolar technique) and in a range of tool types – small soapstone net sinkers (Figure 3.4c), and the use of grinding slabs and polished slab knives. Divisions in material culture can be traced both at Stad (Norway's West Cape) and between the north and south in Hordaland. There is reason to believe that a wider perspective will present a picture of greater regional variation in material culture. One example is the stylistic variations in LMC rock-art (Hagen 1976, Hesjedal 1994, Lødøen 2003, Ramstad 2000a, Mandt and Lødøen 2005).

There are also clear commonalities cutting across these differences. The blade-technique appears to have a rather broadly parallel development in South Norway. An interesting detail is the synchronous changes in platform preparation demonstrated by D. Sanger (1981). The use of handle-cores seems however to be more widespread in East Norway and displays a link towards central areas of Sweden (Knutsson et al. 2003: 419). The presence of transverse points in the LM4–5 also charts supraregional differences. The transverse points are *common* in the coastal areas of East Norway (Mikkelsen 1975a, Ballin and Jensen 1995: 188, Jaksland 2001a: 37, Glørstad 2004: 28), in southern highland areas (Indrelid 1973a), in eastern forest areas (Fuglestvedt 1995: 99) and on the coast and in the hinterland of Finnmark (B. Olsen 1994:34, Hesjedal et al. 1996: 166, Schanche 1988: 108). Transverse arrows seem however to be *rare* in West Norway (Bergsvik 2002: 293). These examples illustrate the necessity of examining regional differentiation in material culture *across* the boundaries of museum catchments, regional and national borders, and other modern barriers that constrain current archaeological research.

The conclusions are, then, an increasing regional differentiation in the material culture throughout the Mesolithic that becomes even more obvious during the Neolithic (e.g., Søborg 1988, Bergsvik 2003a, 2003b). The catalysts behind this process were multifacetted and complex. One of the more mundane is variation in the availability of lithic materials, which probably became increasingly decisive as settlement-patterns stabilised during the LMC. Another catalyst was the large geographical variations in environmental variables, which were greater in the LMC than in the EMC. Both these factors probably stimulated a diversity of subsistence patterns (as also indicated by the faunal remains) and greater variation in the need for tools and equipment. All this had the potential to accelerate regional diversity, but the bottom line is that this trend must be related to the dynamics and increased complexity of the Mesolithic societies, with more clear-cut territorial affinity, social identity and ethnic grouping (Skjelstad 2003: 128, Bergsvik 2003b, 2004, Gundersen 2009).

Mesolithic Trends

Throughout the whole Late Glacial period, a broad skerry/fjord coastal landscape existed on the west side of the waning Baltic ice sheet. During the four-thousand-year-long Late Glacial period, both the sea and land teemed with an arctic fauna, but at present no certain evidence of human settlement has been uncovered prior to c. 9500 cal BC. The fact that late-glacial shorelines have been preserved lends credence to this notion. Shining through this absence of settlement along the Scandinavian coastal-strip is perhaps the lack of specialised, sea-hunting maritime adaptations among the Late-Glacial hunting groups of the Continent. Of course, one cannot rule out the possibility that people may have strayed into this landscape, either by accident or driven by the need to discover new land. However, without seaworthy vessels, this seascape would have been nearly as inaccessible as the moon. The apparent absence of Palaeolithic groups from Late-Glacial Ireland may be an indication of a similar phenomenon.

Marine resources in littoral areas are likely to have played some role in late Palaeolithic subsistence patterns, for example the clubbing of basking seals. The various species of seal represent easy access to quantities of blubber that were probably attractive. An integration of this resource may have been important in the development of specialised arctic maritime subsistence patterns, encompassing the hunting of seal in the open sea.

The pioneer settlement of Norway and West Sweden has several interesting features. In fact, the colonisation of the whole of this 3000-km-long coast appears to have been rapid and extensive. The process seems to have taken place within five to ten generations during the EM1, which, in archaeological terms, must be characterised as an event. The location of sites reflects the use of seaworthy vessels and indicates a clear maritime orientation. The earliest finds from highland areas date to the EM1–2 transition, but it is likely that reindeer hunting is as old as the settlement along the coast. However, whether reindeer hunting was economically important, or more connected to social or cultural factors, is uncertain. The archaeological material offers little that can add detail to this picture. Tanged points are traditionally linked to archery and terrestrial hunting. Their ample numbers on coastal sites may suggest a wider use, perhaps as points in composite barbed projectiles. The only tool element that can be directly connected to sea hunting is the large tanged points occurring on some EMC coastal sites, which may represent lances employed in the killing of harpooned sea mammals (Waraas 2001: 112). Seemingly, the use of flake adzes is also confined to coastal sites, and may be related to procurement of sea mammals, for example, cutting/scraping of blubber without damaging skins.

Regional homogeneity in material culture, generally small sites, and the lack of permanent dwelling structures support the idea of a population based on small, mobile social groups, organised in family-based residential units. The pan-regional and gradual change in the fundamental blade-technique from EM3 and MM1–2 may be related to high mobility and extensive social interaction without distinct social territories.

From the MMC onwards, a more permanent and organised pattern of sites can be traced. Solid house constructions are established in North Norway. The houses signalise a level of investment that implies an increased reuse of sites, indicating a more structured network of sites. The absence of MMC dwellings in South Norway may relate to a different tradition in the construction of houses, less visible in the archaeological record. The structure of interrelated sites documented at Vega in MMC is hardly unique. The impression of increased residential stability is also profoundly reflected in extensive cultural layers at LMC sites, affirmed by abundant traces of dwellings and other constructions both in South and North Norway.

The general impression of the MMC is one of increased regional differentiation with regard to subsistence patterns. The EMC groups appear to have continued their long traditions of high mobility and specialised hunting of large mammals. This scenario changes during the MMC, with the emergence of a subsistence strategy based on a broader spectrum of resources, probably by way of widespread and organised seasonal migrations. Both the faunal remains and the location of the sites seem to point in this direction. In addition to the hunting of reindeer in the mountain plains, there are clear indications of hunting activities in forest areas of the interior in North, Central, and South Norway. Faunal remains from MM1 and MM3 in the coastal sites at Viste (and Tørkop) demonstrate an emphasis on large forest mammals, and bear the hallmarks of seasonal sites. However, the ^{13}C content of the MM1 human remains from nearby Søgne affirms a marine-oriented diet. There are many factors, cultural and natural, which may contribute to an under representation of marine resources, especially fish, in the refuse layers. Nevertheless, the marked presence of large terrestrial mammals cannot be overlooked, and is probably indicative of logistical mobility in organised seasonal activity patterns.

Evidently, hazelnuts are an important element in the diets of South Norway, perhaps an indication of greater emphasis on plant-based foods. Hazelnuts can be gathered and stored in large numbers for long periods and their increased presence on sites may indicate more stable movements within a set structure of sites.

This trend is parallel to a more elaborate regional differentiation in material culture, notably variations in the chubby adze tradition, the demise of blade-technique in Finnmark, and the tradition of polished rock art in Nordland. It is reasonable to believe that differences in material culture and the emergence of more pronounced regional biodiversity throughout the MMC encompass substantial variations in both social organisation and subsistence patterns. The distribution patterns of the Mesolithic chubby adzes seem to outline social territories that probably correspond with communities of a number of residential units.

Towards the LMC and increasingly throughout this period, a trend towards a further elaboration of regional diversity in material culture is evident. This is probably an indication of more distinct groupings in Mesolithic societies, with pronounced regional affiliations. At the same time, sites with thick cultural deposits appear at locations that are particularly favourable for marine foraging, for example, near tidal currents and fjord-mouths, optimal locations for easy access to a wide range of resources. These sites indicate long-lasting occupation of larger social units, residential stability, and a closer relationship to rich and stable biotopes. The subsistence patterns appear to be based on a widening spectrum of species (mammals, plants, birds, fish, and shellfish) within more limited areas. Measured from the amount of hazelnuts, plant-based foods seem to be more significant. Equivalents to South Scandinavian LMC shell-middens are not known, meaning that shellfish can hardly have been a dominant element in Mesolithic subsistence. The location of LMC coastal sites and their organic components indicate subsistence strategies with a greater emphasis on stable fish resources, along with sea birds and sea mammals. Combined with a semisedentary settlement pattern, one can imagine that the smoking and drying of large catches of fish in insect-free seasons made it possible to accumulate substantial food reserves, reflecting the innovative and energetic harnessing for human benefit of the ever-present cold winds.

The combination of increasingly stable settlement patterns in more confined areas, and the distinct patterns of regional biodiversity, probably imply a diversity of economic strategies between regions. This is perhaps most obvious in interior East Norway, where the archaeological record suggests a development of a specialised terrestrial adaptation in LMC, with year-round settlement patterns in the forest/mountain areas. This tradition is closely related to similar Mesolithic groups in interior Northern Fennoscandia documented in Sweden and Finland. There is no reason to doubt the existence of a great variety of adaptive strategies in the changing landscapes and biotopes along the 3000 km of coastline in Western Scandinavia.

All this outlines a picture of more residential stability, stronger regional ties, the establishment of socially defined territories, increased social complexity and probably social formations that may be labelled as ethnic groups. There is reason to believe that there was still great seasonal variation in settlements, social composition and subsistence activities, but increasingly organised by a structure of task groups based in more stable residential units.

Large parts of the hunter-gatherer rock art, found in all parts of Norway, seem to originate within the LMC. This may relate to an intensification of the use of symbols, accompanied by regional differences in style perhaps related to more distinct social identities and increased symbolic interaction between social groups.

Despite all its failings and mysteries, the archaeological material of the Mesolithic forms an image of great dynamism both in time *and space*. These developments include processes that are normally associated with the Mesolithic/Neolithic transition. Of course, the trend towards a greater diversity in human societies would have been even clearer if we had chosen to include the Neolithic. However, this would probably have overshadowed the less prominent but still distinct dynamics of the Mesolithic. It is imperative to emphasise that the social developments that eventually led to the emergence of agriculture are rooted in processes reaching backwards through many generations into societies of the Mesolithic period.

Research Challenges

If we place ourselves in the centre of a large circle that sweeps a hundred years back and a hundred years forward in the scientific landscape, one can expect substantial advances in Mesolithic research in the near future. If there still exists an activity known as archaeology a hundred years from now, changing theoretical perspectives, research focus, and methodological innovations will probably have turned the structures of archaeological research upside down, perhaps several times. Given the possibilities of today's digital tools that are as yet only applied on a limited scale as analytical aids, it might be possible by way of 3D scanning to identify individuals from combinations of flake scars in the well-preserved lithic material. A cool head and the mere press of a button is all it might take to undertake refit studies and complementary analysis of activity patterns. Combinations of digital maps together with information from sites might be combined in models that contain detailed information on biology in the successive landscape settings linked to shoreline displacement. These are all possibilities we can imagine based on today's technology.

In the short term, I believe that an orientation towards chronological frameworks that display a greater capacity to allow for regional diversity will be important, that is, the proposed structure based on chronozones. At a local level, this will simplify research from north to south and from east to west, which is crucial for a deeper understanding of the dynamics of Mesolithic societies.

Digital tools also have the potential to break up today's problematic typology, which creates an unrealistic image of homogeneous artefacts groups that at present restrict our understanding of interregional variation and gradual change. The archaeological material that already exists in collections has not been utilised to the extent that it should. There is too much emphasis on the need for new material and contexts. This is also true of the limited collections of organic material, which through reanalysis and direct dating could contribute important new information.

New excavations should have greater focus on the gathering of organic components. The most obvious is charcoal material, which could reveal activity patterns not visible in the present selective focus on structures and lithic material. Even greater possibilities lie in the decomposed and transformed organic tracers that may be analysed by way of chemical analysis. These are fields that are the scene of some activity today, and which hold enormous potential for the future.

Acknowledgments

I wish to express my gratitude for a variety of constructive contributions from Knut Andreas Bergsvik, Hans Peter Blankholm, Terje Brattli, Lars Forsberg, Håkon Glørstad, Geir Grønnesby, Lasse Jaksland, Arne B. Johansen, Trond Lødøen, Asle Bruen Olsen, Bjørnar Olsen, Morten Ramstad, Kalle Sognnes, Leif Inge Åstveit, Martin Callanan (translation), and Theo Gil (illustrations). This review is born out of and nourished by the ever-generous readiness of these individuals to discuss thoughts and share information.

Chapter 4

Southern Scandinavia

Hans Peter Blankholm*

Introduction

Southern Scandinavia comprises an area of approximately 60,000 km² between 54 degrees and 58 degrees North and 8 degrees to 16 degrees East, and comprises Denmark proper, Scania in Sweden, and Schleswig-Holstein in Germany. It is characterised by gently undulating moraines of Weichselian origin below 100 m. a.s.l., the three straits, Øresund, Storebælt, and Lillebælt connecting the Baltic Sea with the Kattegat Sea, and a great number of river and fjord systems, and smaller islands. To the west is the North Sea; to the north the Skagerak separates it from Norway (Figure 4.1).

At the beginning of the Postglacial, about ten thousand years ago (Table 4.1) there was a rapid increase in temperature, from a July mean of approximately 10 degrees C in the Late Glacial Younger Dryas to approximately 15 degrees in the early postglacial Preboreal, that is slightly below the present-day temperature of 16 degrees. The mean July temperature in the Boreal period was around 18–20 degrees C and the mean January temperature between −1 degrees and −1.5 degrees C. At the Boreal/Atlantic transition, the climate changed from dry to humid and the mean July temperature rose to a Postglacial maximum of 21 degrees C. The Early Neolithic mean July temperature was approximately the same or slightly lower.

The ameliorating climate also fostered a forest succession from open birch and pine forests in the early Preboreal, through pine and hazel dominated forests in the Boreal to the Atlantic Period natural climax forest, characterised by elm, lime, and oak. There were corresponding changes in mammals, fish, shellfish, birds, and plant foods (see Blankholm 1996).

Major changes in land-sea relationships accompanied deglaciation following the last Ice Age (e.g., K. S. Petersen 1985, Christensen 1993). During the peak of the glaciation (20,000–13,000 BP), the sea level was at least 90 m lower than today. It then gradually rose through the Late Glacial,

---

* Institute for Archaeology, University of Tromsø, Norway.

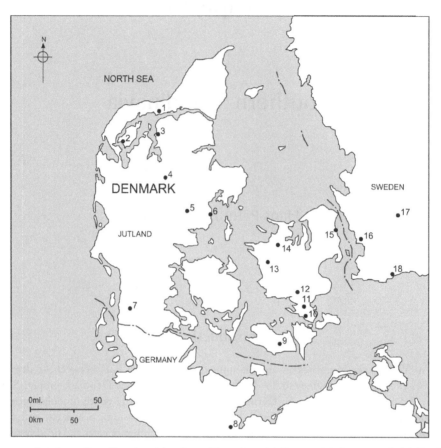

Figure 4.1. Southern Scandinavia with selected key sites: (1) Brovst; (2) Aggersund; (3) Ertebølle; (4) Klosterlund; (5) Ringkloster; (6) Norsminde; (7) Draved; (8) Duvensee; (9) Skottemarke; (10) Sværdborg; (11) Lundby; (12) Holmegård; (13) Mullerup; (14) Ulkestrup; (15) Vedbæk/Bøgebakken; (16) Segebro; (17) Ageröd; (18) Skateholm.

Preboreal, and Boreal periods to approximately 30 m below the present level. The final rise up to about the present level took place within only about six hundred years from 9000 BP onwards, that is, at an average rate of 5 m per one hundred years (Figure 4.2, Christensen 1993). These were drastic changes that might be seen and felt within a lifetime. The once extensive plains of the North Sea bed were gradually submerged, and the freshwater Baltic (Ancylus Lake) was linked to the ocean through the straits of Øresund, Storebælt, and Lillebælt, and eventually reached its present form some time during the Neolithic.

After this major rise in sea level, there followed the so-called Littorina fluctuations with climatically determined changes between 0.5 and 2 m. The shoreline displacement curve for Vedbæk (Eastern Zealand), for example, shows four transgressions of a magnitude of about 1m occurring periodically at approximately five-hundred-year intervals – at 7200, 6700, 6200, and 5700 BP, respectively (Christensen 1993).

These eustatic changes in sea level must be seen in relation to contemporary isostatic movements of the land. Southern Scandinavia lies within the area of isostatic rebound following ice removal.

Table 4.1. Late Glacial and Postglacial pollen zones, fauna, cultures, and chronology (after N. Noe-Nygaard 1995)

^{14}C years B.P.	Faunal Assemblages	Chrono-zones	Pollen zones	Cultural periods	^{14}C years B.P.
0					0
1,000	Cultural landscape fauna	Subatlantic — Late / Middle / Early	Beach time	Historical time / Viking time / Iron age: German Iron age / Roman Iron age / Pre-Roman Iron age	1,000
2,000			XI		2,000
3,000	Domestic cattle, pig, sheep, and goat	Subboreal — Late / Middle / Early	Younger lime time	Bronze age: Younger Bronze age / Older Bronze age / Neolithic cultures: Later Neolithic / Single-grave culture / Middle Neolithic / Early Neolithic	3,000
4,000			VIII		4,000
5,000			VII		5,000
6,000	Red deer, roe deer, wild boar	Atlantic — Late / Middle / Early	Older lime time	Mesolithic cultures: Ertebølle culture / Kongemose culture	6,000
7,000			VI		7,000
8,000	Urus, elk	Boreal — Late / Early	Hazel/pine time Vb / Va	Maglemose culture	8,000
9,000	Bison, wild horse	Pre-boreal — Late / Early	Birch/pine time IV		9,000
10,000		Younger Dryas	Younger Dryas III	Palaeolithic cultures: Ahrensburg culture	10,000
11,000	Reindeer	Allerød	Allerød II	Bromme culture	11,000
12,000		Older Dryas / Bølling	Older Dryas / Bølling Ib	Hamburg culture	12,000
13,000					13,000

Left margin: Postglacial / Late glacial

109

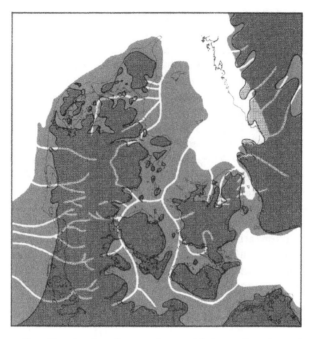

Figure 4.2. Southern Scandinavia nine thousand years (dark grey) and six thousand years (grey) ago (after C. Christensen 1993).

North of a diagonal tilt-line running from the island of Falster to the west coast of Jutland south of Limfjorden, the land has been uplifted by as much as 50–60 m above the present sea level. To the south, southern Jutland and the southern part of some of the Baltic islands have moved at a slower rate and sea-level rise has partly inundated the ancient coastline and archaeological sites associated with it. The present-day coast, fjord systems, and belts are a result of this process, which is still ongoing, albeit at a much reduced rate.

In terms of general cultural chronology, the Late Palaeolithic Hamburgian, Bromme and Ahrensburgian cultures were followed by the Mesolithic Maglemose, Kongemose, and Ertebølle cultures in what appears to be a linear, unbroken sequence, covering a time span of approximately six thousand calibrated radiocarbon years from approximately 9,600 to 3800 cal BC (Tables 4.1 and 4.2). The beginning of the Mesolithic has traditionally been technologically defined by the introduction of the core axe, whereas the boundary with the Neolithic has been defined in economic terms by the introduction of agriculture. This is neither consistent, nor entirely useful for a social perspective, but may nevertheless serve as a rough frame of reference.

Material Culture

Material culture served many purposes and needs, practical, symbolic, and ritual. Some items apparently were chiefly practical, geared to the manufacture of other implements. Other items were probably symbolic markers of status, whereas others again, although practical in appearance, may have served to link the spheres of economic production and social reproduction, and of life and

Table 4.2. Radiocarbon dates for sites mentioned in the text

Site	Lab. No.	BP	Cal BC 2σ
Ageröd I:B	Lu-599	8020 ± 80	7180–6680
Ageröd I:B	Lu-598A	6040 ± 70	5210–4780
Ageröd I:D	Lu-751	7949 ± 80	7060–6640
Ageröd I:D	Lu-760	7680 ± 80	6660–6390
Aggersund	K-2638	3470 ± 95	2030–1530
Aggersund	K-2640	3510 ± 95	2150–1600
Barmose I	K-1359	9240 ± 150	9200–8000
Bjørnsholm	K-5304	6090 ± 100	5300–4750
Bjørnsholm	K-5721	4760 ± 90	3710–3350
Brovst	K-1614	6590 ± 130	5740–5300
Brovst	K-1613	5610 ± 100	4700–4260
Bøgebakke (Vedbæk) Burials	K-2880	6340 ± 80	5480–5070
Bøgebakke (Vedbæk) Burials	K-2784	5810 ± 105	4950–4400
Ertebølle	K-4318	6010 ± 95	5210–4700
Ertebølle	K-4307	5070 ± 90	4040–3650
Halskov Øst	K-5310	5850 ± 100	4950–4460
Halskov Syd	K-5309	6320 ± 100	5480–5040
Lavringe Mose	K-4801	9040 ± 125	8600–7750
Lavringe Mose	K-4800	8690 ± 120	8250–7500
Møllegabet II	K-5640	5910 ± 75	4990–4590
Møllegabet II	K-1165	4590 ± 120	3650–2900
Norsminde	K-5199	3840 ± 95	2600–2000
Norsminde	K-2188	2450 ± 100	810–370
Ringkloster	K-4367	5820 ± 95	4910–4450
Ringkloster	K-4372	4800 ± 65	3710–3370
Skateholm I	Lu-1834	6240 ± 85	5500–4950
Skateholm I	Lu-1848	5790 ± 70	4800–4460
Skateholm II	Lu-2114	6910 ± 70	5980–5660
Skateholm II	Lu-2115	6380 ± 70	4350–4040
Skateholm III	Lu-2156	5850 ± 90	4940–4490
Skottemarke	K-2075	9400 ± 140	9150–8300
Tybrind Vig	K-4150	6390 ± 100	5550–5070
Tybrind Vig	K-6177	5090 ± 140	4250–3600
Ulkestrup I	K-2174	8140 ± 100	7500–6750
Ulkestrup I	K-2175	8370 ± 130	7600–7050
Ulkestrup II	K-2176	8180 ± 100	7500–6800
Ulkestrup II	K-1508	8030 ± 140	7450–6550

Only the earliest and latest date is given for sites with more than two dates. All radiocarbon determinations are given as uncalibrated BP and calibrated ranges at 2 sigma as cal BC. Dates have been calibrated using OxCal v3.10 (Bronk Ramsey 1995, 2001).

death. Some richly decorated and well-maintained items were apparently personal status markers, others, such as large-scale fish-trap systems, communally owned.

Preservation bias has to some extent skewed the picture of material culture. Artefacts of flint and stone can be found everywhere within the study area. Favourable preservation conditions for organic remains such as bone, antler, skin, wood, fruits, and nuts are only found in waterlogged conditions with high alkaline content or in anaerobic marine deposits. This essentially means Scania and the eastern Danish islands, and to a much lesser extent certain parts of the Jutland peninsula. Shell middens may by their very content of shells preserve organic material that would otherwise not survive in the local soil (Blankholm 1996).

Underwater excavations of some of the approximately two thousand registered submerged sites such as Tybrind Vig (S. H. Andersen 1985), and Møllegabet I (Skaarup 1993, Skaarup and Grøn 2004) and a number of sites recovered in connection with the construction of the Storebælt and Øresund bridges, for example, Halskov Syd and Halskov Øst (Pedersen, Fischer and Aaby 1997), have added significant new information.

The southern Scandinavian Mesolithic continues the core-blade-flake technology of the Late Palaeolithic Hamburgian, Bromme, and Ahrensburgian cultures in the area (e.g., Holm and Rieck 1983, S. H. Andersen 1973b, P. V. Petersen and L. Johansen 1993). Yet, the tool repertoire becomes more varied and definitely microlithic in character. This has often been interpreted as a reflection of a change to a broader spectrum of subsistence strategies associated with Postglacial climatic amelioration (e.g., Mithen 1987).

The Maglemosian is first and foremost characterised by its wide repertoire of microlithic armatures (Figure 4.3), core and flake axes, and its micro blade technology (Blankholm 1990, 1991, 1996 with references). Other artefacts include flake scrapers and end-of-blade scrapers, burins, borers, backed blades and axes of greenstone. Tools made from elk and red deer antler include axes, adzes, picks, chisels, and punches for working flint, whereas fishhooks were made from roe deer antler. Pendants were made from teeth of aurochs, elk, red deer, and pig, and occasionally from amber. Pig tusks were used for knives and chisels. Another key artefact of the Maglemosian, the barbed bone point, was made from the ribs, metacarpals, and metatarsals of red deer in particular. Axes and picks were made from the humerus and radius of aurochs, and daggers from the ulna bone of elk, red deer, and pig. Slotted bone points and daggers were made from the metatarsals and metacarpals of elk, red deer and roe deer (ibid., Figure 4.4). Axes, picks, and slotted equipment are often richly decorated in geometric patterns and well curated, and may well have served as personal gear and status markers. Wooden artefacts include bows (Figure 4.5), arrows, paddles, and shafts of various types.

With a few exceptions (e.g., the diagnostic microliths and the barbed bone points), the basic repertoire generally remains the same for the following Kongemose culture. The microliths of the Maglemosian (as in most of Europe) are swiftly replaced by trapezoid and rhombic armatures (Figure 4.3), and these, together with a preeminent core-and-blade technology, become the new diagnostics. A regional division between Western (Jutland and Funen) and Eastern (Zealand and Scania) Scandinavia is indicated by the distributions of rhomboid and broad trapezes, respectively (S. H. Andersen 1983, Blankholm 1990). Tools and blades generally tend to become larger, occasionally reaching sizes suggesting symbolic rather than practical significance. As in the Maglemosian, some items such as the often highly decorated antler axes and slotted equipment may very well have served as symbols of power and prestige.

Although some of the symbolism of the Kongemose material culture disappears with the Ertebølle, the latter culture retains high quality techniques of artefact manufacture. Types become more standardised, and towards the end of this period the manufacture of flake axes is sometimes

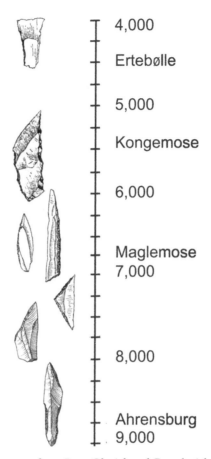

Figure 4.3. Microlithic armatures from Late Glacial and Postglacial Southern Scandinavia (after S. H. Andersen 1981). Dates are cal BC.

reminiscent of production-line techniques. The transverse arrowhead (Figure 4.3) and the specially trimmed core axe are key artefacts. Otherwise, the Ertebølle is characterised by a series of new additions, notably pottery in the form of pointed base vessels and blubber lamps (Figure 4.6), T-shaped antler axes, bone combs, and rings (Figure 4.4), and imported shoe-last adzes. Among the tools for sea-mammal hunting are various types of harpoons. In fact, a very differentiated sea-mammal hunting technology was used (S. H. Andersen 1995). Adornments such as pendants of amber and animal teeth, and necklaces of teeth and shells are occasionally preserved as single finds or in graves. Wooden artefacts include bows (Figure 4.5), arrows, decorated paddles, canoes, and a multitude of shafts, for instance, for leisters. In addition, there are extensive systems of coastal wooden fishing traps, some of which may have been made from managed forests (Pedersen, Fischer and Aaby 1997). The earliest of these, such as Halskov Syd and Halskov Øst, from the Early Ertebølle culture, extended as much as 15 m out from the beach, and were probably communally owned.

It is within the Ertebølle that we see the strongest regional trends in the Mesolithic, trends that may well have had social connotations. There are marked regional distributions of axes of Limhamn greenstone and antler and bone combs and rings (S. H. Andersen 1980, P. V. Petersen 1984). In addition, there are smaller regions, such as Eastern and Central Jutland, denoted by

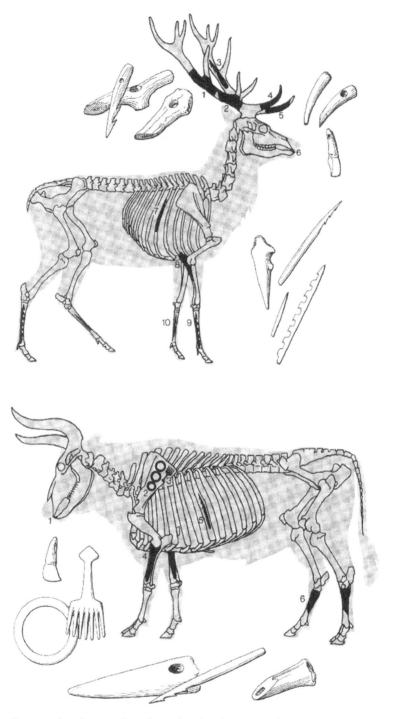

Figure 4.4. Bone and antler artefacts from the Southern Scandinavian Mesolithic (after S. H. Andersen 1981).

Figure 4.5. Bows from the Southern Scandinavian Mesolithic (after S. H. Andersen 1981). Approximate scale 1:20.

distinctive pottery motifs, such as rhombic patterns, and incisions on bone implements like the 'sheaf-of-wheat' motif (S. H. Andersen 1980). P. V. Petersen (1984), by contrast, has suggested a regional pattern for Eastern Zealand based on the differential distribution of various types of flake axes. However, these regional groupings are not constructed according to the same basic criteria and are not necessarily contemporaneous.

The Early Neolithic is chiefly characterised by regional pottery types and styles of decoration (Figure 4.7). Some of the types are also made from wood. Another diagnostic is the heavy thin-butted or point-butted flint axe (polished or unpolished), occasionally reaching large dimensions that suggest symbolic significance or use as prestige items. Towards the end of the period, these are also found in caches. As Kristiansen (1984) notes, it is the only artefact in the Early Neolithic that symbolically links economic production and social reproduction. Although much care and attention was devoted to the pottery and axes, the remaining repertoire of flint tools was quite simple. Flake scrapers usually occur in large quantities, and the first real harvesting tools, sickle blades, begin to appear (Juel Jensen 1994).

Finely made battle-axes and clubs of carefully selected stone, often mimicking contemporary types of copper or bronze from central and eastern Europe are another feature of the late Early Neolithic TRB. Some of these types were even imported by trade or exchange. Among copper

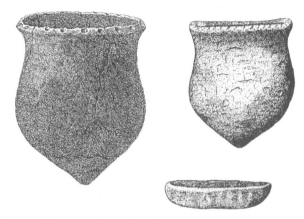

Figure 4.6. Typical pointed base vessels and blubber lamp from the Ertebølle culture (after Tilley 1996). Approximate scale 1:6.

products are coils of fine copper wire, buckles, finger rings, and daggers. Amber became widespread for beads, pendants and bracelets in a variety of shapes, and raw amber often has been interpreted as a trading or exchange commodity of Southern Scandinavian origin.

Economy and Land Use

Maglemosian subsistence data confirms the picture of a hunter-fisher-gatherer culture (Blankholm 1996). The 'big game' at sites such as Mullerup, Ulkestrup I and II, Sværdborg I, Lundby I and II, and Holmegård were aurochs, elk, red deer, roe deer, and pig, but at the site level of investigation, the number of animals killed was generally small (minimum number of individuals typically recorded are red deer 1–7, roe deer 1–18, pig 1–17, elk 1–7, and aurochs 1–7, respectively). Generally, newborn animals, juveniles, and adults of both sexes were hunted during the summer season from March/April through October (Blankholm 1996). A 'conserving' hunting strategy may have been employed for red deer in some places (Bay-Petersen 1978), but mostly it seems that the broader strategy, based on several species, was followed and could make up for temporarily unbalanced culls of any single species' local population. Hunting systems, such as pit traps or extensive fish-traps are unknown.

The exploitation of large game followed general trends, but these varied between species, and for elk even within species (Blankholm 1996). All five species were hunted for their meat and for raw materials for tool manufacture. Field butchering seems evident for the largest species: red deer, elk, and aurochs (ibid.).

Among red deer the emphasis was on antlers and on front and rear legs, which makes sense both in terms of tool manufacture and food supply. The axial skeletal elements and skull are generally poorly represented and may indicate that they were abandoned in the field or taken (possibly with preserved meat) to other locations. Roe deer commonly show a more uniform representation of skeletal elements. Again limb bones may have been selected for tools in greater quantities, but otherwise it seems as if they, and particularly the young animals, were brought back to the habitation sites complete or in sections amounting to complete animals. Pig displays the most uniform representation of skeletal elements altogether. The pig was a very valuable meat resource and the middle limb bones were frequently used for tools. Again, the evidence suggests that pigs

Figure 4.7. Early Neolithic pottery forms (after Tilley 1996). Approximate scale 1:6.

generally were brought in as complete or near complete carcases. Elk was sometimes exploited as a single species, sometimes as one among several species. At Skottemarke, it was hunted as a single species and almost the entire skeleton (save for metapodials) is well represented. When exploited as one of several species, the use pattern is to some degree similar to that of red deer. The exploitation of aurochs was most similar to that of elk when hunted as one of several species (Blankholm 1996).

Other animals were hunted for their fur, for instance, brown bear, beaver, otter, wolf, fox, pine marten, polecat, badger, and wild cat. Birds included grebe, swan, goose, mallard, goosander, white-tailed eagle, crane, and coot. Fishing was probably of major importance and comprised, for example, pike, tench, bream, and eel and probably also salmon and trout. Hazelnuts and probably water lily seeds were major vegetal resources.

The Kongemose culture seems to reveal the same *general* picture, save for the addition of a coastal component, involving the hunt for sea mammals such as seal and porpoise, salt water fishing for species, such as cod, hunting of waterfowl (notably ducks), crane and white-tailed eagle, and the collection of shellfish, such as oysters, cockles, and clams (e.g., S. H. Andersen 1970, Noe-Nygaard 1995, L. Larsson 1982, 1983).

The Ertebølle economy has been studied in some detail and shows exploitation of both land and sea. The composition of species and their relative frequency depends on the type of site, its season of occupation, and the local environment. However, despite an overemphasis on coastal sites (see also later), it should be borne in mind that regardless of site location, the exploitation of terrestrial mammals generally was very substantial compared to that of marine resources. Red deer, roe deer, and pig were the most sought after land mammals; elk and aurochs were less often the prey, or were slowly disappearing from the biotope. Again wild cat, otter, badger, marten, fox, wolf, beaver, bear, and lynx were hunted for their fur. The sea-mammals comprised grey and ringed seal, and small whales such as porpoise, dolphin, and killer whales.

Inland fishing included the same species as in the Maglemose and Kongemose cultures such as pike, perch, bream, eel, catfish, roach, and salmon, whereas saltwater species included cod, plaice, piked dogfish, mackerel, and garfish. Birds hunted included waterfowl such as ducks, swans, and gulls, whereas forest species apparently were of little interest. Shellfish collection was a major endeavour in some, but definitely not all, coastal locations (see later) and involved the collection in various proportions of such species as the common oyster, cockle, and common mussel.

What seemingly sets the Ertebølle economic schedule apart is the character of its specialised hunting or kill-sites, such as Aggersund for swans (S. H. Andersen 1979) and Ringkloster for the hunting or trapping of pigs and pine marten in winter and spring (S. H. Andersen 1998, Rowley-Conwy 1998b). Most interpretations of prehistoric economies emphasise prey species and food content. But it should not be forgotten that taboos and socially imposed directions may well have existed. For example, why were most of the faunal remains thrown back into the water? This may just as well have been a spiritual and ritual act rather than merely an act of cleaning and sweeping the habitation area (Aaris Sørensen 1988).

Although domestication of plants and animals cannot be proved for Ertebølle contexts (and if they had been, those contexts would probably have been coined Neolithic!), abrupt and probably ecologically conditioned changes in the composition of gathered molluscs can be observed on some sites, such as Norsminde, Ertebølle, and Bjørnsholm (S. H. Andersen 1991a, 1991b, 1993, and E. Johansen 1987, Fischer 2002).

In fact, essentially all aspects of the Neolithic subsistence economy around 5000 BP seem to be a continuation of Ertebølle practices (S. H. Andersen 1991a). The 'elm decline', formerly attributed much significance as an indicator of various new economic practices, has now rather convincingly been argued to be the result of disease in combination with climatic and hydrological changes, in essence an ecological phenomenon (Berglund 1991, Rasmussen 1991, Fischer 2002). Much emphasis has been placed on grain impressions in pottery as evidence of cultivation of cereal crops. This has raised a number of questions. First, it is not self-evident that the grain was grown by its ultimate users or consumers. If the idea of growing and using grain was transmitted through trade or exchange, so could the very substance itself (e.g., Jennbert 1984). Also, plough-marks under Early Neolithic earthen long-barrows, if not entirely symbolic or ritual, may indicate cultivation of plants other than cereals. Even if grain impressions are taken as an indication of local cultivation, it is not straightforward to estimate the relative significance of the various species (let alone noncereals). Contrary to butchering debris, lost grains indicate an economic failure – they were those *not* used and were in all likelihood residuals from the process of threshing (Rowley-Conwy pers. comm.). Also, Tilley (1996) has noted that the fact that grain impressions are present does not necessarily mean that grain production was of great economic significance.

Thus, the evidence for Ertebølle or Early Neolithic cereal growing so far is at best circumstantial. It seems certain that grain was used in one way or another, but its value seems to have been less as a source of food and more as a symbolic and manipulative resource and a means for social storage and intensification (see also Fischer 2002).

Evidence for Early Neolithic animal domestication is equally sparse. Hunting, fishing and gathering continued to be significant. Claims for the domestication of pigs (Tilley 1996, Zvelebil 1995b) seem largely derived from circumstantial ecological considerations and are not reflected in the kill-off patterns derived from the actual skeletal evidence (Rowley-Conwy, pers.

comm.), but some form of pig husbandry that fell short of biological domestication remains possible (Zvelebil this volume). Kill-off patterns of cattle and sheep/goat also interestingly indicate that secondary products came into favour before meat production (Rowley-Conwy, pers. comm.).

Although the economic and settlement evidence is fragmentary and elusive, it seems reasonable to suggest that agriculture and domestication were not introduced wholesale from the south, freshly packed and ready to serve to the Ertebølle people.

Settlement

Maglemosian inland sites vary in size. At the small end of the spectrum are sites covering an area approximately 5–9 m × 3–5 m (e.g., Stallerupholm, Ulkestrup Lyng I and II, Sværdborg II, and Barmose I). These were probably occupied by only a small, single social unit (i.e., a group of close relatives) or a detached unit of either or both sexes. The largest sites are about 150 m × 100 m such as Sværdborg I, Lundby I, and II, and were used by several such social units, the contemporaneity of which, however, is still unresolved (Blankholm 1984, 1987a, 1990, 1996). At Duvensee 1 and 5, Ulkestrup I and II, and Holmegård IV, rectangular or subrectangular hut floors were made from interlaced bark sheets and/or split logs mainly from pine and birch, with a single, circular hearth made from sand and/or loam, and measuring 6–7 m × 3–5 m. These hut floors are generally oriented NW–SE, and at Duvensee, five such layers were stratified on top of one another. Hut floors and other activity areas based on the spatial distribution of flint artefacts have been identified on sites such as Stallerupholm, Barmose I, Sværdborg I and II, Lavringe mose, and Ageröd I (Blankholm 1984, 1987a, L. Larsson 1978b, S. A. Sørensen 1988).

Only a few submerged sites, mostly coastal and generally dating to the Late Maglemose Culture or the transition between the Maglemose and Kongemose cultures have been recorded, including Fløjstrup Skov, Musholm Bugt, Blak I and II, and Pilhaken (L. Larsson 1978b, Fischer 1993, S. H. Andersen 1993, 2000). Other types of sites include the so-called Maglemosian fishing sites in the Åmose and Barmose basins characterised by large quantities of barbed bone points (K. Andersen 1983, A. D. Johansson 2006), sites on higher ground with good visual control of the landscape such as Sønder Hadsund and Rude Mark (Boas 1987), and a number of probable kill-sites or hunting stands at some distance from major stream courses or bodies of water (E. B. Petersen 1986, V. J. Pedersen 2006).

The inland sites were generally used from March/April through to September/October, save for Skottemarke, a butchering/kill site for elk, which was used in December/January (Blankholm 1996). Hints of winter activity also may be present at Lundby I and Holmegård I (Blankholm 1996) and possibly Holmegård V (Fischer 1993, but see also Blankholm 1996). Less intensive or sporadic use of the two former sites may well have occurred, but the seasonal determination is uncertain as it is based almost entirely on the evidence of tooth eruption in older pigs, and at Holmegård V, the single find of a bone of a young beaver.

A few seal bones have been found on the inland sites of Ageröd I and Sværdborg I, respectively, suggesting direct or indirect connection with the coast (Møhl 1971, Noe-Nygaard 1971, L. Larsson 1978b). A tentative sketch of a settlement pattern would suggest summer base camps involving a broad range of activities, on the one hand, and hunting stations or kill sites used in the middle of the winter, on the other, but with both lying inland. Larger winter aggregation camps may have existed along the now mostly submerged coastlines, while spring sites for the exploitation of migrating fish may be indicated by the numerous smaller sites along the main river systems. Sites on higher ground may be transit camps, kill sites, hunting stands, or simply observation posts (Blankholm 1996).

Kongemose sites used by a single social unit appear (mostly from the estimates of surface finds) to be of the same general size as in the Maglemosian or possibly slightly larger (K. Andersen 1983, Fischer 1993). The Kongemose site (*locus classicus*) from the older part of the culture (Noe-Nygaard 1988, 1995, Fischer 1993) appears to have been subject to many short-term occupations at varying seasons, including winter, for the purpose of 'big game' hunting and, to a lesser degree, for fishing and fowling. A coastal element involving the collection of shellfish is seen in the shell midden of Brovst (S. H. Andersen 1970, 1993), which dates to the younger Kongemose culture.

Ertebølle culture coastal sites and settlements have been a major field of research for the last couple of decades. However, the emphasis on coastal settlement should be treated with caution (Newell 1984, Blankholm 1987). Apart from a handful of excavated submerged sites, virtually all coastal sites are only preserved north of the tilt line running NW–SE across the study area (see earlier and, for example, Jensen 1982). Moreover, sites with oyster shells only occur where salinity was high enough for oyster survival, that is, mostly in the North and Northeast of the study area.

The focus on these surviving coastal areas and fjords has led to a corresponding neglect of the hinterland. There is, in fact, a great abundance of inland sites from all Mesolithic periods, including the Ertebølle, and the Early Neolithic. In sheer numbers, inland settlement seems not to be very different from coastal settlement. The truth is that very few of these inland sites have been systematically investigated, so any general notions about site size, economy, sedentism, and so on are problematic.

Despite the commonly acknowledged fact that most coastal Early Mesolithic sites (i.e., Maglemosian and Kongemosian) are now submerged (apart from those mentioned earlier), some scholars almost routinely continue to disregard this fact, and compare the Early Mesolithic inland with the Late Mesolithic coast. Thus, it is no wonder that many have come to see the Ertebølle culture as more affluent than its predecessors. However, a study of marine charts would probably show that the former, but now submerged, coastal areas of the Early Mesolithic are just as (if not more) estuarine and productive and full of islands and reefs as in the Ertebølle period (see also Fischer 2002).

The thrust of all this is that for the present we are prevented from evaluating the distinctiveness of the Ertebølle in relation to earlier periods of the Mesolithic, except for some aspects of the use of the hinterland, and these are also the most neglected aspect of Ertebølle research (S. H. Andersen 1998).

Nevertheless, the recent regional 'fjord-investigations' (e.g., S. H. Andersen 1976, E. B. Petersen et al. 1982) have yielded many interesting results. Many of the shell middens (probably only observed in the first place because of the conspicuous bulk of the discarded shells, and of which now only 480 remain) have been shown to have accumulated piecemeal horizontally and vertically over sometimes up to nearly a thousand years (S. H. Andersen, 1993). This indicates continuity in site location, and possibly reuse, on a large scale. This goes, for example, for sites such as Ertebølle (*locus classicus*) (c. 235 m × 3–55 m), Bjørnsholm (c. 335 m × 10–50 m), Norsminde (c. 30 m × 12 m), and Visborg near Mariager (reaching an astonishing 750 m in estimated length, S. H. Andersen pers. comm.).

Other important observations are that even in the areas of Southern Scandinavia where the accumulation of shell middens was possible, there are regionally speaking always more sites *without* shells than shell middens (S. H. Andersen, 1993). Also, it is interesting that certainly not all of the larger shell middens or ordinary sites, on which extensive surface-stripping excavation has taken place, are associated with graves (e.g., Bjørnsholm, Ertebølle, and see later), and that there is a conspicuous lack of convincing dwelling remains (but see Karsten and Knarrström (1999) for a presumed 15 × 7 m dwelling at Tågerup, Scania). Other types of sites include both ordinary base camps (some with large fish-trap systems, e.g., Halskov Ø and S) and specialised sites for fishing or sea-mammal hunting (Ølby Lyng), fowling (Aggersund), or the hunting of animals for their fur, notably pine marten (Ringkloster).

Inland settlements in the Åmosen basin generally seem as broad based in their economy as their Maglemosian equivalents. The seasonality of the inland sites appears equally varied: at Ringkloster November to May, and at Præstelyng April to September. In the Åmose basin, there are also traces of intensive collection of freshwater mussels.

The evidence may be interpreted to suggest several different forms of settlement pattern. One of the more popular interpretations is that each local group covered a fjord area and its adjacent islands and inland river system or hinterland. Each group also had its own centrally located base camp or central site from which groups (or perhaps sometimes the entire community) went out to special purpose camps or sites at specific times of the year (S. H. Andersen 1976, 1981, E. B. Petersen et al. 1982, P. V. Petersen 1984, Blankholm 1987b).

The evidence for widespread sedentism or semisedentism is equivocal. Much of the evidence can be interpreted in this way, or at the least as evidence for frequent reoccupation of the same site. Yet, there also seems to be a conceptual bias in favour of sedentism, maybe simply because this fits well with the various models advanced in the 1980s. Rowley-Conwy's (1998a) recent research has, however, revealed that, for instance, Skateholm I was not used all the year round, whereas several sites in Eastern Jutland probably were. Thus, demographic calculations and claims for demographic stress also remain uncertain (S. H. Andersen 1973a, Blankholm 1987b, Fischer 2002).

Early Neolithic subsistence and settlement in Southern Scandinavia appears to be varied. The picture pertaining to the coastal areas is one of direct settlement continuity from the Ertebølle, but with notable regional variation (S. H. Andersen 1991a). Some scholars claim an increase in site numbers and expansion into the inland in the Early Neolithic. This may be so for some areas (Tilley 1996), but disregards the potential significance of the large numbers of Ertebølle sites recorded during regional and valley surveys, few of which unfortunately have been excavated. Early Neolithic settlement has often been described as one of small and dispersed households living in flimsy, short-lived dwellings on sites or occupation areas of generally smaller size than in the Ertebølle (e.g., Madsen 1987). A general comparison of the sizes of house structures and associated debris from a short time span with the sizes of shell mounds, when the latter are rarely differentiated into their constituent units and have no trace of dwellings is, however, problematic.

Although many claimed Early Neolithic dwellings do not seem to have been substantial or impressive others do, notably the examples of long houses, which have begun to appear in recent years (e.g., L. Larsson and M. Larsson 1986, M. Larsson 1992, Buus Eriksen 1992, F. Nielsen 1989). Tilley (1996) sees a symbolic link between these long houses and the shapes of the earthen long-barrows, long dolmens, and the long polished flint axes. These, however, could all be the expression of an additional common factor, namely, the first expression of a domus of power.

Cemeteries and the Burial of the Dead

Since the discovery of Bøgebakken (Figure 4.8, S. E. Albrethsen and E. B. Petersen 1976) and Skateholm (L. Larsson 1984), the burial of the dead has played a major role in the formulation

of models for Southern Scandinavian Late Mesolithic hunter-fisher-gatherer social complexity and the transition to the Neolithic (e.g., Price 1985, Blankholm 1987b, Tilley 1996, Strassburg 2000).

Burials have now been found at some fifty locations and show considerable variability including both inhumation and cremation graves. Burials are not linked to a specific type or size of site, but are often clearly mixed with habitation debris at settlement sites. Significantly, several of the large shell middens have yielded no Late Mesolithic burials at all (S. H. Andersen 1998). This has led to the rejection of the very concept of 'cemetery', meaning a formal and delimited disposal ground, for the Southern Scandinavian Mesolithic (E. K. Nielsen and Brinch Petersen 1993, Meiklejohn et al. 1998, see also Zvelebil this volume). Generally, it seems that settlement and burial places cannot be separated as distinct types of locale in the landscape.

Most of the burials are dated to the Kongemose/Ertebølle transition at around 6500 BP and not to the end of the Mesolithic as has often been assumed. Some are late, however, and some may even be Early Neolithic (Meiklejohn et al. 1996, Milner et al. 2004, Fischer 2002). L. Larsson (1995) maintains that very few of the traits associated with the disposal of the dead are entirely new, and most can be traced back to the Early Mesolithic, as is also true in the wider European context. The large sample of skeletons allows inferences both about issues of physical status and health and about social organisation.

The skeletal evidence reveals that height throughout the Mesolithic and Early Neolithic averaged 154 and 166 cm for women and men, respectively, compared to 162/175 cm for the Iron Age, 154/165 cm for the mid-nineteenth century, and 168/180 cm at the present day. Bones and skulls, however, generally become less sturdy and teeth smaller (Bennike 1985, 1993). The general state of the health was good with only relatively low rates of caries, arthritis, porotic hyperostosis, and enamel hypoplasia (ibid., Meiklejohn and Zvelebil 1991, Alexandersen 1993).

Stable carbon isotope composition of a very limited number of human skeletons (and dogs as proxy for humans) has formerly led to the conclusion that the Late Mesolithic population primarily subsisted on marine foods, whereas the Neolithic primarily subsisted on terrestrial resources, regardless of location (e.g., Tauber 1981, Noe-Nygaard 1988, Meiklejohn and Zvelebil 1991, Richards et al. 2003). However, a recent, critical review of the evidence by Milner et al. (2004, see also Lidén et al. 2004) clearly shows that this needs further investigation of larger and geographically broader and more diverse samples of both people and places, that refinement is needed in the methodology of studying isotope diet signals, and, one might add, analysis of the role of anadromous fish resources. Thus, although most scholars seem to agree that there is a consistent trend over time towards a more terrestrial-oriented diet among individuals in the course of the Neolithic, neither the actual bulk remains from the consumption of marine resources, nor the isotope evidence from the Early Neolithic seem to corroborate a rapid change in diets from the Late Mesolithic. Following Hedges (2004) that ' . . . we cannot, on current understanding, rule out that the level of marine resource consumption which is indistinguishable from terrestrial values from a bulk collagen measurement may, under some conceivable circumstance, be as high as 30 per cent', it would be reasonable to allow for considerable dietary variation among both individuals and populations.

Palaeopathological studies indicate both sex and/or age trends. For example, wear on the teeth of adult women generally corresponds to the working of hides, whereas tooth wear in men is associated with the holding of working material. Tooth wear becomes more pronounced with age in both sexes, but appears earlier in women (Alexandersen 1993). Constandse-Westermann and Newell (1989) found differences in limb lateralization according to rank and gender.

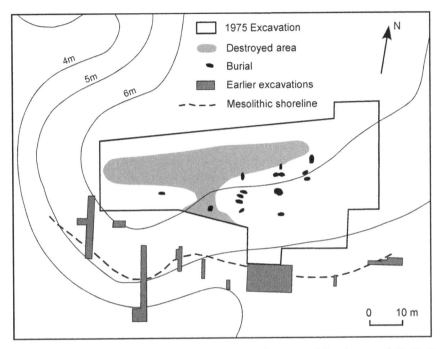

Figure 4.8. The Bøgebakken site and burial ground (after S. E. Albrethsen and E. B. Petersen 1976).

Late Mesolithic evidence of violence and premature death, notably blows to the skull and embedded projectile points may indicate territorial behaviour related to increased population density (e.g., Newell et al. 1979, Price 1985, Meiklejohn and Zvelebil 1991) or social competition between and among ranks, or simple rivalry in the form of jealousy (see also Fischer 2002).

Turning to more detailed analysis of individual sites and association with grave goods, we begin with Bøgebakken near Vedbæk (S. E. Albrethsen and E. B. Petersen 1976). Here eighteen graves were found containing twenty-two individuals (five children, seven females, eight males, and two undetermined). Most were buried separately, but two graves contained two young women with newborn babies, and one contained two adults and a child. Sex/gender differences are apparent from the grave goods, with a certain status accorded to older women and young fertile women, on the evidence of associated tooth pendants. However, although four of the individual female burials had no grave goods, blade knives were commonly deposited in the male graves, whereas the individual child burials had no goods at all.

At the roughly contemporaneous site of Skateholm I (L. Larsson 1984), sixty-five graves were found, of which fifty-seven contained people, and eight contained dogs. Five of the human graves were double, mostly with an adult and a child. Altogether, six child burials, eighteen female, and twenty male burials were found, the rest being too poorly preserved for sex determination. Most graves have no preserved artefacts, but it generally seems as if most of the grave goods are associated with younger females and older males.

At Skateholm II, slightly older than these sites, twenty-two graves were found with twenty-two people and two dogs. Four of the graves contained young children. There also were nine women and nine men. Most were buried individually, but two double graves contained two young men, and two young children, respectively. There is much variability in number, type, and position of the grave goods, but most burials have at least one offering. Age, gender, and status differentiation do not seem to be particularly well marked or standardised. It may be that individual differences and preferences were played out, rather than differences of rank or status (Tilley 1996), or simply that codes were followed that we have not so far been able to decipher.

At the Early Ertebølle site of Strøby Egede (E. B. Petersen 1987), there is a mass grave with eight individuals: three newborns, a boy and a girl, an eighteen-year-old woman, a thirty-year-old man, and a woman approximately fifty years old. The females were in the southern part of the grave and the males in the northern part. All were furnished with grave goods: the two infants with knives, the girl and young woman with red deer tooth pendants around their hips, the two adult women with single flint knives, and the man with five knives, an antler axe, and a bone spatula. There is no sign of violence, so disease or famine may have been the cause of death.

Generally, the Mesolithic burials only represent a small, selected fragment of the population and burial practice and ritual probably followed codes we are only beginning to understand, and this goes for the early Neolithic as well. Hence, wider conclusions on demography following standard calculations would seem futile at present.

However, despite the great variability in mortuary practices, the evidence may be interpreted to suggest weak patterns of social diversity at both local and regional scales along the dimensions of age, sex/gender, and status (e.g., Price 1985, Blankholm 1987b, Meiklejohn et al. 1996, Tilley 1996, Zvelebil this volume). The various methodologies for ageing and sexing skeletons (or cremations) and for relating grave goods to age, sex/gender, and status have not been widely applied within Scandinavian Mesolithic research. Lars Larsson (1989) has pointed out that if the presence of grave goods is used as a simple indicator of social rank, then the highest-ranking grave at Skateholm II belongs to a dog! This cautions against oversimple interpretations, particularly when grave goods of organic materials such as wood, leather, and textiles are also missing (e.g., Tilley 1996).

At the core of the problem lies the fact that we have little way of identifying the symbolic value, or 'exchange rate', of different types of goods. Possibly the only candidate for a plausible symbolic link between age, sex/gender, status, subsistence, life, death, and biological and social reproduction is the flint blade or flint knife, generally regarded as the most simple item of all (Blankholm 1996)!

In essence, people were treated differently according to age, sex/gender, and status. Goods were taken out of circulation and graves apparently were not marked in such a way as to leave lasting visible features in the landscape. Burial and ritual practices show considerable variation locally, regionally, and through time, and together with other evidence provide insights into social relations.

Social Relations

Some scholars (e.g., Price 1981a) have suggested a general European Mesolithic trend from open mating networks (band society) to closed mating networks (tribal society). Although a lineage-based society may well have been the case for the Late Mesolithic in our study area, the burial evidence with its range of single and multiple graves and varying male and female associations may indicate more intricate (and possibly regionally variable) connotations of gender and age than usually envisaged for the standard Mesolithic core or extended family (Tilley 1996, Strassburg 2000).

Following the various social interpretations by the excavators of Bøgebakken and Skateholm I and II (S. E. Albrethsen and E. B. Petersen 1976, Nielsen and Brinch Petersen 1993, Meiklejohn et al. 1998, L. Larsson 1984, 1989b, 1995), new finds have been recovered, and new insights and interpretations have been inspired by various theoretical perspectives.

Tilley (1996), for example, suggests that gender and status are not related to social rank, but to the activities and biographies of individual people during their life, and that marked differences between the cultural roles and customary behaviour of women and men may only have occurred at reproductive age. Thus, he creates an affluent Garden-of-Eden–like image of what he describes as 'primitive communism', in which men and women hunted and gathered and were responsible for childcare and education, with little gender differentiation in terms of roles, status, prestige, or power.

Rowley-Conwy (1998a) has suggested a strong linkage between cemeteries, territoriality, and unilinear descent groups in the Ertebølle, founded on predictable and dense concentrations of resources.

Considering the wide range of burial practices and their dates, and the rather weak evidence for regional groupings, the above interpretations need to be treated critically, although unilinear descent groups could well have been an aspect of social organisation even in the absence of formal cemeteries or territories. Social structures are constructions, not givens, and thus open to change by the actions of individuals or groups. Gender and social diversity form the fundamental sources of social variation. Differences may not be pronounced, but both ascribed and inherited power and status may be present, even if they are not expressed through overt, symbolic means.

In conclusion, the burial evidence may be interpreted to suggest the existence of leadership and competition for power within and between networks of lineage-based groups. These lineages with extended networks were structured internally and externally in relation to other such groups. Thus, the burial evidence reflects, not whole societies, but leading lineages or leading personal configurations within them. In this light, the grave goods are not only structured along the common dimensions of age, sex/gender and status, but also along the dimensions of kin (relatives), that is, brothers, sisters, uncles, aunts, and relations through marriage. Because there were no designated cemeteries and people were probably buried where they died, it is not to be expected that all dimensions will be readily apparent from the burials at any single site. Moreover, it is not to be expected that within local and regional groups all the evidence will reveal a clear, readily interpretable pattern. The wide range of variation also may suggest competition in which contemporaneous groups or individuals deliberately disrupted societal constraints and added what today may be looked upon as oddities or 'noise', but that also might be looked on as a driving force of social dynamics.

The lack, or decline, of extensive and elaborate burial practices in the Middle and Late Ertebølle may be 'masking behaviour' geared to downplay social differentiation but also may indicate more settled or established conditions with more or less fixed social structures, and more concern with restructuring material culture and displaying power in life rather than death. It is interesting that none of the few available graves from the Middle and Late Ertebølle display any of the new items of material culture: ceramics, shoe-last adzes, grain, or cattle. Those were all literally and symbolically kept apart from the realm of death. Two reasons may be suggested for this. Either these categories lend themselves better to substantive and symbolic displays of power in actual or transformed conditions (ritual feasting, cattle-herds, etc.). Or, with increasing manifestations of power, it became more appropriate to retain prestige items in circulation amongst the living. Insofar as prestige items were no longer buried with the dead as a measure of merit and credit, they also may indicate inherited rank or power.

Hans Peter Blankholm

The Transition to the Neolithic

From the 1940s to the early 1970s, two opposing ideas dominated Southern Scandinavian research on the transition to farming (Mahler et al. 1983, Blankholm 1987b):

1. Agriculture was brought in fully developed by the TRB (or Funnel Beaker) people, who gradually ousted or absorbed the Ertebølle population and culture by means of their supposedly superior means of production (e.g., Becker 1947, Brøndsted 1957).
2. The Ertebølle people learned about farming from their Linearbandkeramik neighbours and related groups to the south by means of diffusion of ideas, and established a mixed hunter-fisher-gatherer and food-producing economy. Only after this stage was Southern Scandinavia invaded by the TRB people (e.g., Troels-Smith 1953: 42ff.).

With the development of the economic and processual archaeology of the 1970s, new ideas, theories and models were proposed, for example, by S. H. Andersen (1973a, 1981), Paludan-Müller (1978), Rowley-Conwy (1981, 1983, 1984b), Zvelebil and Rowley-Conwy (1984), and Jensen (1982). Generally these works emphasise a single, usually external, agent coupled with a triggering factor as the dominant cause of change, for instance demographic pressure or ecological and environmental change (Blankholm 1987b, Fischer 2002). In essence they offer a largely monocausal, if not deterministic, interpretation. In reaction to this endeavour, other scholars have pursued a greater concern with internal, dynamic agents and social factors, as reflected in the works of Mahler et al. (1983), Jennbert (1984), and Blankholm (1987b). This, in turn, was followed by postprocessual works such as those of Thomas (1988) and Hodder (1990) emphasising 'ideological' changes, and a comprehensive reinterpretation by Tilley (1996). This is not the place for an extensive review of these works. However, the changing theoretical perspectives and the rapidly accumulating and increasingly varied evidence has led to re-assessments of some of the components of the debate, notably the following:

1. Concepts of affluence and complexity have been shown to be ill-defined and obsolete and have been more or less abandoned (Binford 1983, Hood 1992, Zvelebil 1986a, Renouf 1995). Certainly, treating the Ertebølle as either complex, or as an example of 'the original affluent society' (e.g., Tilley 1996), would seem problematic.
2. The burial evidence, as noted earlier, has been critically revised and the cemetery concept itself discarded as inappropriate to the Ertebølle evidence. It is also evident that the burial practices are only part of a wider repertoire of European Mesolithic practices in general.
3. Ertebølle sedentism has been called into question and it has been suggested that the role of shell middens has been over-emphasised at the expense of other types of sites (S. H. Andersen 1993).
4. There is at best only a weak basis of evidence for assessing territoriality and demography.

A crucial point of departure for much work on the transition is the notion of a 'delayed introduction of farming'. For more than twenty-five years, many scholars have wondered why the Ertebølle people persisted with their way of life for a thousand years or more, whereas fully Neolithic Linearbandkeramik and related groups, with whom they apparently shared ideas and possibly trade, were well established in Northern and Central Germany (S. H. Andersen 1973a, Rowley-Conwy 1983, Zvelebil and Rowley-Conwy 1984, Newell 1984, Blankholm 1987b, Fischer 1993, Tilley 1996).

In fact, the concept of a long delay in the introduction of farming is fraught with problems. For example, there is only one well-excavated inland Ertebølle site that can be successfully subjected to assessment of the primary evidence, across the whole of central and eastern Jutland and indeed well into northern Germany – in fact there are only three well-excavated inland Ertebølle sites in Jutland altogether (Andersen 1998) – and the number of well-excavated coastal sites in the same area is hardly greater. It is little wonder, then, that huge (but most likely spurious) gaps appear in the record. Also, when comparisons are made, it is not always clear which of the many Linearbandkeramik and related groups to the south are involved (e.g., Barker 1985, Zvelebil et al. 1998; but see Fischer 2002 for a more specific view). This leaves a very 'woolly' picture. Rather than resisting farming or cattle-rearing in whatever form, people, or groups of people, might well simply have adapted selected elements of the new resources to their own ends and needs, including maintaining a sense of difference or 'otherness' from their neighbours to the south.

Moreover, the literature seemingly operates with a mixture of critically and uncritically assessed dates from different kinds of datable material. For instance, the distortion of dates on shell by the marine reservoir effect has only recently been taken into account (e.g., the dating of the early TRB burials, Meiklejohn et al. 1998).

It also seems inappropriate to blame the Ertebølle people for ignoring what they probably did not know about. As indicated by Gamble (1986) and Rowley-Conwy (1998a), *we* know that agriculture was introduced eventually, but *the Ertebølle people* probably did not know this until shortly before it was about to happen. If we take ceramics as the earliest sign of some sort of contact, this would leave a gap before the Early Neolithic of about five hundred to seven hundred years, which is rather less than the usually postulated one thousand to twelve hundred years, and really quite a small interval given the margins of error in radiocarbon dating.

The supposed novelty of communication networks with southern neighbours and beyond at the Mesolithic/Neolithic transition has also been questioned. L. Larsson (1995) argues that in principle the introduction of the handle-core and microblade technique in the early Mesolithic is no different from the introduction of pottery or new ways of dealing with the dead or domestication. One could add that the rapid spread of the broad trapeze over most of Europe around 8000 BP may be just as good a candidate for being associated with the spread of the Indo-European language as the domestic mode of production (Renfrew 1988, Zvelebil 1995a).

Again, 'delay' is relative to which definitions we use. The beginning of the Ertebølle is defined in purely technological terms; the transition to farming (irrespective of whether it is stock-rearing or plant agriculture) is defined in economic and cultural terms. Depending on how the limits are more or less arbitrarily set, the 'delay' will vary accordingly.

Finally, some allowance should be made for variability at the expense of normative description. The latter presupposes that when change occurs it affects the whole range of cultural and social behaviour for all people simultaneously, resulting in the replacement of an Ertebølle norm by a Neolithic one. It leaves no room for the entirely plausible idea that some people continued traditional hunting, fishing, and gathering, that others ventured into cattle-rearing, and yet others again into plant agriculture (or any realistic combination of these various subsistence activities).

When we turn to exchange networks, it is probably true that certain ideas and their material manifestations must have been adopted from other groups, but the evidence for *extensive* exchange systems is not altogether convincing.

In the first place, the evidence for exchange is highly variable through time, and for the most part indicated by relatively few material remains. There is almost no evidence for trade and contact in the early part of the Ertebølle. In the classical Ertebølle stage the idea of ceramics was widely diffused, whereas T-shaped antler axes had a more restricted regional distribution. Both appeared later than the majority of the richly varied burials. Later there are a few scores of shoe-last adzes left in relatively few, often unsealed, artefact scatters (Pedersen, Fischer, and Hald 1997, Klassen 2002). Later again, we have a few dozens of copper items and the idea of farming. Given the time spans involved, these indications are very few in number. If this was the result of exchange or trade operated by extended networks, they do not seem to have been very active! Probably what mattered more was symbolic and ideological meaning and value, not bulk material manifestations (see also Fischer 2002).

Next is the question: With whom did they practise exchange or get their ideas from? The common scenario is one of direct contact with some unspecified fully Neolithic groups 'to the south', for instance, via the Oder River (e.g., Fischer 2002). Such contacts, however, could have been filtered through social groups of possibly quite different social structures and ideological settings than those found within the Linearbandkeramik, Stickbandkeramik, or the Ertebølle. Also in this perspective, the notion of an 'integrated ideological package' seems unlikely (Hodder 1990, Thomas 1988).

Several authors have noted that the polished flint axes became a central symbolic and utilitarian resource appearing in settlements, graves, votive deposits and hoards (e.g., Kristiansen 1984). They also may have been exchanged, but not necessarily to any great extent. What was probably valuable in the first place was the raw material. The more raw material of the right size and quality that could be controlled at its source or accumulated, the more axes could be produced and displayed, offered, buried, traded, or given away. The networks controlling raw material and distribution were probably among the more powerful ones.

It is the widening of contextual and symbolic associations and connotations in the setting of communities, landscapes, and networks that is new. Even low-intensity networking may have been important, but valuables and goods need not necessarily have gone through the same channels or in the same directions. Copper axes and trinkets, like shoe-last adzes, were a rare phenomenon in Southern Scandinavia. Made of nonrenewable raw material, they were probably the only real objects to have been traded over long distances through several networks, and because of this were also of high prestigious and symbolic value and significance.

Some authors also have expressed the view that the subsistence economy was probably among the least important aspects in the changing situation (e.g., S. H. Andersen 1993, Tilley 1996). Food from domesticated plants and animals was probably considered, at first, to be an exotic item with high prestigious and symbolic value (Tilley 1996). Yet, once in place, and in contrast to the shoe-last adzes and imported copper, but similar to clay and flint, these resources became renewable ones that could be intensified and expanded through increased production and converted into social storage, in turn convertible into ever more increasing wealth and power.

The introduction of cultigens and domesticated animals thus provided resources that could be more easily controlled, produced and turned into surplus. But we should not overlook the possibility that Ertebølle practices of forestry, fish traps, exploitation of natural shell banks, or even the right to hunt specific kinds of animals might have been equally amenable to restriction and control by the powerful. What probably changed most were connotations of *land* and the *landscapes*. With farming must have come the appropriation of fixed areas of land under the control of particular social groups, although permanent fish traps made of coppiced wood from maintained forests may also be similarly interpreted.

The first deliberately constructed monuments built to impose meaning on the landscape and to link mortuary practice and death with economic production, power, and material culture, were the earthen long-barrows, round barrows, long-dolmens, and timber mortuary houses of the Early

Neolithic (e.g., Liversage 1992, Ebbesen 1992). These were probably meant to last indefinitely and create an enduring impression. As in the Ertebølle, some sites contain burials, a vast number do not, but often the Neolithic monuments were built either over the settlements, or in close proximity to, them. However, it seems, unnecessary (contra Tilley 1996), to link the shape and orientation of earthen long barrows or long-dolmens to the Ertebølle shell mounds. The latter are highly varied in shape and size, and were usually accumulated over many centuries, presumably without any intentional predetermined form. Moreover, there is only a slight geographical overlap between the distributions of shell mounds, on the one hand, and earthen long-barrows and dolmens, on the other. It is not entirely obvious why those building earthen long barrows in interior southern Jutland should ideologically or symbolically relate their constructions to something they most likely had never had any experience of, that is, the discard of bulky oyster shells in gradually accumulating heaps. There is, in fact, more similarity in outline between these monuments and the polished stone axes.

Some scholars have interpreted the long mounds and mortuary houses as evidence for a social elite (e.g., Randsborg 1975), whereas others claim that 'the grave goods are no richer, numerous, or varied than those occurring in the flat graves' (Tilley 1996 in partial agreement with Ebbesen 1992) and view the monuments as social symbols of local groups.

The one thing, however, does not necessarily preclude the other. Given that flat graves and earthen long-barrows were contemporaneous, one could ask: 'Were they both used by the same social group(s), or was each associated with a group of its own?' It is not entirely obvious that the common Neolithic social-geographical units of North and South Jutland, Funen, and Zealand are appropriate for answering the question. In fact, there is very little difference among grave goods, and if both mortuary practices were in use within the same society (network), then difference would be marked out by the very construction of the monument itself. And because the monuments are too few to have contained more than a minor, selected portion of the population, both they and the flat graves must have had social significance, but with different meanings.

The earthen mounds could then be both social symbols and elite burials, in which case local community/group prestige and leadership would have been simultaneously displayed in one and the same phenomenon and manifest the foundation or consolidation of a developing ancestral cult. These monuments require an unprecedented amount of organised work. If this was not done on the demand of a leader before his or her death, or by their successors, then there must have been at least some degree of communal consensus on who should receive such mortuary treatment, and that must have been a very highly esteemed person.

If we maintain a link of leadership (not necessarily elite) to earthen mounds, then the flat graves must mean something different, unless they were simply a different expression of burial for leaders in other communities. They may reflect the burials of (constituted) lower ranks and/or the burials of associated kin of a leader according to age, sex/gender, or siblings graded into various classes.

There is thus considerable variation in the Early Neolithic burial evidence, including indicators of graded status. Tilley (1996) interprets an apparent dichotomy (based on two-artefact combinations with axes and pots) between flat graves and long dolmens as a regional phenomenon. Insofar as axes and pots have been repeatedly interpreted as symbolic keys linking subsistence, production, reproduction, and death, this is interesting as it may simultaneously reflect two ideologies of regional networks or groups exchanging with one another, but restructuring material culture to set themselves apart. However, it may also indicate a gradual shift from one set of beliefs to another, or live-stock farming (axes) versus grain-cultivation (pots).

The scenario that can be pictured in general is one of a series of transformations through restructuring of old and new ideas through material culture:

> ...the new ideology was primarily to do with restructuring notions of time and space, death and the body, prestige and social competition. Many of the individual components of their ideology were present within *different* Ertebølle communities. The development of extensive exchange systems between Ertebølle groups and with the Continental farmers acted as an integrating and crystallising catalyst gradually bringing initially disparate sets of ideas together into a coherent totality which eventually radically altered the Ertebølle lifeworld on a wholesale basis (Tilley 1996: 73, emphasis in original).

Although transformations were swift in some places, others were slow. To assume that all those changes were something that everyone wanted or were just waiting for is probably too optimistic. Some changes may have been peacefully negotiated, others less so. Unfortunately, it is exactly at this point that the record is too muted to give more detailed indications. Even if we retain the concept of lineage-inherited power, it does not necessarily follow that the power of one lineage or its head could not be replaced by that of another. Indeed, in a segmentary lineage system with competition one would expect just that.

Vertical and horizontal social structures in the early stages of the Early Neolithic do not appear much different from the Ertebølle. The building of monuments would, however, have required mobilisation and coordination of labour at a much larger scale. Some social groups built small round mounds, others earthen long-barrows, others again long dolmens, and still others did not construct monuments at all. It is possible that the construction of monuments was based on the power to control the redistribution of (surplus) agricultural produce. But there is no need to economically or socially downgrade those groups who did not construct monuments or plant crops. The choice *not* to engage in such practices could just as well be interpreted to suggest resistance to, or action against, dominance imposed by other groups attempting to monopolise land or people. For example, hunter-fisher-gatherers, crop planters, and cattle farmers do not necessarily have the same interests and this goes both for within-group and between-group relationships. There is some difference of opinion as to whether these monuments represent the burials of high-ranking, powerful people or whether they symbolised group affiliation with the land and its ancestors (see earlier and Tilley 1996). If those involved in the construction were all affiliated through kinship (lineage) ties, the monuments could mark out both.

As noted, very few individuals ended up in the monuments, In fact, long-term and discontinuous construction may have been politically convenient as it more frequently sets the stage for repeated rallying of people for both practical and ritual display and legitimisation of power than in a comparatively short-lived event. If the power to decide, mobilise, and organise was not inherently vested in one or a few influential people (specialised knowledge of how to construct monuments may also have been an asset), some choices would have had to be made on who was going to be buried in which manner, who would end up as sacrifices, and who should direct and coordinate building and other tasks. Whichever scenario we propose, some individuals would have been disappointed, resulting in latent conflict.

Status or leadership in the Ertebølle may have been ascribed or achieved through success in acquiring prestige food, in material resource production and exchange, or with reference to specific knowledge or ties to the spiritual world. And this also may have been true for the Early Neolithic, but with the addition that claims would have been made with reference to a longer line of descent and monopolised knowledge plus the success in growing and managing food production and controlling networks.

Leadership may well have been contested, however. There is no reason to assume a peaceful just-so story without competition and rivalry. For instance, when several megaliths are found close together they may not necessarily represent one single influential family, but possibly a succession of different leaders. Even if power was inherited or acquired with reference to particular claims to the spiritual world, it may be argued that it only lasted as long as the person was successful. That leaders could face replacement or premature death should not be ruled out. At any rate, the fact that some were buried without grave goods, others with some goods, and others again with substantial amounts of goods in either flat graves, round- or long-barrows, or dolmens *is* indicative of some vertical and horizontal differentiation. The very fact that monuments came into existence may signify incipient institutionalised leadership. Thus, generally speaking, the entire time span from the Early Ertebølle to the end of the Early Neolithic may be viewed as an ever-changing mosaic of structuration and restructuration.

Conclusion

All of this only serves as a brief synthesis of facts and interpretations. There is no need to emphasize that the evidence will continue to be interpreted and reinterpreted according to the continuing accumulation of data and the development of theory and methods. It may serve as a testimony to the quality of Southern Scandinavian Mesolithic research that many an elusive aspect of prehistoric society can in fact be dealt with. To penetrate deeper will, however, require both long-term and more integrated research strategies, and programs that not only provide for better regional and temporal coverage through the entire Mesolithic but also confront the social issues.

Acknowledgments

The author wishes to thank Peter Rowley-Conwy, University of Durham, and Søren Andersen, the National Museum of Copenhagen, for readily sharing their opinion on a number of issues, and the editors and three anonymous reviewers for all of their helpful comments.

Chapter 5

Mesolithic Britain

Chris Tolan-Smith*

Introduction

In conventional terms, the Mesolithic Period in Britain (Figure 5.1) is defined by the presence of microliths, small flint blades, and bladelets, usually considered to be the armatures in composite hunting weapons. Since the earlier part of the last century, a distinction has been acknowledged between Early Mesolithic assemblages characterised by microliths fashioned on rather broad blades and later assemblages, in which narrow blades provided the blanks for microlith manufacture (Clark 1932, Radley and Mellars 1964, Jacobi 1976). Also, with the passage of time, microliths became increasingly geometric in shape and smaller in size so that assemblages ascribed to the Late Mesolithic are often characterised by large numbers of very small geometric microliths (Radley et al. 1974). However, like most subdivisions of the archaeological record the term 'Mesolithic' is an artificial construct that, while functioning as a useful tool in some respects, also imposes constraints on research when the focus is lifted above that of technological development. This realisation has led to a redefinition of the term, taking its meaning beyond that of the literal 'Middle Stone Age' and including a specific span of time and way of life.

The possibility of giving the Mesolithic an objective chronological framework rather than one simply based on artefact typology has been provided by radiocarbon dating. On the basis of several hundred radiocarbon dates (Smith 1997: 182–9), the Mesolithic in Britain is regarded as spanning the period from 10,000 BP to 5000 BP (9,500 cal BC to 3,800 cal BC), although many issues still remain to be resolved. One of the most serious arises from the realisation that the radiocarbon timescale is not the same as that derived from other sources such as tree rings and ice cores that more closely approximate conventional calendar years. Radiocarbon years are not only of different duration to calendar years, they also vary over time. This leads to anomalies, such as periods when the timescale is compressed so that samples separated by several centuries may produce the same

---

* School of Historical Studies, University of Newcastle upon Tyne, UK.

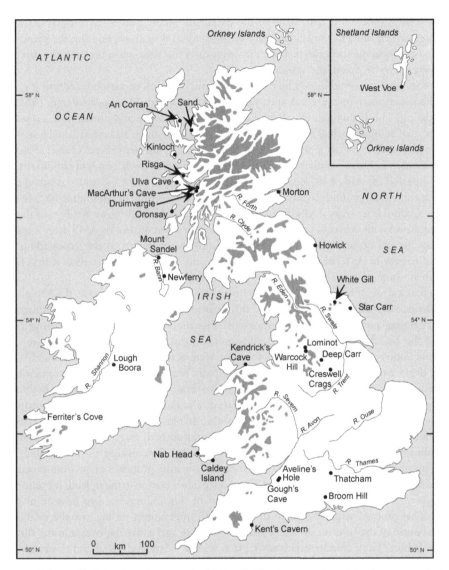

Figure 5.1. Map of Britain showing principal Mesolithic sites mentioned in the text and selected Late Glacial sites listed in Table 5.1. Druimvargie rockshelter is close to MacArthur's Cave, and Broomhead Moor, Dunford Bridge and March Hill are upland sites in the south Pennines in the vicinity of Warcock Hill and Lominot (not shown on the map for reasons of space). Creswell Crags includes the sites of Mother Grundy's Parlour, Robin Hood's Cave, Church Hole Cave and Pin Hole Cave. Shaded areas indicate land above 350 m (© G. N. Bailey).

radiocarbon date. Four such compressions of the timescale are of particular relevance to studies of the British Mesolithic, at 10,000 BP, 9600 BP, 9200 BP, and 8750 BP (Becker et al. 1991: 22–4, Reynier 1994: 536, 2000: 33). There is as yet no practical solution to this problem and it is unfortunate that the conventionally accepted beginning of the Mesolithic at 10,000 BP coincides with one of these compressions.

A less serious problem is that many of the dates still widely quoted were obtained while the technique was still in its infancy. Some have wide standard deviations, limiting the precision with which the events in question can be dated; in other cases the association between the dated sample and the event can be called into question.

Both concerns can be addressed by the more careful selection of samples, accepting only those where the association is unequivocal, and by the use of Accelerator Mass Spectrometry (AMS) radiocarbon dating. This technique, which has been available since the mid-1980s, makes it possible to date very small samples such as individual hazelnuts, human remains and cut-marked bones. In particular, it has been possible to apply the technique to a range of distinctive types of artefact made from bone and antler, hitherto considered too valuable to sacrifice to the demands of radiometric dating.

Over a period of nearly two decades, sixty-seven artefacts of bone and antler ascribed on typological or contextual grounds to either the Late Upper Palaeolithic or Mesolithic have been dated using the Oxford University AMS system (Tolan-Smith and Bonsall 1999). Analysis of these dates, and comparison with others obtained by association with conventional or AMS dates, suggests that significant changes occurred in bone and antler technology around 7700 cal BC, coinciding with the advent of narrow blade technology (ibid.:253, fig. 2 and 255). AMS radiocarbon dates (Table 5.1) are the main source for the chronological framework of this study.

As well as a stage of technological development and a distinct span of time, the Mesolithic also can be defined as the period that witnessed the adaptation of anatomically modern humans to the rapidly changing post-Pleistocene environment. The theme of environmental change has often provided the backdrop against which developments during the Mesolithic can be viewed. The Mesolithic hunter-gatherers of the early Holocene were at first confronted with a largely open and recently deglaciated landscape but one that was rapidly becoming mantled with coniferous forests and deciduous woodland. At first, sea levels were low but, with the inundation of the North Sea, low-lying lands were lost and population displaced, a major factor influencing the demographic development of Britain during the Early Mesolithic (Coles 1998). At the same time, coastlines lengthened and the relative altitude of the uplands diminished, increasing the opportunities for a diversification of economic pursuits. It is also apparent that, during the Mesolithic, humans became significant active agents in the environment, initiating processes of environmental change, particularly through the manipulation and disturbance of vegetation in the uplands (Simmons 1996).

However, the developments that form the focus of this volume need to be seen as part of a process. That process, which began in the thirteenth millennium cal BC, saw the establishment, over the course of the next six thousand years, of hunting and gathering communities throughout the British Isles. These developments took place within a dynamic social and economic context that has hitherto received less attention than it merits. Earlier studies, when they have ventured beyond the realm of stone tool typology, have focused on the ecological, as opposed to the social, relations of production (Smith 1997, Simmons 1996).

Drawing extensively on the work of Binford (1980), Woodburn (1980) and Ives (1990), I have proposed that the socioeconomic strategies pursued by such groups lie on a continuum (Tolan-Smith 2003a). At one end of this continuum are relatively egalitarian bands of residential foragers pursuing strategies designed to produce more-or-less immediate returns and with kinship systems that limited local group size and promoted the formation of alliance networks. At the other end are communities that pursued strategies leading to delayed returns as a consequence of the logistic deployment of specialist task groups, and with kinship rules that promoted local population growth and, axiomatically, social complexity. In the paragraphs that follow the socioeconomic status of the communities of Mesolithic Britain will be assessed along with their temporal stage and technological characteristics.

Table 5.1. Radiocarbon dates

Site	Material	Lab. No.	BP	Cal BC 2σ
Lowland England				
Gough's Cave, Somerset	Bone	OxA-3413	12,940 ± 140	13850–12950
Gough's Cave, Somerset	Bone	OxA-4106	12,670 ± 120	13400–12300
Gough's Cave, Somerset	Bone	OxA-3411	12,650 ± 120	13300–12300
Robin Hood's Cave, Derbyshire	Bone	OxA-1616	12,600 ± 170	13400–12100
Robin Hood's Cave, Derbyshire	Bone	OxA-3416	12,580 ± 110	13200–12250
Gough's Cave, Somerset	Bone	OxA-3414	12,570 ± 120	13200–12250
Gough's Cave, Somerset	Bone	OxA-4107	12,550 ± 130	13200–12200
Pin Hole Cave, Derbyshire	Bone	OxA-3404	12,510 ± 110	13100–12200
Gough's Cave, Somerset	Bone	OxA-3412	12,490 ± 120	13100–12150
Robin Hood's Cave, Derbyshire	Bone	OxA-1618	12,480 ± 170	13200–12000
Robin Hood's Cave, Derbyshire	Bone	OxA-1619	12,450 ± 150	13100–12000
Kent's Cavern, Devon	Bone	OxA-7994	12,430 ± 80	13000–12150
Robin Hood's Cave, Derbyshire	Bone	OxA-1617	12,420 ± 200	13200–11900
Poulton-le-Fylde, Lancs	Bone	OxA-150	12,400 ± 300	13400–11700
Gough's Cave, Somerset	Bone	OxA-3452	12,400 ± 110	13000–12100
Aveline's Hole, Somerset	Bone	OxA-1121	12,380 ± 130	13000–12050
Three Holes Cave, Devon	Bone	OxA-1500	12,350 ± 160	13100–11900
Pin Hole Cave, Derbyshire	Bone	OxA-1467	12,350 ± 120	13000–12000
Robin Hood's Cave, Derbyshire	Bone	OxA-3415	12,340 ± 120	12950–12000
Kent's Cavern, Devon	Bone	OxA-1789	12,320 ± 130	12950–11950
Robin Hood's Cave, Derbyshire	Mammoth ivory	OxA-1462	12,320 ± 120	12950–11950
Gough's Cave, Somerset	Bone	OxA-1071	12,300 ± 180	13000–11800
Robin Hood's Cave, Derbyshire	Bone	OxA-1670	12,290 ± 120	12900–11900
Mother Grundy's Parlour, Derbyshire	Tooth	OxA-5698	12,280 ± 110	12850–11900
Three Holes Cave, Devon	Bone	OxA-3208	12,260 ± 140	12900–11800
King Arthur's Cave, Gloucs	Bone	OxA-6844	12,250 ± 100	12750–11850
Church Hole, Derbyshire	Antler	OxA-3718	12,250 ± 90	12700–11900
Kent's Cavern, Devon	Bone	OxA-8002	12,240 ± 100	12700–11850
Three Holes Cave, Devon	Bone	OxA-3209	12,180 ± 130	12700–11800
Mother Grundy's Parlour, Derbyshire	Tooth	OxA-8739	12,170 ± 80	12280–11860

(*continued*)

Table 5.1. (*continued*)

Site	Material	Lab. No.	BP	Cal BC 2σ
Gough's Cave, Somerset	Mammoth ivory	OxA-1890	12,170 ± 130	12750–11850
Three Holes Cave, Devon	Bone	OxA-3890	12,150 ± 110	12500–11750
Church Hole Cave, Derbyshire	Bone	OxA-4108	12,110 ± 120	12400–11700
Church Hole Cave, Derbyshire	Antler	OxA-3717	12,020 ± 100	12150–11730
Fox Hole Cave, Derbyshire	Antler	OxA-1494	12,000 ± 120	12200–11650
Three Holes Cave, Devon	Bone	OxA-3891	11,980 ± 100	12120–11680
Mother Grundy's Parlour, Derbyshire	Tooth	OxA-8738	11,970 ± 75	12060–11730
Fox Hole Cave, Derbyshire	Antler	OxA-1493	11,970 ± 120	12200–11600
Gough's Cave, Somerset	Antler	OxA-2797	11,870 ± 110	12050–11500
Mother Grundy's Parlour, Derbyshire	Charcoal	OxA-5858	11,790 ± 90	11880–11470
Leman and Ower Banks, North Sea	Antler	OxA-1950	11,740 ± 150	11950–11300
Gransmoor, E. Yorks	Wood	SRR-4920	11,475 ± 50	11480–11280
Porth-y-Waen, Shropshire	Antler	OxA-1946	11,390 ± 120	11550–11050
Broken Cavern, Devon	Bone	OxA-3887	11,380 ± 120	11520–11040
Kinsey Cave, N. Yorks	Antler	OxA-2456	11,270 ± 110	11380–10980
Coniston Dib, Yorkshire	Bone	OxA-2847	11,210 ± 90	11310–10980
Dowel Cave, Derbyshire	Antler	OxA-1463	11,200 ± 120	11340–10940
Torbryan Six Cave, Devon	Bone	OxA-3894	11,130 ± 100	11260–10930
Sproughton 2, Suffolk	Antler	OxA-518	10,700 ± 160	11000–10200
Earl's Barton, Northants	Antler	OxA-803	10,320 ± 150	10800–9400
Sproughton 1, Suffolk	Bone	OxA-517	10,190 ± 150	10700–9300
Waltham Abbey, Essex	Antler	OxA-1427	9790 ± 100	9700–8800
Thatcham IV, Berkshire	Antler	OxA-732	9760 ± 120	9700–8750
Thatcham V, Berkshire	Bone	OxA-5191	9510 ± 90	9200–8600
Thatcham V, Berkshire	Bone	OxA-5190	9430 ± 100	9200–8450
Thatcham V, Berkshire	Charred hazelnut	OxA-5192	9400 ± 80	8950–8350
Badger Hole Cave Two, Somerset	Human bone	OxA-1459	9360 ± 100	8850–8300
Earl's Barton, Northants	Antler	OxA-500	9240 ± 160	9200–7900
Aveline's Hole, Somerset	Human bone	BM-471	9144 ± 110	8700–7950
Greenham Dairy Farm, Berkshire	Charred hazelnut	OxA-5194	9120 ± 80	8570–8210
Aveline's Hole, Somerset	Human bone	OxA-799	9100 ± 100	8650–7950
Gough's New Cave, Somerset	Human bone	OxA-814	9100 ± 100	8650–7950
Aveline's Hole, Somerset	Human bone	Q-1458	9090 ± 110	8650–7950
Badger Hole Cave, Somerset	Human bone	OxA-	9060 ± 130	8650–7800
Wandsworth, London	Antler	OxA-3736	9050 ± 85	8550–7950

Site	Material	Lab. No.	BP	Cal BC 2σ
Mother Grundy's Parlour, Derbyshire	Bone	OxA-3453	8960 ± 95	8350–7750
Marsh Benham, Berkshire	Charred hazelnut	OxA-5195	8905 ± 80	8300–7750
Mother Grundy's Parlour, Derbyshire	Charred hazelnut	OxA-3397	8900 ± 90	8300–7750
Aveline's Hole, Somerset	Human bone	OxA-800	8860 ± 100	8300–7650
Kew Bridge, London	Antler	OxA-1160	8820 ± 100	8250–7600
Aveline's Hole, Somerset	Human bone	OxA-1070	8740 ± 100	8250–7550
Mother Grundy's Parlour, Derbyshire	Charred hazelnut	OxA-3394	8730 ± 95	8200–7550
Broomhead Moor, W. Yorks		Q-0800	8573 ± 110	8000–7350
Iping Common, Sussex	Charred hazelnut	OxA-5193	8565 ± 80	7820–7470
Broom Hill, Hampshire		Q-1528	8540 ± 150	8200–7150
Mother Grundy's Parlour, Derbyshire	Charred hazelnut	OxA-3396	8500 ± 110	7800–7150
Kent's Cavern, Devon	Human bone	OxA-1786	8070 ± 90	7350–6650
Broom Hill, Hampshire		Q-1460	7830 ± 120	7050–6450
Broom Hill, Hampshire		Q-1128	6534 ± 125	5710–5220
Three Holes Cave, Devon	Bone	OxA-4491	6330 ± 75	5480–5070
Three Holes Cave, Devon	Bone	OxA-4492	6120 ± 75	5290–4840
March Hill, W. Yorks		Q-1188	6020 ± 220	5500–4400
March Hill, W. Yorks		Q-0788	5850 ± 80	4910–4500
Dunford Bridge, W. Yorks		Q-0799	5380 ± 80	4360–4030
Wales				
Upper Kendrick's Cave. N. Wales	Tooth	OxA-5862	9945 ± 75	9760–9260
Nab Head, Dyfed	Charred hazelnut	OxA-1495	9210 ± 80	8630–8280
Nab Head, Dyfed	Charred hazelnut	OxA-1496	9110 ± 80	8600–8200
Worm's Head Cave, S. Wales	Human bone	OxA-4024	8800 ± 80	8250–7600
Daylight Rock, Caldey Island	Human bone	OxA-7686	8655 ± 60	7840–7570
Ogof-yr-Ychen, Caldey Island	Human bone	OxA-7741	8415 ± 65	7590–7330
Ogof-yr-Ychen, Caldey Island	Human bone	OxA-7690	8290 ± 55	7510–7170
Ogof-yr-Ychen, Caldey Island	Human bone	OxA-7691	8210 ± 55	7360–7060
Nab Head, S. Wales	Charcoal	OxA-860	7360 ± 90	6420–6050
Nab Head, S. Wales	Charcoal	OxA-861	6210 ± 90	5370–4930
N. England and Scotland				
Victoria Cave, N. Yorks	Antler	OxA-2455	11,750 ± 120	11890–11380
Victoria Cave, N. Yorks	Antler	OxA-2607	10,810 ± 100	11020–10680

(*continued*)

Table 5.1. (*continued*)

Site	Material	Lab. No.	BP	Cal BC 2σ
Victoria Cave, N. Yorks	Antler	OxA-2453	10,220 ± 110	10450–9450
Seamer, N. Yorks	Antler	OxA-1176	9700 ± 160	9700–8600
Star Carr, N. Yorks	Wood	Q-14	9557 ± 210	9500–8200
Seamer, N. Yorks	Antler	OxA-1154	9500 ± 120	9250–8450
Star Carr, N. Yorks	Wood	C-353	9488 ± 350	10100–7800
Howick, Northumberland	Charred hazelnut	OxA-11829	8890 ± 45	8240–7910
Howick, Northumberland	Charred hazelnut	OxA-11801	8734 ± 37	7940–7600
Howick, Northumberland	Charred hazelnut	OxA-11830	8715 ± 50	7940–7590
Kinloch, Isle of Rhum		GU-2040	8560 ± 75	7760–7470
Druimvargie Rockshelter, Argyll	Bone	OxA-4608	8340 ± 80	7580–7170
Kinloch, Isle of Rhum		GU-2150	8310 ± 150	7650–6800
Howick, Northumberland	Charred hazelnut	OxA-11806	8278 ± 35	7460–7180
Auchareoch, Isle of Arran	Charred hazelnut	OxA-1601	8060 ± 90	7350–6650
Loch Doon Flint Site, Scotland	Charcoal	OxA-1598	8000 ± 100	7250–6600
Druimvargie Rockshelter, Argyll	Bone	OxA-4609	7890 ± 80	7050–6590
Kinloch, Isle of Rhum		GU-2147	7880 ± 70	7040–6590
Auchareoch, Isle of Arran	Charcoal	OxA-1600	7870 ± 90	7050–6500
Druimvargie Rockshelter, Argyll	Bone	OxA-1948	7810 ± 90	7050–6450
An Corran, Isle of Skye	Bone	OxA-4994	7590 ± 90	6610–6240
Kinloch, Isle of Rhum		GU-2149	7570 ± 50	6510–6340
Morton T, Fife		NZ-1302	7330 ± 200	6600–5800
Auchareoch, Isle of Arran	Charred hazelnut	OxA-1599	7300 ± 90	6380–6010
MacArthur's Cave, Argyll	Antler	OxA-1949	6700 ± 80	5730–5480
Cumstoun, Kircudbrightshire	Antler	OxA-3735	6665 ± 70	5710–5480
Morton T, Fife		NZ-1193	6400 ± 125	5650–5050
Smittons, Dumfries and Galloway	Charred hazelnut	OxA-1595	6260 ± 80	5380–5000
Starr I, Scotland	Charcoal	OxA-1596	6230 ± 80	5370–4980
Caisteal nan Gillean I, Oronsay	Charcoal	Q-3008	6190 ± 80	5320–4930
Caisteal nan Gillean I, Oronsay	Charcoal	Q-3007	6120 ± 80	5230–4840
Morton T, Fife		Q-0928	6115 ± 110	5350–4750
Caisteal nan Gillean I, Oronsay	Charcoal	Q-3009	6035 ± 70	5080–4730
Isle of Risga, Argyll	Antler	OxA-2023	6000 ± 90	5250–4650
Isle of Risga, Argyll	Antler	OxA-3737	5875 ± 65	4910–4550

Site	Material	Lab. No.	BP	Cal BC 2σ
Priory Midden, Oronsay	Charcoal	Q-3001	5870 ± 50	4850–4590
Shewalton, Ayrshire	Antler	OxA-1947	5840 ± 80	4900–4490
Priory Midden, Oronsay	Charcoal	Q-3000	5825 ± 50	4800–4540
Morton B, Fife	Bone	OxA-4612	5790 ± 80	4830–4450
Ulva Cave, Argyll	Antler	OxA-3738	5750 ± 70	4780–4450
Cnoc Coig, Oronsay	Human bone	OxA-8004	5740 ± 65	4730–4440
Priory Midden, Oronsay	Charcoal	Q-3002	5717 ± 50	4690–4450
Cnoc Coig, Oronsay	Human bone	OxA-8019	5615 ± 55	4550–4340
Cnoc Sligeach, Oronsay	Marine shell	Birm-465	5606 ± 155	4800–4050
Cnoc Coig, Oronsay	Charcoal	Q-1354	5535 ± 140	4700–4000
Priory Midden, Oronsay	Charcoal	Q-3003	5510 ± 50	4460–4260
Cnoc Coig, Oronsay	Charcoal	Q-1351	5495 ± 75	4500–4220
Cnoc Coig, Oronsay	Human bone	OxA-8014	5495 ± 55	4460–4240
Caisteal nan Gillean I, Oronsay	Charcoal	Q-3010	5485 ± 50	4450–4240
Casteal Nan Gillean II	Human bone	OxA-8005	5480 ± 55	4450–4230
Morton B, Fife	Bone	OxA-4611	5475 ± 60	4460–4220
Smittons, Dumfries, and Galloway	Charred hazelnut	OxA-1594	5470 ± 80	4470–4050
Priory Midden, Oronsay	Charcoal	Q-3004	5470 ± 50	4450–4230
Cnoc Coig, Oronsay	Charcoal	Q-1353	5465 ± 80	4460–4050
Caisteal nan Gillean I, Oronsay	Charcoal	Q-3011	5450 ± 50	4450–4160
Cnoc Coig, Oronsay	Charcoal	Q-1352	5430 ± 130	4550–3950
Cnoc Sligeach, Oronsay	Charcoal	BM-670	5426 ± 159	4650–3800
Carding Mill Bay, Argyll	Antler	OxA-3740	5190 ± 85	4240–3790
Morton B, Fife	Bone	OxA-4610	5180 ± 70	4230–3790
Carding Mill Bay, Argyll	Bone	OxA-3739	4765 ± 65	3660–3370
Ireland				
Mount Sandel, N. Ireland		UB-2362	8990 ± 80	8340–7830
Lough Boora, Ireland		UB-2199	8475 ± 75	7610–7340
Mount Sandel, N. Ireland		UB-2008	8440 ± 65	7590–7350
Lough Boora, Ireland		UB-6400	8350 ± 70	7550–7180
Mount Sandel, N. Ireland		UB-2359	7885 ± 120	7100–6450
Newferry, N. Ireland		UB-496	7485 ± 115	6570–6070
Mount Sandel, N. Ireland		UB-2358	6980 ± 135	6100–5620
Newferry, N. Ireland		UB-505	6605 ± 170	5900–5200
Ferriter's Cove, Ireland		BM-2228AR	5850 ± 130	5050–4350
Newferry, N. Ireland		UB-508	5795 ± 105	4950–4350

(continued)

Table 5.1. (*continued*)

Site	Material	Lab. No.	BP	Cal BC 2σ
Ferriter's Cove, Ireland		BM-2227R	5400 ± 220	4750–3700
Newferry, N. Ireland		D-36	5290 ± 170	4500–3700

Preference has been given to dates produced on identifiable archaeological specimens (bone and antler artefacts, cut-marked animal bone and human bone) by the Oxford AMS system. An additional selection of dates is included from sites mentioned in the text. Sites and dates are organised by region and in date order within each region. Sites in northern England north of latitude 54 degrees North are grouped with sites in Scotland (see text for discussion). Dates of Late Upper Palaeolithic materials from the Late Glacial period are included to demonstrate the broad distinction between an early occupation of lowland England and Wales and the later spread of settlement to the north and in Ireland. Sources: Bronk Ramsey et al. 2000a, 2000b, 2002, Gillespie et al. 1985, Gowlett et al. 1986, 1987, Hedges et al. 1987, 1989, 1994, Hedges, Housley et al. 1996, Hedges, Pettitt et al. 1996, Tolan-Smith 1997, Tolan-Smith and Bonsall 1999, Waddington et al. 2003. All radiocarbon determinations are given as uncalibrated BP and calibrated ranges at 2 sigma as cal BC. Dates have been calibrated using OxCal v3.10 (Bronk Ramsey 1995, 2001).

The Early Mesolithic

The Early Mesolithic in the British Isles is conventionally defined by the presence of broad-blade microliths, frequently obliquely blunted points (Figure 5.2), and by the absence of narrow-blade geometric microliths (Figure 5.3). However, it has for long been appreciated that this is an oversimplification. Broad-blade microliths are often found as a component of narrow-blade assemblages. What do change are the proportions of the different types present and their sizes (Smith 1997: 5). Also the observation that the debitage of broad-blade manufacture tends towards narrow-blade proportions and vice versa (Pitts and Jacobi 1979: 166) is a further argument for exercising caution in the classification of assemblages on typological grounds. A rather firmer chronological basis is provided by the direct dating of implements made of bone and antler, as discussed later.

A range of diagnostic traits makes it possible to subdivide the broad-blade assemblages of the Early Mesolithic, and Reynier (1994) has suggested that the compressions in the radiocarbon timescale can be used as a means of dividing the period into three 'stages', each of about four hundred years' duration. Reynier (1994: 537) points out that there is little dated evidence of Early Mesolithic settlement during his 'Stage 1', which spans the period between 9,600 cal BC and 9000 cal BC. Substantial evidence only begins to appear in the period between 9000 cal BC and 8400 cal BC, his 'Stage 2' (Reynier 1994: 537). 'Stage 2' assemblages consist of those of the 'Star Carr' and 'Deepcar' types. Both are dominated by obliquely blunted points and the differences between them are of a statistical rather than a fundamental nature. However, a characteristic of 'Deepcar' assemblages is that about 20 percent of their obliquely blunted points have light additional retouch applied to their opposing edge. It also seems to be the case, where dates are available, that 'Deepcar' assemblages appear on the scene rather later than those of 'Star Carr' type (Reynier 1994, 2000). Reynier's 'Stage 3' marks the final part of the Early Mesolithic from 8400 cal BC down to about 7750 cal BC. Both 'Star Carr' and 'Deepcar' type assemblages persist through 'Stage 3' and are joined in the early eighth millennium cal BC by assemblages of 'Horsham' type (Reynier 1994: 537). Obliquely blunted points continue to be the dominant microlith form in 'Horsham' assemblages, a significant

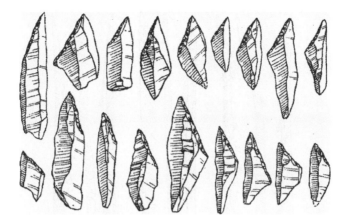

Figure 5.2. Obliquely blunted points (after Clark 1971: 101). Scale 2:3.

number having additional 'Deepcar' style retouch along their leading edge. However, the diagnostic component of 'Horsham' assemblages is the presence of hollow-based points. It is also the case that 'Horsham' assemblages are largely confined to southeast England (Reynier 1994: 530–1).

Turning attention to bone and antler technology, the application of radiocarbon dating has established that the Early Mesolithic was characterised by slender, uniserial barbed points (Figure 5.4) manufactured by the 'groove-and-splinter' technique and a type that had been current in southern Britain from the Late Glacial Interstadial (Smith 1997: 6, fig. 1.2). Another implement type, elk antler mattocks (Figure 5.5), appears to have been confined to the Early Mesolithic with no Late Upper Palaeolithic antecedents, unless a comparison is made with the reindeer antler club or 'Lyngby Axe' from Earl's Barton (Cook and Jacobi 1994).

Although there may have been some technological developments during the tenth millennium cal BC, the way of life of the Early Mesolithic communities of Britain was a continuation and development of a process that had been underway since the thirteenth millennium. Conventionally part of the Late Upper Palaeolithic, the early stages of this process lie outside the scope of this volume, though if the Early Mesolithic is to be understood they cannot be ignored completely.

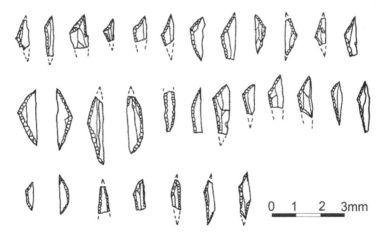

Figure 5.3. Narrow blade geometric microliths (after Radley, Tallis, and Switzur 1974: 6).

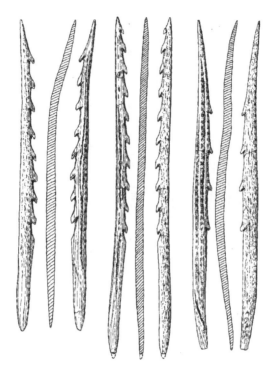

Figure 5.4. Uniserial barbed points (after Clark 1971: 139). Scale 1:3.

From the maximum extent of the ice sheets during the Dimlington Stadial at 19,500 cal BC, Britain had become deglaciated by 14,750 cal BC and, following a period of total abandonment, was beginning to be brought back within the realm of human settlement by the mid-thirteenth millennium. In a series of publications (Smith and Openshaw 1990, Smith 1997, Tolan-Smith 1998, Tolan-Smith and Bonsall 1999), I have proposed that the spatial and temporal distribution of the radiocarbon-dated records of an initial human presence in the British Isles allows several distinct phases of settlement to be identified. The first I regard as the phase of initial colonisation. This began around 12,700 cal BC, towards the end of the Late Glacial Interstadial (Dryas Ib, Ic, and II), and was marked by the rapid and widespread dispersal of human groups into the lowlands of central, southern, and eastern England.

During this initial phase, people moved into Britain overland from adjoining areas of the north European plain. The world they encountered in southeast and central Britain differed little from the one they were familiar with and is unlikely to have presented many challenges. One area in which unfamiliarity may have exerted a premium is in the availability of raw materials. As groups move into unfamiliar territory it may take some time before a full appreciation of raw material availability can be established, leading to a tendency, during the initial stages of occupation, for raw materials to be transported over long distances (Kelly and Todd 1988: 237–8). In a recent analysis of Late Upper Palaeolithic material from southern Britain, Barton and Dumont (2000: 155) have noted that their initial phase of settlement, dated to the middle part of the Late Glacial Interstadial and termed by them the 'Creswellian', is characterised by the use of nonlocal (>160 km distant) sources or raw material.

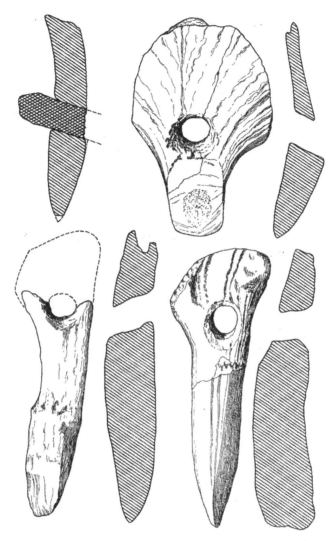

Figure 5.5. Elk antler mattocks (after Clark 1971: 159). Scale 1:4.

This phase can be viewed ecologically as a case of a population expanding to fill its niche. The radiocarbon dates for a human presence across the north European plain, from the shores of the Baltic to the English Midlands, a spread of 12 degrees of longitude, are barely distinguishable, and the spread of communities throughout this area need have involved no more than a barely perceptible adjustment of annual hunting ranges of 20 km per generation. Simulation studies by Surovell (2000) of the North American case have shown that regions can be populated very rapidly as a result of the accumulation of numerous small-scale moves.

The second, or consolidation, phase corresponding to the Loch Lomond Stadial (Dryas III) and the Preboreal (Godwin Zone IV) and dating from approximately 10,950 to 8250 cal BC, is one during which little further expansion occurred and population growth was accommodated by the infilling of areas already occupied. Archaeologically, this is reflected regionally by an increase in the evidence for a human presence in southern Britain (Tolan-Smith 1998: 23–5 and figs. 2b and 3) and on a site-by-site basis by a greater interest in the use of locally available raw materials (Barton and Dumont 2000: 157). The latter is precisely what would be expected as communities became familiar with the resources of a newly occupied region. In asking why the recolonisation of Britain stopped at around 10,950 cal BC, I do not think we can avoid an explanation that is, at least in part, environmental or ecological, though in practice it was limitations of the social structures and practices of the groups involved that actually called a halt to expansion. They were confronted with two adverse sets of circumstances. First, by the middle of the fourteenth millennium cal BC, the climate in northern Europe had begun to deteriorate with the onset of the Dryas III cold stage, in Britain represented by the return to glacial conditions in much of the north. At just the time when groups were beginning to extend their ranges west and north, conditions in those areas began to deteriorate. Second, even without the problems presented by a deteriorating climate, the way of life that had developed during the Late Glacial on the north European plain had reached its geographical limit in the west and north. The people that had so successfully extended that way of life were confronted with very different and unfamiliar landscapes in the mountains of western and northern Britain and on the shores of the Atlantic Ocean. The west and north were *terra incognita* in the most literal sense, and knowledge could only be acquired by trial and error.

The earlier part of the consolidation phase corresponds to the Final Upper Palaeolithic of Barton and Dumont (2000: 155–60), and the Early Mesolithic belongs to its latter part. Although Early Mesolithic and Late Upper Palaeolithic assemblages can be distinguished on typological grounds, there is little to suggest other radical changes in the way of life pursued by the population of southern Britain at this time, and northern Britain remained unoccupied.

An understanding of the way of life of the Early Mesolithic communities of the British Isles is best obtained from a consideration of the evidence from a number of key sites. Lakes, the residue of the melted ice sheets, dominated the landscape of the early Postglacial in southern Britain, accompanied by forests composed of a nearly continuous mantle of birch, pine, oak, elm, and hazel. The well-known sites of Star Carr and Thatcham, both hunter-gatherer encampments beside early Postglacial lakes, have produced rich assemblages of finds and animal bones from which it is possible to make generalisations about aspects of economic behaviour.

At *Star Carr*, excavations carried out intermittently over half a century offer a vivid picture of a range of aspects of hunter-gatherer life (Mellars and Dark 1998). Stone tools were manufactured on the dry slopes immediately above the lake margins, which were kept open through the frequent burning of reed growth, either to facilitate hunting or simply to improve the visibility of and access to the open water. The latter was further facilitated by the construction of a walkway of split aspen and birch logs, while part of the lake margin may have been deliberately consolidated through the dumping of logs and branches. Excavations undertaken in the 1950s detected evidence for a range of activities on this 'platform', the most notable of which was the manufacture of barbed points made from antler, nearly two hundred examples of which were recovered. Faunal remains suggest that a range of species was hunted, the most important of which were aurochs, elk, red, and roe deer. Incomplete skeletal representation has been taken to imply that the site was mainly the scene of butchery activity with the main meat bearing joints being removed for consumption elsewhere. The faunal remains also indicate that Star Carr is unlikely to have been occupied on a year round basis. Which seasons were favoured is a topic about which there has been some disagreement. The original excavator's interpretation of winter occupation (Clark 1954) has been superseded by a view that the site was mainly occupied during the summer but with intermittent visits throughout the year (Legge and Rowley-Conwy 1988). The recent research at Star Carr has produced evidence for occupation during two distinct episodes of 80 and 130 years' duration, both in the early ninth millennium cal BC and separated by an interval of several decades (Mellars and Dark 1998: 224). It is possible to envisage a scenario in which a band of hunter-gatherers made regular visits to Star Carr over a period of several generations. These visits were interrupted before being resumed again about a generation later. The reason for this interruption is unknown but the dating suggests that it may have occurred within the span of a single lifetime, and the return to Star Carr may have been initiated by an individual or individuals who remembered visits to the site in their childhood. This is, of course, all speculation, but it is very rare in Mesolithic archaeology that we are able to consider events at this level of resolution.

At the broadly contemporaneous site of *Thatcham*, the excavations concentrated on the dry-land surfaces above the lake margins, leading to the recovery of over eighteen thousand Early Mesolithic flints (Wymer 1962). Recent reanalysis of the assemblage suggests that it may be comprised of two components; a small, spatially concentrated assemblage of 'Star Carr' type and a more widely scattered assemblage of 'Deepcar' type, the former being heavily patinated (Reynier 2000). This suggests two distinct phases, or episodes, of occupation. Apart from a number of hearths, the excavations at Thatcham produced no clear evidence of structures although it has been suggested that abrupt variations in the density of finds might mark the position of one or more shelters (Smith 1997: 124, 126, fig. 7.10).

Limited excavations undertaken in the waterlogged deposits at the lake margin led to the recovery of a faunal assemblage similar to that from Star Carr with red and roe deer well represented along with elk, aurochs, wild pig, and horse. A skeletal analysis of the most numerous species, red deer, revealed a preponderance of limbs suggesting that carcasses were butchered elsewhere, with only the most useful joints being brought back to the site (Smith 1997: 121). This may be contrasted with the situation at Star Carr, where there was more evidence for in situ butchery. The implication of this is that the Thatcham site may have been a residential location or 'base camp', to use the conventional terminology. This interpretation is supported by an analysis of the stone tool assemblage, which includes significant numbers of tools associated with maintenance activities (Healey et al. 1992: 61).

Analysis of bird remains suggests that Thatcham, like Star Carr, seems to have been occupied mainly in the summer (Smith 1997: 122), which raises the question of what these communities did at other times of the year.

An insight into the degree of mobility experienced by some Early Mesolithic hunter-gatherers is provided by the distribution of raw materials. A particularly clear case of this is provided by the site of Deepcar, near Sheffield, from which 95 percent of the raw materials recovered came from sources up to 80 km away in east Yorkshire. As noted earlier, in the case of the initial settlement of southern Britain during the Late Upper Palaeolithic, the use of remote sources of raw material is a characteristic of the early stages of the colonisation process.

The site at *Deepcar*, like Star Carr and Thatcham, also overlooks a former lake. Although no radiocarbon dates are available, the stone tool assemblage is sufficiently distinctive for it to be dated to the Early Mesolithic. Indeed, assemblages of 'Deepcar' type are ascribed by Reynier to the latter part of his 'Stage 2', dated to the mid-ninth millennium cal BC. Although at the relatively modest altitude of 150 m OD, Deepcar is surrounded by bleak, upland moors and fells rising to well over 300 m OD. It was probably a temporary encampment at which parties of hunters made brief halts in order to repair their equipment before moving deeper into the uplands. Evidence of this deep penetration is provided by a number of sites at significantly higher levels such as *Warcock Hill* at 380 m and *Lominot* at 426 m. This is one of the earliest indications we have of the logistic deployment of specialist task groups.

The consolidation phase of the Late Upper Palaeolithic and Early Mesolithic settlement of the British Isles was characterised by infilling of the areas already occupied, with little further extension of settlement (Tolan-Smith 1998, Tolan-Smith and Bonsall 1999: 256), and Reynier has specifically referred the spread of 'Deepcar' type assemblages into the interior as part of such an 'infilling' process (Reynier 1994: 539).

It is a widely held view that hunter-gatherers, of necessity, pursued a mobile way of life that was largely governed by the cycle of the seasons. This was almost certainly the case during the Late Upper Palaeolithic and Early Mesolithic in Britain, though it may have been less so as the Mesolithic period drew to a close. It is, however, necessary to consider what is meant by mobility and seasonality; they are not the same. The view often taken is that Early Mesolithic hunters moved on a seasonal basis between ecological zones, with moves taking place between the coast and interior valleys and uplands (Darvill 1987: 42, Simmons 1996: 194–222, Smith 1997: 131). The results of recent stable isotope analyses of diet suggest that this model may need to be reevaluated. To date only a few specimens have been studied, but examination of δ^{13}C and δ^{15}N ratios has failed to produce any evidence that Early Mesolithic people living in Britain had a significant marine component in their diets, irrespective of how close they lived to the sea (Richards and Hedges 1999a, 1999b, Richards et al. 2000, Schulting and Richards 2000: 56–8; but see also Milner et al. 2004, Hedges 2004). This implies less movement than expected between inland areas and the coast, and there is little other evidence for the use of coastal resources during the Early Mesolithic. Although this may be partly because of the loss of sites to rising sea levels, the absence of a marine component in the diets of communities living within less than a day's trek from the coast is probably significant.

Steep rocky shorelines and cliffs have been less affected by rising sea levels, and Early Mesolithic sites have been found in such situations. Unfortunately, such sites are mainly represented by scatters of stone tools and lack the faunal and human remains that make economic and dietary analyses possible. However, unlike the shallow lagoons and estuarine flats of elsewhere, such coastlines are not usually abundant in resources and it may be that these communities maintained a predominantly terrestrial orientation in spite of their proximity to the sea.

Nab Head in Dyfed is one of the best-known examples of an Early Mesolithic site in a coastal location (David 1989). Here, research at a later Iron Age cliff-top promontory fort has led to the recovery of a large assemblage of stone tools attributed by Reynier to his 'Star Carr' type (Reynier 1994: 530 and fig. 1 no. 18). Two AMS dates from this site place the Early Mesolithic occupation there during the final part of the ninth millennium cal BC and make Nab Head one of the earliest coastal sites in Britain. Apart from the charred hazelnuts used to provide the dates, no organic remains have been recovered from Nab Head and the economic basis of the community there must remain a matter of speculation. Although shallow embayments and estuarine zones were available within a two-hour foraging range, Nab Head itself is not particularly well-situated for the exploitation of marine resources, given the present-day shoreline topography, and some other motivation must underlie the choice of site – perhaps a greater focus on terrestrial resources at a time when sea level was still well below the present level and the shoreline more distant.

Given the nature of the archaeological record, Mesolithic studies usually have to focus on aspects of technological and economic behaviour. All too rarely is it possible to glimpse aspects of the symbolic life of these early communities. Nab Head provides a rare exception in that, in addition to the numerous stone tools, the excavators have also recovered 690 perforated shale discs, or beads. Such finds usually occur singly or in twos or threes, and the recovery of such a large number suggests that Nab Head may have been a production and distribution centre. We can only conjecture what the significance of these beads may have been, but as items of ornamentation their use may have, at least implicitly, communicated messages of identity and status. Two other items from Nab Head have also attracted attention. Both are pebbles that exhibit varying degrees of modification that have led to them being interpreted as figurines, a view more convincing in one case than the other. At all events, the unusual finds from Nab Head serve as a useful reminder of the richness of life outside the sphere of primary subsistence.

A further insight into the noneconomic aspects of life in the Early Mesolithic is provided by the cemetery at *Aveline's Hole* in Burrington Comb in the Mendip Hills (Smith 1997: 137–8, 171, 180). This cave is believed to have contained the remains of over seventy individuals but most were found over 150 years ago and even those discovered in the earlier part of the twentieth century were destroyed during an air raid in the Second World War. A few surviving fragments have been dated to around 8300 cal BC. Assuming that this dating can be applied to the group as a whole, an intriguing question arises. Does this large number of burials represent a very conservative and persistent pattern of funerary ritual by a small coresident group or the cemetery of a larger social unit, comprised perhaps of several such groups? Estimates of the rate of demographic growth in southern Britain during the late tenth millennium cal BC favour the latter explanation (Smith 1992: 39–40) and suggest that Aveline's Hole was a funerary aggregation site for several co-resident groups linked by ties of kinship and lineage. As such, it may be seen as the physical manifestation of the emergence of a far-reaching alliance network.

Like their forebears in the Late Upper Palaeolithic, the communities of Early Mesolithic Britain probably developed socioeconomic systems that tended towards the residential foraging mode (Binford 1980) with economic activity geared towards supplying more-or-less immediate returns (Woodburn 1980) and with kinship systems that prohibited local group growth and promoted alliance formation (Ives 1990). However, from the very beginning of the period it is possible to detect the beginnings of developments such as the logistic deployment of specialist task groups, which would lead towards a modification of that system to one more suited to the ecological and demographic circumstances of the Postglacial.

The Late Mesolithic

The Late Mesolithic is conventionally defined by the widespread occurrence of narrow-blade assemblages, the earliest of which occur simultaneously in Northeast England and Ireland early from about 8000 cal BC. However, the trend towards a reduction in size and the adoption of increasing geometric forms had been underway during the Early Mesolithic; conversely, forms diagnostic of that period, such as obliquely blunted points, continued to be a component in Late Mesolithic assemblages. Attempts have been made to subdivide Late Mesolithic geometric microliths into a number of typological classes (Radley et al. 1974, Jacobi 1976), but, except as a descriptive device, this has proved largely unsuccessful and the types identified appear to have little, if any, chronological significance.

Turning to bone and antler working, the distinction between the Early and Late Mesolithic seems rather more clear-cut. Late Mesolithic barbed points, which tend to be both uniserial and biserial, are flat and squat (Figure 5.6) and manufactured on blanks produced by splitting lengths of antler beam or long bone shaft, as opposed to the 'groove-and-splinter' technique favoured in the Early Mesolithic. The elk antler mattocks of the earlier period are replaced by similar implements made from the beam of red deer antlers (Figure 5.7), a factor probably to be attributed to the

Figure 5.6. Late Mesolithic barbed points (after Anderson 1895: 223). Scale 2:5.

demise of elk early in the Postglacial. Another implement diagnostic of the Late Mesolithic, but of uncertain function, is the bone or antler bevel-ended tool (Figure 5.8), although examples made from stone are also known. None of these implements are known from Early Mesolithic contexts and the fact that all three types became widespread after approximately 7700 cal BC (Tolan-Smith and Bonsall 1999) underlines the distinction between the Early and Late Mesolithic in a more effective manner than the rather gradual changes noted in the stone tool assemblages.

Classic Late Mesolithic geometric microlith assemblages are best known from sites in the southern Pennines such as **Broomhead Moor Site 5**, **Dunford Bridge** and **March Hill** (Radley et al. 1974) and on the North York Moors as at **White Gill** (Radley 1970). Dates range from the mid-eighth through to the mid-fifth millennium cal BC. These sites are all situated at relatively high altitude, usually above 300 m, and consist of scatters of flints of which microliths are the dominant types. In some cases they were found with hearths and irregular arrangements of stake holes that might mark the position of light shelters (Radley et al. 1974, Smith 1997: 135–7). Studies of pollen from nearby peat deposits have identified what appear to be episodes of vegetation disturbance, often associated with an increase in the input of charcoal into the soil profile. This suggests that Late Mesolithic communities in the uplands were deliberately modifying the vegetation through fire management, either to suppress the elevation of the tree line, to maintain open clearings or to promote the growth of browse attractive to prey animals such as red deer (Mellars 1976, Simmons 1996). The restricted inventories from these sites and their high exposed locations suggest the activities of hunting parties operating away from the main residential location, an activity already identified during the Early Mesolithic.

Complementing these upland hunting camps, a number of lowland sites in river valleys provide evidence for a more diverse range of activities. The site at **Broom Hill**, occupied during the mid-eighth millennium cal BC, produced a large number of microliths but also significant quantities of burins and scrapers indicating a range of maintenance activities. Over 100 axes or adzes imply a significant investment of energy in forest clearance and perhaps also carpentry. A series of hollows, each about 4 m across and in one case surrounded by stake-holes, may mark the position of shelters (Smith 1997: 131–3).

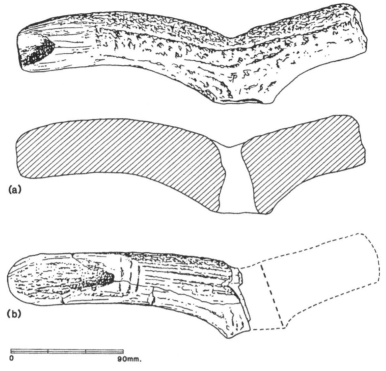

Figure 5.7. Late Mesolithic antler mattocks (after Lacaille 1954).

The hollows at Broom Hill were shallow scoops filled with occupation debris and should not be confused with the 'pit dwellings', which were a feature of Mesolithic settlement studies during the middle part of the twentieth century. At a number of sites in southern England quantities of Mesolithic flints were recovered from irregular hollows which, at the time, were taken to be primitive shelters, perhaps roofed over with branches, for example, from Farnham, Selmeston, and Abinger (Clark 1934, Clark and Rankine 1939, Leakey 1951). However, reviews of this evidence by Newell (1981) and Woodman (1985) have established that most of these features were tree-falls,

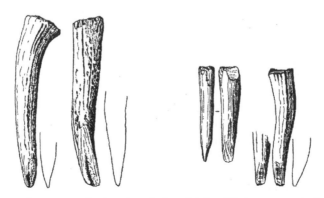

Figure 5.8. Bone or antler bevel-ended tool (after Clark 1971: 155). Scale 1:5.

with fortuitous accumulations of Mesolithic material. Such tree-falls are a natural feature of mature deciduous woodland. Whereas in the uplands Late Mesolithic communities appear to have been attempting to suppress tree growth, in the lowlands it was more a question of adapting to the prevailing conditions and making the most of what opportunities presented themselves in the form of natural clearings.

This aspect of the Late Mesolithic of mainland Britain, the extension of settlement throughout the lowlands and, via the major river valleys, into the uplands offers no marked break with what has been identified during the Early Mesolithic. It was, in effect, a continuation of the infilling which was a feature of the second or 'consolidation' phase (Tolan-Smith 1998; see also Reynier 1994: 540) in the Late Glacial and Postglacial recolonisation of the British Isles.

An aspect of the Late Mesolithic that does mark a departure from patterns established previously is the renewed expansion of settlement into hitherto unoccupied areas. Up until the late ninth millennium cal BC, there is little evidence that settlement had extended beyond latitude 54 degrees North in mainland Britain, and no clear evidence that people had yet reached Ireland. By about 6000 cal BC, most of the British Isles had been brought within the realm of human settlement (Tolan-Smith 1998, 2003a, 2003b). As with the halt to expansion that occurred towards the end of the Late Upper Palaeolithic, both environmental and social considerations need to be taken into account when assessing why expansion was resumed.

The northward migration of the Polar Front to the latitude of Iceland during the ninth millennium cal BC (Housley 1991, Tolan-Smith 1998: 26) produced a significant improvement in the climate of the British Isles. This was further enhanced when eustatic sea level rise led to the establishment of fully maritime conditions during the course of the eighth millennium cal BC. A further concomitant of sea level rise, although not widely remarked on, was an effective reduction in the altitude of upland areas by an equivalent amount with a consequential amelioration of conditions above 300 m. In short, conditions conducive to further expansion developed during the course of the ninth millennium cal BC.

Two early examples of this renewed wave of expansion are the site of Howick in Northumberland on the northeast coast of England and the site of Mount Sandel in northeast Ireland during the early to mid-eighth millennium cal BC. The site of **Howick** is eroding out of a low sandy cliff above the present-day beach, and recent excavations have yielded evidence of a timber-framed structure dated to c. 7,850 cal BC with a number of associated pit features. Some eighteen thousand stone tools made from local beach pebbles of flint were recovered. These include cores and debitage, and a wide range of tool types with typical narrow-bladed pieces, geometric microliths, small scrapers and amorphous retouched pieces (Waddington et al. 2003, Waddington 2007). Preservation of organic materials was very poor a, but the subsistence remains include charred hazelnut shells, a few burnt bones of seal, pig, fox, and canid, and marine shells of limpets and dogwhelks. The wide range of tools and the complex and robust nature of the dwelling structure suggest repeated use as a residential base.

Mount Sandel in the valley of the River Bann (Woodman 1985, Smith 1997: 124–31) is the earliest evidence for the settlement of Ireland. Excavations carried out in the 1970s led to the recovery of over 44,000 flint artefacts, including 1,179 microliths, most of which were typical Late Mesolithic geometric forms but which included a few obliquely blunted points. Finds of scrapers and knapping debris indicate that a range of activities had taken place at the site. Only burnt bones survived the acid soil conditions, but 80 percent of those identified were of fish, mainly salmon, sea trout, and eel, all of which could be caught in the narrows on the River Bann near the site. Of the mammals identified, only pig occurred in significant numbers, probably reflecting the impoverished state of Ireland's early Postglacial fauna. Of particular importance is the recovery at Mount Sandel of the ground plans of a series of 'D-shaped' huts, each about 6 m across with a central hearth and a door on the 'flattened' south side. The plans of six huts were identified but four were rebuildings, suggesting that at any one time a maximum of three were in use, each accommodating a single family and providing an indication of the size of the coresidential group. The biological evidence from the site suggests occupation during the late summer and autumn when supplies were abundant, perhaps enabling groups normally living separately to aggregate. Where they were at other times of the year is unknown, although the contemporaneous site of **Lough Boora** in the Irish Midlands indicates that settlement was widespread (Smith 1997: 128–9, 172). The main activity at Mount Sandel appears to have been fishing the runs of migrating salmon and eel in the narrows close to the site. This could have been with spears but may have involved the use of fixed facilities such as fish weirs.

A similar interpretation has been offered for the site of **Newferry** about 40 km upstream (Woodman 1977). Here, activity took place on seasonally flooded sand and gravel banks within the course of the braided river channel a short distance down stream from where it leaves Lough Beg. The finds are unusual in that they include over forty polished stone axes and several hundred flakes and blades with trimmed butts, the so-called Bann Flakes (Figure 5.9). Microliths were very few and occurred only in the earliest levels. The polished stone axes and 'Bann Flakes' are suggestive of woodworking, and the location of the Newferry site, actually within the channel of the river, makes it likely that the activity represented there was the construction of weirs and fish-traps. Bones of salmon and eel were also recovered, and fishing with fixed facilities continued in the area until the relatively recent past. Newferry exhibits all the signs of being a specialized extraction camp visited by logistically deployed task groups and may be contrasted with Mount Sandel, where there is evidence for a greater range of activities and, by inference, the presence of an entire coresidential group.

Activity at Newferry took place over more than two millennia from the late ninth to the mid-fifth millennium cal BC. As such, this is rather later than the evidence from Mount Sandel and Lough Boora, but this is likely to be a fortuitous accident of recovery as Newferry lies between these sites and it is unlikely that it was settled at a significantly later date. However, the butt-trimmed 'Bann Flakes; found in such numbers at Newferry have a widespread distribution on later Mesolithic sites in Ireland. This return to a more 'macrolithic' industry stands in sharp contrast to most of the rest of the British Isles, where microliths continued to be the diagnostic artefact type until the end of the Mesolithic period.

To get to Ireland in the mid-eighth millennium cal BC involved a sea crossing, and it is reasonable to assume that the passage was made from Southwest Scotland, from which the coast of Ireland is visible on most days. Even though the distance involved is relatively short, these are some of the most hazardous stretches of water around the British Isles and it seems unlikely that the colonisation of Ireland was accomplished by the crew of a dugout canoe fortuitously blown off course. The arrival of humans in Ireland is the first evidence we have of the development of a maritime technology capable of facilitating the exploitation and settlement of the Atlantic coasts of the British Isles. These technological developments did not take place within a social vacuum and it was developments in social organisation that made them possible.

Although the pattern of socioeconomic organisation typical of the Early Mesolithic was very adept at replicating itself across relatively homogenous and isomorphic landscapes of lowland Britain and the upland margins, it had begun to reach its natural limit of expansion in northern and western Britain and on the shores of the Atlantic Ocean. It became necessary to learn about unfamiliar landscapes and to apply that knowledge. Although a form of adaptation in the conventional ecological sense, the acquisition of landscape knowledge and the ability to use it are also social processes and take place within a social arena in which both become socially privileged commodities.

The principal characteristic associated with the communities who colonised the coasts of western Britain during the Late Mesolithic is the use of logistically deployed task groups on a wider scale than noted hitherto. We know from ethnography that the deployment of task groups involves an acceptance of delayed returns; task groups may have to be away from the main residential location for prolonged periods and they need provisioning before they set out. The activities undertaken by these task groups, such as the collection of resources in bulk or movement along the coast, up river valleys and between islands, also require investment in fixed facilities such as fish traps or the construction of boats. Such developments in economic organisation entail a social cost. The deployment of task groups has to be organised and an individual or individuals need to make the investment, the return on which is delayed. These circumstances create opportunities for social differentiation leading to the accumulations of wealth, power, and status that are necessary for the system to operate. Population growth is a concomitant of such developments and such groups typically develop inward looking patterns of kinship that stress endogamy and promote local group growth, often at the expense of alliance formation.

Archaeological evidence for developments of this kind can be both explicit and implicit. Explicit evidence is usually found in cemeteries and occurs in the form of variability in funerary rites, nutritional status, and dietary history. Evidence for elaborate ritual, high nutritional status and specialised diet is often taken as a proxy indication of status differentiation. The Late Mesolithic cemeteries of western France, southern Scandinavia, and the Baltic region provide good examples of this type, and also include not infrequent evidence for interpersonal violence, also considered to be a concomitant of increasing social complexity. Explicit evidence of this kind has not yet been found anywhere within the British Isles and it is necessary to document the process of social development through other kinds of evidence.

Foremost in my view is the evidence for a developed maritime technology implied by the occupation of Ireland, the Isle of Mann and the Hebridean archipelago. Indeed, the entire Late Mesolithic settlement of north western Britain seems to have been a mainly maritime venture (Tolan-Smith 2001: 165–8). As was the case with the settlement of Ireland and the Isle of Mann, the colonisation of Islay, Jura, Colonsay, Oronsay, Mull, Ulva, Rhum, and Skye, and the mooted but as yet unconfirmed Late Mesolithic settlement of the Outer Isles and Orkney (Edwards 1996, Mithen 2000, Saville 1996, Smith 1997: 158–80, Tolan-Smith 2001, Tipping 1996, Wickham-Jones 1997, Wickham-Jones and Firth 2000), entailed significant sea crossings of a kind unlikely to be attempted in a dugout canoe (see also Bjerck this volume for Norway). The recently reported shell midden of West Voe at Sumburgh on the southern tip of the Shetland Islands, some 80 km by sea from the Orkneys, with a date of 4320–4030 cal BC (Melton and Nicholson 2004), further emphasises the maritime skills of populations in this region. This implies the construction and management of sea going craft (Smith 1997: 139–43), and the high status of boat owning and handling is well known among hunter-gatherers in the ethnographic record. In these terms the colonisation of northwestern Britain needs to be seen as a social, as well as a geographical, event.

Further evidence for the emergence of new patterns of socioeconomic organisation comes from evidence for the activities of logistically deployed specialist task groups at a range of special activity locations. Probably the best-known sites in this category are the shell middens that are such a feature of the Late Mesolithic in Northwest Britain and Ireland although, to date, few have been studied in sufficient detail to provide more than an indication of their date.

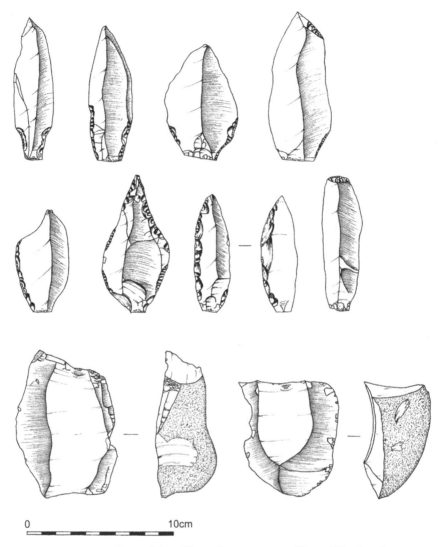

Figure 5.9. Bann flakes (illustration courtesy of Peter Woodman).

The best-known group of Late Mesolithic shells middens is on the small island of **Oronsay** in the Inner Hebrides. Known to archaeologists for over a century, the five middens on Oronsay, which have been dated mainly to the mid-fifth millennium cal BC, were the subject of a detailed study by Paul Mellars in the 1970s (Mellars 1987, Smith 1997: 147–57). The most conspicuous components of the middens are the shells of marine molluscs, mostly limpets in the case of the Oronsay middens, and it appears that one of the specialist activities undertaken on the island was the collection of shellfish along its rocky shore. Less conspicuous but probably of greater economic significance are the remains of a range of marine mammals including grey and common seals, dolphins, porpoises, and a large cetacean, probably a rorqual. The latter species probably represents fortuitous strandings rather than targeted prey whereas the seals were probably systematically hunted (Smith 1997: 150). Indeed, the skerries off the southwest end of the island are known as Eilean nan Ron, or 'seal island', and are the home each autumn to a thousand or more grey seals (Haswell-Smith 2000: 18). However, almost certainly the most important economic activity represented in the Oronsay middens is fishing, particularly for saithe, abundant remains of which were recovered. Detailed studies of seasonal indicators have made it possible to suggest that the various middens on Oronsay were the scene of activity at different times of the year extending from the early summer through to the late autumn. It seems likely that specialist task groups came to the island to hunt seals and fish for saithe. Traces of hearths and timber structures may be an indication that some of the catch was smoke-dried in order to ensure preservation while it was transported to another location, perhaps on the mainland or on the larger nearby islands of Jura or Islay. One group of anomalous finds that is difficult to explain is the small collection of bones of men, women, and children from the middens. These consist mainly of extremities – fingers and toes – and do not represent distinct burials. Perhaps the remains of task group members who died 'on active service' were removed for burial elsewhere but after decomposition had begun. An alternative explanation would be that the island was the theatre for specific funerary rituals, offering an interesting prehistoric parallel for the later Early Christian practice of burial on remote Hebridean islands.

Few other Late Mesolithic middens have been studied in such detail as those on Oronsay although some offer interesting comparisons and contrasts. At **Ferriter's Cove** on the Dingle Peninsula in southern Ireland a group of small middens, dating from the mid- to late-fifth millennium cal BC, are scattered along the foreshore of a sheltered bay (Woodman et al. 2000). Each accumulation may represent no more than a single collecting episode and contrasts with the more intense activity documented at the Oronsay sites. However, although a number of mollusc species are represented in the Ferriter's Cove middens, the parties who periodically visited the locality specifically targeted the common dogwhelk. Shell middens are usually composed of limpets, periwinkles, cockles, mussels, or oysters. Dogwhelks are relatively rare. As carnivores, they occupy a higher tropic level than the common edible species and, although not difficult to find, are relatively less numerous and require additional effort to collect large numbers. This seems good evidence for task specific logistic deployment.

Small shell middens are also a common feature of caves occupied during the Late Mesolithic and later periods in Scotland. Several caves situated around Oban Bay, such as **MacArthur's Cave** and the **Druimvargie Rockshelter**, have been taken to represent, along with the Oronsay sites and a similar midden on the island of **Risga**, a distinct maritime aspect of the Mesolithic in Scotland known as the 'Obanian' (Lacaille 1954: 198–245, Pollard 2000, Smith 1997: 150, 153–7, 178–9). Although these sites were originally thought to be a very late phenomenon, recently obtained radiocarbon dates from the Druimvargie Rockshelter, and from newly discovered 'Obanian' type sites at **Ulva Cave** on the island of Ulva, at the **An Corran Rockshelter** on Skye and the **Sand Rockshelter** at Applecross, have extended this dating back to the later part of the eighth millennium cal BC (Tolan-Smith and Bonsall 1999, Hardy and Wickham-Jones 2002). The 'Obanian' now spans virtually the whole of the Mesolithic period in western Scotland.

The middens at these caves and rockshelters are often very small and probably represent only short-term episodes of collecting. As such there has been a tendency to refer to them as 'dinnertime camps' (Russell et al. 1995: 286). The use of this term derives from work by Meehan (1982) in Australia, who studied the activities of parties of Aboriginal shellfish collectors, usually women, whose normal practice was to sustain themselves while on collecting expeditions by having 'dinnertime' picnics in the vicinity of the shellfish beds.

In some cases, task groups may have targeted a specific species of shellfish, as appears to have been the case at Ferriter's Cove. In other cases, shellfish meat may have been used to sustain the party while engaged in other activities, such as fishing or sealing, as in the example of the Oronsay middens; it may even have been collected as bait (Smart 2000). A further example is provided by the late sixth millennium cal BC midden at **Morton** in Fife on the east coast of Scotland (Coles 1971, 1983, Smith 1997: 143–7). Here, an elongated midden extending for 30 m along the foreshore was dominated by bivalve species, chiefly cockle and Baltic tellin, representing the collection of bivalves from the sandy and muddy shores of the creeks immediately to the south of the site. Fish remains also were well represented, and over 90 percent of those that could be identified were of cod. As cod are difficult to catch from the shore their presence in large numbers implies the use of boats. Nesting sea birds also were harvested. Seasonal indicators led Deith (1983a, 1986, 1989) to suggest that the site was visited throughout the year to obtain raw material for stone working, rather than to target specific food resources at the season of optimum availability. More than thirteen thousand stone artefacts were recovered during excavations that employed a wide variety of raw materials, most of which could be picked up as pebbles on the beaches around the site. During the sixth millennium cal BC, the main focus of interest at Morton seems to have been the acquisition of raw materials suitable for stone tool manufacture. While at Morton, the task groups engaged in this activity sustained themselves from whatever resources were available, which varied from season to season. Boats would have been necessary for the cod fishery but also would have provided a convenient means of transporting quantities of bulky raw materials.

The acquisition of raw materials is another activity likely to have been undertaken by specialist, logistically deployed, task groups, as at Morton. Good quality workable stone is not abundant in northern Britain and learning about the landscape and the resources it offered was one of the features of the renewed phase of expansion that took place during the Late Mesolithic. A particularly clear example of this is provided by the exploitation of a hydrothermal chalcedony known as bloodstone. This material occurs naturally at a single location, Bloodstone Hill on the island of Rhum, yet is found on Mesolithic and later prehistoric sites within a radius of about 70 km (Clarke and Griffiths 1990: 149–65). Excavations undertaken by Caroline Wickham-Jones (1990) on the east side of the island at **Kinloch** have established that the exploitation of bloodstone was underway by the mid-eighth millennium cal BC. From an early stage in the settlement of the region, groups seem to have been making visits to Rhum with the specific aim of acquiring raw materials. However, the finds from Kinloch are not confined to those associated with stone tool manufacture but include a range of types associated with maintenance activities, implying visits to the island of some duration. These visits were, nevertheless, focused on the specific task of acquiring bloodstone.

Conclusion

The dates obtained for the Kinloch site remain the earliest firm evidence for a human presence in Scotland. They are virtually indistinguishable from those obtained for Mount Sandel in Northeast Ireland and imply that once the colonisation of Ireland and Northwest Britain got underway, it was a rapid event (Smith 1997: 158–80). The initial recolonisation of the British Isles after the Last Glacial Maximum was originally accomplished during the Late Upper Palaeolithic, whereas the Early Mesolithic was mainly characterised by the infilling of areas initially occupied during the Late Glacial Interstadial. By the end of the seventh millennium cal BC, virtually the whole of the British Isles had been brought within the realm of human settlement and it is this renewed phase of expansion that characterises the Late Mesolithic. In terms of hunter-gatherer adaptations to mid-latitude temperate environments, the population may have begun to approach the maximum that the region could sustain by this way of life (Smith 1992), and if territorial expansion ceased to be an option population growth could only be accommodated by economic or technological innovation.

In this review of the archaeology of the Mesolithic period in Britain, I have employed a particular model of socioeconomic organisation. It is proposed that the initial settlement of lowland Britain during the Late Upper Palaeolithic and Early Mesolithic periods was accomplished by groups who mainly followed a residential foraging pattern of economic activity designed to produce more-or-less immediate returns. Such groups are particularly well-suited to the colonisation of relatively homogeneous, isomorphic landscapes, having patterns of economic behaviour capable of almost infinite replication until radically different ecological circumstances are encountered. They characteristically have kinship structures that accommodate population growth through exogamy. This in turn leads to the formation of wide ranging alliance networks, a pattern of social organisation that further facilitates noncompetitive territorial expansion through information exchange and social storage.

During the Mesolithic, radically different ecological circumstances were being encountered in the uplands of western and northern Britain and, in particular, on the shores of the Atlantic Ocean. An economic pattern better suited to coping with these new challenges was one in which the logistic deployment of specialist task groups replaced the more generalised pattern of residential foraging that had prevailed hitherto. Much of the evidence for the Mesolithic in northern and western Britain appears to arise from the activities of such specialist task groups.

Hunter-gatherer communities who deploy logistic task groups and accept a delayed return pattern of economic activity commonly have kinship structures that promote endogamy and accommodate population increase through local group growth. Almost by definition, they tend to be inward-looking and hostile to the encroachments of outsiders. The most clear-cut example of these processes at work is to be found on the Pacific Northwest Coast of North America, where the early European explorers and traders encountered a dense population of maritime hunter-gatherers living in large communities with complex social hierarchies who deployed task groups of logistic collectors engaged in a range of delayed return pursuits. Warfare between these communities was endemic and prisoners of war, converted into slaves, were an important economic commodity. As such, warfare was a delayed return strategy and a war party a logistically deployed task group.

The archaeological record of Late Mesolithic Britain offers no evidence of anything on this scale or level of complexity but it does provide evidence, through indications of the logistic deployment of specialist task groups, for the emergence of a delayed return system of economic behaviour that must also have had implications for levels social organisation. It is the emergence of this new pattern of socioeconomic organisation during the Mesolithic that enabled the settlement of the British Isles to be completed.

This process of socioeconomic development documented in the British Isles during the Mesolithic period is a trajectory followed by anatomically modern humans at various times throughout the world and with varying end results. Why the process that can be documented in Britain did not lead to the emergence of societies as complex and developed as those on the Pacific Northwest Coast is a complex and fascinating topic, but it is one that lies mainly outside the scope of the present discussion. In both regions, the process began at a similar time in the millennia following the maximum stage of the Last Glaciation but whereas on the Pacific Northwest Coast it continued unabated until the arrival Europeans in the eighteenth century AD, in Britain and elsewhere in Europe it was overtaken by other developments. A hint as to the nature of these developments is provided by several Late Mesolithic middens in Ireland such as Ferriter's Cove and Dalkey Island, the faunal assemblages from which include representatives of domesticated species, chiefly sheep and cattle. The social development of the hunter-gatherer communities of the British Isles was overtaken by the spread of food production, the ultimate delayed return strategy, and by the social changes concomitant on this new pattern of economic activity. The communities of the British Isles did reach levels of social complexity comparable to those found on the Pacific Northwest Coast, but during the Neolithic rather than the Mesolithic period.

Acknowledgments

The assistance of Robert Hedges and the Oxford Radiocarbon Unit is gratefully acknowledged in the production and discussion of radiocarbon dates. Geoff Bailey compiled Table 5.1 and produced the map in Figure 5.1.

Chapter 6

New Developments in the Study of the Mesolithic of the Low Countries

Leo Verhart*

Introduction

Despite the fact that the Low Countries are small and flat, it is not easy to review recent developments in the study of the Mesolithic, because of the volume and complexity of the archaeological data. The area has a long research tradition, with differing approaches, research intensity, and archaeological potential, making a short and comprehensive summary of the entire Mesolithic an impossibility. Moreover, there are no recent overviews of the entire area, the latest being the three volumes by J. Rozoy (1978). Reviews are almost exclusively limited to specific countries, smaller regional studies and excavation reports of individual sites. Quite clearly the difference in languages, French and Dutch, often constitutes a not inconsiderable barrier. The archaeological material is also not as rich as in other regions of Northwest Europe, offering less scope for the examination of social issues. As a result, the following approach has been adopted. First, an outline of the Mesolithic is provided, based on geography and environment, history of research, archaeological data and dates. Next, I describe developments in more detail in chronological sequence, as illustrated by a number of recent case studies from the Netherlands and Belgium, with the emphasis on settlement system and economy. Finally, I will examine the issue of the Mesolithic-Neolithic transition.

Geography and Environment

The Low Countries consist of the Netherlands and Belgium, both mainly extensions of the Northwest European Plain, as are the neighbouring areas of northern France, Luxembourg and northwest Germany. This geographical unit (Figure 6.1) is bordered in the northwest by the North Sea and is largely characterized by a relatively flat coastal plain gradually rising to a maximum of approximately 700 m above sea level to the southeast. Broadly speaking, it consists of a lowland and an

* National Museum of Antiquities, Leiden, Netherlands.

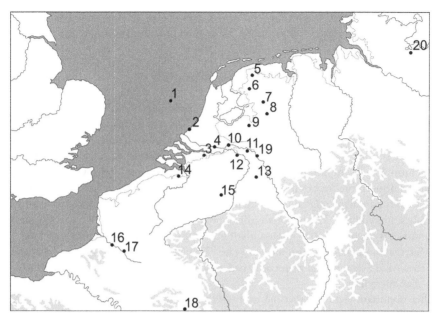

Figure 6.1. Generalised geographical terrain of the Low Countries and the most important Mesolithic sites mentioned in the text. 1: Brown Bank (NL), 2: Europoort (NL), 3: Willemstad (NL), 4: Hardinxveld-Giessendam (NL), 5: Bergumermeer (NL), 6: Jardinga (NL), 7: Pesse (NL), 8: Mariënberg (NL), 9: Zutpen (NL), 10: Den Bosch (NL), 11: Merselo (NL), 12: Geldrop (NL), 13: Posterholt (NL), 14: Verrebroek (B), 15: Wommersom (B), 16: Hangest-sur-Somme (F), 17: Tirancourt (F), 18: Noyen-sur-Seine (F), 19: Bedburg-Königshoven (G), 20: Duvensee (G) (drawn at the National Museum of Antiquities, Leiden, the Netherlands).

upland zone. Within these zones, large contrasts occur. In the west of the Netherlands and part of Belgium, there is a dynamic and complex system of Holocene delta deposits. In the south and east, there are continuous Pleistocene coversands interrupted by peat bogs and fluvial deposits of varying extent. The north of the Netherlands and the northwestern part of Germany are dominated by glacial deposits, with differences in substrate and relief in higher areas. In addition, the flatness of the coversand area and the glacial deposits is relative. The mountains and hills perceived by Belgians and Dutch, particularly in the low-lying areas in the west, are dismissed by many foreigners as insignificant. Nevertheless, these often turn out to be pivotal in the selection of settlement locations.

A second important factor is the post-Pleistocene warming, leading to a rise in sea levels in the period 9200–7000 cal BC (9600–8000 BP) (Coles 1998, Jelgersma 1979, Louwe Kooijmans 1971–72, Verhart 1995). Initially, the Low Countries were not by the sea, but far inland. That situation changed dramatically over a period of two thousand years. Large stretches of low-lying coastal land were inundated, the North Sea basin was filled and by about 5800 cal BC (7000 BP) the coastline was almost at its present location. The rise in sea level also affected the hinterland. Groundwater levels rose, drainage stagnated, and extensive peat bogs came into existence (Casparie and Bosch 1995, Groenendijk 1997). The effects on climate, flora and fauna were equally large. Climate changed from continental to more Atlantic conditions. The open parkland of the early

159

Holocene with its herds of reindeer and horse was replaced by dense forests and more sedentary game: aurochs, elk, red deer, roe deer, brown bear, wild boar, beaver, otter, and marten.

History of Research

Research into the Mesolithic of the Low Countries has a long tradition, particularly in Belgium (De Puydt 1885). As early as the late nineteenth century, caves were being explored and excavations carried out in the Kempen coversands. In the Netherlands, research started later. Until 1965, both countries were strongly influenced by French and Scandinavian examples. This meant that typology and typochronology were important issues (Bohmers and Wouters 1956, G.E.E.M. 1969, 1972, Gob 1985). Furthermore, research was mainly aimed at excavating artefact concentrations, often resulting in only partial investigation of settlements and failure to excavate those areas of a site with more thinly scattered finds. The reason for this approach was mainly practical. The Mesolithic of the Low Countries is characterized by thousands of sites consisting almost exclusively of concentrations of flint. Sites with organic remains are very rare. This 'poverty' forced us to focus on the much richer French and Scandinavian material in order to provide an image of the Mesolithic consisting of more than mere flint.

Another important feature is that the study of the Mesolithic was mainly carried out in a site-related context. The excavation results of an individual site were compared to those of other sites or to examples from abroad.

The arrival of American archaeologists in the Netherlands changed this situation. They brought a more Anglo-Saxon approach that gradually found favour in Belgium as well. Recently, a domestic research tradition has come into existence that blends the strong points of Anglo-Saxon archaeology with our native research tradition. One of its most conspicuous features is the emphasis on investigation of sites within their regional context. Until the late 1960s, site-oriented investigations were prevalent. In Scandinavia, regional Stone Age research goes back a long way (Mathiassen 1943, 1948, 1959), and for other periods in the Netherlands regional investigations were already popular (Waterbolk 1962), but the arrival of Ray Newell and Douglas Price marked a change in attitudes towards the Mesolithic. The key new elements were the theories of the New Archaeology combined with the application of regional research agendas.

Newell started a regional project around the Bergumermeer in Friesland (Huiskes 1988, Newell 1973), but the most extensive study involved the Mesolithic on the Drents Plateau (Price 1975, Price 1980). This approach was not to be continued, because of the intractability of the Dutch material. The Dutch Mesolithic has long suffered the dilemma of a plethora of relatively easy to discover sites that taken together nevertheless provide a heavily distorted picture. This distortion is caused by four factors:

1. In the eastern part of the Netherlands, the Pleistocene deposits are on the surface, whereas in the west they are covered by Holocene deposits. In the east, finds can be collected easily on the surface, leading to overrepresentation in the distribution pattern.
2. Mesolithic people did not dig much, as a result of which all finds occur in the top 30 cm of the soil profile; these are consequently highly susceptible to disturbance, particularly by agricultural activities.
3. Location and intensity of archaeological research determine to a large extent the nature of distribution patterns. Clusters in the distribution pattern are often artefacts of research intensity rather than reflections of habitation intensity.

4. As it turns out the localities visited by Mesolithic people have been favoured over long periods, as a consequence of which it is almost impossible to distinguish between activities over time. This severely hampers research into settlement typology and settlement patterns.

Price was disappointed in his hope that the results of his investigations would lead to firm conclusions, but a few Dutch archaeologists made a fresh start in the middle of the 1980s. In the north of the Netherlands, research was carried out in Groningen (Groenendijk 1997, Niekus and Reinders 2002) and Friesland (Huiskes 1988). In the south of the Netherlands, two projects took shape. Arts and Deeben (Arts 1987, 1989, Arts and Deeben 1981, Deeben 1988) concentrated mainly on the Late Palaeolithic and Mesolithic, while a Leiden group focused on the transition from Mesolithic to Neolithic (Verhart 2000, Wansleeben and Verhart 1990, 1995, 1998). The latter investigation, the Meuse Valley Project, attempted to locate as many sites as possible that had been short-lived and used only once, in order to get a clear picture of the range of hunter-gatherer activities. The results of that investigation in particular will be discussed here. Recently, the river dunes in the west of the Netherlands have once more become objects of investigation. It had long been known that well-preserved Mesolithic traces were hidden beneath thick layers of Holocene deposits, but excavation costs exceeded most research budgets. Recently, however, funds have become available for archaeology as a result of large-scale industrial developments. This has led to interesting new results at Hardinxveld-Giessendam, where two Mesolithic sites deeply buried beneath metres of sediments have been excavated (Louwe Kooijmans 2001a, Louwe Kooijmans 2001b), greatly adding to our knowledge of the Late Mesolithic.

Belgium followed a slightly different path under the impetus of P. M. Vermeersch, who started a long series of excavations in the early seventies in the coversand regions of the Kempen in northern Belgium (Vermeersch 1982, 1984, 1989, 1996). Peter Gendel's pioneering study of social territories (1984, 1987, 1989) also may be considered a sequel to this project. Recently, the emphasis has shifted to western Belgium (Crombé 1998, Crombé, Perdaen, and Sergant 2003).

In the Ardennes, André Gob did much work in the 1970s, notably in the regional investigation of the Ourthe valley (Gob 1981). Later research has become more site-focused, with the main emphasis on investigation of caves (Crombé and Cauwe 2001).

In the neighbouring western part of Germanys there is little current research, at least as reflected in publications. In the 1970s and 1980s, Surendra Arora (1976, 1979, 1981) studied the Mesolithic, with special emphasis on typology and the exchange of raw materials. A dramatic discovery was the Early Mesolithic site of Bedburg-Königshoven (Street 1989, 1991, 1999), where a large amount of organic material was discovered in the bed of the river Erft. Important research has been carried out to the north and to the south. In the north Bokelmann has been investigating the Duvensee region for a number of years. Beautifully preserved short-lived Early Mesolithic encampments have been uncovered there, yielding a wealth of new details about the behaviour of hunter-gatherers (Bokelmann 1971, 1991, Bokelmann et al. 1981, 1985). Recently new research has started in the Baltic coastal regions (Lübke 2005). In southern Germany, Michael Jochim has been active now for a number of years in the Federsee area. This investigation is especially important for its application of anthropological models and the introduction of various innovative research techniques (Jochim 1976, 1993 this volume).

In northern France, various large, developer-funded projects have lent a new impetus to Mesolithic research. Here, too, surface sites lacking organic materials are prevalent. In recent years, this picture has changed thanks to excavations in the valleys of the Seine and Somme and in the path of the TGV railway (Ducrocq 1990, 1999, Ducrocq et al. 1996, Mordant and Mordant

1992, Verjux 2003, Valdeyron this volume). However, large-scale regionally inspired research does not occur here.

Site Potential and Dating

The great majority of Mesolithic sites are open-air sites, thousands of which are located on the coversands and glacial deposits. This is in stark contrast to the areas of Holocene sedimentation and the loess lands, where few sites are known. This is mainly a result of geological processes. In the areas of Holocene deposition, sites have been covered by sediments several metres thick, and are only exposed as the result of accident or intensive investigation. In the loess areas, agricultural activities over the past two thousand years have led to heavy erosion and the consequent disappearance of sites on hills and slopes, whereas sites in valleys have been covered by colluvial deposits sometimes several metres thick. The dense forest growing here in the Atlantic period, offering little attraction for Mesolithic activity, is another – and perhaps more plausible – explanation for the absence of sites in this area. Conditions of preservation on surface sites are also poor. Only stone and flint are preserved, and the organic component has disappeared. An additional factor hampering research into these sites is the phenomenon of multiple habitation. As it turns out, locations of settlement sites have been repeatedly favoured over time, resulting in the creation of palimpsests, and making it virtually impossible to distinguish between all aspects of the various periods of use of a settlement.

Contrasting sharply with these thousands of surface finds are the sites discovered in caves, peat bogs and the Holocene delta. Their numbers are much smaller, but conditions of preservation are often much better. From these locations comes most of our knowledge on food supply and other aspects of Mesolithic society. Some of the finds are out of context, but in recent years research has increasingly focused on the wetlands, as exemplified by the investigations in the Scheldt/Meuse/Rhine Delta (Crombé, Perdaen and Sergant, 2003; Louwe Kooijmans 2001a, 2001b, 2003) and peat bogs like the Duvensee and Federsee. The large-scale investigation of caves mostly occurred in the nineteenth and twentieth centuries. Now research is limited to small-scale observations, often in the lower unexplored parts of caves, and with surprising results. For example, Mesolithic and Neolithic burials have recently come to light (Cauwe 1988, 1995, 1998, Cauwe et al. 1993).

Dating the various phases within the Mesolithic has long been a problem. Although ever more radiocarbon dates have become available, time and again samples from open-air sites prove to be highly unreliable (Crombé, Groenendijk and Van Strydonck 1998, Crombé and Van Strydonck 2004). This has to do with repeated prolonged use of settlement areas and 'natural' charcoal ending up in the soil as a result of bioturbation. This repeatedly raises the question of whether the sample really does belong to what is to be dated and to what extent bioturbation has played a part in the composition of the sample, in other words, what is the share of old and/or recent charcoal.

The development of AMS dating now offers new possibilities. Organic artefacts can now be dated, and this should make it possible in future to acquire a better grip on chronology, in combination with spatial analysis of settlement areas.

A final problem concerns the geographical distribution of the data. Well-dated sites or longer stratigraphic complexes do exist, but usually these are located on the periphery of the Low Countries or even beyond their borders, for example, in Germany in the Duvensee area (Bokelmann 1971, 1995) and the Schwabian Alb (Taute 1972, 1974), and in France the Somme valley (Ducrocq 1990, 1999, Ducrocq et al. 1991, 1996) and northern France (Fagnart 1991).

Because of all these problems it is no wonder that various – often highly refined – typochronological schemes have been developed (Rozoy 1978, Thévenin 1999a). These schemes are often conflicting and moreover often do not correspond with the expected radiocarbon dates. In recent years, new data have been obtained, in particular by Crombé, that allow the distinction of regional groups in the west of Belgium within the Early and Late Mesolithic (Crombé 1998, 2002). Only a small number of sites have been investigated and dated and there remain uncertainties about the functional differences between them, so that it remains to be seen whether this typochronology is valid for a larger area as well. Like Crombé, we have decided here in favour of a simple, quite rough, division into Early, Middle, and Late Mesolithic, linked to the most recent survey of radiocarbon dates (Table 6.1, Lanting and Van der Plicht 2000).

Early Mesolithic c. 8500–7700 cal BC (9200–8700 BP)

The beginning of the Early Mesolithic is traditionally equated with the beginning of the Holocene, with its dramatic climatic changes, when temperatures gradually rose to an average in winter of 0 degrees C and in summer of 17 degrees C. Forests also expanded, comprising at first pine and birch, and later hazel, oak, and elm. Strong regional differences, however, occurred in the development of the vegetation, the result of relief and local topography (Van Leeuwaarden 1972). Animal life greatly changed in this period as well with the disappearance of the large herds of the Late Palaeolithic.

The traditional beginning of the Early Mesolithic as a cultural phenomenon is dated to approximately 8500 cal BC (9200 BP) (Lanting and Van der Plicht 1996, 2000), coinciding with the transition from Late Dryas to Preboreal. However, this is an arbitrary boundary, since many traditions of the Early Mesolithic are rooted in the material culture of the Late Palaeolithic. Moreover, quite a number of Ahrensburgian sites have been dated to the Preboreal (Fischer and Tauber 1986, Lanting and Van der Plicht 1996, Street et al. 1994).

It is therefore no surprise that the Early Mesolithic flint industry closely resembles the Ahrensburgian. In the absence of characteristic artefacts like the tanged point of the Ahrensburgian, or the unilaterally retouched A and B points typical of the Early Mesolithic, it is almost impossible to tell the industries apart. Ahrensburgian points and B-points occur simultaneously, in differing ratios. On the basis of the flint technology, relations with the Federmesser also can be discerned (De Bie and Caspar 2000). There is, however, an increase in microlithization in the Early Mesolithic.

The introduction of projectile points with surface retouch is considered to mark the end of the Early Mesolithic and the start of the Middle Mesolithic, even though this process has been identified at some Early Mesolithic sites (Crombé 1998, 2002).

In a material sense, the strong cultural homogeneity in the Early Mesolithic is remarkable. All over northwest Europe assemblages can be identified that are dominated by unilaterally retouched points and triangles. In addition core axes, scrapers, burins and retouched blades and flakes occur. In the Low Countries, the pattern is similar. A and B points are prevalent on most sites. In addition, microliths are common, and include specimens with two retouched sides and a retouched base, segments and triangles. Yet there are regional differences as well. In the southern part of the Low Countries, south of the Rhine, there are relatively more points with retouched bases and segments than in the north of Europe, for instance in the north German Duvensee group (Bokelmann 1971, Crombé 1998). In this respect, the southern part of the Low Countries is more closely related to southern and central European traditions, at least for certain subphases of the Early Mesolithic. Other notable features are the use of the microburin technique in the production of microliths and the early presence of core axes.

Table 6.1. Recent radiocarbon dates from the Netherlands and Belgium

Location	Object	Lab No.	BP	Cal BC 2σ
Netherlands				
Almere-Hoge Vaart	Hearth pit	UtC-4623	6112 ± 45	5220–4930
Almere-Hoge Vaart	Hearth pit	UtC-5706	6200 ± 60	5310–5000
Almere-Hoge Vaart	Hearth pit	UtC-5707	6208 ± 47	5310–5040
Almere-Hoge Vaart	Hearth pit	UtC-5708	6135 ± 49	5220–4940
Almere-Hoge Vaart	Hearth pit	UtC-5709	7800 ± 60	6820–6470
Almere-Hoge Vaart	Hearth pit	GrN-24982	6370 ± 40	5470–5220
Archem	Bone point	OxA-1942	8330 ± 90	7570–7140
Dalfsen	Hearth 4	GrN-7283	7760 ± 130	7050–6400
Dalfsen	Hearth 7	GrN-7431	8830 ± 45	8210–7750
Europoort	Bone point MS-64	OxA-1944	8060 ± 250	7600–6400
Europoort	Bone point MS-164	OxA-1945	8180 ± 100	7500–6800
Hardinxveld-Polderweg	Human bone (grave 1)	GrA-9804	6820 ± 50	5810–5620
Hardinxveld-Polderweg	Dog (grave 3)	GrA-9807	6650 ± 50	5650–5480
Hardinxveld-Polderweg	Dog (grave 4)	GrA-10920	5880 ± 60	4910–4580
Hardinxveld-Polderweg	Human bone	GrA-11830	6170 ± 70	5310–4940
Jardinga	Aurochs-1	GrA-9640	6180 ± 50	5300–4990
Jardinga	Aurochs-1	GrA-9643	6240 ± 50	5320–5050
Jardinga	Aurochs-1	GrA-9644	6260 ± 50	5340–5050
Jardinga	Aurochs-1	GrA-9650	6210 ± 50	5310–5030
Jardinga	Aurochs-3	GrA-9645	6520 ± 50	5610–5370
Jardinga	Aurochs-2	GrA-9646	6420 ± 50	5480–5310
Jardinga	Red deer	GrA-9649	6410 ± 50	5480–5310
Pesse	Canoe	GrN-486	8270 ± 275	8000–6500
Pesse	Canoe	GrN-6257	8825 ± 100	8250–7600
Merselo-Haag	Hearth	GrN-17406	8225 ± 50	8210–7740
Merselo-Haag	Hearth	GrN-17407	5120 ± 60	4050–3770
Nieuw Schoonebeek	Hearth IVA	GrN-14533	7725 ± 50	6650–6460
Nieuw Schoonebeek	Hearth IVD	GrN-14532	6175 ± 35	5220–5010
Nieuw Schoonebeek	Hearth VB	GrN-14534	6070 ± 40	5210–4840
Nieuwe Pekela	Hearth pit 22884 D	GrN-13750	8230 ± 45	7450–7080
Nieuwe Pekela	Hearth pit 22884 K	GrN-13751	9110 ± 45	8460–8240
Nieuwe Pekela	Hearth pit 22884 E	GrN-15313	8090 ± 30	7180–7030
Nieuwe Pekela	Hearth pit 11	GrN-18821	8090 ± 35	7180–6840
Nieuwe Pekela	Hearth pit 20189 C	GrN-18822	8260 ± 30	7460–7170
Nieuwe Pekela	Hearth pit 20189 D	GrN-18823	8115 ± 25	7180–7050
Nieuwe Pekela	Hearth pit 20189 E	GrN-18824	8185 ± 30	7310–7070
Nieuwe Pekela	Hearth pit 20189 F	GrN-18825	8300 ± 50	7500–7180
Nieuwe Pekela	Hearth pit 20189 I	GrN-18826	8110 ± 50	7310–6840
Nieuwe Pekela	Hearth pit 25189 D	GrN-18827	8135 ± 25	7180–7050
Nieuwe Pekela	Hearth pit 25189 E	GrN-18828	8110 ± 50	7310–6840
Nieuwe Pekela	Hearth pit 25189 S	GrN-18829	8145 ± 25	7290–7050

Location	Object	Lab No.	BP	Cal BC 2σ
Nieuwe Pekela	Hearth pit 26 N	GrN-18830	7920 ± 50	7030–6650
Nieuwe Pekela	Hearth pit 26 O	GrN-18831	8230 ± 25	7250–7140
Nieuwe Pekela	Hearth pit 34	GrN-18832	7955 ± 45	7040–6690
Nieuwe Pekela	Hearth pit 35	GrN-18833	8115 ± 35	7190–7040
Nieuwe Pekela	Hearth pit 36	GrN-18834	8260 ± 50	7480–7130
Nieuwe Pekela	Hearth pit 37	GrN-18835	8320 ± 50	7520–7180
Nieuwe Pekela	Hearth pit 39	GrN-18837	7870 ± 50	7030–6590
Nieuwe Pekela	Hearth pit 40	GrN-18838	8020 ± 50	7080–6750
Nieuwe Pekela	Hearth pit 219	GrN-18839	8490 ± 50	7600–7480
Nieuwe Pekela	Hearth pit 220	GrN-18840	8415 ± 40	7580–7360
Oirschot V	Cremation grave	GrN-14506	7790 ± 130	7050–6400
Posterholt-HVR 164	Hazelnut shell	UtC-4914	8800 ± 60	8250–7650
Posterholt-HVR 164	Hazelnut shell	UtC-4916	9160 ± 80	8600–8240
Posterholt-HVR 164	Hazelnut shell	UtC-4917	9100 ± 50	8460–8230
Posterholt-HVR 164	Hazelnut shell	UtC-4920	9080 ± 50	8440–8220
Waubach	Feature	GrN-6000	8020 ± 95	7300–6600
Waubach	Feature	GrN-6025	8370 ± 50	7550–7310
Willemstad	Wooden statuette	GrN-4922	6400 ± 85	5530–5210
Zutphen	Bone	GrA-12904	9090 ± 120	8650–7900
Zutphen	Bone red deer	GrA-16811	9380 ± 60	8810–8470
Zutphen	Bone red deer	GrA-16813	7510 ± 60	6460–6240
Zutphen	Bone	GrA-16814	8870 ± 60	8240–7780
Zutphen	Bone red deer	GrA-16815	9240 ± 60	8620–8300
Zutphen	Antler red deer	GrA-16817	8880 ± 60	8240–7790
Belgium				
Anseremme-des Autours	Human bone	OxA-4917	9500 ± 75	9200–8600
Freyer-Margaux	Human bone	Lv-1709	9190 ± 100	8700–8240
Freyer-Margaux	Human bone	OxA-3533	9530 ± 120	9250–8550
Freyer-Margaux	Human bone	OxA-3534	9350 ± 120	9150–8250
Freyer-Margaux	Human bone	Gif A-92354	9590 ± 110	9300–8600
Freyer-Margaux	Human bone	Gif A-92355	9530 ± 120	9250–8550
Freyer-Margaux	Human bone	Gif A-92362	9260 ± 120	8800–8250
Loveral, Sarassins	Human bone	Lv-1506	9090 ± 100	8600–7950
Loveral, Sarassins	Human bone	Gif A-94536	9640 ± 100	9300–8750
Malonne-Petit Ri	Human bone	OxA-5838	9090 ± 140	8700–7800

Dates are given as uncalibrated BP (see Lanting and Van der Plicht 2000 for a recent review) and calibrated ranges at 2 sigma as cal BC. Dates have been calibrated using OxCal v3.10 (Bronk Ramsey 1995, 2001).

Less is known about the organic component of the material culture. Tools of bone and antler are known from the submerged North Sea plain (Louwe Kooijmans 1971–72, Verhart 1988, 1995), from riverbeds and peat bogs and from several Belgian caves. There is a wide range of tools: points of bone and antler, axes and axe sleeves. The Pesse canoe from the Netherlands is well known, although some doubt that it is actually a canoe (Beuker and Niekus 1997). Recently for

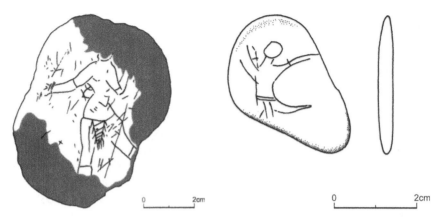

Figure 6.2. Stone engravings from the Netherlands. Left: the so-called 'dancers of Geldrop'. Right: the so called 'dancer of Wanssum' (drawn at the National Museum of Antiquities, Leiden, the Netherlands).

the first time organic remains have been discovered in a stream valley near Zutphen (Groenewoudt et al. 2001). Here bones were found in a Preboreal peat deposit, including brown bear, wild boar, red deer, roe deer, wild cat, and beaver, as well as some tools. In Bedburg-Königshoven in Germany (Street 1989, 1991, 1999) abundant bones of aurochs, red deer, roe deer, and horse, together with some flint, were recovered from river sediments.

Until recently, burials were rare. Individual human bones have been recovered but more recently actual burials have come to light. Occasionally this is an individual burial, but the majority are collective in nature. In the Belgian caves of Margaux at Freyer, Abri des Autours at Anseremme, and Loveral and Petite at Malonne, collective graves have been found, whereas individual burials occur at Anseremme and Dinant in Belgium and at the Abri du Loschbour in Luxembourg, among others (Cauwe 1998, Lanting and Van der Plicht 2000). Incidentally, it is often quite difficult to determine the individual nature of a burial. What appear to be collective graves may rather be palimpsests of individual burials. As yet, no Early Mesolithic burials have been identified from the sandy areas.

Examples of art are also rare in the Low Countries. In most cases these are stone objects with some engraving, sometimes in overlapping patterns, as exemplified by retouchoirs from Remouchamp-Station Leduc in Belgium (Lejeune 1984) and Venray in the Netherlands. Two stones portraying a human figure have been recovered from Geldrop (Bohmers and Wouters 1962) and Wanssum (Verhart and Wansleeben 1990), both in the Netherlands (Figure 6.2). In an entirely different class are the red deer antlers with several perforations in the skull (Figure 6.3), which are considered to have been masks (Street 1989), but because of the poor preservations condition in the Low Countries, such finds are rare.

Early Mesolithic Research: Two Examples

Waaspolders: Belgium

During construction of extensive docks to the west of Antwerp, it became obvious that in the Waaspolders a vast, almost intact Pleistocene terrain lies beneath a clay layer between 0.5 and

Figure 6.3. The red deer antler mask from Bedburg-Königshoven, Germany (Römisch-Germanisch Zentrallmuseum, Mainz, Germany).

4 m thick, where habitation traces from the Late Palaeolithic to the Early Neolithic have been preserved (Crombé 1998, Crombé, Perdaen, and Sergant 1998, 2003, 2008). Flint concentrations from the Early Mesolithic are most numerous. At Verrebroek, a large Early Mesolithic activity area has been discovered and excavated on an eastern spur of a coversand zone. In all, approximately 6,000 m² have been uncovered, but the overall size of the Early Mesolithic activity area is estimated to have been over 3 ha.

In the excavated area, clusters of flint, pits, tree falls and hearths (both surface and deeply dug hearths) can be distinguished (Figure 6.4). The function of the pits is not known. The deep hearths contain charcoal, mainly from pine (*Pinus* sp.), and occasionally some charred hazelnut shells and flint. Some shallow hearths also have been found.

The flint artefacts form discrete clusters that only rarely overlap. In size, these range from tiny structures (>1–2 m²) to very large ones (50–100 m²). Although detailed spatial analysis has not yet been undertaken, some patterns are already clear. The connection between burned flints, charred hazelnut shells, and burnt bone makes it likely that surface hearths did occur as well. There is usually one hearth per cluster, but several hearths are present in the larger clusters. Most flint clusters can probably be interpreted as traces of small living areas. The small size of most of these reinforces their interpretation as single-family dwellings. The differences in tool composition by cluster indicate a wide range of activities. All clusters are characterized by the predominance of points, ranging from 40 percent to 75 percent of the tools.

There are some clusters in which a single tool type is predominant; these are considered to have been special activity areas. The relationship between living areas and these special activity areas is still unclear. Some spots are likely to have been dumps.

The flint used is of inferior quality and appears to have been collected locally. Quartzites from Wommersom and Tienen (approximately 75 km as the crow flies) are present, but only in limited

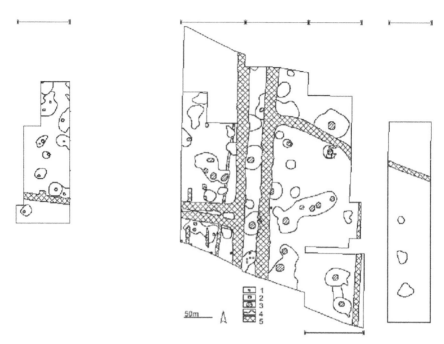

Figure 6.4. Verrebroek 'Dok', Belgium: simplified distribution map of high-density artefact units. Key: 1 Hearth-pit; 2 Bone cluster; 3 Surface-hearth; 4 Artefact locus; 5 Medieval ditch (drawn at the University of Gent).

amounts. Some slabs and 'percuteurs' have been manufactured from micaceous sandstone (so-called psammites) originating from the Condroz area, more than 100 km south of the site.

Typologically, the clusters are quite different in microlithic composition. At present, three groups can be distinguished. The first two groups (the Ourlaine and Verrebroek groups) have an almost equal percentage of A and B points. In the first group many segments occur, whereas in the second triangles are predominant. Both groups appear to have been exactly contemporaneous, in the second half of the Preboreal. The third group (the Chinru group) is characterized by a predominance of asymmetric triangles and points with retouched bases. This group is younger, dating from the first half of the Boreal.

The available radiocarbon dates, mainly from surface hearths and obtained by using charred hazelnut shells, clearly demonstrate that the site has a long history of habitation. The sixty-eight dates range from 8710 and 7570 cal BC (including 2 standard deviations). Three younger dates indicate that the site was occasionally reused during the Late Mesolithic.

Vlootbeek: Netherlands

From 1986 onwards, field investigations have been carried out in the valley of the Vlootbeek, near Posterholt, southeast of Roermond (Verhart 2003). The valley of the Vlootbeek is actually the late glacial stage of the Roer River. Early in the Holocene the river changed its course, thereby preserving almost the entire valley. Field investigations recovered twenty-five Early Mesolithic sites (Figure 6.5). Younger Mesolithic sites are absent. This creates a situation unique for the Netherlands.

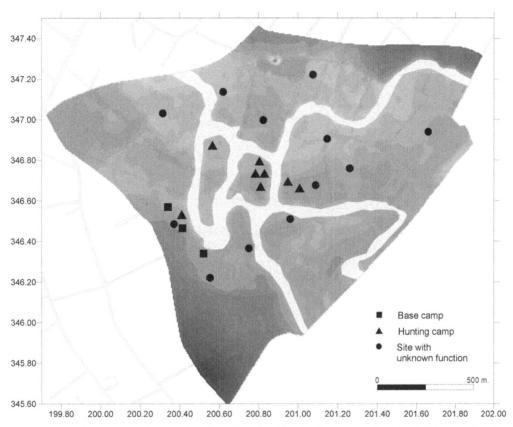

Figure 6.5. The former river valley showing the distribution of Early Mesolithic sites in the modern Vlootbeek valley near Posterholt, the Netherlands (drawn at the National Museum of Antiquities, Leiden, the Netherlands).

Sites, however tiny, are not mixed and provide excellent opportunities for insight into the behaviour of Early Mesolithic hunter-gatherers.

The distribution data from the surface sites soon made it clear that there are relatively small find assemblages with a predominance of projectile points as well as large assemblages yielding a wide range of tools. The location of the sites is distinctive as well. The small sites (hunting camps) are located on old sand and gravel banks in the valley, whereas the larger sites (base camps) are situated on the higher embankments, presumably related to functional differences. To test this hypothesis, two sites have been excavated.

In 1993–1995, a small camp with a total area of 250 m² was investigated. Approximately six thousand pieces of flint were found in undisturbed soil, only fourteen hundred of which are larger than 15 mm. The major part of the finds therefore consists of small flint debris. The spread of finds clearly shows a small cluster with a diameter of approximately 6 m. The finds consist for the most part of debris from flint processing: some hammer stones, cores, blocks, flakes, and blades.

The relationship between tool types is remarkable (Table 6.2). Scrapers, always abundant on Stone Age sites, are almost completely absent, while the percentage of points and micro burins is high at 81 percent. Among the arrowheads the simply retouched projectile points, the A and B points, are predominant. Many points are broken, with base fragments the most numerous. The

169

Table 6.2. Relationship between tool types and settlement types in the Vlootbeck Valley, the Netherlands

	Hunting Camp		Base Camp	
Tool type	n	%	n	%
Points	61	54.0	15	21.7
Microburins	31	27.4	1	1.5
Scrapers	3	2.7	11	15.9
Burins	3	2.7	20	29.0
Retouched blades/flakes	15	13.3	22	31.9
Total	113	100.1	69	100.0

number of scrapers is small, as is the number of flakes and blades with retouch. Despite the presence of charcoal and burned hazelnut shells a hearth could not be identified.

Radiocarbon dates have produced surprising results (Table 6.3). From identical site locations, four charred hazelnut shells and four pieces of charcoal have been dated. The results demonstrate the unreliability of charcoal for site dating. The charcoal turns out to be in part recent and in part old charcoal brought in with river sediments. Only hazelnut shells are reliable indicators of the age of the site.

The distribution of the artefacts suggests a surface on which remains of activities have been preserved intact with little subsequent disturbance. There is a sharp boundary between areas with finds and those without. Outside the cluster there is almost no material, whereas on many other sites clusters appear as concentrations within a larger and more diffuse spread of finds. Differential distribution of different artefact classes also points to the same conclusion. It does not appear likely that there has been a hut or tent in the area, as the artefact distribution does not reflect the presence of such a shelter. It appears more likely that activities took place in the open air.

Although the data have not yet been completely worked out, some conclusions may already be drawn. The overall distribution of finds, the sharpness of the pattern and the artefacts themselves

Table 6.3. Radiocarbon Dates from the Early Mesolithic site of Posterholt, the Netherlands

Excavated Square	Material	Lab. No.	BP	Cal BC (AD) 2σ
59.50/203.00 B1	Charcoal	UtC-4918	237 ± 31	1520–1960 (AD)
56.75/198.50 B2	Charcoal	UtC-4919	$22,570 \pm 150$	20950–20300
61.00/200.75 B1	Charcoal	UtC-4915	$28,020 \pm 220$	26550–25600
61.00/202.75 B2	Charcoal	UtC-4921	$40,100 \pm 800$	40000–36600
61.25/200.00 B2	Hazelnut	UtC-4914	8800 ± 60	8250–7650
56.75/198.50 B2	Hazelnut	UtC-4920	9080 ± 50	8440–8220
59.50/203.00 B1	Hazelnut	UtC-4917	9100 ± 50	8450–8230
61.75/201.00 B1	Hazelnut	UtC-4916	9160 ± 80	8600–8240

Dates are given as uncalibrated BP (see Lanting and Van der Plicht 2000 for a recent review) and calibrated ranges at 2 sigma as cal BC. Dates have been calibrated using OxCal v3.10 (Bronk Ramsey 1995, 2001).

all suggest a single, short-lived use of the area. The site can be interpreted as a hunting camp by the large number of points, the abundance of notches and the small number of scrapers. Various activities appear to have taken place in spatially distinct areas. Most striking is the overlap between points and microburins, indicating the manufacture of points and repair of hunting gear. The small size of the site is a sign that the group staying here must have been small. If ethnographic studies of recent hunter-gatherers are applicable to the Dutch Mesolithic, then the data may indicate a small group composed of men and boys.

From 1996 to 1999, a larger camp was investigated. In an area of 90 m by 70 m, three clusters were found. One of these has been investigated in detail. The area turned out to have been used repeatedly in the Early Mesolithic and various activity zones can be distinguished. For example, an old tree-fall contained many burins and burin spalls, there was a small hunting camp in the western part and in the middle an accumulation of material was found that appears to be the result of overlapping activities. The tool composition is quite different from that of the hunting camp. Points are much less numerous and microburins are almost completely absent. Moreover, tools that can be linked to domestic activities are quite abundant. Within the excavated area, at least five deep hearths have been found.

The valley of the Vlootbeek demonstrates a remarkable pattern of small, short-lived hunting camps on islands in the valley and on the shores. Base camps, however, occur exclusively on the higher embankments. This striking dichotomy can be explained in two ways. The sites could have been used in a yearly cycle, which would require us to demonstrate 'synchronicity'. This appears impossible. Alternatively, the sites represent chronologically distinct stages in the exploitation of the valley, separated by, perhaps, fifty years. This, too, is impossible to substantiate, because of the limitations of the radiocarbon method and our typological framework.

Middle Mesolithic c. 7700–6500 cal BC (8700–7700 BP)

The Middle Mesolithic is a period we know little about. The exact duration is unclear and the number of excavated sites is small. There is an additional problem. If the Middle Mesolithic is considered a stage in a typochronological development, it is remarkable that the points with surface retouch characteristic of this period are already present on older sites. The question is whether these early finds are genuine or whether they represent younger, intrusive material. This question is hard to answer because there are so lamentably few intact Middle Mesolithic sites and not much refitting research has been performed. The beginning of this stage can be dated after 7700 cal BC at the site of Hangest-sur-Somme in France, on the basis of the absence of points with surface retouch and the presence of C points with ventral retouch on the base (Ducrocq 1992).

Because of the small number of sites, little is also known about the settlement system and economy. Geographically and climatically there is little change. The forests became denser and sea levels continued to rise, albeit at a slower rate. The coastal area with its low dunes was being formed and slowly stabilised during this period.

There is a clear dichotomy in this period in the Low Countries. In the south we find points with surface retouch in combination with the more intensive use of Wommersom quartzite. Points with surface retouch suggest links with the Sauveterrian/Tardenoisian tradition. Another notable feature is the use of microblades, in the shape of backed blades. These seem to make their first appearance in this period (Ducrocq 1999, Vermeersch 1984).

To the north, the situation is quite different. Points with surface retouch are absent and Wommersom quartzite barely occurs north and east of the Rhine. The clear break in the south is not visible in the north. There, more continuity appears to exist between Early and Middle Mesolithic. In this stage, older types remain in use, but the percentage of triangles among the microliths increases (Groenendijk 1997). In striking contrast to the south, perforated stones, the so-called Geröllkeule, put in an appearance in this period. Such artefacts are extremely rare south of the Rhine and the Meuse (Hulst and Verlinde 1976).

The small number of investigated sites and the few radiocarbon dates make it almost impossible to create a general impression of this period. The site of Helchteren-Sonisseheide in Belgium is considered to have been a short-lived encampment with a high percentage of microliths (Gendel et al. 1985). This site is also notable for the large percentage of Wommersom quartzite. Microwear analysis demonstrates that some blades were used for processing hides.

The site of Le Petit Marais de la Chaussée-Tirancourt in France is also from this period. Unlike the Belgian and Dutch sites, preservation conditions here are optimal, and flint, bone, pits, and two burials, one a cremation the other an inhumation, have been discovered (Ducrocq et al. 1991, 1996).

A burial is also known from the sandy soils in the south of the Netherlands, in this case a quantity of cremated bone found in a small pit at Oirschot. A small amount of flint was associated with this pit, including points with surface retouch. The cremated bone comprised human material and a single piece of animal bone (Arts and Hoogland 1987). An AMS date of the cremated material has yielded an age of 7400 cal BC.

The Late Mesolithic c. 6500–5250/4400 cal BC (7700–6200/5600 BP)

Climate and terrain are subject to some change in the Late Mesolithic. As sea levels rose, the continental climate gave way to a more strongly maritime climate. In general, temperatures rose somewhat and vegetation cover thickened. The dense forest would have hampered the human search for vegetable foods, and animals would have found foraging in this terrain difficult as well. Some areas became extremely wet. Consequently some previously inhabited areas were now abandoned, for example, Oost-Groningen in the Netherlands (Groenendijk 1997).

The Late Mesolithic is typologically quite homogeneous. Trapezes, both broad and narrow, dominate the points. These first appear to be used in the Mediterranean (Clark 1958, Gronenborn 1997, Thévenin 1999b). In the north, they make their appearance somewhat later: in the Low Countries around 6500 cal BC; further to the north around 6200 cal BC. In the Late Mesolithic, the strong regional differences of the previous period seem to have disappeared, but this is probably misleading. Although the use of trapezes appears to indicate homogeneity, there are striking differences in style, use of raw materials and other types of tools.

Because of the uncertainties surrounding the association between hearths and trapezes in sandy areas, stratified finds in caves are important for pinpointing the first appearance of trapezes. Even in the oldest layers of Jägerhaus-Höhle (Germany), trapeze-like artefacts occur (Taute 1972, 1974). These are blades with oblique truncations on both ends. From the Beuronien D (approx. 6500 cal BC) onwards, trapezes occur regularly. A greater age cannot be ruled out.

A second source of information on the use of trapezes is northern France. The fauna on the site of Thennes-le Grand-Marais I yielded an age of 6400 cal BC (Fagnart 1991). From the Dutch-Belgian coversands, older ages are known, but the association between dating samples and trapezes is problematical, so these older ages should be discounted.

Even further north, in south Scandinavia, the appearance of trapezes is dated around 6200 cal BC. They appear first at Seedorf in Germany (Bokelmann 1999), and in Denmark at Blak 2 (Sørensen

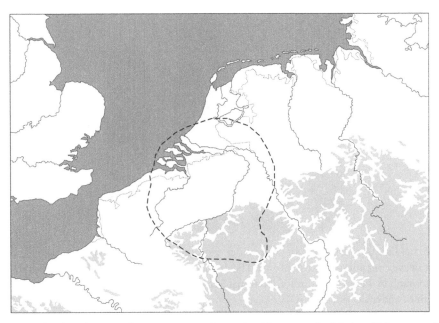

Figure 6.6. The distribution of Wommersom Quartzite (drawn at the National Museum of Antiquities, Leiden, the Netherlands; source: Gendel 1984 with additions).

1996), and Musholm (Fischer 1994). In line with Crombé (1998, 2002) the beginning of the Late Mesolithic may be dated around 6500 cal BC.

Regional differences are also obvious in style and in the use of raw materials. In France south of the Seine trapezes occur with left lateralization, whereas to the north the right hand side is retouched (Figure 6.6, see also Valdeyron this volume). The use of Wommersom quartzite occurs mainly between the Seine and the Meuse, and is almost completely absent north and east of the Rhine (Arora 1979).

Flake axes also come into use in this period, which is particularly well-documented in the north of the Netherlands. The flake axes in the south of the Netherlands and Belgium may be Late Mesolithic, but a large number belong to the younger Michelsberg Culture. The distribution of the Geröllkeule shows a similar pattern as in the preceding period. They are found more frequently, but exclusively north of the Rhine and the Meuse. In the south, they remain rare.

Finds of organic material that can clearly be linked to Late Mesolithic flint were until recently extremely rare in the Low Countries, in contrast with the large number of examples in northern Germany (Harz 1991, Schwabedissen 1981). The majority of the organic artefacts in the Low Countries are stray finds from secondary contexts that can be attributed to the Late Mesolithic on typological grounds or on the basis of radiocarbon dates. In recent years, discoveries in stream and river valleys have yielded more material. In addition, we now know a small number of sites where bone material has been recovered in primary contexts, for instance, Jardinga in the Netherlands (Prummel et al. 1999) and Place Saint Lambert at Liege in Belgium (Van der Sloot et al. 2000, 2003).

A splendid example of such an accidental find occurred at the construction of an artificial lake near 's-Hertogenbosch in the Netherlands. A large number of artefacts made of bone and antler

Figure 6.7. Finds from Den Bosch: bone chisel, perforated and decorated antler sleeve, perforated antler sleeve containing the tusk of a wild boar, and a fragment of red deer antler with decoration (photograph by Peter-Jan Bomhof, National Museum of Antiquities, Leiden, the Netherlands). Length of antler sleeve 215 mm.

came to light. Exceptional finds are an antler axe sleeve with pointillé decoration and an axe sleeve still containing a small axe blade made of a worked wild boar tooth (Figure 6.7).

Really spectacular are the finds of wood, bone and antler discovered during excavations in the wake of large developer-funded projects in the western part of the Netherlands (Louwe Kooijmans 2001a, Louwe Kooijmans 2001b, Louwe Kooijmans 2003). At a depth of c. 9 m below sea level, Late Mesolithic settlements were investigated on two river dunes at Hardinxveld-Giessendam. Most important is Polderweg, with an age of 5500–5300 cal BC. Here remnants of fishing nets and rope, wooden bows, paddles, axe shafts, spears, digging sticks, axe blades of antler, axe sleeves, and adzes were discovered (Louwe Kooijmans 2001a, Louwe Kooijmans 2003). Some of the artefacts are decorated. Nearby is a second, somewhat younger site, De Bruin (5100–4800 cal BC), which has produced a similar range of finds, and also a 5.5-m long canoe made of limewood (Louwe Kooijmans 2001b).

Recent excavations and stray finds make it clear that bone and antler industries, always highlighted as a distinctive feature of the Late Mesolithic of southern Scandinavia, are also present elsewhere. It becomes ever more obvious that the Low Countries had a bone industry of their own, much more influenced by northern France. Two good examples of this are the axe blades made of red deer antler, particularly the nonperforated T-shaped antler axes (Crombé et al. 1999) and antler axe sleeves, often decorated with pointillé. Parallels for these artefacts can be found in the Oise valley (d'Acy 1893, Blanchet and Lambot 1977, Fagnart 1991).

A unique item is the small wooden statuette from Willemstad (Figure 6.8), which was found during the construction of a large system of locks (Van Es and Casparie 1968). This depicts a human face and the bottom appears to have been made into a kind of handle. At present no parallels are known from Europe. The depth at which the statuette was found, 8 m below sea level, the results of pollen analysis and the age of the oak (5300 cal BC) are all in agreement.

The number of burials from the Late Mesolithic is small. So far none are known from caves. In the eastern sandy area near the Dutch Mariënberg, six pits have been found that are considered to

Figure 6.8. Wooden statuette from Willemstad, height: 12.5 cm (photograph by Peter-Jan Bomhof, National Museum of Antiquities, Leiden, the Netherlands).

be inhumation graves (Van Es et al. 1988, Verlinde 1982). In the cylindrical pits, the dead would have been buried in a sitting position. The dead had been showered with ochre and had received arrow shaft polishers and unworked long blades as burial gifts. As a result of the poor preservation condition of the soil, no remains of the bodies themselves have been preserved, only large amounts of red ochre and the stone artefacts (Figure 6.9).

Burials are also known from the recent excavations in the west of the Netherlands at Hardinxveld-Giessendam, where bone is well preserved. There are three graves at the site of Polderweg: an adult woman stretched out on her back, a man buried in a sitting position in a cylindrical pit and an adult whose burial pit has been disturbed (Smits and Louwe Kooijmans 2001a). The dead had not been provided with any burial gifts. In addition three burials of dogs have been uncovered here. At the site of De Bruin, two graves have been discovered, as well as stray skeletal material. These are an adult man in outstretched position and an adult man in a sitting position (Smits and Louwe Kooijmans 2001b). Here, too, the dead had not been provided with any artefacts. Clearly, if graves without gifts are characteristic of the Late Mesolithic, they will not be recognizable in the dry coversands.

At Hardinxveld, it was possible for the first time to gain some insight into the exploitation of the wetlands in the Late Mesolithic. The bone remains and seeds indicate that the sites, being elevated, dry areas in the wetlands, were used in midwinter. Hunting and fishing were the main activities, in particular the capture of pike and trapping. The finds, graves and pits, the latter considered by the excavators to have been dwellings, are indications that these were base camps on the river dunes.

The recent finds in the west of the Netherlands provide a highly detailed picture of life in the Late Mesolithic. The problem, however, is that these data stem from a single site in a highly specific terrain: the wetlands. The question remains whether these data are representative of a larger area.

175

Leo Verhart

Figure 6.9. Cross-section of a grave pit from Mariënberg, the Netherlands. At the bottom a layer of red ochre is visible (photograph: National Service for Archaeological Heritage, Amersfoort, the Netherlands).

Late Mesolithic Research: An Example

The Venray Region

Within the framework of the Meuse Valley Project, an area of c. 150 km² was investigated between 1988 and 1992 around Venray in the Netherlands (Verhart 2000, Wansleeben and Verhart 1990, 1995, 1998). By means of an inventory of amateur collections, systematic field survey and an excavation, the groundwork has been laid for reconstructing the behaviour of Late Mesolithic hunter-gatherers in the sandy regions of the Netherlands, an area where no organic material has been preserved.

Geographically, the area is characterized by three large units: to the east a narrow zone with Late Pleistocene and Holocene Meuse deposits, in the middle the coversands and to the west the peat of the Peel, by now largely dug away. From the Peel, two streams flow to the east and discharge into the Meuse. A palaeogeographic reconstruction of the terrain provides a picture of dense forest vegetation on the coversands, slightly more open vegetation in the eastern Meuse valley and a much more open area to the west: the high peat bogs of the Peel (Figure 6.10).

The distribution of Late Mesolithic sites shows a striking pattern. There is a cluster of sites at the transition between coversands and the Meuse valley in the east. A second cluster is located in the west at the source of the streams, at the exact transition between the Peel peat bogs and the coversand area.

The tool composition of the surface sites dating from the Late Mesolithic is almost identical. At all sites points, scrapers, backed blades, and retouched blades/flakes are present in almost equal

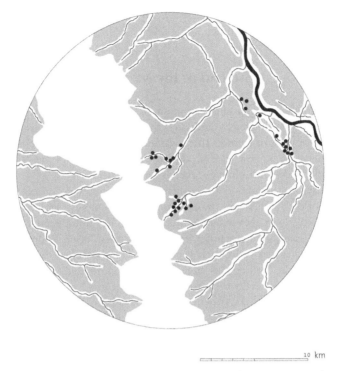

10 km

Figure 6.10. The Venray region: simplified reconstruction of the terrain in the Late Mesolithic with the distribution of Late Mesolithic sites. White: peat and open areas along streams and rivers; grey: forest (drawn at the National Museum of Antiquities, Leiden, the Netherlands).

proportions. Projectile points are often present in somewhat greater numbers. There is no single dominant tool category.

In order to gain insight into the nature of on-site activities, an excavation took place at Merselo-Haag. Within an area with a low find density three clusters could be identified. Two of these are almost identical in artefact composition, with large amounts of small flake material, cores and a limited number of tools, indicators of small areas used for flint processing. The third cluster contained many implements, such as retouched flakes and blades, trapezes, scrapers, and a remarkable amount of backed blades. Analysis of the distribution of different raw material groups and refitting demonstrate that the three clusters are part of a single episode of use, which can be dated in the Late Mesolithic. Traces of earlier activities also have been recovered: in the west a small cluster of Early Mesolithic material and more to the east a stray find of a Middle Mesolithic point with covering retouch (*feuille de gui*). This means that the location has been a favoured settlement area over a long period. The Late Mesolithic site can be interpreted as a small, relatively short-lived base camp, where hunting was the most important activity, beside a wide range of domestic activities.

The similarities in tool composition and size make it likely that the other sites in the region had more or less similar functions. This means that the larger and longer-lived settlements that are generally assumed to have existed in this period (Newell 1973, Price 1975, 1978) are absent in this region. These may be located outside the region, but it is much more likely that many of the larger base camps from the Late Mesolithic are actually accumulations at a single favoured location of various settlement activities over time.

The End of the Mesolithic

The end of the Mesolithic, the transition from an economy dominated by hunting, fishing and gathering to an economy dominated by agrarian activities, is a complicated process. The older view that with the arrival of the first farmers there was an immediate end to the hunter-gatherer way of life has been superseded by new research during the past decade. In this chapter, the emphasis will be on the Netherlands, with some excursions further afield.

Archaeological data for this period are qualitatively divergent and quite far apart in space and time. In the south of the Netherlands, Bandkeramik (LBK) colonists arrived around 5250 cal BC and settled on the fertile loess plateaux along the Meuse. They introduced a sedentary lifestyle in small villages, domesticates, such as emmer, einkorn, legumes, linseed, poppy, cattle, pigs, sheep, and goats, and pottery and new tools, such as grindstones and polished stone adzes.

In the western part of the Netherlands, hunter-gatherers continued to live their traditional lives. Around 4950 cal BC, pottery is for the first time apparent in a younger phase at Hardinxveld-Giessendam (Louwe Kooijmans 2003), which might have been inspired by Late LBK examples. In this phase some sherds of Blicquy pottery, from southern Belgium/northern France, have been found as well. Another indication for more frequent contacts with the south is the use of imported long blades of Rijckholt flint. At a later stage, around 4650–4400 cal BC, the first domesticates appear. These are bones of cattle, pig, goat, and sheep. Except for the pig bones, these are all limb bones, indicating that meat was brought to the site. It is not clear whether these bones mean that the people at Hardinxveld-Giessendam raised their own cattle on the higher sands some distance to the south or whether this represents an exchange with cattle breeders. Grain appears much later and has been dated in the west to as late as around 4200 cal BC (Louwe Kooijmans 1993a, 1993b, 2003, Raemaekers 1999).

What happened in the Belgian area in the west has long been a mystery. Early Neolithic finds were known from Melsele (Flanders) but these were few in number and, moreover, from a site with a strong mixture of older Mesolithic material and younger Late Neolithic artefacts (Van Roeyen et al. 1991). Recently however Swifterbant pottery has been discovered near Antwerpen as well (Crombé et al. 2000), so a development somewhat comparable to the west of the Netherlands may be assumed.

What happened, meanwhile, between the loess region and the coastal area? In other words, how did the transition from hunter-gatherers to farmers occur? Evidence for traditional explanations for the transition from Mesolithic to Neolithic, such as economic superiority, violence, worsening climate and population growth, is absent or cannot be demonstrated. An ethnographic comparison between modern hunter-gatherers and prehistory is not very feasible. In order to gain insight into the processes involved in this transition, it was decided to study socially and economically highly divergent societies that come into contact (Verhart 2000). This makes it apparent that in contacts between farmers and hunter-gatherers two stages can be distinguished.

In the first stage, contacts strongly influence the social subsystem but do not as yet lead to structural changes. In this stage, there is an exchange of, among other things, artefacts, food, and raw materials and services are provided that play a part in a competitive social system. These do not yet lead to structural economic changes.

Then a second stage of contact occurs, where as it were the 'decision' has been made to continue the relationship. At this stage, it is also possible for hunter-gatherers to make a different decision, distance themselves from the newcomers and avoid all contact.

The differences in distribution patterns of various Early Neolithic artefacts point to a heightening of contacts and indicate the growing importance of these implements in the prestige system. This process can be observed at two geographical scales. The first is the northwest European zone of contact between LBK and Mesolithic hunter-gatherers. When comparing the distribution maps of LBK and Rössen artefacts it is apparent that objects of low value (pottery and sherds) have a limited distribution, exclusively in the immediate contact zone. The more valuable adzes and Breitkeile are spread over a much wider area. In the LBK phase, this is still limited to a thin scatter, but in the Rössen phase a strong clustering and expansion can be discerned (Merkel 1999, Verhart 2000). The explanation that these items would have been left by LBK or Rössen farmers is not very plausible; exchange is more likely (Verhart 2009).

The second scale is the southern Netherlands. From the data of the Meuse Valley Project and other investigations, mainly excavations, it may be inferred that the presence of LBK settlers and their successors of the Rössen Culture, had hardly any economic effects on the local population (Louwe Kooijmans 1993a, 1993b, Verhart 2000, Wansleeben and Verhart 1990, 1995). There is no continuity of habitation between the LBK and the Rössen, which occupy different regions (Figure 6.11), although there is continuity just over the border at the Aldenhovener Platte in Germany (Lüning 1982a, 1982b, Stehli 1989). The general impression is that the transition to a farming way of life in the southern Netherlands did not occur until the Michelsberg phase, which succeeded the Rössen, and even then the farming economy has strong Mesolithic overtones.

The archaeological evidence for the second stage of contact is based mainly on data from excavations in the west and middle of the Netherlands. In this phase, economic transformations become apparent as demonstrated by the use of pottery, domestic crops and animals in combination with hunting, gathering and fishing. The Mesolithic characteristics still visible in certain parts of the material culture, the settlement pattern and the various types of settlement, lead to the conclusion that these are local groups of Mesolithic origin who have adopted agricultural elements of increasing importance in the economy.

Similar well-documented data are not available for the coversands in the south, where organic remains are not preserved. It is possible, with some effort, to demonstrate Mesolithic origins in the flint industry. The few data on settlement pattern and settlement types suggest a way of exploiting the terrain that is still strongly Mesolithic in character, in combination with farming and husbandry. Indications for this are provided by the settlement pattern in the core region of Venray (Wansleeben and Verhart 1995). During the middle Neolithic, a pattern is discernible here that is still highly similar to the preceding Late Mesolithic pattern, but the increase in agricultural components in the economy may clearly be deduced from the choice of location. During the Neolithic, a shift occurs towards locations best suited for agriculture and increasingly less oriented towards hunting, gathering and fishing. By the end of the Neolithic, these last components no longer appear to play any significant part.

Final Remarks

Within the Low Countries, a wide range of research has taken place. This range, with its variable intensity and depth, make it hard to provide a clear review. This will have been obvious from

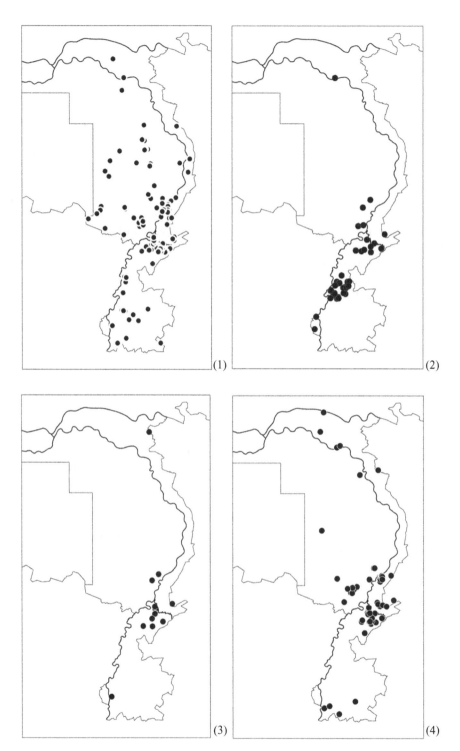

Figure 6.11. Distribution pattern of (1) Late Mesolithic, (2) Linear Band Ceramic (Linearband-keramik), (3) Rössen, and (4) Michelsberg sites in the Dutch Meuse valley (drawn at the National Museum of Antiquities, Leiden, the Netherlands).

this chapter, but I would like to make some final remarks. This is a region with a distinctive development, which should be studied in its own context. The strong reliance on the Mesolithic in the south of France as well as that in the south of Scandinavia should diminish, as more detailed local data become available. This is exemplified by research on the settlement system. A Danish (Ertebølle) model is still being used that assumes an increasing specialization in the exploitation of food resources, a more sedentary way of life, larger settlements and increasing complexity at the end of the Mesolithic (Fischer 2002, Price 1985, Rowley-Conwy 1983, Zvelebil 1986c, 1998). Research in the southern Netherlands appears to point to the exact opposite: more specialization in the Early Mesolithic, and smaller settlements in the Late Mesolithic that also appear to have been used for shorter periods. Investigation of the river dunes in the western Netherlands indicates strong relations with southern regions, like the north of France (Louwe Kooijmans 2001a, 2001b, 2003).

It would therefore be worthwhile if research were concentrated in the Low Countries themselves, in which the study of small regions should be the first priority. These could be integrated later. More attention should be paid to the investigation of sites with a high potential. These should be short-lived sites that have been used only once, and sites where organic material has been preserved. It is obvious that this will be very expensive, but this difficulty appears to have lost some of its importance with the adoption of the Valetta treaty.

Another important factor for the future is international cooperation. Many of the (spatial) patterns we think we have identified in our archaeological material might well stem from contemporary cultural barriers. More cooperation between archaeologists involved in the Mesolithic in the Low Countries and neighbouring areas might put a different perspective on these patterns and in time render them obsolete.

Acknowledgments

I would like to acknowledge the various kinds of assistance I have received in writing this article from the following people (in alphabetical order): Nico Arts, Phillipe Crombé, Jos Deeben, Henny Groenendijk, Bert Groenewoudt, Jan Lanting, Leendert Louwe Kooijmans, Martin Street, Ad Verlinde, and Milco Wansleeben. Hetty Otten-Vogelaar provided the translation.

Chapter 7

The Mesolithic in France

Nicolas Valdeyron*

Historical Framework

The Mesolithic period traditionally lacks a sense of identity. It can easily appear insignificant compared to the Palaeolithic with the arrival of anatomically modern humans in Europe and the flourishing of art, or the Neolithic with the first farming societies and the construction of monuments. In France, the problem is made worse by the unspectacular nature of Mesolithic artefacts. It took some time for the Mesolithic even to be recognised and even then it was seen as a period of regression. Although the Mesolithic *is* now seen as a period in its own right, ideas have moved forward only gradually as new research has slowly changed perspectives.

In the mid-1800s noone considered that a period might even exist between the Palaeolithic and the Neolithic. The 'Mesolithic', as we know it today, was absent from Lubbock's model of 1865 (Lubbock 1865). Neither was there any mention of the period at the Paris World Fair in 1867. In fact, a rather symbolic empty corridor separated the Palaeolithic and Neolithic rooms. Research into prehistory was in fact only in its very early stages. It was only ten years later that the first Mesolithic arrowheads, termed 'pygmies' because of their small size, were identified (Rozoy 1978).

A few years later, it became clear that some time had elapsed between the Palaeolithic and the Neolithic. However Cartailhac's 'hiatus theory' was the most popular explanation for what had happened between the two periods. Cartailhac (1870) proposed that Europe was depopulated at the end of the last glaciation. He supposed that the famous Magdalenian hunters would have moved north following the last reindeer herds and it was not until the arrival of the Neolithic that the abandoned territories were once more populated.

Doubts began to arise about the hiatus theory in 1874, first voiced by de Mortillet (1874). By 1887 it was seriously undermined by new evidence for occupation during the supposed 'hiatus'. Piette

---

* Département Histoire de l'art et archéologie, Université Toulouse-Le Mirail, France.

led excavations at Mas D'Azil and identified the Azilian (Piette 1889, Piette 1895). The Azilian is now recognised as an Epipaleolithic industry but certainly at the time provided irrefutable evidence for occupation between the Palaeolithic and the Neolithic levels. Further evidence came from G de Mortillet's work at La Tourasse (Saint-Martory, Haute-Garonne), which also testified to human presence at the time (de Mortillet 1894).

Problems with dating deposits meant that there was still a perceived gap between what might be termed Epipalaeolithic and Neolithic industries. In 1885, the recognition of the Tardenoisian by de Mortillet based on deposits excavated by Taté in the Sablonnière of Coincy in the Paris Basin might have closed the issue (de Mortillet 1885). However, although the Tardenoisian covers much of the Mesolithic sequence in the Paris Basin, it was still widely regarded as more of a pre-Neolithic industry. To complicate matters, the term 'Tardenoisian' took on a rather general nature and began to mean pre-Neolithic assemblages with trapezes, therefore including assemblages from the South of France, Belgium, Spain, North Africa, and even India. Further Mesolithic deposits continued to be identified in the rest of France, but they were typically so mixed that their chronological position as part of the Mesolithic was not clear.

It was not until the 1930s that Mesolithic studies took off in France, rather later than in other countries. This timing related to interest in new excavations and new interpretations. The first decisive contribution was made by Saint-Just Péquart, with the excavation of the cemeteries of the Breton islets of Téviec (Péquart and Péquart 1929) and Hoëdic (Péquart and Péquart 1934). These cemeteries provided clear evidence for elaborate social organization, rich material culture and a previously unsuspected complex symbolic and ideological universe in the Mesolithic. Other evidence from stratified deposits provided a clear idea of cultural sequences. The excavation by L. Coulonges of the Sauveterre-la-Lémance deposits in the Lot-et-Garonne (the shelters of Le Martinet and Le Roc Allan), that of Cuzoul de Gramat (Lot) by R. Lacam and A. Niederlender (1941) also marked an essential turning point (Coulonges 1928, 1935, Lacan et al. 1944). Coulonges identified an ancient phase, characterised by the presence of microlithic triangular arrowheads and attributed to a culture that he named Sauveterrian from the Sauveterre deposits (which Niederlender and Lacam confirmed with the Cuzoul excavation), and a more recent phase, marked by the development of trapezes, which he included under the Tardenoisian label.

Further research and excavations continued to be carried out in the Mesolithic. The period between 1945 and 1970 was marked by the exploration of the large deposits in the Paris basin – Chaville, Rochers d'Auffargis, the Sablonnière of Coincy (Rozoy 1978), and in the south of France – Rouffignac in the Dordogne, Montclus in the Gard and Châteauneuf in the Bouches-du-Rhône (Barrière 1973, 1974, Escalon de Fonton, 1976a, 1976b). However, public and academic perceptions of the period continued to be poor. In fact, the dominant theory saw the Mesolithic as a time of regression – a kind of Prehistoric Dark Ages. Mesolithic populations were described as degenerate savages, scouring the coastlines for shellfish and barely managing to survive on the scarce resources available (Rozoy 1978). Mesolithic technology, economy, and social structure were viewed as backward. The arrival of the Neolithic was in turn seen as a time when dynamic colonists pushed back impoverished and unstructured Mesolithic communities.

It was not until the 1960s that the importance of the period was recognised. The revision of ideas was brought about largely through the work of one man – J. G. Rozoy. Rozoy began his research in the 1960s, culminating in the publication of *Les Derniers Chasseurs* in 1978. The volume was a monumental work and marked an important change in perspective. Microliths, the distinctive and apparently uninspiring technology of the period, were now instead seen as a mark of the flexibility and innovation of Mesolithic groups. Rozoy demonstrated that microliths were used as projectiles, the points and barbs of arrows used with a bow. The use of bows thus marked an important technological development. Earlier ideas about scarce resources also were revised and the economy was now seen as dominated by plentiful food resources from game animals, although Rozoy failed to recognise that plant foods also might have been important. Rozoy also made a detailed study of Mesolithic lithic industries, which was the basis for his substantial reevaluations. Rozoy based his analysis on the classic methods of Bordes and the 'type fossil' approach, and proposed the existence of coherent cultural groups stretching over territories a few tens to a few thousands of square kilometres, which he supposed were geographically stable and conservative. Ironically, although Rozoy revised ideas about the period and set the Mesolithic within its place as an important stage in prehistory, he did not use the term Mesolithic, but instead preferred 'Epipalaeolithic', seeing Mesolithic populations as following a strict Palaeolithic tradition.

Rozoy's publication made a significant impact on French Mesolithic research. However, his cultural models generated strong criticism. Alternative models based partly on new research and partly on changing approaches were developed. The earliest models were the most radical. In 1985, Roussot-Larroque (1985) proposed the theory of the 'Roucadourian cycle'. This model suggested that a major change had taken place during the Mesolithic sequence with later arrowheads being substantially influenced by the beginning of the Neolithic, to the point where the Mesolithic once again lost its identity, becoming according to some authors a kind of 'pre-Neolithic' phase (Philibert 1988). This theory has lost support through recent work; however, a more significant and detailed criticism of Rozoy's cultural groups comes from recent excavations. Barbaza (Barbaza et al. 1991) working with the deposit of Fontfaurès in the Lot amongst others, has demonstrated a complex picture of technological variation and change in the south, which runs contrary to Rozoy's model. Although some divisions proposed by Rozoy are still recognised, important parts of Rozoy's model have now been refuted (Valdeyron 1994, Marchand 1999, Ducrocq 2001).

Palaeoenvironmental Framework

The Postglacial (beginning at about 9700 cal BC) saw the first appearance of Mesolithic societies in Europe. The Postglacial immediately followed the Tardiglacial, the last cold phase at the end of the Ice Age. This cold phase witnessed marked fluctuations in climate, the gradual decline of the extensive Palaeolithic steppes and steppe communities of gregarious herd animals, and the onset of a temperate climate similar to that of the present.

The Postglacial period is traditionally divided into a series of phases based on pollen sequences. These phases show the gradual spread of woodland and associated plant and animal species into Europe with the stabilisation of warmer and wetter environments. The precise nature of woodland change varied in different regions, as between the Atlantic and Mediterranean coasts, for example, and in different topographic conditions, as between the foot of the Pyrenees or the heart of the Massif Central, although there is a broadly similar pattern throughout the country.

A brief summary illustrates these major environmental transformations. The first phase, the *Preboreal* period (between 9700 and 8000 cal BC) was still cold, although wetter than previous periods. A sparse forest of birch and juniper, joined later by hazel and oak, began to develop. Rising temperatures and rainfall towards 8000 cal BC mark the beginning of the *Boreal* during which pine and hazel became the dominant tree species in an increasingly dense and widespread forest. Towards 6900 cal BC at the beginning of the *Atlantic* phase, temperatures and rainfall reached a maximum – the 'Climatic Optimum'. During this phase temperate forests dominated by oak developed and reached their maximum extent (Magny 1995).

The palaeoenvironmental context and how this changed through the Mesolithic is a key to understanding the period. Mesolithic populations adapted to entirely different environments from those typical of the Palaeolithic. These major transformations undoubtedly influenced many individual and collective behaviours as well as ways of looking at the world.

Chronology and Culture

Most authorities agree on a division of France into two large cultural provinces, one in the South and one in the North (Valdeyron 1994). A series of distinct facies can be identified within these provinces. Nonetheless, although Rozoy made very rigid divisions between lithic traditions on a small scale, it is clear that in reality the components and limits of these facies are fluid and subject to change through time. Locations of sites are show in Figure 7.1, and a selection of radiocarbon dates in Table 7.1.

Throughout both 'provinces', there are several apparent chronological phases, which are common to the whole country. Three or four phases can be identified, based on lithic typology, particularly microlith types. The only major variations between regions are seen at the beginning of the Neolithic, when sequences are affected by variations in the timing of arrival of the Neolithic, its rate of spread and its relationship to indigenous Mesolithic groups.

General Features

The early and middle phases of the Mesolithic (tenth–eighth millennia cal BC) belong to the Preboreal and Boreal periods. They are marked by a distinctive change in stone tool production compared to the Palaeolithic. Whereas Palaeolithic industries are based on blades made by rigorously controlled systematic techniques of knapping, those of the early Mesolithic have different characteristics, particularly a dominance of bladelet production using a rather opportunistic knapping strategy and differences in the types and frequencies of retouched tools – most particularly the dominance of geometrical microliths, triangles, segments, and/or varieties of backed points. These differences are reflected not only in the final form of stone tools but also in changes of production techniques, including selection of nodules and general and specific knapping techniques.

In terms of raw material selection, nodules were typically chosen for the production of bladelets. In fact it is only in rare cases where abundant availability of raw material favoured blade production that blades were produced in any quantity. One such case is at Rouffignac (Dordogne), where the source of flint was large flint nodules found within the rockshelter (Barrière 1973, Barrière 1974).

Knapping techniques were also simple or opportunistic. Cores were normally unipolar with evidence for multiple platforms being largely a result of reorientation of the core. Platforms were in fact rarely produced in a systematic manner, with new platforms judiciously selected rather than deliberately prepared. Bladelets were typically created using soft hammers made of bone, wood or even soft stone. The small bladelets produced by these techniques were primarily used for making microliths, particularly geometric microliths, although other diagnostic tools were also made. They were frequently obtained using the 'microlithic' technique, which leaves a diagnostic blank called a microburin. In other cases, bladelets were simply made from breaking bladelets in two locations or by simply retouching a bladelet to produce the desired form.

A great diversity of microlithic forms typifies the French Mesolithic (Valdeyron et al. 2009). Isosceles triangles are the most frequent geometric form in the earliest phase. However, these disappear almost completely in the middle phase, giving place to thinner and increasingly scalene forms

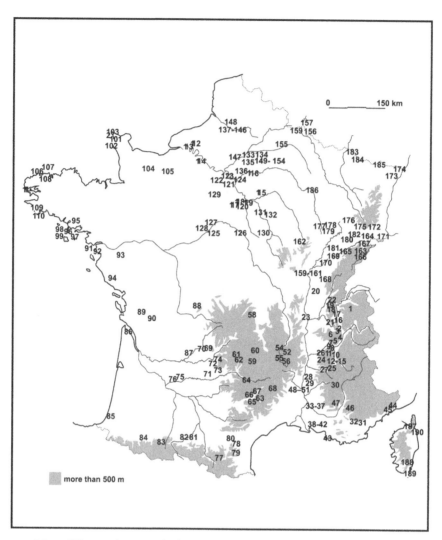

Figure 7.1. Map of France showing the location of selected Mesolithic sites. Only those sites are shown which are listed in Table 7.1 or mentioned in the text. The site names corresponding to the numbers are in Table 7.1. Additional sites not listed in Table 7.1 are: 12: Pas de l'Aiguuille; 13: La Grange; 59: Ventecul; 72: Le Cuzoul de Gramat; 74: Les Fieux; 89: La Vergne; 90: Pierre-St.-Louis; 93: Les Etangs de la Brenière; 95: Kerhillio; 97: Hoédic; 98: Téviec; 100: Kerjouanno; 109: Kervouyen; 115: Noyen-sur-Seine; 121: Sonchamp III; 122: Rochers d'Affargis; 124: Chaville; 156: Allée Tortue.

with a more acute point. Aside from geometric microliths, there are points without retouched bases such as Sauveterre points and linear backed points, or those with retouched bases such as Tardenois points and Rouffignac points, as well as narrow backed bladelets. The classic tools of the typical industries, such as scrapers, burins, and borers, are less common in relation to the microliths, although there is no strict rule and percentages vary according to site function. Classic tools are nonetheless rare or represented by rather atypical pieces, particularly burins, which are much less

Table 7.1. Selected radiocarbon dates from Mesolithic sites in France

No.	Site Name	Commune	Type	Lab. No.	BP	Cal BC 2σ
1	Grotte de la Vielle Eglise	La Balme-de-Thuy	C	Ly-1936	8170 ± 160	7350–7040
2	Jean-Pierre I	St. Thibaud-de-Couz	C	Ly-428	9050 ± 260	9200–7500
3	La Fu	St. Christophe	C	Ly-2913	8580 ± 20	7605–7575
4	Aulp-du-Seuil	St. Bernard-du-Touvet	C O	Ly-7093	8160 ± 70	7500–7000
4	Aulp-du-Seuil			Ly-692	8740 ± 60	8200–7550
7	Grande-Rivoire	Sassenage	C	Ly-5433	8278 ± 680	9200–5800
9	Abri de L'Echelle	Rovon	C	Ly-7095	8050 ± 95	7350–6650
9	Abri de L'Echelle			Ly-7094	6940 ± 70	5990–5700
10	Coufin 1 et2	Choranche	C	Ly-2106	8200 ± 140	7550–6750
10	Coufin 1 et2			Ly-3648	7810 ± 140	7100–6400
11	Abri Pas-de-la-Charmate	Châtelus	C	Ly-4204	8240 ± 260	7460–7070
11	Abri Pas-de-la-Charmate			Ly-3786	7820 ± 120	7050–6450
14	Grotte-du-Campagnol	Gresse-en-Vercors	C	Ly-2814	9010 ± 200	8700–7600
14	Grotte-du-Campagnol			Ly-3649	8980 ± 220	8700–7500
16	Abris de Thoys	Arbignieu	C	Ly-270	9350 ± 300	9500–7700
17	Abri de Sous-Balme	Culoz	C	Ly-286	9150 ± 160	8800–7800
17	Abri de Sous-Balme			Ly-289	7360 ± 1080	9500–3500
17	Abri de Sous-Balme	Culoz	C B	Ly-1668	8640 ± 380	8700–6600
20	Les Charmes	Sermoyer	O	Ly-863	8490 ± 170	8000–7000
21	La Côte-de-Mopard	St Benoit	C	Ly-4789	7240 ± 125	6480–6020
32	Baume de Fontbrégoua	Salernes	C	Gif-2992	8400 ± 110	7600–7050
32	Baume de Fontbrégoua			Gif-2991	7600 ± 100	6640–6240
33	Les Mians	Gordes	C	Ly-2200	8620 ± 380	8700–6600
34	Gramari	Méthamis	C	KN-386	8730 ± 55	7960–7600
34	Gramari			Gif-752	7740 ± 190	6830–6420
38	Cornille	Istres	C B	Ly-413	8100 ± 130	7500–6650
39	La Font des Pigeons	Châteauneuf-lès-Martigues	C	Ly-438	7830 ± 170	7200–6350
39	La Font des Pigeons			KN-182	7520 ± 240	7100–5900
39	La Font des Pigeons			Ly-2830	7260 ± 120	6400–5900
39	La Font des Pigeons			Ly-2833	7630 ± 150	7050–6100
40	Mourre Poussiou	Fos-sur-Mer	C	Ly-706	8980 ± 200	8700–7500
42	Cap Ragnon	Lle Rove	C	MC-500	7650 ± 150	7050–6200
43	L'Ile Riou	Marseille	C	MC-441	7400 ± 100	6440–6060
44	Pendimoun	Castellar	C	Ly-5338	8920 ± 220	8700–7500
45	Caucade	Nice	C	MC-2343	7590 ± 160	7350–6450

(continued)

Table 7.1. (*continued*)

No.	Site Name	Commune	Type	Lab. No.	BP	Cal BC 2σ
46	Ravin de Mouresse-Molines	Puimoisson	C	Gif-8930	7760 ± 80	6820–6440
47	St Mitre	Reillane	C	MC-266	7950 ± 150	7300–6450
48	Baume de Montclus	Montclus	C B	KN-58	8130 ± 240	7600–6500
48	Baume de Montclus			Ly-542	7540 ± 160	6700–6000
49	Baume de Ronze		C	Ly-2178	8480 ± 190	8200–7000
50	La Pécoulette	Orgnac	C	Ly-2364	8450 ± 350	8400–6500
51	La Vessignée	Ste Remèze	C	Ly-4460	7820 ± 180	7200–6250
52	Longetrave	St. Marcel-d'Ardèche	C	Ly-410	8420 ± 280	8300–6700
52	Longetrave	Freycenet-la-Cuche		Ly-617	7320 ± 140	6500–5900
55	Abri de Baume/Loire	Solignac-sur-Loire	C	Ly-539	7100 ± 180	6400–5600
58	Pontcharaud	Clermont-Ferrand	O	Ly-7625	7095 ± 50	6070–5880
61	Les Baraguettes 1	Velzic	C	Beta-108631	8700 ± 50	7940–7590
61	Les Baraguettes 4	Velzic	C	Gif-10005	8750 ± 80	8200–7550
61	Les Baraguettes 4			Ly-7004	9040 ± 80	8460–7960
62	Lavernière I	Velzic	C	Ly-399	9360 ± 65	8810–8430
63	Abri des Usclades	Nant	C	Gif-8744	8220 ± 70	7460–7060
63	Abri des Usclades			Gif-8745	7290 ± 60	6340–6020
64	Roquemissou	Montrozier	C	Ly-4100	7040 ± 200	6400–5550
67	Les Salzets	Mostuejouls	C	Gif-443	8770 ± 200	8500–7300
69	Chez Jugie	Cosnac	C	Ly-1331	8040 ± 260	7600–6400
70	La Doue	St. Cernin-de-Larche	C	Ly-2233	8750 ± 150	8250–7550
71	Fontfaurès	Lentillac-Lauzès	C	Ly-4448	9140 ± 160	8800–7800
73	Grotte du Sanglier	Reilhac	C	Ly-5687	7753 ± 235	7300–6000
73	Grotte du Sanglier			OxA-4551	6915 ± 70	5930–5660
75	Roc Allan et Martinet	Sauveterre-la-Lemance	C	Ly-4545	8160 ± 90	7500–6800
75	Roc Allan et Martinet			4931	7626 ± 79	6650–6270
77	Abri du Roc de Dourgne	Fontanès-de-Sault	C	MC-1108	8620 ± 100	8000–7450
80	Gazel	Sallèles-Cabardes	C	Grn-6704	7880 ± 75	7040–6590
81	Buholoup	Montberaud	C	Ly-5642	8346 ± 66	7540–7180
83	Abri du Moulin	Troubat	C	Ly-5273	8622 ± 81	7940–7520
84	Grotte du Poyemaü	Arudy	C	Ly-1381	8620 ± 250	8300–7000
84	Grotte du Poyemaü			Ly-1784	7830 ± 200	7300–6200
85	Grotte d'Olaskoa	St. Michel	C	Gif-8426	8210 ± 80	7460–7050
86	La Lède de Gurp	Grayan et l'Hopital	O	Ly-5325	8758 ± 98	8250–7550
86	La Lède de Gurp			Ly-6045	7360 ± 85	6410–6060
87	Cluzeau, Cro de Grainville	Rouffignac	C	Gr-2895	8590 ± 95	7940–7480
87	Cluzeau, Cro de Grainville			Gr-2889	7800 ± 50	6770–6480
88	La Roche-aux-Fées	Cieux	C	Ly-4707	8860 ± 270	8800–7300
88	La Roche-aux-Fées			Ly-4704	7360 ± 80	6400–6060

No.	Site Name	Commune	Type	Lab. No.	BP	Cal BC 2σ
91	Pointe St Gildas	Préfailles	O	Gif-3531	7520 ± 140	6650–6050
103	Roc de Gite	Auderville	O	Gif	8460 ± 170	8000–7050
114	La Balastière de l'Onglais	Acquigny	O	Gif-7700	8150 ± 460	8300–6000
114	La Balastière de l'Onglais			Ly-2837	9140 ± 300	9200–7500
116	Le Fossé de Travers	Chelles	O	Gif-7708	8870 ± 140	8300–7600
129	Parc du Château	Auneau	O B	Ly-5606	8350 ± 105	7590–7130
137	Le Petit Marais	La Chaussée Tirancourt	O	Gif-8422	7140 ± 110	6230–5770
137	Le Petit Marais			Gif-7886	7360 ± 130	6460–6000
138	Fosse 4	La Chaussée Tirancourt	B	Gif-9253	9020 ± 100	8550–7800
139	Fosse aux restes humains	La Chaussée Tirancourt	B	Gif-9329	8460 ± 70	7600–7350
140	Couche archéologique	La Chausée Tirancourt	O	Gif-9330	8420 ± 70	7590–7320
141	Autre secteur	La Chaussée Tirancourt	O	Gif-9331	7770 ± 80	6830–6440
142	Fosse sans restes humains F2	La chaussée Tirancourt	O	Gif-8913	7840 ± 90	7050–6450
143	Marais	Cagny	O	Gif-7994	7060 ± 150	6250–5650
144	Le Petit Marais	Picquigny	O	Gif-9330	8420 ± 70	7590–7320
144	Le Petit Marais			Gif-9331	7770 ± 80	6830–6440
145	Gravière III 2	Hangest-sur-Somme	O	Gif-9277	8160 ± 90	7500–6800
145	Gravière III 2			Gif-9276	8290 ± 70	7520–7140
146	Gravière II Nord	Hangest-sur-Somme	O	Gif-8911	8740 ± 80	8200–7550
146	Gravière II Nord			Gif-8912	8830 ± 90	8250–7650
147	Gravière II Nord			Gif-9328	9100 ± 80	8600–8000
148	Le Grand Marais	Thennes	O	Gif-8421	7470 ± 130	6600–6050
149	Le Marais de Berny	Ailly-sur-Noye	O	Gif-8522	8520 ± 60	7650–7470
150	Belloy	Belloy-sur-Somme	O	Gif-8705	8240 ± 100	7520–7050
155	Saleux	Saleux	O	Ly-6881	8600 ± 100	7970–7470
157	Sablonnière I, II, III	Coincy-l'Abbaye	O	Gif-1266	8190 ± 190	7600–6650
159	Montbani 12, 13	Mont Notre Dame	O	Gif-355	8060 ± 350	8000–6200
171	Gigot	Bretonvillers	C	Ly-1112D	8500 ± 95	7740–7320
172	Abri sous roche de Bavans	Bavans	C	Ly-1456	8560 ± 100	7950–7350
172	Abri sous roche de Bavans			Ly-1455	8210 ± 80	7460–7050
172	Abri sous roche de Bavans			Ly-1015	7810 ± 120	7050–6450
172	Abri sous roche de Bavans			Ly-1415	7130 ± 70	6210–5840
175	Abri-des-Prés-Mourey	Villers-le-Lac	C	Gif-9097	8230 ± 70	7460–7070
177	Daupharde	Ruffey-sur-Selle	O	Ly-7352	8230 ± 95	7510–7050
178	Les Cabônes	Ranchot	C	Ly-2297	8730 ± 170	8300–7500

(continued)

Table 7.1. (*continued*)

No.	Site Name	Commune	Type	Lab. No.	BP	Cal BC 2σ
178	Les Cabônes			Gif-8395	8510 ± 90	7740–7350
178	Les Cabônes			Gif-8394	8280 ± 70	7510–7080
178	Les Cabônes			Gif-8397	7820 ± 60	7000–6450
180	Unnamed	Choisey	O	Ly-244	9175 ± 70	8570–8270
181	Mannlefelsen	Oberlarg	C B	Gif-2387	9030 ± 110	8550–7800
181	Mannlefelsen			Ly-1297	8230 ± 300	8000–6400
197	Strette,c. XXIV	Barbaggio	C	Ly-2837	9140 ± 300	9200–7500
198	Curacchiaghju,c. VI	Levie	C	Gif-795	8560 ± 170	8300–7100
199	Araguina-Sennola,c. XV	Bonifacio	C B	Gif-2705	8520 ± 150	8200–7100
200	Abri de Monte Leone	Bonifacio	C	ETH-8305	8225 ± 80	7470–7060
202	Abri de Torre d'Aquila	Pietracorbara	C B	LGQ-507	7840 ± 310	7500–6000

Dates are given as uncalibrated BP (see Lanting & Van der Plicht 2000 for a recent review) and calibrated ranges at 2 sigma as cal BC. Dates have been calibrated using OxCal v3.10 (Bronk Ramsey 1995, 2001). Key to site types: C, cave or rockshelter; O, open-air site; B, burial. Site numbers refer to the map in Figure 7.1. *Note that sites are sometime referred to by the commune in which they occur rather than by the site name.*

varied than in earlier industries and are less clearly formed. Retouched flakes or bladelets are often present alongside bashed blades. Massive tools on blocks or large flakes, with apparent use on the point or distal edge, are a unique element of industries in the north of France, and are absent from the southernmost industries.

The later Mesolithic sequence is poorly understood. This is largely because of a lack of reliable stratified deposits and assemblage sequences. In fact, there is still some discussion over the division of the period into two phases. Nonetheless recent evidence does support a 'Late Mesolithic' phase, beginning in the first half of the seventh millennium cal BC, followed by a 'Final Mesolithic phase', the precise chronological position of which is still under discussion. This sequence is marked by the appearance of trapeze arrowheads – symmetrical or asymmetrical with rectilinear truncations – often accompanied by scalene triangles in the earlier part of the sequence, continuing from the middle phase. The Final Mesolithic marks a distinct change in the microlithic component of assemblages. In this phase, we see the appearance and development of broad pieces made on broader and longer bladelets, even blades, and the disappearance of trapezes. There are less marked changes in other tools, with an increase in tools on blades, such as retouched blades, and notched and denticulated blades with irregular retouch. The Final Mesolithic also sees the appearance of a new technique – indirect percussion by punch. The punch blade technique (debitage type Montbani in the Paris basin, type Montclus in the South) produces very regular long standardised blanks (Marchand 1999, Pelegrin 2000). This technique may have brought significant advantages. It is less certain that the use of punch blades presents a cultural change, but it does nonetheless illustrate the ability of Mesolithic populations to develop innovative solutions. It also suggests a large degree of long distance contact and communication as the spread of the technique appears to be synchronous, at least on a scale that can be identified.

In contrast to the lithic artefacts, bone and antler artefacts are scarce throughout the Mesolithic sequence, especially in settlement contexts. Pieces that have been recovered tend to be roughly made and are not very varied in form. The most common pieces are awls of bone or wild boar tusk, and saws and polishers of bone. Some more distinctive pieces are also found, particularly in cemetery contexts, such as decorated bone spear points from Téviec and Hoëdic (Morbihan), eyed needles and deer antler harpoons from L'Abeurador (Hérault), a pick from le Cuzoul de Gramat (Lot), a red deer antler axe from the shelter of Cabônes (Jura), and axes and red deer antler sheaths from the Somme (Rozoy 1978, Vaquer and Barbaza 1987, Richard et al. 2000, Ducrocq 2001).

Personal ornaments are also very rare in settlement contexts, but they can be numerous in funerary contexts, where they can make up a significant component of grave goods. As in the Palaeolithic, personal ornaments tend to be made of bone, teeth, shells or stone. Perforated or grooved animal teeth are quite common, with ornaments made of red deer canines or incisors, and blades made of wild boar tusk being the most numerous. Marine or freshwater shells, sometimes fossilized, were also used, predominantly those of *Dentalium* and especially *Columbella rustica* in the South, whereas in northern and eastern France there was a larger variety, with the possible use of very remote sources (Taborin 1974, Rozoy 1978). Even human teeth have been used as ornaments. Perforated human teeth were found at les Fieux cave (Lot) (Champagne et al. 1990) and in the Cabônes rockshelter (Jura) (Cupillard and Richard 1998).

It is likely, of course, that many ornaments would have been made of perishable materials, such as wood. In fact, we must be missing a vast array of important items of material culture that have not survived. Finds made of plant materials are extremely rare, especially in French contexts with unfavourable preservation conditions. A few exceptional examples demonstrate what is missing, such as pine canoes and nets found in the bed of the Seine upstream of Paris, at Noyen-on-Seine and Nandy (Mordant and Mordant 1989).

Many items of material culture made on perishable materials may have had an important role in demonstrating cultural identity, though none have survived. Bone and antler tools or personal ornaments were probably also important in this context, although there are so few of these artefacts that they provide little evidence for group identities. In fact, our ideas about the cultural landscape of Mesolithic France have been completely dominated by the record of lithic industries and their change through time. Analysis of these industries has led to a model of broad cultural homogeneity in the Early Mesolithic, cross-cut by a major division between North and South of France, followed by a greater diversification through time.

Cultural Landscapes

Southern France

The first phase of industries in Southern France, the Sauveterrian, shows a remarkable homogeneity across this vast region. The origins of these first industries are marked by the appearance of triangular geometric microliths. Although Rozoy defined several groups, such as the classic Sauveterrian, Causses, and Montclusian, these are now grouped together into one large entity, which spreads from the Atlantic to the Alps and from the foothills of the Pyrenees to a line broadly connecting the Loire to the Vercors. Although there are variations within this area, none are significant enough to call into question the uniformity of the tradition (Barbaza 1991, Valdeyron 1994).

Industries of the earliest phase of the Sauveterrian are predominantly concentrated in the Aquitaine Basin – Rouffignac in Dordogne, Fontfaurès and les Fieux in Lot, les Usclades in Aveyron, in Languedoc – l'Abeurador in Hérault, and in Provence – Saint-Mître in Alpes-de-Haute-Provence

Nicolas Valdeyron

Figure 7.2. Montclus triangles from Félines-Minervois and Balma de l'Abeurador (Hérault), excavations of J. Vaquer and M. Barbaza. Microlithic arrowheads of typical Sauveterrian type (drawn by M. Barbaza). Match head on the right provides the scale.

and Roquefure in Vaucluse (Valdeyron 1994). Sites tend to be found in low altitude areas or in zones where access was facilitated by important rivers. Industries at these sites are characterised by typical geometrical triangles as well as isosceles or scalene microliths, the latter with points that are not particularly acute, and various types of point, in particular Sauveterrian and obliquely truncated points.

The sphere of influence of the Sauveterrian broadens at the end of the earliest phase and during the middle phase. This latter phase is known as the *Montclusian* – a term used by Rozoy but recently adopted as a generic chronological term rather than a regional industry (Barbaza et al. 1991). Peripheral facies illustrate the arrival of new tool types. The Montclus triangle, a finely made microlith which is retouched on all three edges, for example, diffuses west as far as Brittany and north to the Paris Basin (although not extending beyond the Seine) and into the Northern Alps and beyond via the Rhone Valley (Figure 7.2). This type appears in unusual forms at sites in Vercors (Kozlowski 1976, Kayser, 1988, Bintz et al. 1991).

The dynamism of the period is reflected not only in changing lithic assemblages but also in the exploitation of new environments. There is increasing evidence of the use of medium- and even high-altitude mountain slopes. The best evidence for high upland exploitation comes from the Sauveterriano of northern Italy (Bagolini et al. 1983) and was until recently only recognized at sites in the northern Alps of France such as the Vercors region, with the open-air sites of le Pas de l'Aiguille and l'Aulp du Seuil, and the shelters of le Pas de la Charmatte and the Couffin I cave (Bintz et al. 1988, 1991) or in the Massif Central at the shelters of Ventecul and les Barraquettes (Surmely et al. 2003), and in the immediate surrounding regions, notably the Limousin, with the sites of Lake Neuvic (Buisson 1988). However, recent discoveries have shown similar exploitation of high uplands in the Basque mountain area of the French Pyrenees (Valdeyron 2000b).

On the coast of Provence, a different microlithic industry – the Montadian – developed. This is characterized, particularly in the earliest phases, by the presence of a significant number of segments, and these are always noticeably more numerous than triangles. Nonetheless, there are significant

192

similarities between the Montadian and the Sauveterrian, with Montclus triangles appearing in Montadian assemblages from the Middle Phase onwards.

The late and final phases of the Sauveterrian in southern France are less well documented. Sequences tend to be derived from sites which were excavated early, such as Rouffignac in Dordogne, le Martinet in Lot-et-Garonne, le Cuzoul de Gramat in Lot, Montclus in Gard and Châteauneuf-lès-Martigues in Bouches-du-Rhône (Valdeyron 2000a). Nonetheless, the small number of recent excavations, such as Dourgne and Gazel, in Aude, and Buholoup in Haute-Garonne, are likely to bring important new information.

During these later phases, the Sauveterrian industry breaks up into what could be seen as a cultural mosaic. In the southwest, we see a persistence of the Sauveterrian tradition. Elements from previous phases, particularly triangular microliths, continue to be important in assemblages following the arrival of trapeze industries. In western Languedoc, however, it is nongeometrical points that are retained in the later phases and here trapezes, when they appear, are still rare. An ultimate and probably very late phase is characterised by the appearance of 'Gazel points' with invasive final retouch, a type of arrowhead (Barbaza 1993). In Eastern Languedoc and Provence, there appear to be two partially contemporaneous industries. The Late Mesolithic at Montclus has affinities to the Sauveterrian and is marked by the appearance of symmetrical trapezes in layer 16 (Rozoy 1978). However there is a marked change in subsequent levels (layer 14) to what have been termed the 'Castelnovian' industries at this site. The Castelnovian may have developed from the Montadian. The industry first appears in coastal Provence, its appearance in Montclus being seen as a possible sign of territorial expansion, further extended into the Rhone Valley up to the Vercors massif. The debitage of the Castelnovian is similar to that from Montbani assemblages, being characterised by blade tools. The trapeze arrowheads from this tradition show a clear development from those with rectilinear truncation and concave bases, to trapezes with two concave truncations (Montclus trapezes), to triangles resulting from the evolution of these trapezes, and finally to arrowheads with transverse edge and covering retouch (Montclus arrowheads).

Corsica

Although an earlier settlement of Corsica remains possible, it seems mostly likely that the earliest colonisation occurred during the Mesolithic. In fact the Mesolithic colonisation of the island provides clear proof that watercraft capable of traversing the open sea were in use before the Neolithic. Colonisation of the island appears to have been rapid, with the principal early sites – Strette in the North, Curacchiaghiu in the South and Araguina-Sennola in the southernmost end – distributed throughout the island (David 2005). However, it is difficult to discern the origins of colonising populations as the lithic assemblages lack diagnostic types that might link them to continental French or Italian traditions.

Northern France

The picture of different lithic industries in northern France is rather more complex than in the south. There does not appear to have been any large-scale homogeneity comparable to the Sauveterrian of the south. In fact, there are clearly several distinct facies, which share several features. These industries commonly have few triangles and abundant points, initially without and later with a retouched base. A number of factors constrain our understanding of these industries, however – limited new excavations, a scarcity of well-stratified deposits and difficulties in inter-preting the large number of open-air sites.

To the north of the Seine, the industries are clearly influenced by broader technocomplexes of northwestern Europe, such as the Epi-Ahrensburgian as demonstrated in the synthesis of Ducros (Ducrocq 2001). At the start of the Boreal, the influences are clearly from the East. Features such as the appearance of points with retouched bases associated with segments link the region with the Beuronian (see Jochim this volume). In the second half of the Boreal and at the beginning of the Atlantic period, the Tardenoisian appears. Recent research by Ducrocq has extended the limits of this tradition. The Tardenoisian is now seen as including separate groups identified by Rozoy (Ardennian, Somme culture, northern Tardenoisian, and southern Tardenoisian) and extending into Belgium and the Netherlands. The Tardenoisian is defined by a diverse range of arrowhead types. In the earlier phases, triangles, backed bladelets and points with covering retouch (*feuilles de gui*) appear. Later, trapezes associated with regular debitage similar to the Montbani style appear. The most famous deposits of the Paris basin, the Allée Tortue, Montbani, Coincy 2, and Sablonnière (Rozoy 1994), belong to this last phase (Ducrocq 2001).

South of the Seine, the mixed nature of assemblages deriving from sandy deposits makes inter-pretation difficult. Nonetheless, there appears to be a major difference between this region and the north of the Seine, with the river forming a clear cultural barrier. Assemblages here show a number of similarities with industries from southern France such as the high proportion of triangles, also common in the Sauveterrian, and the presence of large points known as Chateaubriand points, which are similar to Sauveterrian points. But there are also differences from southern France, notably the presence of broad points with unretouched bases and the types of arrowheads in the late and final phases.

In Brittany, evidence for the earliest phase of the Mesolithic is very limited. No deposits can be clearly dated to the Boreal with any certainty although some assemblages probably date to this period, for example, at Kerjouanno in Morbihan, where isosceles and scalene triangles are associated with concave-based points and irregular debitage of Coincy type (Kayser 1988). The evidence for the middle phase is better documented. This phase is characterised by the almost complete disappearance of isosceles triangles and the parallel development of scalene triangles (sometimes linked to Montclus triangles) and is seen in Finistère as being related to the Bertheaume group. The sites of Kergalan and Kervouyen are good examples of these industries (Kayser 1988). The final stage corresponds to the development of the Téviecian identified by Rozoy from the sequences at Hoëdic, Téviec, and Kerhillio and recently revised by Marchand (1999). This industry occupies the end of the Mesolithic sequence at least in the south of Brittany. The Téviecian evolves from assemblages marked by the presence, in about equal proportion, of asymmetrical trapezes and symmetrical trapezes, associated with scalene triangles with small concave sides, to assemblages in which the symmetrical trapezes become more dominant, finally becoming the only microlith type present. The style of the debitage is irregular. The recently explored site of Beg-er-Vil, where excavations were carried out between 1985 and 1988 by O. Kayser, complements the list of the most representative Téviecian deposits. In Finistère, the presence of a regular Montbani type debitage and some pieces with opposing flat retouch mark differences from the classic Téviecian.

In the Centre-West region, research in the past fifteen years, particularly by Gouraud and Marchand in the Pays-de-la-Loire, has changed interpretations (Gouraud 1996, Marchand 1999). Although difficult to date precisely, the oldest phase, probably from the Preboreal period, shows clear affinities with the south. This phase is characterised by isosceles and scalene triangles in similar proportions, points with transverse bases and obliquely truncated points. This phase is present at the site of les Etangs de la Breniere (the Loire-Atlantique) where it bears many similarities to the Sauveterrian in layer 6 of the Fontfaurès rockshelter (Lot) (Gouraud 1992).

In the second half of the Boreal these industries become more distinctive, with the presence of unique elements. Sauveterrian influences are still detectable but differences are clearly apparent, with the absence of Sauveterre points and the presence of a type of point with a preserved trihedral point (la Majoire point), which is unknown in the south.

The Late and Final phases are more complex and better documented despite the dominance of surface collected material. Marchand (1997) tentatively proposed four to five phases, which need to be confirmed by further excavations. The first phase is the recently identified 'Gildasian' from the site of la Pointe Saint-Gildas in Loire-Atlantique. The following three to four phases (the fourth being more conjectural) describe the development of the 'Retzian'. The Retzian was identified by Rozoy but was at the time only poorly sequenced. From the second half of the sixth millennium cal BC and during the fifth millennium, Retzian arrowheads show a series of changes. Initially these arrowheads are characterised by a type of trapeze (Payré trapeze), then by a variety of arrowhead forms (spur arrowhead, Châtelet) associated with trapezes and finally by the trapezes alone.

Because of its geographical position, the East of France lies at an intersection between different lithic traditions. Unfortunately, the evidence to date is too patchy to reconstruct a complete picture of changing styles. General characteristics are evident from some recent excavations such as Mannlefelsen shelter in Alsace and Bavans cave in the Jura (Aimé 1993). However, very recent detailed excavations reveal a much more specific and complex picture. Good examples are provided by the open-air site at Choisey 'Aux Champins' and the nearby deposits of Ruffey-sur-Seille (Séara et al. 2002). At the former, industries from layer 2 have points with non-retouched bases and isosceles triangles, suggesting a Preboreal date. They are very similar to the Epi-Ahrensburgian and would mark the southernmost limit of this assemblage type. The most recent phase (layer 1) is characterised by the absence of isosceles triangles and the presence of points with transverse bases and many segments, characteristics common to deposits of the middle Mesolithic at sites in the Jura, such as the Cabônes shelter in Ranchot (Cupillard and Richard 1998). The deposits at Ruffey-sur-Seille present a different picture of influences. In spite of their geographical proximity to Choisey, the lithic industries appear to be related to different traditions. Here an exceptionally well-stratified sequence covers almost all the Mesolithic, from the earliest phases to the late phase (Séara et al. 2000). The first occupation phase is dated to the second half of the Preboreal. The lithic industries are characterised by the presence of isosceles triangles and points with transverse bases and by the extreme scarcity of segments, and are similar to the Beuronian A like the contemporaneous Alsace deposits. The second occupation belongs to the end of the Preboreal and the beginning of the Boreal and documents an early phase of the middle Mesolithic. Lithic industries, based on local raw materials, show very clear southern affinities (isosceles triangles, varieties of scalene pieces similar to Montclus triangles and Sauveterre points), which relate them closely to the Sauveterrian. The following phase, from the first half of the Boreal, yields an industry that parallels the middle Sauveterrian. Finally, at the beginning of the Atlantic, a last phase can be distinguished, with trapezes (the only arrowheads present) and a series of retouched bladelets knapped by indirect percussion, and has convincing equivalents in certain Swiss deposits.

The development and diffusion of different lithic industries illustrates the complexity of the cultural landscape in the Mesolithic. Different lithic styles probably represent groups and regions with distinct identities. Even so, there would have been extensive contact between groups, which were likely to have been mobile, exogamous bands. The complexity of influences on lithic traditions is illustrated by the differentiation of the Sauveterrian in the late and final phases and the emergence of distinct microliths and assemblage characteristics. It is not until the beginning of the Neolithic that we see a return to homogeneity over large areas and a basic contrast between the north and the south of France, which characterised the earlier phases of the Mesolithic.

Whatever the relationships between populations or 'cultures' and the diffusion of ideas in the Mesolithic, we can be certain that the end of the period and the beginning of the Neolithic was a time of culture contact. The timing of the transition varies across different regions although for most areas there was probably a lengthy period of contact. Interpretations of this critical period tend to be based on ideas rather than actual evidence, with a paucity of remains that can be clearly dated to the transition itself.

Particularly interesting evidence for what might have occurred at the Mesolithic-Neolithic transition is provided by La Hoguette ceramics. This ceramic type is contemporaneous with or even precedes the LBK of the Paris Basin, placing it in the second half of the sixth millennium cal BC. However, La Hoguette pottery is completely different from that produced by LBK populations, not only in form and style of decoration but also in the way in which the pottery was produced. Analyses of the stylistic elements has led to a suggestion that the ceramics may have been produced by Mesolithic groups influenced by contact with the Mediterranean Neolithic populations to the south before the arrival of the LBK (Manen 1997). This interpretation is certainly credible, and attractive, given its recognition of an autochthonous component to Neolithic developments. However, there is a paucity of evidence to support the model. There is a lack of chronological control over the timing of development of the ceramic types, a lack of evidence for exchange between the southern and northern zones and various problems with interpretations of Mesolithic-Neolithic contact in the southern areas. For example, at sites such as Châteauneuf-lès-Martigues in the Bouches-du-Rhône, Gramari in Vaucluse and Dourgne in Aude, relationships between Mesolithic and Neolithic populations have been suggested on the basis of evidence for sheep and goat in Mesolithic contexts (Poplin et al. 1986). However these associations rarely stand up to scrutiny, with errors in dating or with problems of postdepositional disturbance and mixing of deposits.

Alternative interpretations of the transition have been proposed. Binder (1987) suggested that Mesolithic trapeze industries were the result of diffusion of ideas from Neolithic populations. Once again there are problems with the chronological control of assemblages, which limits the possibilities for testing these ideas. In a reversal of ideas about cultural influences, Jeunesse (1997) proposed that elements of LBK lithic traditions and funerary practices were derived from contacts with Mesolithic populations. In this scenario cultural and technological influences at the transition were more a matter of reciprocal exchange of ideas and ideologies rather than of one-way traffic from Neolithic to Mesolithic.

Subsistence Practices

It is perhaps the study of subsistence practices more than any other field that has seen the most marked transformation in recent years. There have, of course, been improvements in excavation techniques, particularly with the introduction of systematic sieving leading to more widespread recovery of carbonised plant remains. However, it has not been changes in the nature of the evidence but changes in ideas and perceptions about the period that have most changed interpretations. The early stages of a change in perception of Mesolithic subsistence practices began with Rozoy's research. Rozoy focused on Mesolithic hunting practices, seeing Mesolithic populations as continuing the great Palaeolithic hunting tradition, in contrast to the rather meagre image of

Mesolithic subsistence popular at the time. However, Rozoy ignored the role of plant foods, and we are now much more aware of the importance of plant foods in Mesolithic diets, and moreover of the complexity of the plant exploitation practices that mark the Mesolithic as distinctive from preceding and subsequent periods (Barbaza 1999). Of course, Mesolithic populations continued to hunt (at least until the beginning of the Neolithic) but showed a remarkable ability to adapt to the new subsistence opportunities of Postglacial environments. Thus Mesolithic economies are now seen as 'broad spectrum' economies in which hunting, although the most visible subsistence practice archaeologically, does not necessarily have a dominant role.

The clearest evidence of hunting practices comes from exploitation of large game animals, particularly the three species typical of Postglacial forests – red deer, roe deer, and wild boar – with the occasional addition of aurochs. There is also evidence of exploitation of other species such as badger, wolf, beaver, rabbit, and hare, and species particularly hunted for their fur such as marten, weasel, and squirrel (Brugal and Desse 2004). Alongside this typical hunting spectrum are a number of regional variations. In the uplands of the Pyrenees or the Alps there is evidence for specialised hunting of chamois, ibex or marmot (Barbaza 1999). In Gramari (Vaucluse), the spectrum of hunted species is particularly unusual, including horse and aurochs as well as deer and ibex (Paccard et al. 1971). Although in general terms most sites show a wide range of exploited species, there is evidence for marked specialization in some areas. The Montadian deposits of Montagne in Senas, for example, are dominated by aurochs, which make up 90 percent of the faunal remains (Rozoy 1978). In l'Abeurador (Hérault), as in the rockshelter of Bavans (Doubs), lynx, probably killed for their fur, have been recorded. A particularly rare and interesting case is that of hunting of brown bear, notably from the final Mesolithic at la Baume de Montandon (Doubs) (Cupillard et al. 2000).

The hunting of brown bear provides an interesting example of the complexity of human-animal relationships in the Mesolithic. Evidence of a remarkable hunting incident is preserved at the cave of Bichon, in Switzerland (Morel 1993). Here a bear appears to have been wounded by several projectiles (a point was found deeply planted in a cervical vertebra) and taken refuge in a small cavity within the cave. A hunter appears to have tried to move the dying animal and was mortally wounded – a striking snapshot of the way of life of Mesolithic hunters. In the Vercors massif, in contrast, evidence of a bear maintained in captivity has been recovered at Grande Rivoire (Chaix et al. 1997). Here two half mandibles belonging to the same individual show a deformation characteristic of having been tied using rope inserted between the first and second molar. Further evidence of close relationships between people and animals comes from evidence for domesticated dogs, as at Cuzoul de Gramat, in Lot, the Montandon cave in Doubs and le Petit Marais in the Somme (Rozoy 1978, Ducrocq et al. 1991, Cupillard et al. 2000). The relationship between hunters and dogs/wolves not as prey but as partners in the hunt may even date to Palaeolithic times.

Small prey animals were also important in Mesolithic subsistence economies. Various species of birds were exploited. In l'Abeurador in Hérault, for example, there is evidence for the exploitation of water birds, as well as pigeons, probably trapped with a net during their annual migration (Vilette 1999). Fish also were exploited from rivers, ponds, lakes, or the sea. Exploitation could be local or systematically organized, as in Montclus in Gard, a site considered as a possible smokery (Rozoy 1978), and organized fishing may have been a seasonal activity providing food which could be preserved. Shellfish are also an important resource. Shell middens were once seen as a sign of a poverty of subsistence resources in the Mesolithic. However, these middens, which can comprise several million shells, point instead to a seasonal exploitation of a varied resource base and a diversified economy. Marine shell middens, such as those in Brittany, at Téviec, Hoëdic, and at the recently excavated site of Beg-er-Vil, remain poorly understood, whilst terrestrial shell middens, as in Troubat in Hautes-Pyrénées, or Poyëmau in Pyrénées-Atlantiques, are almost a symbol of the Pyrenean Mesolithic. Although they were highly skilled hunters, Mesolithic populations also were clearly substantial collectors.

Animal protein was nonetheless undoubtedly complemented by plant foods. The development of temperate forest led to the arrival of a range of plant resources such as hazel nuts, roots and tubers, fern rhizomes, mushrooms, and various fruits. It is difficult to quantify the importance of plant foods although there is some evidence of an intensive exploitation. At l'Abeurador, several thousands of wild leguminous carbonised plants and hazelnut shells were recovered (Vaquer and Barbaza 1987). This type of exploitation, however, is not necessarily a prelude to the Neolithic but perhaps more rightly seen as evidence for the innovative use of storage.

In fact it is perhaps in the relationship between exploitation patterns and mobility that the distinctiveness of the Mesolithic is most apparent. Groups undoubtedly moved within a seasonal cycle to exploit different resources at different times of the year. The small surface area of occupation levels, in particular those within rockshelters, suggests that group sizes were small, perhaps limited to a few families, though research into the frequency of reoccupation of sites and raw material sourcing might in the future provide better opportunities for reconstructing actual group movements and territories. Bridault and Chaix (1999) have recently put forward general models based on this type of evidence for the Alps and the Jura. Although exploitation of various food resources was in some cases specialised or intensive, it is clear that mobility rather than sedentism was the dominant characteristic.

Site Organisation and Structure

Although there are large numbers of Mesolithic sites in France, our understanding of intra-site organisation is poor. This paradoxical situation is explained by several factors. The most obvious constraint is that most excavations were carried out many years ago before modern recording techniques. Additionally preservation conditions in many areas are poor, particularly in regions such as the Paris Basin where there is extensive postdepositional mixing because of sandy deposits. However, it also is clear that there has been little interest until recently in social interpretations of intra-site organisation.

Site-based research follows noticeably different trends between the north and south of France. In the south, caves and rockshelters are the dominant type of excavated site and research concentrates on these locations to the detriment of open-air deposits. The only notable open-air site explored in early work was Gramari in Vaucluse (Paccard et al.), where evidence for some type of structure was identified. However there has recently been an attempt to focus more clearly on open-air sites with excavations at la Pierre-Saint-Louis at Geay in Charente-Maritime (Foucher et al. 2000), la Grange at Surgères (Marchand et al. 2000) in the same département, the deposits of le Camp de Jouanet (Tarn-et-Garonne) (Amiel and Lelouvier 2002) and Al Poux (in Lot). On this last site, Mesolithic hearths have been excavated and a probable rectangular shaped hut identified. In the North, open-air sites are dominant, as in the Paris Basin and in Brittany. Evidence for site structure is limited by preservation conditions, although recent fieldwork has yielded interesting insights, as at le Petit-Marais de la Chaussée-Tirancourt in the Somme, Choisey and Ruffey-sur-Seille in the Jura or early work at Bavans in Doubs, and Mannlefelsen at Oberlarg in Alsace.

Most excavations throughout the country yield stratified deposits with variations in how clearly occupation levels can be defined. There is rarely evidence of much structure to the occupation.

Typically, occupation levels are made up simply of scatters of ash, charcoal, and stones from hearths associated with discarded tools, knapping debris, and faunal remains. Finely superimposed lenses of occupation often provide evidence for frequent reoccupations, which in many cases may be quite short-lived. The most common features are hearths, which can be flat or in a small depression, or structured hearths with a stone filling or stone border. They also may be evidence for pits used for storage, or the remains of stake holes or supportive structures of some kind. Only in very unusual circumstances do good preservation and limited reoccupation make it possible to reconstruct site organisation and structure more precisely.

An example of the problems of interpretation comes from two sites in the Jura: Choisey 'Au Champins' and Ruffey-sur-Seille 'A Daupharde' (Séara 2000, Séara et al. 2002). Each has resulted in a very different interpretation of settlement organisation. At Choisey there is a clear distinction between 'domestic' and sleeping space. The artefacts and evidence for domestic activities are distributed around an external hearth where there is a concentration of knapping and faunal remains. Although artefact densities are highest around this hearth there appear to be several activity areas that intersect each other, with small scatters of knapping debris in the more marginal zones. Sleeping and perhaps other domestic activities appear to have taken place within what is interpreted as a hut structure, about 4 m², with an internal hearth and stone border and artefacts spread around and outside this zone. The main distinction between this pattern and the famous site of Pincevent in the Magdalenian of the Paris Basin (Julien et al. 1988) is that at Choisey this sleeping area/hut structure is almost completely bare of artefacts.

At Ruffey-sur-Seille, different activities – domestic, knapping, tool production and use, and food consumption – concentrate primarily around a principal hearth. The concentration of knapping and food debris spread over an area of around 50 m² at the start of the sequence in the Early Mesolithic, and a smaller area of 15 m² in the Late Mesolithic. Throughout the sequence, larger discarded objects such as cores and burnt stones lie at the edge of the occupation area. The dense distribution of knapping debris and debitage appears to suggest an absence of discrete activity areas and makes it difficult to identify or distinguish domestic and sleeping space. It has been suggested that the use of space here also provides an example of a continuity of cultural norms as the same type of distribution is repeated throughout the sequence (Séara et al. 2002). It is not clear whether the contrasts between these two exceptional sites are the result of cultural or social differences, or whether they relate to differences of preservation or functional factors.

Other sites provide further evidence for the nature of site use, although none provide as detailed a picture as these two sites in the Jura. In fact, only a few record structures more complex than a few simple pits. Of these the most notable are Sonchamp III (Yvelines) (Bailloud 1967) and Mannlefelsen (Oberlag, Alsace) (Thévenin and Santy 1977). At Sonchamp III in the Paris Basin, a probable oval-shaped hut, approximately 12 m², was reported. At Mannlefelsen, the remains of several structures were recovered. A stone dam was constructed, apparently designed to hold back the water of a small stream. Alignments of posts or stake holes also provide possible evidence of a palisade, and groups of stake holes and stones form an oval area of 6 m², which may be evidence for a tent supported by the wall of the shelter.

In spite of these recent examples, wider European research into intra-site distributions, such as that typical of Italy, Portugal, or Denmark, for example (see Pluciennik this volume, Straus this volume, Blankholm this volume), reveals a need to progress further in developing the theoretical models of site organisation in France. Multidisciplinary research, such as that carried out over twenty years in the northern Alps (Bintz et al. 1999) provides a model of what needs to be developed and extended elsewhere.

Nicolas Valdeyron

Symbolism and Burial Practices

Of all the categories of evidence, burial practices show the greatest variability. This may be because burials or other evidence for symbolic behaviour are extremely rare, and so our understanding is naturally patchy and can be biased by a few cases. Alternatively variability may reflect genuine cultural distinctiveness in the past.

Burials can take many different forms. They may be simple, multiple or collective, primary or secondary, and inhumations or in rare cases cremations. There may also be differences in grave goods or funerary architecture or in the location of graves. Burials may be isolated, either associated with a domestic site or in a separate location, or part of a larger group of burials or even a cemetery.

A few classic sites, such as the cemeteries of Téviec and Hoëdic in Brittany, and single burials as at le Cuzoul de Gramat in Lot, traditionally dominated our understanding of burial practices in the Mesolithic. Perhaps the most important of these are the cemetery sites of Téviec and Hoëdic. Both comprised several graves, each housing several individuals – ten graves in Téviec and nine in Hoëdic contained twenty-three and fourteen individuals, respectively – and appear to have been reorganized on successive occasions. The burials were essentially earth-cut pits, with borders made up of stones, and covered by deer antlers, which functioned as a capping for the burials. Bodies were extended, in sitting positions or leaning against the wall. Grave goods comprised ornaments of marine shells, large bone points, some of which were decorated, and stone tools. From the time of their discovery, Téviec and Hoëdic have played an important role in the recognition of Mesolithic social practices.

The range of burial evidence has however been broadened in recent years by the excavations of several important groups of burials. The cemetery at la Vergne (Saint-Jean-d'Angély, Charente-Maritime) discovered in 1995 is one example, which provides evidence for rather different burial practices. Four burials (dating to the earliest Mesolithic) were recovered, although only three were well preserved. There were no surface structures or cappings. In general terms, the burials were similar, being single inhumations in pits of varying depths, associated with ochre deposits, stone tools, perforated wolves' teeth, and many perforated and coloured marine shells. However, several of the burial details reveal some variation. The burial positions vary, with some bodies in a sitting position with bent knees, others extended on their left side. In one case, a young child rested on its stomach in a contracted position. The representation of grave goods also varies. Although all burials contained marine shells, in one there were more than two thousand. Additionally, the anklebones of aurochs were present in two tombs and a deer anklebone was present in the third.

Further evidence for distinctive burial practices comes from the cemetery at Le Petit-Marais de la Chaussée-Tirancourt (Somme) excavated in 1990, with several burials of final Mesolithic date (Ducrocq and Ketterer 1994). The burials comprised inhumations and cremations, although all were secondary burials with body parts having been redeposited. Grave goods include faunal remains, flint artefacts and body ornaments with many perforated marine shells. Interestingly, there had clearly been a process of selection of body parts, with long bones and crania selected for rather haphazard disposal in the burial pit.

At the end of the Mesolithic there is evidence for a re-use of a burial pit at Parc du Château in Auneau (Eure-et-Loir). One individual was buried in a sitting position with the back against the wall of the grave and two further bodies were added later (Figure 7.3). One of these was buried in a contracted position on a stone floor whilst the other was placed on the back with the lower limbs folded. The grave goods were limited to a fragment of a bone awl, pieces of shell beads and flint blades (Verjux 1999).

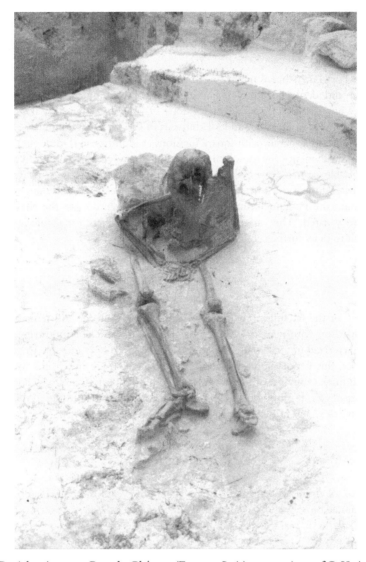

Figure 7.3. Burial at Auneau, Parc du Château (Eure-et-Loir), excavations of C. Verjux. The burial relates to an early phase of the Mesolithic. Note the position of the individual, buried in sitting position with the back against the wall of the burial pit (drawn by C. Verjux).

Ruffey-sur-Seille in Jura provides evidence for a different and distinctive funerary rite (Séara et al. 2002). Here in the Middle Mesolithic levels, a small midden of burnt human bone was found 1 m from the main hearth and associated with an ochre ball and a flint flake. Analyses of the human bones revealed that selection of particular skeletal elements had once again taken place, with a preponderance of cranial and long bones and almost complete lack of vertebrae and peripheral bone elements.

Evidence for a remarkable and perhaps shocking treatment of the dead comes from Agris, in Charente, in les Perrats cave (Boulestin 1999). Many human bones, from eight individuals (both adults and children) were recovered in archaeological deposits dominated by domestic refuse, including in particular a large deposit of animal bones. Butchery marks on the human bones are characteristic of disarticulation and defleshing, and the site has been seen as probable evidence for cannibalism.

Although the burial evidence is interesting and varied, it is difficult to draw general conclusions about symbolism and ideology from such a limited dataset. We might typically look to art items to complement the picture. There is evidence for body ornaments such as tiny fragments of incised bones, as in l'Abeurador in Hérault and les Escabasses in Lot, decorated points from the burials of Téviec and Hoëdic and a spatula with square incisions at Rouffignac (Dordogne) (Barrière 1973, 1974). However, the evidence for Mesolithic art is unfortunately very limited and this suggests that much of the portable art may have been made on perishable materials, perhaps wood. Parietal art would add a further dimension. It has been suggested that parietal art from the series of decorated rockshelters within the Fontainebleau forest in the Paris basin dates to the Mesolithic, but this cannot be securely dated. The variability and scarcity of evidence for ideology and symbolism makes it difficult to draw further conclusions.

Conclusion

As this overview of the Mesolithic era in France shows, knowledge still remains rather patchy, at least by comparison with neighbouring countries. If the stone tool industries are well known today, well characterized in terms of technology as well as typology, and able to generate detailed cultural syntheses, this is not the case for other topics, which are much less well documented. Recent research marks a revival of interest in the Mesolithic period, and new approaches related to settlement organisation, mobility, and a range of activities, are beginning to fill out the picture and finally to give the Mesolithic era a proper place in French Prehistory.

Acknowledgments

Many thanks for all those who created, a few thousands years ago, the material to write this prehistory, and for all those who have contributed in recent decades to recovering it. Special thanks are due to M. Barbaza, F. Séara and C. Verjux, and to K. Gernigon, whose help was invaluable.

Chapter 8

The Mesolithic of the Upper Danube and Upper Rhine

Michael A. Jochim*

Introduction

The heart of central Europe is a region of relatively uniform material culture during the Late Glacial and Postglacial periods and can be distinguished from surrounding areas by a number of criteria. This region (Figure 8.1), which comprises the southern German states of Baden-Württemberg, Bavaria, Rheinland-Pfalz, and Saarland, together with neighbouring portions of eastern France and northern Switzerland, is characterised today by farms, meadows, and forests in a mostly gentle landscape of hills and valleys. Most of this region lies between 200 and 700 m above sea level, but it includes the upper drainages of the Danube and Rhine and is punctuated topographically by the higher elevations of the Black Forest and the karstic limestone plateau of the Franconian and Schwabian Alb and the Swiss Jura. South of this plateau are the rolling, morainic plains of the Swiss Mittelland and the German areas of Oberschwaben and Oberbayern, which are dotted with lakes and bogs. Throughout history (and prehistory), this region has had relatively easy travel and communication links to other parts of the continent: along the Danube to the east and the Black Sea, down the Rhine to the North Sea, and via the Belfort Gap to the headwaters of the Rhone and south to the Mediterranean. The role of these links in prehistoric exchange, diffusion, and migrations has been much debated.

Because a number of characteristics of both the natural environment and prehistoric behaviour appear to be broadly similar between the Late Glacial and Postglacial periods, and distinguish these periods from the preceding Magdalenian of the Upper Palaeolithic, attention is here focused on both the late Pleistocene and the early Holocene. In other words, 'Postglacial' adaptations seem to have begun in the Late Glacial (Stewart and Jochim 1986, Bolus 1992). Among the features uniting this region during the Late Palaeolithic and Mesolithic are:

* Department of Anthropology, University of California, Santa Barbara, USA.

Michael A. Jochim

1. A prehistoric environment that was very similar throughout, and that underwent successional changes in vegetation and animal communities at much the same rate.
2. An archaeological record that is overwhelmingly dominated by surface lithic scatters, but which also includes a relatively few key sites with organic preservation and features located in caves and rockshelters or sealed in riverine or lacustrine sediments.
3. Morphologically similar sets of stone points and geometric microliths.
4. A similar pattern of change through time in the types and frequencies of certain retouched tools.
5. An array of ornaments that differ from those of neighbouring areas (Newell et al. 1990).
6. A special attention given to the treatment of human skulls that has given rise to the notion of a 'skull cult' during the Mesolithic.
7. The notable lack of certain implements, particularly chipped stone axes and perforated stones, that are common components of assemblages to the north.

Archaeological Database

The number of known sites of definite or probable Late Palaeolithic or Mesolithic age in this region is enormous. In the Rheinland-Pfalz, for example, there are now more than one hundred (Cziesla 1998); the hills east of Stuttgart have more than two hundred (Kvamme and Jochim 1990), northern Bavaria has more than seven hundred (Naber 1970), the Federsee and Bodensee have more than two hundred (Jochim 1998), the Donaumoos along the Bavarian Danube has another one hundred (Rieder and Tillman 1989), and the north-central portion of the Swiss plain has more than two hundred (Nielsen 1996). Despite this abundance of data, however, three factors limit the quality of information they provide. First of all, the sites are unevenly distributed, with concentrations reflecting, at least in large part, the focused investigations of individuals. In the southern Rheinland-Pfalz, for example, few sites were known until intensive research began in 1980. Clusters of sites in the western Bodensee, the Federsee, the Donaumoos, and the northern Franconian Alb similarly reflect the activities of a few persistent individuals. As a result, our knowledge of Mesolithic land use and population distribution may be severely biased.

Second, the vast majority – more than 90 percent – of these sites are surface lithic scatters. Not only do such sites lack preserved organic materials and features. They also frequently lack clear chronological diagnostics or contain such diagnostics from several time periods, reflecting mixed occupations. A few examples demonstrate this well. A study of six sites in the southeastern Federsee basin revealed that all contained materials from both Late Palaeolithic and Mesolithic occupations, apparently in differing proportions (Eberhardt et al. 1987). In his study of 746 sites in the Franconian Alb, Naber (1970) was forced to disregard 362 sites because they lacked clear temporal diagnostics. Our recent surface surveys in Oberschwaben located 282 surface sites, but only 55 could be attributed to specific periods (Jochim et al. 1998). These characteristics of the surface sites pose serious problems for studies of both site contents and patterns of land use.

A third factor limiting the utility of the data available is the fact that many of the excavated sites were investigated relatively early in this century. Excavation methods of that period now appear severely lacking by today's standards. The excavations by Peters (1935) in Falkenstein Cave, for example, distinguished only one occupation layer that is more than 1 m in thickness. Moreover, after two world wars, much of the material and excavation notes from such sites have been lost (e.g., Peters 1946). This is especially true of the most visible and rich cave sites and limits their contribution to our knowledge.

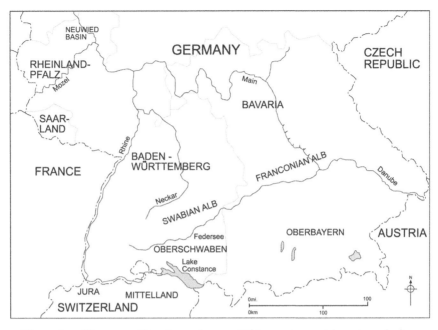

Figure 8.1. The upper Danube and upper Rhine region, with major subareas.

Until we can develop methods for extracting more information from surface lithic scatters, the burden of interpretation falls largely on the few excavated sites with organic preservation, despite their limitations (Figure 8.2). Most of these are caves and rockshelters: Weidental cave in the Rheinland-Pfalz, a series of sites in the Schwabian Alb (including Jägerhaus, Falkenstein, and Malerfels caves and Inzigkofen, Helga-Abri and Felsställe rockshelters), another cluster in the Franconian Alb (most notably, Steinbergwand and Schräge Wand caves), and several sites in the Birs Valley of northeastern Switzerland (Birsmatten cave and Tschäpperfels rockshelter, among others). In addition, there are now several more recently excavated open-air sites that have proved quite informative, including several sites in the Neuwied Basin of the central Rhineland (Niederbieber, Kettig), three sites in the Neckar Valley (Rottenburg-Siebenlinden I, II, III), five sites in the Federsee Basin (Henauhof Nord I and II, Henauhof Nordwest, Henauhof Nordwest 2, and Henauhof West), and the site of Schötz 7 on the former Wauwiler Lake in Switzerland.

Chronology and Technology

At the height of the Last Glacial Maximum, approximately eighteen thousand years ago, the southern portions of this region were covered by the Alpine glaciers. The unglaciated regions to the north experienced long, dry winters and high winds that, despite the warmth of the short summers, created a landscape of sparsely vegetated steppe-tundra (Frenzel 1983). Over the course of succeeding millennia, temperatures rose rather rapidly, although episodically, reaching modern levels perhaps as early as 13,300 BP and continuing to a Postglacial maximum around eight thousand years ago. One cool phase during this process, the Younger Dryas (10,800–10,300 BP), followed the warm Alleröd period (11,800–10,800 BP), but seems not to have been as pronounced as in northern Europe, although the elevation of the tree line in the Black Forest decreased by 100–200 m

205

Michael A. Jochim

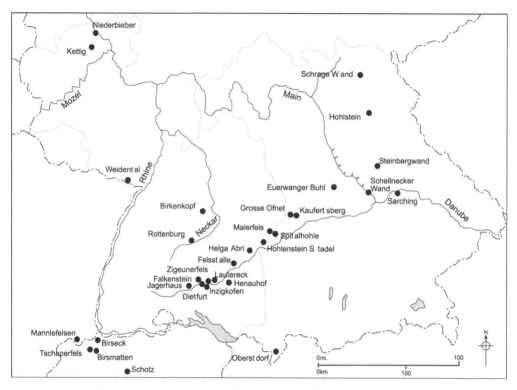

Figure 8.2. Major sites in the Upper Danube and Upper Rhine.

during this time (Frenzel 1983). Responding to the glacial melting and changing temperatures, river regimes underwent profound and fluctuating changes, varying according to their location. For example, the upper Rhine down cut its bed considerably due to glacial run off, whereas the Neckar and Danube showed a predominance of depositional processes, creating thick layers of Postglacial sediments. Across the morainic areas of Oberschwaben and Oberbayern, the numerous lake basins began a process of infilling, but at variable rates, so that this entire region was characterised throughout the Last Glacial and Postglacial by numerous lakes, marshes, and bogs at different stages of development.

With the rising temperatures, reforestation began relatively early, dramatically altering the Ice Age environments. By the Alleröd period, pine and birch were widely distributed, but in the north and the higher elevations of the south, tree density was lower with mosaic landscapes of grassland and forest. A unique record of largely aspen stands is preserved from this time in the low areas of the Neuwied Basin in the Rhineland beneath the volcanic pumice of the Laacher See eruption (Baales et al. 1999). Thermophilous trees such as oak, elm, ash, and lime followed, together with hazel, displacing pine to drier soils and creating a more varied patchwork of vegetation. Regional differences are apparent, with hazel more abundant in the west and southwest and spruce more common in the southeast (Kuster 1995). These changes had many implications for the region's inhabitants: a decrease in grassy fodder for large herds of animals such as reindeer and horse; an increase in the diversity of potential plant foods for both humans and other animals; an increase in the seasonal contrasts of shade and vegetational cover; and increased problems of visibility and travel.

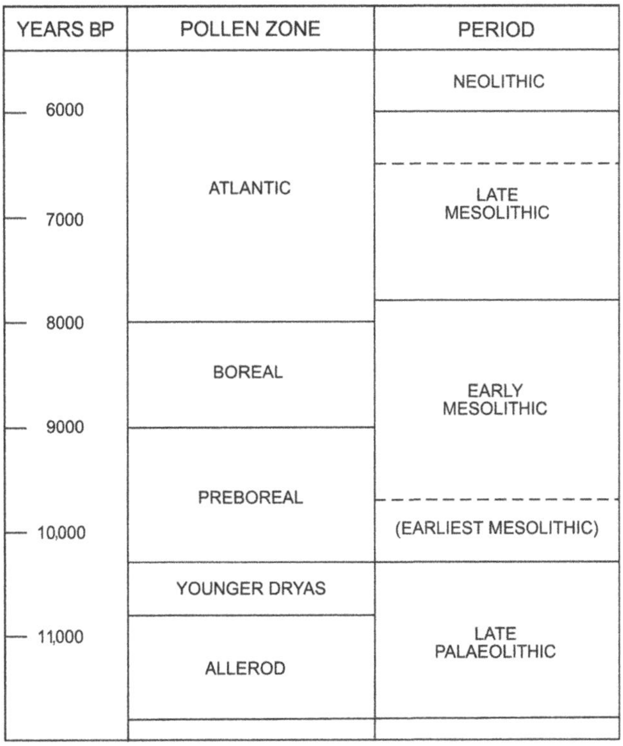

YEARS BP	POLLEN ZONE	PERIOD
― 6000	ATLANTIC	NEOLITHIC
― 7000		LATE MESOLITHIC
― 8000	BOREAL	EARLY MESOLITHIC
― 9000	PREBOREAL	
― 10,000		(EARLIEST MESOLITHIC)
	YOUNGER DRYAS	LATE PALAEOLITHIC
― 11,000	ALLEROD	

Figure 8.3. Chronology of the Late Palaeolithic and Mesolithic.

The archaeological chronology for the area is presented in Figure 8.3. Against the background of climatic and vegetational changes marked by a succession of pollen stages there is a series of changes in certain key artefacts, primarily projectiles. The major periods recognized are the Late Palaeolithic, the Early Mesolithic (subdivided into substages) and the Late Mesolithic.

The Late Palaeolithic, which dates to the periods of the Allerød and Younger Dryas (11,800–10,300 BP), is similar to the contemporary Azilian in France and the largely contemporary Federmesser of the North European Plain (Valdeyron this volume, Verhart this volume). Diagnostics of these assemblages are backed points and backed blades, together with short scrapers, round scrapers, and burins. In comparison to the preceding Magdalenian, from which it is often difficult to distinguish, the Late Palaeolithic has smaller artefacts and fewer distinct types of retouched tools, as well as far fewer objects of portable art and adornment. Organic artefacts are also rare.

The Early Mesolithic, or Beuronien, lasted for approximately twenty-five hundred years until 7800 BP and is characterised above all by its abundance of microlithic points and triangles (Taute 1974b). Three primary stages were initially defined for this period, based on stratigraphic sequences in cave sites and supported by radiocarbon dates:

1. Beuronien A, characterised by isosceles triangles with obtuse angles, narrow irregular trapezes, and lanceolate points with convex, dorso-ventrally retouched bases;
2. Beuronien B, with isosceles triangles with acute angles and lanceolate points with concave, dorso-ventrally retouched bases;

207

Michael A. Jochim

3. Beuronien C, typified by backed bladelets, very small and narrow scalene triangles, bilaterally backed micropoints, and lanceolate points with concave, dorsally retouched bases.

In addition, a poorly defined and scarce 'Earliest Mesolithic', characterised largely by obliquely retouched points, has been claimed at several sites. Subsequent research has suggested that the distinctions between stages A and B are not clear, and it is now common to use a two-part division of the Early Mesolithic into Beuronien A/B and Beuronien C. Moreover, studies in the Rheinland-Pfalz have suggested both regional differentiation in some microlithic styles and a further chronological subdivision of the Beuronien B (Cziesla and Tillman 1984). One technological hallmark of the Early Mesolithic is the frequent heat-treating, or tempering, of stone to improve its workability.

With the beginning of the Late Mesolithic around 7800 BP, there is a major technological change in lithic production. Extremely regular blades made by pressure-flaking come to dominate assemblages and the heat-treating of stone raw material declines in importance. Trapezes made from regular blades become a common microlithic form, as is true in many other parts of the continent at this time. Cziesla (1992), however, has suggested that these technological changes were not universal, and that certain areas, such as the southern Rheinland-Pfalz and the Ardennes, retained earlier techniques and forms. In addition to the changes in blade technology and microliths, notched blades and long endscrapers occur in greater numbers among the retouched tools. This period ends between 6500 and 6000 BP, not long after the appearance of true agricultural villages in the area, and the possibility and implications of a contemporaneity between Mesolithic hunter-gatherers and Neolithic farmers have been much debated (Cziesla 1992, Gronenborn 1990, 1994, Kind 1992, Nielsen 1994).

The use of materials other than stone is rather sparsely documented. Bone implements are known from both Early and Late Mesolithic contexts and include scrapers made from long bones and smooth bone points, which occur in several caves in the Alb and are particularly numerous in the lakeside site of Henauhof Nordwest (Jochim 1993). Animal teeth were perforated as jewellery, and, in the case of boars' tusks, for carving tools. Red deer antler was used to fashion perforated and unperforated axes and adzes, retouchers, hide-scrapers, and barbed harpoons, primarily in the Late Mesolithic. Except for a possible wooden spear dating to the Boreal (Wall 1961), wooden implements are not known. However, the antler axe-heads and microlithic arrow points imply the existence of wooden handles and shafts. Moreover, use-wear studies on blades from the Late Mesolithic site of Henauhof Nord II have identified wood polish (Owen and Pawlik 1993). Furthermore, the existence of sites on islands in the Federsee of Oberschwaben suggests the presence of watercraft, perhaps dugouts like those found elsewhere in Europe (Probst 1991). In the forested environments of central Europe, wood was certainly an abundant material, and no doubt found many uses. Consequently, the lack of stone axes throughout much of the Mesolithic of this area is puzzling, particularly because such tools were common in the north. The antler axes known from the Late Mesolithic may, however, have been used to fell trees (Nielsen 1997). The use of hides can also only be inferred, both from the presence of bone and antler scraping tools and from the identification of hide polish on lithics (Owen and Pawlik 1993). Red ochre has been found on a number of sites, but its use is unknown, except in the case of one find of a possible painting of a bovid on a rock slab in the Early Mesolithic of Felsställe (Campen et al. 1983). No finds of cordage like those known from the northern European Mesolithic have been made in this region, although it, too, may be inferred from the presence of perforated ornaments that were presumably strung together or sewn onto clothing.

Subsistence

Not surprisingly, the information about subsistence activities in this region is overwhelmingly dominated by evidence for hunting. Bones of large herbivores form the majority of faunal remains in those sites where organic materials are preserved. Recent chemical analyses of human bone from the Late Mesolithic skull burials of Ofnet Cave support this interpretation. They document a high intake of animal protein and lead to the conclusion that "the people buried in the Ofnet cave might even be considered 'carnivores' within the system of human omnivorous and opportunistic dietary behaviour" (Bocherens et al. 1997: 128). These studies also suggest that infants were nursed until about the age of three, a practice particularly common among hunter-gatherers for whom hunting provides a major part of the diet, as few weaning foods are available. Dental studies of these same Ofnet materials document wear patterns consistent with a generalized foraging diet, similar to Eskimo and other groups (Baum 1991).

Tables 8.1–8.3 present a summary of many of the important faunal assemblages of southern Germany and northern Switzerland from the Late Palaeolithic, Early Mesolithic, and Late Mesolithic. Most of the sites tabulated are caves or rockshelters, the few exceptions being the Rottenburg sites in the Neckar Valley, the Henauhof sites in the Federsee, and Schötz 7 in Switzerland. Throughout all three time periods, red deer was the major prey (found at 88 to 100 percent of the sites per period), followed by roe deer, aurochs, and, in the Late Palaeolithic, horse, or, in the Mesolithic, boar. Four or five other species of large herbivores, however, were taken during each period, including elk, chamois, ibex, bear, and reindeer. Except for the reindeer, interpreted as part of a remnant population in the refuge of the Black Forest during the early Holocene (Hahn et al. 1993), these species reflect the forested environment, broken by mountain slopes or small grassland patches. That such grasslands became scarcer over the course of these periods as reforestation progressed, however, is evidenced both by pollen diagrams and by the declining role of horse (Jochim 1998).

A variety of smaller mammals also appear among the faunal assemblages, although their economic role is uncertain, given the propensity for caves to accumulate such bones naturally. Nevertheless, it seems likely that a good number of these animals were, indeed, human prey, as many of them (beaver, marten, fox, wildcat, wolf, badger) are found in the assemblages of open-air sites as well. The relative importance of the meat and furs from these species, however, is unknown.

Other faunal resources included a variety of birds, both aquatic (ducks, swans) and terrestrial (capercaillie), eggs, fish (including pike, catfish, huchen, and bream), and freshwater mussels. Remains of plant foods are scarce. Charred hazelnut shells do appear in a number of sites in some numbers, and concentrations of pollen in certain layers of Jägerhaus Cave have been interpreted as indicating the gathering of round-leafed sorrel (Hahn 1983). Rottenburg-Siebenlinden in the Neckar Valley was also reported to contain remains of wild raspberry, apple, and cabbage (Hahn and Kind 1991).

Hunting technology included the bow and arrow, as witnessed by the numerous microliths, one of which was found embedded in the skeleton of an aurochs found in the Neckar Valley (Ströbel 1959). Other implements probably used for hunting, such as spears, clubs, nets, or traps, are poorly documented, and the one wooden spear found in the peat of the Federsee was probably used for fishing (Wall 1961). One important aid in hunting may have been the domestic dog, bones of which were found in the Early Mesolithic level of Rottenburg-Siebenlinden III (Kind 1995), at the Euerwanger Bühl Cave in Bavaria (Probst 1991), and at the Late Mesolithic site of Henauhof

Table 8.1. Presence/absence of fauna at Late Palaeolithic sites

Site	1	2	3	4	5	6	7	8	9	10	11	12	13	14	15	16	17	18
Large Mammals																		
Red deer	x	x	x	x	–	x	x	–	x	x	x	x	x	x	x	x	x	x
Roe deer	–	–	x	–	–	–	x	x	x	x	–	x	–	–	–	x	–	–
Boar	x	x	–	–	–	–	–	–	x	–	–	–	–	–	x	–	–	–
Aurochs	x	–	–	–	–	x	–	–	–	–	–	–	x	x	x	x	–	–
Elk	–	–	–	x	–	–	–	–	–	–	–	–	–	x	x	–	–	–
Horse	x	–	x	–	–	–	–	–	–	–	–	–	–	–	x	x	x	x
Ibex	–	–	–	x	x	–	–	–	–	–	–	–	–	–	x	–	x	–
Chamois	–	–	–	–	–	–	–	–	–	–	–	–	–	x	–	x	–	–
Bear	–	–	x	x	–	–	–	–	–	–	–	–	–	–	x	–	–	–
Small Mammals																		
Beaver	–	–	–	x	–	–	–	–	x	–	–	x	–	x	x	x	–	–
Hare	–	–	x	x	x	–	–	–	–	–	–	x	–	–	–	–	x	x
Wolf	x	–	x	–	–	–	–	–	–	–	–	–	–	–	x	–	–	–
Fox	–	x	–	–	–	–	–	–	–	–	–	–	–	–	x	x	x	–
Ermine	–	–	x	–	–	–	–	–	–	–	–	–	–	–	–	–	x	–
Marten	–	–	–	–	–	–	–	–	–	–	–	–	–	–	x	–	–	–
Badger	–	–	–	–	–	–	–	–	–	–	–	–	–	–	x	–	x	–
Weasel	–	–	–	–	–	–	–	–	–	–	–	–	–	–	–	–	x	–
Fish	x	–	–	x	x	x	x	–	–	–	–	x	–	x	x	x	–	–
Birds	x	–	–	–	–	–	–	–	x	–	–	x	–	–	x	x	x	x

1: Henauhof NW, level 6; 2: Henauhof West; 3: Fohlenhaus; 4: Zigeunerfels, level D; 5: Zigeunerfels, level E; 6: Helga Abri; 7: Isteiner Klotz, cave 8; 8: Isteiner Klotz, cave 9; 9: Isteiner Klotz, cave 10; 10: Isteiner Klotz, cave 11; 11: Isteiner Klotz, cave 12; 12: Isteiner Klotz, cave 14; 13: Urbar; 14: Andernach; 15: Niederbieber; 16: Kettig; 17: Neumühle; 18: Steinbergwand, level VIII.

Nord II (Kind 1997). In addition to the wooden spear, other finds of possible fishing gear include the barbed antler points of the Late Mesolithic, at least some of the smooth bone points from throughout the Mesolithic, a composite fishhook of wood and bone, complete with a small fish as bait (Torke 1993), and a possible net weight made from a roll of birchbark and containing gravel and clay (Kind 1992). All but the antler points were found, or were most numerous, in the lakeside sites of the Federsee.

Except for groves of hazel and seasonal aggregations of red deer, food resources were relatively dispersed. Most of the big game occurred in small or medium-sized groups and were often scattered for at least part of the year. This is quite different from the situation during the Magdalenian of the Upper Palaeolithic in the region, when the more gregarious reindeer and horse formed the major prey. Consequently, during the Late Palaeolithic and Mesolithic, no faunal assemblages show evidence of communal kills or group hunts. Hunting must have occurred largely on an encounter basis and taken the form of single kills. In the Danube drainage, there also were no large runs of fish; again, the major aquatic prey were relatively dispersed. The Rhine drainage probably had salmon runs, but there is no concrete evidence that these were exploited.

Table 8.2. Presence/absence of fauna at Early Mesolithic sites

Site	1	2	3	4	5	6	7	8	9	10	11	12	13	14	15	16	17	18	19	20	21	22	23	24	25
Large Mammals																									
Red deer	x	x	x	x	x	x	x	x	x	x	x	x	x	x	–	x	x	–	x	x	x	x	x	–	x
Roe deer	x	x	x	x	x	–	x	x	x	x	x	x	x	x	x	–	x	x	x	x	x	x	x	x	x
Boar	x	x	x	x	x	x	x	x	x	x	x	–	x	–	–	x	–	x	x	x	–	x	–	x	–
Aurochs	–	x	x	x	x	–	–	–	–	–	–	–	–	–	x	–	x	–	x	x	x	x	–	–	–
Elk	–	–	x	–	–	–	–	–	–	–	–	–	–	–	–	–	–	–	x	–	–	x	–	–	–
Horse	–	–	–	–	–	–	–	–	–	–	–	–	–	–	–	–	–	x	x	–	–	–	–	–	–
Reindeer	–	x	–	–	–	–	–	–	–	–	–	–	–	–	–	–	–	x	–	–	–	–	–	–	–
Bear	–	–	–	–	–	–	–	–	–	x	–	–	–	–	–	–	–	–	–	–	x	–	–	–	–
Small Mammals																									
Beaver	x	x	x	–	x	–	x	x	x	x	x	x	–	–	–	x	x	–	–	–	x	x	x	–	–
Hare	x	–	–	–	–	–	–	–	–	–	x	–	x	x	–	x	x	x	x	–	x	–	x	x	x
Badger	–	–	–	–	–	–	–	x	–	–	–	–	–	x	–	–	x	–	x	x	x	–	–	x	x
Otter	–	–	–	–	–	–	–	x	–	x	–	x	–	x	–	–	x	–	–	–	x	–	–	–	–
Wolf	–	–	–	–	–	–	–	–	–	–	–	–	–	–	–	–	x	x	–	–	x	–	x	–	–
Fox	–	x	x	–	–	–	–	–	–	x	–	x	x	x	–	x	x	x	x	x	x	x	–	x	x
Wildcat	–	–	x	–	–	–	–	–	–	–	x	x	x	–	–	–	x	x	x	x	x	–	–	–	–
Lynx	–	–	–	–	–	–	–	–	–	–	–	x	–	–	–	–	–	–	–	–	–	–	–	–	–
Marten	–	–	x	–	–	–	–	–	–	x	x	x	–	–	–	–	x	–	–	–	x	–	–	x	x
Weasel	–	–	–	–	–	–	–	–	–	–	–	x	–	x	–	–	–	x	x	–	–	–	–	–	x
Polecat	–	–	–	–	–	–	–	–	–	–	–	–	–	–	–	–	–	–	–	–	–	–	x	–	–
Fish	x	–	–	–	–	–	–	–	–	x	x	x	x	x	x	x	x	x	x	x	x	–	x	–	x
Shellfish	–	–	x	–	–	–	–	–	x	–	x	–	x	–	–	–	–	–	–	–	–	–	–	x	–
Birds	x	x	x	–	–	–	–	–	x	x	x	x	–	x	x	x	x	x	x	x	–	–	–	x	x

1: Isteiner Klotz; 2: Rottenburg: Siebenlinden I; 3: Rottenburg: Siebenlinden II; 4: Rottenburg: Siebenlinden III, level 3; 5: Rottenburg: Siebenlinden III, level 4; 6: Jägerhaus, level 13; 7: Jägerhaus, level 11; 8: Jägerhaus, level 9; 9: Jägerhaus, level 10; 10: Jägerhaus, level 8; 11: Falkenstein, lower third; 12: Inzigkofen, lower third; 13: Zigeunerfels, level C; 14: Felsställe; 15: Schuntershöhle; 16: Helga Abri; 17: Malerfels; 18: Spitalhöhle; 19: Henauhof NW, level 5; 20: Henauhof NW, level 4; 21: Birsmatten, levels 3–5; 22: Kleine Kalmit; 23: Dietfurt; 24: Bettelküche; 25: Steinbergwand, level IV.

Table 8.3. Presence/absence of fauna at Late Mesolithic sites

Site	1	2	3	4	5	6	7	8	9	10	11	12	13	14	15	16	17
Large Mammals																	
Red deer	x	x	x	x	x	x	x	x	x	x	x	x	x	x	x	x	x
Roe deer	x		x	x	x	x	x	x	x	x	x	x	x	x	x	x	x
Boar	x	x	x	x	x	x	x	x	x		x	x	x	x	x	x	x
Aurochs	x	x	x		x			(x)	(x)				x	x	x	x	x
Elk	x														x		x
Horse	x												x				x
Ibex																	x
Chamois						x	x						x	x			x
Bear								(x)	(x)				x		x		x
Small Mammals																	
Beaver	x	x				x		x		x	x	x	x	x	x	x	x
Hare						x	x	x					x			x	
Badger	x					x					x	x	x				x
Otter						x					x	x					x
Wolf	x			x						x	x	x	x	x	x		
Fox						x			x			x	x				x
Wildcat	x					x				x	x	x	x	x			x
Marten	x					x	x	x	x	x	x	x	x		x	x	x
Weasel											x						
Polecat													x				
Fish	x	x	x			x	x	x	x	x	x	x	x			x	x
Shellfish						x		(x)	(x)	x	x						
Birds	x	x	x			x			x	x	x	x		x	x	x	x

1: Henauhof NW, level 3; 2: Henauhof West; 3: Henauhof NW 2; 4: Henauhof Nord II; 5: Rottenburg: Siebenlinden III, level 2; 6: Jägerhaus, level 7; 7: Jägerhaus, level 6; 8: Falkenstein, middle third; 9: Falkenstein, upper third; 10: Inzigkofen, middle third; 11: Inzigkofen, upper third; 12: Lautereck; 13: Birsmatten, levels 1: 2; 14: Tschäpperfels; 15: Schötz 7; 16: Zwingen; 17: Liesbergmühle VI.

Environmental changes over the course of the Late Palaeolithic and Mesolithic may have had a number of effects on the subsistence economy. Progressive reforestation certainly must have increased travel costs and hampered visibility, making hunting a more costly endeavour through time. At the same time, the increasing diversity of the vegetation probably led to a more mosaic, patchy environment in which the distribution of major food resources may have become more differentiated and predictable. Thus, although hunting may have become increasingly costly, it may also have become more predictable as well.

Reactions to these changes seem to have taken the form of increasing subsistence diversity. Table 8.4 (summarizing the information from Tables 8.1–8.3) indicates the following changes through time in the economy: increasing diversity of big game species; increasing diversity of small game species; and increasing number of sites with fish, birds, and shellfish alongside the mammalian prey. Other possible coping mechanisms, such as food storage, may have had little importance, given

Table 8.4. Summary of time trends in faunal representation, showing the average percentage of large mammal species per site, the average percentage of small mammal species per site, and the percentage of sites with fish, shellfish, and birds, by time period

	Sites N	Big Game Species/Site %	Small Game Species/Site %	Sites with Fish %	Sites with Shellfish %	Sites with Birds %
Late Pal.	18	31	16	50	0	39
Early Meso.	25	39	27	56	16	60
Late Meso.	17	49	38	76	29	71

the lack of large kills or harvests. Weidental Cave in the Rheinland-Pfalz has a horseshoe arrangement of stones interpreted as a meat cache (Cziesla 1997), but otherwise little evidence has been found.

Settlement

In light of the predominance of surface lithic scatters among the sites, there is very little information about intrasite features and patterns. Nevertheless, even from the more limited sample of excavated cave and open-air settlements there is relatively little evidence of structures and features. If this evidence is at all representative, it suggests a lack of substantial energy investment in particular sites, indicative perhaps of relatively high mobility.

Oval depressions interpreted as huts have been reported at lakeside, open-air sites on the Federsee (Reinerth 1929) and the Obersee (Reinerth 1956) in Oberschwaben, as well as on the Wauwilermoos in Switzerland (Nielsen 1997). In at least one case, however, more recent interpretations suggest these to be tree falls (Paret 1961, see also Tolan-Smith this volume). Along the Bavarian Danube, sites near Sarching were reported to have structural remains in the form of depressions and postholes (Gronenborn 1997, Schönweiss and Werner 1977). Somewhat more reliable are the finds at the Helga-Abri rockshelter of two depressions, one of which contained a rock-lined hearth and a pit (Hahn and Scheer 1983), and in the cave of Spitalhöhle, where a small depression of about 5 m² was found near the back wall (Hahn 1984). Other reported structural remains include a rock alignment in front of the rockshelters of Schräge Wand in Bavaria (Naber 1968), a 2 m × 1 m sheet of bark flooring in the moist peat of the site of Henauhof Nord II (Kind 1992), a sandstone pavement at the open-air site of Birkenkopf near Stuttgart (Peters 1941), and a few postholes at Oberstdorf 5 in the Alpine foothills (Reinerth 1956). These few remains come from all three periods considered here, with no obvious trends through time.

The most commonly reported features at sites in this region are hearths. Some are visible as concentrations of charcoal or patches of reddened clay (Oberstdorf 1, Rottenburg-Siebenlinden I, II, III, Felsställe, Weidental Cave, Henauhof Nordwest 2, Henauhof Nord I, II); a few are stone-lined (Helga-Abri, Rottenburg-Siebenlinden III). Several are associated with large anvil stones (Oberstdorf 2, Henauhof West, Henauhof Nordwest) or pits (Rottenburg-Siebenlinden III, Helga-Abri). In most cases, the hearths are surrounded by concentrations of debris suggesting their focal role in the placement of activities.

Site locations are quite variable. Throughout the limestone of the Jura/Alb plateau, inhabited caves and rockshelters are found primarily in smaller tributary valleys, but vary in elevation above the valley floor, orientation, and size (Eriksen 1991). Lakeshore locations are common, particularly in northern Switzerland, around Lake Constance, and the Federsee and other lakes in Oberschwaben and Oberbayern (Reinerth 1929, 1953, Gehlen 1988, Nielsen 1992). Numerous sites have been found on low-lying sand dunes and terraces in the floodplains of the Rhine and Danube (Gersbach 1951, 1968, Rieder and Tillman 1989) and smaller streams (Reinerth 1956). Another common location is on the edges of plateaux and hills high above river valleys (Stoll 1932, Stoll 1933, Kvamme and Jochim 1990). It seems likely that this wide variety of locations reflects, in part, a similar variety of site functions. In some cases, there is evidence to support this interpretation. At least two of the well-excavated sites in the Neckar floodplain at Rottenburg-Siebenlinden, for example, appear to be residential camps, characterised by a diverse set of tools and features (Hahn and Kind 1991, 1992, Hahn et al. 1993, Kieselbach and Richter 1992, Kind 1995). By contrast, a number of surface sites on hilltops on the eastern edge of the Black Forest less than 20 km from the Neckar sites are overwhelmingly dominated by microliths and appear to be largely specialised hunting camps (Stoll 1932, 1933). On the other hand, there is ample evidence within each locational category for variation in artefacts and activities to suggest that gross location alone is a poor indicator of site function. For example, two Late Palaeolithic sites on the Federsee appear to represent a residential camp on the one hand (Henauhof Nordwest, level 6) and a short-term hunting camp on the other (Henauhof West), yet are only 200 m apart on the former shoreline (Jochim 1995). Similarly, the Late Mesolithic sites of Henauhof Nordwest, level 3 and Henauhof Nord II differ substantially, again suggesting a contrast between residential and specialised functions (Jochim 1998, Kind 1992). Among the cave and rockshelter sites along the upper Danube, Kind (1996) argues for the presence of both hunting camps (Jägerhaus Cave) and residential camps (Inzigkofen Shelter).

Seasonality of occupation also does not seem to correlate neatly with general site locational characteristics. Within the site of Henauhof Nordwest, for example, there are indications of a shift from predominantly summer occupation during the Early Mesolithic to autumn during the Late Mesolithic (Jochim 1998). Similarly, the evidence at Jägerhaus Cave has been interpreted as indicating shifts between predominantly spring/summer and autumn or autumn/winter occupations in the different levels (Hahn 1983). If true, these changes in the seasonality of individual sites illustrate well Binford's (1982) argument that places in the landscape can change in use and economic meaning depending on their location within the seasonal range of a group.

Nevertheless, there are indications of gross seasonal patterning in the distribution of sites. I have elsewhere suggested that a cluster of rather high elevation Late Palaeolithic sites in the Alpine foothills to the east of Lake Constance may, because of their location, represent largely warm weather occupations. The same might be true of some sites in the eastern Alb, based on finds of birds' eggs at Helga Abri (Jochim 1998). If so, then cold season occupations may have occurred around the lakes of Oberschwaben, although evidence is currently lacking for this. On similarly slim evidence, it might be argued that Late Palaeolithic sites along the upper Rhine west of Lake Constance were occupied largely in autumn and winter, the periods when low water levels facilitated fish-spearing and when fish runs were greatest. Warm seasons, by contrast, may have witnessed a move into the swampy regions of the Rhine floodplain to the north. For the Early Mesolithic, I have argued for a general seasonal axis of mobility linking warm season residential occupations in the eastern Alb and Oberschwaben with cold season camps higher along the Danube to the west (Jochim 1998).

Such frankly speculative suggestions about seasonal movements receive some support from the distribution of stone raw materials. In all sites from these time periods, materials from the immediate locality dominate the assemblages, but frequently, stones from up to 50–100 km away occur in these assemblages as well (Naber 1970, Arora 1978, Hahn 1983, 1998, Gehlen 1988, Rieder and Tillman 1989, Baales and Street 1996, Karle 1998, Kind 1998). If these materials were obtained during the course of annual movements, then they may help in the identification of annual ranges. During the Late Palaeolithic, the Alpine sites contain some Jurassic chert from the Alb to the north, the sites in the Alb have some radiolarite from Oberschwaben, and sites in Oberschwaben have both. Thus, these three areas may be linked in the most frequent patterns of seasonal movement during this period. Along the Rhine, sites in the south contain some jasper from farther north in the valley and sites in the northern Rhine lowlands have some material from the south, again suggesting that patterned seasonal movement linked these two areas. Sites in the northern Rheinland-Pfalz are linked by raw materials primarily to sources up to 80–100 km to the north and northwest (Baales and Street 1996). During the Mesolithic, sites in Oberschwaben continue to contain substantial amounts of chert from the Alb, again linking these two areas in a likely annual range.

A remarkable feature of the archaeological record of most of this region is the changing pattern of site numbers through time. Late Palaeolithic sites are relatively abundant, at least in certain areas like Oberschwaben and the Swiss Plain; in fact, reanalysis of collections in these areas has led to the recognition that many traditionally 'Mesolithic' sites are, indeed, primarily Late Palaeolithic in age (Eberhard et al. 1987; Nielsen 1997). Smaller concentrations are known in the Birs Valley of Switzerland (Wyss 1968), the upper Danube (Albrecht 1983), the Alpine foothills (Reinerth 1956) and northern Bavaria (Naber 1970). During the Early Mesolithic, the number of known sites increases dramatically, as does their distribution. In virtually every area where people have looked, Early Mesolithic sites are the most numerous sites of these three periods, and the diversity of topographic positions occupied is also the greatest. During the Late Mesolithic, however, this pattern changes, and the number of known sites decreases precipitously in most areas (Gehlen 1988, Rieder and Tillman 1989, Jochim 1990, Cziesla 1998). Even if one allows for the fact that the Late Mesolithic was of shorter duration than the Early Mesolithic (Nielsen 1994), this decrease appears significant in many regions. Whole areas like the hills east of Stuttgart and western Lake Constance appear to have been virtually abandoned.

A number of interpretations for this pattern has been offered. Both Hahn (1983) and Cziesla (1998) question the reality of the decrease in site numbers, but on different grounds. Hahn suggests that changes in the forces of erosion and sediment deposition have simply destroyed or masked the Late Mesolithic sites to a greater degree. Cziesla, by contrast, hypothesizes that, in looking only for trapezoidal microliths, we are missing many Late Mesolithic sites lacking these supposed diagnostics. Taute (1974a) and Rieder and Tillman (1989) accept the pattern as real and suggest that it reflects a population decline, perhaps related to the progressive reforestation and the increased difficulty of hunting. Finally, Müller-Beck (1983) offers the suggestion that settlement locations shifted during the Late Mesolithic, leading to concentrations in areas of poor modern site visibility.

I have argued a position most in agreement with that of Müller-Beck, that a change in settlement pattern occurred in the Late Mesolithic (Jochim 1990). This change may not only have concentrated sites in less archaeologically visible locations, but also may have led to the creation of fewer sites altogether, without a decline in population levels. In brief, I believe a case can be made for a change from a highly mobile pattern of residential mobility during the Late Palaeolithic and

Early Mesolithic to a more logistically organised system of lower residential mobility during the Late Mesolithic.

The progressive reforestation of the Postglacial led to both increasingly dense forests and increasingly diverse vegetational communities. The relatively uniform pine and birch forests of the Late Glacial were gradually transformed into mosaics of different vegetational patches as the immigrating plants competed and adapted to different microenvironments. This must have led to a more differentiated distribution of animal species as well. Differences among microenvironments in resource productivity must have been magnified. A previous pattern of high-mobility foraging, which worked well in the more homogeneous forests, would have become less effective as important food resources became differentially distributed. Increasingly, only the most productive areas of the landscape may have attracted and supported residential occupations; other resources, in different locations, may have been more effectively procured through logistical forays.

Such an organisational change would have had a profound impact on the archaeological record. The number of residential camps created would have decreased considerably. The possibility of reoccupation of such camps in increasingly restricted areas would have increased, leading to fewer, but archaeologically more visible sites in certain productive areas. Late Mesolithic sites appear to be concentrated in locations offering high resource productivity and diversity, particularly certain lakeshores (the Federsee, Wauwilermoos) and the narrow upper Danube valley of the western Alb. Although these sites lack obvious evidence of major investments in the construction of features, as might be expected in residential camps of longer duration and more frequent use, they do show quite thick cultural layers (e.g., Falkenstein Cave, Inzigkofen Shelter) or purposeful discard areas and caches of bone (Henauhof Nordwest) indicative of more intensive use.

In this context of more logistic organisation, careful core preparation and blade manufacture may have increased in importance as 'gearing up' took place in the residential camps for logistical forays (Fisher 1990). Henauhof Nord II on the Federsee seems to represent such a logistic camp to which previously manufactured blades were carried. Tool reliability may have become more important in artefact design at the expense of maintainability (Bleed 1986) if limited periods of animal movements were anticipated and targeted. This would have led to a decline in the use of arrows with multiple stone barbs (and fewer microliths) and the development of some larger, complex implements, carefully made with redundant parts, such as the barbed antler harpoons, which would have been difficult to repair.

Exchange

It is difficult to distinguish exchange of materials from their direct procurement in the archaeological record of mobile hunter-gatherers. General, intuitive rules of thumb seem to guide most interpretations. Exchange is considered more likely as the distance between source and archaeological occurrence increases, as the proportion of retouched tools or blades (in contrast to cores and primary reduction debris) increases, and as the similarity in seasonal resource offerings between source and destination areas increases (making it less likely that they will be linked in patterned seasonal movements). These 'rules', of course, are problematic in several ways. None provides a quantitative threshold – in distance, proportions, or ecological similarity – to guide interpretations. There are still many debates in the literature about the size of home ranges of prehistoric hunter-gatherers, and no precise ecological models to allow us to predict them, with the result that ethnographic analogies still inform many interpretations, and these can vary. Exchange could involve the transport of either raw nodules or finished products, creating uncertainties in the use of this criterion (e.g., Auffermann 1996). Finally, the determination of seasonal movements is, as discussed earlier, difficult, and rendered more complex by the possibility of use of areas in multiple seasons (but perhaps in different ways) and of varying degrees of repetitiveness in seasonal movements (Jochim 1991).

The occurrence of stone raw materials at sites from sources 50–100 km away is not uncommon in this region, and was used above to suggest some gross patterns of seasonal movement that linked areas of considerable ecological differences. The underlying assumption is, of course, that such distances are reasonable to expect in the course of annual mobility. What is interesting is that a number of sites also contain very small amounts of materials deriving from greater distances – 200 km or more. This greater distance, together with the fact that the materials involved include not only stone but also fossils (hence, 'nonutilitarian' goods), suggests that these items are likely candidates for interpretations as exchange items.

During the Late Palaeolithic and Early Mesolithic, fossil shells from the area near the confluence of the Rhine and Main occur in sites on the upper Danube and in Oberschwaben (Rähle 1978, Jochim 1993, Gietz 1998). Banded chert from Bavaria has also been found in sites in these same areas (Jochim 1998). During the Late Mesolithic, these same patterns are found, but are supplemented by a few finds from even more distant sources. Shells from the Mediterranean have been found in the sites of Birsmatten in Switzerland, Falkenstein Cave in Baden-Württemberg, and Grosse Ofnet in Bavaria, and fossils in Grosse Ofnet and in Zigeunerfels in Baden-Württemberg derive from sources to the east along the Danube (Rähle 1978). These materials seem to have moved along routes of communication along the Rhone and Danube corridors.

It may be that these expanded networks of the Late Mesolithic reflect growing regional alliances in an increasingly competitive environment. It was during this period that hunting appears to have become more difficult, requiring some subsistence diversification, and that resource distributions became sufficiently differentiated so as to encourage a possible reorganisation of settlement to focus on locations of particular resource abundance and diversity. If such locations were relatively scarce, then competition over their use may have developed or intensified. Alliances among local groups may have been encouraged and maintained in part through exchange.

Burials

Human skeletal material is not abundant in this region (Newell et al. 1979, Probst 1991). A few sites of all three periods have been reported to contain isolated human teeth or bones in the assemblages, Dietfurt and Henauhof West in the Late Palaeolithic, Falkenstein and Steinbergwand Caves in the Early Mesolithic, and Inzigkofen Shelter and Jägerhaus Cave in the Late Mesolithic. True burials have been reported for only two sites, both from Early Mesolithic contexts, although their dating has been disputed. Birsmatten in Switzerland contained the burial of an adult woman associated with the lowest of its Mesolithic levels (Bandi 1963). A double burial of an adult woman and a child was found at Schellnecker Wänd in Bavaria, and the bodies were accompanied by a few stone artefacts and the beak of a bird (Naber 1977).

In addition, however, there are four finds in this area that have led to the interpretation of a 'skull cult' during the Late Mesolithic. The finds occur in eastern France (Mannlefelsen), Baden-Württemberg (Hohlenstein-Stadel), and Bavaria (Grosse Ofnet, Hexenküche by Kaufertsberg), and consist of skulls with associated vertebrae, but no additional body parts. The dating of some of them has been much disputed, but recent radiocarbon dating has confirmed the Late Mesolithic age of all but the Kaufertsberg find (Orschiedt 1998). The finds at Grosse Ofnet are the most impressive, consisting of two shallow pits, each containing a number of skulls, jaws, and vertebrae. A third pit between these two contained charcoal and charred bone fragments, which may represent the postcranial skeletons. The skulls face west and are covered with ash and red ochre. Originally, twenty-seven skulls were reported to be in one depression and six in the other, for a total of thirty-three, but more recent analyses suggest totals of thirty-four (Orschiedt 1998) and thirty-eight (Frayer 1997). Because of this discrepancy in numbers, it is difficult to ascertain the exact age and sex distribution of the skulls, but it is clear that children outnumber adults, and females outnumber males (in the original analysis there were twenty subadults, nine adult females, and four adult males). Evidence of bludgeon wounds to the head has been found on eighteen of the skulls, but differentially distributed by age and sex: they occur on 100 percent of the adult men, 23 percent of the adult women, and 58 percent of the children (Frayer 1997). As these wounds show no signs of healing growth, they are assumed to have occurred around the time of death, and to be the likely cause of death. A number of the skulls also show cut marks suggesting defleshing. The vertebrae also bear cut marks indicating decapitation by slitting the throat. Goods accompany many of the skulls, perhaps originally as part of necklaces or caps: 215 perforated deer teeth and 4,250 shells (Orschiedt 1998). In contrast to original reports in which only women had such associated ornaments, men appear to have some as well, although not as abundantly as adult women and children.

At the cave of Hohlenstein-Stadel, three skulls and associated vertebrae were found on a stone pavement in a depression together with red ochre and accompanied by perforated fish teeth (Orschiedt 1998). These skulls belong to an adult man, an adult woman, and a two-year-old child to four-year-old child, all facing southwest. Here, too, the vertebrae show evidence of decapitation and all three skulls bear signs of blows to the head. An interesting detail is the determination of hydrocephalus in the child's skull.

The finds at the other two sites are similar (Probst 1991). At Kaufertsberg an adult man's skull and two vertebrae were found in a depression, covered with red ochre. An adult male skull was also found at Mannlefelsen, together with jaw and vertebrae, on an arrangement of stones and surrounded by a stone alignment. Cut marks were found on the jaw and possibly on the base of the skull.

As might be imagined, these finds have fuelled much speculation. That they were intentionally buried is not in dispute, and it is clear that it was heads, not skulls, that were buried, as the jaws and vertebrae were usually in articular position, presumably held there by soft tissue. In the case of Ofnet, however, whether they were buried in one episode or many is debated. Frayer (1997) argues that they were interred in one episode, based on the undisturbed articular positioning and lack of evidence for rodent gnawing that might result from prolonged exposure. Consequently, he also suggests that they represent an example of a 'Mesolithic massacre' in order to account for such a large number of simultaneous deaths. By contrast, Orschiedt (1998) suggests that they were buried over a long period, and that, although some individuals certainly may have died a violent death, this need not imply a group massacre.

In either case, these finds document both a burial practice (and set of rituals?) distributed across this entire region and a high incidence of interpersonal violence. Their appearance during the Late Mesolithic may confirm the development of increasing levels of competition and conflict during this time, as well as a growing tendency to establish spiritual claims to particular areas by the burial of kin. Both may reflect an increasingly differentiated and disputed economic and social landscape.

Art and Ornaments

Items of adornment comprise the majority of nonutilitarian artefacts in this region. Many of these were obtained by exchange (shells, fossils) and, as perforated ornaments, were found accompanying burials. Perforated animal teeth are also common ornaments and include fish teeth, boar tusks, and canines of deer, wolf, and fox. The fish teeth are a unique type of ornament in the European Mesolithic. Consequently, in their study of the distribution of ornaments throughout the continent, Newell et al. (1990) defined a 'Fish Tooth Band' centred on the upper Danube, where most of these artefacts have been found. Perforated bone pendants, both plain and engraved, have been found in both Early and Late Mesolithic contexts at Schellnecker Wänd, Zigeunerfels, and Lautereck (Taute 1967, Taute 1972, Naber 1977).

Objects of 'art' are scarce. From the Late Palaeolithic, red-painted pebbles are known from Birseck-Ermitage in Switzerland, and two engraved stones from Niederbieber in the central Rhineland (Probst 1991, Baales and Street 1996). Mesolithic finds include an engraved antler fragment from Falkenstein Cave, an engraved stone from Ingendorf in the Rheinland-Pfalz, engraved bone fragments from Henauhof Nordwest in Oberschwaben and from Hohlstein Shelter in Bavaria, and a stone slab with a red-painted outline of a bovid from Felsställe (Campen et al. 1983, Probst 1991, Jochim 1998).

The End of the Mesolithic

A lively debate about the end of the Mesolithic and the beginning of the Neolithic in this region currently rages, and this chapter can do little justice to the complexities of the various arguments (see Lüning et al. 1989, Gronenborn 1990, 1994, Kind 1992, Tillman 1993, Nielsen 1994, Jochim 2000). Among the major points of contention are the following:

1. The role of immigration versus acculturation in the spread of economies based on domesticated plants and animals.
2. The role of southeastern versus southwestern Europe in the initial spread of such economies.
3. The degree of continuity in lithic typology and technology between the Late Mesolithic and the Early Neolithic.
4. The degree of chronological overlap between Late Mesolithic and Early Neolithic sites.

Until relatively recently, it was accepted that agricultural economies were introduced into this area by immigrants of the Linearbandkeramik Culture (LBK) from the east/southeast, with the local hunter-gatherers of the Late Mesolithic either displaced or absorbed. This scenario has been complicated by a number of discoveries. The La Hoguette Culture, characterised by ceramics, domesticated animals (but not plants), and a Mesolithic stone assemblage, is now known from sites both east and west of the Rhine (see also Valdeyron this volume). Its pottery, which bears many resemblances to that in southern France, is often found together with early LBK pottery at sites in Baden-Württemberg. One interpretation of this phenomenon is that La Hoguette represents a population of acculturated hunter-gatherers with contacts or origins in southern France. In addition, both certain microlith types and the method of preparing platforms for blade manufacture show continuity across the Mesolithic/LBK transition in this area. Furthermore, a number of radiocarbon dates for Late Mesolithic sites overlap those of early LBK sites, implying contemporaneity. Finally, a number of palynological and geological studies suggest that some degree of forest clearance occurred before the appearance of Neolithic sites in the archaeological record (Kossack and Schmeidl 1975, Semmel 1995, Haas 1996, Erny-Rodman et al. 1997).

From such evidence, it is clear that the processes underlying the transition to the Neolithic were not simply immigration and displacement. At the same time, however, the existing data are insufficient to provide a clear alternative interpretation. At the very least, it seems that the local Late Mesolithic groups, as bearers of a long-lasting cultural tradition, played a more active role in this transition than had previously been accepted.

Chapter 9

The Mesolithic of the Middle Danube and Upper Elbe Rivers

Jiří A. Svoboda*

Geographic Characteristics

The hilly regions of central Europe south of the North European Plain form a territory fragmented into subregions by highland barriers but unified by plains and large rivers such as the Danube and the Elbe (Figure 9.1). The Danube, the largest river, passes to the north of the Alps (present-day Austria), and subsequently enters the Carpathian Basin in the southeast, which is divided by the modern boundaries of Slovakia and Hungary. To the north, the present-day Czech Republic is composed of two geographic regions, Moravia and Bohemia. The Morava river, a tributary of the Danube, passes through the Moravian geomorphological corridor separating the Carpathian mountains in the east from the Bohemian massif in the west, and provides further access to the North European Plain (present-day Poland). The Bohemian massif, as an independent geomorphological unit, encircles the Upper Elbe Basin.

Mesolithic occupation, as reflected in the present-day archaeological record, demonstrates a change of settlement strategies compared to both the Upper Palaeolithic and the Neolithic. This is reflected in all three types of sites encountered in the region: open-air sites, karstic caves, and pseudokarstic rockshelters.

The distribution of open-air sites shows that in lowland regions, Mesolithic populations settled at elevations considerably lower than their Upper Palaeolithic predecessors, typically along rivers and lake edges. At the same time, previously unsettled or sparsely settled highland areas were also colonised, as on the Bohemian/Moravian Highland or in southern Bohemia, and, as extreme cases, in the high mountainous environments of the Alps.

Karstic landscapes such as the Moravian Karst, the Bohemian Karst or the Slovakian Karst usually form large peneplains of folded limestone cut by river valleys or penetrated by subterranean streams. These larger karstic areas are supplemented by smaller outcrops of limestone, also with

* Institute of Archaeology, Academy of Sciences of the Czech Republic.

221

Jiří A. Svoboda

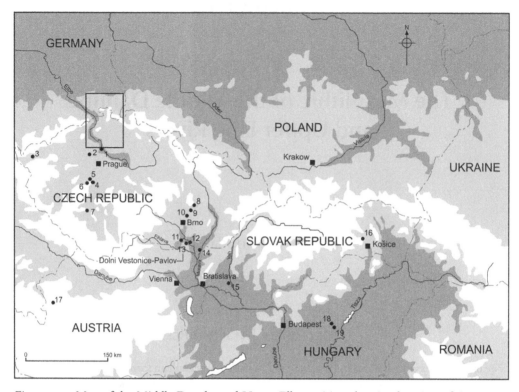

Figure 9.1. Map of the Middle Danube and Upper Elbe regions, showing location of sites men-
tioned in text. Oblong area: North Bohemian sandstone region (shown in detail on Figure
9.2). 1: Hořín, 2: Velká Bučina – Chržín, 3: Tašovice, 4–6: Bohemian karst (Martina, Bacín,
Za křížem, Na skalici), 7: Putim, 8: Průchodice Cave, 9: Kůlna Cave, 10: Barová Cave, 11:
Smolín, 12: Šakvice, 13: Dolní Věstonice, 14: Mikulčice, 15: Sered', 16: Medvedia Cave, 17:
Zigeunerhöhle Rockshelter, 18–19: Jászberény and Jásztelek.

caves, distributed throughout the region. Compared to the Upper Palaeolithic, some of the caves
selected for Late Palaeolithic and Mesolithic occupation are of smaller dimensions, some are only
partly sheltered (forming overhangs or abris), and some are located at higher elevations both
absolutely and in relation to the local valley floor. Presumably, most of these shelters functioned as
short-term hunting posts.

A typical feature of the North Bohemian landscape are sandstone plateaus cut by a network
of steep gorges with rockshelters (Figure 9.2). Whereas Upper Palaeolithic occupation has not
been recorded here, some of these "rock-cities" have recently provided evidence of systematic
Mesolithic settlement. These include the Polomené Mountains with several west–east and north–
south oriented valleys entering the adjacent Dubá basin, the Hradčanské Rocks, which is a compact
sandstone massif penetrated by east–west oriented gorges, the Peklo valley drained from south to
north by the Robečský River, the Bohemian Paradise, and the Elbe River Sandstones (Bohemian
Switzerland Natural Park) extending to the east of the Elbe River gorge and traversed from west
to east by the Kamenice River and its tributaries.

As a result of its favourable location in the European continent and to its geomorphological
characteristics enabling passage and communication to both hunters and animals, the Middle

222

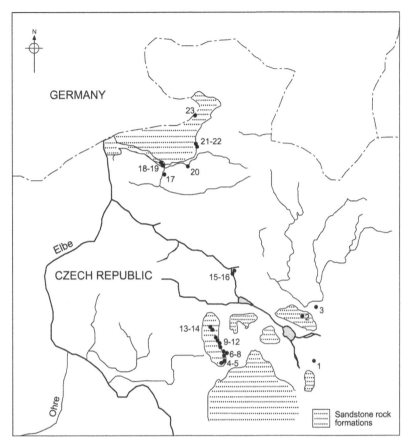

Figure 9.2. Detailed map of the North Bohemian sandstone region. 1: Bezděz, 2: Uhelná Gorge, 3: Donbas, 4–5: Vysoká and Nízká Lešnice, 6–8: Proškův Rockshelter, Strážník, Stará skála, 9–12: Máselník, Černá Louže, Pod Černou Louží, Šídelník, 13–14: Heřmánky, Hvězda, 15–16: Pod zubem and Pod křídlem Rockshelters, 17: Arba, 18–19: Dolský Mlýn, Okrouhlík, 20: Sojčí Rockshelter, 21–22: Švédův and Jezevčí Rockshelters, 23: S. Vencl's Rockshelter.

Danube region played a central role during the Upper Palaeolithic. By the end of the Pleistocene and during the earlier Holocene, as the North European Plain and Baltic opened up to more systematic human occupation, the Middle Danube region appears to have become more peripheral. This trend is reflected in the history and intensity of Late Palaeolithic/Mesolithic research in the North European Plain, representing present-day Germany and Poland, which profits from a longer tradition and larger sites compared to Hungary, Austria, Slovakia, and the Czech Republic. Most researchers in the latter countries would agree that the Mesolithic is the least well-known period of their local prehistories.

By contrast, the Middle Danube region was open to movements of people and ideas arriving from the southeast at an earlier date, which is the expected source area for the introduction of agriculture and farming populations. In southern Hungary, the early Neolithic radiocarbon dates of the Körös culture extend back to about 7000 years BP (i.e., about 6000 cal BC), whereas most of the remaining territory was colonised by Linear Pottery settlement about five hundred years later.

223

Jiří A. Svoboda

The earliest radiocarbon dates for Linear Pottery are similar to the latest for the Mesolithic, around 6500 BP (5500 cal BC), thus raising the issue of Mesolithic-Neolithic contact and interaction.

History of Research and Mesolithic Concepts

By the end of the nineteenth century, the first generations of researchers focusing on exploration of karstic caves suspected a kind of transitional period somewhere between the Diluvial and Alluvial layers, but without a solid stratigraphic background (e.g., Maška 1886). Early in the twentieth century, the spread of surface research in open-air landscapes revealed a number of lithic assemblages, some of which were Mesolithic (Limberg and Burgschleinitz in the Danube valley, Kozly in the Elbe valley), but some were later labelled Neolithic or later (Skutil 1940: 89–99, Dobosi 1972, Antl-Wieser 1993). In addition, the misused "Campignian" concept, interpreted as a Mesolithic facies of crude stone tools, led to mistaken classification of a number of Palaeolithic artefacts and Post-Mesolithic workshop sites as Mesolithic. The result was a general scepticism shared by some leading authorities about the very existence of the Mesolithic in this region.

It is interesting to note that, as early as the 1930s, local German amateurs working in the sandstone regions of North Bohemia correctly recognised the finds there as representing a 'Middle Stone Age'. The first excavation of Mesolithic rockshelters was undertaken by J. Laufka at four sites around Lhota near Dubá, but the results were only published as a newspaper note, and the precise location of the sites is not known. At the same time, K. Stellwag surveyed Mesolithic open-air sites around Stvolínky in the same region (Franz 1933). Later, unfortunately, the sites were attributed to the Neolithic, and the finds were almost forgotten.

Systematic research of Mesolithic open-air sites was initiated after World War II by K. Žebera (1958), F. Prošek (1951, 1959), B. Klíma (1953), K. Valoch (1978, 1981), S. Vencl (1971), Vencl and colleagues (2006), J. Svoboda (1977), J. Bárta (1981), Kértész et al. (1994), and others. Simultaneously, a methodological improvement in the field investigation of cave archaeology brought to light Late Palaeolithic and Mesolithic layers from karstic caves, first from Kůlna (Valoch 1988) and later from a number of smaller cave sites (Bárta 1990, Horáček et al. 2002). Because of better conditions for organic preservation, cave sites provide important biostratigraphic and environmental evidence (Ložek and Cílek 1995). However, as a result of intensive early research in the karstic regions, the sedimentary fill of these caves was largely dug out, and little remains today. In contrast, the hitherto almost unexplored sandstone rockshelters in North Bohemia (Prošek and Ložek 1952), which have been the subject of a systematic excavation and survey project since the 1990s (Svoboda et al. 1998, 2000, Svoboda 2003), are especially promising for the archaeology of the last foragers, with good opportunities for contextual studies of Holocene palaeoclimatology, environment, settlement strategies, and resource exploitation.

Since the definition of the Mesolithic in a modern sense about half a century ago, the question of its boundaries with the preceding and subsequent periods has been addressed. Concerning the origins of the period, an important step was the definition of the regional Late Palaeolithic (Vencl 1970, Valoch 1981) as a one-thousand-year period of Late Glacial adaptation prior to the Mesolithic but showing clear trends towards the microlithisation of artifacts. More complex is the question of the relationship with the Neolithic. M. Mazálek (1954), using comparative studies of lithic typology, interpreted certain tool types of transcultural occurrence such as trapezes and certain arrowheads as indicators of Mesolithic-to-Neolithic continuity, reaching as late as later Neolithic and Chalcolithic periods. This theory faced strong criticism from Vencl (1960), who argued for a total population change at the Mesolithic-Neolithic boundary (see also J. K. Kozlowski 1981, Vencl

1986). Later studies of lithic technologies also suggest that a general change in core preparation and reduction strategies was more important than a morphological similarity visible in individual tool types. To clarify this question, however, a solid chronological framework is necessary, with emphasis on data from the latest Mesolithic and the earliest Neolithic, and the possibility of overlap of the two.

Environmental Change and Chronology

Chronological questions may be addressed by biostratigraphic evidence, archaeological typology, and radiocarbon dating. Vegetation reconstructions are mostly based on pollen-analytical records from peatbogs in various geographic contexts in the Middle Danube and Upper Elbe regions, notably in Hungary (Kértész et al. 1994), in South Moravia (Svobodová 1997, Rybníček and Rybníčková 2001) and in Northwest Bohemia (Jankovská 1992, 2000), but never directly from archaeological sites and layers. Another type of terrestrial record are stratigraphic sections in karstic cave entrances (Valoch 1988, Ložek and Cílek 1995, Horáček et al. 2002), and in pseudokarstic rockshelters (Svoboda et al. 1998, 2000, Svoboda 2003), with palaeobotanical macroremains, molluscs, and other faunal remains in archaeological context and with relatively high-resolution chronology. The correlation between these types of record poses a notable problem.

The Late Glacial (13,000–10,000 BP) was marked by milder climate with warmer and moister oscillations such as the Bölling and Alleröd. In the early part of the Late Glacial, loess ceased to accumulate and began to show initial pedogenesis or to be replaced by shallow colluvial deposits. The formation of chernozem soils in arid loess areas began, and rendsina soils appeared for the first time in karst areas. As the landscape changed, lightly wooded taiga dominated by *Pinus sylvestris* and *Betula* expanded during warmer fluctuations, whereas thermophilous trees like oak probably made their first appearance as isolated stands. Areas of marshes and shallow lakes appeared and meadows replaced steppe vegetation. Large areas were still open. In the northern part of the Moravian Karst, areas characterised by scree slopes and sparse vegetation were recolonised. Generally speaking, the landscape acquired a mosaic configuration and showed a much higher diversity in both habitat and species than the preceding pleniglacial. However, there is not sufficient evidence at the moment to identify the impact of the last colder oscillation of the Upper Dryas.

The Preboreal (10,000–9000 BP) was a period of dramatic climatic change, with mean annual temperatures about 3 degrees lower than today, but the vegetation composition did not respond immediately. We observe a growing density and extent of the previous birch-pine stands and a simultaneous retreat of steppe vegetation.

The Boreal (9000–7500 BP) saw a further temperature increase, with mean annual values 2–3 degrees higher than today. *Quercus*, *Ulmus*, and *Corylus* invaded the birch-pine forests. Heliophilic and montane plants disappeared.

The Atlantic (7500–4500 BP) is characterised by continuity of warm and humid conditions. Thermophilous oak forest and mesophilous mixed lime-oak forest spread in the lowlands, with new trees such as *Tilia*, *Acer*, *Fraxinus*, *Ulmus*, and *Taxus* spreading over the whole territory.

In the individual subregions, there is considerable variability within this general picture. This is especially visible if we compare pollen diagrams from the Hungarian Plain, showing a larger extent of open areas alternating with deciduous forests (Kértész et al. 1994), with those from Northern Bohemia, dominated by coniferous forests (e.g., Jankovská 1992). This pattern of variation is also supported by analysis of palaeobotanical macroremains, especially charcoal.

Jiří A. Svoboda

Table 9.1. Review of Magdalenian, Late Palaeolithic, and Mesolithic radiocarbon dates from Hungary, Austria, Slovakia, and the Czech Republic (except North Bohemia)

Site	Layer	Material	Lab. No.	Date (BP)	Cal BC 2σ
Pekárna	Layer gh	Bone	Ly-2553	12,940 ± 250	14200–12300
Pekárna	Layer 6–7	Bone	GrN-14828	12,670 ± 80	13350–12500
Pekárna	Layer 6–7	Antler	OxA-5972	12,500 ± 110	13100–12200
Kolíbky	Cultural layer	Antler	OxA-5973	12,680 ± 110	13400–12350
Nová Drátenická		Bone	OxA-1953	13,870 ± 140	15100–14050
Nová Drátenická		Bone	OxA-1954	12,900 ± 140	13850–12850
Nová Drátenická		Bone	OxA-1952	11,670 ± 150	11900–11250
Kůlna	Layer 6		GrN-5097	11,590 ± 80	11700–11320
Kůlna	Layer 6		GrN-11053	11,450 ± 90	11530–11170
Kůlna	Layer 4		GrN-6102	11,470 ± 105	11620–11180
Kůlna	Layer 3		GrN-6120	10,070 ± 85	10050–9300
Koněprusy	Proškův dóm	Human bone	GrA-13696	12,870 ± 70	13600–12950
Hostim	Cultural layer		Ly-1108	12,420 ± 470	13900–11400
Moča	Danube River	Human bone	OxA-7068	11,225 ± 80	11310–11000
Zigeunerhöhle		Human bone	ETH Zürich	8020 ± 125	7350–6600
Jászberény	II-C	Molluscs	Deb-1966	8030 ± 250	7600–6400
Jászberény		Carbonate	Deb-2466	7350 ± 80	6400–6050
Bacín	Base of a fissure	Human femur	OxA-9271	9490 ± 65	9150–8600
Martina	Vesmírná corridor sector C	Charcoal	Praha	8219 ± 219	7700–6500
Smolín		Bone	GrN-7662	8315 ± 55	7520–7180

Dates are given as uncalibrated BP (see Lanting & Van der Plicht 2000 for a recent review) and calibrated ranges at 2 sigma as cal BC. Dates have been calibrated using OxCal v3.10 (Bronk Ramsey 1995, 2001).

Compared to later prehistoric and present-day conditions, the environmental evidence from the North Bohemian rockshelters shows that Mesolithic conditions were more favourable in a number of aspects. The soils were more calcareous and moister, and the vegetation and fauna more diverse. The relatively dense Mesolithic settlement was probably related to these favourable environmental conditions.

Our archaeological chronology is based on the appearance of diagnostic points and microliths, such as curved-backed points and backed blades for the Late Palaeolithic, triangles for the earlier Mesolithic and trapezoids for the late Mesolithic. However, a number of open-air sites show the simultaneous appearance of these types, probably because of stratigraphic mixing. The evidence from cave and rockshelter sections, if correlated to biostratigraphy and radiocarbon dating, potentially provides a more secure and fine-grained framework (Tables 9.1 and 9.2). However, at present, chronological boundaries (as given here, in uncalibrated dates) remain provisional.

The Late Palaeolithic (11,000–10,000 BP) is characterised by the first appearance of microlithic artefacts, although there is also considerable variability, with at least three industrial variants. An Epimagdalenian tradition with backed microblades is found mainly in caves, such as Kůlna, Barová Cave, Tří volů Cave, and Dolní Cave. Second, there are assemblages with backed curved points, which appear in the northwest (the Federmessergruppe of Northern Bohemia and the Tišnovian

Table 9.2. Review of Mesolithic radiocarbon dates from the North Bohemian rockshelters

Site	Context	Depth	Material	Lab No	Date BP	Cal BC
Pod zubem	Hearth	75	Charcoal	GrN-23332	6790 ± 70	5990–5720
Pod zubem	Charcoal	80	Charcoal	GrN-23333	6580 ± 50	5620–5470
Bezděz	Charcoal	140	Charcoal	GrN-25772	6930 ± 120	6030–5620
Dolský mlýn	Charcoal	175	Charcoal	GrN-26557	6720 ± 120	5890–5460
Dolský mlýn	Hearth	210	Charcoal	GrN-26558	7020 ± 50	6010–5780
Dolský mlýn	Hearth	240	Charcoal	GrA-19156	7770 ± 70	6780–6450
Dolský mlýn	Charcoal	260	Charcoal	GrA-19157	6910 ± 60	5980–5670
Okrouhlík I	Hearth		Charcoal	GrA-19158	7300 ± 60	6350–6020
Okrouhlík II	Hearth		Charcoal	GrA-19161	7940 ± 70	7050–6650
Šídelník I	Charcoal	76–79	Charcoal	GrA-11456	7120 ± 80	6210–5810
Šídelník I	Charcoal	90	Charcoal	GrN-24213	7830 ± 170	7200–6350
Černá Louže	Charcoal	c.230	Charcoal	GrN-21558	7950 ± 80	7060–6650
Pod Č. Louží	Charcoal	120–125	Charcoal	GrA-11455	7620 ± 80	6640–6260
Vys. Lešnice	Charcoal	c.240	Charcoal	GrN-24217	7930 ± 160	7300–6450
Pod zubem	Charcoal	115–120	Charcoal	GrN-23335	7660 ± 130	7000–6200
Pod zubem	Charcoal	115	Charcoal	GrN-23334	8110 ± 240	7600–6500
Pod křídlem	Charcoal	50–70	Charcoal	GrN-23331	8160 ± 80	7500–6800
Švédův rock	Charcoal	120–130	Charcoal	GrN-25170	8180 ± 110	7550–6800
Šídelník III	Hearth	80	Charcoal	GrN-24214	8300 ± 150	7600–6800
Uhel. rokle II	Hearth	70	Charcoal	GrN-25776	8410 ± 65	7590–7330
Hlavatá rock	Hearth	90–125	Charcoal	GdA-531	8480 ± 50	7600–7480
Jezevčí rock	Hearth 3	240	Charcoal	GrN-25170	8530 ± 150	8200–7150
Máselník I	Charcoal 6	110	Charcoal	GrN-21556	8560 ± 70	7740–7490
Máselník I	Charcoal 7	130	Charcoal	GrN-21557	8790 ± 70	8250–7600
Okrouhlík I	Pit 5	–	Charcoal	GrA-19162	8680 ± 70	7950–7580
Okrouhlík I	Pit 6	–	Charcoal	GrA-19163	9170 ± 70	8570–8260
Nízká Lešnice	Charcoal	120	Charcoal	GrN-24210	10,160 ± 190	10700–9200

Dates are given as uncalibrated BP (see Lanting & Van der Plicht 2000 for a recent review) and calibrated ranges at 2 sigma as cal BC. Dates have been calibrated using OxCal v3.10 (Bronk Ramsey 1995, 2001).

in Moravia). Finally, there are rare tanged points (Vencl 1970, Valoch 1981, Svoboda et al. 1996). An "exotic" typological feature, hitherto without parallel elsewhere, is the appearance of Helwan segments, typical of the Natufian, on the surface site of Šakvice in south Moravia (Figure 9.3). From all these sites, radiocarbon dates are very rare.

The earlier Mesolithic (10,000–7000 BP), with a dominance of microlithic triangles, segments and Tardenoisian points as diagnostic tool types, was originally labelled Tardenoisian and more recently Beuronian, or the Beuron-Coincy culture (S. K. Kozlowski 1981). Radiocarbon dates are available from Jászberény and Smolín in the southeastern plains (Table 9.1), and from a number of North Bohemian rockshelters (Table 9.2, Figure 9.4).

The later Mesolithic (7000–6500) is predominantly characterised by geometric trapezes and blades longer than before. In the southeast, several sites on the Hungarian plain and in south Moravia may fall into this interval, for example, Jásztelek, Mikulčice (cf. Kértész et al. 1994, Škrdla et al.

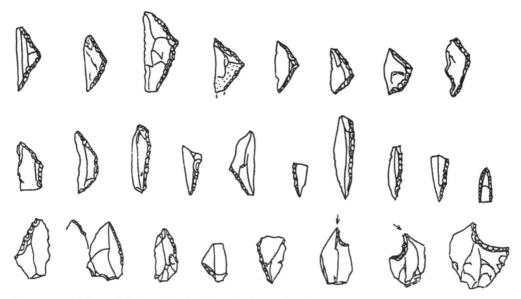

Figure 9.3. Arba rockshelter, North Bohemia. Example of an earlier Mesolithic industry. Full size.

1997), even if these assemblages may not be culturally uniform. If the expected dates are correct, these sites are contemporaneous with the earliest Neolithic of the Körös culture, expanding from the southeast, for example, Gyálarét-Szilágyi at 7090 ± 100 BP (see also Horváth and Hertelendi 1994). In Northern Bohemia, the youngest Mesolithic dates from Pod zubem, Bezděz and Dolský Mlýn rockshelters (Table 9.2) are as young as 6500 BP, and could theoretically represent the persistence of a foraging population in an agriculturally unfavourable rocky highland. In all of the rockshelters excavated so far, Linear Pottery is absent or only represented by a few potsherds (Heřmánky, for example). However, the Stroked Pottery of the succeeding period forms a clear horizon in a network of rockshelters, as in open-air sites in the vicinity. In the Bezdez rockshelter, the late Mesolithic and Stroked Pottery layers are separated by a thick sterile layer.

Resources, Economy, and Subsistence

Lithic Resources

One of the dominant trends observed in European Mesolithic economies is an emphasis on local lithic raw materials for tool production, only partly supplemented by imports (Vencl 1990). This picture is in contrast to previous, labour-expensive Upper Palaeolithic economies, where we observe a clear dominance of imports from distances reaching hundreds of km (e.g., Svoboda et al. 1996).

The most important imports are flint nodules of morainic origin from areas covered by the Pleistocene glaciations (the North European Plain generally). However, some flint nodules could have been distributed further to the south by rivers such as the Ploučnice or Morava, so that when found in the northern parts of Bohemia or Moravia, this material is still considered as virtually local, or transported over relatively short distances.

Figure 9.4. Dolský Mlýn Rockshelter, North Bohemia (excavation 2001).

Local materials form a true mosaic following the individual subregions. In the southeast, the Carpathian Basin supplied quartzites, especially limnoquartzites, and menilites, whereas obsidian sources were available in the volcanic areas of the northeastern part of the Basin and radiolarites in the Carpathians and Alps. Moravia supplied several types of cherts (Krumlovský Les-type, Olomučany-type, etc.), and Bohemia various fine-grained quartzites (Bečov, Tušimice and Skršín types), jasper, porcelanite, and serpentinites. Materials of south German (Bavarian) origin are also recorded in the western part of the region. The emphasis on the nearest available material may be explained by relatively small territories at a subregional level, whereas the ubiquitous presence of imports indicates contact at a larger geographical scale.

In addition, coarse-grained sedimentary rocks and volcanites were used for a variety of other purposes (hammerstones, grinding stones, polishing and polished stones, heat accumulators in hearths), and such materials were usually locally available.

Vegetational and Faunal Resources

K. Valoch (1977) initially suggested the possibility of plant food exploitation on the basis of two grinding stones found at Smolín, although supporting palaeobotanical evidence was not available at the time. Recently, however, flotation of Mesolithic deposits in the Jezevčí rockshelter by P. Pokorný has revealed palaeobotanical macroremains, mainly seeds, of the following species: *Sambucus nigra, Picea abies, Rubus idaeus, Chenopodium album, Rubus* sp., *Pinus sylvestris, Coryllus avellana, Poaceae*. These results suggest gathering of plants, as in the case of *Sambucus nigra*, or berries such as *Rubus*. Other plant remains include hazelnut shells recovered from several North Bohemian rockshelters.

A further source of evidence comes from preliminary analysis of the residue and use-wear data from the Pod zubem and Pod křídlem rockshelters (Hardy 1999). These analyses indicate that stone tools were used to exploit a wide range of resources. Plant materials are represented by possibly starchy material, wood, and other plants. Traces of hair and feathers on lithic implements indicate that both avian and mammalian resources were being exploited, most probably for food, which, of course, does not exclude other purposes.

Unfortunately, relatively little faunal evidence is available from open-air sites, probably because of factors affecting bone preservation. At the Hungarian Plain sites of Jászberény and Jásztelek, Kértész et al. (1994) record the dominance of bovids (aurochs), supplemented by red deer, deer, horse, pig, and individual finds of turtle and birds' eggs. Another faunal spectrum is available from Smolín in south Moravia (Valoch 1978), with a dominance of horse (based on teeth), accompanied by bovids, beaver, elk, wild pig, fox, and red deer. The North Bohemian rockshelters follow a similar pattern, but in the Pod zubem rockshelter, the larger species are outnumbered by smaller forest animals such as marten, wild cat, beaver, fox, wolf, and hare (Horáček 1999). In addition, some rockshelters yielded individual specimens of turtle, frog (*Bufo* cf. *bufo*), and birds. In the faunal assemblage from Dolský Mlýn, a rockshelter located on the bank of the Kamenice River, I. Horáček (in Svoboda 2003) also noted the presence of fish vertebrae, some representing individuals up to 1 m long, but of undetermined species.

In the inner parts of the Medvedia Cave near Ružín, east Slovakia, J. Bárta (1990) discovered the skeletal remains of two bears (*Ursus arctos*) together with two bone projectiles. According to Bárta, at least one of the bears was killed by the projectile, which was found directly among the ribs. This provides a rare piece of direct evidence for bear hunting in caves.

Initially, it was thought that the pattern of settlement in North Bohemia was one of seasonal movements between the open-air sites in the lowlands and the rockshelters in the surrounding sandstone plateaus (Svoboda 1977). However, additional research has provided only limited evidence to test this seasonal model. In some of the North Bohemian rockshelters, as at Pod zubem, the faunal composition shows a dominance of fur-bearing animals, and the characteristics of the bone industry, with a dominance of awls, suggest working of furs and hides, possibly in expectation of the approaching winter. Finds of hazelnuts at the same site also suggest a late summer or early autumn occupation. Overall, however, there is little evidence to support or reject specific models of settlement patterns involving links between these different types of sites.

Open-Air Settlement, Caves, and Rockshelters

Although a relatively large number of Mesolithic sites is recorded from the Middle Danube and Upper Elbe region (Figure 9.1), most of them are small in terms of size and artefact numbers. This is particularly evident in comparison with larger sites in the North European Plain and Baltic. In addition, certain sites form structured regional clusters, as in various parts of Bohemia. Some authors have argued that this distribution reflects the selection of areas for survey in accordance with preconceived hypotheses about settlement patterns (Vencl 1971, 1989). However, most of the regional clusters were not discovered by problem-oriented surveys but result from general field research and can be considered as more or less representative. Therefore, the observed distribution of sites, their relatively small size, and interregional variations can all be used as starting points for discussing Mesolithic social organisation and settlement strategies.

Open Air Sites

Vencl (1971) has critically examined the so-called law of sand as applied to Mesolithic settlement in general and equally in central Europe. However, his argument that association of sites with sand deposits is merely a result of a better visibility of artefacts during field surveys appears to be only partially justified. The distribution of sites detected by surface surveys really demonstrates that an important portion of Mesolithic settlement is located on low elevation (100–200 m a.s.l.) sandy deposits and dunes along rivers and lake edges. The formation of dunes, a favourite human habitat, was one of the important developments within the lowland regions during the Late Glacial and Early Holocene. Dune sites are known in western Slovakia, for example, at Mačanské vršky near Sered' (Bárta 1981) and south Moravia, where a number of the sites coincide with lowland fortifications and cemeteries of early Medieval age, for example, at Mikulčice, Staré Město, Pohansko, Strachotín, and Dolní Věstonice (Klíma 1953, Škrdla et al. 1997). Unfortunately, the dune stratigraphy is not fine enough to supply good quality contextual and archaeological data. Besides dunes, other important sites are Barca in east Slovakia (Prošek 1959), Jászberény in Hungary (Kértész et al. 1994), and Kamegg in Lower Austria (Antl-Wieser 1993).

The site of Smolín in the Dyje and Svratka lowlands of south Moravia is the only one known more widely in the western literature (Valoch 1985). Here, K. Valoch (1977) conducted a complex excavation of two Mesolithic features described as large oval-shaped pits, which produced a rich lithic industry with geometric triangles, faunal remains and radiocarbon dates (Table 9.1). A smaller site with a smaller circular pit and a lithic assemblage was excavated at Dolní Věstonice V (Svoboda 1992).

In Bohemia, open-air sites were excavated on the shores of the Řežabinec Lake at Putim in south Bohemia (Mazálek 1953), albeit in the context of earlier Palaeolithic occupations, above the Ohře River at Tašovice in western Bohemia (Prošek 1951) and on the banks of the Elbe River at Hořín in central Bohemia (Sklenář 2000). All these sites have features and pits of various shapes and dimensions, although there are unfortunately no radiocarbon dates. Most recently, large-scale rescue excavations by I. Sýkorová and J. Fridrich at Velká Bučina and Chržín, central Bohemia, have provided new evidence of settlement ground plans with features and Mesolithic industries.

Certainly, a critical approach to the interpretation of features at open-air sites is necessary (Newell 1981). It seems that some of these pits are Mesolithic and man-made structures, but we have to be cautious in explaining them either as dwellings or refuse pits, or in other terms, and each site should be analysed with respect to its own depositional and postdepositional history.

Mesolithic settlement patterns show a trend towards the occupation of previously unoccupied or sparsely occupied highland areas, up to 500 m a.s.l., with the Bohemian/Moravian Highland and the hill regions of south Bohemia as typical examples of such landscapes. The extreme cases of high altitude Mesolithic locations are the south Bohemian sites in the Šumava Mountains, with altitudes of 725 m (Vencl 1989) and especially the Alpine sites in the Austrian Tirol, reaching altitudes of 2300 m (e.g., Stadler 1991). Other mountainous sites are known from the Italian side of the Alps. A plausible explanation is increasing population pressure together with favourable environmental changes by the end of the Pleistocene and in the earlier Holocene, opening the highlands for more permanent settlement, resource exploitation and exploration of extreme altitudes.

Karstic Caves and Rockshelters

During earlier excavations in karstic caves, before the systematic application of sieving and flotation, it is highly probable that scattered Mesolithic artefacts of small size, stratified between easily visible Neolithic and Magdalenian layers, would have escaped attention. Thus, we are probably currently dealing with only a fragment of the real settlement system in the karst. Biostratigraphic chronology provides a substitute for radiocarbon dates but, given the mosaic and patchy character of the early Holocene landscapes, chronological relationships are not always clear. It is especially difficult to draw a clear stratigraphic boundary between Late Palaeolithic and Mesolithic occupation on the basis of the karstic record. Man-made features and hearths are difficult to recognise in cave sediments, with the notable exception of a pit burial in the Zigeunerhöhle in Austria (Rettenbacher and Tichy 1994).

In Moravia, stratified Late Palaeolithic and Mesolithic material was first recorded during systematic excavations at Kůlna Cave in the Moravian karst (Valoch 1988), and at a smaller site with important stratigraphy in the Barová Cave (Horáček et al. 2002). A few other smaller sites, always with a few artefacts, were recorded from Moravia, at altitudes of 350–520 m a.s.l., at Soutěska rockshelter in the Pavlovlské Hills (Late Palaeolithic or early Mesolithic), Pruchodice I cave in central Moravia (Svoboda and Ložek 1993), and Velká Kobylanka rockshelter (Ložek et al. 1959), and from Slovakia (Bárta 1990). In the Bohemian karst, Late Palaeolithic occupation has been documented in the small caves of Tří volů and Dolní, and Mesolithic in the caves of Martina, Za křížem, and Na Skalici. At the entrance section of the Martina Cave, the Mesolithic assemblage is dominated by a perforated axe of deer antler (Vencl 1996) and a charcoal layer deeper in the cave supplied a Mesolithic radiocarbon date (Table 9.1, Žák and Melková 1999). The environment of these smaller caves comprised landscapes of forest and scrub and open rocky and steppe areas during the Preboreal and Boreal periods (Horáček et al. 2002). Finally, a karstic fissure on the top of the Bacín Hill included human skeletal fragments, dated to the Mesolithic (Matoušek 2002). With the exception of Kůlna, these Late Palaeolithic and Mesolithic cave sites are just episodic hunting posts. Stone artefacts are scarce, and with almost no use-wear traces (A. Šajnerová in Horáček et al. 2002).

Pseudokarstic (Sandstone) Rockshelters

The sandstone regions, especially in Northern Bohemia, remained unexplored by earlier researchers until recently (Svoboda 2003, Svoboda et al. 2007). Proving Mesolithic occupation in the adjacent region of Bohemian Paradise, where the sites were known but some were misinterpreted, is another issue that has recently come into focus (Šída and Prostředník 2007). Current work aims to investigate a representative sample of sites rather than to explore them in totality (Figure 9.2, Figure 9.4). Compared to the predominantly episodic occupation of karstic caves, some of the pseudokarstic rockshelters include rich cultural layers, labour-intensive stone-built hearths, and lithic industries with evidence of use-wear traces. Larger oval-shaped or circular pits, comparable to the ones discovered at open-air sites, also were excavated in some of the rockshelters (Heřmánky, Pod zubem). Evidence from rockshelters also provides an opportunity to analyse spatial relationships between natural features, such as the rock walls and sheltered areas, and man-made features such as hearths, post-holes, and artefact densities. In this site context, it seems that we are dealing with artificial structures, and the ground plans suggest dwelling facilities. The quantity of artefacts varies from tens to thousands of pieces, but there is no correlation between the number of pieces and the complexity of features. The richest sites are in the north (Okrouhlík, Arba, Švédův rockshelters) near the German border, suggesting possible relationships north of the modern border and onto the North European Plain. Some of the southern sites, by contrast, offer better conditions for organic preservation, thus supplying better faunal evidence and some bone industries, and these seem to be related rather to the open-air sites of Central Bohemia.

Technology

Recent excavation has revealed new evidence for hearth construction at certain rockshelters, and for pyrotechnology in general. Some of the hearths are elaborate, filled with blocks of sandstone (Pod zubem, Šídelník III rockshelters) and ferrous sandstone (Stará skála rockshelter), both available locally, or with basalt cobbles brought in from nearby river deposits (Dolský Mlýn, Okrouhlík rockshelters). The stones are interpreted as heat accumulators. In some cases, pan-shaped pits, filled with ash, were recovered below the covering of stone blocks. A system of adjacent kettle-shaped pits were hollowed out around some other hearths, and some still included heated pebbles around, suggesting use as a boiling pit (Figure 9.5). Interestingly, whereas the 'normal' hearths, composed only of charcoal and reddened and burnt sand, are located in central parts of the sheltered areas (and the stratigraphic sequences illustrate that such optimal places have repeatedly been selected for founding hearths until recent times), the more elaborate hearths with stone blocks or pebbles tend to be located at the peripheries. These hearths and related facilities have clearly been used both for warmth and for cooking of food. Similar types of associations of hearths and pan-shaped and kettle-shaped pits have been recorded at complex Upper Palaeolithic sites such as Dolní Věstonice.

Lithic raw materials were mostly available as nodules from glacial moraines, from primary sources of quartzite and chert, and as pebbles from secondary fluvial deposits. Mining is unknown during the Mesolithic, but the evidence from the chocolate flint outcrops in Poland, such as Tomaszów, suggests at least an intensive exploitation, and an adjacent burial at Janislawice has been ascribed to someone who worked in a mine (Cyrek 1995). At Stvolínky I, North Bohemia, some of the stone artefacts and larger cores were made from large quartzite blocks, which are scattered around the site, whereas the majority of artefacts were made from imported flint (Svoboda 1977). Generally, the cores at Mesolithic sites are mostly smaller than 3 cm, and some show remains of pebble cortex on the surface, which means that secondary sources in glacial and fluvial sediments were relied on more than primary outcrops. As in other parts of Europe, the technology of cores, microblades, and small flakes demonstrates an emphasis on microlithic implements used as inserts in composite tools.

Figure 9.5. Hearths with basalt pebbles from the 2005 excavations at the Okrouhlík Rockshelter, North Bohemia.

Two bilaterally grooved bone projectiles, with stone blades ready to be inserted, were found in the Medvedia Cave near Ružín in association with bear skeletons (Figure 9.6, Bárta 1990). In addition, the preliminary analysis of the residue and use-wear traces on lithic artefacts from Pod zubem and Pod křídlem rockshelters (Hardy 1999) confirms that stone tools were being hafted. Resin appears to have been used as a mastic to help hold some tools into a haft, whereas the wood tissue found on some artefacts may be actual remnants of such a haft.

Unfavourable conditions for organic preservation at most of the sites limit the possibilities of recovering any bone industry. Nonetheless, from the North Bohemian Mesolithic, we have a whole series of simple bone awls, supplemented by a chisel-shaped artefact from the Pod zubem rockshelter, and the cave of Martina in the Bohemian karst has yielded a pierced axe of deer antler (Figure 9.6). Recently, longitudinal wooden objects, clearly worked, were recovered from Early Holocene peat-bog deposits at the Švarcenberk pond in South Bohemia (Šída et al. 2007).

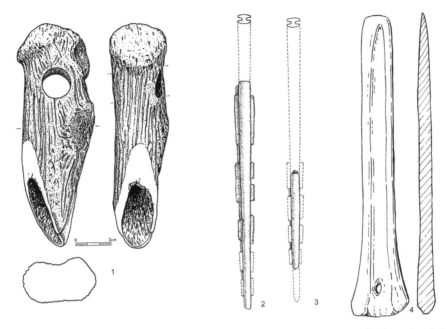

Figure 9.6. Bone implements. 1: Martina Cave, 2–3: Medvedia Cave, 4: Pod zubem Rockshelter.

Finally, some Mesolithic industries are supplemented by larger hammerstones, stone plaques, and polishing stones, including typical grooved polishers, as at Smolín and Nizká Lešnice.

Symbolism, Burials, and Other Human Remains

In general, the evidence of symbolism is extremely poor. Two cases of engraved stones were found at the Mesolithic surface sites of Přibice (Valoch 1981, Abb.3) and Putim 3 (Vencl 2001), but, given the context, their Mesolithic age and symbolic significance remains unproven. From the later Mesolithic layers at the Bezděz rockshelter, we found a polished and finely pierced deer canine, and an unfinished pierced artefact was recovered from the same context.

Mithen (1994: 120), mapping the Mesolithic cemeteries in Europe, noted a preference for coastal locations (see also Blankhom this volume, Straus this volume, Zvelebil this volume). Although this pattern may be produced by discovery bias, the absence of cemeteries in central Europe does seem to confirm these observations. The only evidence for human remains comes from a small number of burials, and some isolated finds or burials of somewhat uncertain age. The only complete burial was discovered in a large, approximately 50 m long, south-facing rockshelter, Zigeunerhöhle, near Elsbethen in the Salzburg basin, Austria (Figure 9.7, Rettenbacher and Tichy 1994). Here the body of a two- to three-year-old child was buried most probably in a crouched sitting position, facing south, inside a circular pit 0.4 m deep. A charcoal layer indicates that a fire was built over the burial after filling up the pit. The related fauna and lithic artefacts are of earlier Mesolithic date. Geographically, this burial belongs to the Upper Danubian Mesolithic burials of south Germany (Altmühl valley, etc.). A radiocarbon date obtained from the child's rib dates the burial to 8020 ± 125 BP.

Jiří A. Svoboda

Matoušek (2002) has documented another type of funerary behaviour at the top of the Bacín Hill, Bohemian karst, where remains of an adult male (twenty to thirty years old) were found in a filling of a vertical karstic fissure. The radiocarbon date from the bones was 9490 ± 65 BP. During research in the North Bohemian sandstone rockshelters, four isolated human teeth also were discovered at the sites of Pod zubem, Vysoká Lešnice and Šídelník I (two specimens). They all belong to older individuals and are heavily worn. A small fragment of a human skull with evident cutmarks was found in the rockshelter of Nízká Lešnice (Svoboda et al. 2000).

Finally, open-air burials in pits, with no directly associated archaeological material but possibly of middle or early Holocene age, were discovered at Staré Město, Obříství, and Františkovy Lázně. However, their Late Palaeolithic/Mesolithic age remains unproved. At Obříství, a date obtained from burial 4, a fragment of a mesial part of a rib, 20 mm long (4650 ± 50 BP, GrA-13710), points to a later Neolithic or Eneolithic age, which is also consistent with the geological situation (Svoboda et al. 2002).

Conclusion

Mesolithic occupation in the Middle Danube and Upper Elbe regions covers a wider range of landscape types and altitudes, compared to both the Upper Palaeolithic and Neolithic, a pattern that suggests a higher variability in resource exploitation strategies. At the same time, the individual sites become smaller and show less evidence of internal complexity. The rarity of large and complex sites may partly result from less intensive Mesolithic research in the past (as some researchers have proposed), but it may also reflect a real state of demographic and settlement patterns. Compared to other areas, especially to the north and to the west of Europe, it seems that the geographic centre of the continent lost the central role it held during the Upper Palaeolithic. To a certain extent, it regained this role with the appearance of Neolithic farming populations.

The scenarios of interaction between the last hunters-gatherers and the first farmers are still a matter of discussion. In archaeology in general, approaching any interaction between two different entities, interpreted in terms of various populations, requires a solid chronological framework and geographic dispersal maps before opening the more theoretical questions. In Czech archaeology, traditionally, there has been a lack of dialogue between specialists on the Mesolithic and the Neolithic, partly because of different methodology. As a result, the boundary between the two periods may seem more exaggerated than was really the case.

In the southeast (Hungary), we have uncalibrated dates for the Körös culture around 7000 BP, whereas the earliest dates for the Linear pottery in Moravia (Mohelnice: 6200–6400 BP) and Bohemia (Bylany: 6000–6300 BP) are slightly later. Dates for the latest Mesolithic in North Bohemia, usually from sites with trapezoid microliths (Dolský Mlýn, Bezděz, Pod zubem), lie between 6500 and 7000 BP. In terms of calibrated radiocarbon years, it seems that the first farmers were present in Hungary by 6000 cal BC and in Bohemia and Moravia after 5500 cal BC. At the moment (and contrary to the situation in Poland and eastern Germany), we have no solid Mesolithic dates later than this that would suggest an overlap between the two stages.

An area where Late Mesolithic and Neolithic layers are found at the same sites and in the same stratigraphic sequences is North Bohemia. The rockshelters there repeatedly show evidence of an occupational hiatus between the two periods. It seems that this region remained almost uninhabited during the Linear Pottery period, with major reoccupation later, during the Stroked Pottery period.

In general, this spatial and temporal structure suggests an influx of farming populations from the southeast to the northwest with new technologies, perhaps resulting in some regions even

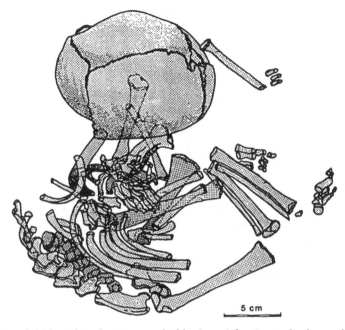

Figure 9.7. The child burial in the Zigeunerhöhle Cave (after Rettenbacher and Tichy 1994).

in an extinction of the indigenous populations. This model, however, does not mean that the local population had no impact on future developments, be it in terms of genetics, technology, or behaviour, or that archaeologists should not search for evidence of such contact in their record, as has been found further to the north.

Acknowledgments

This chapter incorporates recent results of the National Geographic Society excavation project 98–6330, 'The Last Foragers of Northern Bohemia' (1999–2001).

Chapter 10

The Mesolithic of the Iron Gates

Clive Bonsall*

Introduction

The Iron Gates region may be defined as the 230-km-long section of the Danube valley that forms the border between Romania and Serbia. Marking the beginning of the 'lower Danube', it comprises two distinct physiographic zones with contrasting geology and relief.

The first corresponds with the Iron Gates 'gorge' where the Danube breaks through the Carpathian–Balkan mountain chain. Also known as Djerdap (Serbia) and Clisura (Romania) it is really a system of gorges, some narrow and canyon-like, separated by small basins, which extends for over 130 km. The gorge is developed in rocks of mainly Palaeozoic and Mesozoic age, which include limestone formations in which caves and rockshelters occur. The terrain on either side of the gorge is mountainous, rising to over 700 m above the river on the Serbian side. The average gradient of the river within the gorge is much steeper than elsewhere along the middle or lower Danube. Before it was impounded, strong currents, turbulent flow, rapids and rock reefs characterized this section of the river, impeding navigation; current velocity varied between 3.5 and 18 km per hour.

Downstream from the gorge, the Danube valley broadens out as the river enters a landscape of more moderate relief, underlain by mainly Quaternary sediments, at the western edge of the Wallachian Plain. Here the river is flanked by a broad alluvial plain consisting of several terraces varying in age from mid-Holocene to pre-Last Glacial maximum. The river gradient in this lowland zone is much shallower, current velocity being less than 4 km per hour.

The Iron Gates is the 'jewel in the crown' of the Southeast European Mesolithic, renowned for its exceptional record of human occupation during the Late Glacial and the earlier part of the Holocene between approximately 13,000 and 5500 cal BC – a time segment that encompasses the whole of the Mesolithic and the beginning of the Neolithic[1].

* School of History, Classics and Archaeology, University of Edinburgh, UK.

Elsewhere in Southeast Europe, the Mesolithic has proved difficult to find. There are some notable cave and rockshelter sites scattered through the Balkans, such as Franchthi and Theopetra (Greece), Crvena Stijena, Medena Stijena, and Odmut (Montenegro), Pupićina and Vela Spila (Croatia), and Mala Triglavca (Slovenia). But open-air sites are mostly surface sites on which only stone artefacts have survived.

The existence of Mesolithic sites in the Iron Gates was recognized only in the 1960s. This was a consequence of the decision by the Romanian and Yugoslav governments to build two dams across the Danube for power generation. The first dam, which became operational in 1971, was built where the Danube leaves the Iron Gates gorge, and was designed in part to improve navigation through the gorge. The second dam (operational in 1984) is located 80 km downriver at the island of Ostrovu Mare.

Archaeological surveys and rescue excavations were undertaken prior to construction of the dams. However, these were quite limited in their extent, focusing on valley floor areas on both sides of the river that would eventually be submerged beneath the reservoirs created by the dams, and very little archaeological exploration took place in areas farther from the river.

More than fifty sites with traces of Mesolithic and/or Early Neolithic occupation were identified (Figure 10.1). The majority are situated in the gorge sector. They include several cave and rockshelter sites, all on the Romanian side of the river, and a larger number of open-air sites. Open-air sites also have been found downriver, in the more open section of the Danube valley between the Iron Gates I and II dams. The open-air sites are on low terraces along the Danube or small islands in the river. In spite of the contrast in physical setting between the gorge and the downstream sector, the archaeological records of the two zones show many similarities. Although small in number, the range and quality of the information from the Iron Gates sites bearing on Mesolithic architecture, art, burial practices, bone and stone technology, and subsistence, is superior to that from most other areas of Europe.

'Mesolithic' and 'Epipalaeolithic' in the Iron Gates

Because of its relative archaeological 'isolation' – surrounded by vast areas where evidence of Late Glacial and early Holocene settlement is sparse – the Iron Gates Mesolithic is often viewed in its own terms, without close reference to events in other regions of Europe. Hence, its subdivisions and terminology tend not to conform to the conventions and criteria adopted elsewhere. In many parts of Europe changes in stone technology provide the basis for subdividing the Mesolithic, but these play little or no role in subdividing the period in the Iron Gates.

Opinion is divided over when the Mesolithic of the Iron Gates begins and ends, but almost no one places its beginning at the onset of the Holocene, as is the convention elsewhere. Some authors prefer the term 'Epipalaeolithic' to Mesolithic, arguing for continuity with the local Upper Palaeolithic. Others make a clear distinction between Epipalaeolithic and Mesolithic and use the terms accordingly. Because of the generally microlithic character of the lithic assemblages, some authors regard the whole of the period from the beginning of the Late Glacial to the adoption of farming in the Middle Holocene as 'Mesolithic' (e.g., Jovanović 1969a) or 'Epipalaeolithic' (e.g., Boroneanţ 1973). Boroneanţ (1989) divided the period into two cultures – 'Clisurean' dating to the Late Glacial, and 'Schela Cladovei' dating to the Holocene. The latter he equated with the Lepenski Vir culture identified by Srejović on the Serbian bank of the Danube. Interestingly, in his earlier work, Srejović did not describe the Lepenski Vir culture as Mesolithic, but as 'Epipalaeolithic' in

Clive Bonsall

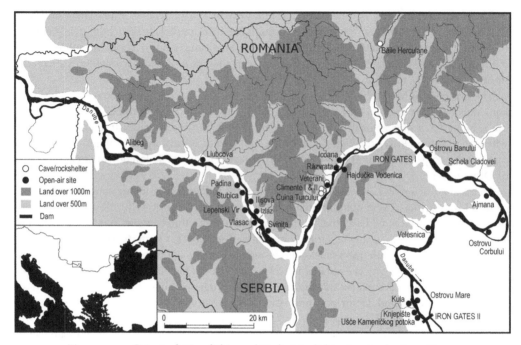

Figure 10.1. Principal Mesolithic and Early Neolithic sites in the Iron Gates.

its early phase, and 'Proto-Neolithic' in its later phase, reflecting his belief in an indigenous origin of farming and pottery manufacture in the region (Srejović 1969).

As research progressed, it became the conventional view that the hunter-gatherer sites of the Late Glacial–Holocene show evidence of increasing social complexity and sedentism with time, and that an important shift in residential mobility patterns and subsistence practices occurred in the early Holocene approximately 7600 cal BC – when, supposedly, people abandoned the caves and rockshelters they had used as residential sites during the Late Glacial and initial Holocene, and began to establish permanent or semipermanent settlements on the banks of the Danube based on intensive exploitation of riverine resources. Many researchers have argued that the establishment of open-air settlements on the Danube approximately 7600 cal BC should be regarded as the beginning of the 'Mesolithic' in the region, and that what came before is 'Epipalaeolithic' (e.g., Voytek and Tringham 1989).

The Iron Gates sites contain some of the largest concentrations of Mesolithic burials in Europe. Burials have been recorded from at least twelve sites[2], and four of these, Lepenski Vir, Padina, Schela Cladovei and Vlasac, each contained very large numbers of graves. Ivana Radovanović has attempted to redefine the Iron Gates Mesolithic in terms of changes in burial practice, arguing that the Mesolithic can be distinguished from the preceding Epipalaeolithic by the appearance of 'formal disposal areas' for burial of the dead. These she defines as 'areas of continuous, ceremonial, mortuary disposal' (Radovanović 1996: 14).

Chronology

Field investigations in the Iron Gates took place mainly between 1965 and 1984. Many were short campaigns, conducted under rescue conditions, often with very limited resources. Comparatively

	PERIOD	CULTURE	DANUBE LEFT BANK	DANUBE RIGHT BANK
7000	EARLY NEO.	PROTO-STARČEVO		
			Cuina Turcului IIIa–c	Lepenski Vir IIIa
7500				
			Schela Cladovei II	Padina I
				Hajdučka Vodenica I
				Lepenski Vir II
8000	PROTONEOLITHIC	LEPENSKI VIR CULTURE — LATER (L. VIR — S. CLADOVEI)	Schela Cladovei I	Vlasac III
8500			Icoana II / Ostrovu Banului III	Lepenski Vir Ic–e / Vlasac II
	EPIPALAEO.	EARLY	Icoana I / Ostrovu Banului I–II	Lepenski Vir Ia–b / Vlasac Ib
				Proto-Lepenski Vir
10000			Cuina Turcului IIa–b	Vlasac Ia
	LATE PALAEO.	EPIGRAVETTIAN	Cuina Turcului I	
			Veterani / Climente II	
14000				

Srejović (1969) (a)

Figure 10.2. Chronology and 'periodisation' of the Iron Gates sites according to different authors: (a) Srejović 1969; (b) Jovanović 1969; (c) Voytek and Tringham 1989; (d) Radovanović 1996; (e) Boroneanț 2000. Dates are uncalibrated radiocarbon years BP.

few radiocarbon measurements were carried out at the time. Excavators relied mainly on stratigraphy and artefact typology to date their sites, often proposing quite complex relative chronologies. In many sites, more than one Mesolithic occupation layer was recognized, sometimes stratified below one or more Early Neolithic layers.

Various attempts were made to correlate the individual site sequences, using the small number of ^{14}C dates available and type comparisons of artefacts (especially architectural features) to produce an integrated chronology for the Iron Gates region as a whole (Figure 10.2).

There are many differences of detail between the various schemes, but the major point of controversy has been the dating of Lepenski Vir and Padina. Srejović (1969, Srejović and Letica 1978) interpreted Lepenski Vir I–II and Padina A and B as Mesolithic, antedating 7500 BP (6400 cal BC). Jovanović (1969a) assigned Padina A to the Mesolithic, and Padina B and the whole of the Lepenski Vir sequence to the Early Neolithic after c. 6400 cal BC. The debate turned on the validity of the ^{14}C ages for Lepenski Vir I–II, and the cultural/chronological significance of the presence of pottery in the buildings of Lepenski Vir I–II and Padina B.

The inherent weakness of all of these chronologies is that they rely heavily on the original stratigraphic interpretations of individual sites proposed by their excavators. In very few cases, however, have the individual site stratigraphies been adequately tested against independent dating methods. Two exceptions are Lepenski Vir and Vlasac, both of which have large series of

241

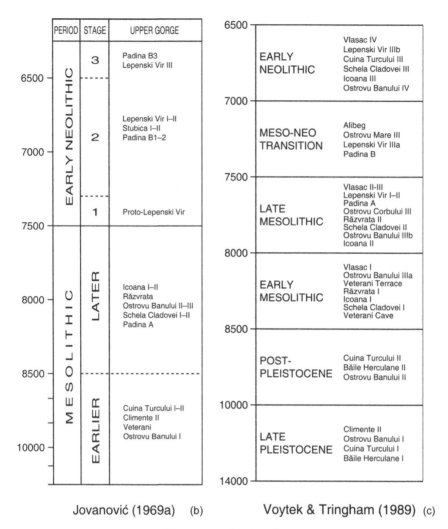

Figure 10.2 *(continued)*.

radiocarbon ages. At both sites the results of ^{14}C dating were inconsistent with the stratigraphic interpretations.

At Lepenski Vir, Srejović (1972) identified a stratigraphic sequence of five occupation phases: Proto-Lepenski Vir (Early Mesolithic), Lepenski Vir I and II (Late Mesolithic), and Lepenski Vir IIIa and IIIb (Early Neolithic). A series of charcoal samples from contexts associated with LV I–II buildings gave ^{14}C ages between c. 7430 and 6560 BP (6300 to 5500 cal BC) (Quitta 1972), but no dates were obtained at that time for the earlier (Proto-LV) or later (LV IIIa–b) phases. Subsequent AMS dating of human remains assigned to LV III gave ages, which, after reservoir correction, were indistinguishable from the charcoal dates for LVI–II (Bonsall et al. 1997, 2000, Cook et al. 2002). Thus, unless phases LV I–IIIb occupy a very short time-span, the radiocarbon evidence is in conflict with Srejović's stratigraphic dating of the burials and architectural remains.

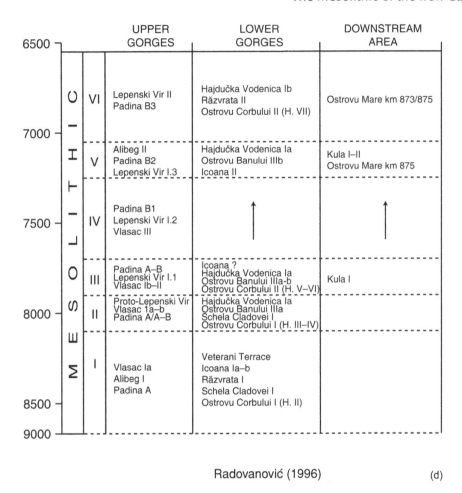

Radovanović (1996)   (d)

Figure 10.2 (*continued*).

The occupation at Vlasac was divided into four phases: Vlasac I (Early Mesolithic), Vlasac II–III (Late Mesolithic) and Vlasac IV (Early Neolithic) (Srejović and Letica 1978). Again, the radiocarbon evidence is in conflict with the relative chronology based on stratigraphy. Radiocarbon ages of the majority of charcoal samples from phase I lie within a range from c. 7010 to 6865 BP (5900 to 5750 cal BC) and are significantly *younger* than the age range of c. 7930 to 7440 BP (6800 to 6300 cal BC) for the charcoal samples from phases II and III (Srejović and Letica 1978). Subsequent AMS dating of five human skeletons assigned to phases I and III yielded (reservoir corrected) ^{14}C ages that are generally older than the charcoal ages for phase I (Bonsall et al. 1997, 2000).

Similar problems have since emerged at Schela Cladovei, where Boroneanț identified a stratigraphic sequence of two Mesolithic phases, which he assigned to stages II and III of his Schela Cladovei culture, followed by two Early Neolithic phases, dubbed 'proto-Sesklo' and Criş (Boroneanț 1989). The Romanian–British excavations at Schela Cladovei between 1992 and 1996 (Boroneanț et al. 1999; Bonsall et al. 2002) confirmed the presence of Mesolithic and Early Neolithic (Criş) occupations, but found no stratigraphic or radiocarbon evidence to support the subdivision of either occupation.

243

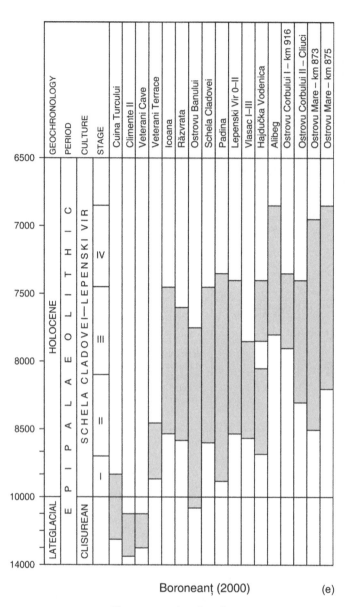

Boroneanț (2000)   (e)

Figure 10.2 (*continued*).

In an effort to explain away the discrepancies between stratigraphic and radiocarbon dating at Lepenski Vir and Vlasac, Srejović, and Letica (1978) suggested that the charcoal samples from the lower levels of both sites had been contaminated owing to groundwater penetration, resulting in erroneous ^{14}C ages. However, as noted earlier, new AMS measurements on human bone are equally at variance with the stratigraphic interpretations of Lepenski Vir and Vlasac, as well as Schela Cladovei, which suggests it is the stratigraphic interpretations that are in error. This in turn raises concerns about the validity of the stratigraphic sequences proposed for other sites in the Iron Gates and, by extension, all of the regional chronologies illustrated in Figure 10.2.

The alternative to a chronology based on dubious interpretations of 'stratigraphy' is one based on radiocarbon dating. Although the vast majority of the sites are no longer available for investigation owing to impounding of the Danube by the Iron Gates dams, large collections of animal and human bones are preserved in museums and are suitable for direct dating by AMS. Detailed ^{14}C dating programmes using these materials have the potential to: (i) establish the period or periods of occupation of individual sites; and (ii) suggest chronological subdivisions of the Mesolithic based on changes in bone technology and burial practices. This work is at a very early stage. At the time of writing, AMS dates on human bones and/or bone artefacts are available only for Hajdučka Vodenica, Lepenski Vir, Padina, Schela Cladovei and Vlasac (Table 10.1). From these data, coupled with critical use of previous radiometric ^{14}C measurements, a provisional radiocarbon-based chronology may be proposed (Tables 10.2 and 10.3).

Early Mesolithic, 13,000–7200 cal BC

The early stages of the Iron Gates Mesolithic are poorly documented. Use of caves and rockshelters on the Romanian bank of the Danube can be traced back to the Late Glacial period. The most extensively excavated site, and the most securely dated, is Cuina Turcului – a rockshelter situated close to the Danube, approximately 12 m above the pre-dam river level. In excavations undertaken between 1964 and 1969, two 'Epipalaeolithic' layers (Cuina Turcului I and II) were identified, separated by a thick stony layer containing no archaeological materials.

The artefact assemblages from both layers – described as 'Romanello-Azilian' by Păunescu (1970) and 'Clisurean' by Boroneanţ (1989) – have been regarded as Late Glacial in age, based on the presence among the chipped stone tools of convex-backed blades and bladelets and 'unguiforme' end-scrapers. Similar tool-making traditions characterized other regions of Europe at the end of the Pleistocene, for example, the Azilian in southwest France and northern Spain, the Romanellian in Italy, and the 'Federmesser' technocomplex of the North European Plain.

Radiocarbon dating of bulk samples of pine charcoal from the Cuina Turcului I layer gave ages of $12,600 \pm 120$ BP (Bln-803) and $12,050 \pm 120$ (Bln-804) BP, suggesting use of the rockshelter at a time equivalent to the first half of the Late Glacial Interstadial of northwestern Europe. The presence of woodland species (e.g., red deer, wild pig) among the mammalian remains from this layer is consistent with this interpretation (Bolomey 1970, 1973).

Dating of the Cuina Turcului II layer is less secure, being based on a single ^{14}C measurement with a large error – $10,125 \pm 200$ BP (Bln-802) – also on pine charcoal. This could indicate use of the site either towards the end of the Late Glacial or early in the Holocene. Proxy environmental indicators from this layer present a confusing picture. The avifauna and pollen spectra suggest temperate conditions, consistent with a Holocene age (Pop et al. 1970, Păunescu 1970), whereas the mammalian remains are a mixture of temperate woodland (e.g., red deer, wild pig) and more open hilly habitat (e.g., chamois, ibex) species. These data can be explained in several ways. The

Table 10.1. List of radiocarbon dates for Mesolithic and Early Neolithic sites in the Iron Gates

Site	Context	Material	Lab. No.	BP	cal BC (2σ)
Cuina Turcului	Hearth, layer I, 5.90–5.95 m	C	Bln-803	12,600 ± 120	13221–12275
	Hearth, layer I, 6.20–6.40 m	C	Bln-804	12,050 ± 120	12232–11711
	Hearth, layer I, 5.70–5.85 m	C	GrN-12665	11,960 ± 60	12023–11754
	Hearth, layer II, 3.68–3.85 m	C + B	Bln-802	10,125 ± 200	10639–9251
Hajdučka Vodenica	Burial 8	H	OxA-11128	*8165 ± 90*	7477–6833
	Burial 15 ('younger')	H	OxA-11126	*7524 ± 77*	6503–6227
	Burial 12	H	OxA-11127	*7522 ± 82*	6561–6222
	Burial 20	H	OxA-11109	*7389 ± 84*	6419–6078
Icoana	Trench IV, 2.10 m, horizon Ib	C	Bln-1078	8605 ± 250	8287–7075
	Trench IV, 0.50 m, horizon Ia	C	Bln-1077	8265 ± 100	7518–7070
	Trench II, 1.60 m, horizon Ia	C	Bonn no. 2	8070 ± 130	7448–6647
	Trench II, 1.20 m, horizon Ib	C	Bonn no. 3	8010 ± 120	7306–6610
	Trench II, 2.00 m, horizon Ib	C	Bonn no. 4	7660 ± 110	6750–6247
	Trench III, 1.00 m, horizon II	C	Bonn no. 1	5830 ± 120	4993–4402
Lepenski Vir	Burial 60 ('LV Ic')	H	OxA-11715	*9020 ± 80*	8445–7953
	Burial 69 ('Proto-LV')	H	OxA-11703	*8784 ± 72*	8202–7609
	Under house 23	B	OxA-8610	8770 ± 60	8180–7605
	House 62 ('LV Ib')	C	KN-405	7430 ± 160	6592–6006
	Burial 61 ('LV Ic')	H	OxA-11698	*7374 ± 80*	6406–6071
	Burial 14 ('LV I–II')	H	OxA-11704	*7368 ± 75*	6396–6072
	House 36 ('LV Ia')	C	Bln-740b	7360 ± 100	6425–6049
	Burial 54d ('LV Ib')	H	OxA-11700	*7353 ± 72*	6385–6067
	Burial 54c ('LV Ib')	H	OxA-11696	*7346 ± 57*	6365–6074
	Burial 45b ('LV I')	H	OxA-11701	*7337 ± 79*	6388–6053
	House 36 ('LV Ia')	C	Bln-740a	7310 ± 100	6392–6010
	Burial 31a ('LV III')	H	OxA-5827	*7308 ± 108*	6401–5997

Burial 79a	H	OxA-11705	**7312 ± 79**	6366–6029
House 54 ('LV Ib–c')	C	Z-143	7300 ± 124	6426–5928
Burial 26 ('LV I')	H	OxA-11693	**7284 ± 47**	6233–6056
House 54 ('LV Ib–c')	C	KN-407	7280 ± 160	6445–5845
Burial 54e ('LV Ib')	H	OxA-11697	**7250 ± 59**	6227–6017
House 54 ('LV Ib–c')	C	Bln-738	7225 ± 100	6354–5896
Burial 7/1 ('LV I')	H	OxA-11692	**7218 ± 81**	6243–5917
House 27 ('LV Id–e')	C	KN-406	7210 ± 200	6445–5720
Rear of house 51, under level of house XLIV	B	OxA-8618	7200 ± 60	6217–5986
Burial 7/1 ('LV I') [repeat]	H	OxA-12979	**7157 ± 77**	6215–5892
Burial 44 ('LV III')	H	OxA-5830	**7152 ± 106**	6233–5797
Burial 89a ('LV II')	H	OxA-11702	**7133 ± 75**	6208–5845
Between houses 20 and 33 ('LV Ia–b')	F	OxA-8725	**7060 ± 114**	6207–5721
House 54 ('LV Ib–c')	C	Bln-653	7040 ± 100	6081–5719
Burial 32a ('LV III')	H	OxA-5828	**7036 ± 95**	6066–5728
House 54 ('LV Ib–c')	C	Z-115	6984 ± 94	6028–5676
Burial 9 ('LV IIIb')	H	OxA-11695	**6982 ± 50**	5983–5747
Burial 88 ('LV III')	H	OxA-5831	**6980 ± 92**	6023–5677
House 47 ('LV Id–e')	C	UCLA-1407	6970 ± 60	5983–5735
Burial 8 ('LV III')	H	OxA-11694	**6942 ± 47**	5972–5729
House 37 ('LV Id')	C	BM-379	6900 ± 150	6055–5544
House 37 ('LV Id')	C	Bln-678	6900 ± 100	5984–5636
House 1 ('LV Id')	C	Bln-575	6860 ± 100	5982–5572
House 9 ('LV Id')	C	Bln-647	6845 ± 100	5978–5565
House 16 ('LV Ie')	C	Bln-576	6820 ± 100	5972–5554
House 34/43 ('LV I?')	C	Bln-650	6820 ± 100	5972–5554
House 32 ('LV Ie')	C	P-1598	6814 ± 69	5867–5571

(continued)

Table 10.1. (*continued*)

Site	Context	Material	Lab. No.	BP	cal BC (2σ)
	House 37 ('LV Id')	C	Bln-649	6800 ± 100	5899–5526
	Burial 35 ('LV III')	H	OxA-5829	*6718 ± 93*	5777–5480
	House IX ('LV II')	C	Bln-654	6630 ± 100	5723–5378
	House 51 ('LV Ie')	C	Bln-652	6620 ± 100	5718–5376
	House XXXII ('LV II')	C	Bln-655	6560 ± 100	5657–5324
Ostrovu Banului	Trench IV, horizon III, hearth 2	C	Bln-1080	8040 ± 160	7455–6593
	Trench I, horizon III, hearth 1	C	Bln-1079	7565 ± 100	6606–6227
Ostrovu Corbului	Hearth, level I, 4.50–4.53 m	C	SMU-587	8093 ± 237	7567–6503
	Hearth, level II, 4.02–4.12 m	C	SMU-588	7827 ± 237	7350–6228
	Hearth, level I, 4.20–4.38 m	C	Bln-2135	7710 ± 80	6692–6423
	Hearth, level I, 4.20–4.38 m	C	Bln-2135a	7695 ± 80	6681–6421
	Level I, 4.23 m	C	GrN-12675	7640 ± 80	6647–6368
Padina	Under house 14	B	OxA-11102	9990 ± 55	9760–9307
	Burial 21	H	OxA-11106	*9729 ± 73*	9314–8839
	Burial 11	H	OxA-11104	*9700 ± 72*	9292–8835
	Burial 15	H	OxA-11105	*9138 ± 71*	8547–8247
	Midden – profile 3, segment 1, excavation level 3	B	OxA-9055	8445 ± 60	7590–7357
	Bear (*Ursus arctos*) bone	B	BM-1403	8138 ± 121	7477–6710
	Burial 1a (antler artefact)	B	OxA-11108	7750 ± 50	6654–6471
	Burial 1a	H	OxA-11107	*7525 ± 77*	6504–6227
	House 17, hearth (bone artefact)	B	OxA-11103	7315 ± 55	6353–6053
	'Occupation layer' (?) ('Padina B2')	C	GrN-8230	7100 ± 80	6203–5778
	Trapezoidal building (?) ('Padina B3')	C	GrN-7981	7075 ± 50	6047–5845
	Padina B1	C	GrN-????	7065 ± 110	6206–5725
	House 18, floor	B	OxA-9052	6965 ± 60	5983–5732
	Under floor of house 15 (bone artefact)	B	OxA-9054	6790 ± 55	5784–5574

Site	Sample	C	Lab code	Date (BP)	Cal range
Răzvrata II	Hearth (in trapezoidal building?) ('Padina B1')	C	GrN-8229	6570 ± 55	5625–5390
Schela Cladovei	'Hut'	C	Bln-1057	7690 ± 70	6645–6434
	Bone artefact, Area VI	B	OxA-9140	8105 ± 60	7312–6830
	Bone artefact, Area VI	B	OxA-9135	8085 ± 60	7302–6818
	Burial, Area III	H	OxA-4385	**8090 ± 118**	7448–6681
	Bone artefact, Area VI	B	OxA-9139	8075 ± 60	7293–6775
	Burial, Area III	H	OxA-4379	**8070 ± 122**	7442–6649
	Burial, Area VI	H	OxA-9007	**8055 ± 86**	7296–6690
	Burial, Area III	H	OxA-4380	**8046 ± 122**	7338–6644
	Burial, Area III	H	OxA-4382	**8046 ± 124**	7345–6642
	Bone artefact, Area VI	B	OxA-9138	8040 ± 60	7162–6701
	Bone artefact, Area VI	B	OxA-9137	8010 ± 60	7072–6699
	Bone artefact	B	OxA-9207	8000 ± 80	7128–6654
	Burial	H	OxA-8502	**7988 ± 72**	7072–6665
	Bone artefact	B	OxA-9374	7980 ± 60	7055–6696
	Burial, Area III	H	OxA-4378	**7971 ± 115**	7282–6536
	Burial, Area VI	H	OxA-8583	**7960 ± 97**	7126–6601
	Bone artefact, Area VI	B	OxA-9132	7950 ± 55	7044–6687
	Burial, Area III	H	OxA-4381	**7932 ± 130**	7173–6499
	Bone artefact, Area V	B	OxA-9131	7925 ± 60	7033–6656
	Bone artefact, Area III	B	OxA-8582	7880 ± 290	7515–6227
	Bone artefact, Area VI	B	OxA-8584	7915 ± 85	7050–6608
	Burial, Area III	H	OxA-8581	**7904 ± 93**	7060–6573
	Bone artefact, Area VI	B	OxA-8549	7905 ± 60	7032–6644
	Burial	H	OxA-8547	**7886 ± 92**	7051–6532
	Bone artefact, Area VI	B	OxA-9136	7895 ± 55	7030–6641
	Burial, Area III	H	OxA-4383	**7834 ± 120**	7041–6472

(continued)

Table 10.1. (continued)

Site	Context	Material	Lab. No.	BP	cal BC (2σ)
	Bone artefact	B	OxA-8580	7770±240	7314–6106
	Bone artefact, Area VI	B	OxA-9143	7825±60	7020–6485
	Bone artefact	B	OxA-8579	7790±100	7028–6451
	Bone artefact, Area VI	B	OxA-8550	7805±70	7016–6468
	Bone artefact, Area VI	B	OxA-8585	7780±75	6905–6454
	Burial, Area VI	H	OxA-8548	**7762±90**	7002–6432
	Bone artefact, Area VI	B	OxA-9142	7745±60	6679–6464
	Bone artefact, Area VI	B	OxA-9209	7720±70	6678–6441
	Bone artefact, Area VI	B	OxA-9141	7700±60	6642–6451
	Bone artefact, Area VI	B	OxA-9205	7570±90	6593–6243
	Bone artefact, Area VI	B	OxA-9208	7530±70	6492–6235
	Bone artefact, Area VI	B	OxA-9206	7460±75	6461–6110
	Bone artefact, Area VI	B	OxA-9355	7100±50	6064–5886
	Bone artefact, Area VI	B	OxA-9210	7010±80	6019–573
	Bone artefact, Area VI	B	OxA-9356	6900±50	5895–5674
	Bone artefact, Area VI	B	OxA-9357	6890±60	5964–5661
	Bone artefact, Area VI	B	OxA-9597	6880±50	5878–5667
	Bone artefact	B	OxA-9134	6865±55	5876–5645
	Bone artefact, Area VI	B	OxA-9385	6770±50	5740–5571
	Bone artefact	B	OxA-9133	6715±55	5720–5539
	Bone artefact	B	OxA-9358	6695±55	5713–5523
Vlasac	Burial 72 ('Vlasac I')	H	OxA-5824	**9850±130**	9861–8838
	Burial 72 ('Vlasac I') [repeat]	H	OxA-5825	**9750±168**	9799–8647
	Burial 51a ('Vlasac I')	H	OxA-5822	**8376±121**	7594–7083
	Square C/III, layer 15 ('Vlasac II')	C	Bln-1050	7935±60	7041–6659
	Square A/II, layer 14 ('Vlasac II – beginning')	C	Lj-2047b	7930±77	7048–6645
	Square C/III, layer 22 ('Vlasac II')	C	Lj-2047a	7925±77	7049–6643

Context	Material	Lab code	^{14}C age BP	Cal BC (2σ)
Dwelling 5 – square BC/V, layer 18 ('Vlasac Ib')	C	Bln-1170	7840 ± 100	7034–6486
Square d/5, layer 9 ('Vlasac Ib – end')	C	Bln-1171	7830 ± 100	7030–6478
Burial 83 ('Vlasac III')	H	OxA-5826	*7804 ± 104*	7028–6461
Burial 54 ('Vlasac I')	H	OxA-5823	*7756 ± 113*	7028–6421
Square c/9, layer 14 ('Vlasac II')	C	Bln-1169	7665 ± 60	6632–6429
Square b/18, layer 13 ('Vlasac II')	C	Bln-1052	7610 ± 60	6594–6379
Burial 24 ('Vlasac III')	H	OxA-5825	*7598 ± 113*	6653–6227
Square b/9, beneath hearth 16 ('Vlasac II')	C	Z-267	7559 ± 93	6591–6236
Square b/9, layer 6 ('Vlasac II – end')	C	Bln-1168	7475 ± 60	6439–6233
Square A/II, Layer 13 ('Vlasac III')	C	Bln-1954	7440 ± 60	6438–6125
Dwelling 1 – square C/III, layer 26 ('Vlasac Ib')	C	Z-262	7000 ± 90	6032–5718
Dwelling 1 – square C/III, layer 26 ('Vlasac Ib')	C	Bln-1951	6905 ± 100	5984–5638
Dwelling 2 – square a/18, layer 18 ('Vlasac Ib')	C	Bln-1053	6865 ± 100	5983–5617
Dwelling 2 – square a/18, layer 18 ('Vlasac Ib')	C	Bln-1014	6805 ± 100	5964–5532
Dwelling 1 – square C/III, layer 26 ('Vlasac Ib')	C	Bln-1051a	6790 ± 100	5891–5522

Dated material: B = terrestrial mammal bone; C = charcoal; F = fish bone; H = human bone. Calibration was performed with CALIB 5.0.2 (Stuiver and Reimer 1993, Stuiver et al. 2005) using the IntCal04 curve (Reimer et al. 2004). The ^{14}C ages of human bones have been corrected for the Danube freshwater reservoir effect using Method 1 of Cook et al. (2002). A 100 percent reservoir correction was applied to the ^{14}C age of a fish bone from Lepenski Vir. Reservoir corrected ^{14}C ages are shown in **bold italics**. The reservoir age corrections were applied prior to calibration using the terrestrial calibration curve. Data from: Bonsall et al. (1997, 2008), Borić and Miracle (2004), Boroneanţ (2000), Burleigh and Živanović (1980), Quitta (1975), Radovanović (1996), Srejović and Letica (1978), Whittle et al. (2002).

Table 10.2. *Provisional chronology for the Iron Gates based on radiocarbon dating*

Time-range (cal BC)	Notional Period	Representative Sites
13,000–7200	Early Mesolithic	Cuina Turcului, Lepenski Vir, Padina, Vlasac
7200–6300	Late Mesolithic	Hajdučka Vodenica, Icoana, Ostrovu Banului, Ostrovu Corbului, Schela Cladovei, Vlasac
6300–6000	Final Mesolithic	Lepenski Vir
6000–5500	Early Neolithic	Cuina Turcului, Lepenski Vir, Padina, Schela Cladovei, Vlasac

Cuina Turcului II layer may relate to a short-lived occupation at the beginning of the Holocene when the surrounding landscape consisted of a mosaic of habitats. Alternatively, the archaeological remains may derive from a series of occupations over a longer period, which began in the Late Glacial and continued into the Holocene.

Bone tools, including a number of decorated items, were found in the Cuina Turcului I and II layers. According to Srejović (1969: 14) there are important differences in the decorative motifs that characterize the two layers. In the earlier layer a distinctive motif is a zig-zag pattern of parallel incised lines; whereas in the Cuina Turcului II layer cross-hatched and net-like motifs occur, which are characteristic of later Mesolithic sites in the Iron Gates including Lepenski Vir, Schela Cladovei, and Vlasac. The time-ranges of the various decorative motifs applied to antler and bone (and sometimes stone) artefacts from sites in the Iron Gates have yet to be established through direct AMS radiocarbon dating of the artefacts themselves, but the presence of cross-hatched and net-like designs on some of the pieces from Cuina Turcului II raises the possibility that this layer includes material from later Mesolithic occupations.

A final Late Glacial age has been inferred from typological evidence for the earliest occupation at an open-air site on Ostrovu Banului, an island in the Danube just below the Iron Gates I dam (Boroneanţ 2000, Păunescu 2000). However, there is no independent dating evidence to support this interpretation, and both the geological context and the character of the lithic assemblage are quite consistent with an early Holocene age.

Indications of cave use in the Late Glacial and the lack of contemporaneous open-air sites are usually interpreted as evidence of a mobile population that relied on hunting large land mammals. According to some authors, this lifestyle continued into the early Holocene until c. 7600 cal BC, when open-air settlements, based on intensive exploitation of aquatic resources, were established along the Danube. However, there is no doubt that the aquatic resources of the Danube were already being exploited during the Late Glacial period. Fish bones were recovered from the Cuina Turcului I and II layers, although they were much more abundant in the later horizon.

The notion of cave dwelling during the Late Glacial and very early Holocene is overly simplistic. It is unlikely that any society has ever lived exclusively in caves, and prehistoric peoples often made use of caves for economic or ritual purposes whilst living in open-air settlements (Tolan-Smith and Bonsall 1997). In the Iron Gates cave use continued until quite late in the Holocene; although Cuina Turcului is noted especially for its Late Glacial occupation remains, the rockshelter was used at various times during the Holocene when open-air sites are also known to exist.

Table 10.3. Radiocarbon date calibration table for the
period 6500–10,000 BP

Age in ^{14}C Years BP	Approximate Calibrated Calendar Age
6500	5500 BC
6600	5550 BC
6700	5600 BC
6800	5700 BC
6900	5800 BC
7000	5900 BC
7100	6000 BC
7200	6050 BC
7300	6150 BC
7400	6300 BC
7500	6400 BC
7600	6450 BC
7700	6500 BC
7800	6600 BC
7900	6700 BC
8000	6900 BC
8100	7100 BC
8200	7200 BC
8300	7400 BC
8400	7500 BC
8500	7600 BC
9000	8200 BC
9500	8800 BC
10,000	9500 BC
10,500	10,600 BC
11,000	11,000 BC
11,500	11,400 BC
12,000	11,900 BC
12,500	12,700 BC
13,000	13,400 BC

Radiocarbon ages have been converted into approximate calendar ages using the CALIB (rev. 5.0.2) calibration program
(see Table 10.1 for details).

The lack of open-air settlements along the Danube older than 9500 cal BC is perhaps better explained in terms of the Late Glacial river environment. During the Younger Dryas, in particular, higher seasonal discharges associated with snowmelt and glacial meltwater are likely to have been a deterrent to settlement of the riverbank. People probably lived on higher ground, such as older river terraces, above the level of flooding – areas that were not surveyed archaeologically in the 1960s to 1980s! Occupation of the riverbank would have been possible during periods of low discharge, for example, in midsummer and midwinter, but such sites are likely to be underrepresented in the archaeological record. Repeated, seasonal flooding and high rates of flow during the Younger Dryas would tend to result in deep burial or erosion of any riverbank sites occupied during this phase or earlier in the Late Glacial.

For much of the Holocene, the Danube was characterized by smaller annual variations in discharge, which allowed settlements to be established closer to the river. That people occupied sites along the riverbank very early in the Holocene is demonstrated by ^{14}C dating of human remains from several sites. One burial from Vlasac has a ^{14}C age of c. 9850 BP (9300 cal BC) (Bonsall et al. 1997, 2000, Cook et al. 2002) and there are burials from Lepenski Vir, Padina and Vlasac with ^{14}C ages ranging between c. 8400 and 9750 BP (7500 to 9250 cal BC) (Burleigh and Živanović 1980, Bonsall et al. 1997, 2004, Borić and Miracle 2004).

A variety of body positions is represented among these Early Mesolithic burials. They include individuals who were buried (i) lying on their back, extended, with legs and arms straight, (ii) lying on one side with the legs slightly flexed, (iii) lying on their back with the legs flexed and splayed and the soles of the feet together (the famous burial 69 from Lepenski Vir: Srejović 1972: fig. 56), and (iv) in a 'sitting' position with the legs splayed and crossed. What social or religious significance these different burial positions may have had is a matter for speculation.

The character and duration of the Early Mesolithic occupations at Lepenski Vir, Padina, and Vlasac is unclear. None of the architectural remains at these sites is securely dated to this period; in fact the vast majority of the surviving structural features appear to belong to later Mesolithic and/or Early Neolithic occupations[3]. There are a few AMS ^{14}C dates on animal bones which show that they derive from early occupations (Table 10.1), but as yet there are no direct age measurements for antler/bone artefacts or art objects that would allow any of them to be assigned to the Early Mesolithic.

In the absence of well-dated faunal and archaeobotanical assemblages, the economic basis of these early riverside settlements must be inferred from stable isotope analysis of dated human remains. Skeletons from Lepenski Vir, Padina and Vlasac dated between c. 9850 and 8400 BP (9300 to 7500 cal BC) all exhibit very high bone collagen C- and N-isotope values, reflecting a diet in which a large proportion of the protein must have been obtained from freshwater fish or animals that consumed freshwater fish (Figure 10.3). These data suggest that already by the beginning of the Holocene the inhabitants of the Iron Gates gorge were heavily reliant on the Danube for their subsistence needs. It is interesting that the averages of the $\delta^{13}C$ and $\delta^{15}N$ values are lower than the Late Mesolithic averages. Average $\delta^{15}N$ for 7 Early Mesolithic burials is 14.3‰, while the average for 21 Late Mesolithic burials is 15.2‰. A Student's t-test shows the difference between the two groups to be statistically significant at the $p \leq 0.05$ level of probability. The lower average $\delta^{15}N$ value of the Early Mesolithic skeletons may indicate that riverine resources were marginally less important in the period before 7200 cal BC than later on in the Mesolithic.

Given that the C- and N-isotope composition of bone collagen in adults reflects average diet over a period of years to decades (for discussion, see Ambrose 1993: 110–11), the results from Lepenski Vir and Vlasac imply that consumption of fish was not just a seasonal activity for the Early Mesolithic inhabitants of these sites. Regardless of whether fishing was carried out year round or undertaken intensively at a particular time, or times, of year and the surplus stored for later consumption, the stable isotope evidence implies that these foraging communities were in some degree sedentary.

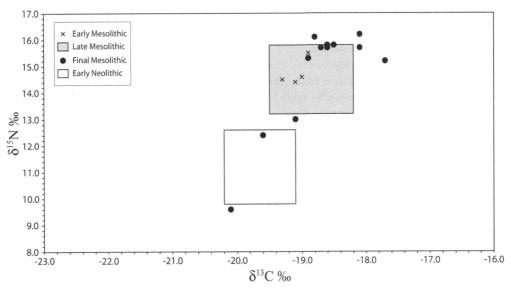

Figure 10.3. Stable isotope (δ^{13}C and δ^{15}N) values for Early and Final Mesolithic skeletons from Lepenski Vir and Vlasac plotted against the Late Mesolithic and Early Neolithic ranges. The Late Mesolithic range is based on data from Schela Cladovei and Vlasac. The Early Neolithic range is based on data from Lepenski Vir.

Late Mesolithic, 7200–6300 cal BC

Eight sites have radiocarbon dates in this time range: Hajdučka Vodenica, Icoana, Padina, Răzvrata, and Vlasac in the gorge, and Schela Cladovei, Ostrovu Banului, and Ostrovu Mare in the downstream section (Table 10.1, Figures 10.1–10.2). But only Schela Cladovei and Vlasac have large series of dates more or less spanning the period.

The Romanian–British project at Schela Cladovei (Bonsall et al. 1997, Bonsall et al. 2002, Boroneanţ et al. 1999) has so far produced 45 AMS ^{14}C dates, all from secure contexts. Thirty-six dates span the period from c. 8100 to 7450 BP (7100 to 6300 cal BC), and no evidence of earlier Mesolithic occupation was found.

The situation at Vlasac is less satisfactory. As noted previously, the relative chronology proposed by Srejović and Letica (1978) is suspect and should be disregarded. Of a total of 18 radiocarbon dates, 11 cluster between c. 7950–7450 BP (6900–6300 cal BC), suggesting an important Late Mesolithic component in the site. However, not all of the ^{14}C ages are from well-defined contexts. Moreover, other dates show there was also earlier Mesolithic occupation at Vlasac and suggest that some features regarded by the excavators as 'Mesolithic' are, in fact, of Early Neolithic age. Hence, isolating the Late Mesolithic component at Vlasac is problematic.

Nevertheless, Schela Cladovei and Vlasac together provide the clearest indication of the character of settlement in the Iron Gates region between 7200 and 6300 cal BC.

The Late Mesolithic societies of the Iron Gates are often described as complex hunter-gatherers, characterized by sedentism, construction of substantial houses, intensive use of local resources for food and tools, food storage, exchange, and social ranking (e.g., Voytek and Tringham 1989, Radovanović and Voytek 1997). However, several aspects of this interpretation are open to question.

Architecture

A variety of structural remains were recorded at Schela Cladovei and Vlasac. The most conspicuous were those described by the excavators as 'hearths' and 'houses'.

The majority of the hearths were rectangular features, up to a metre long, with a border of large tabular stones set on edge. There were also a few simple hearths lacking stone borders. Some of the stone-bordered hearths were associated with traces of house floors. Others were isolated features and may have been constructed in the open, unless the original house floors have not survived or were simply not recognized.

The better-preserved houses had a trapezoidal ground plan, and it is generally supposed that the entrance was at the broader end. They appear to have been semisubterranean structures ('pit houses') in which the sides of the pit formed the walls (or the lower part of the walls) of the house. The house pits varied in depth and diameter. One example at Schela Cladovei was excavated at least 0.30 m below the contemporaneous Mesolithic ground surface (Bonsall, unpublished data); while Srejović and Letica (1978) report house pits at Vlasac up to 0.82 m deep. Following abandonment of the houses, the pits were often infilled with refuse from domestic and industrial activities.

All the houses at Schela Cladovei and Vlasac appear to have been small, single-room structures; the largest house pit at Vlasac (house 2) measured approximately 5 m from front to back, although the habitable space was probably less. Some houses contained a stone-bordered hearth set into the floor; others apparently lacked hearths. The form of the roof and the means of access to the houses are unknown. Postholes were identified in house 2 at Vlasac and presumably held posts that formed part of the superstructure. The excavators of Vlasac conjectured that the houses there had pitched roofs and were entered by means of a stair or ramp, but could present no strong supporting evidence (Srejović and Letica 1978: 146–7).

The remains of an estimated forty-three houses were excavated at Vlasac (Srejović and Letica 1978: 146)[4]. Not all of these, it seems, relate to Late Mesolithic occupation of the site. To judge from the radiocarbon evidence, some of the structures are of Early Neolithic date. Conventional ^{14}C ages on charcoal were obtained for three houses (Table 10.1). Only one – house 5 (Srejović and Letica 1978: fig. 13) – gave an age consistent with a Late Mesolithic dating. The other two structures – houses 1 and 2 (Srejović and Letica 1978: figs. 7–8) – have much younger ^{14}C ages suggesting they belong to the Early Neolithic[5]. These last-mentioned structures were the largest recorded at Vlasac and had their broader ends facing toward the river like the trapezoidal buildings of Lepenski Vir and Padina B, which date to the Final Mesolithic and Early Neolithic.

Burials

Large numbers of burials were recorded at both Schela Cladovei and Vlasac. Eighty-five graves containing the remains of more than one hundred individuals were found at Vlasac, and more than sixty graves have been excavated at Schela Cladovei. Direct AMS ^{14}C dating suggests that the majority belong to the Late Mesolithic, although some of the burials at Vlasac undoubtedly belong to the earlier Mesolithic (Bonsall et al. 1997, 2000, 2002, Boroneanţ et al. 1999, Cook et al. 2002).

Single inhumation was the norm; the dead were placed in simple earthen graves, often lying extended on their backs, but sometimes lying on one side with the legs and arms flexed. There is persuasive evidence for the deliberate disposal of individual human bones, groups of disarticulated bones, and body parts still held together by soft tissue. In some cases, they may represent bones

Figure 10.4. A typical Late Mesolithic extended inhumation burial uncovered during the Romanian-British excavations at Schela Cladovei (Romania). Other human bones, possibly resulting from the practice of excarnation, have been carefully placed in the grave along the left side of the primary burial (© Clive Bonsall).

from a previous burial that were uncovered when a new grave was dug and reburied with the corpse (e.g., Figure 10.4). Other instances suggest the practice of excarnation – removal of the flesh from a corpse leaving only the bones. It is unclear what method of excarnation was used. The corpse may have been exposed, perhaps on a specially constructed platform, to allow the flesh to either rot away or be removed by scavengers. However, removal of flesh by mammalian and some avian scavengers would be expected to leave marks on the bones. To the author's knowledge, such evidence has not been reported from either Vlasac or Schela Cladovei. Excarnation can also be achieved by 'burying' the corpse (i.e., covering it with earth or stones) until the soft tissue has decayed completely, and then exhuming the bones. Whatever the method practised, excarnated bones were sometimes buried separately and sometimes added to graves containing an intact body.

Special treatment appears to have been given to the skull. Some, otherwise intact, adult skeletons from both Schela Cladovei and Vlasac were lacking the skull or cranium and there is evidence of separate burial of crania either individually or in small clusters (e.g., Boroneanţ et al. 1999). At Schela Cladovei, the absence of cut-marks associated with skull removal suggests burials were revisited and the skulls removed after the flesh had decayed. Skull removal and skull caching are known from late Epipalaeolithic (Natufian) sites in the Levant and were especially characteristic of the ensuing PPNA phase (c. 9500–8800 cal BC), where they have been linked with the veneration of ancestors and the creation of social memory (Kuijt 2000, 2001). When such practices first appeared in the Iron Gates is unclear; at Schela Cladovei the context is clearly Late Mesolithic, but at Vlasac and elsewhere the evidence remains largely undated.

The presence of cemeteries (formal burial areas) is thought by archaeologists to indicate full or partial sedentism. There has been some debate as to whether cemeteries existed in the Late Mesolithic of the Iron Gates (Radovanović 1996). At both Schela Cladovei and Vlasac people were buried within the confines of the settlement. At first sight, it seems the burials are scattered across the settlement area, with a tendency to occur near houses. This has created the impression that graves were deliberately placed around or adjacent to the houses (Srejović and Letica 1978). But the relationship may be fortuitous. The Late Mesolithic occupations at Schela Cladovei and Vlasac span several centuries, and there is evidence from Schela Cladovei that the same areas were not used simultaneously for burial and habitation. Rather houses were built on ground that had previously been used for burial, and vice versa (Bonsall, unpublished data). The excavations at Schela Cladovei exposed several small areas with particular concentrations of burials. One area of just approximately 4 × 4 m contained eight more or less intact extended inhumations with approximately the same orientation, parallel to the Danube (Boroneanţ et al. 1999). This could be interpreted as a small formal burial area that remained in use for a limited period, before it was abandoned and a new burial plot established in another part of the site. Periodic relocation of burial and habitation areas is to be expected during the five-hundred- to seven-hundred-year lifespan of the Late Mesolithic settlements at Schela Cladovei and Vlasac, especially if the sites were not occupied continuously during their respective lifespans.

Convincing evidence for the existence of cemeteries in the Late Mesolithic of the Iron Gates comes from the site of Hajdučka Vodenica. An area approximately 4 × 2.5 m at the rear of the site, lying partly within a recess in the bedrock (the so-called chamber tomb), contained the remains of at least twenty-two individuals (Jovanović 1967, 1969b, 1984, Radovanović 1996, Borić and Miracle 2004). They comprised articulated skeletons, lying in the extended supine position and orientated parallel to the Danube, and groups of disarticulated bones. The arrangement of the burials suggests careful and deliberate placement within a cemetery. Two burials from the cemetery have (reservoir corrected) AMS ^{14}C ages of c. 7400–7500 BP (6300–6400 cal BC) (Table 10.1, Borić and Miracle 2004: fig. 11, table 3).

Cemeteries, it seems, did not just appear in the Late Mesolithic. At Padina, at least twelve burials were found in an area of approximately 12 × 1.75 m in sector III in the downstream part of the site. Large stones had been heaped up over the burials forming an elongated cairn, known as the 'stone construction of the necropolis' (Jovanović 1969a, Radovanović 1996, Borić and Miracle 2004). Radiocarbon dating of three skeletons (Table 10.1; Borić and Miracle 2004: tables 1 and 3) indicates an Early Mesolithic age for the cemetery. Differences in the ^{14}C ages suggest the cemetery was in use over a long period. In fact the cairn may be a composite feature resulting from the piling up of stones over individual burials emplaced at different times. The construction of stone heaps over corpses or graves appears to have been a common practice throughout the Mesolithic in the upper gorge. At Lepenski Vir, there are instances of stones heaped up over bodies or redeposited bones dating to the Early Mesolithic and the Final Mesolithic (see Radovanović 1996: figs. 4.2 and 4.6). Cairns may have served as markers or memorials and, as such, may have been maintained over many generations; in some cases, they may have been associated with the practice of excarnation (see Bonsall et al. 2008: 190).

Some archaeologists (e.g., Chapman 1993, Radovanović 1996, Zvelebil 2004) have looked for evidence of status differences among the Late Mesolithic burials of the Iron Gates, but with inconclusive results. Ethnographic studies show there is often a connection between the treatment of the body and the status of that person in life. Accordingly, Radovanović (1996) suggested that excarnation was reserved for individuals of higher status. However, apart from the presence of red ochre in many graves, burial goods are few and provide no clear evidence of social distinctions within the communities. Distinctions according to sex or age are difficult to discern. Ochre was associated with the burials of men, women, and children, and the practice of excarnation seems to have applied to adults and children alike. A few of the burials at Schela Cladovei and Vlasac were accompanied by cyprinid pharyngeal teeth and/or marine shell beads, but again there are no clear associations according to sex or age. Arguably the 'richest' burial at Vlasac is that of a young child (Burial 21) with cyprinid teeth in the stomach area and approximately fifty perforated shells of the marine mollusc, *Cyclope neritea*, on the chest – the shells were perhaps originally strung as a necklace (Srejović and Letica 1978: 58, pl. CVI). Archaeologists working on hunter-gatherer sites in other parts of the world, such as the Pacific Northwest Coast of North America, have sometimes taken the presence of shell beads in graves as an indicator of high social status (cf. Ames and Maschner 1999: 181). However, this is perhaps overstating the evidence. Ethnographically, shell beads are known to fulfil a variety of purposes. Often they serve as tokens of social relationships (Binford 1983) or simply as personal ornaments, rather than as symbols of wealth and social rank. In the Iron Gates shell beads appear to have been used throughout the Mesolithic, and in Europe as a whole their manufacture dates back to the early Upper Palaeolithic at least.

Some interesting examples of mortuary ritual have been recorded from the Iron Gates sites. Bones of dogs, the only domestic animal of this period, were found in association with human remains at Vlasac, and there is one possible example of the separate burial of a dog (Radovanović 1999). The ritual burial of dogs appears to have been widespread among Postglacial hunter-gatherers. The practice is well documented in the Late Mesolithic of the circum-Baltic region (Larsson 1989c, Larsson 1990a), and examples are known from Germany (Street 2003) and Israel (Davis and Valla 1978) as early as c. 12,000 cal BC.

Subsistence

The Late Mesolithic economy appears to have been relatively diverse. Faunal remains show that the inhabitants of Schela Cladovei and Vlasac harvested a broad spectrum of animal resources. Large herbivores (red deer, roe deer, wild pig, and aurochs) were exploited for meat and raw materials. Fur-bearing mammals such as brown bear, wolf, otter, and badger were taken, as were several species of birds including eagles (probably sought for their feathers). Fish and shellfish (especially freshwater mussels, *Unio* sp.) also figure very prominently in the faunal inventories of both sites, and shells of edible land snails (*Helix* spp.) occur (Pickard and Bonsall in preparation).

In the Romanian–British excavations at Schela Cladovei, where wet sieving was employed, fish bones far outnumbered those of other animals in Late Mesolithic contexts. Carp, sturgeon, and catfish (*Siluris glanis*) dominate the assemblage, although several other species are represented (Bartosiewicz et al. 1995). Many of the fish caught were of very large size; Bartosiewicz et al. (2008) estimate individual specimens of sturgeon to have weighed as much as 150 kilograms.

Curiously, there is no mention of sturgeon in the Vlasac excavation report (Bökönyi 1978), but probably they were present[6]. Acipenserid bones have been reported from other sites upstream of

Schela Cladovei, including several sites within the Iron Gates gorge. Sterlet and great sturgeon (beluga) were reported from 'Mesolithic' contexts at Ostrovu Banului and Icoana, and bones of sterlet and Russian sturgeon were identified in layer II at Cuina Turcului (Nalbant 1970, Păunescu 2000). Sturgeon remains are also reported from Early Neolithic contexts at Padina (Clason 1980).

The role of plant foods in Late Mesolithic subsistence in the Iron Gates is debatable. Among ethnographically known hunter-gatherers in temperate environments, plants usually made some contribution to diet though often more in terms of weight than calories, as most plants are poor sources of food energy compared to animals (Bonsall 1981, Kelly 1995). Moreover, the costs of processing plant food in terms of time and specialized equipment are often high. Late Mesolithic people would have had access to a broad array of plant foods in the early Holocene woodlands of the Iron Gates region (Mišic et al. 1972). It is likely that wild plants were collected for dietary and other (e.g., medicinal and manufacturing) purposes, but there is no evidence that they made a major contribution to subsistence. There are no artefacts from Mesolithic contexts that can be related specifically to plant collecting or processing, and even when fine sieving and flotation have been used, as in the Romanian–British excavations at Schela Cladovei, plant remains have been recovered only in very small quantities (Mason et al. 1996). The prevalence of oak in pollen assemblages from several sites led Prinz (1987) to suggest that acorns could have been a dietary staple in the Iron Gates Mesolithic, as they were for some North American aboriginal groups (Driver 1961), but the apparent absence from the Iron Gates sites of the technology necessary for intensive processing of acorns argues against this idea.

Stable isotope analysis of human remains from Vlasac and Schela Cladovei provides a good indication of the relative importance of terrestrial and freshwater resources. Bonsall et al. (1997, 2000, 2004) examined a number of skeletons dating between c. 7100 and 6600 cal BC. All showed elevated C- and N-isotope values, suggesting diets in which the greater part (approximately 60–85 percent) of the protein was derived directly or indirectly from freshwater food sources. The averages of the δ^{13}C and δ^{15}N values are slightly heavier than those of skeletons dating to the earlier Mesolithic.

The stable isotope data are thought to reflect mainly protein consumption rather than the whole diet (Bonsall et al. 1997), but they do not reveal the exact source of the protein. Fish are likely to have been considerably more important than either shellfish or aquatic mammals such as otters, although eating the meat of any animal that regularly consumed fish could have contributed to the 'aquatic' signal (see later).

In theory, food sources high in carbohydrate or fat but low in protein (e.g., certain plant foods) could have contributed significantly to diet without affecting bone collagen stable isotope values. Other evidence is against this. Bonsall et al. (1997) noted a lack of caries and the presence of heavy calculus on the teeth of Late Mesolithic individuals buried at Schela Cladovei, suggesting diets low in carbohydrate and high in protein. The oil in sturgeon and other fatty fish, and caviar from sturgeon which is especially rich in fat, may have compensated for the lack of carbohydrate in the diet.

Was Food Storage Practised in the Iron Gates Mesolithic?

The role of storage in the Late Mesolithic of the Iron Gates is an important issue. Food storage is generally seen as crucial to the development of complex hunter-gatherer societies, and some archaeologists (e.g., Voytek and Tringham 1989) have argued that it was central to the Late Mesolithic economy of the Iron Gates.

As Ames and Maschner (1999: 127) have observed, basic techniques for preserving fish and shellfish – sun and wind drying and smoking – have probably been known since at least the Late Pleistocene, and it is reasonable to suppose that they were also familiar to the Mesolithic foragers of the Iron Gates. The sunny, dry summers that characterize this part of Europe would have provided ideal conditions for drying (at least small) fish on outdoor racks, and it is likely that some food storage occurred. But was storage practised on a large scale?

The most obvious reason for storing food is to be able to survive periods when fresh food is in short supply. Although the Iron Gates was a rich environment especially in terms of aquatic resources, it was not a constant source of plenty; there were undoubtedly times of scarcity, especially during the winter. Fishing along the Danube is considerably more productive during the warmer months of the year (March/April to September/October). The main food fish are either not available during the winter or are difficult to capture. Catfish become less active as water temperature decreases and may cease to feed, carp tend to move into (comparatively warmer) deeper waters where they are less accessible, while sterlet also congregate in bottom holes and show little activity. Before dam construction effectively cut off their migration route, anadromous sturgeon were common in the Iron Gates reach of the Danube, but could only be taken in significant numbers during spring/early summer and autumn on their way to and from their spawning grounds (Bartosiewicz et al. 2008).

The problems of catching fish during the winter months would have been exacerbated in some years by freezing of the Danube. In recent times, freezing of the river across its entire width has been rare, but freezing at the margins is more frequent. Regardless, the presence of surface ice would have made fishing and the use of boats, if not impossible, certainly more hazardous. Historical records suggest that winter freezing of the Danube occurred more often during the 'Little Ice Age' c. AD 1500–1850 than in the period since then. Similar cooling phases occurred during the time-range of the Iron Gates Mesolithic c. 7300 cal BC and c. 6200 cal BC, each lasting several hundred years. A reduction of 2 degrees C in mean summer and annual temperatures across mid-latitude Europe characterised the second of these episodes, known as the '8200 cal BP cold event' (Magny et al. 2003). The more rigorous climatic conditions of these cooling phases may have had the effect of reducing the numbers of carp and catfish available in the Danube, as these species require a water temperature of at least 18 degrees C to reproduce (Bartosiewicz and Bonsall 2004: 268, table 7). The timing of sturgeon migrations along the Danube also may have been affected.

Thus Mesolithic communities in the Iron Gates may not have been able to survive some (i.e., very long or severe) winters without food storage methods. Yet there are no structural remains from the Iron Gates sites that would indicate large-scale preservation and storage of fish or other food items. This in itself is not conclusive, as certain kinds of storage facilities may leave few or no traces in the archaeological record. Containers made of basketry, bark, wood, or animal skin/tissue are highly unlikely to have survived in the free-draining, calcareous soils of the Iron Gates sites, while small pits and the postholes of fish-drying racks or raised caches could have been erased by pedogenetic alteration of the sediments since the Mesolithic, or simply overlooked during excavations that for the most part were conducted rapidly under rescue conditions. Voytek and Tringham (1989) suggested that some of the rectangular stone-bordered pits, widely interpreted as hearths, could have been used for storage, and there is some evidence to support this interpretation. The soil infilling one such feature at Schela Cladovei contained large numbers of small fish bones. None of these were obviously fire-damaged and magnetic susceptibility readings on soil samples from the stone-bordered pit failed to identify it as a hearth (Bonsall et al. 1992).

Although it is likely that some food storage occurred, people may have been able to survive most winters without heavy reliance on stored foods. Even in winter, the Danube is still a source of food in the form of freshwater mussels[7] and waterfowl[8]. Certain species of fish, including barbel, pike, and pikeperch, also can be taken quite readily during the winter[9], and opportunistic fishing for carp, catfish, and sturgeon cannot be ruled out, especially in milder weather. There are historical records of winter catches of sturgeon in the Hungarian section of the Danube (Bartosiewicz et al. 2008: table 7) and sturgeon will occasionally over-winter in the *accessible* reaches of the Danube today, that is, between the Black Sea and the Iron Gates II dam. Hunting of wild herbivores may have made some contribution to winter food supply, but the stable isotope data (discussed earlier) would appear to rule this out as a major source of food.

Dogs were the only domesticated animals kept by Late Mesolithic communities in the Iron Gates, and would have been a very convenient source of food during the winter months when other resources were scarce. Dog bones were particularly numerous at Vlasac. Among the 9,831 bone fragments of the three most important mammals consumed at the site dog accounted for 20 percent and was second in importance to red deer (68 percent) and more numerous than wild pig (12 percent) (Bökönyi 1975: table 1)[10]. The fact that the dog bones were often disarticulated and fragmented, like those of deer and wild pig, suggests that dogs were regarded as a food source; and the breakage patterns exhibited by long bones and skulls indicated to Bökönyi (1975: 168) that dogs were eaten. Clason (1980) drew similar conclusions from the large numbers of dog bones found at Padina and the state of fragmentation and charring of the bones.

Use of dogs as food would not be inconsistent with the stable isotope evidence of human diet from the Iron Gates Mesolithic. Dogs are omnivores and a large proportion of their diet may consist of left-over human food. Bone collagen stable isotope values of (probably) Mesolithic dogs from Vlasac (Grupe et al. 2003) suggest they ate significant amounts of fish, and regular consumption of dog meat may have contributed to the even higher levels of ^{13}C and ^{15}N present in the bones of Mesolithic humans.

Consumption of dog meat is widely reported among ethnographically-known hunter-gatherers, and also has been demonstrated from several Mesolithic sites in Europe (Benecke and Hanik 2002). The evidence for human consumption of dog flesh at some sites in the Iron Gates is sufficiently strong as to suggest that dogs were reared primarily for eating – a practice that has occasionally been documented among recent hunter-gatherers (e.g., Powers 1877) and was widespread among farming societies in ancient and historical times, especially those who, like the Aztecs and Polynesians, lacked large domesticated animals (Diamond 1997)[11].

In general terms, the larger the dog the greater its food value and it is interesting that the Vlasac dogs were larger on average than those from Early Neolithic (Starčevo-Körös-Criş culture) contexts in the Iron Gates and surrounding regions (Bökönyi 1975: 175–6). This size difference may reflect a change in the uses to which dogs were put between the Mesolithic and the Neolithic when domesticated livestock became available, and lends support to the suggestion that dogs were reared for eating during the Mesolithic. The keeping of dogs for human consumption may have been part of a deliberate strategy for coping with seasonal (especially winter) food shortages, and as such could be regarded as a form of indirect storage.

Ethnographic studies suggest that winter scarcity is not the only, nor necessarily the primary, reason for large-scale food storage by hunter-gatherers. Storage can be an important component of exchange systems; surplus food may be traded and dried foods, especially, which weigh less and preserve longer, can be transported over large distances. People also stored food for 'social' reasons – storage facilitated social gatherings and the allocation of time to nonsubsistence activities. For example, many aboriginal peoples of the Northwest Coast of North America regarded winter as a 'ceremonial season, when people should not have to search for food' (Suttles 1968: 64). Among Northwest Coast society generally food surpluses ultimately were converted into prestige.

To what degree these were also factors in the Iron Gates Mesolithic, thousands of years before the emergence of complex hunter-gatherer societies on the Northwest Coast, is difficult to gauge from the archaeological record and remains a source of debate.

If sites such as Vlasac and Schela Cladovei represent permanent or semi-permanent base camps, then individual Mesolithic communities were probably relatively small, numbering tens rather than hundreds of people – especially within the gorge where settlement space adjacent to the river was limited. Such small communities would not be reproductively or socially viable, and their survival would depend on participation in wider social networks (cf. Chapman 1989, Bonsall et al. 1997). People from different communities may have gathered together periodically for purposes of social intercourse, finding mates, sharing information, trade, ceremonial, and worship. Such gatherings would have required a food supply but may not have necessitated heavy reliance on storage, especially if they were timed to coincide with seasonal concentrations of migrating sturgeon.

Technology

The lithic technology of the Late Mesolithic is hard to characterize. At Vlasac concerns over the reliability of the stratigraphic interpretation of the site make it difficult to distinguish 'Late Mesolithic' from earlier or later material. At Schela Cladovei, Late Mesolithic features excavated between 1992 and 1996 produced only small assemblages of lithic artefacts, in spite of the use of wet sieving. The raw materials used were flint, radiolarite, and quartz, all apparently obtained locally mainly in the form of river pebbles. Bipolar débitage is much in evidence. Retouched pieces are few, comprising mainly scrapers and truncated bladelets.

In contrast, both sites produced an array of tools made from bone, red deer antler, and boars' tusks. Those that can be assigned to the Late Mesolithic with a fair degree of confidence include heavy duty 'hoes' or 'mattocks' made from red deer antler, boar tusk scrapers, awls, and distinctive bone arrowheads with a double-bevelled base.

A few decorated items were recovered from Schela Cladovei, and a much larger number from Vlasac. They consist mainly of bone, antler and stone objects engraved with geometric motifs, typically bands or areas filled with oblique hatching or cross-hatching. The chevron motif, which is well represented in layer I at Cuina Turcului, also occurs at Vlasac. However, it remains to be established through direct AMS ^{14}C dating how much of the artwork from Vlasac belongs to the Late Mesolithic.

External Relations

Evidence that the inhabitants of Vlasac and Schela Cladovei engaged in trade or other forms of exchange with neighbouring groups is the presence in some of the graves of the shells of marine molluscs (Srejović and Letica 1978, Boroneanţ et al. 1999), which could have originated in the Black Sea, Aegean, or Adriatic. These almost certainly were acquired through exchange rather than procured directly from the source. The shells were made into 'beads' using various techniques.

There is evidence that relations with other groups were not always peaceful. A significant proportion of the adults buried at Schela Cladovei (nearly 15 percent of those examined) died violently, shot by arrows equipped with bone points (Figure 10.5). Others suffered broken bones, including skull fractures, which also may have been the result of violence (Boroneanț and Nicolaescu-Plopșor 1990, McSweeney et al. in preparation). The high incidence of arrow wounds at Schela Cladovei is unusual, but such evidence is not unique in the Iron Gates. One instance of a bone arrow-head embedded in the pelvis of a juvenile male has been reported from Vlasac (Roksandić 2000), although the burial in question (Burial 4a) is undated and so cannot be assigned with confidence to the Late Mesolithic.

Bone arrowheads were also common as individual finds at both sites. At Schela Cladovei they were nearly always found with burials, in positions suggesting they were originally embedded in the soft tissue surrounding the skeleton and could have been the cause of death. At Vlasac, the pattern of occurrence is less clear. Bone arrowheads were found with at least four burials – Burials 9, 11a, 40, and 63 (Srejović and Letica 1978). In most cases, more than one arrowhead was present, and from their positions in relation to the skeletons they are likely to have been associated with arrow injuries. Also, because fine sieving was not employed in the Vlasac excavations, such small items could have been overlooked in other burials. Judging from published illustrations (Srejović and Letica 1978: pl. CI), some of the bone arrowheads from Vlasac show fractures which may have resulted from impacts against bone. Similar evidence was found at Schela Cladovei.

We can only speculate on the causes of the violence at Schela Cladovei and whether it reflects conflict within the community or between communities. Both are likely, although the frequent use of the bow and arrow is suggestive of intergroup conflict ('warfare'). Ethnographic studies suggest that hunter-gatherers engage in raiding and warfare primarily for reasons of revenge or material benefit[12], and warfare to protect or acquire important resource areas is widely reported (e.g., Heizer 1978, Suttles 1990). In the Iron Gates, ownership of, or access to, prime fishing spots may have been a frequent source of conflict. Schela Cladovei lies just a few kilometres downriver from the rapids that once marked the exit of the Danube from the Iron Gates gorge but that ceased to exist when the river was impounded by the Iron Gates I dam (Bartosiewicz and Bonsall 2004: fig. 8). The rapids created a bottle-neck in the upriver migration of sturgeon, leading to a seasonal concentration of these fish below the rapids. It is tempting to link the signs of warfare at Schela Cladovei to competition with neighbouring groups for control of this valuable resource.

Does the level of violence at Schela Cladovei tell us anything about mobility patterns in the Iron Gates Mesolithic? Among recent hunter-gatherers warfare appears to have been more frequent and more intense among sedentary peoples, presumably because they had more possessions to defend, but it was by no means unknown among non-sedentary foragers (cf. Divale 1972: table 2). In both cases, casualties caused by warfare could account for a significant proportion of all adult male deaths.

Final Mesolithic, 6300–6000 cal BC

There is a conspicuous gap in the radiocarbon dates for both Schela Cladovei and Vlasac between c. 7450 and 7100 BP (6300 and 6000 cal BC), and very few other sites in the Iron Gates have ^{14}C dates in this time-range (Figure 10.6a–c). This implies a significant decrease in activity at the sites or a change in the nature of that activity.

Proxy climate records show this to have been a period of cooler and wetter climate affecting much of western and central Europe, when the Danube and other river systems experienced more frequent and more extreme flooding (Bonsall et al. 2002, Magny et al. 2003).

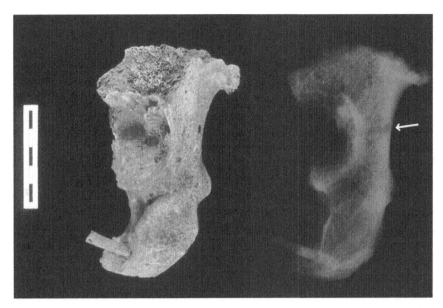

Figure 10.5. Part of a human pelvis from Schela Cladovei with an embedded bone arrowhead. On the x-ray the hole made by a second arrow is also visible. Around 15 percent of Late Mesolithic adults buried at Schela Cladovei had arrow injuries and probably died from their wounds (© Clive Bonsall).

Sites on the banks of the Danube would have been vulnerable to big floods, and it is possible that people chose to relocate their settlements, or at least their houses and living areas, onto higher ground further away from the river. Any sites located on higher terraces or on the plateau above the valley are likely to have escaped detection during the archaeological surveys of the 1960s to 1980s, as those areas were not surveyed systematically. It is unlikely that activity ceased altogether at the riverbank sites. Probably they continued to be used as places from which to conduct fishing activities and at which to land boats.

The only site that can be shown to have remained in regular use during this period is Lepenski Vir. Occupying a unique position facing the imposing Treskavac Mountain on the opposite bank of the Danube (Figure 10.7), Lepenski Vir has a number of features that set it apart from other Iron Gates sites. These only become apparent in the archaeological record after c. 6300 cal BC and include: buildings with lime plaster floors, the apparently deliberate placement of burials within or beneath some of the buildings, an unusually high frequency of decorated objects including the famous sculptured boulders which were often placed on the floors of buildings, and the deposition of parts of animal carcasses inside some of the buildings which suggest symbolic, and in some cases sacrificial, acts (Bökönyi 1972, Dimitrijević 2000, 2008).

These distinctive features of Lepenski Vir suggest that it was a 'sacred site' used primarily as a centre for burial and ritual, and some archaeologists have speculated that the plaster-floored structures served as temples or shrines, rather than houses (e.g., Srejović 1972, Gimbutas 1991). The religious character of Lepenski Vir may explain why this site remained in use throughout the period from 6300 to 6000 cal BC when other riverbank sites in the Iron Gates ceased to be occupied on a regular basis. It was perhaps regarded as hallowed ground inhabited by the spirits

Clive Bonsall

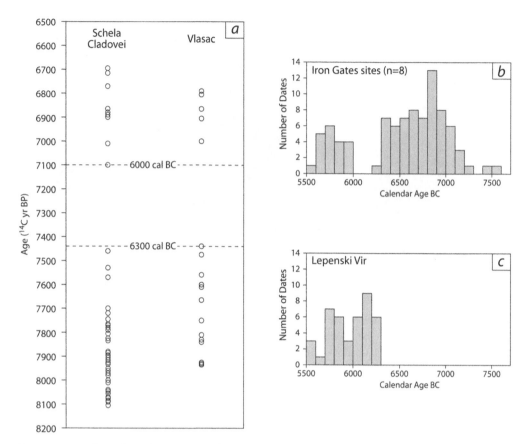

Figure 10.6. The radiocarbon 'gap' in the Iron Gates: *a*. ¹⁴C mean ages for Schela Cladovei and Vlasac; *b*. Calibrated (median probability) ages per 100-year period between 5500 and 7700 BC from Hajducka Vodenica, Icoana, Ostrovu Banului, Ostrovu Corbului, Padina, Răzvrata, Schela Cladovei, and Vlasac; *c*. Calibrated (median probability) ages per 100-year period between 5500 and 7700 BC from Lepenski Vir. The radiocarbon dates listed in Table 10.4 have been excluded.

of the ancestors, and by continuing to use it as a burial place the group could maintain rights of ownership and inheritance of the land, the river and resources (Bonsall et al. 2002).

Although Lepenski Vir between 6300 to 6000 cal BC shows some novel features compared to the preceding period, the underlying cultural tradition is still clearly 'Mesolithic'. Burial practices remain essentially the same, with extended supine inhumation as the norm (Figure 10.8). Bone chemistry analyses reveal that the majority of individuals who were buried at Lepenski Vir between 6300 and 6000 cal BC placed the same heavy emphasis on aquatic food sources as their Late Mesolithic predecessors at Schela Cladovei and Vlasac. In fact, median human bone collagen $\delta^{13}C$ and $\delta^{15}N$ values are even heavier, which may indicate that dependence on the aquatic food web increased still further during this final phase of the Mesolithic (Figure 10.3, Bonsall et al. 2004).

Table 10.4. List of 'unsatisfactory' radiocarbon dates from Mesolithic and Early Neolithic sites in the Iron Gates

Site	Context	Material	Lab. No.	BP
Alibeg	Trench II, horizon II	C	Bln-1193	7195 ± 100
Ogradena-Icoana	'Criş hut', horizon III (?)	C	Bln-1056	7445 ± 80
Padina	Burial 12	H	BM-1146	9331 ± 58
	Burial 39 (?)	H	BM-1404	9292 ± 148
	Burial 14	H	BM-1147	9198 ± 103
	Burial 7	H	BM-1144	8797 ± 83
	Above house 12	D	OxA-9034	7755 ± 65
	Burial 2	H	BM-1143	7738 ± 51
	House 18, floor	D	OxA-9053	7685 ± 60
	House 9	D	OxA-9056	7625 ± 55
Schela Cladovei	Burial, Area III	H	OxA-4384	8570 ± 105
	Bone artefact, Area VI	B	OxA-9211	6250 ± 450
Vlasac	Grave 54	C	Z-264	6335 ± 92
	Grave 11	C	Z-268	6713 ± 90

Dated material: B = terrestrial mammal bone; C = charcoal; D = dog bone; H = human bone. The dates from Alibeg and Ogradena-Icoana are single measurements from dubious contexts. The dates on bones of dogs and humans from Padina most likely require correction for the freshwater reservoir effect; however, for the humans, there are no associated $\delta^{15}N$ measurements, which would allow a correction to be applied (the same applies to OxA-4384 from Schela Cladovei), and for the dogs there is insufficient information on the dietary end members to perform a reservoir correction. OxA-9211 from Schela Cladovei has a very large error. Z-268 and Z-264 from Vlasac appear to be from grave fills; hence the charcoal may be redeposited and comprise material of differing ages. Data from: Bonsall et al. (1997, unpublished), Borić and Miracle (2004), Boroneanţ (2000), Burleigh and Živanović (1980), Srejović and Letica (1978), Whittle et al. (2002).

When Did the Neolithic Transition Occur in the Iron Gates?

The Downstream Area

According to the radiocarbon evidence the Late Mesolithic occupation at Schela Cladovei came to an end c. 6300 cal BC. The site was reoccupied c. 6000 cal BC and, from the outset, a change in cultural patterns is apparent. Livestock keeping is indicated by abundant remains of domestic cattle, pigs and sheep/goats, although hunting and fishing still contributed to the economy. There were clear changes in material culture and technology, reflected in the appearance of pottery, ground stone artefacts, and new forms of bone tools (Figure 10.9). There are traces of buildings with a rectangular ground plan in contrast to the trapezoidal structures of the Late Mesolithic, as well as evidence for trade or exchange in exotic materials such as obsidian and high-quality 'Balkan' flint (Figure 10.10). No burials dating to this period have been identified at Schela Cladovei, but evidence from other sites in the downstream area such as Velesnica (Vasić 2008) suggests a change in funerary practices around this time with the appearance of burials in which the body is almost invariably placed in the crouched position.

Figure 10.7. The distinctive trapezoidal mountain of Treskavac on the Romanian bank of the Danube, opposite Lepenski Vir (© Clive Bonsall).

These new elements can all be paralleled in early farming settlements of the Starčevo-Körös-Criş complex, which by 6000 cal BC occupied a large area of southeast and central Europe surrounding the Iron Gates. Thus, there seems little doubt that the part of the Danube valley that lies immediately downstream of the Iron Gates gorge had been assimilated into the Starčevo-Körös-Criş complex by 6000 cal BC.

But when was agriculture introduced to downstream area? AMS ^{14}C dates from Blagotin in Serbia (Whittle et al. 2002: 107) suggest Neolithic farmers were already present in the Morava catchment, approximately 150 km to the southwest of Schela Cladovei, by 6200 cal BC. However, farming settlements are not recorded along the Danube or in its catchment area beyond for a further 150–200 years. The earliest ^{14}C dates for Early Neolithic (Körös) settlements on the Pannonian Plain (Whittle et al. 2002) are no older than the date of the appearance of agriculture at Schela Cladovei. The same applies to the first Neolithic settlements in Romania north of the Danube. Sites attributed to the earliest phase of the Cris culture ('Pre-Criş' [Paul 1995] or 'Criş I' [Lazarovici 1993]) on the Banat plain and in Transylvania have ^{14}C ages clustering around 7100 BP (6000 cal BC) (Biagi et al. 2005), which are statistically indistinguishable from the earliest ^{14}C dates for Neolithic activity on the Pannonian Plain and at Schela Cladovei.

Figure 10.8. Final Mesolithic burial inserted through the floor of House 21 at Lepenski Vir (© Archaeological Institute, Beograd).

One interpretation of the radiocarbon evidence is that the spread of agriculture through the Balkan Peninsula came to a standstill c. 6200 cal BC to the south of the Danube, and a new phase of expansion began c. 6000 cal BC when agriculture spread rapidly along the Danube and its tributaries in northeast Serbia, Hungary, and Romania. The apparent delay in the appearance of Early Neolithic settlements on the floodplains and lower terraces of the Danube and its northern tributaries has been attributed to severe flooding associated with the distinct global cooling phase between 6300 and 6000 cal BC (Bonsall et al. 2002). Frequent, large-scale, and unpredictable floods would have been a deterrent to farming of valley bottoms and may have excluded large areas from the possibility of cultivation and stockraising.

The Iron Gates Gorge

The Iron Gates gorge offered a very different environment from the fertile alluvial plains on either side of the Carpathian Mountains, and the timing of the Neolithic transition within the gorge has been the subject of intense debate. Central to this debate is the site of Lepenski Vir, which shows evidence of frequent, perhaps continuous, use between c. 6300 and 5500 cal BC. Arguably, this is the only site in the entire Iron Gates region where the events of that time range can be studied as a more or less uninterrupted process.

Fragments of pottery, and occasionally whole pots, were found lying on the floors of some of the trapezoidal buildings at Lepenski Vir (Srejović 1969, 1972, Borić 1999, 2002, Radovanović 2000, Garašanin and Radovanović 2001). The buildings with pottery seem to be among the latest in

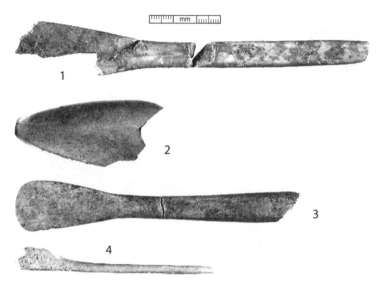

Figure 10.9. New forms of bone tools appeared in the Iron Gates from approximately 6000 cal BC. These examples from Schela Cladovei (Romania), comprising fragments of spoons (1–3) and an awl with a distinctive worked base (4), can be paralleled in sites of the Early Neolithic Starčevo-Körös-Criş complex throughout the central and northern Balkans (© Clive Bonsall).

the sequence with ^{14}C ages ranging between 7083 ± 73 and 6814 ± 69 BP (c. 5950 to 5700 cal BC) (Figure 10.11, Bonsall et al. 2002: fig. 6, Bonsall 2005).

A new form of burial also appeared. The traditional Mesolithic burial rite of extended supine inhumation was replaced by crouched inhumation characteristic of the Starčevo-Körös-Criş complex. The latest example of a burial in the Mesolithic tradition has a reservoir-corrected ^{14}C age of 7133 ± 75 BP (c. 6000 cal BC), and the earliest dated instance of a Neolithic-type burial is 7036 ± 95 BP (c. 5950 cal BC) (Bonsall et al. 2004, Bonsall et al. 2008, Bonsall 2005).

This evidence implies that two key Neolithic traits – pottery manufacture and crouched inhumation – became firmly established at Lepenski Vir at about the same time as they did at sites in the lowland plains on either side of the Iron Gates gorge. It does not prove that they were introduced simultaneously, nor does it preclude the possibility of Starčevo culture elements, especially portable items such as pottery, ground stone tools and artefacts made from Balkan flint, infiltrating the gorge during the Final Mesolithic as a result of initial contacts with farmers[13].

By contrast, it is clear that *some* 'Mesolithic' traditions survived at Lepenski Vir and other sites within the gorge into the period after 6000 cal BC. For example, buildings with a trapezoidal ground plan continued to be erected at Lepenski Vir, Padina, and Vlasac, and carved boulders continued to be deposited inside buildings at Lepenski Vir implying continuity of religious traditions.

Bones of domestic livestock (cattle, pig and sheep/goat) were found at Lepenski Vir and other sites in the gorge in contexts that also produced Starčevo ceramics ('Lepenski Vir III', 'Padina B', 'Hajdučka Vodenica II'), which suggests the livestock remains and the pottery are contemporaneous. In all cases, however, it seems the bones of livestock are far outnumbered by the remains of wild animals and fish (e.g., Bökönyi 1972, Clason 1980, Greenfield 2008).

The dating of the livestock remains at Lepenski Vir is especially problematic. Neither Bökönyi (1972), nor Dimitrijević (2000, 2008) have reported bones of domestic animals other than

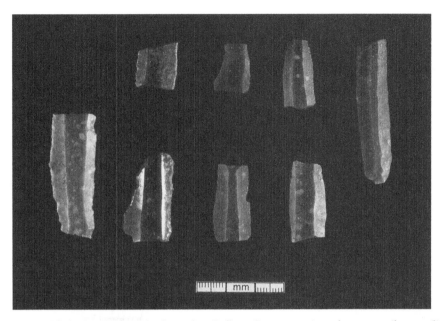

Figure 10.10. Blades made from high-quality Balkan flint, sometimes known as 'honey flint' or 'yellow-spotted flint', from the Romanian-British excavations at Schela Cladovei. This type of flint is common in Early Neolithic Starčevo-Körös-Criş culture contexts in the central and northern Balkans, often in the form of complete blades. Thought to originate from sources on the Pre-Balkan Platform, it is one of several 'exotic' materials that enter the Iron Gates through exchange c. 6000 cal BC (© Clive Bonsall).

dogs from the trapezoidal buildings, and because Garašanin and Radovanović (2001) and Borić (2002) have effectively reassigned the features originally attributed to 'Lepenski Vir III' to the same period as the trapezoidal buildings ('LV I–II'), it is not clear how the livestock remains relate to the architectural features on the site. It is possible to suggest a 'ritual' explanation for the absence of the bones of livestock from the later ('ceramic') buildings at Lepenski Vir (Bonsall 2005), but the chronological context of the livestock remains will only be reliably established by direct ^{14}C age measurements on the bones.

The persistence of Mesolithic traditions and the preponderance of wild over domestic animal remains in the period after 6000 cal BC have led some authors to propose that the inhabitants of the Iron Gates gorge remained hunter-gatherers for centuries after a Neolithic economy based on cereal cultivation and stockraising had been established in the surrounding areas (e.g., Clason 1980, Voytek and Tringham 1989, Radovanović 1996, Radovanović and Voytek 1997, Zvelebil and Lillie 2000). According to this theory, the presence of pottery and bones of livestock is the result of trade or exchange with neighbouring farmers.

Other evidence contradicts this interpretation. The appearance of new burial practices around this time implies more than mere trade contacts, and can only be explained in terms of either acculturation or immigration. Moreover, bone collagen stable isotope analysis suggests that the people buried at Lepenski Vir after 6000 cal BC did not subsist mainly on fish and other aquatic foods like their Mesolithic predecessors, but derived a large proportion of their dietary protein from terrestrial sources (Figure 10.3). It is difficult to see how such a major change in diet

271

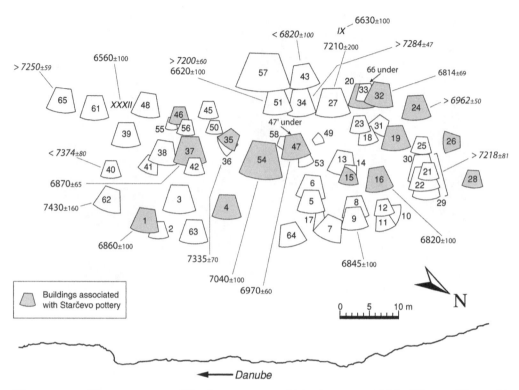

Figure 10.11. The occurrence of Starčevo pottery within the trapezoidal buildings of Lepenski
Vir. Dates shown are in ¹⁴C years BP – the dates assigned to individual buildings are either the
¹⁴C ages of associated charcoal samples, or based on the stratigraphic relationship of a building
to another radiocarbon dated feature (animal bone, building, or burial).

could have been accomplished without an economy in which agriculture played a significant role
(cf. Bonsall et al. 1997, 2000, Bonsall 2003).

From these lines of evidence, it can be argued that the later Stone Age people of the Iron Gates
gorge made the transition to agriculture and adopted other facets of Early Neolithic culture at
roughly the same time as their neighbours on the Pannonian and Wallachian plains. However, in
all three areas to varying degrees fishing and hunting continued to be part of the Early Neolithic
economy (cf. Clason 1980, Bonsall et al. 1997, Bartosiewicz et al. 2001, Whittle et al. 2002).

The riparian sites within the gorge seem unlikely places from which to have conducted farming
activities, and the possibility exists that after 6000 cal BC they were used not as primary residential
sites, but as seasonal fishing camps, perhaps maintained in order to take advantage of the sturgeon
migrations in late spring/early summer and autumn. This would explain the much smaller numbers
of Early Neolithic (vs. Mesolithic) burials and the low frequencies of bones of domestic livestock
in the sites.

As suggested earlier, the spread of farming may have come to a temporary standstill c. 6200 cal BC
to the south of the Iron Gates. By that time a farming settlement had been established at Blagotin
in the catchment area of the West Morava river (Whittle et al. 2002). However, the agricultural
frontier may have extended further north along the Morava and other southern tributaries of the
Danube. This raises the possibility that the hunter-gatherers of the Iron Gates were in contact with

Figure 10.12. Trapezoidal buildings with carefully laid plaster floors, stone-bordered 'hearths', and other stone fixtures are a conspicuous feature of Lepenski Vir. In this example so-called altars – large tabular stones with artificially ground hollows in the upper surface – can be seen set into the floor behind the hearth and adjacent to the near side of the building. Such buildings began to be erected on the site during the Final Mesolithic around 6300 cal BC, but their construction continued throughout the Early Neolithic between 6000 and 5500 cal BC when pottery and farming were introduced to the region (© Archaeological Institute, Beograd).

farmers to the south for a time before the eventual establishment of farming in the Iron Gates region. Some authors have argued that there was contact between the two populations by 6300 cal BC if not earlier (e.g., Radovanović 1996, Tringham 2000, Whittle et al. 2002, Borić and Miracle 2004) although these claims are often based on 'data', such as the supposed early appearance of pottery at Lepenski Vir and Padina, which have yet to be verified.

For reasons already discussed, Lepenski Vir is the site most likely to furnish evidence of forager–farmer contacts.

The appearance of lime plaster floors (Figure 10.12) at Lepenski Vir c. 6300 cal BC might be interpreted as evidence of contact with farmers, since the technique is otherwise unknown in the European Mesolithic. The earliest evidence of lime plaster pyrotechnology is from the Late Epipalaeolithic (Natufian) period in the Levant. Buildings with plaster floors proliferate in the Near East during the PPNB phase (8800–6900 cal BC) (Gourdin and Kingery 1975, Kingery et al. 1988, Thomas 2005) and are first encountered in Europe in the Greek Early Neolithic (Perlès 2001). However, the earliest Greek examples are no older than those at Lepenski Vir. Moreover, to date, there are no clearly documented finds of lime plaster floors from Early Neolithic sites in the region between Greece and the Danube – an area in which limestone abounds – and this raises doubts that the use of the technique at Lepenski Vir was inspired by contact with farmers. An equally plausible case could be made for an independent invention of lime plaster pyrotechnology in the northern Balkans, or its transmission from the Near East to southeast Europe before the Neolithic (Bonsall 2005).

An unusual feature of Lepenski Vir highlighted by Borić and Stefanović (2004) is the occurrence of burials of neonates beneath the floors of some of the trapezoidal buildings. Because this practice is not clearly represented in earlier Mesolithic contexts at neighbouring Vlasac, but is known from Epipalaeolithic and Neolithic sites in the East Mediterranean, Borić and Stefanović have implied that it spread with farming from the Near East to southeast Europe, and thus reflects contact between the inhabitants of Lepenski Vir and nearby farmers in the period between c. 6300 and 6000 cal BC. However, none of the infant burials from Lepenski Vir has been ^{14}C dated and so it is not certain that they all belong to the time-range from 6300 to 6000 cal BC. Moreover the lack of Mesolithic house remains in southeast Europe outside the Iron Gates means we cannot be sure that the practice of burying infants under house floors was not practised by indigenous hunter-gatherers before the arrival of farming. As with the lime plaster floors, it may be that the presence of sub-floor burials at Lepenski Vir and their (apparent) absence from Late Mesolithic Vlasac and Early Neolithic Padina is simply a reflection of the special significance of Lepenski Vir for the Final Mesolithic inhabitants of the region, and not a marker of culture change.

The evidence of symbolic behaviour at Lepenski Vir has also been linked to contact with farmers. According to Radovanović and Voytek (1997) trade relations with neighbouring farmers led to the intensification of an already complex social and ideological system within Iron Gates gorge, which enabled the inhabitants to resist assimilation and preserve their cultural identity and hunter-gatherer lifestyle longer than was the case in the area downstream of the gorge.

Bonsall et al. (2002) have offered an alternative explanation which links the proliferation of stone sculptures at Lepenski Vir after c. 6300 cal BC with climate change and a concomitant increase in flood frequency, magnitude and unpredictability along the Danube. Accepting Srejović's (1972) interpretation of the figural sculptures as apotropaic representations of mythical ancestors or 'fish-gods', Bonsall et al. (2002) suggested they were intended to protect against the growing threat from flooding by the Danube, rather than the advancing tide of agriculture.

Arguably, the strongest evidence for the presence of farmers close to the Iron Gates in the centuries before 6000 cal BC is provided by bone chemistry analyses. Stable isotope data indicate that the people buried at Lepenski Vir during the Final Mesolithic (6300–6000 cal BC) generally had diets that were very high in aquatic protein, higher even than during earlier phases of the Mesolithic (Figure 10.3). However, three adults from this period show diets that were unusually high in terrestrial protein, similar to those of the Early Neolithic after 6000 cal BC. All three had been accorded the traditional Mesolithic burial rite of extended supine inhumation. Various explanations have been proposed (Bonsall et al. 2004, Bonsall et al. 2008). Of these, arguably the most convincing are that the three individuals with more 'terrestrial' diets were (i) local people who lived within the Lepenski Vir catchment at a time when farming started to make a significant contribution to the economy, (ii) incomers who originated among farmers in the hinterland, or (iii) locals who moved to live with farmers and on death were returned to the ancestral home for burial. The corollary of each of these hypotheses is that the Lepenski Vir population had at least *knowledge* of agriculture and, by implication, contacts with farmers around or before 6000 cal BC.

Other questions follow on from this. What was the nature of the forager–farmer interactions? If intermarriage did occur, does this indicate that external relations with farmers were generally peaceful? Ruth Tringham (2000), drawing on the work of Chapman (1993) and Zvelebil and Lillie (2000), painted a compelling picture of contacts across the agricultural frontier as a two-way process that involved exchanges of goods and personnel, leading to population increase and intensification of production among foragers and farmers alike, then to social competition and status differentiation among the hunter-gatherers and their eventual adoption of farming. She went on to argue that interactions with the foragers of the Iron Gates gorge stimulated a perceived change in subsistence practices in the later stages of the Starčevo-Körös-Criş culture (*viz.* greater emphasis on local animal and plant resources) and were an important factor in the formation of the Middle Neolithic Vinča culture. These last-mentioned aspects of Tringham's hypothesis, however, are difficult to accept in the light of reappraisal of the chronology of the Iron Gates Mesolithic, especially the dating of Lepenski Vir (see earlier), and Bartosiewicz's demonstration that 'local' animal resources (wild ungulates and domesticated cattle and pigs) were of secondary importance to sheep/goat herding throughout the Early Neolithic of the Carpathian Basin (Bartosiewicz 2005).

Summary and Conclusions

The Iron Gates is a key area within southeast Europe for studying the Mesolithic and the transition to farming. Yet after more than four decades of research the archaeological evidence continues to generate intense debate and disagreement among scholars.

The prevailing view of the Iron Gates Mesolithic, based on excavations conducted in the 1960s, is of a foraging society, which, in the course of its long development from the Late Glacial to the mid-Holocene, exhibited an increasing degree of social complexity and sedentism. In this scenario, there was an initial period of cave occupation when people followed a nomadic lifestyle based on hunting terrestrial herbivores. Then, around 7600 cal BC, the foragers began to intensify their exploitation of aquatic resources, which made possible a reduction in residential mobility leading to the establishment of semipermanent or permanent settlements on the banks of the Danube. According to some archaeologists, so successful was this foraging adaptation that the Mesolithic inhabitants of the Iron Gates were able to resist the adoption of agriculture for centuries after it became established in the surrounding regions, even though they traded with neighbouring farmers for pottery and other goods.

A new phase of research began in the 1990s with the Romanian-British excavations at Schela Cladovei and the systematic application of AMS ^{14}C dating and stable isotope analysis to bone remains from the Iron Gates sites. AMS dating of animal and human bones and bone artefacts from Lepenski Vir, Schela Cladovei, and elsewhere has exposed flaws in the traditional chronological framework of the Iron Gates Mesolithic and has laid the foundations of a more secure radiocarbon-based chronology. Stable isotope analysis of human remains has provided a new perspective on the economic basis of the Mesolithic and the transition to farming in the Iron Gates region, which in key respects is at variance with previous ideas drawn from osteoarchaeological data.

The degree of 'social complexity' exhibited by the Mesolithic inhabitants of the Iron Gates and whether they became more socially complex with time remain contentious issues.

Sedentism and *storage* feature prominently in ethnographic descriptions of hunter-gatherer complexity. A case can be made for sedentism or substantially restricted residential mobility in the Iron Gates Mesolithic. The Danube provided an important concentration of food resources and bone chemistry studies suggest there was focal exploitation of these resources from at least the beginning of the Holocene. Formal burial areas also were in existence by that time. Some food storage is likely in the Iron Gates Mesolithic, but there is no evidence that direct storage was practised on any significant scale. On the other hand, there is good evidence that dogs were eaten and that they were fed surplus food including fish; in effect, dogs may have served as food-storing repositories.

Based on a study of seventy-four ethnographically known societies, Kent (1990) found a close correlation between social complexity and the internal partitioning of houses. Judged on this criterion, the Mesolithic people of the Iron Gates rank fairly low on the scale of complexity. From the limited data available, their houses appear to have been relatively small – on average they were larger than those of nomadic societies such as the San (cf. Yellen 1977) but substantially smaller than the houses of the sedentary hunter-gatherers of the Northwest Coast (cf. Maschner 1991) – and lacking clear internal partitions.

Most ethnographic studies of complex hunter-gatherers rely on data from the Northwest Coast of North America. In documenting the emergence of cultural complexity on the northern Northwest Coast, Maschner (1991, Ames and Maschner 1999) identified a number of archaeologically observable trends, including: (i) economic intensification, (ii) growth in population and settlement size, (iii) intensification of warfare, and (iv) the emergence of hereditary social ranking and craft specialization. There are few signs of similar processes taking place over the time-range of the Iron Gates Mesolithic.

Average stable C- and N-isotope ratios in human bone collagen can be seen to increase during the Mesolithic. This may indicate an increase in the importance of aquatic *versus* terrestrial resources with time, which could be interpreted as economic intensification. Equally, however, it could reflect other factors such as changes in the food web.

Tringham (2000) argued for a population explosion among the hunter-gatherers of the Iron Gates after c. 6500 cal BC as a result of contact with farmers. In reality, however, there are too few data on which to base estimates of group size or overall population density for any stage of the Iron Gates Mesolithic.

Warfare certainly occurred during the Iron Gates Mesolithic, on the evidence of arrow injuries from Schela Cladovei and Vlasac. But there is no evidence of increasing levels of conflict through time. The unusually high percentage of arrow injuries at Schela Cladovei possibly relates to a very restricted phase within the Late Mesolithic, while a recent study by Roksandić (2000) of the many Final Mesolithic and Early Neolithic burials at Lepenski Vir apparently revealed no individuals with arrow injuries. Moreover, there is no direct evidence of perimeter defence and the construction of fortifications in the Iron Gates at any stage of the Mesolithic or Early Neolithic.

The stone sculptures from Lepenski Vir may be the work of craftsmen, but the fact that they are virtually confined to that site argues against the idea that craft specialisation was a general feature of the Iron Gates before the introduction of pottery manufacturing.

Also, it is difficult to argue for the existence of social ranking in the Iron Gates Mesolithic using the standard' archaeological indicators of burial goods or house size variability. Almost the only items from graves which can be termed 'prestige goods' (luxury items or items of special value) are marine shell beads and necklaces. Archaeologically, shell beads are widely distributed in time and space (back to the early Upper Palaeolithic in Europe) and ethnographically they are known to have served a variety of purposes. So it would be naïve to assume that their occurrence in Mesolithic burials in the Iron Gates is proof of inherited status.

Rather than exhibiting increasing complexity, in many respects the Iron Gates Mesolithic shows remarkable stability. Between c. 9500 and 6300 cal BC, there appears to have been little change in subsistence patterns or the complexity of material culture. Mortuary practices are fairly consistent throughout the period. The trapezoidal house form is not clearly documented before the Late Mesolithic; although such structures may have been built earlier, and they continued to be erected at sites in the Iron Gates gorge with no major change in form or size until the end of the Early Neolithic c. 5500 cal BC.

New features appear at Lepenski Vir in the gorge between 6300 and 6000 cal BC, which contrast sharply with what had gone before. They include figural stone sculptures, the placement of burials beneath house floors, and new architectural elements such as lime plaster floors and stone-built façades. The challenge for archaeologists is to determine to what extent these features reflect real culture change perhaps stimulated by contact with farmers or by environmental stress, and to what extent the special character of Lepenski Vir has created a 'false' impression of change.

The florescence of Lepenski Vir during the last few centuries of the Iron Gates Mesolithic occurred at a time when many sites along the banks of the Danube were either abandoned or ceased to be occupied on a regular basis. This event coincided with a period of distinctly cooler and wetter climate across middle Europe, which was accompanied by a marked increase in riverine floods. It is possible that, faced with an increased threat from flooding, people chose to relocate their settlements onto higher ground away from the river.

The climatic downturn and increased flooding in the Danube catchment may have forced a temporary halt in the advance of agriculture through the Balkans. Between 6200 and 6000 cal BC, the agricultural 'frontier' probably lay to the south but within 100 km of the Iron Gates. It is likely that contacts between the foragers within the Iron Gates region and farmers to south were established sometime during this period, and stable isotope data from Lepenski Vir suggest there may have been movement of personnel (and by implication goods and ideas) between the two populations.

The view that the hunter-gatherers of the Iron Gates gorge resisted the adoption of agriculture for many centuries is not supported by the available evidence. Paired ^{14}C and stable isotope analyses of human remains from Lepenski Vir show a marked reduction in average δ^{15}N and δ^{13}C values c. 6000 cal BC suggesting a shift to a diet that included a much higher proportion of protein from terrestrial food sources than the average Mesolithic diet. The fact that this dietary shift broadly coincided with the appearance of pottery (and, probably, ground stone tools and 'exotic' raw materials such as Balkan flint and obsidian) and new burial practices all with clear parallels in the Starčevo-Körös-Criş complex, strongly implies that farming had begun to play an important role in the subsistence economy of the Iron Gates region, and that the 'neolithization' of the gorge occurred at more or less the same time as in the surrounding regions. Fishing continued to be practised during the Early Neolithic throughout the Iron Gates, and sites that were 'abandoned' around 6300 cal BC were reoccupied c. 6000 cal BC. In some respects, the changes within the gorge appear less dramatic than those in the downstream area, in that 'Mesolithic' traditions of architecture and religion continued for a time at sites in the gorge, although not, it seems, elsewhere.

It is difficult to imagine the sites located on narrow alluvial benches at the foot of the gorge acting as bases from which farming activities were conducted – farmers normally must remain close to their crops and livestock. This raises the question of whether sites such as Hajdučka Vodenica, Padina, and Vlasac continued to be occupied on a permanent or semipermanent basis after 6000 cal BC or whether they became seasonal fishing camps. This latter hypothesis may explain the scarcity of Early Neolithic burials and bones of livestock at these sites.

This is one of many questions about the Mesolithic-Neolithic transition in the Iron Gates that remain unresolved. Other questions that readily come to mind are: Did more severe winters or territorial pressure from farmers during the 'Little Ice Age event' of 6300–6000 cal BC lead to a greater reliance on stored foods? And did this contribute to the heavier δ^{15}N values seen in the bones of many Final Mesolithic people buried at Lepenski Vir? Did pressure on natural resources linked to climate change and/or competition from farmers encourage the hunter-gatherers to adopt agriculture?

Although many of the sites excavated in the 1960s and 1980s are now under water as a result of the impounding of the Danube by the Iron Gates I and II dams, there is still considerable scope for further research in the region, which may help to resolve these and other issues discussed in this chapter. Some sites in the downstream area, such as Schela Cladovei and Ostrovu Banului, are still accessible and would repay more extensive excavation. Archaeological investigation of older (higher) terraces along the Danube offers the best hope for the discovery of new sites, including sites belonging to the crucial period between 6300 and 6000 cal BC. In addition, finds from previous excavations now in museum collections remain a potentially rich source of new data. Using this material there is scope for seasonality studies of mammalian, fish, and shellfish remains bearing on questions of residential mobility and site function. The application of AMS ^{14}C dating to human and animal bones, bone artefacts, and organic temper and residues from pottery sherds would provide valuable information on the development of art, burial practices, technology, and the timing of the introduction of animal domesticates and ceramic technology. DNA and stable isotope analyses of human remains could be used to address questions relating to the movement of people into the Iron Gates region and between communities within the region, an aspect of the Iron Gates Mesolithic that remains poorly understood.

For archaeologists involved in this research the Iron Gates remains an immensely rich repository of information about the Mesolithic and the transition to farming, and one of the most remarkable cultural landscapes of European prehistory.

Acknowledgments

The author would like to thank Paolo Biagi, Joni Manson, Ivana Radovanović and Barbara Voytek for information about Early Neolithic sites in Southeast Europe, Gordon Thomas for information on lime plaster pyrotechnology, and Geoff Bailey, Gordon Cook, Mark Macklin, Robert Payton, Catriona Pickard, Penny Spikins, László Bartosiewicz, and two anonymous referees for their comments on a preliminary draft of the paper.

Postscript: Since 2005, when this chapter was written, more than eighty new AMS ^{14}C measurements on animal and human bones from seven sites have been reported (Borić and Dimitrijević 2007, Dinu et al. 2007, Borić et al. 2008); there are 36 new dates from Lepenski Vir, 21 from Vlasac, 19 from Icoana, 8 from Schela Cladovei, 2 from Răzvrata, and one each from Ostrovu Banului and Ostrovu Mare. To assimilate all these new data would have been a major task, involving re-writing several sections of the chapter and updating tables and figures. It was decided not to attempt this, because full details of the dates are not available. The majority of the new ^{14}C dates from Lepenski Vir have been presented only in graphical form (Borić and Dimitrijević 2007: fig. 3), whereas these and the dates for Icoana, Răzvrata, Schela Cladovei, Ostrovu Banului, and Ostrovu Mare have been reported without the associated δ^{13}C and δ^{15}N values, which limits discussion. Nevertheless, the new data have a bearing on some of the issues discussed in this chapter. For example, (i) Borić and Dimitrijević (2007) have reported the first direct dates on bones of domestic livestock from Lepenski Vir, which show that domesticates were present by $c.$ 5900 BC (cf. p. 271), and (ii) the new dates for Lepenski Vir and Vlasac (Borić and Dimitrijević 2007, Borić et al. 2008) have implications for the dating of the trapezoidal structures at those sites (cf. pp. 256 and 276), although the relationships between the samples dated and the structures is a complex issue – for discussion of the Lepenski Vir data, see Bonsall and colleagues (2008). It is interesting to note, however, that the new ^{14}C dates would not appear to alter significantly the bimodal distribution pattern evident in Figure 10.6b (p. 266).

Notes

1. In this chapter, original ^{14}C measurements are quoted in years 'BP'; calibrated calendar ages are given as 'cal BC'. Calibrations were carried out using the CALIB (rev. 5.0.2) radiocarbon calibration program (Stuiver and Reimer 1993; Stuiver et al. 2005) – see Table 10.1 for further details. A basic calibration table is provided in Table 10.3. Human bone ^{14}C ages quoted in the text have been corrected for the

freshwater reservoir effect that characterizes the Iron Gates reach of the Danube (Cook et al. 2001, Cook et al. 2002).

2. Burials dated, or presumed to date, to the Mesolithic and/or Neolithic have been found at a number of sites in the Iron Gates: Ajmana, Climente II, Cuina Turcului, Hajdučka Vodenica, Icoana, Kula, Lepenski Vir, Padina, Schela Cladovei, Ušće Kamenickog potoka, Velesnica, and Vlasac (see Figure 10.1).

3. Srejović believed that the earliest architectural remains at Lepenski Vir were a series of stone bordered hearths found in the lowest part of the site adjacent to the Danube (Srejović 1972: 45–46). These structures were the main evidence for his 'Proto-Lepenski Vir' settlement, which he assigned to the beginning of the Holocene ('Preboreal period') despite the lack of supporting radiocarbon evidence. This interpretation was disputed by Bonsall et al. (2002), who suggested the hearths were remains of buildings that were contemporaneous with the trapezoidal buildings upslope but had been destroyed during extreme flood events. This may explain the (apparent) absence of charcoal from the 'Proto-Lepenski Vir' hearths; such buoyant materials could easily be washed away by flood waters. Srejović assigned at least one grave – burial 69 (Srejović 1969, plate 64) – to his 'Proto-Lepenski Vir' phase, and this was subsequently dated to c. 8800 BP (7900 cal BC) (Bonsall et al. 2004), but contemporaneity with the hearths near the river was never demonstrated.

4. It is not clear how Srejović and Letica (1978) arrived at the total of forty-three houses. For the 'Mesolithic levels' of Vlasac (I–III), they describe fourteen 'dwellings', twenty-six built 'hearths' (some of which were inside the dwellings, others 'in the open'), two simple hearths, and at least fifteen other structures some of which were interpreted as remains of tented structures.

5. In spite of the 'late' ^{14}C dates for Houses 1 and 2, the excavators attributed them to the earliest occupation phase at Vlasac (phase Ia), partly because they lacked hearths and thus could "be regarded as representing the beginning of the Vlasac architecture" (Srejović and Letica 1978: 146).

6. Bökönyi, who was a mammalian specialist, may have overlooked the presence of sturgeon in the samples he analyzed from both Vlasac and Lepenski Vir. More recent work by Vesna Dimitrijević (cited in Borić 2002: 1030) has identified sturgeon (mainly beluga) bones from the floors of some of the trapezoidal buildings at Lepenski Vir.

7. Native Americans living along the Missouri and other major rivers relied heavily on mussel meat during the winter months when other food was scarce.

8. The Iron Gates reach of the Danube today is an important wintering area for wildfowl, especially ducks.

9. The remains of these species are not abundant in the Iron Gates sites. All three were recovered from Mesolithic contexts in the Romanian–British excavations at Schela Cladovei (Bartosiewicz et al. 1995, Bartosiewicz 2001, Bartosiewicz unpublished data), but the season of capture was not determined.

10. Antler was included among the red deer remains in the faunal report for Vlasac, but is unlikely to have changed the overall ranking of the three species discussed here.

11. Consumption of dog meat was not uncommon in Europe in historical times. The slaughter of dogs for human food was only finally prohibited in Germany in 1986 (Geppert 1992) and dogs are still eaten as a delicacy in parts of Austria, former Czechoslovakia, Moravia, and Switzerland today.

12. Under these broad headings many specific causes of conflict between hunter-gatherer communities have been reported: previous attacks, murder, suspected witchcraft, jealousy over women, theft/poaching, abduction of women and children, rape, insult, trespass, infringement of territorial rights, access to resource areas or high priority goods, nonpayment of bride price, capture of slaves, and so on.

13. Ground-edge implements and Balkan flint artefacts have been reported from trapezoidal buildings at Lepenski Vir (Kozłowski and Kozłowski 1983, Borić 2002, Antonović 2006). Both are characteristic of Early Neolithic Starčevo-Körös-Criş culture contexts in the central and northern Balkans. Antonović (2006: 39-43) has provided details of the ground-edge implements from the Lepenski Vir buildings, but, at the time of writing, there is no published information on the occurrence of Balkan flint.

Chapter 11

The Mesolithic of European Russia, Belarus, and the Ukraine

Pavel Dolukhanov*†

Introduction

The area discussed in this chapter includes the greater part of the East European Plain stretching from the Black Sea in the south to the Arctic Ocean in the north. This huge segment of the Eurasian Plate with flat or slightly undulating relief ranges in altitude from 100 to 300 m above sea level. The Carpathian and Crimean Mountains, both belonging to the Alpine folded system, form its southwestern and southern limits. The climate of the whole area is continental with cold winters and hot summers, and frequent summer droughts in the south. The vegetation cover reflects latitudinal zonality, comprising boreal coniferous forests in the north and mixed coniferous–deciduous forests in the south. Steppe or treeless grassland consisting of drought-resistant herbs dominate further south, and tundra, with cold-resistant plants, mosses, and lichens, in the coastal regions of the Arctic in the far north.

In the Russian Empire, later to become the USSR, authentic Mesolithic sites were first discovered in the late nineteenth century (Merezhkovskii 1880). Yet the term 'Mesolithic' only came into general use much later (Rudinskii 1929). Following the typological-stylistic concepts that became established in Soviet Archaeology, the Mesolithic was viewed as an archaeological period featuring the wide use of projectile points and especially geometric microliths. Essentially similar definitions of the Mesolithic may be found in more recent post-Soviet publications (Kol'tsov 1989a, Stanko 1997). Soviet scholars attached paramount importance to the invention and introduction of bows and arrows, which, in accordance with the concepts of Lewis Morgan and Friedrich Engels, constituted the basic feature of a 'later stage of savagery' (Formozov 1966: 35). The end of the Mesolithic period was marked by the introduction of pottery. S. N. Bibikov (1950) developed a different approach, which viewed the Mesolithic as a period of crisis of Palaeolithic-style hunting

---

* School of Historical Studies, University of Newcastle upon Tyne, UK.

subsistence triggering a diversification of food-gathering strategies with an eventual emergence of early forms of stock-breeding and agriculture.

The cultural-typological approach remains to this day the leading paradigm in Russian and Ukrainian Mesolithic studies. Discussing the typological criteria of the Mesolithic, Stanko (1982: 95–6) mentions the improvement of prismatic core reduction technique, the general microlithisation of the inventory and the emergence of composite tools. Mesolithic society is viewed as a mosaic of 'archaeological cultures' defined as 'a set of synchronous sites sharing common attributes and clearly distinct from all others.' Telegin (1985: 87) argues that these attributes include typological features such as specific types of cores, types of blanks (flake/blade ratio), and specific frequencies and types of 'secondary trimmed tools': endscrapers, burins, arrowheads, retouched blades, and, especially, microliths. In consequence, the analysis of the Mesolithic is all too often restricted to the discussion of interrelations between 'archaeological cultures' and their evolution in time and space. Here, the Mesolithic is viewed as the period of hunter-gatherer economies adapted to the environment and resources of the early and middle Holocene.

The lower boundary of the Mesolithic coincides with the beginning of the Preboreal vegetation zone, c.10,400–9200 cal BC. Radiocarbon dates of that order have been obtained for several early Mesolithic sites in Russia and the Ukraine (Tables 11.1–11.3). The upper limit of the Mesolithic is usually considered by East European archaeologists as corresponding to the introduction of pottery. In various parts of the East European Plain pottery making started between 8000 and 500 cal BC. In contrast to other parts of Europe, the appearance of pottery and the adoption of agriculture were separated on the East European Plain by a long time interval. The intermediate period, often referred to as 'Sub Neolithic' lasted in various areas from two thousand to three thousand years.

During the maximal stages of the Last Glaciation (LGM), 20,000–18,000 BP, the climate on the East European Pain was excessively cold and dry with cold-resisting 'periglacial' forest-steppe vegetation (Grichuk 1992). At that time, a network of Upper Palaeolithic settlements with subsistence based on hunting of large herbivores arose in the basins of major rivers (Soffer 1985). This period marked a maximum regression of the Black Sea and the emergence of the 'Neoeuxinian' basin, a brackish megalake with water levels 100–120 m below the present level (Chepalyga 2002, Konikov 2007). The greater part of the north Pontic shelf, including the Azov Sea, was exposed as a low-lying plain with lakes and meandering rivers.

Beginning c. 18,000 BP, an increased influx of meltwater from glaciers led to a gradual rise in lake-level resulting in the 'Neoeuxine transgression' (Fedorov 1982, Konikov 2007). As the Black Sea level reached that of the 'Bosphorus sill' (−60 m) at c. 12,000 BP, the excess water started spilling into the Aegean Sea via the Straits of Dardanelles and Bosporus. The rising Mediterranean Sea reached the sill level at about 8400 BP (7600–7300 cal BC), resulting in the establishment of the two-level current in the Straits and the colonisation of the Black Sea by Mediterranean molluscs (Hiscott et al. 2005).

An alternative scenario was suggested by Ryan et al. (1997) and Ryan and Pitman (1998). According to these writers, following the Postglacial sea-level rise, the Mediterranean Sea catastrophically breached the Bosphorus Strait at c. 6100 cal BC (reported as 7150 BP.) and rapidly refilled the Black Sea basin, flooding the shelf. In a later publication (Ryan et al. 2003), the flood date has been pushed still earlier, to 8400 BP or 7500 cal BC. The alleged 'flood' led to drastic environmental changes, and stimulated the transition to farming in Europe. Current geologic investigations in the Marmara Sea and on the Black Sea shelf (Aksu et al. 2002, Hiscott et al. 2005, Yanko-Hombach 2007, Balabanov 2007) have found little or no evidence supporting this scenario. The 'flood' could

Table 11.1. Radiocarbon chronology: the Steppe and the Crimea

No.	Site name	Lat.	Long.	Material	Lab. No.	BP	Cal BC 2σ
1	Vasylievka 3	48°22'	35°10'	Human bone	OxA-3807	10,060 ± 105	10,400–9200
2	Vasylievka 3	49°22'	35°10'	Human bone	OxA-3808	9980 ± 100	10,100–9200
3	Vasylievka 3	49°22'	35°10'	Human bone	OxA-3809	10,080 ± 100	10,400–9200
4	Senchicy 5a	25°50'	51°53'	Animal bone	Ki-6263	9580 ± 70	9100–8900
5	Rirzhski Ostrov	50°38'	29°44'	Charcoal	Ki-6261	7875 ± 50	7100–6600
6	Rirzhski Ostrov	50°38'	29°44'	Charcoal	Ki-6260	7800 ± 60	7100–6600
7	Vyazivok-4a	49°57'	32°56'	Charcoal	Ki-5220	9310 ± 70	8750–8300
8	Vyazivok-4a	49°57'	32°56'	Charcoal	Ki-5221	9530 ± 80	9100–8800
9	Vyazivok-4a	49°57'	32°56'	Charcoal	Ki-5222	9600 ± 50	9200–8800
10	Vyazivok-4a	49°57'	32°56'	Charcoal	Ki-6255	9260 ± 90	8650–8250
11	Igren'-8	48°24'	34°36'	Shells	Ki-956	9290 ± 110	8800–8200
12	Igren'-8	48°24'	34°36'	Charcoal	Ki-368	8860 ± 470	9400–6600
13	Igren'-8	48°24'	34°36'	Charcoal	Ki-950	8650 ± 100	8200–7450
14	Igren'-8	48°24'	34°36'	Shells	Bln-1707-1	8575 ± 70	7800–7500
15	Igren'-8	48°24'	34°36'	Charcoal	Ki-805	8080 ± 210	7600–6500
16	Igren'-8	49°22'	34°36'	Shells	Ki-850	7300 ± 130	6450–5980
17	Igren'-8	49°22'	34°36'	Shells	Ki-806	6930 ± 130	5940–5850
18	Igren'-8	25°50'	34°36'	Shells	Ki-2169	6650 ± 200	6000–5100
19	Igren'-8	50°38'	34°36'	Shells	Ki-2168	6520 ± 95	5600–5300
20	Igren'-8	50°38'	34°36'	Shells	Ki-2170	6920 ± 120	6000–5600
21	Igren'-8	49°57'	34°36'	Shells	Ki-1569	7850 ± 100	7050–6450
22	Igren'-8	49°57'	34°36'	Shells	Ki-2171	6500 ± 200	5800–4950
23	Igren'-8	49°57'	34°36'	Shells	Ki-1206	7120 ± 100	6120–5750
24	Igren'-8	49°57'	34°36'	Animal bone	Ki-6256	7080 ± 60	6080–5800
25	Igren'-8	48°24'	34°36'	Animal bone	Ki-6257	6963 ± 60	5900–5700
26	Igren'-8	48°24'	34°36'	Animal bone	Ki-6258	6910 ± 50	5900–5700
27	Igren'-8	48°24'	34°36'	Animal bone	Ki-6259	6860 ± 45	5850–5650
28	Storunya-1	48°24'	24°33'	Charcoal	Le-1417	5200 ± 70	4200–3800
29	Molodova-5	48°24'	27°05'	Charcoal	GIN-54	10,940 ± 150	11,450–10,650
30	Girzhevo	49°22'	29°42'	Animal bone	Le1703	7050 ± 60	6030–5770
31	Mirnoe	49°22'	39°32'	Animal bone	Le-1648	7200 ± 80	6250–5900
32	Vishennoe-1	25°50'	34°36'	Animal bone	Ki-6264	9680 ± 70	9300–8800
33	Vishennoe-1	50°38'	34°36'	Animal bone	Ki-6265	9740 ± 60	9300–8800
34	Buran-Kaya	50°38'	34°36'	Animal bone	Ki-6266	5070 ± 40	3960–3760
35	Buran-Kaya	49°57'	34°36'	Animal bone	Ki-6267	8750 ± 55	8000–7600
36	Buran-Kaya	49°57'	34°36'	Animal bone	Ki-6267a	11,460 ± 70	11,900–11,200
37	Buran-Kaya	49°57'	34°36'	Animal bone	Ki-6269	10,650 ± 65	10,050–10,350
38	Trinity Cape-1	49°57'	34°36'	Shells	Ki-6340	7450 ± 70	6450–6100
39	Trinity Cape-1	48°24'	34°36'	Animal bone	Ki-6341	7800 ± 60	6900–6450
40	Shan-Koba	48°24'	33°50'	Animal bone	Ki-5821	7600 ± 45	6500–6380
41	Shan-Koba	48°24'	33°50'	Animal bone	Ki-5822	6780 ± 40	5750–5620
42	Shan-Koba	48°24'	33°50'	Animal bone	Ki-5823	10,210 ± 80	10,710–9300
43	Shan-Koba	48°24'	33°50'	Animal bone	Ki-5824	9890 ± 80	9750–9200

No.	Site name	Lat.	Long.	Material	Lab. No.	BP	Cal BC 2σ
44	Shan-Koba	49°22′	33°50′	Charcoal	GIN-6277	8240 ± 150	7600–6750
45	Kukrek	49°22′	33°55′	Charcoal	Ki-954	9600 ± 150	9400–8400
46	Kukrek	25°50′	33°55′	Charcoal	Bln-1799-1	7320 ± 65	6260–6020
47	Kukrek	50°38′	33°55′	Charcoal	Bln-1799-2	7285 ± 70	6260–6000
48	Laspi-7	49°22′	33°44′	Shells	Ki-951	9100 ± 130	8750–7800
49	Laspi-7	49°22′	33°44′	Charcoal	Bln-1921	9085 ± 100	8600–7950
50	Laspi-7	25°50′	33°44′	Charcoal	Ki-953	8930 ± 100	8300–7700
51	Laspi-7	50°38′	33°44′	Charcoal	Ki-952	8870 ± 230	8900–7200
52	Laspi-7	50°38′	33°44′	Shells	Ki-876	8680 ± 250	8500–7000
53	Laspi-7	49°57′	33°44′	Shells	Bln1795-1	8570 ± 120	8000–7300
54	Laspi-7	49°57′	33°44′	Shells	Bln-1795-2	8760 ± 70	8200–7550
55	Laspi-7	49°57′	33°44′	Charcoal	Ki-957	8340 ± 250	8000–6800
56	Laspi-7	49°57′	33°44′	Charcoal	Ki-637	8080 ± 210	7600–6500
57	Laspi-7	48°24′	33°44′	Charcoal	Ki-704	8030 ± 190	7450–6400
58	Laspi-7	48°24′	33°44′	Shells	Ki-638	7620 ± 230	7100–6000
59	Laspi-7	48°24′	33°44′	Charcoal	Ki-863	7500 ± 380	7400–5600
60	Laspi-7	48°24′	33°44′	Charcoal	Le-1326	6940 ± 140	6100–5550
61	Soroca-2	48°24′	28°11′	Charcoal	Bln-588	7515 ± 120	6600–6050
62	Soroca-2	49°22′	28°11′	Charcoal	Bln-587	7420 ± 80	6430–6070

Dates are given as uncalibrated BP (see Lanting and Van der Plicht 2000 for a recent review) and calibrated ranges at 2 sigma as cal BC, except for those in excess of 12,000 years BP. Dates have been calibrated using OxCal v3.10 (Bronk Ramsey 1995, 2001). Sources: Timofeev and Zaitseva (1998), ORAU Datelist 11 (Hedges et al. 1990), and ORAU Datelist 19 (Hedges et al. 1995).

not have had any impact on the spread of farming, as agricultural sites appeared in the Balkans much earlier than the alleged catastrophe and in the Black Sea area much later.

Recent estimates show that at the Younger Dryas to Preboreal transition, c. 10,500 cal BC, summer temperatures in Europe rose by at least 6 degrees C (Isarin and Bohnke 1999). In northern Russia, as elsewhere in northern Eurasia between 8,500 and 2,500 cal BC, summer temperatures were higher than now by values ranging from 2.5 to 7.0 degrees C (MacDonald et al. 2001). The spread of mixed forests with a considerable presence of thermophilous species occurred during the Atlantic period. This period lasted from c. 7000 until 3500 cal BC and comprised several warmer and colder episodes.

According to Balabanov (2007), at the beginning of the Holocene, 10,500 cal BC, the level of the Black Sea was 40–50 m lower than now. The Neoeuxinian transgression finally brought sea level up to −25 m by 9350–9200 cal BC. The end of the Neoeuxinian stage (8650–8300 cal BC) was marked by a substantial regression. Three transgressive phases followed. At 7330–7050 cal BC, the sea level rose to −16–17 m. Later, at 7050–5400 cal BC, the sea rose to −9 or −10 m. A regression occurred at 6000–5600 cal BC, when sea level fell to −20 m. Three transgressive phases occurred at 4600, 4200, and 3800 cal BC, followed by a maximum rise at 3000 cal BC, when the sea level reached the present-day position.

Vegetation changes, in addition to hunting pressures during the Late Glacial period, led to the nearly total extinction of bison, the principal Palaeolithic hunting prey. Large settlements

Pavel Dolukhanov

Table 11.2. Radiocarbon chronology: Mixed Forest Region (calibration as for Table 11.1)

No.	Site name	Lat.	Long.	Material	Lab. No.	BP	Cal BC 2σ
63	Lanino	57°11′	33°00′	Charcoal	Le-1229	7150 ± 70	6200–5840
64	Ivanovskoe 2	56°51′	39°02′	Wood	Le-2176	8510 ± 90	7750–7300
65	Ivanovskoe 3	56°51′	39°02′	Wood	Le-1934	7400 ± 80	6430–6060
66	Ivanovskoe 3	56°51′	39°02′	Peat	IGAN-81	8900 ± 100	8300–7650
67	Ivanovskoe 3	56°51′	39°02′	Peat	IGAN-80	8370 ± 50	7550–7300
68	Ivanovskoe 3	56°51′	39°02′	Wood	Le-3098	8130 ± 80	7500–6800
69	Ivanovskoe 3	56°51′	39°02′	Peat	IGAN-161	7500 ± 70	6420–6220
70	Ivanovskoe 3	56°51′	39°02′	Wood	Le-3095	7310 ± 70	6260–6000
71	Ivanovskoe 3	56°51′	39°02′	Wood	Le-1980	7630 ± 40	6530–6400
72	Ivanovskoe 3	56°51	39°02′	Wood	Le-1979	7510 ± 80	6500–6200
73	Ivanovskoe 3	56°51′	39°02′	Charcoal	Le-1983	7310 ± 80	6380–6000
74	Ivanovskoe 3	56°51′	39°02′	Wood	Le-1905	8430 ± 90	7600–7300
75	Ivanovskoe 3	56°51′	39°02′	Charcoal	GIN-242	8850 ± 70	8250–7750
76	Ivanovskoe 3	56°51′	39°02′	Wood	Le-1912	7470 ± 80	6460–6100
77	Ivanovskoe 7	56°51′	39°02′	Peat	Le-1260	7490 ± 100	6500–6100
78	Ivanovskoe 7	56°51′	39°02′	Peat	Le-1261	7375 ± 170	6450–6000
79	Berendeyevo 3	56°34′	39°10′	Wood	Le-1556	7770 ± 100	7050–6400
80	Berendeyevo 2a	56°34′	39°10′	Charcoal	Le-1572	7860 ± 80	7050–6000
81	Berendeyevo 2a	56°34′	39°10′	Wood	Le-1571	7430 ± 80	7450–6100
82	Berendeyevo 2a	56°34′	39°10′	Wood	Le-1570	6990 ± 80	6000–5700
83	Berendeyevo 1	56°34′	39°10′	Wood	Le-1557	7830 ± 80	7050–6450
84	Ozerki 5	56°42′	36°41′	Wood	GIN-7216	6930 ± 70	6000–5650
85	Ozerki 5	56°42′	36°41′	Charcoal	GIN-6659	7410 ± 90	6450–6050
86	Ozerki 5	56°42′	36°41′	Charcoal	GIN-6660	7190 ± 180	6200–5980
87	Ozerki 5	56°42′	36°41′	Wood	GIN-7217	7120 ± 50	6080–5870
88	Ozerki 5	56°42′	36°41′	Wood	GIN-7218	7310 ± 120	6400–6000
89	Ozerki 5	56°42′	36°41′	Wood	GIN-6662	6970 ± 120	6080–5600
90	Ozerki 9	56°42′	36°41′	Wood	MGU-133	8050 ± 40	7200–6750
91	Ozerki 16	56°42′	36°41′	Wood	GIN-6654	8770 ± 40	8000–7600
92	Ozerki 17	56°42′	36°41′	Wood	GIN-6655	8830 ± 40	8200–7750
93	Vodysh	58°08′	41°32′	Charcoal	Le-1229	7150 ± 70	6200–5850
94	Malaya Lamna	56°34′	41°55′	Charcoal	Le-2610	8800 ± 90	8250–7600
95	Sukontsevo 7	56°28′	34°50′	Wood	GIN-4950	8870 ± 70	8250–7750
96	Sukontsevo 7	56°28′	34°50′	Wood	GIN-4734	8900 ± 110	8300–7650
97	Sukontsevo 7	56°28′	34°50′	Wood	GIN-4733	8710 ± 150	8200–7550
98	Sukontsevo 7	56°28′	34°50′	Charcoal	Le-3015	9650 ± 100	9300–8700
99	Sukontsevo 7	56°28′	34°50′	Charcoal	GIN-3902	9220 ± 50	8600–8300
100	Sukontsevo 7	56°28′	34°50′	Charcoal	GIN-5441	9220 ± 50	8600–8300
101	Butovo	56°43′	35°21′	Charcoal	GIN-5441	9310 ± 110	8800–8250

Table 11.3. Radiocarbon chronology: Coniferous (Boreal) Forest Region and Tundra (calibration as for Table 11.1)

No.	Site name	Lat.	Long.	Material	Lab. No.	BP	Cal BC 2σ
102	Kolovaty	67°18′	58°40′	Wood	Le-4000	6985 ± 250	6400–5400
103	Lek-Lesa	64°47′	53°24′	Charcoal	Le-3604	9010 ± 70	8330–7960
104	Pindushi-19a	63°12′	34°51′	Charcoal	TA-1521	7280 ± 80	6250–7960
105	Vis	63°07′	52°30′	Wood	Le-616	7820 ± 80	7050–6450
106	Vis	63°07′	52°30′	Wood	Le-684	7150 ± 60	6100–5900
107	Vis	63°07′	52°30′	Wood	Le-685	7090 ± 80	6100–5760
108	Vis	63°07′	52°30′	Wood	Le-776	8080 ± 90	7350–6650
109	Vis	63°07′	52°30′	Wood	Le-713	7090 ± 70	7350–6750
110	Parch-1	61°36′	54°40′	Charcoal	Le-4033	7165 ± 150	6400–5700
112	Orovnavolok-9	62°46′	35°05′	Charcoal	TA-1092	7720 ± 100	7050–6350
113	Yavronga	62°39′	46°24′	Charcoal	Le-853	8530 ± 60	7680–7460
114	Pegrerma-8	62°35′	34°26′	Charcoal	TA-677	7140 ± 80	6120–5800
115	Pegrerma-8	62°35′	34°26′	Charcoal	TA-721	7050 ± 150	6250–5600
116	Pegrerma-8	62°35′	34°26′	Charcoal	TA-672	7050 ± 150	6250–5600
117	Reindeer Island, Grave 100	62°03′	35°22′	Human bone	GIN-4836	9910 ± 80	9750–9200
118	Reindeer Island, Grave 89	62°03′	35°22′	Human bone	OxA-1972	9020 ± 450	9600–7000
119	Reindeer Island, Grave 109	62°03′	35°22′	Human bone	OxA-1973	7750 ± 110	7050–6400
120	Reindeer Island, Grave 80	62°03′	35°22′	Human bone	OxA-1669	7560 ± 90	6600–6200
121	Reindeer Island, Grave 80	62°03′	35°22′	Human bone	OxA-1668	7560 ± 90	6600–6200
122	Reindeer Island, Grave 85	62°03′	35°22′	Human bone	OxA-2125	7510 ± 90	6500–6100
123	Reindeer Island, Grave 70	62°03′	35°22′	Human bone	GIN-4450	7470 ± 240	7000–5700
124	Reindeer Island, Grave 57	62°03′	35°22′	Human bone	OxA-2266	7350 ± 90	6400–6000
125	Reindeer Island, Grave 80	62°03′	35°22′	Human bone	OxA-1667	7330 ± 90	6400–6000
126	Reindeer Island, Grave 89	62°03′	35°22′	Human bone	OxA-2124	7280 ± 90	6180–5960
127	Reindeer Island, Grave 57	62°03′	35°22′	Human bone	OxA-1665	7280 ± 80	6180–5960
128	Reindeer Island, Grave 142	62°03′	35°22′	Human bone	GIN-4451	7220 ± 110	6250–5850
129	Reindeer Island, Grave 84–85	62°03′	35°22′	Human bone	GIN-4839	7210 ± 50	6200–5950

(continued)

Table 11.3. (*continued*)

No.	Site name	Lat.	Long.	Material	Lab. No.	BP	Cal BC 2σ
130	Reindeer Island, Grave 152–153	62°03′	35°22′	Human bone	GIN-4452	7140 ± 140	6100–5880
131	Reindeer Island, Grave 158	62°03′	35°22′	Human bone	GIN-4454	7130 ± 170	6400–5700
131	Reindeer Island, Grave 71	62°03′	35°22′	Human bone	GIN-4449	7130 ± 140	6250–5700
131	Reindeer Island, Grave 118	62°03′	35°22′	Human bone	GIN-4840	7080 ± 80	6080–5760
131	Reindeer Island, Graves 108–109	62°03′	35°22′	Human bone	GIN-4838	7070 ± 100	6100–5700
132	Reindeer Island, Grave 151	62°03′	35°22′	Human bone	GIN-4453	6980 ± 200	6250–5450
133	Reindeer Island, Grave 73	62°03′	35°22′	Human bone	GIN-4841	6960 ± 100	6000–5650
134	Reindeer Island, Grave 10	62°03′	35°22′	Human bone	GIN-4456	6950 ± 90	6000–5650
135	Reindeer Island, Grave 19	62°03′	35°22′	Human bone	GIN-4457	6870 ± 200	6250–5350
136	Reindeer Island, Grave 3-3a	62°03′	35°22′	Human bone	GIN-4459	6830 ± 100	5930–5540
137	Reindeer Island, Grave 16	62°03′	35°22′	Human bone	GIN-4458	6790 ± 80	5850–5540
138	Reindeer Island, Grave 57	62°03′	35°22′	Human bone	OxA-1666	6100 ± 90	5800–4700
139	Reindeer Island, Grave 57	62°03′	35°22′	Human bone	OxA-1664	5700 ± 80	4720–4360
140	Nizhnee Veret′e I	61°13′	38°58′	Charcoal	GIN-4031	9050 ± 80	8122–7994
141	Nizhnee Veret′e I	61°13′	38°58′	Peat	GIN-4869	8790 ± 100	7935–7690
142	Nizhnee Veret′e I	61°13′	38°58′	Wood	GIN-2552u	8310 ± 120	7490–7100
143	Nizhnee Veret′e I	61°13′	38°58′	Wood	GIN-2452d	8270 ± 130	7430–7050
144	Nizhnee Veret′e I	61°13′	38°58′	Charcoal	Le-1469	9600 ± 80	8954–8620
145	Nizhnee Veret′e I	61°13′	38°58′	Wood	Le-1472	8750 ± 70	7899–7698
146	Nizhnee Veret′e I	61°13′	38°58′	Charcoal	Le-1470	8270 ± 100	7430–7090
147	Nizhnee Veret′e I	61°13′	38°58′	Charcoal	Le-1471	7960 ± 100	7000–6660
148	Nizhnee Veret′e I	61°13′	38°58′	Wood	Le-1773	7700 ± 80	6554–6422
149	Popovo, Grave 8	61°17′	38°57′	Human bone	GIN-4857	7150 ± 160	6160–5810
150	Popovo, Grave 9	61°17′	38°57′	Human bone	GIN-4856	9730 ± 110	9050–8660
151	Popovo, Grave 6	61°17′	38°57′	Human bone	GIN-3887	7290 ± 150	6340–5960
152	Popovo, Grave 3	61°17′	38°57′	Human bone	GIN-4442	9520 ± 130	8930–8440
153	Popovo, Grave 2	61°17′	38°57′	Human bone	GIN-4446	5400 ± 300	4550–3810
154	Popovo, Grave	61°17′	38°57′	Human bone	GIN-4447	9430 ± 150	8920–8260

disappeared and much smaller sites appeared in the southern part of the Pontic Lowland (such as Bol'shaya Akkarzha, near Odessa). The lithic inventory acquired a microlithic character (Stanko et al. 1989).

Mesolithic sites appeared in a range of Holocene environments (Figure 11.1), and varied in their subsistence and cultural manifestations. For that reason, the following review is organised according to geographical divisions into four main categories: (1) the Mountainous Fringe (the Crimea and the Carpathians); (2) the Steppe; (3) Mixed Forests; and (4) Boreal Forests.

The Mountainous Fringe

The Crimea

Mesolithic sites in the Crimea are identified by their topographic position (predominantly in mountainous valleys), their subsistence (hunting of forest and forest-steppe animals, with an increased role of gathering and fishing), and their lithic inventories. Stanko (1982: 99) stresses that in most cases the stone tools retained their Upper Palaeolithic character, the main distinctions being the refinement of core-reduction technique, resulting in the increased production of regular prismatic blades and bladelets. Retouched tools are dominated by small endscrapers with varying frequencies of geometric microliths.

Settlement Pattern. Mesolithic levels are known in at least twenty caves and rockshelters located in the canyons of small rivers and streams draining the northern range of the Crimean Mountains. The thickness of Mesolithic deposits varies from a few cm to 4–6 m. Based on the stratigraphy of the deposits, Bibikov et al. (1994) conclude that at least several sites bear evidence of prolonged habitations.

Subsistence. Animal remains in stratified rock shelters show a gradual transition from the Late Palaeolithic to the Mesolithic. According to Vekilova (1971: 160–5), the early Mesolithic ('Azylian') saw the disappearance of mammoth, reindeer, cave bear, and cave hyena. The Mesolithic hunting prey included grassland species (wild horse, antelope-saiga, aurochs, wild sheep, and goats, increasingly supplemented by those adapted to forests (red deer, roe deer, wild boar, and brown bear) (Bibikov et al. 1994). Mesolithic deposits include numerous bones of large-size fish, both freshwater (salmon, trout and roach), and brackish-water ones (pike-perch and catfish). Several sites (Shan-Koba, layer 3, Fatma-Koba, and Kurzak-Koba) include large concentrations of the shells of edible common snails (*Helix aspera*). This snail forms the shell-midden site of Laspi 7 located on the seashore in Sebastopol Bay. Earlier reports suggested the occurrence of domesticated pig at the Mesolithic site of Tash-Air (Krainov 1960). Tsalkin (1970: 261–6) has convincingly demonstrated that the bones identified as pigs either penetrated from the younger deposits, or belong to wild boar.

Material Culture. Several archaeological cultures are distinguished from differences in typology of lithic tools (Figure 11.2, Telegin 1982, 1989). The Shan-Koba Culture, typified by several cave sites and the coastal site of Laspi 7, has industries manufactured on small-size prismatic blades, with a high proportion of backed blades, end-scrapers, burins and geometrics (lunates and trapezes). The Murza-Koba industries are found at Crimean cave-sites above the Shan-Koba levels. They include notched and backed blades and end-scrapers made on truncated blades. Geometrics

287

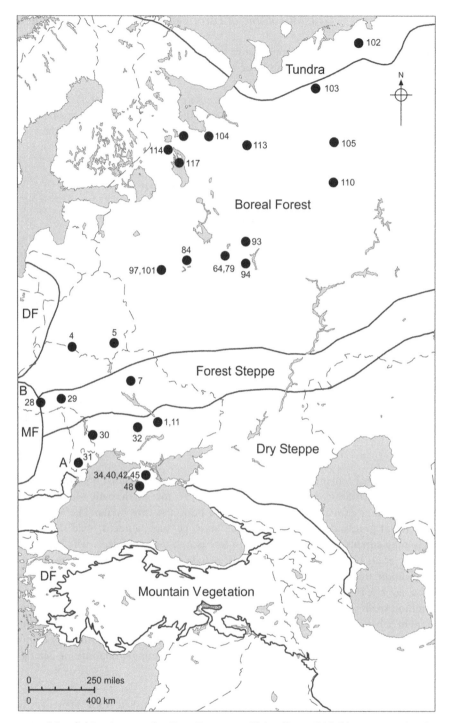

Figure II.I. Mesolithic sites on the East European Plain (from Dolukhanov 2002). Vegetation zones correspond to the position at the climatic optimum, 7000–6000 cal BC. A: the Danube-Dniestr interfluve; B: the Kamenitsa area. MF: Mixed Forest; DF: Deciduous Forest. For the names of sites that correspond to the numbers on the map, see Tables II.I–II.3.

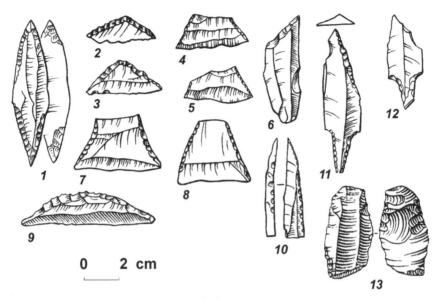

Figure 11.2. Stone tools in the Ukraine Mesolithic (Telegin 1989). 1: point (Syuren 2); 2: triangle (Shan-Koba); 3: segment (Vodopadny); 4, 5: trapezes (Oskorivka); 6: asymmetrical point (Syuren 2); 7: trapeze (Sursky); 8: trapeze (Shan-Koba); 9: segment (Zamil Koba); 10: Gravettian point; 11: point (Nobel 1); 12: point (Korost); 13: Kukrek armature (Kukrek).

are rare, but include a diagnostic *fossil directeur*, the Murza-Koba trapeze. Bone and antler tools are not numerous, but include characteristic small-size harpoons. The small rockshelter of Syuren' 2 in the middle chain of the Crimean Mountains occupies a special position. The inventory of the lower level includes tanged points with direct analogies in the Polish Swiderian.

Burials. Level 3 of Murzak-Koba rock shelter includes a double burial of a male and a female. Partly preserved skeletons were found beneath stone slabs, side-by-side, in an extended posture, facing the east. The age of the female is estimated as twenty to twenty-five years old, that of the male as forty to fifty years old (Bibikov et al. 1994: 105–8).

A burial of an adult male, with an estimated age of about forty years, was also found in the Fatma-Koba rockshelter. This skeleton was found in a contracted posture lying on the right side in a shallow grave.

Chronology. Telegin, in his earlier publication (1982: 49), using typological criteria and stratigraphic evidence, divided the Crimean Mesolithic into two stages: the Shankobian, 9000–7000 cal BC, and the Murzakobian, 7000–5000 cal BC. Since that time, a large series of radiocarbon dates has become available for the site of Laspi 7, placing it in the time-range of 8900–6000 cal BC (see Table 11.1).

The Carpathians

Settlement Pattern. In the Carpathian Mountains, the sites are small, less than 500 m², usually located on lower river terraces (Table 11.3). One of the largest sites, Starunja 1, includes an oval-shaped hollow with a hearth flanked by a wall of limestone blocks. In the majority of cases thin archaeological layers are found superimposed, which make their strict delimitation difficult. The Middle Dniester catchment is the only area where Mesolithic sites are found on higher elevations. A group of sites at Nezvizka lies on the terrace 120–160 m above the river.

Subsistence. Animal remains at Mesolithic sites include reindeer, boar, and dog, as well as numerous shells of terrestrial snail *Helix*, and freshwater pearly mussels (*Unio sp.*). Yet in view of the stratigraphic uncertainties, attribution of these finds to the Mesolithic is in doubt.

Material Culture. Matskevoi (1991) has distinguished at least three cultures in the local archaeological sequence, the Kunin-Nobel, Nezvizko-Oselivka, and Vorotsev-Starunja. Yet in view of their stratigraphic uncertainty, the authenticity of these cultures is in doubt, as their inventories combine obviously heterogeneous materials ranging from Late Palaeolithic to Neolithic. Based on the lithic typology, J. Kozlowski (2004) identified in the East Carpathian Mesolithic the elements of Janislawician supposedly stemming from the north (see later), and those of Erbiceni, stemming from the south. The latter shows common technological features with the Grebenikian in the steppe area.

Chronology. The Mesolithic layer at the Molodova 5 site on the middle Dniestr, yielded a date of 11,050–10,750 cal BC (Table 11.1). The average date for the earliest pottery-bearing Bug-Dniester sites is 6114 ± 101 cal BC (Dolukhanov and Shukurov 2004). These limits may be accepted as an estimate of duration of the Carpathian Mesolithic.

The Steppe

Settlement Pattern. Numerous Mesolithic sites occur on the Danube-Dniestr interfluve in the western segment of the Pontic Lowland (Figure 11.3). They form a hierarchy of settlements linked to topographic position. The largest sites (Mirnoe 1 and Beloles'e are on the shores of estuaries in the coastal area. They are seen as base-camps inhabited on a year-round basis. Based on the size and number of dwelling structures and using ethnographic evidence, Stanko (1982) argues that the Mirnoe community consisted of twenty to twenty-five individuals, representing three or four nuclear families each with four to six individuals. Smaller sites in a similar setting supposedly belong to task groups budding off from the main centre. The location of several sites at higher elevation in the foothills implies seasonal transhumance.

Mesolithic settlements are also located in the terraced valleys of the major rivers (the Dniepr, Dniestr, and Severskiy Donets). A dense cluster of sites is found in the middle reaches of the Dnieper at Igren', Oskorivka, Vasylievka, Yamburg, and others.

Subsistence. The Mesolithic economies developed in an environment of growing scarcity of hunting resources, bison, the principal Palaeolithic hunting prey, which had been largely exterminated by that time. Mesolithic groups targeted the less numerous herds of wild horse (or tarpan) and antelope-saiga, or more solitary animals such as aurochs. Fishing and gathering increasingly supplemented the hunting of land mammals. Stable isotope analysis of human bone from Mesolithic cemeteries on the Dniepr shows shifts occurring at the transition from the earlier Mesolithic (Vasylievka III) to its later stage (Vasylievka II), as signalled in the concentration of barium and strontium and increased ^{13}C values indicating a greater consumption of plant food (Jacobs 1994, Lillie 1996). Lillie and Richards (2000) later questioned this conclusion, but appear to have misinterpreted the archaeological context. They found no dietary shift based in the stable isotope evidence stemming

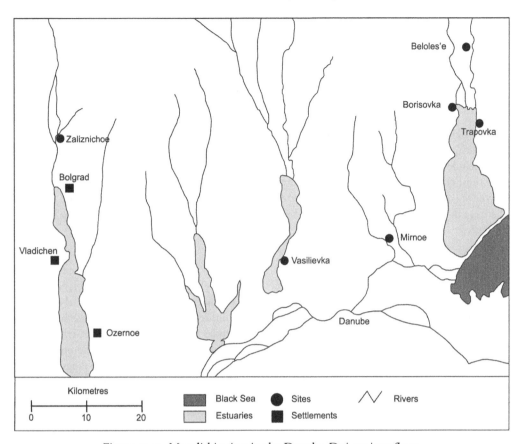

Figure 11.3. Mesolithic sites in the Danube-Dniestr interfluve.

from the cemeteries of Dereivka I, Mar'evka, Ospovka, Vasylievka V, and Yasinovatka. But all of these belong to the single Dniepr-Donets cultural entity (the 'Mariupol' type and the 'Supra-Rapids' variety). Hence, this evidence by definition cannot reflect a long-term trend in dietary preferences. Korobkova (1993) has identified at Mirnoe prismatic blades with microscopic traces of linear use-wear, which she and Stanko (1982) view as evidence of 'reaping knives' used for harvesting edible plants. Pashkevich (1982: 136) has found the grains of several potentially edible plants in the deposits of Mirnoe: white goosefoot (*Chenopodium album*), black bindweed (*Polygonum convoluvulus*), vetch (*Vicia hirsuta*), and sorel (*Rumex acetosa*).

Material Culture. Based on stylistic and technological grounds, two 'archaeological cultures' were identified in the steppe area. The Kukrekian is typified by the 'Kukrekian armature,' a truncated, notched and ventrally retouched blade (Figure 11.2: 13), and was first recognised at the open-air site of Kukrek in the Crimean steppe. Later, implements of this type were identified at other sites in the Crimea, on the Dniepr River (Igren 8) and in various areas of the Pontic Lowland. The Grebenikian, as exemplified by Mirnoe, Girzhevo, and other sites, is yet another culture grouping, predominantly in the Odessa District. The inventory includes endscrapers and microliths consisting exclusively of trapezes.

291

Burials. Large communal cemeteries, unknown in earlier periods, reflect new social developments in the Ukrainian Mesolithic. A group of impressive cemeteries, Vasylievka, Volos'ke, and others, lies near the Dniepr Rapids, south of Dnipropetrovsk (Stolyar 1959, Telegin 1982). Individuals within the same cemeteries are associated with distinct burial rites, suggesting cultural homogeneity: most were buried in a contracted position, and some in an extended supine position. Still more important, the skeletons belong to at least three distinct physical types (Gokhman 1966, 1986, Potekhina 1999). A first group of individuals with broad and high-relief faces is viewed by Gokhman (1966: 187) as belonging to the autochthonous 'Cro-Magnon' population stemming from the Upper Palaeolithic of Central and Eastern Europe. A second group was found only at Volos'ke cemetery and includes individuals with very narrow and long faces typical of the 'Mediterranean race.' The third type, found at Vasylievka 1 and among the dead buried in extended supine postures at Vasylievka 3, features narrow faces and protruding jaws. At Volos'ke, and at Vasylievka 1 and 3, there are numerous cases of ribs and vertebrae penetrated by flint arrowheads, indicating death by violence.

Chronology. AMS measurements (Anthony 1994, Jacobs 1994, Lillie 1996) suggest the age of Vasylievka 3 cemetery as 10,400–9200 cal BC (Table 11.1). Stanko (1982) and Telegin (1982, 1989), using typological criteria, distinguish in the Ukrainian steppe Mesolithic an early stage (as exemplified by Beloles'e with an essentially Late Palaeolithic technology, regular prismatic blades and a limited number of geometrics. The later stage includes Grebenikian (Mirnoe, Girzhevo, and others) and also Kukrekian sites. There are several radiocarbon dates available for the eponymous site and Igren' 8 on the Dniepr. Existing radiocarbon dates for Igren' 8 lie in a wide range between 8800 and 6000 cal BC (see Table 11.1). The oldest evidence of pottery is from the lower levels of the Rakushechnyi Yar site located on a small island in the lower stretches of the River Don, with radiocarbon dates indicating an age of 6400–5600 cal BC (Aleksandrovsky et al. 2009).

Mixed Forests

Northern Ukraine-Southern Belarus

Settlement Pattern. Dense concentrations of Mesolithic sites are found in the Polissya Lowland of northern Ukraine and southern Belarus. The sites usually lie on the lower terraces of rivers and lakes belonging to the Upper Dniepr catchment, often on sand dunes. These sites are usually small and recognisable only by accumulations of lithics. The largest site, Nobel, in the upper part of the Pripet River basin, a tributary of the Dniepr, covers 500 m² and includes traces of a rectangular dwelling with hearths in each corner (Matskevoi 1991). The sites in the Volyn-Podilsk Upland in the Northwest of the Ukraine are similar to those in Polissya: accumulations of lithics on the lower terraces of rivers and lakes. Only one site, Vorotsev 2, is of any size or complexity, with seven structural complexes, each comprising two to four oval-shaped dwellings 5–10 m², a flint 'workshop', hearths, and several smaller hollows supposedly used as storage pits (Matskevoi 1991: 99). Zalizniak (1991) distinguishes two types of dwelling sites, winter ones, larger in size and located at higher elevations, and summer habitations of much smaller size, close to rivers and lakes.

Subsistence. The rare animal bones belong exclusively to reindeer. Zalizniak (1991: 138) suggests a wider spectrum of subsistence including the hunting of land mammals (elk, aurochs, red deer, roe

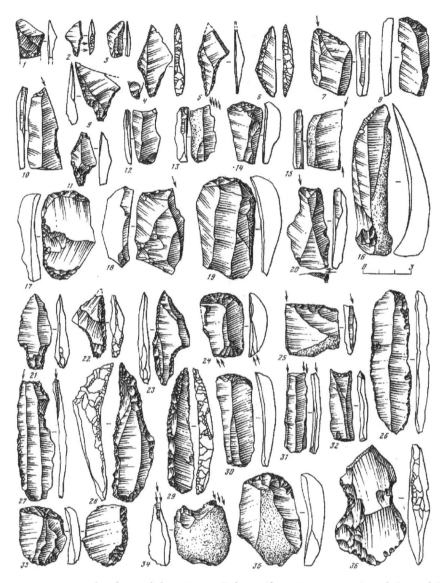

Figure 11.4. Stone tools of Mesolithic sites in Belarus (from Gurina 1989) and Central Russia (from Koltsov 1989b). 1: borer; 2–8 arrowheads (Koromka); Butovian: 9, 10, 17: arrowheads; 11, 12: backed points; 13, 16, 20, 21, 23: armatures; 19, 20: retouched blades; 14: endscraper; 15: sidescraper (Sobolevo 5); 26, 27: Ienevian trapezes; 28, 33: Ienevian retouched blades; 29, 30, 32, 34: Ienevian arrowheads.

deer, and boar), fishing and gathering of edible plants. At a later stage, as typified by Janislawician sites, the hunting prey consisted of aurochs, boar, wild cat, and beaver (Kol'tsov 1989).

Material Culture and Chronology. The lithic tools (Figure 11.4: 1–8) were manufactured on small-size flint blades, and include two main categories: projectile points and geometrics. The

293

earlier sites with tanged points (Nobel, Perevoloka, Senchitsy, and others) are viewed as the local variant of the Polish Swiderian (Matskevoi 1991). Available dates for Swiderian sites in Poland place them into the Younger Dryas, c. 11,000–10,500 cal BC (Schild 1998). The later stage, supposedly of Preboreal and Boreal age (10,500–7000 cal BC) and referred to as Kudlevian (Zalizniak 1991), is marked by a high proportion of backed knives. Its climax is in the Early Atlantic, when rare trapezes appear. This line of development was interrupted in the later Atlantic by an intrusion of the Janislawician. This cultural unit first identified in Poland (S. Kozlowski 1965) and includes in its inventories so-called Janislawicy-type points and triangles combined with commonly occurring trapezes. In Belarus and in neighbouring Lithuania, the sites attributable to the Janislawician are found mostly in the Nieman catchment and on the Sozh River (the tributary of the Upper Dnieper), where the important site of Grensk was located. In contrast to the western sites, the eastern ones feature the occurrence of 'heavy-duty' axe-like tools and the absence of trapezes (Koltsov 1989). Simultaneously, a distinct Pisochnyi-Riv Culture developed in the Northeast, with tanged points of Ahrensburg and Lyngby type combined with asymmetrical trapezes. Several sites (Teterev and others) include the 'Kukrekian armature' (see earlier). Zalizniak (1991: 42–3) views this as an indication of yet another migration coming from the Black Sea via the Dniepr basin.

Central Russia

Settlement Pattern. The sites in this area are usually found in the catchment of the Upper Volga, and the Oka, its largest tributary. One may distinguish, first, sites located on upper and middle river terraces, often on dunes, and, second, wetlands sites, often embedded in peat deposits. In the former case, three oval-shaped dwellings were found at the site of Sobolevo 5. These dwellings are approximately 5 m by 3 m in plan, with one or two hearths inside and potholes along the periphery. At the wetland site of Berendeyevo 3, in the Yaroslavl District, a large platform consisting of several layers of birch bark and wooden logs has been found. In several cases (Ugol'novo 1 and Petrushino), storage pits were located in the immediate vicinity of the dwellings (Kol'tsov 1989b).

Subsistence. Animal remains are better preserved at wetland sites and are predominantly of elk and beaver. Red deer, brown bear, hare, and wolf are present in lesser quantities. The bones of fish and waterfowl are numerous (Krainov and Khotinsky 1984).

Material Culture. Kol'tsov (1984, 1989b) has identified two Mesolithic archaeological cultures in the area: Butovian and Ienevian. The former (Figure 11.4: 9–26) contains a high proportion of arrowheads, which include Ahrensburgian, Swiderian, and Post-Swiderian varieties. Other tools are endscapers, mainly circular and 'unguiforme', and burins, mostly made on broken blades. Microliths are rare and consist mainly of retouched bladelets. Ienevian industries (Figure 11.4: 26–34) include various strategies of flint splitting techniques reflected in the greater variety of core types. Flakes are the most commonly used blanks. Endscapers include circular and irregular varieties, and burins are manufactured on broken blades. Numerous microliths comprise variegated trapezes, truncations, isosceles triangles, and also micropoints, backed points, and 'bi-truncated' points. Heavy-duty tools include several varieties of axes and adzes. The wetland sites have a rich bone and antler industry, which includes spearheads and arrowheads, axes of Kunda type, harpoons, and personal adornments made of animal teeth and bones.

Chronology. Kol'tsov (1989b) distinguishes two stages in the development of the Butovian. The earlier stage, featuring the occurrence of Ahrensburgian, Swiderian and Post-Swiderian arrowheads, may be dated by analogy with the sites further west to the Younger Dryas-Preboreal transition, c. 10,500 cal BC. The later Butovian is exemplified by the Ivanovskoe-Berendeyevo sites, with radiocarbon dates in the range of 8300–6000 cal BC (Table 11.2).

Boreal Forests

Northern Russia

Settlement Pattern. Sites are found on the lower terraces of rivers, notably the Northern Dvina, Pechora, Sukhona, Vychegda, and their tributaries. The larger sites are found on the wetland shores of the Kubenskoye, Vozhe, and Lacha lakes and several smaller lakes. Nizhnee Veret'e I, which lies in the catchment of the Lacha Lake, is the largest site in the whole area with a total area of 1500 m^2, with evidence of three rectangular postframed houses with one or two hearths inside, two hearths outside the dwellings, storage pits, and a 'ritual pit' which included a birch trunk 35 cm long, with an attached elk skull (Oshibkina 1989a, 1989b, 1997).

Subsistence. Because of the longer occurrence of tundra-like landscapes, reindeer remained an important hunting prey in the Mesolithic of Northern Russia, along with elk, beaver, waterfowl (especially swan), and fish. The bones of pike are the most common fish remains. The dog, the only domesticated animal, was fairly common. Burned and broken dog skulls were found at the site of Nizhnee Veret'e I (Oshibkina 1989a, 1989b).

Material Culture. The stone industry includes endscrapers, burins (mostly on broken blades), tanged arrowheads, and backed bladelets. There is also a variety of heavy-duty tools, including axes, adzes, chisels, and 'hoe-like' instruments. A rich industry in bone, antler and wood includes a large variety of spear- and arrowheads, harpoons, scrapers and barbed points (Figure 11.5, Oshibkina 1989a, 1989b, 1997).

The Mesolithic layers at the Vis peat-bog in the Vychegda River catchment yielded a large collection of wooden implements, which included ornamented bows, skis, sledge runners, an oar, a bark float, a bark vessel, a fishing basket, and a net made of sedge fibre (Burov 1989, Oshibkina 1989a, 1989b).

Burials. Reindeer Island (Olenii Ostrov) Cemetery on the Onega Lake is the largest in Europe (see also Zvelebil this volume). It includes 174 burials, and before its partial destruction is thought to have had no less than four hundred graves (Gurina 1956). The funerary remains suggest that the cemetery belonged to a large and stable community with considerable internal differentiation in wealth and status (O'Shea and Zvelebil 1984). Four individuals in the northern part of the cemetery (the 'shamans') were interred in a standing position facing west in funnel-shaped shafts 1.3–1.8 m deep. The richest graves contain sculptured or ornamented objects with representations of elk, snakes, and humans carved in stone, wood, and bone. Hunting equipment is more common in male graves, and comprises bone and stone points, bone daggers, slate knives, harpoons, fishhooks, and quivers. Female graves generally had fewer grave goods than the male examples, and these comprise household artefacts, flint blades, awls, polishers, burins, and scrapers, as well as perforated beaver incisors and snake effigies. A smaller cemetery consisting of ten burials was discovered at Popovo on the river Kinema, 1.5 km upstream from the site of Nizhnee Veret'e I. The grave goods include several complete fish skeletons, two complete dog skeletons, and a necklace made of dog teeth (Oshibkina 1989a, 1989b).

Chronology. The large series of radiocarbon dates for the Reindeer Cemetery on Lake Onega indicate a time span of 9,600–6,000 cal BC. A series of dates for Nizhnee Veret'e I suggests an age of 8100–6400 cal BC. These may be viewed as providing a reliable age estimate of the Mesolithic for the entire area of Northern Russia (Table 11.3). Mesolithic sites occurred at about the same time in the Higher Arctic, as one may judge by the dates for Lak-Lesa, Vis and other sites, which lie in the range of 8,300–5,600 cal BC (Table 11.3).

Discussion

The evidence cited here supports a view of the Mesolithic as a protracted period of hunter-gathering settlement, with subsistence adapted to the early and middle Holocene environments, and showing both continuities and contrasts with the preceding Palaeolithic period and the succeeding Neolithic.

The origins of the Mesolithic on the East European Plain are sought in the collapse of an extensive Upper Palaeolithic network. This network, which had arisen in the 'periglacial area', formed a main refugium for the Palaeolithic population during the Last Glaciation Maximum (Dolukhanov et al. 2001). During the Late Glacial period 12,000–10,000 cal BC, rising temperature and humidity combined with hunting pressure depleted the rich big game resources, on which the livelihood of Palaeolithic groups basically depended. After c. 12,000 cal BC, the principal hunting prey, first the mammoth and later the bison, disappeared, and large sites vanished in the Upper Palaeolithic core area of the Dniepr and Don Basins.

This led to an outflow of human groups both to the north and to the south, as well as an infiltration from the west. At that time, a new network consisting of smaller sites arose along the banks of small rivers and lakes, apparently oriented to the pursuit of seasonally migrating ungulates (initially reindeer). These movements are documented in the distribution of industries with a component of tanged points (the Ahrensburgian and Swiderian), which are present over the entire area of the East European Plain, extending as far as the Crimea.

The beginning of the Holocene was marked by the further depletion of hunting resources in an environment where increased temperatures and humidity led to the expansion of forests. At this stage, a gradual reorientation in subsistence activities of local groups proceeded without any large-scale immigrations from outside. In contrast to the Upper Palaeolithic, the Mesolithic strategies of food-quest increasingly relied on the hunting of solitary animals adapted to the forest and forest-steppe environments (elk, roe deer, red deer, and wild boar). The reindeer, which was the principal hunting prey during the Late Glacial period, disappeared from the greater part of the East European Plain in the early Holocene. Northern Russia, which included tundra-like landscapes, was a notable exception, where reindeer remained an important hunting prey. Hunting was increasingly complemented by the use of aquatic resources and harvesting of plant food. An increasing role for plant food in the Mesolithic diet became apparent in the steppe area (Jacobs 1994, Lillie 1996).

In contrast to Upper Palaeolithic settlements, which are restricted to loess soils in the periglacial area, Mesolithic sites are found in all landscape zones, including those that had been only recently freed from ice-sheets. The northernmost Mesolithic site in Eurasia dated to 7100–6700 cal BC

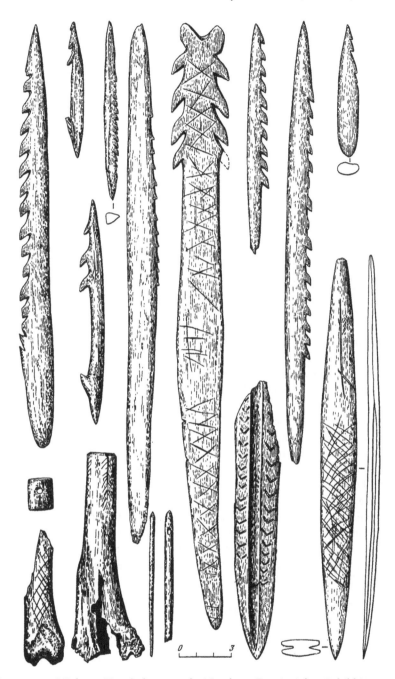

Figure 11.5. Nizhnee Veret'e bone tools, Northern Russia (after Oshibkina 1989b).

is found on Zhokhov Island (The New Siberian Archipelago, 76 degrees North latitude), on the exposed shelf of the Arctic Ocean (Pitul'ko 1998).

Palaeolithic settlements consisted of several dwellings made out of large mammoth bones, were apparently habitable on a year-round basis, and were principally located on higher elevations above the wider stretches of large rivers (Soffer 1985, Dolukhanov 1996). Mesolithic sites were concentrated in selected landscapes with diverse and predictable resources, and especially in wetland environments near marine estuaries, lakes, and in river basins, both on the plain and in the mountains.

Still more important differences between the Late Palaeolithic and Mesolithic are apparent in social structures. Soffer (1985) argues that Late Palaeolithic society on the East European Plain consisted of residential groups, varying in size between twenty and sixty persons. These groups displayed a social hierarchy, with 'high-status' individuals allegedly located at 'cold-weather base camps'. The latter is exemplified by the site of Sunghir in Central Russia where the burials of several individuals indicate clear signals of wealth and inherited power such as spears of mammoth tusk in the infants' graves (Bader 1978). The occurrence of figurative art with the apparent prominence of female ivory figurines is yet another feature of the East European Upper Palaeolithic. This is often viewed as an indication of a prominent position held by women in Late Palaeolithic society. The Mesolithic lifestyle featured an increased sedentism combined with limited-scale seasonal transhumance. In several cases, there is clear evidence for larger permanent base-camps associated with a network of smaller seasonal occupations. Jacobs (1992), based on the analysis of dental data from Mesolithic burials, views Mesolithic society as consisting of large 'mating networks' of a closed or semiclosed type.

Principal changes in social organisation are signalled by the appearance of large 'communal' cemeteries, which were unknown in the Palaeolithic. The largest known cemetery on the Reindeer Island (Lake Onega, Russian Karelia) with at least four hundred graves (Gurina 1956) is particularly significant. The occurrence of social hierarchy within an apparently large and stable community is highlighted by the burials of male individuals ('shamans') in vertical shafts with clear signals of wealth and status. No less important, Mesolithic cemeteries were found in the steppe area, near the Dniepr Rapids. Their most significant element was the evidence of warfare. In several cases the deceased at these cemeteries bear witness to violent death, with flint arrowheads embedded in ribs and vertebrae.

The evidence from cemeteries clearly signals gender distinctions. At Reindeer Island cemetery, hunting equipment and armaments are found in male graves. Female graves are normally poorer in funerary goods, which were commonly restricted to household artefacts and artworks (for further discussion, see Zvelebil this volume). The Dniepr Rapids cemeteries with evidence of warfare contain almost exclusively male individuals.

This suggests a society consisting of large male-dominated social aggregations, which included an important segment of military-oriented bands (particularly in the steppe, where food resources were scarce).

There is strong evidence of cultural segregation within Mesolithic societies. This is particularly apparent in the Dniepr Rapids cemeteries, where the deceased were often buried following distinct burial rites within the same burial ground (Stolyar 1959, Telegin 1982). The fragmentation of cultural space becomes apparent in the form of 'archaeological cultures' with more locally restricted distributions manifesting their identity in similar material symbols. Following an ethnocultural approach, Russian and East European archaeological schools traditionally link up stylistic variations observable in artefactual assemblages with 'archaeological cultures' often identified with ethnic and/or linguistic entities (Dolukhanov 1996: 3–6). In contrast, Western scholars tend to visualise artefactual variability in terms of the *chaîne opératoire*, translated as an operational sequence that reflects 'the different stages of tool production from the acquisition of raw material to the final abandonment of the desired and/or used objects, and dictated by the choices made by . . . humans.' (Bar-Yosef et al. 1992: 511).

Stylistic variables which lie at the base of both 'archaeological cultures' and '*chaînes opératoires*' may include both *fossils directeurs*, such as 'Swiderian points' or 'Kukrekian armatures', and general technological characteristics, such as the proportion of flake versus blade blanks, the proportion of microliths, 'heavy-duty' tools, and so on. At least in some cases, the stylistic and technological characteristics may be seen as a signal of a common cultural tradition, and their changes through time as reflecting transcultural interaction and displacement of Mesolithic communities. Thus the occurrence of 'Swiderian points' in Late Glacial assemblages might identify the expansion of reindeer-hunting communities on the East European Plain, who originated in the Vistula-Pripyat core area. The occurrence of similar points in later Mesolithic contexts is an indication of a genetic relationship between their makers and the earlier communities of the Late Glacial. In the steppe area, two distinct archaeological cultures, the Kukrekian and Grebenikian, with sites that are often found in similar landscape settings, obviously denote different cultural affiliations and origins. By contrast, the common occurrence of 'heavy-duty' tools and the almost total absence of geometric microliths at Mesolithic sites in the Boreal zone clearly signal the impact of the local forested environment.

Another important issue relates to residential mobility. Older views of Mesolithic groups as peripatetic hunter-gatherers are no longer tenable. The occurrence of Mesolithic cemeteries persisting over considerable periods of time (such as at Reindeer Island) is an obvious indication of the stability of these communities and their territorial control. The Mesolithic life-style included a limited number of permanent or semipermanent (apparently cold season) base camps and a network of much smaller sites resulting from a seasonal transhumance.

There are also indications of larger-scale directional migrations. The original peopling of the northern Boreal zone, previously covered by ice-sheets, occurred during the Late Glacial period, resulting from a migration from the Vistula-Pripyat area. At the same time, the influx into the steppe area proceeded from the north. The steppe area with its vulnerable and rapidly changing environment remained an arena of repeated human displacement. Significantly, at the Dniepr Rapids cemeteries, the skeletons buried according to different burial rites belong to at least three distinct physical types (see earlier). Even allowing for the caution with which morphological data should be treated in the absence of molecular genetic analyses, these groupings may be seen as proxy evidence of demographic dynamics.

Another issue concerns the prolonged survival of hunter-gatherer pottery-making communities in the greater part of the forested East European Plain (the 'Sub-Neolithic'). These communities are normally viewed in the West as belonging to the Mesolithic (Zvelebil and Lillie 2000, Zvelebil this volume). However, recent archaeobotanic studies (Hather and Mason 2002: 4–5) show that it is often impossible to draw a clear distinction between agricultural and hunter-gatherer communities, as hunter-gatherers may undertake agricultural practices and vice versa. The limited importance of cereal agriculture in most areas in Neolithic Britain, for example, is widely accepted (Edmonds 1999, Whittle 1999, Richmond 1999, Robinson 2000), although this view has been recently contested (Rowley-Conwy 2004).

The appearance of ceramic vessels at certain types of sites, notably shell-middens in the coastal areas of Europe, as in the upper levels of the Portuguese shell mounds (Straus this volume) and in the Ertebølle of southern Scandinavia (Blankholm this volume), apparently failed to modify a Mesolithic life-style based on marine resources and wild plants (Stiner et al. 2003, Andersen and Johansen 1987, Robinson and Harild 2002). By contrast, pottery-making hunter-gatherers in the boreal forests of Eurasia display several attributes of complex societies, such as sedentism, high population density, intensive food procurement, technological elaboration, development of exchange networks (that may include their agricultural neighbours), social differentiation, and territorial control (Zvelebil 1996b: 331).

Recent studies in Northwestern Russia (Dolukhanov et al. 2004) identified evidence of swidden-type agriculture in the local Mesolithic-Neolithic context starting at c. 5000 cal BC. It becomes increasingly clear that the distinction between an agricultural and a nonagricultural Neolithic is rather blurred, and the dominant manifestations of Neolithic are different in different parts of the world and even in different parts of Europe (Séfériadès 1993, Tringham 2000, Thomas 2003).

Recent studies show that large-scale pottery making combined with elements of stockbreeding started in the steppe area much earlier than had been previously thought. The sites of the Yelshanian and North-Caspian cultures (Vybornov 2008) have been identified in the Middle Volga basin and the North Caspian Lowland. Small, presumably seasonal occupations are found close to water channels. Subsistence was based on the hunting of a wide range of animals (wild horse, aurochs, elk, brown bear, red deer, fallow deer, saiga antelope, marten, and beaver), food collecting (tortoise and edible molluscs, mostly *Unio*), and fishing. Remains of domestic animals (horse, cattle, sheep, and goat) were found at several sites, yet the penetration from the later levels cannot be ruled out. Radiocarbon dates obtained for the earlier sites give a time range of 8000–6500 cal BC (Vybornov, Dolukhanov, et al. 2009, Vybornov, Kovalyukh, et al. 2009). The remaining three dates lie in the span of 8025–7475 cal BC.

Rakushechnyi Yar is a clearly stratified Neolithic settlement located on a small island in the lower stretches of the River Don, which includes twenty-three archaeological layers (Belanovskaya 1995). The deepest levels (23–6) are deemed as 'Early Neolithic' with animal remains consisting of both wild animals (red deer, roe deer, fox, hare, numerous birds) and domesticated (sheep, goat, cattle, dog, horse – either wild or domestic). Numerous shells of edible molluscs (mostly *Viviparus*) indicate the importance of food gathering. Radiocarbon dates obtained for the early pottery-bearing strata give a time range of 6400–5600 cal BC (Aleksandrovsky et al. 2009).

The Early Neolithic in the western Ukraine and Moldova is usually associated with the sites of the Bug-Dniestrian Culture (Danilenko 1969, Markevich 1974). At early sites, about 80 percent of animal remains belong to wild species, mostly roe deer and red deer. Among the domestic animals, pig, cattle, and (on later sites) sheep/goat have been identified. Archaeological deposits contain huge amounts of *Unio* molluscs and tortoise shells. Roach, pike, sturgeon, and catfish are found among numerous fish bones. Birds such as sparrow hawk, honey buzzard, and wood pigeon have been recorded. Remarkably, impressions of three varieties of wheat were found on the pottery: emmer, einkorn, and spelt. Radiocarbon dates obtained for the earlier sites are 6400–5600 cal BC (Dolukhanov et al. 2009).

Vasil'ev (1981) and Vasil'ev and Sinyuk (1985) have distinguished a 'Mariupol' cultural entity stretching from the Dniepr in the west to the Urals in the east, from which several cultures, including the Sredni Stog, Samarian and Khvalynian later developed. The Khvalynian has been recently dated by a series of radiocarbon measurements to a time span of 5200–4500 cal BC, so that the Mariupol cultural entity should predate this. Mariupol-related sites, which shared several common stylistic and symbolic features, were uniformly based on cattle-dominated stockbreeding with early evidence for the domestication of the horse. One may reasonably suggest that in an environment of increasing scarcity in water supply in the areas east of the Dniepr, the 'agricultural revolution' predominantly took the character of stockbreeding. Significantly, all skeletal remains from Mariupol-type burials, for which stable isotope and dental evidence are available (Lillie and

Richards 2000: 967), indicate diets in which 'the majority of protein came from terrestrial-based resources with a significant amount of river fish'. In terms of the model suggested by Zvelebil and Rowley-Conwy (1986), the 'Sub-Neolithic' pottery-making societies may be viewed as belonging to the 'substitution phase' in which stockbreeding and (possibly) agriculture provided 5–50 percent of the diet.

Fully-fledged agricultural communities appeared in the south of the East European Plain in the form of the sites of the Linear Pottery Culture: on the middle Dniestr and smaller rivers of Moldavia and south-western Ukraine, presumably stemming from the Carpathian basin. The Bug-Dniestrian sites on the Southern Bug River included imported Linear pottery ware with 'music-note' ornament.

According to Dumitrescu et al. (1983: 108–9), the fully agricultural Tripolye-Cucuteni Culture was a later development of the Boian Culture in Rumania, which spread east of the Prut as a result of population movement. Yet the interaction with local groups is equally in evidence. The impact of the Bug-Dniestrian is especially visible in the flint technology of early Tripolye sites (Bibikov and Zbenovich 1985).

In the boreal forests further north, the elements of farming first appeared at 5,000 cal BC. They gradually grew in importance until plough-type farming and stock rearing became fully dominant in the first millennium cal BC.

Chapter 12

The Mesolithic of Atlantic Iberia

Lawrence Guy Straus*

Introduction

The subject of this chapter is the Mesolithic of the southwest corner of Europe, the Atlantic façade of the Iberian Peninsula: Portugal and the narrow zone between the Cantabrian Cordillera and Sea that stretches from Galicia to the Basque Country. There are thus two geographic aspects that define the study area: western (the open Atlantic) and northern (the Bay of Biscay). The scarcity or lack of post-Palaeolithic/pre-Neolithic archaeological sites in the interior, Atlantic-drained regions of Spain (Castile, León, Extremadura) or even of Portugal, means that our knowledge of Mesolithic foraging adaptations is significantly limited to coastal and near-coastal areas (Figures 12.1 and 12.2). This is probably the result of a combination of factors: a shorter, less intense history of prehistoric research in the interior, a lesser visibility of Mesolithic sites relative to Palaeolithic ones, and an actual concentration of early Holocene human populations in the favourable coastal habitats. It is quite possible that the latter explanation is the most valid and that human use of the interior of the Iberian Peninsula during the Holocene was fairly scant until the introduction of food production economies in the period between 7000–6000 BP, whereas it was precisely the Atlantic façade, with its relatively rich and diverse resources, which saw the latest survival of foraging lifeways in the Peninsula. This was in many ways similar to the situation along the shores of the Baltic (Zvelebil this volume, Bjerck this volume) or in the Iron Gates Gorge of the Danube (Bonsall this volume), with late adoption of agriculture resulting from the relative prosperity of local hunting, gathering and fishing subsistence strategies.

The study area extends from Cape St. Vincent (at 37°N and 9°W) northward to Cape Finisterre (at 43°N and 9°20′W) and then eastward to the crotch of the Bay of Biscay at the Franco-Spanish border between San Sebastián and Biarritz (at 43°20′N and 1°45′W). Varying amounts of information on the Mesolithic are available from several Portuguese regions – from south to

* Department of Anthropology, University of New Mexico, USA.

This chapter has been updated with new information and new radiocarbon dates that have become available since the publication of the hardback edition.

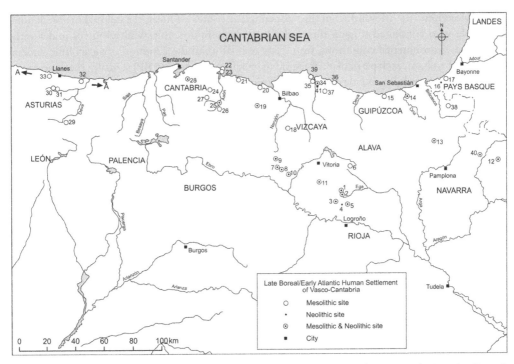

Figure 12.1. Human settlement of Asturias, Cantabria, Euskadi, and Navarra during the Boreal and Early-Middle Atlantic Phases. Sites: 1. Atxoste Kanpanoste (M+N); 2. Kanpanoste Goikoa (M+N); 3. Montico de Charratu (M+N); 4. Peña Larga (N); 5. La Peña de Marañón (M+N); 6. Kukuma (M); 7. Socuevas (M+N); 8. Fuente Hoz (M+N); 9. Berniollo (M+N); 10. La Renke (M+N); 11. Mendandia (M+N); 12. Zatoya (M+N); 13. Abauntz (M+N); 14. Marizulo (M+N); 15. Herriko Barra (M); 16. Mouligna (N); 17. Moura (M); 18. Urratxa (M); 19. Arenaza (M+N); 20. Pico Ramos (M); 21. La Trecha (M); 22. La Fragua (M); 23. El Perro (M); 24. La Chora (M); 25. El Mirón (M+N); 26. Tarrerón and Las Pajucas (M); 27. Cubio Redondo (M); 28. La Garma (M+N); 29. La Calvera (M); 30. Los Canes (M); 31. Arangas (M); 32. Mazaculos (M); 33. La Riera (M); 34. Santimamiñe (M+N); 35. Atxeta (M); 36. Lumentxa (M); 37. Kobeaga (M); 38. Berroberría (M); 39. Pareko Landa (M); 40. Aizpea (M+N); 41. Kobaederra (N); A to A = Main concentration of Asturian concheros; 'M' = Mesolithic; 'N' = Neolithic; Principal sources: Alday 1998, Arias 1991, Arias et al. 1999, Clark 1983, Fano 1998, González Morales 1982.

north: Algarve, Alentejo, Estremadura, Ribatejo, Douro, and Minho – and from the Spanish regions that border the Cantabrian Sea (also known as the Bay of Biscay) – from west to east: Galicia, Asturias, Cantabria (ex-Santander), and Euskadi (Basque Autonomous Region), hereafter globally referred to as 'Cantabrian Spain', except when individual regional or provincial sectors are specified. Galicia has both west-facing (provinces of Pontevedra and La Coruña) and north-facing (province of Lugo) coasts, and a landlocked interior province (Orense). Euskadi consists of the coastal provinces of Vizcaya and Guipúzcoa and the interior provinces of Alava and Navarra, the latter drained by the Ebro River to the Mediterranean, and these inland provinces are included here as necessary, particularly with regard to the spread of the food production economy at the end of the Mesolithic. By 'Mesolithic' in this subpeninsular context, I mean the cultural manifestations of people who continued to gain their subsistence only by foraging wild resources under early Holocene environmental conditions, from c. 10,000 BP until the adoption of agriculture and/or animal husbandry in each particular subregion (generally c. 6000–5500 BP). Usually, the appearance of pottery more or less coincides with the adoption of a food production economy in the regions under consideration, although there are some suggestions that the latest Mesolithic inhabitants may have acquired their first ceramic vessels (through emulation or, more likely, trade or theft) from neighbouring Neolithic groups before actually abandoning their foraging lifeways. In terms of characteristic lithic technology, there are three general types of industries of Mesolithic age in the study area:

1. 'Epipalaeolithic' industries rich in backed bladelets and backed points with varying quantities of (generally small) endscrapers and other Upper Palaeolithic tool types.
2. Geometric microlithic industries sometimes with fairly few other formal lithic tool types.
3. Macrolithic industries dominated by cobble picks, choppers, and/or large flakes, which can be found either essentially alone or associated with varying amounts of microliths.

The microlaminar 'Epipalaeolithic' industries (which include the early Holocene phases of the late Cantabrian Azilian) precede the geometric microlithic industries, which in turn can be contemporaneous with the macrolithic ones. The microlaminar to geometric succession is also characteristic of other European regions, including Mediterranean Spain and Southwest France (e.g., Aura et al. 1998, Thévenin 1990–91, see also Pluciennik this volume, Valdeyron this volume), although the timing of this technological transition does vary slightly.

The terminal Magdalenian developed unevenly and almost imperceptibly into the Azilian, the latter characterised by flat-section, basally perforated, very rarely decorated antler harpoons, over the course of the last millennium and a half of the Würm Tardiglacial in Asturias, Cantabria and Euskadi (Fernández Tresguerres 1980, Fernández Eraso 1985, González Sainz 1989, Aura et al. 1998, Straus 1991a), with the Azilian continuing throughout the course of the Preboreal to be replaced by a variety of more localized industries ('cultures'?) from the Asturian to the geometric Mesolithic of the Basque Country in the Boreal and Atlantic periods. However there is no Azilian *per se* in Mediterranean Spain or Portugal, but the regional Upper Magdalenian (without harpoons in Portugal) displayed a high degree of continuity in assemblages rich in backed or 'nibbled' (Dufour) bladelets and small nongeometric backed points. These Epipalaeolithic assemblages predominated during the Preboreal period, only to give way to geometric microlith-dominated ones made by means of the microburin technique during the course of the Boreal and especially Atlantic phases (Bicho 1993, 1994, 1998, Zilhão 1995, Aura et al. 1998). The technological transition is little known in Galicia, but initial indications suggest a local sequence from a terminal Magdalenian to an Azilian-like Epipalaeolithic under conditions of rapid reforestation (e.g., Llana et al. 1992, Ramil 1997). Radiocarbon dates are listed in Tables 12.1 and 12.2.

Chronological and Palaeoenvironmental Background

The Mesolithic of the Iberian Atlantic façade took place entirely under conditions of a reestablished, northeasterly flowing Gulf Stream, although temperatures were still somewhat cooler than at present during the Preboreal phase (Duplessy et al. 1981, Ruddiman and McIntyre 1981, COHMAP 1988). The amelioration in conditions at c. 10,000 BP was as swift and dramatic as had been the Dryas III

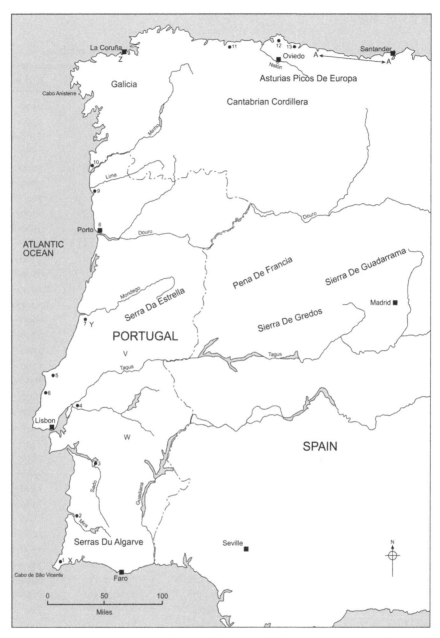

Figure 12.2. Boreal and Early Atlantic Mesolithic (and Initial Neolithic) human settlement of Portugal, Galicia, and Asturias. 1. Sagres Area Sites; 2. Alentejo Coast and Mira Valley Sites ('Mirian'); 3. Sado Valley Sites; 4. Muge and Magos (Tagus Estuary) Sites; 5. Rio Maior and Bocas Area Sites; 6. Torres Vedras Area Sites; 7. Mondego Estuary Sites; 8. Douro Estuary Sites ('Portuguese Asturian'/'Ancorian'); 9. Minho Coast Sites ('Portuguese Asturian/'Ancorian') (?); 10. Fiales and other Minho Estuary Sites ('Camposanquian') (?); 11. Luarca ('Asturian') (?); 12. Cabo de Peñas (Avilés-Gijón) Area, including Bañugués ('Asturian'); 13. Villaviciosa Area ('Asturian'). A to A = Main concentration of Asturian concheros in E. Asturias and W. Cantabria; V, W, X, Y = Areas of Cardial Neolithic Settlement in S. Portugal; X = Early Neolithic (?) Site of O Reiro at Barrañan (Galicia); (?) = Mesolithic age of all or some sites in area may be problematic. Principal sources: Bicho 1994, Clark 1983, Fano 1998, González Morales 1982, González Morales and Arnaud 1990, Vázquez 1988, 2004, Zilhao 1993, 1998.

Table 12.1. Radiocarbon dates for the Holocene Mesolithic of Vasco-Cantabria

Site	Level	Lab No.	BP	Cal BC 2σ
Arenaza*	IID	CSIC-173	9600 ± 180	9500–8300
La Fragua*	3	GrN-20966	9600 ± 140	9300–8550
La Fragua	1 lower	GrN-20965	7530 ± 70	6500–6230
La Fragua	1 mid	GrN-20964	6860 ± 60	5880–5630
La Fragua	1 upper	GrN-20963	6650 ± 120	5780–5360
El Mirón	10.1	GX-24464	9550 ± 50	9160–8750
El Mirón	10.1	GX-25852	8700 ± 40	7840–7590
El Mirón	10.1	GX-24463	8380 ± 175	8000–6800
Ekain*	II	I.1 1666	9540 ± 210	9500–8200
Ekain*	IVbs	I-9239	9460 ± 185	9250–8300
Los Azules*	3d	CSIC-260	9540 ± 120	9300–8550
Los Azules*	3a	CSIC-216	9430 ± 120	9200–8300
Abauntz*	D	Ly-1964	9530 ± 300	10,100–7900
Mazaculos	3.3	GaK-6884	9290 ± 440	10,100–7400
Mazaculos	1.1	GaK-8162	7280 ± 220	6600–5700
Mazaculos	A3	GaK-15222	7030 ± 120	6250–5650
Cueva Oscura*	IIA	Ly-2938	9280 ± 230	9300–7900
El Perro	1.3	GrN-18115	9260 ± 110	8770–8270
Morín	Conchero	I-5150	9000 ± 150	8600–7650
La Riera	29 lower	Gak-2909	8650 ± 300	8600–7000
La Riera	29 upper	GaK-3046	6500 ± 200	5850–4950
Penicial	Conchero	Gak-2906	8650 ± 180	8250–7350
Berroberría	C	GrN-16619	8510 ± 90	7740–7350
Berroberría	Bbase	GrN-16619	8470 ± 80	7610–7320
Arangas	3	OxA-6887	8300 ± 50	7500–7180
Arangas	4	OxA-6888	8280 ± 55	7490–7140
Arangas	3	OxA-7149	8195 ± 60	7450–7050
Arangas	2B	OxA-7160	8025 ± 80	7180–6680
Arangas	E2	UBAR-465	7150 ± 470	7200–5000
Jaizkibel 3	16	GrN-23733	8300 ± 50	7500–7180
Jaizkibel 3	16	GrN-27984	8190 ± 100	7550–6800
Jaizkibel 3	16	GrN-28008	7780 ± 130	7050–6400
Zatoya	Ib	Ly-1457	8260 ± 550	8700–6000
Zatoya	Ib	Ly-1398	8150 ± 170	7550–6650
Fuente Hoz	III	I-12985	8120 ± 240	7600–6500
Fuente Hoz	III	I-13496	7880 ± 120	7100–6450
Fuente Hoz	III	I-12083	7840 ± 130	7100–6450
Fuente Hoz	III	I-12778	7140 ± 120	6240–5740
La Peña de Marañón	d	BM-2363	7890 ± 120	7100–6450
Kanpanoste Goikoa	III lower	GrN-20455	7860 ± 330	7600–6000
Kanpanoste Goikoa	III lower	GrN-20215	7620 ± 80	6640–6260
Mendandia	IV	GrN-22744	7810 ± 50	6780–6500
Mendandia	IV	GrN-22745	7780 ± 60	6770–6460
Aizpea	I	GrN-16620	7790 ± 70	6830–6460

Site	Level	Lab No.	BP	Cal BC 2σ
Aizpea	I	GrN-16621	7160 ± 70	6220–5900
Aizpea	II	GrN-16622	6830 ± 70	5880–5620
Aizpea	II	GrA-779	6600 ± 50	5620–5480
Espertín	2	Gif-10053	7790 ± 120	7050–6400
La Garma A	2	OxA-7495	7710 ± 90	6770–6390
La Garma A	2	OxA-7284	7685 ± 65	6640–6430
La Garma A	2	OxA-6889	6920 ± 50	5970–5710
La Garma A	2	OxA-7150	6870 ± 50	5880–5660
Sierra Plana	Upper	UGRA-209	7550 ± 190	7000–6000
La Trecha	1	URU-0083	7500 ± 70	6470–6230
La Trecha	Conchero	URU-0039	6240 ± 100	5500–4900
La Trecha	Conchero	URU-0051	5600 ± 310	5300–3700
La Trecha	Conchero	URU-0050	5430 ± 70	4450–4050
Coberizas	Conchero	GaK-2907	7100 ± 170	6400–5650
Urratxa	?	Ua-11435	6955 ± 80	6010–5700
Urratxa	?	Ua-11434	6940 ± 75	5990–5700
Los Canes	K	AA-6071	6930 ± 95	6000–5650
Los Canes	D	AA-5295	6860 ± 65	5890–5630
Los Canes	D	AA-5296	6770 ± 65	5790–5550
Los Canes	F	AA-5294	6265 ± 75	5470–5010
Los Canes	6I	OxA-7148	6160 ± 55	5300–4940
Sierra Plana	Paleosol	OxA-6916	6830 ± 55	5840–5630
Bricia	Conchero	GaK-2908	6800 ± 160	6050–5450
Pareko Landa**	Arm k-5	GrN-22429	6650 ± 130	5800–5320
Kanpanoste Goikoa	III	GrN-20289	6550 ± 260	6000–4900
Kanpanoste Goikoa	III	GrN-20214	6360 ± 70	5480–5210
La Chora	Conchero	GrN-20961	6360 ± 80	5490–5110
Herriko Barra**	Upper	Ua-4821	6010 ± 90	5210–4710
Herriko Barra**	Upper	Ua-4820	5960 ± 95	5250–4550
Herriko Barra**	Upper	I-15351	5810 ± 170	5100–4300
Herriko Barra**	Upper	I-15350	5730 ± 110	4800–4350
Pico Ramos**	4	Ua-3051	5860 ± 65	4900–4540
Tarrerón**	III	I-4030	5780 ± 120	4950–4350
Les Pedroses	Conchero	GaK-2547	5760 ± 180	5100–4200
Cubio Redondo	Conchero	Beta-106050	6630 ± 50	5850–5300
Cubio Redondo	Conchero	Beta-106049	5780 ± 50	4730–4490
La Poza l' Egua	Conchero	TO-10222	8550 ± 80	7520–7130
Tito Bustillo	Burial	Beta-197042	8470 ± 50	7590–7470
Colomba	Conchero	TO-10223	7090 ± 60	5740–5530
El Truchiro	Conchero	TO-10912	6470 ± 70	5560–5310

* Azilian or possible Azilian; **Aceramic Neolithic or 'Terminal Mesolithic'

Principal Sources: Straus 1992, González Morales 1995, Alday 1998, Arias et al. 1999, González Morales and Straus 2000, Arias, Armendariz, et al. 2009. All radiocarbon determinations are given as uncalibrated BP and calibrated ranges at 2 sigma as cal BC. Dates have been calibrated using OxCal v3.10 (Bronk Ramsey 1995, 2001).

Table 12.2. Radiocarbon dates for the Holocene Mesolithic of Portugal

Site	Level	Lab No.	BP	Cal BC 2σ
Bocas I*	Fund.o	ICEN-901	10,110 ± 90	10,100–9350
Bocas I*	O	ICEN-900	9880 ± 220	10,200–8600
Bocas I*	01-Feb	ICEN-903	9900 ± 70	9670–9240
Casal Papagaio	Base	ICEN-369	9710 ± 70	9300–8830
Casal Papagaio	–	ICEN-372	9270 ± 90	8720–8290
Casal Papagaio	–	Hv-1351	8870 ± 105	8300–7650
Magoito	Concheiro	ICEN-80	9970 ± 70	9800–9250
Magoito	Concheiro	ICEN-82	9910 ± 100	9900–9200
Magoito	Concheiro	ICEN-81	9790 ± 120	9700–8800
Magoito	Concheiro	GrN-11229	9580 ± 100	9250–8650
Magoito	Concheiro	ICEN-52	9490 ± 60	9150–8600
Cabeço do Porto Marinho*	IIISW/Upper	SMU-2666	9270 ± 170	9200–8000
Cabeço do Porto Marinho*	Area V/Lower	ICEN-688	9100 ± 160	8750–7750
S. Julião	Area A	?	8800–7500	–
Areeiro III	Test Vib	ICEN-547	8860 ± 80	8250–7700
Areeiro III	Area I/hearth 2	ICEN-494	8850 ± 50	8220–7780
Areeiro III	Area I/hearth I	ICEN-546	8570 ± 130	8200–7300
Areeiro III	Area 2	ICEN-688	8380 ± 90	7590–7180
Palheirões do Alegra	Flint hearth	ICEN-136	8400 ± 70	7590–7300
Palheirões do Alegra	–	GX-16414	8800 ± 100	8250–7600
Castelejo	–	?	>7600	–
Ponta de Vigia	Hearth	ICEN-51	8730 ± 110	8250–7550
Curral Velho	–	ICEN-270	8040 ± 70	7180–6690
Curral Velho	–	ICEN-269	8050 ± 100	7350–6650
S. Julião	Area B	?	8250–7900	
Fonte Pinheiro	–	ICEN-973	8450 ± 190	8200–7000
Castelejo	–	Beta-2276	7620 ± 100	6650–6250
Castelejo	–	Beta-2908	7450 ± 90	6460–6090
Montes de Baixo	4B	ICEN-720	7550 ± 70	6510–6230
Montes de Baixo	2	ICEN-718	7230 ± 70	6240–5980
Arapouco	Middle	Q-2492	7420 ± 65	6430–6100
Forno da Telha	2	ICEN-417	7360 ± 90	6420–6050
Forno da Telha	2	ICEN-416	7320 ± 60	6360–6050
Moita do Sebastião	Base/Skeleton 6	Sa-16	7350 ± 350	7100–5500
Moita do Sebastião	Skeleton 22	TO-131	7240 ± 70	6240–5990
Moita do Sebastião	Skeleton 29	TO-133	7200 ± 70	6230–5920
Moita do Sebastião	Skeleton 24	TO-132	7180 ± 70	6220–5910
Moita do Sebastião	Skeleton 41	TO-134	7160 ± 80	6220–5880
Moita do Sebastião	Skeleton CT	TO-135	6800 ± 70	5850–5560
Bocas	01-Feb	ICEN-899	7130 ± 120	6230–5740
Poças de S. Bento	Lower	Q-2493	7040 ± 70	6030–5750
Poças de S. Bento	Middle	Q-2495	6850 ± 70	5890–5620
Poças de S.Bento	Middle	Q-2494	6780 ± 65	5810–5560

Site	Level	Lab No.	BP	Cal BC 2σ
Fiais	–	TO-806	7010 ± 70	6010–5740
Fiais	–	TO-705	6840 ± 70	5880–5620
Fiais	–	TO-807	6260 ± 80	5470–5000
Fiais	–	ICEN-141	6180 ± 110	5400–4800
Cabeço da Arruda	–	TO-10216	7040 ± 60	6030–5770
Cabeço da Arruda	Skeleton III	TO-360	6990 ± 110	6060–5670
Cabeço da Arruda	Skeleton A	TO-354	6970 ± 60	5990–5730
Cabeço da Arruda	Skeleton 42	TO-359a	6960 ± 60	5990–5720
Cabeço da Arruda	Skeleton D	TO-355	6780 ± 80	5840–5540
Cabeço da Arruda	–	TO-10217	6620 ± 60	5640–5470
Cabeço da Arruda	Skeleton N	TO-356	6360 ± 80	5490–5110
Cabeço da Arruda	71–83	Sa-197	6430 ± 300	6000–4700
Medo Tojeiro	–	BM-2275R	6820 ± 140	5990–5490
Medo Tojeiro	–	BM-2275	6150 ± 120	5400–4750
Cabeço do Pez	Middle	Q-2497	6730 ± 75	5750–5490
Cabeço do Pez	Middle	Q-2496	6430 ± 65	5520–5290
Cabeço do Pez	Upper	Q-2499	5535 ± 130	4700–4050
Cabeço da Armoreira	2	TO-11860	5710 ± 170	5000–4150
Cabeço da Armoreira	3	TO-11861	5960 ± 70	5040–4700
Cabeço da Armoreira	3–4	Sa-194	6050 ± 300	5700–4300
Cabeço da Armoreira	–	HV-1349	6430 ± 65	5520–5290
Cabeço da Armoreira	2–3	TO-10225	6550 ± 70	5630–5370
Cabeço da Armoreira	–	TO-10218	6630 ± 60	5650–5470
Cabeço da Armoreira	Skeleton 7	Beta (?)	6850 ± 40	5840–5650
Cabeço da Armoreira	39	Sa-195	7030 ± 350	6700–5200
Vale da Fonte da Moça	50/60	TO-11863	6650 ± 60	5670–5480
Vale da Fonte da Moça	100/120	TO-11864	6890 ± 140	6030–5550
Vidigal	3	Ly-4695	6640 ± 90	5730–5380
Vidigal	2	GX-14557	6030 ± 80	5210–4720
Samouqueira	–	?	7160 ± 70	6220–5900
Samouqueira	–	TO-130	6370 ± 70	5480–5210
Barca do Xerez de Baixo	1/P41/C2	Beta-120607	8640 ± 50	7870–7535
Barca do Xerez de Baixo	2/G53/2A/14	OxA-13406	8150 ± 40	7310–7060
Barca do Xerez de Baixo	2/H53/2A/8	OxA-13265	8250 ± 35	7450–7085
Barca do Xerez de Baixo	5/AS46/-/231	OxA-13266	8730 ± 35	7940–7605
Barca do Xerez de Baixo	2/G52/2A/22	OxA-13264	8250 ± 35	7450–7085
Barranco das Quebradas III	F21(n.a.2)	Wk-12133	7995 ± 60[†]	7060–6695
Barranco das Quebradas III	T2, n.a. 0–22	Wk-8940	7980 ± 85[†]	7305–6640
Barranco das Quebradas V	M7. 15b	Wk-13693	8035 ± 80[†]	7315–6690
Barranco das Quebradas III	T2, n.a. 60–70	Wk-8951	8400 ± 65[†]	7580–7325
Barranco das Quebradas IV	L18(n.a.2)	Wk-12134	8490 ± 65[†]	7600–7375
Barranco das Quebradas I	T2, n.a. 40–50	Wk-8939	8580 ± 75[†]	7815–7485

(continued)

Table 12.2 (*continued*)

Site	Level	Lab No.	BP	Cal BC 2σ
Barranco das Quebradas I	T2, n.a. 110-120	Wk-8950	8640 ± 75[†]	7940–7540
Rocha das Gaviotas	R32, c. 3a	Wk-13690	8295 ± 60[†]	7520–7085
Rocha das Gaviotas	S33, c. 3c	Wk-13691	8585 ± 60[†]	7745–7525
Castelejo	Middle levels	ICEN-743	7170 ± 70[†]	6220–5900
Castelejo	Middle levels	ICEN-745	7550 ± 70[†]	6510–6230
Castelejo	Middle levels	BM-2276R	7840 ± 120[†]	7050–6450
Castelejo	c. 4	ICEN-215	7880 ± 40	7030–6610
Castelejo	c. 4	ICEN-213	7900 ± 40	7030–6645
Castelejo	c. 5	ICEN-211	7970 ± 60	7060–6690
Armação Nova	c. 2	ICEN-1229	7120 ± 70[†]	6210–5840
Armação Nova	c. 2	ICEN-1230	7150 ± 70[†]	6210–5890
Armação Nova	c. 4	ICEN-1227	6970 ± 90[†]	6020–5700
Armação Nova	c. 4	ICEN-1228	7740 ± 70[†]	6690–6440
Val Boi	C2 (human)	TO-12197	7500 ± 90	6530–6100
Rocha das Gaviotas	2c, hearth 1	Wk-13692	6710 ± 60[†]	5730–5520
Rocha das Gaviotas	2c, hearth 2	Wk-14797	6860 ± 40	5850–5660
Rocha das Gaviotas	2c, hearth 3	Wk-14798	6820 ± 50	5810–5620
Rocha das Gaviotas	2c, base	Wk-14793	6340 ± 50[†]	5730–5550
Rocha das Gaviotas	2c, base	Wk-14794	6280 ± 50[†]	5810–5620
Rocha das Gaviotas	T1, 1.10	Wk-6075	6890 ± 75[†]	5980–5640
Cabeço das Amoreira	Burial 7	Beta-127450	6850 ± 40	5540–5480
Cabeço das Amoreira	CAM-00-01	TO-11819-R	7300 ± 80	5990–5820
Cabeço das Amoreiras	Burial 5	Beta-125110	7230 ± 40	6200–6030
Cova da Onça	Burial	Beta-127448	7140 ± 40	5840–5740
Moita do Sebastião	Burial 16	Beta-127449	7120 ± 40	5800–5710
Arapouco	Burial 2[a]	Sac-1560	7120 ± 40	5970–5730
Cabeço do Pez	Burial 4	Sac-1558	6740 ± 100	5670–5520
Cabeço do Pez	Burial 4	Beta-125109	6760 ± 40	5690–5630
Fiais		ICEN-110	6870 ± 220	5560–5985
Fiais		ICEN-103	7310 ± 90	5500–5660

* 'Terminal Magdalenian', [†] Marine Reservoir Correction of −380 ± 30 years

Sources: Bicho 1994, Rolão et al. 2006, Lubell et al. 2007, Arias, Armendariz, et al. 2009, Bicho 2009, Meiklejohn et al. 2009. All radiocarbon determinations are given as uncalibrated BP and calibrated ranges at 2 sigma as cal BC. Dates have been calibrated using OxCal v3.10 (Bronk Ramsey 1995, 2001).

'crisis', which had seen the abrupt southerly readvance of the Polar Front at c. 11,000 BP. Although attenuated in Cantabrian Spain and, especially, in Portugal vis-à-vis more northerly latitudes of Western Europe, the Dryas III caused a setback to the reforestation of Atlantic Iberia, even though there were no significant repercussions in terms of available animal resources. Red deer and ibex had always been the mainstays of late Upper Palaeolithic subsistence, supplemented by horse and chamois in both Cantabrian Spain and Portugal, and by bison in the former region and by aurochs in the latter. Despite the largely open vegetation of the Tardiglacial, reindeer was only a rare and sporadic presence in northern Spain (with trace quantities in Magdalenian archaeofaunas from Guipúzcoa westward to Asturias) and has never been found in Portugal.

Conventional dates for the Preboreal are c. 10,200–8700 BP, for the Boreal c. 8700–7500 BP, and for the Atlantic (the 'Postglacial Optimum', with highest temperatures and sea levels), c. 7500–5000 BP, although the distinctions between Preboreal and Boreal are far from clear in these oceanic, southerly latitudes. The Preboreal was still relatively cool, but humid, with some decrease in humidity in the Boreal, and major increases in both humidity and temperature in the Atlantic (e.g., Mateus 1985, Dupré 1988).

The reforestation of Portugal, not only with various species of pine but also with various deciduous mesophilous and thermophilous taxa, was well underway in Bölling/Alleröd times (Bicho 1994, Aura et al. 1998 with refs.). Mixed oak woodlands became more important throughout the early Holocene, culminating in the climax Atlantic phase (Mateus and Queiroz 1993). These woodlands were populated by red and roe deer, aurochs and boar, as well as a variety of smaller game. The rising sea levels created large estuaries (especially of the Minho/Miño, Douro/Duero, Tejo/Tagus, Sado, and Mira rivers), teeming with both resident and migratory fish and birds, as well as many species of shellfish. The importance of these estuaries and their extraordinarily abundant, diverse food resources cannot be underestimated – especially, from a forager's perspective – in comparison to the far less rich interior of Portugal, Castile, and Spanish Extremadura.

Under the temperate, humid conditions of Alleröd times in Cantabrian Spain, reforestation was well underway, with the dominant taxa being pine and birch (Straus 1992, Aura et al. 1998 with refs.). The effect of Dryas III was only limited. The Preboreal saw an increase in hazel but, over time, dense, mixed deciduous forests, dominated by both hazel and oaks, came to characterize at least lower elevations of the rugged Cantabrian relief. Although rich in mast (including acorns, hazelnuts, beechnuts, and chestnuts), the forests that developed would have made human movement difficult, especially given the mountainous terrain. Smaller, less gregarious game (e.g., roe deer and boar) also became much more important under these conditions, as bison disappeared and horse became rare. The marine transgression at the end of the Last Glacial and during the early Holocene had a particularly dramatic effect in Vasco-Cantabria in terms of reduction of the useable land surface, due to the narrowness of the strip of land (often itself very hilly or even mountainous) between the shore and the Cordillera – generally no more than 25–50 km under interglacial conditions – with a loss of approximately 6–16 km of formerly exposed continental shelf. Also in contrast to Portugal, few large estuaries were created by the transgression in Cantabrian Spain, although numerous small inlets came into being. In contrast, Holocene western Galicia is known for its many long, broad estuaries, and thus was endowed with many rich habitats and littoral ecotones. The Galician and Vasco-Cantabrian shores and rivers were rich in fish, molluscs, crustaceans, echinoderms, and fowl, in part offsetting the loss of some of the larger game.

The Portuguese Epipalaeolithic (Preboreal/Early Boreal Periods)

The archaeological record of southern Portugal (Estremadura, plus west-coastal Alentejo and Algarve) for the period c. 10,500–8500 BP, variously labelled as 'Terminal Magdalenian' or 'Epipalaeolithic' by N. Bicho (1998: 39), is characterized by industries rich in Dufour or backed bladelets, with microlaminar blanks produced from carinates (keeled 'core-scrapers') or small prismatic cores respectively. Aside from the armatures (including backed points), many of the formal tools (endscrapers, burins, notched and denticulated pieces, etc.) were made on flakes.

The Preboreal period sees a dramatic increase in the number of sites relative to the millennia of the Tardiglacial, and now there is more diversity of locations (both coastal and upland) and presumed site functions. Shell middens with radiocarbon dates of c. 10,000 BP have been found in the vicinity of Sintra-Magoito on the Atlantic littoral of the Lisbon Peninsula, Estremadura – and at the mouth of the Rio Mira estuary – Pedra do Patacho/Eira da Pedra in Alentejo (González Morales and Arnaud 1990, Arnaud 1993). Associated lithics are often large, unretouched flakes, and the malacofauna include limpets (*Patella*) and periwinkles (*Littorina littorea*). There are hints of possible mollusc gathering at the undated terminal Magdalenian site of Vale da Mata near the mouth of the Sizandro River in Estremadura (Zilhão 1995). There are also inland shell middens in Estremaduran caves (Bocas, Papagaio) of this early Preboreal period, clearly indicating human movements between the shore and the near-interior, up to at least 30 km one way (González Morales and Arnaud 1990, Bicho 1993). A major cluster of open-air sites – including significant lithic workshop localities – exists in the flint-rich Rio Maior basin of central Estremadura. This apparent concentration of sites is in part a result of favourable geomorphological conditions of preservation and visibility, and to intensive recent research by a team directed by A. Marks and J. Zilhão (Marks et al. 1994, Zilhão 1995), following on the work of M. Heleno in the 1930s–1940s.

Although these Rio Maior sites (especially the several loci at Cabeço do Porto Marinho) have yielded a wealth of high-quality lithic technological information, they do not have much pre-served material, so what little we know about Epipalaeolithic subsistence comes from the few excavated caves and shell middens, none of which yet have definitive publications. It is apparent that subsistence was highly diversified and had actually since earlier Magdalenian times included a significant aquatic component. Red deer, aurochs, boar, roe deer, and occasionally ibex, chamois, and horse were hunted, supplemented by a wide variety of littoral and estuarine molluscs, as well as (as yet poorly documented) marine and riverine fish (González Morales and Arnaud 1990, Bicho 1993, 1994, Aura et al. 1998). The diverse types of small, lightweight 'armatures' of Dufour and backed bladelets, backed points (presumed projectile tip and barbed elements) imply the existence of the bow and arrow. Plant foods such as acorns, hazelnuts, roots, and berries were no doubt also gathered, but we have no direct evidence for them at this time.

There is as yet no evidence for structures in this period, except for small, circular, stone-lined hearths uncovered during salvage excavations at Magoito (González Morales and Arnaud 1990: 456, Arnaud 1993). Similarly, evidence of 'artistic' expression or ornamentation is lacking, except for ten shell beads in the inland midden of Casal Papagaio Cave (González Morales and Arnaud 1990: 457).

The Late Azilian of Vasco-Cantabria

The Holocene-age Azilian of Vasco-Cantabria is of course much better known than the contem-poraneous cultural traditions of Portugal (or Galicia, where although there are possible Azilian sites [Peña de Xiboi, Peña Grande, Prado do Inferno], none have the diagnostic harpoons or radiocarbon dates). At present there are some fifty-eight known Azilian or Azilian-like sites in north-central Spain (including a few in Galicia, Navarra, Castilla and León), but most of these are undated. Fifteen have radiocarbon dates that place them within the Preboreal time range, and I have argued (Straus 1985) that many of the Azilian deposits that have been assigned to the Alleröd on solely palynological grounds, could reasonably be attributed to the Preboreal. The most recent radiocarbon dates are a group of eight at 9500–9400 BP, with a single (but reasonable) outlier at 9280 ± 230 BP at Cueva Oscura de Anía in Asturias (Straus 1979, 1985,

1991a, 1992, González Morales 1982, 1995, 1996). (A determination of 8700 ± 170 BP on shell from an Azilian level at Urtiaga in Guipúzcoa is now believed by most specialists to be too young.)

The distribution of Azilian sites (including 'late' ones) follows the same pattern as that of the Upper Magdalenian and the total numbers of sites are virtually identical. Azilian levels almost always overlie late Magdalenian ones, and the Azilian technology (lithic and osseous) is a clear development from and simplification of the late Magdalenian technology. Azilian lithic assemblages are usually dominated by backed bladelets and points (including the characteristic curved backed type known as 'Azilian' points, but that in reality can be quite common in late Magdalenian assemblages too) and small flake and 'thumbnail' endscrapers, but few (and generally very simple) burins, perforators or other specialised lithics. Geometric microliths are generally rare or absent, although there are some exceptions that seem to herald the coming of 'true' Mesolithic technologies a few centuries later, for example, at El Piélago and El Valle (Breuil and Obermaier 1912, Fernández Tresguerres 1980, Garcia Guinea 1985, Straus 1992, Aura et al. 1998). The truly distinctive hallmarks of the Azilian of Vasco-Cantabria (and southern France) are the flat-section harpoons. In northern Spain these often have a basal 'buttonhole' perforation, presumably for lanyard attachment, and derived from the more elegant, cylindrical-section Magdalenian harpoons, as demonstrated by the classic 'developmental' sequences of pieces from El Valle, El Otero, and now Los Azules (Breuil and Obermaier 1912, Fernández Tresguerres 1994).

There are Azilian sites near the coast, in the coastal hill ranges and on the very edges of the Cordillera and Picos de Europa. In fact, the upward trend in the location of the highest known settlements, begun in the Lower Magdalenian and even Solutrean, continued in the Azilian, as the montane glaciers retreated and finally disappeared. Some Azilian sites are at quite high elevations, up to or even above 1,000 m a.s.l., for example Antón Koba in Guipúzcoa, Urratxa in Vizcaya, La Calavera, and possibly Abrigo de la Mina in Cantabria and even on the south side of the Cordillera, on the edge of the northern Meseta, from Zatoya in Navarra to Espertín and La Uña in León (e.g., González Morales et al. 2004, Bernaldo de Quirós and Neira 1996, Armendáriz 1997, Muñoz and Berganza 1997, Barandiarán and Cava 1989a). In several better-explored cases, there are Azilian sites along the whole course of individual river valleys from the coast to the mountains, for example, Río Asón in Cantabria (González Morales 1990, Straus and González Morales 1998). The coast includes evidence of intensive exploitation of shellfish and fish as well as of terrestrial game and birds, for example, at La Riera in Asturias, while inland there is evidence of specialized ibex-hunting locations, for example, at Rascaño in Cantabria, much as in the Magdalenian (Straus 1992). It is easy to imagine settlement systems that involved both logistical and residential mobility to exploit all the habitats and resources of particular drainage basins. Although seasonality data are still few, there is evidence of both specialized warm-season and multiseason uses of different upland sites, for example, Ekain and Abauntz versus Rascaño, and evidence for multiseason use of major base camps in the coastal zone, for example, La Riera, as had been the case in the Magdalenian. Certain sites seem to have been intensively occupied during the Azilian, for example, Los Azules in Asturias, El Piélago and El Valle in Cantabria, and Ekain in Guipúzcoa, with multiple levels, relatively rich inventories of artefacts, some investment in structured hearths and pits, and, in the case of Los Azules, an intentional human burial with ochre staining, a stone slab covering and apparent grave offerings including a concentration of otherwise unusual *Modiolus* shells (Fernández Tresguerres 1980, 2004). Yet even Los Azules is a very small cave, and most Azilian occupations seem to have been on a smaller scale than many Magdalenian ones even when using the same cave – an observation that squares with what we know of the Azilian in the French Pyrenees – a very few major sites, notably le Mas d'Azil, La Tourasse, Troubat, and many small, ephemeral camps, often capping rich, spatially extensive Magdalenian occupation layer, as at Isturitz, Duruthy, Dufaure, and several other famous sites. It remains to be seen how any of this might translate into changes in actual human population numbers between the Tardiglacial and initial Holocene.

As noted earlier, Azilian subsistence in Vasco-Cantabrian Spain was clearly a continuation of the intensified strategies that had been developing in the antecedent Magdalenian (and indeed Solutrean) periods, with ever greater exploitation of marine, estuarine, and riverine resources – ocean, anadromous and fluvial fish, molluscs, notably limpets and periwinkles, crustaceans echinoderms, and waterfowl – as well as red and roe deer, boar, chamois, ibex, and limited quantities of horse and aurochs, plus other birds (Straus and Clark 1986, Straus 1992, Altuna 1995). The broad-spectrum diversification in subsistence that characterized the Magdalenian probably increased even further to include ever more plant foods in the Preboreal, although direct or even indirect archaeological proof of this is so far absent. Among other potential vegetal foods, acorns, and hazelnuts would have been abundant. The presence of fire-cracked rock, as in late Upper Palaeolithic contexts, could indicate roasting of a variety of foods, in this case including vegetal ones, although potential grinding/pounding stones are not particularly more abundant than before.

Azilian 'art' and ornamentation is very scarce, and some of it actually seems to date to the early (Dryas III) range of this 'transitional' culture. There are virtually identical flat-section harpoons with geometric engraved decorations from early Azilian levels at Los Azules, Cueva Oscura de Aria, and La Lluera, all in central Asturias (Fernández Tresguerres 1994, Adan et al. 1999). Also suggesting some continuity from the Magdalenian before its artistic tradition disappeared, there are seven bone pendants from both terminal Magdalenian and early Azilian contexts that have intricate engraved geometric designs consisting of fine parallel lines adorned with perpendicular tick marks (González Sainz 1989: 255–6). Finally, although far fewer than in France (Pluciennik this volume), some Cantabrian Azilian sites have yielded one or more non-representational painted cobbles, notably at Los Azules with twenty-nine such cobbles, nineteen of which were found in the context of the burial, which dates to 9500 BP (Fernández Tresguerres 1980). Engraved cobbles with clear Azilian provenience are absent and there are very few simply engraved bone objects besides those noted earlier. There are simply no examples of representational portable art in the Azilian and none of the cave art of the Vasco-Cantabrian region can be attributed to this period either. The *youngest* credible AMS-dated cave drawings are an ibex and horse in Las Monedas (Cantabria) both at c. 12,000 BP, that is, Upper Magdalenian (Moure et al. 1996). Ornaments (in addition to the few pendants mentioned earlier) are far rarer in Azilian than in Magdalenian contexts, and include some perforated red deer canines and shells, particularly in the unusual Los Azules site (Fernández Tresguerres 1980, 2004).

Boreal-Age Portugal

Relatively little is known about the specific period between 8700 and 7500 BP in Portugal, but facts are accumulating fast (González Morales and Arnaud 1990, Bicho 1994). The known sites are mainly situated along the coast of Estremadura, Alentejo and Algarve: Sâo Juliâo above Sintra (twelve dates on a long-forming shell midden between 8800 and 7500 BP), Ponta da Vigia near Torres Vedras (8730 BP), Curral Velho between Sintra and Torres Vedras (two dates of c. 8000 BP), Palheiroẽs do Alegra near Milfontes (dates of 8800 and 8400 BP), Montes de Baixo near Aljezur (corrected shell dates of 7550 and 7230 BP on two levels bracketing the Boreal-Atlantic boundary) and Castelejo, 15 km north of Cape St.Vincent (three dates between 8200 and 7500 BP). Extreme southwestern Portugal, near Cape Saint Vincent, has also recently revealed a series of sites whose occupations span the period between the early Mesolithic and the early Neolithic. The Boreal phase is well represented. The earliest small shell middens are at Rocha das Gaviotas and Barranco das Quebradas (the latter with multiple loci along a stream valley above the imposing cliffs of the Atlantic shore). These are dated between 8640 ± 75 BP and 7980 ± 85 BP (7735–6711 cal BC) by nine assays on mollusc shells, corrected for the reservoir effect (Bicho 2009, Valente and Carvalho 2009). The molluscan faunas are very diverse, but the deposits are suggestive of short-lived and repeated human occupations. Almost all the lithic artefacts are simple pieces made on local raw materials, with few formal geometrics. Projectile elements may have been used elsewhere, even if manufactured in this area. Hearths with rock fill are found in several of the sites, with evidence of shellfish cooking.

An emergency survey of the vast interior area of the Guadiana River valley in Alentejo (south-central Portugal) up to the Spanish border yielded evidence of early Mesolithic human occupation. One of the most intensively studied sites is Barca do Xerez de Baixo, with large numbers of refits (Araújo and Almeida 2007, 2008, Araújo et al. 2009). The five loci of this open-air site are dated (by five assays) between 8729 ± 36 and 8150 ± 40 BP (7936–7076 cal BC) and are characterized by numerous hearths with fire-cracked rocks and burnt lithic artefacts and faunal remains. Most of the artefacts are on local quartz and quartzite; these include many flake cores, some of which may also have been choppers, hammers, core-scrapers and other heavy-duty tools. Bladelets and formal tools are few, and retouched microliths are lacking. The site is interpreted as a butchering camp, where simple tools were locally produced, primarily to process aurochs, horse, and red deer carcasses for meat and hides. The bones are heavily fragmented. Woodworking may also have been carried out. This site bears similarities to the coastal Alentejo site of Palheiroes do Alegra in terms of age and lithic assemblages (see below). In the near interior of Estremadura there are only a couple of dated sites in the Rio Maior area: Areeiro, with dates ranging between 8800 and 8400 BP for different loci, and Fonte Pinheiro at 8450 BP.

The 'carinated' technology for the production of bladelets (often converted into Dufour nibbled pieces) continued for a brief time at the beginning of this period in the flint-rich Rio Maior basin, but other, new technologies begin to appear in the record elsewhere. At Ponte da Vigia (Zilhão et al. 1987) and other sites, for example, Escravalheira (Carvalho et al. 1989) in the sand dunes of the coast near Torres Vedras, there are flake-rich assemblages with limited numbers of bladelets (including a few backed or pointed ones) and small tools such as thumbnail endscrapers, perforators, notches and denticulates, but no geometrics certainly associated with them. There are also some macrolithic core-tools (choppers). Whether the association of a few geometric microliths from surface collections with excavated materials found alongside hearths at Ponte da Vigia is genuine is an open question, given the dune blowout nature of the site; there could be a palimpsest problem at this and other open-air coastal sites in central and southern Portugal.

Macrolithic industries are well-known at coastal sites in Alentejo and western Algarve, notably the so-called Mirian culture, with cobble 'axes' or 'hoes', sometimes apparently associated with 'Asturian-like' picks (Penalva and Raposo 1987), as in the vicinity of Milfontes at the Rio Mira estuary, where we have found them ourselves. Choppers and large flakes are also common at some of these sites, few of which have been professionally excavated. A recent revision of the grab bag of lithic assemblages lumped within the so-called Languedocian culture of H. Breuil and G. Zbyszewski (characterized by macroliths such as choppers and picks, plus abundant flakes and flake tools such as notches), now places many of these Portuguese assemblages in the early Postglacial period (Raposo and Silva 1984). One interesting case that has been carefully studied is Palheiroẽs do Alegra, which, unfortunately, is also a coastal dune blowout. The site, a major knapping workshop locality, has yielded *both* characteristic Mirian macroliths made on greywacke *and* flint bladelets of leptolithic 'tradition' in apparent association with radiocarbon-dated hearths (Penalva and Raposo 1985, Raposo et al. 1989, González Morales and Arnaud 1990, Arnaud 1993). Although the function of the Mirian macroliths, which absolutely dominate the lithic inventories of certain sites, for example, Vale da Telha at Aljezur, Algarve (Penalva and Raposo 1987), is unknown, an hypothesis relating them to the exploitation of *both* shellfish *and* vegetal foods and wood would seem reasonable.

Apart from the growing dependence on highly diverse aquatic resources attested to by shell middens and by the littoral and estuarine locations of many sites, we have few data on subsistence for the Portuguese early (Boreal-age) Mesolithic. Certainly the forests were rich in mast, which probably supplemented wild game dominated by red and roe deer, aurochs and boar, together with smaller animals such as lagomorphs. We lack evidence on structures (other than simple hearths), art, ornamentation, or burials for this period.

The issue of northern Portugal and Galicia should be raised at this time, although there are no radiometric dates or other chronological indicators for the Ancorian 'culture' of the Minho region or the so-called Galician Asturian or Camposanquian. The most extensive reviews of this material (at least to my knowledge) are still those of G. A. Clark (1976, 1983, 2004) and J. Maury (1977). The majority of these sites are located on terraces of the lower Minho (Miño in Spanish), as well as along the open northern Portuguese littoral, with a separate concentration around the mouth of the Douro at Oporto. It seems probable that the macrolithic collections, including many 'Asturian-like' cobble picks, choppers, and handaxes, may be the product of mixtures (in some cases mechanical) of Lower and Middle Palaeolithic, and Mesolithic assemblages at open-air coastal and riverine terrace sites. As Clark (1983: 48) puts it: 'the morphological similarity between the Cantabrian picks and the unifacial implement of the Luso-Galician sites is fortuitous.' Any efforts to establish chronological or 'phylogenetic' relationships between the latter and the Cantabrian Asturian are not supported by present evidence. Cobbles have been used as expedient tool-making materials in all periods – including the Roman era – so without any datable materials, these surface finds are virtually impossible to place in secure chronological context, although Maury (1977) believes that some of these artefacts are of Postglacial age. Clark's opinion has received support recently from the Galician archaeologist, J. M. Vázquez Varela (2004). Citing a doctoral dissertation by J. Meireles, Vázquez states that the worked cobble collections of the northern Portuguese coast pertain to a variety of Acheulean, Mousterian, Upper Palaeolithic, Mesolithic, and even recent periods. Without excavations and finds in stratigraphic context, it is difficult to work out a more precise sequence or to categorise artefacts really typical of specific periods. Yet it is likely that there is a Mesolithic component here, as well as in coastal Galicia. It is nonetheless also clear that the northern Portuguese/western Galician coast is rich in Acheulean materials that sometimes do mimic (and are sometimes mixed with) macrolithic Mesolithic ones, especially in beach contexts.

According to Vázquez Varela (2004), two recently excavated sites on the north coast of Galicia illustrate some of the problems of distinguishing Mesolithic from *more recent* materials. At Fiales a pick, a cleaver and various other worked cobbles, flakes, and flake tools were found in a sedimentary context that was, by geological and palynological extrapolation, attributed to the late Tardiglacial/initial Preboreal. But recent revision has cast serious doubts on this dating, throwing the age of the site (and of 'Asturian' picks in the region in general) into doubt. Another site, O Reiro, on the shore near the city of La Coruña, has yielded marine and terrestrial faunal remains and a scanty lithic assemblage, including a unifacially worked cobble, a backed blade and a few other tools, plus some blades, flakes, and cores – none really diagnostic. The site produced a radiocarbon

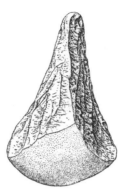

Figure 12.3. Asturian pick from La Riera (after Vega del Sella 1930: fig. 6). Approximate scale 1:2.

date of 6590 ± 70 BP on organic-rich sediments. But it also has cereal pollen and some sherds of poor quality, undecorated pottery. Either this is the result of disturbance and mixing, or the site is in reality a very early Neolithic location. There are simply no unambiguous, radiometrically dated Mesolithic sites in the region. And Vázquez Varela stresses that cobble picks and other expedient tools can be found in sites of virtually any pre- or proto-historic period in Galicia. Shell middens, too, although common, are not at all necessarily of Mesolithic age; some are as recent as the Iron Age or Roman period. Many true Mesolithic sites, he argues, may actually have been inundated in some coastal areas because of Holocene sea-level rise.

Boreal-Age Northern Spain: The 'Asturian' and Other Mesolithic Traditions

As the classic Azilian ends in Vasco-Cantabrian Spain late in the Preboreal, it seems to be replaced by a variety of perhaps more localized technological traditions, all of which represent breaks with the Upper Palaeolithic. The best-studied, best-characterised of these 'cultures' is the Asturian, first discovered and defined by the Conde de la Vega del Sella in the first two decades of the twentieth century and exhaustively analysed by G. A. Clark (e.g., 1976, 1983, 1989, 2004) and M. González Morales (e.g., 1982, 1989, 1995, Fano and González Morales 2004), from whom most of the information here is derived. Now abundantly dated by radiocarbon, the Asturian phenomenon is known to have spanned the period from about 9200/9300 to about 6500 BP, but there are later shell middens, some with apparently associated ceramics as recent as c. 5700 BP. Thus, the Asturian covers the late Preboreal, all of the Boreal and the early Atlantic.

The Asturian is principally characterised by sites that are mostly coastal, the Boreal coastline essentially being the same as the present one, with a slight modification during the Flandrian transgression of the Atlantic phase, and shell middens (*concheros*) in cave mouths, with very few artefacts, the most distinctive of which is the unifacially worked cobble pick (Figure 12.3). The main molluscan taxa are limpets (mainly *Patella vulgata* and *P. intermedia*) and topshells (*Monodonta lineata*, also known as *Trochocochlea crassa*), but they are accompanied by a wide variety of other species, as well crabs, sea urchins, and fish (especially *marine* taxa). The artefacts, besides the picks and some other heavy-duty cobble implements (choppers, chopping tools), include small numbers of flake tools – endscrapers and sidescrapers, notches, denticulates, burins, perforators – and a very few backed bladelets (some of whose provenience is controversial). The heavy-duty tools are mostly made of quartzite, whereas the light-duty ones are mainly on flint. There are at least eighty known (certain and likely) Asturian sites, mostly located in eastern Asturias and western Cantabria, with a few outliers toward both the West and East (Straus and Clark 1986). Almost all Asturian shell middens are within about 3 km of the present shore, the average distance being 1.4 km (Clark 2004, see also Fano 1998), and the maximum 8 km, at Meré on the Río Bedón.

In addition to the 'crude-looking' lithic industry, which has at times led the Asturian to be misdiagnosed as a Lower Palaeolithic tradition, as in the case of so many nonmicrolithic Portuguese Mesolithic industries, there are only a few osseous implements: some bone awls or 'points', a couple of perforated antlers (both of problematic provenience) and several bipointed bone pieces that are reasonably classified as fish gorges. But there are no harpoons; nor are there ornaments or works of portable art. In that respect, the 'Asturian' certainly does project an image of 'cultural impoverishment', coming as it does from an area extraordinarily rich in Upper Palaeolithic mobile and rupestral art and in some cases from the same sites that have this upper Palaeolithic material. Although there are a few other human remains associated with the Asturian, there is only one known intentional burial, and that unfortunately is from a site that was poorly excavated early in the twentieth century. This is the Abrigo del Molino de Gasparín (Asturias), where a possible older adult female was interred within a massive layer of shells, surrounded by a line of stones and closely associated with three typical picks, the whole of which was covered by a mound of stone and dirt capped by a hearth (Clark 1976, Newell et al. 1979, González Morales 1982). We know of no other Asturian structures or even 'living floors', with the notable exception of such a surface at the base of the *conchero* in Mazaculos Cave (Asturias), where the cave seems to have been lived in before being converted into a shell dump. The early Asturian deposit has substantial numbers of red deer remains, including many young animals – as is the case in other sites such as La Riera, which may be evidence of resource stress and subsistence intensification. There are smaller numbers of roe deer, boar, aurochs, and chamois. The later Asturian faunal assemblage is smaller but also dominated by red deer, with traces of roe deer and boar. Human use of Mazaculos Cave became more sporadic in the later Asturian, but the ungulate fauna suggests intensive warm-season hunting in the earlier period, whereas oxygen isotope analysis of shellfish indicates cold-season occupation, suggesting a degree of permanency to human presence along the coast in the Preboreal (Marín and González Morales 2009).

Mazaculos has yielded human mandibles from disturbed contexts. A skeleton (probably buried) at the entrance of Tito Bustillo Cave near the mouth of the Sella River (also in eastern Asturias) has recently been radiocarbon-dated to 8470 ± 50 BP (7620–7470 cal BC) (Beta-197042). There were no grave goods except for some red ochre (Arias, Armendariz, et al. 2009). Also near the shore of eastern Asturias is the small, recently rescue-excavated cave of Poza l'Egua, which produced another isolated mandible dated to 8550 ± 80 BP (7470–7260 cal BC) (TO-10222). Stable isotope analyses indicate that the individual had a diet that was roughly half marine and half terrestrial ($\delta^{13}C = -16.724‰$, $\delta^{15}N = 12.180‰$) (Arias 2005–06, Arias, Fernández-Tresguerres, et al. 2007). The associated faunal remains included red deer with traces of roe deer, boar, chamois, and ibex, as well as fish and molluscs (mainly *Patella*).

In addition to the vast quantities of limpets and topshells, the latter replacing the colder water adapted periwinkles of the Upper Palaeolithic, plus urchins, crabs, and fish, subsistence consisted of red and roe deer, aurochs, and boar, all generally in fairly small quantities. Plant foods were undoubtedly important and there are some apparent grinding/pounding stones in Asturian contexts, but direct evidence of nuts is thus far absent. This should change with the current introduction of flotation methods. Pollen and macrobotanical evidence, the latter from Mazaculos and La Llana concheros, is indicative of the presence of fruit- and nut-bearing trees, notably oak but also hazel, beech, and chestnut. Although the Asturian picks could possibly have been used to grub for vegetal foods (Straus 1979), their generally coastal distribution and almost exclusive association with *concheros* does tend to suggest that their (main or sole?) function was in shellfish gathering – as limpet hammers – as Vega del Sella originally thought (González Morales 1982, Fano and González Morales 2004).

In parallel with the classic Asturian, there are coastal shell midden sites in eastern Cantabria, notably in El Perro Cave level 1.3, at 9260 ± 110 BP, with neither characteristic Asturian nor Azilian artefacts, but overlying a sequence of two Azilian levels and one late Magdalenian (González Morales 1995) and Vizcaya (Santimamiñe, with an undated, oyster-rich *conchero* containing geometric microliths, but no true Asturian picks, and overlying an Azilian deposit [Altuna 1972]).

I. Gutierrez Zugasti (2009) has recently surveyed the utilization of molluscan resources in the terminal Pleistocene and early Holocene in the Cantabrian region. This supports the idea of intensified subsistence, including diversification and increased exploitation of limpets to the point of local overexploitation, originally derived from analyses of the late Upper Paleolithic, Azilian, and Asturian record in La Riera Cave (Ortea 1986, Straus and Clark 1986). A detailed analysis of the macro-mammalian faunal records from the small La Fragua Cave at the mouth of the Asón River in eastern Cantabria shows that the Azilian and Mesolithic assemblages are virtually identical (Marín 2004). Red deer dominate, followed by roe deer, ibex, and aurochs. The Mesolithic level contains boar, which is absent in the Azilian. Juvenile individuals are well represented, as is often the case in early Holocene faunas. Overall, the picture of early Holocene human subsistence, as postulated in the La Riera monograph, is one of great diversification under the possible stress of relatively high population packing in this narrow coastal strip between the Cantabrian Sea and Cordillera.

A central issue in debate over the Asturian during the last two decades has been the question as to what may have been going on during all or parts of this time in the interior areas of the Asturo-Cantabrian region during the formation of the *concheros*. The debate was originally stimulated by a hypothesis put forth by G. N. Bailey (1973) in 1971, by which shellfish would have only been seasonal and secondary resources. Interdisciplinary research at La Riera Cave during the second half of the 1970s, published in final form by Straus and Clark (1986), was in part designed to help test this and other hypotheses concerning the nature of site functions in eastern Asturias. An alternate hypothesis argued for full-time human residence of the coastal zone (Clark 1983). The idea was that molluscs could have been used as tiding-over resources during seasonal periods of subsistence stress (e.g., late winter/early spring). The test involved oxygen isotope analyses of shells, conducted by M. Deith and N. J. Shackleton (Deith 1983b, Shackleton and Deith 1986), using my modern control samples picked on the shore closest to La Riera and Asturian-age limpets and topshells not only from La Riera, but also from the nearby sites of Penicial and Mazaculos. The first results concluded that Asturian mollusc-gathering did not take place in summer, but this did not preclude the possibility that people may have stayed near the coast subsisting on other foods during the warm season as well as during the rest of the year, when shells were taken. Later, oxygen isotope analyses of more shells from other Asturian sites in eastern Asturias, including La Llana, Cordoveganes and El Toralete, produced similar results, that is, no evidence of summer mollusc-gathering (Fano and González Morales 2004). The small sample of mammals from the living surface at the base of the Mazaculos shell heap included young individuals killed in late spring or summer, whereas the acorns, hazelnuts, and other nuts presumably exploited would have been ripe in the autumn (Fano and González Morales 2004). These facts and suppositions have been used by González Morales to argue for year-round human residence near the coast, and new seasonality data recovered from limpet shells point to the same conclusion (Bailey and Craighead 2003).

In a now infamous article (Straus 1979), I suggested that the concheros, far from representing 'full-service' residential sites, may have been dumps in caves often no longer actually habitable, as the middens often actually ended up reaching – and finally becoming cemented to – the cave-mouth ceilings. I argued that people might have been elsewhere doing other kinds of subsistence activities when they were not camped in front of the conchero caves. I went so far as to suggest a partial temporal overlap between the late Azilian and early Asturian, with the two cultural manifestations being functionally complementary, that is, respectively, the hunting and shellfish-gathering components of a wider regional adaptive system. In short, I had difficulty seeing the rather impoverished *concheros* as representing the sum total of the adaptations of at least late Preboreal people in this region. Subsequently, as more – and more accurate and precise – radiocarbon dates were obtained for Azilian and Asturian deposits, it became clear that there was little or no real chronological overlap between the two cultural phenomena (González Morales 1995, 1996, Fano and González Morales 2004). This development led some to argue that the interior may have been abandoned, perhaps due to the density of forestation and consequent difficulty of movement. Recent archaeological discoveries are, however, beginning at least partially to challenge this view (see Straus and González Morales 2003).

First of all, it is necessary to discuss the non-Asturian record from the Basque Country and eastern Cantabria. The Basque Azilian includes several sites in the mountains, as well as others near the coast. Some assemblages, for example, Zatoya in upland Navarra, are referred to as 'non-geometric Epipalaeolithic', as they fall within the Azilian time range, but lack the typical 'fossil director' artefacts (harpoons, decorated pebbles, curved backed points); there are even open-air sites of Preboreal age on the south side of the Cantabrian Cordillera in Alava, for example, Berniollo (Berganza 1990). Both the Azilian *per se* and the nongeometric Epipalaeolithic technological traditions are characterised by many backed bladelets and backed points (some Sauveterrian-like, as at Abauntz also in upland Navarra or the upper level of Ekain in Guipúzcoa). They change unevenly into geometric Mesolithic industries in the Boreal period. Such sites are found in the interior south of the Cordillera in Alava (Kukuma, Fuente Hoz, Socuevas, Montico de Charratu) and Navarra (Zatoya), as well as in the northern Basque Country, for example, Santimamiñe (Baldeón and Berganza 1997, Barandiarán and Cava 1989b). But not all sites of Boreal age have geometric microliths; at Kanpanoste Goikoa in southern Alava the basal cultural level dated to 7700 BP has a heavily specialized assemblage dominated by denticulates, notches, and endscrapers, but no geometric microliths (Alday 1998). These appear only in a later – mid-Atlantic age – layer. The point is, however, that the Spanish Basque Country – from the upper Ebro Basin south of the Cordillera to the shore of the Bay of Biscay – seems to have been fairly broadly occupied by foraging groups throughout the Preboreal and Boreal. The environmental conditions of the Postglacial seem not to have posed insurmountable problems for human settlement even in the upland interior. The *apparent* lack of sites in the interior of Cantabria and Asturias during the Boreal, apart from the recently excavated site of Peña Oviedo 'Cabin 2', at approximately 1,000 m a.s.l. in the Picos de Europa, with a radiocarbon date of c. 8600 BP (González Morales et al. 2004) has yet to be explained (if it is real), in contrast to the Preboreal, when there are many Azilian sites in the interior alongside coastal sites with sometimes abundant shellfish. This is perplexing, especially because sites reappeared in the high, montane interior of Asturias and Cantabria during the Atlantic period, and *continued* to be present in the interior uplands of the Basque Country in that period, although they never were absent during the Boreal.

The Basque Country Boreal-age faunal record is limited, but interesting. Littoral sites are less well known than in Asturias and Cantabria, but there are shell middens in Santimamiñe and Lumentxa (Vizcaya) and near Biarritz in the coastal French Basque province of Labourd. Recently, the skeleton of an adult male has been found buried within an aceramic shell midden in a rockshelter ('J3') on the shore of Jaizkibel mountain between San Sebastian and the French border (Iriarte et al. 2005). Charcoal from immediately below the skeleton was dated to 8190 ± 100 BP, while bone from the burial yielded a date of 8300 ± 50 BP. There were apparently no associated grave goods. Stable isotope analyses of the J3 skeleton indicate a diet that contained both marine and terrestrial components ($\delta^{13}C = -16.68‰$, $\delta^{15}N = 11.48‰$) (Arias 2005–06). Overlying deposits did contain ceramics. As for well-studied ungulate faunas, the interior Alavés site of Kukuma, unfortunately with unclear dating, has a small assemblage associated with boar, red deer, aurochs, chamois, and, especially, ibex, which is not surprising given the cave's location on the steep, rocky slopes of the Sierra de Alzania (Mariezkurrena 1997). In the securely dated Level Ib of Zatoya at 900 m a.s.l. on the southern edge of the Pyrenees in Navarra (two determinations of c. 8300 BP), a geometric microlithic industry with backed bladelets and backed points (Barandiarán and Cava 1989a), is associated with a mammalian faunal assemblage dominated by boar and red deer, together with small numbers of remains of ibex, roe deer, and chamois, and traces of aurochs and horse (Mariezkurrena and Altuna 1989). Six animals were killed in the warm season and one possibly in mid-autumn. These cases add to the evidence from the (earlier excavated) site of Marizulo in steep hills above San Sebastián. Level III at this site, with a small, rather banal lithic assemblage, is thought to date perhaps to the Boreal (Cava 1978). The small mammalian faunal assemblage is absolutely dominated by red deer, but also includes some roe deer, boar, and ibex (Altuna 1990). The undated Mesolithic levels of Arenaza, in low hills above Bilbao, are similarly dominated by red deer, but these far more abundant assemblages have more ungulate taxa, including traces of chamois, horse, and aurochs, as well as the more common roe deer, boar, and ibex (Altuna 1990). All in all, it is clear that Mesolithic 'Basques' were hunting game from woodland areas and rocky slopes. And they were doing it *both* near the coast *and* in the high, mountainous interior.

The Mesolithic 'Highwater' in Portugal

The early Atlantic period, corresponding to the Flandrian marine transgression, saw the zenith and then downfall of Mesolithic lifeways in Portugal, where (to date) almost all the known sites are from the coastal/estuarine zone, especially the famous shell middens of the Muge and Sado rivers, as well as several recently excavated sites along the littoral of Alentejo. In this period, Mediterranean woodlands dominated by holm, cork, and other oaks together with alder, under a subhumid, very warm climate, spread throughout the country, as ocean water pushed up into the lower courses of all the rivers (notably the Tejo, Sado, and Mira). Sites not on the coast or along estuaries are virtually unknown. The beginning of the Atlantic phase was punctuated by the 8200 cal BP cold event, which may have seen significant changes in oceanic conditions. These in turn may have caused a decline in open coastal resources but may have favoured deep estuarine habitats such as those of the Muge (Tagus) and Sado rivers as areas for concentrated human settlement (N. Bicho, pers. comm. 2009).

An exception to the 'rule' of estuarine settings is Forno da Talha, near a flint source in the Rio Maior area of Estremadura, possibly seasonally used to obtain lithic raw materials and to hunt mammals, mainly red deer, plus some aurochs, boar, roe deer, rabbit and horse (Rowley-Conwy 1993) by people who otherwise were based at Tagus midden sites as much as 35 km distant. Forno da Telha, radiocarbon dated by two corrected shell determinations to 7000 BP, contains marine molluscs and spurred 'Muge/Cocina' type microlithic triangles, all of which point to connections with the coastal Mesolithic (Araújo 1993).

The classic studies of the Muge shell middens, located on a tributary of the huge Tagus estuary (Figure 12.2) first excavated in the mid- to late nineteenth century, were published by J. Roche during the 1960s and synthesized by him in 1972 (Roche 1972a). Roche, together with O. da Veiga Ferreira, excavated at Moita do Sebastião, Cabeço da Amoreira, and Cabeço da Arruda. Many other such sites have been recorded along the Muge and the nearby Magos stream, both of which during the early Atlantic phase had major estuarine marshes. There have been significant recent studies of materials from these sites: by an interdisciplinary Canadian research team led by D. Lubell, M. Jackes, and C. Meiklejohn (e.g., Lubell and Jackes 1988, Lubell et al. 1986, 1989, 1994) and by Belgian zooarcheologist A. Lentacker (1986, 1994). The Sado shell middens, originally dug in the 1950s and 1960s, have been recently restudied and published in preliminary form (e.g., Arnaud 1989,1993) and two (Poças de Sao Bento and Amoreiras) have been re-excavated by a Swedish-Portuguese team directed by L. Larsson and J. Arnaud and by Arnaud, respectively. Further south, in Alentejo a coastal Mesolithic site (Vidigal) of similar age was tested by Straus (Straus et al. 1990); nearby, also on the Alentejo coast both north and south of the Rio Mira estuary, the Canadian team excavated two sites (Samouqueira and Medo Tojeiro) with Mesolithic components in the same early-mid Atlantic time range (Lubell et al. 1989). Upstream by some 20 km, along the Rio Mira valley (but near estuarine waters at the time of occupation in the Atlantic phase) Arnaud and Lubell have excavated another such site, at Fiais. The ensemble of Atlantic-age shell middens from the Muge-Magos (Tagus estuary) and Sado and Alentejo coast/Mira Valley clusters now boasts a total of some two dozen radiocarbon dates, several of which are AMS determinations (see lists in Zilhão 2004, Vierra 2004, Lubell et al. 1988). They range from 7400–6000 BP, with an outlier of 5500 BP in the upper layer of the shell midden of Cabeço do Pez along the Sado. Early in this time range there was also a pair of possible Mesolithic sites along the Mondego estuary near Figueira da Foz (Zilhão 1998). In the period between 6800 and 6500–6000 BP, there was apparently overlap with the earliest Neolithic occupations of Portugal, which tended to be in the interior as well as around Figueira da Foz and in the extreme southwest corner of Europe at Sagres, away from the extraordinarily productive estuaries of the Tagus, Sado and Mira (Zilhão 1993, 1998, 2004).

The flint industries associated with the *concheiro* sites are characterized by geometric microliths: elongated, spurred Muge/Cocina type triangles dominate at some sites or levels, trapezes at others, and circle segments at still others. All these are made by the microburin technique, so other (unfinished) 'microburins' are also frequent. The relative frequencies of the different microlith forms are seen as changing through time throughout the early Atlantic by some authors. In a recent study by B. Vierra (1995), the shift from microlaminar to geometric microlith-based industries is seen as being related to the development of more diversified subsistence economies in the late Mesolithic of Portugal (as elsewhere in Europe). The highly standardized geometric microliths are argued to be highly efficient and capable of being used interchangeably for a variety of purposes in composite implements and weapons. Other flint tools in the *concheiros* are rare, except denticulates and/or notches and some backed bladelets. Endscrapers, truncated pieces and especially burins are generally few. However, there are also macrolithic implements made of quartzite or greywacke (depending on the region): unretouched flakes, choppers, minimally retouched cobbles, hammer stones and grinding stones, plus cores. Quartz crystal was also deliberately flaked, sometimes for the production of bladelets. The bone industries consist of antler mattocks or axes, handles, and bone and antler awls. Ornaments consist of common perforated shells of a variety of species, perforated bones, teeth, and stones – some of which were found associated with burials.

All these sites are defined by vast quantities of marine and estuarine mollusc shells, either disposed as actual thick heaps, for example, the Muge *concheiros*, or as extensive sheets of shell, for example,

Vidigal and Fiais. The particular species that dominate in the malacofauna vary from site to site, no doubt depending on local aquatic habitats – estuarine versus open littoral, type of bottom such as sand, rock, or mud, and variability in salinity, wave action, and nutrients – with some overwhelmingly dominated by oysters, others by cockles, still others by limpets. Mussels, whelks, furrow shells, and razor clams are also found. But, as has been demonstrated by Lentacker (1986, 1994), Rowley-Conwy (as reported by Lubell and Jackes 1988), and by Arnaud (1989) and LeGall et al. (1994), there was much more to the highly rich and diversified subsistence of coastal and estuarine Portuguese Mesolithic people than molluscs. Especially when fine screening and complete recovery techniques are used, the sites yield not only large, medium, and small mammal remains (boar, red and roe deer, aurochs, horse, otter, rabbit, hare, various carnivores including dog), but also a plethora of migratory and resident birds, crustaceans, estuarine, anadromous, and ocean fish, some seasonally and others perennially available near the sites, depending on local circumstances. The presence of some deep-sea molluscs may suggest the existence of boats, but most of the fish found in the archaeological deposits can be taken from the shore, and nets and/or weirs must have been present. Acorns and other available edible vegetal products such as pine and pistachio nuts, tubers, roots, and berries also may have been major contributors to the overall diet, at least seasonally. And the nuts may have been stored, as suggested by the presence of pits in some of the sites. Recent trace element and stable isotope analyses of human remains from the Muge and Sado Atlantic-age sites by C. Umbelino and colleagues (2007) indicate a great diversity of individual diets but always include a mix of marine and terrestrial animal foods and plants. The marine contribution ranged between 25 and 70%. There are interesting differences between the Muge and Sado humans, with the latter in general having an even more diversified diet that included more plant foods.

Based on a wide variety of data from marine, terrestrial, and avian species, Lentacker has concluded that the vast Muge sites were used at all seasons of the year, although that does not *necessarily* mean permanent, sedentary occupation. For one thing, it is likely that with such intense shellfish collection, local beaches or rocks would become exhausted and would have to be allowed to be replenished from time to time, requiring human movement at least up and down broader stretches of shore. In contrast, at Vidigal the more limited seasonality indicators (from bream, sharks, and rays that approach the shore only during the warm season, as well as from red deer dentition) all point to spring–summer use of this open-coastal location adjacent to a creek that would have been invaded by seawater at the time (LeGall et al. 1994). Fiais, by contrast, in the near interior of the Mira, has cold and warm season indicators (Lubell and Jackes 1988). However, whether people from Fiais would, nonetheless, have made trips to the nearby coast of the Mira estuary in summer to sites like Vidigal (as seems likely) is unproven. There are some indications that among the Sado Valley sites, Arapouco (closest of these sites to the sea) was used preferentially during the warm season and Cabeço do Pez (furthest inland) had cold season occupations (Arnaud 1989). But overall, residential movement may have been restricted to the Sado valley itself – not a very large area. Recent isotopic analyses of human remains have shown that the overall Mesolithic diet at two Muge sites and Samouqueira on the Alentejo coast was indeed a mixture of marine and terrestrial foods, although there was some individual variation dependent on local food availability and on where each of these individuals spent most of their lives (Lubell et al. 1994).

The Muge and Sado sites are famous for their human burials; in fact, the Portuguese Mesolithic cemetery collections are among the largest in Europe. Not counting the numerous nineteenth- and early-twentieth-century discoveries, well over one hundred (Cardoso and Rolão 2003, Cunha and Cardoso 2003), J. Roche's excavations at Moita do Sebastião, Amoreira, and Arruda yielded thirty-four, seventeen, and thirteen burials, respectively – some with multiple skeletons. Just Moita alone produced up to forty-four individuals in Roche's work (Newell et al. 1979). Roche (1972a,

1972b) shows that these were not randomly placed, but carried out in the context of a distinctive funerary ritual within the precincts of definite burial grounds in the middens. The individuals often were accompanied by grave goods of perforated shells, and less certainly of utilitarian tools and cobbles, found in intimate association with the skeleton, which is generally tightly flexed. Some of the same observations pertain to the Sado cemeteries, where at least five of the middens have yielded from six to twenty-seven burials (Arnaud 1989). Men, women, and children are found in these cemeteries. The Muge burials in various collections may total about three hundred individuals (Cunha and Cardoso 2003). Other sites further south in Portugal, for example, Samouqueira and Fiais, have yielded just one or a few burials.

Roche's excavations at Moita do Sebastião revealed a number of post-holes and dug-out structures at the base of the *concheiro*, which he interpreted as a south-facing, semicircular hut, with associated roasting and storage pits, two full of unopened furrow shells, a large paved trench, cobble walls, hearths, some with fire-cracked rocks. Pits and hearths also were found at Amoreira, also at the base of the *concheiro* (Roche 1972a, 1972b). Post-holes also have been found in the new excavations at sites along the Sado (Arnaud 1993).

The vast area and volume of the *concheiros*, the existence of numerous and sometimes multiple burials constituting an actual cemetery area, the presence of structures, and the indications of occupation at all seasons of the year at least for some of the Muge sites all suggest a low degree of residential mobility bordering on sedentism, as argued by Roche (1972a: 100). But Roche also pointed out that these were not closed societies, for they had to procure their flint elsewhere, as it was not locally available at the Muge. In fact, Roche argued that flint would have had to come from the Jurassic limestone hills of the Lisbon Peninsula, between the Tagus and the Atlantic. This makes all the more plausible the likelihood of trips to the Rio Maior area, for example, to Forno da Telha, as suggested earlier. Similarly, we know that the diminutive flint bladelet cores and microliths at Vidigal, in stark contrast to the large cores and flakes of quartzite or greywacke locally available in the form of beach cobbles, came from distant limestone massifs in southern Estremadura or smaller outcrops in the interior of Alentejo (Straus et al. 1990, Vierra and Arnaud 1996). Because the retouched artefacts made of flint, and the cores and bladelet blanks from which they were made, are reasonably relatable to hunting as projectile tips, or barbs in the case of the finished microliths, it is also reasonable to suggest that the flint may have been acquired during the course of (logistical) hunting expeditions to the hills. Even if game were not totally exhausted in the vicinity of the major *concheiro*-related residential base camps, although that might be conceivable for the more sedentary of the Muge or Sado sites, flint acquisition would have been an additional incentive for hunters regularly to travel further afield on their hunting trips. The flint that was transported was necessarily in the form of very small nodules or cores, and it was used to the maximum. There is virtually no evidence of primary reduction of flint, in the form of cortical material, at Vidigal, which is not surprising. The overwhelming majority of flint artefacts are retouched microliths and unretouched bladelets (Figure 12.4), mostly found in areas peripheral to the central shell midden, as if activities relating to gearing up for hunting were kept separate from shell dumping and meat roasting areas of this extensive site. The local, poorer-quality quartzites and greywackes would have been used expediently for chores related to plant gathering and processing, woodworking, butchering, and possibly mollusc collection. Interestingly, quartz crystal, available within 5 km of the site in the Cercal Hills, was sometimes used in place of flint for bladelet production both among the Muge sites and at Vidigal.

The clusters of Mesolithic sites near Cape Saint Vincent continued to see human occupations in the early Atlantic phase. In this period, Rocha das Gaviotas, with several hearths, has been dated by six radiocarbon determinations on shells and charcoal between 6890 ± 75 and 6281 ± 50 BP

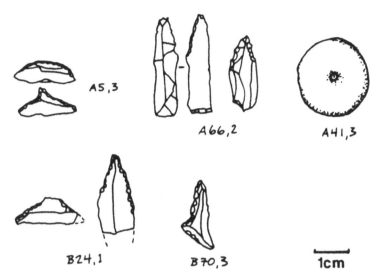

Figure 12.4. Selection of microliths, cores, and a stone 'button' from Vidigal (after Straus et al. 1990: fig. 3).

(5880–5560 cal BC) (Bicho 2009, Valente and Carvalho 2009). Nearby Armação Nova has four reservoir-corrected dates on shell ranging from 7740 ± 70 to 6970 ± 90 BP (6639–5750 cal BC). Castalejo has seven dates on both marine shells and charcoal, ranging between 8220 ± 120 and 7170 ± 70 BP (7050–5920 cal BC) (Bicho 2009). The huge open-air site of Val Boi near Sagres on the southern Atlantic shore, well-known for its long Upper Palaeolithic sequence, yielded human remains dated to the early Atlantic phase: 7500 ± 90 BP (6440–6250 cal BC) (Bicho 2009). All but the latter sites have shell middens and, as before, hearths with fire-cracked rocks. The molluscs are diverse, and other subsistence remains include fish and rabbits. Humans were definitely intensifying their food quest in the years immediately before the appearance of Cardial ware ceramics at these and other sites in the Algarve. Shellfish collection continued, and there is considerable continuity in lithic technology (including the use of local raw materials for making macrolithic tools). Herding was added to a diversified subsistence base of fishing and mollusc collection. The first Cardial pottery in the Algarve dates to about 6500 BP (reservoir-corrected) (ca. 5500 cal BC) at Rocha das Gaviotas, Castelejo, Padrão, and Cabranosa. These ceramics and specific objects of personal ornamentation are highly suggestive of some human movements from and/or contacts with early Neolithic settlements in northwest Africa and Italy (Bicho 2009).

Further north, beyond the Algarve, which is at the gateway between the Mediterranean and the Atlantic, the earliest demonstrable Neolithic sites in Portugal are associated with Cardial pottery after c. 6800–6500 BP, and are apparently all outside the coastal and estuarine zones of Ribatejo and Alentejo, namely at sites in the interior of Portugal – mainly Estremadura (Caldeirão, Almonda caves) – and in coastal areas further north in open air sites around Figueira da Foz (date at 6930 BP) (Zilhão 1998). By c. 6000 BP, later Neolithic materials lacking Cardial wares and often associated with burials are found in several places, including Caldeirao and Casa da Moura (Zilhão 1993, 1998, 2000, 2004). Insistent claims by C. T. Silva and J. Soares (Silva 1997, Soares 1997 [both with references]) for the existence of an early Neolithic at a few sites along the Alentejo coast, notably at Vale Pincel and Medo Tojeiro, not far from Vidigal, have been thoroughly analysed from a taphonomic standpoint by Zilhão and argued to be the result of mixtures between Mesolithic and later Neolithic materials.

At the moment, at least, it looks very much as if Mesolithic foragers, ensconced in their rich coastal and estuarine habitats along the lower courses of the Tagus, Sado, and Mira, continued their successful way of life based on diversified exploitation of a very broad spectrum of wild resources for at least five centuries after food producing economies associated with ceramics had been introduced into areas of Portugal that were less favourable from a hunter-fisher-gatherer perspective. The Portuguese interior seems to have become usable by people on a permanent basis with the introduction of agro-pastoralism, whereas it seems to have been used only logistically by the residents of the coastal *concheiros* for hunting and flint acquisition. One can only wonder if loss of access to the interior eventually contributed to those people abandoning their millennial foraging lifeways to join their 'cousins' (or the 'newcomers'?) who had earlier taken up food production. Introduction of the Neolithic 'package' may well have been via the maritime route from southern Spain and North Africa. But whether this 'introduction' was an actual movement of people or, rather, of ideas, domesticates, and technologies remains to be demonstrated. Although there is some biological evidence for population continuity between the Mesolithic and Neolithic of Portugal, replacement cannot yet be totally ruled out (Jackes and Lubell 1999). It is worth noting that sherds have been found in at least the upper layers of some of the Muge, Sado and Mondego *concheiros*, as well as in Vidigal. If these are not intrusive or deposited at later date, they *might* be indicators of contacts between the last foragers and the first farmers of Portugal. The hypothesis of overlap and contact was actually suggested by Roche in 1972, and remains one of the most fascinating aspects of the study of the extraordinarily rich but geographically limited Late Mesolithic of Portugal. The nature and extent of possible relationships (avoidance/mutualism, raid/trade, antagonism/intermarriage) between foraging and farming groups in the rather small territory of south-central Portugal remains to be elucidated. However it is now becoming clear that the diet of the early-mid Neolithic people, even at Casa da Moura (Straus et al. 1988) and Feteira (Zilhão 1984), not far from the coast of northern Estremadura, was based only on terrestrial foods of meat and cereals (Lubell et al. 1994). The change from 'Mesolithic' to 'Neolithic' diets – and overall adaptations – appears to have been abrupt. The question is: 'why'?

The Atlantic Phase and the Tardy 'Neolithisation' of North-Coastal Spain

The Asturian 'culture' continued into the Atlantic phase, with several uncontroversial radiocarbon dates on *concheros* with typical picks in the time range between 7500 and 6500 BP. In addition, there is a *conchero* without picks that is radiocarbon dated to 5760 ± 180 BP at Les Pedroses, in the heart of the Asturian culture area (Clark 1976). Other post-Azilian shell middens without picks (or pottery) have recently been excavated and/or dated in the Río Asón estuary area of eastern Cantabria (La Fragua, El Perro, El Perro, La Chora, La Trecha). They belong to the period from 7500–5500 BP (González Morales 1995). Slightly further east, near the shore of western Vizcaya, the small cave of Pico Ramos has recently produced a non-ceramic deposit with a mixture of marine and terrestrial molluscs, birds and red deer bones, associated with a pair of geometric microliths and an AMS date of 5860 BP (Zapata 1995). It is conceivable that some or all of the great shell deposit in Santimamiñe Cave near Guernica (Vizcaya) also might date to this period, while a recently excavated open-air site near Santimamiñe, Pareko Landa, with geometric microliths but no ceramics, has a radiocarbon date of 6650 BP (López and Aguirre 1997). The massive exploitation of coastal-zone resources continued during the Flandrian transgression, combining intensive use of molluscs, crustaceans, urchins, and marine fish with hunting of woodland-dwelling animals (especially red and roe deer, boar) and the likely exploitation of mast and other plant foods. Testimony to the continued importance of hunting is the coastal, open-air site of Herriko Barra in western Guipúzcoa, where 92 percent of the eleven hundred identifiable mammalian remains are of red deer (with no domesticated species – or pottery). These are associated with geometric microliths (including segments with double-bevel retouch), evidence of a mixed deciduous forest dominated by alder, hazel and oak, plus elm), and a radiocarbon date of 5810 BP (Mariezkurrena and Altuna 1995).

But what of the mountainous interior (Straus and González Morales 2003)? Until recently, it was believed to have been abandoned, at least in the Asturian and Cantabrian sectors. Then, in the early 1980s, the Cave of Los Canes was discovered, located on the south face of the Sierra de Cuera, a steep range, 600–1375 m high, which dominates the whole narrow coastal strip of eastern Asturias, in the shadow of the Picos de Europa (Arias 1991, Arias and Pérez 1990). Although neither particularly high (325 m) nor very far from the shore as the crow flies (12 km), Los Canes is separated from the coastal zone by a 1000 m crest line with very steep slopes. Access to the coast would have been easier (as it is today) eastward along the intermontane valley of the Río Cares and then northward down the Río Deva, a total distance of some 29 km. First thought to be an aceramic Neolithic site, Los Canes contains a component that falls fully within the range of the latest classic coastal Asturian sites (Arias 1991). The lithic assemblage includes several geometric microliths (triangles, circle segments and trapezes), a few with double-bevel ('Helwan') retouch. Four individual adult burials have been directly dated by five AMS assays between 7025 ± 80 and 6265 ± 75 BP (plus a child) in three graves. These skeletons have yielded δ^{13}C and δ^{15}N values ranging between −20.00 and −19.20‰ and between 9.39 and 7.71‰, respectively, indicating a predominantly terrestrial diet, despite the nearness of the coast on the other site of the ca. 1,000 m-high Sierra de Cuera (Arias 2005–06). This suggests that the Mesolithic inhabitants of Los Canes maintained a territory in the valley between the Picos de Europa and the Sierra de Cuera and did not often exploit the resources of the shore, manifesting low mobility and limited ranges during the Atlantic climatic phase. However, as apparent grave offerings, there are associated perforated shells and a perforated antler (such as were found in two coastal Asturian sites during old excavations, as well as at a little-known non-Asturian site, Logalán, in western Vizcaya). Until recently, Los Canes appeared to be virtually alone as an interior, upland late Mesolithic site in Asturias and Cantabria. But things seem to be changing as research progresses and more interest is paid to the interior. The possibility of increasingly limited human band territories in at least the coastal Mesolithic is supported by evidence for the use of mostly local, non-flint lithic raw materials in the classic Asturian region (Clark 1976, 1983, Arias, Fernández, et al. 2009).

The *conchero* in Colomba Cave on the shore due north of Los Canes recently yielded leg bones of a human male adult dated to 7020 ± 60 BP (5710–5605 cal BC) (TO-10223). The δ^{13}C value for the tibia is −15.784‰, and the δ^{15}N is 12.580‰, indicating a diet with a major marine component, in strong contrast to that of the Los Canes individuals. The age was corroborated by a radiocarbon date on organic sediments of 7020 ± 90 BP (5990–5810 cal BC) (UBAR-833) (Arias 2005–06, Arias, Fano, et al. 2007). The Colomba *conchero* is composed mainly of limpets (*Patella* spp.) and topshells (*Monodonta*). Salmonid and sparid fish remains were also recovered. An even later Mesolithic burial has been found recently in the shell midden of Truchiro Cave, part of the La Garma karstic complex near the eastern shore of the Santander Bay. This is a single individual (a male youth or an adult female) dated directly to 6470 ± 70 BP (5560–5310 cal BC) (TO-10912) and buried with perforated cockle shells and a large group of flint cores (Arias, Armendariz, et al. 2009). Currently ongoing excavations of new shell-midden sites in the easternmost Asturias are yielding additional human remains (I. Gutierrez Zugasti and M. R. González Morales, pers. comm. 2009). Large Mesolithic cemeteries like those of Portugal are absent in Vasco-Cantabrian Spain. However, it is increasingly evident that humans were regularly buried in the shell middens of both Asturian and non-Asturian cave sites throughout the region and during the whole time-span of the Mesolithic (and preceding Azilian) all the way up to the appearance of Neolithic economies and lifeways at ca. 5800 BP.

A recent review of the question of Mesolithic occupation of the Iberian interior by Arias, Cerrillo-Cuenca, and colleagues (2009) indicates that although apparently sparse, there clearly were foraging peoples – probably at very low population densities relative to those of the coastal zones – in areas more than 50 km from the Atlantic and Mediterranean shores of the peninsula in early-mid Holocene times. The largest concentration of interior Mesolithic sites is along the southern flanks of the Pyrenees and Basque Mountains, that is, along the left margin of the Ebro Valley in Catalonia, Aragón, Navarra, La Rioja, and Alava. This string of occupations precedes a similar distribution of early Neolithic occupations (often in the same caves and rockshelters) that connected the Mediterranean world with that of the Atlantic or Cantabrian one. Otherwise, confirmed Mesolithic sites have only been found in significant numbers in the lower Ebro Basin and upper Guadalquivir and Segura valleys in southeastern Spain. There are solitary sites in the upper Minho Valley of Galicia and the lower-middle Guadiana Valley of Portugal, and a pair of sites in the middle Tagus Valley. In addition, there are several problematic sites in Castille and La Mancha. But altogether these are very few sites for such a vast area as the Iberian interior during a period of some four millennia. Arias, Armendariz, and colleagues (2009) show a trend of increase in numbers of interior Mesolithic sites from Preboreal (n = 12) to Boreal (n = 16) to Atlantic (n = 27) times, although all these amounts pale in comparison with the numbers of coastal sites in all these early-mid Holocene phases, especially in Portugal, Galicia, and Vasco-Cantabria.

Another exception to the strictly coastal distribution of Cantabrian Mesolithic sites is Tarrerón, a small cave at an elevation of approximately 400 m a.s.l. on the edge of the Cantabrian Cordillera at the border between Cantabria and Vizcaya. Excavated in the late 1960s by J. M. Apellániz (1971), the lowest cultural layer of Tarrerón yielded very small bone and stone artefact assemblages, the latter including a few endscrapers and retouched blades and a circle segment with double-bevel retouch. This layer was said to be rich in marine molluscs (despite the approximate 26 km distance to the coast at the mouth of the Río Asón estuary), together with some land snails. Remains of fish, deer, and aurochs were also found. The deposit was dated on some of the (abundant) charcoal to 5780 ± 120 BP.

In the last few years, two more sites have been added to the roster of non-ceramic, late Mesolithic localities in the interior of eastern Cantabria: El Mirón and Cubio Redondo. The former is a huge cave only a couple of kilometres downstream of Tarrerón along an Asón tributary, the Río Calera. Situated at approximately 300 m a.s.l., on a steep cliff-face in one of the Cordilleran outer ranges, Mirón was an important site during Upper Palaeolithic and Post-Palaeolithic times, with a series of rich Neolithic, Chalcolithic, and Bronze Age occupations. Between the earliest (ceramic-bearing) Neolithic (c. 5800 BP) and Azilian (11,700 BP) levels is a layer (level 10.1), which has so far yielded only a rather small and undiagnostic lithic assemblage together with a meagre faunal assemblage, but no ceramics. So far, this level is dated to 8300–9500 BP, but further determinations will be required to clarify the ambiguity presented by the three disparate dates now available (Straus and

González Morales 1998). At least visits to El Mirón seem to have occurred during the Mesolithic in the Boreal and/or early Atlantic periods. Cubio Redondo is a small cave in the first foothill range of the Cordillera, approximately 16 km from the shore at the Asón estuary, recently excavated by J. Ruiz Cobo (Ruiz Cobo and Smith 2001, González Morales et al. 2004). The cultural deposit is rich in land snails, and also has a few marine shells, together with red and roe deer, ibex, boar, and bird remains. Lithic artefacts are few but include a backed point and a circle segment with double-bevel retouch. There are no associated ceramics and the midden yielded two disparate AMS radiocarbon dates of c. 6600 and 5800 BP, respectively, on bone and charcoal. The latter date, as well as the one from Tarrerón, overlaps with the Neolithic dates from the current excavations in nearby El Mirón, associated with ceramics and domesticates.

Not far away (55 km from Mirón), at 1,015 m a.s.l. in the Cordillera of south-central Vizcaya and at least forty difficult kilometres from the shore, the small cave site of Urratxa (Muñoz and Berganza 1997) has yielded two AMS dates of 6950 BP. There is a microburin and a trapeze, suggesting attribution to the Mesolithic. Much of the flint comes from some 40 km to the south in Treviño (an enclave of Burgos Province within the Basque province of Alava) and the fauna is dominated by ibex, indicating that this was a specialized logistical hunting camp. Other aceramic sites to the south in Alava date to this early Atlantic period (Fuente Hoz: 7140–8120 BP; Kanpanoste Goikoa: 7620 and 7860 BP for the earliest, nongeometric horizon versus 6360 and 6550 BP for the later, geometric-rich one; Mendandia: 7810 and 7780 BP; Marañón: 7890 BP). And in northern Navarra there are Mesolithic levels in Berroberría that date to 6910–6560 BP, in Zatoya to c.8200 BP, and in Aizpea to 7790–7160 BP and 6830 and 6600 BP for the earlier and later horizons respectively (Alday 1998, 2002). It is right at about 6300 BP that the first ceramics appeared in the upper Ebro Basin of Alava and Navarra. Indeed there seems to be a period of contemporaneity between nonceramic, geometric-rich 'Mesolithic' occupations and ceramic, also geometric-rich 'Neolithic' ones in the region immediately to the south of the eastern Cantabrian Cordillera and western Pyrenees. Both the terminal Mesolithic level at Kanpanoste Goikoa and its contemporary, the earliest Neolithic level (6320 BP) at Zatoya, have yielded *Columbella rustica* shells (Alday 1998, Barandiarán and Cava 1989b). These are of Mediterranean origin and indicate the existence of social contacts among food producing and foraging groups within the greater Ebro Basin at this time. Slightly older dates for Neolithic occupations are found further east down the Ebro, notably in Aragón, for example, Forcas, Chaves, Moros de Olvena (Alday 1998, 2005) – suggestive of the direction of expansion of food production economies and their associated technologies.

It now appears that diversified foraging economies and purely bone and lithic technologies (including variable percentages of geometric microliths, with use of the microburin manufacturing technique and both backing and double-bevel retouch) persisted throughout Asturias, Cantabria, and coastal Basque regions (including their montane zones) until c. 5700–5500 BP. Meanwhile, to the south of the Cordillera in the upper Ebro Basin of Navarra and Alava, the transition from 'Mesolithic' to 'Neolithic' technologies and lifeways was already underway as early as c. 6300 BP. The ecological differences between the drier, warmer Mediterranean environments of the latter region and the wetter, cooler ones of the former may have temporarily retarded and then 'filtered' the expansion of the Neolithic system, as the Vasco-Cantabrian hills would have been more suitable for pastoralism than for early Near Eastern–derived cereal agriculture, at least at first. So, in the terms of the Zvelebil and Rowley-Conwy (1984, 1986) model for the transition from foraging to farming, there was a fairly long 'availability' period and a delayed 'substitution' period for the transition in north-coastal Spain (see Arias 1999).

When that substitution came, it seems to have been accompanied by the first megalithic monuments in Vasco-Cantabria, the oldest in the East (Larrate in Guipúzcoa at 5810 ± 290 BP), with several of c. 5500 BP in Cantabria, and, going westward, others of c. 5200–5000 BP in Asturias (see González Morales 1992, González Morales et al. 2004 with references). The first domesticated animals seem to appear at about the same time. At El Mirón Cave, Level 10 dated to 5700–5600 BP and the stratigraphically equivalent 5500–5800 BP-dated Levels 303–303.3 contain macromammalian faunas dominated by ovicaprines (Altuna et al. 2004), and wheat directly dated to 5600 BP, along with good-quality plainware ceramics. The site is also close to a dolmen dated to 5500 BP (Serna 1997). In Guipúzcoa, the site of Marizulo has yielded possibly domesticated ovicaprines at 5285 ± 65 BP (Altuna 1980).

The oldest megaliths in Galicia are dated to 5400–5000 BP and the oldest ones in northern Portugal are in the same range, with the exception of one site, Maninho, with two dates that average to c. 5700 BP (Alonso and Bello 1997). The oldest megaliths in central Portugal date to c.4900–5100 BP (Senna-Martinez et al. 1997). The first evidence of cereal pollen in Galicia, associated with indicators of deforestation, dates to c. 5500 BP (Fábregas et al. 1997), although the dating of the appearance of ceramics and domesticated animals in this region is still unclear.

Conclusions

Whatever its mode(s) of transmission (migration, trade, exchange, and/or other social contacts) or its route(s) from the Mediterranean world, whether via the Ebro, the Castillian meseta, Portuguese Estremadura, by sea from eastern Spain and/or North Africa (or by sea from Aquitaine?), the Neolithic made a late appearance in North Atlantic Spain. The highly diversified late Mesolithic subsistence strategies of those regions, although they produced less spectacular results than the contemporaneous cultures of estuarine Portugal by way of shell heaps, structures, and especially cemeteries with grave goods, were nonetheless well suited for the littoral and wooded, montane inland environments of greater Vasco-Cantabria. In Portugal, the apparently imported Neolithic adaptation took root relatively early only in areas that were not the core territories of Mesolithic foragers. The process of wild resource-based subsistence diversification in Atlantic Iberia had been an exceptionally long one, dating back at least to early Magdalenian and even Solutrean times. Never in these regions had humans been specialised hunters of large herd game such as reindeer or horses – in contrast to late Upper Palaeolithic France or Germany. Long-standing and very stable adaptations, capable during the transition from the Pleistocene to the Holocene (c. 13,000–8000) of gradually dealing with a retreating coastline (compensated for by retreating mountain glaciers), reforestation, and modest changes in faunal resources, were fine-tuned over time, but they did not undergo revolutions in the peculiar topography of north-coastal Spain. The Mesolithic was heir to a long tradition both in that region and in Portugal; the success of its adaptations along the Atlantic façade is attested by its long survival, well after the Mediterranean façade had become the land of Neolithic cereal farmers, herders, and potters.

Acknowledgments

My work in the Mesolithic, Upper Palaeolithic and Neolithic of Spain and Portugal (as well as in France and Belgium) over the past thirty-two years has been generously supported by grants from the National Science Foundation (USA), the National Geographic Society, the L. S. B. Leakey

Foundation, and the University of New Mexico. I have profited immeasurably from discussions with many European and American colleagues; in the case of the Mesolithic and transition to the Neolithic in Iberia especially with Manolo González Morales, João Zilhão, Nuno Bicho, and Geof Clark, who are, however blameless for my errors of fact or interpretation. Thanks also to Alvaro Arrizabalaga and Mari Jose Iriarte for information on their shell midden site on Monte Jaizkibel in Guipúzcoa.

Chapter 13

The Coastal Mesolithic of the European Mediterranean

Mark Pluciennik*

Introduction

The problem of drawing archaeological boundaries and the related process of categorisation, with all their advantages and pitfalls, is perhaps nowhere more evident than in thinking about the Mesolithic of the Mediterranean. The geographical division is itself, of course, arbitrary. The European Mediterranean coast is contiguous with the coastline of Asia (Turkey and the Levant) and Africa (from Egypt westwards to the Straits of Gibraltar), and there are many islands within the Mediterranean which act as stepping-stones between the north and south. Regional divisions relate as much to modern geopolitics as to any inherent differences within the archaeology (Figure 13.1).

In addition – and in contrast to much of central and northern Europe where the impact of the Last Glacial Maximum was more profound – one can argue for much more continuity from the preceding period, whether in climatic, ecological or cultural terms (cf. Bicho 1994, Straus 1995, 1996, Straus this volume, Araújo 2003). Chronologically, therefore, we could confine ourselves to a Mesolithic *sensu stricto*, starting at the beginning of the Holocene. But there are good arguments for looking some two thousand to three thousand years earlier than this for developments such as a broadening of the subsistence base and a shift towards forest game and aquatic and plant resources, as in central Italy or southern mainland Greece. There are equally good reasons for looking later than the conventional boundary for developments in lithic technologies, as in parts of Iberia. At the other end of the scale, there is a good case to be made for radical sociocultural change not at the Neolithic boundary, meaning here the first evidence of domesticated plants and animals and associated material culture, but rather in the middle or later Neolithic.

The chronology of the Mediterranean Mesolithic is also 'squeezed' in the east by the early appearance of the Neolithic compared to its later spread to the west (see Table 13.1 for radiocarbon

* School of Archaeology and Ancient History, University of Leicester, UK.

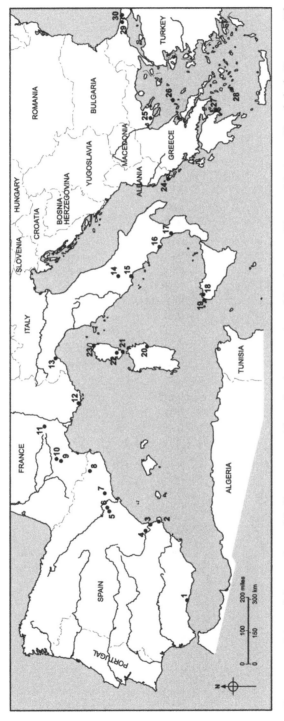

Figure 13.1. Map of the northern Mediterranean with main sites mentioned in the text. Key: 1. Nerja, 2. Tossal de la Roca, 3. El Collado, 4. Cocina, 5. Botiquería de los Moros, 6. Costalena, 7. Filador, 8. Balma del Gai, 9. Grotte de Gazel, 10. Abeurador, 11. Montclús, 12. Châteauneuf-les-Martigues, 13. Arene Candide, 14. Lago Fucino, 15. Riparo Blanc, 16. Grotta Erica, Grotta della Porta, 17. Grotta della Madonna, 18. Grotta dell'Uzzo, 19. Levanzo (Grotta della Cala dei Genovesi), 20. Corbeddu, 21. Araguina-Sennola, 22. Curacchiaghui, 23. Strette, 24. Sidari, 25. Theopetra, 26. Cave of Cyclope, Youra, 27. Franchthi, 28. Melos, 29. Ağaçli, Gümüşdere, 30. Domali.

Table 13.1. *Selected radiocarbon determinations for Mediterranean Europe*

Site Name	Lab. No.	BP	Cal BC 2σ
Spain			
Microlaminar Epipalaeolithic			
Balma del Gai, Catalonia ('Azilian')	MC-2140	11,050 ± 160	11,400–10,650
Nerja, Andalucia	UBAR-153	1,0860 ± 160	11,200–10,450
Mallaetes, Valencia	KNI-915	10,370 ± 105	10,650–9700
Las Forcas, Aragon	GrN-17748	9360 ± 140	8950–8050
Balma Margineda, Catalonia ('Azilian tradition' base)	Ly-2843	10,640 ± 260	11,200–9300
Balma Margineda, Catalonia ('Azilian tradition' top)	Ly-2842	9250 ± 160	8950–7950
Geometric Epipalaeolithic ('Sauveterrian')			
Balma del Gai, Catalonia	MC-2141	10,030 ± 160	10,300–9000
Abri del Filador, Catalonia	ICEN-495	9130 ± 230	9000–7500
Late geometric Epipalaeolithic ('Tardenoisian')			
Botiquería de los Moros	Ly-1198	7550 ± 200	7000–5900
Costalena	GrN-14098	6420 ± 250	5800–4750
Cova Fosca	I-9867	8632 ± 200	8050–7100
Las Forcas II	Beta-59995	7090 ± 340	6600–5200
Balma Margineda, Catalonia	Ly-2840	8390 ± 150	7900–7000
Non-microlithic phases			
Abrigo del Angel (8b)	GrN-15520	8150 ± 170	7500–6600
Forcas II (d)	CAMS-5354	8650 ± 70	7910–7510
'Mesolithic' industries with pottery			
Balma Margineda (level 3)	Ly-2839	6670 ± 120	5740–5330
Las Forcas II (Level b upper)	Beta-60773	6940 ± 90	5960–5620
France			
Grotte Gazel (Layer 6 'Epimagdalenian')	Gif-2654	10,760 ± 190	11,150–10,200
Grotte Gazel (Layer 5)	Gif-2655	10,080 ± 190	10,700–9200
Grotte Gazel (Layer F6) ('Late Sauveterrian Mesolithic')	GrN-6704	7880 ± 75	7040–6590
Grotte Gazel (Layer 4) (Mesolithic with pottery)	Gif-2401	6810 ± 130	5980–5490
Balma de l'Abeurador (late Mesolithic)	MC-2144	8740 ± 90	8200–7550
Abri du Roc de Dourgne ('Montclusian Sauveterrian')	MC-1107	6850 ± 100	5980–5560
Cauna d'Arques (late Mesolithic)	Gif-2415	8920 ± 200	8550–7550
Roc d'en Bertran (late Mesolithic)	MC-594	8100 ± 110	7450–6650
Strette, Corsica	Ly-2837	9140 ± 300	9200–7500
Curacchiughiu, Corsica	Gif-795	8560 ± 170	8300–7100
Araguina-Sennola, Corsica	Gif-2705	8520 ± 150	8200–7100
Italy			
Trentino-Alto Adige			
Riparo di Pradestel (Sauveterrian)	R-1151	9320 ± 50	8740–8350
Riparo di Pradestel (Tardenoisian)	R-1148	6870 ± 50	5880–5660
Riparo di Romagnano III (Sauveterrian)	R-1147	9830 ± 90	9700–8900

Site Name	Lab. No.	BP	Cal BC 2σ
Riparo di Romagnano III ('Tardenoisian/Castelnovian')	R-1147	7850 ± 60	7030–6560
Liguria			
Grotta Arma dello Stefanin ('Epigravettian')	R-145	8800 ± 300	8800–7100
Grotta Arma dello Stefanin ('Final Epipaleolithic')	R-109	7800 ± 100	7050–6450
Emilia-Romagna			
Monte Bagioletto Alto (Castelnovian)	Bln-2839	8260 ± 60	7480–7080
Tuscany			
Isola Santa ('Epigravettian')	R-1524	10,720 ± 140	11,000–10250
Isola Santa (Sauveterrian)	E-90	9370 ± 150	9150–8250
Isola Santa (late Mesolithic)	R-1527α	8590 ± 90	7940–7480
Lazio			
Riparo Blanc	R-341	8565 ± 80	7820–7470
Puglia			
Grotta Scaloria	LJ-5098	9030 ± 120	8550–7750
Grotta Romanelli ('Romanellian')	GrN-2056	9880 ± 100	9850–9150
Calabria			
Grotta della Madonna ('Upper Palaeolithic')	R-185	10,120 ± 70	10,100–9400
Grotta della Madonna ('Mesolithic')	R-187	8735 ± 80	8200–7550
Sicily			
Perriere Sottano	UtC-1424	8700 ± 150	8250–7500
Grotta dell'Uzzo ('Base of Mesolithic')	P-2736	10,070 ± 90	10,050–9300
Grotta dell'Uzzo ('Upper Mesolithic')	P-2556	9030 ± 100	8550–7800
Grotta dell'Uzzo ('Transitional')	P-2734	7910 ± 70	7050–6640
Grotta dell'Uzzo ('Neolithic')	P-2733	6750 ± 70	5770–5520
Greece			
Sidari, Corfu	GXO-771	7670 ± 120	6850–6200
Theopetra (associated with burial)	DEM-315	9274 ± 75	8710–8300
Theopetra (top of Mesolithic)	DEM-576	8060 ± 32	7140–6820
Theopetra: (top of Mesolithic)	DEM-583	8014 ± 49	7070–6750
Cyclop's Cave, Youra	DEM-597	9274 ± 43	8630–8340
Cyclop's Cave, Youra	DEM-524	8791 ± 23	7960–7750
Cyclop's Cave, Youra	DEM-595	8209 ± 47	7360–7060
Franchthi Cave, Argolis	P-2227	9430 ± 160	9250–8300
Franchthi Cave, Argolis	P-1518	8938 ± 100	8300–7700
Franchthi Cave, Argolis	P-2017	8530 ± 90	7760–7350
Franchthi Cave, Argolis	P-1527	7897 ± 88	7060–6590

For Italy, the most comprehensive sources are the compilation and updates by Skeates and Whitehouse (Skeates 1994, Skeates and Whitehouse 1994, 1995–6, 1997–8); see also Pluciennik (1997) for detailed discussion of many Mesolithic (and Neolithic) dates. For Greece, the review by Facorellis (2003) is extremely useful. I am not aware of similar syntheses for either southern France or Mediterranean Spain (but see Cava 1994, Tortosa and Ripoll 1995). Many of the available dates were performed on collected fragments of charcoal and have very large error terms. All radiocarbon determinations are given as uncalibrated BP and calibrated ranges at 2 sigma as cal BC. Dates have been calibrated using OxCal v3.10 (Bronk Ramsey 1995, 2001).

dates). In much of the eastern Mediterranean and Aegean the Mesolithic, defined by the presence of Holocene hunter-gatherers, may only last a millennium or two, with the earliest Neolithic dated at around 7000 cal BC (Perlès 2001: 84–110), whereas in the west the period is typically two or three times as long. But there is also evidence of continuity in practices such as upland hunting and coastal fishing and fowling beyond these dates, whether due to the survival of 'pure' hunter-gatherers, or to new communities of hunter-herder-fisher-farmers of diverse origins. There are also inter- and intraregional differences in responses to the availability of new forms of material culture and subsistence practices.

Thus, the Mesolithic in the northern Mediterranean has an arbitrary beginning and an ending, both of which are time-transgressive and dependent on definitions. In addition, although not a problem confined to the Mediterranean, site preservation is often heavily biased towards caves and rockshelters. Many open-air sites, which may often have been rather insubstantial in the first place, have been masked by subsequent sedimentation, destroyed by agricultural practices, or drowned by postglacial sea-level rise. Thus, we may note the recent discoveries of Grange des Merveilles II in central southern France (Bazile and Monnet-Bazile 1998), an 'EpiPalaeolithic' site only discovered through a section dug to investigate the alluvial record for an adjacent Neolithic site. In Thrace in northeast Greece, a similar find of a probable post-Palaeolithic horizon below three metres of sediment was discovered while exploring the extent of the Neolithic site of Makri (Efstratiou, pers. comm.). Such sites on lake margins, alluvial plains, and in river valleys may be typical of preferred Mesolithic locations, but are obviously prone to burial by subsequent Holocene infilling of depressions. All this means that we are dealing with a heavily biased and fragmented selection of sites and remains, and inevitably see a very partial picture. Given that the relevant archaeological deposits are almost always palimpsests of the material outcomes of events over many generations, it is not surprising that categories and periodisations are always contestable.

The apparent difficulty of doing more than describing tools and subsistence has contributed to the persistence of culture-historical and overly typological approaches to surviving material culture (largely lithics). It also has hindered attempts to frame critical questions concerned with such issues as the meaning of cultural similarities or differences between areas, or the reality of any entity called the 'Mesolithic of the Mediterranean'.

Lithics

The attempt to apply cultural and typological terms derived from elsewhere has often led to both confusion and the proliferation of terms. For example, as Tortosa and Ripoll note (1995: 126), in Iberia the lithic assemblages termed 'Upper Mediterranean Magdalenian' by some, are else-where referred to as Epimagdalenian, Postmagdalenian, Late or Final Mediterranean Magdalenian or Mesolithic, whereas others would include them in a generic Epipalaeolithic, Azilian, or even Aziloid. Nevertheless, we can note broad similarities across much of the area. The apparent conti-nuities in subsistence, technology and sometimes settlement pattern are reflected on the broadest scale by the continuation of Palaeolithic traditions across the Pleistocene-Holocene boundary, to produce assemblages which, in terms of lithic (and in places antler and bone) technology, we may term the Epipalaeolithic. In Iberia and much of southern France, these industries are therefore related to the Magdalenian, though their postglacial manifestations are often called Azilian (after the Mas d'Azil in southwestern France) and can be dated to the eleventh and tenth millennia BP. However, in Mediterranean Spain west of the Ebro these microblade industries appear to continue until about 8500 BP, with the geometric 'Cocina' facies known from a little later at rockshelter sites such as Botiqueria des Moros and Tossal de la Roca. East of the Ebro, in Valencia, Catalonia, and the Pyrenees, Sauveterrian-type assemblages are known from the beginning of the Holocene at around 10,000 BP. However, more 'opportunistic' and macrolithic assemblages dominated by tools such as scrapers and denticulates, of uncertain date and without any microlithic or geometric components, are also known. This microlithic–macrolithic contrast is known elsewhere in Iberia (Straus this volume) and often linked to site-functional differences; there is a tendency for geometric assemblages to be associated with coastal sites in Mediterranean Iberia (Bernabeu et al. 1995: 210).

East from the Pyrenees in Languedoc and Roussillon in southwest France, the late glacial or early postglacial 'Magdalenian' sequences are generally followed by Sauveterrian (or Montclusian) assemblages with a strong component of geometric triangular microliths. The later Mesolithic industries of the 8th millennium BP show a tendency towards the more 'opportunistic' use of local materials and are typologically characterised by triangular points. Further east, in Provence, the Holocene industries show an important geometric component from the beginning, at first characterised by triangles and segments and regionally denominated Montadien and Montclusian, and subsequently by trapezes. The transition to the 'Castelnovian' is seen from around 8000 BP at the important coastal site of Châteauneuf-les-Martigues, for example.

In southeast France, much of Italy and further east in the Mediterranean, the late glacial and early postglacial lithic assemblages are seen as developments of the Epigravettian, which is the type-name used to describe Late Upper Palaeolithic industries of much of Eastern Europe (Gamble 1986). Although these assemblages are often microlithic with high percentages of backed bladelets, many also contain varying though small percentages of geometric microliths. The industries or facies attributed to subsequent millennia typically contain much higher proportions of geometric microliths, beginning with Sauveterrian industries, classically (though not exclusively) with triangles and crescents, followed by the Tardenoisian or Castelnovian, with trapezes (see Binder 2000: 118–27 for recent discussion of the various overlapping facies; Philibert 2002 for recent discussion and analysis of southern French Sauveterrian assemblages; also Valdeyron this volume).

It is generally thought that much of this assemblage variation (Figures 13.2–13.5) relates to changing hunting practices and preferred forms of mounting microliths as armatures in hunting weapons (see Bergman 1993, Fischer 1989, Bicho 1993, 1994, cf. Straus 1993). This in its turn is linked to the increasingly closed nature of the forest cover necessitating different ways of killing medium to large game. However, microwear analysis has shown that unretouched blades and flakes, whether produced intentionally or as debitage, may be as important as the retouched tools that are typically the focus of attention (Juel Jensen 1988). In some areas, there do appear to be broad correlations between game resources and changes in lithic styles, but in places such as southwest France these seem to vary independently (Geddes et al. 1986: 74, Rozoy 1989). In addition, many of these microliths may have been mounted as composite knives or other tools related to plant collection and processing.

Although the general tendency towards 'microlithisation' and 'blade and trapeze' industries may be partly related to functional requirements and efficiency of manufacture, 'ways of doing' are as much social as technical. Typically, and in contrast to the Late Upper Palaeolithic, reliance on high-quality flint derived from relatively distant sources decreases, and there is often more emphasis on the apparently expedient use of local materials. However, it is not clear if we are comparing like with like. There were probably changes in the spatial (and social) organisation of activity as well as the nature of mobility (of people and materials) within communities. Interestingly, in

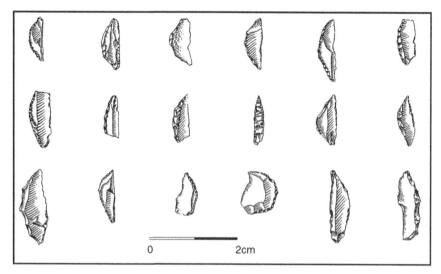

Figure 13.2. Geometric microliths and points from the Azilian horizons, from Balma Margineda, Andorra (after Geddes et al. 1989).

Mediterranean Turkey broadly similar sequences can be observed at the end of the Pleistocene, with a shift from microlithic, non-geometric assemblages made on both local and imported raw materials, to assemblages dominated by geometric microliths of local stone (Otte et al. 1995: 943–4; cf. Adam 1999 for Theopetra, Greece). The invention, spread, and transformation of innovatory practices are cultural processes: in places no doubt people may have arrived independently at similar 'solutions' to changing requirements (and often were working under similar material constraints), but however sparse populations were in comparison to those of later times, Mesolithic communities were not isolated. Nonetheless, at individual sites we can often see continuity as well as change in such things as the types and proportions of raw materials used, often from considerable distances away from where they were acquired. This implies continuity of knowledge in all sorts of ways, of known and named places that shape movement through the landscape, and of how to acquire goods and resources whether tangible, practical, social, or spiritual.

Environment and Subsistence

By convention, the physical geography of the Mediterranean region is often defined in terms of vegetation and climate, especially rainfall, itself reinforced for the Mesolithic by the tendency to treat hunter-gatherers within an ecological framework. A recent call for an appreciation of any Mediterranean unity in terms of interaction predicated upon regional unpredictability, variation, and 'local irregularity' (Horden and Purcell 2000: 13) is attractive but difficult for our period. Many Mediterranean environments are not conducive to the preservation of pollen sequences in comparison to the lakes and peat bogs of northern Europe (Huntley and Birks 1983, Huntley 1990). Although southern French and northern Italian data are relatively abundant, those for southern Greece, southern Italy, Sicily, and southern Iberia are less well known in detail. Many of the pollen cores are at relatively high altitudes, where lake sediments or peats are present, which has led to problems of extrapolation, especially with regard to the probable importance of lowland and coastal

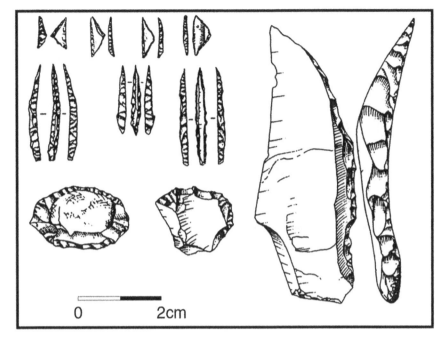

Figure 13.3. Sauveterrian points, geometric microliths, and other tools, from Riparo di Romagno, Italy (after Lanziger 1991).

areas for Mesolithic communities. Although there are sequences from coastal lagoons, these are generally for the later part of the period.

The climate of the preceding millennia was variable with short colder spells, though not as pronounced as in northern Europe, and in general there is a Holocene amelioration of the climate from cold and dry to warmer and generally wetter conditions. However, at many Mediterranean latitudes and beyond, thermophilous vegetation and its associated fauna were present for much of the late glacial (e.g., Follieri 1968, Renault-Miskovsky et al. 1979, Pons and Reille 1988, Bennett et al. 1991, López 1992: 237, Willis 1994, Willis et al. 2000, Bottema 2003). Persistent though variable open forest-steppe landscapes including pine were present in central and southern Italy and southern Spain, for example. In many areas, the limiting factor on the extent and nature of forest may have been rainfall rather than temperature, with forest refugia confined to higher altitude. Thus, in contrast to much of central and northern Europe, in the Mediterranean we can envisage the spread of first pine and then deciduous (e.g., oak, hornbeam, ash) and Mediterranean (e.g., *Phillyrea*, pistachio) forest species downwards as well as outwards around the beginning of Holocene. In northern Greece, central Italy, and southern Iberia, it has been argued that this process began much earlier. At Tenaghi Philippon in northeast Greece, at 40 m a.s.l., a forest expansion (mainly deciduous oak, but also hornbeam, lime, hazel, elm, and pistachio) was said to occur from about 13,500 BP (van Zeist and Bottema 1982: 284–5), following a long period of steppe-dominated vegetation, but this early dating has since been questioned (Bottema 2003: 42). Nevertheless, the increased availability of wood may at least partly explain the decrease in bone and antler points and harpoons noted in final Palaeolithic assemblages, although bone continues to be preferentially used for fishhooks, for example.

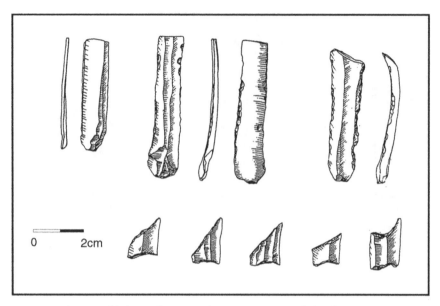

Figure 13.4. Castelnovian blades and trapezoid geometric microliths, from La Font-des-Pigeons, Châteauneuf-les-Martigues (after Binder 1987).

In broad geographical terms, and at the largest scale, there was a general replacement of extensive but open pine forests and juniper at lower altitudes by a mosaic of ecological communities over much of the area eventually dominated by evergreen Mediterranean oak forest (Figure 13.6). Higher up, these forests were variably composed of deciduous oak, beech, ash, hazel, birch, and pine, the latter more extensive at higher altitudes. However, there are and were differences of climate between the eastern and western Mediterranean, which would have had corresponding effects on the vegetation and associated fauna (COHMAP 1988, Huntley 1990, Roberts et al. 2001: 633). In addition, Mediterranean shrubs and trees such as olive, pistachio and the Strawberry Tree were present in places (Mateus 1989, Costantini 1981, Riera i Mora 1993). In the Pyrenees, for example, fir, hazel, birch, and other deciduous trees have been identified through charcoal analysis, for example, at Balma Margineda, Andorra (Geddes et al. 1989). Away from the coast in the semiarid zones of both southern Iberia in the west (Carrión et al. 2001) and Anatolia in the east (Wick et al. 2003), steppe or sparse pine forests seem to have persisted until the mid-Holocene, again suggesting that rainfall patterns have been the primary limiting factor.

Nor should we lose sight of local variation. Pollen analysis from Atlantic Portugal (Mateus 1989: 84–5, Santos and Sánchez Goñi 2003), southern Spain (López 1992, Pantaléon-Cano et al. 2003), southern France (Puertas 1999) and central Italy (Magri 1999: 198–9) and various charcoal studies (Vernet 1997: 89–124) indicate considerable variation within relatively small areas of landscape. Local patterning comprises coastal and estuarine salt marshes and lagoons, alder-dominated forests along river and stream margins, pine forest and heath, steppe, and macchia and variable evergreen and deciduous forests with lime and elm. Some of these plant communities do not now occur in the Mediterranean or elsewhere.

Vertical variation within regions also was important. A comparison of pollen and charcoal analysis near Alicante in southern Spain shows the early Holocene development of mixed oak forests with a low representation of Mediterranean forest species at sites such as Tossal de la Roca

(Bernabeu et al. 1995: 179–80). The nearby coastal site of Nerja seems to show the maintenance of relatively open environments across the Pleistocene-Holocene boundary, with an increase in temperature and aridity leading to the dominance of plants including legumes, wild olive, pistachio, and rosemary. Nevertheless, our current stereotype of the Mediterranean as hot, dry, and bare refers to a relatively recent phenomenon. Under largely forested conditions, extremes would have been much ameliorated: streams and rivers would have been less markedly seasonal, water tables higher, and springs, streams, and standing water more abundant.

The Mediterranean zone today is a generally mountainous area with narrow coastal plains backed by mountains. This typically provides a variety of ecologically distinct zones within a relatively short distance. In resource terms, this is seen within hunter-gatherer studies as conducive to a particular type of settlement pattern of 'vertical' logistic mobility, perhaps in contrast to horizontal and more residential mobility often thought to be more typical of the preceding period. Similarly, relief and character in many of the lower areas, subsequently masked by Holocene alluviation, would have been more pronounced (e.g., the Tavoliere plain in north Puglia), with particularly marked changes in coastal configurations. Many ecologically rich marshlands and lakes have vanished through lowering of the water table by overextraction and drainage. Sea-level rise since the Last Glacial Maximum also has been crucial in changing the topography of the Mediterranean coast, with extensive loss of coastal plains especially in the Levante area of Spain, southern France, southeast Sicily, and in the Adriatic (Shackleton and van Andel 1985). By the beginning of the Mesolithic, relative sea level had risen from a low of about −120 m to −40 m (Pirazzoli 1987), although locally

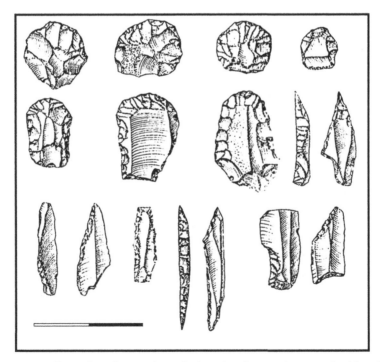

Figure 13.5. Romanellian of southern Italy, including the characteristic circular 'thumbnail' scrapers and various backed points and blades; from the Grotta del Cavallo, Puglia (after Palma di Cesnola 1963).

Figure 13.6. Modern Mediterranean oak forest in Sardinia. A more densely forested version of these landscapes was probably widespread throughout much of the Mesolithic Mediterranean.

variable depending on tectonic activity, which is especially prevalent in the central and eastern Mediterranean. This process continued at a slower rate until the mid-Holocene until it reached a point a few metres above current levels.

Although sea-level rise is often seen in negative terms as the loss of land and resources, in fact, in combination with changing climate, it often led to the development of fringing coastal freshwater, brackish and saltwater lagoons, which were extremely rich and were extensively exploited for food and other resources, for example, Grotta Romanelli, Puglia, Italy (Cassoli et al. 1979), Châteauneuf-les-Martigues, southern France (Desse 1987). In addition, the climatic amelioration allowed the exploitation of higher zones within the mountains and their foothills, a process that is particularly well-documented for the Pyrenees (Geddes et al. 1986, 1989) and the Italian Alps (Maggi 1999). This allows us to 'see' other components of the Mesolithic settlement and subsistence system and to identify a shift in spatial and species emphasis (both faunal and floral) and greater variability. Part of the contrast between 'Mesolithic' and 'Palaeolithic' may be a function of archaeological visibility as well as intrinsic radical change, with many winter and spring lowland and coastal sites from the earlier period now lost beneath the waves. This reading is supported by the increasing evidence of Palaeolithic exploitation of marine resources (Cleyet-Merle and Madelaine 1995). A combination of such changes and consequent responses may be a factor in the notorious invisibility of the Greek Mesolithic.

Although there are sometimes ways of exploring persistent activities and differences in consumption (through bone studies and bone chemistry), little detailed work has been done for the Mediterranean Mesolithic. Isotope analysis at the later Mesolithic midden sites in Portugal suggests that for many people approximately half the diet was from marine sources (Lubell et al. 1994: 213). There are also intriguing suggestions that the marine-terrestrial proportion varied within populations, though the analyses published so far do not allow us to consider this in terms of age or sex, which may have been important axes of variation. Work on dental caries in southern European samples (e.g., Borgognini Tarli and Repetto 1985 for Sicily) shows generally high (but site-variable) incidences, which may be linked to the higher availability and consumption of sugar-rich fruits in comparison with northern Europe.

The loss, movement, or comparative rarity of large herd animals (reindeer, horse and bison), and the trend towards more solitary species (roe deer, boar), it is argued, would encourage individual 'encounter' hunting. At the same time, unpredictability demands flexibility, to which varying types of armatures and ways of mounting armatures are seen as the technical response (see also Zvelebil this volume). However, it is likely that a whole variety of techniques and ways of organising artefact production and foraging practices was used within and across communities. In southern Iberia and southern France, the prevalence of lagomorphs suggests that trapping was often as important as hunting by tracking. Riverine and marine fish (and other animals) could have been caught with nets; and fish traps, spearing and 'tickling' are all possible. From later Mesolithic coastal sites such as the Grotta dell' Uzzo in Sicily (Figure 13.7) and Cyclope Cave on Youra in Greece, there are numerous bone fishhooks indicating individual angling from the coast or from boats. Large fish that come close to shore to spawn such as tuna (also found at Franchthi in Greece) could have been speared and other fish collectively driven into nets. Shellfish, crabs, and sea urchins were collected, and waterfowl and other birds caught by a variety of means. At many sites, an increase in terrestrial as well as marine shells can be seen in the final Late Upper Palaeolithic and the Mesolithic (Lubell 2004a, b). Most of these resources and techniques were available before the Mesolithic, but their distribution and abundance changed. With the growth in the variety of ecozones, the importance of plant foods such as acorns, nuts, and wild fruits increased, along with techniques for harvesting, processing and even ways of managing them, although we have little or no direct evidence of the latter.

Figure 13.7. Grotta dell'Uzzo, Sicily. The coast is a short distance to the left of the picture.

Finally, however, we might characterise the environment for the people of the time: landmarks such as the sea, rocks, rivers and lakes, cliffs, hot springs, gorges, plateaus, isolated trees, volcanic islands, and mountains would have delineated places, paths, and orientations, and perhaps boundaries and access to other communities and resources. Many of these places would have been named and incorporated into stories. Travel would often have been difficult and a sense of orientation crucial. Although Mesolithic (and Neolithic) people were undoubtedly capable of altering their surroundings with clearance of forests and undergrowth by ring barking, felling, or fire, there is so far little evidence of this in Mediterranean pollen sequences until the Bronze Age (Magri 1995, but see, for example, Mateus 1989: 73). Daily and embodied familiarity with immediate surroundings would have shaded off, though differently for different members of any one community, into regions known much less well, or only through hearsay, lore and the cosmological frameworks which no doubt told how the world and the beings within it arose.

Settlement Patterns and Mobility

One of the more useful models for thinking about the ways in which people may have moved around and utilized their landscape is the contrast between residential and logistical mobility. In the former pattern, communities as a whole move in relation to resource abundance and availability; in the latter, mobility is in effect transferred to particular specialised task groups. This contrast should be evident in particular archaeological signatures such as the number of tool types (with high variability suggesting multipurpose and perhaps long-term occupation, as opposed to short-lived single-activity sites) and the nature of the faunal remains (in terms of seasonality, processing, consumption, and discard). However, these ideal types are rarely so clearly distinguished in practice (see, e.g., Tortosa and Ripoll 1995: 137–9, Milliken 1998a: 76–9). Furthermore, we have to consider that archaeological assemblages are usually palimpsests accumulated over periods of time within which practices may have varied.

Site size, seasonality of faunal data, and the presence of large numbers of burials have been used to argue that the later Mesolithic southern Portuguese middens represent classic 'logistical mobility' base camps from which foraging groups went to particular locations such as estuaries and woodlands (Lubell and Jackes 1988), but comparable sites are rare in the Mediterranean. In other parts of Iberia and in the French Pyrenees, many of the caves and rock shelters seem to relate to summer–autumn occupation, although the range of subsistence evidence from some excavations shows that these were not necessarily simply hunting sites (Geddes et al. 1986, Cava Almazura 1994). Winter and spring sites could have been in the valley bottoms or in coastal locations, but both may have involved whole communities, and Rozoy (1998) argues that some upland sites also may have been 'residential'.

Another general pattern of movement may have been for relatively small and flexible dispersed groups to aggregate at certain types of locations at certain times of the year, but without the formal sense of territory and rootedness implied by the term 'base camp'. On the steep coastline of eastern Liguria and further east, relatively large open-air sites are found at medium altitudes in the earlier Mesolithic, perhaps linked to vanished coastal sites, whereas in the later Mesolithic high-altitude and probably more specialized summer-autumn hunting sites were occupied (Maggi 1999). In southern Puglia, Milliken (1998) has found very little evidence of specialized activities in the very late Pleistocene and early Holocene lithic assemblages. The transhumant winter–summer, lowland–upland settlement pattern proposed by Barker (1981) for Late Upper Palaeolithic central-southern

Figure 13.8. Franchthi Cave, Greece.

Italy may have been replaced by flexible semisedentary groups tending to keep near coastal lagoons and rare water sources, a 'network of loosely-defined social groups and communities linked by a variety of social relationships [which] extended over vast areas' (Milliken 1998a: 78, 1998b). Such networks would have facilitated both direct and indirect procurement of flint. The combination of ibex and shellfish at coastal Tyrrhenian sites of Italy such as the Grotta Erica and Grotta La Porta is perhaps suggestive of winter exploitation in connection with unknown inland sites, or different types of coastal sites further north or south. For example, rare marine shells at Latronico 3 in nearby Basilicata and in the Abruzzo show Mesolithic movement from coasts at least 100 km into the hills (Mussi et al. 2000).

At the Grotta dell' Uzzo, Sicily, a variety of evidence including fish otoliths has led Taglia-cozzo (1993) to propose that the Mesolithic sequence demonstrates increasingly lengthy seasonal occupations of the site perhaps culminating in year-round sedentism for at least part of the group (Figure 13.7). Initially, subsistence evidence is dominated by the remains of red deer and pig; in the later Mesolithic fish, shellfish and birds were added, together with gathered plant resources (e.g., wild olives, pulses) from a 'classic' Mediterranean landscape with evergreen oak, Strawberry Tree, and *Phillyrea* (Costantini 1989). This can be contrasted with the pattern at Franchthi in Greece, where occupation becomes much more sporadic in the latest Mesolithic (Figure 13.8). Rather than conforming to rigid types, such evidence of opportunism, dynamism, and chronological differentiation suggests that regionally specific social and environmental conditions governed the ways that people inhabited their landscapes.

In addition to attempting to categorise patterns of group movement, it may also sometimes be helpful to think in terms of mobility as inhering in certain types of goods and people. The movement of flint over several hundred kilometres during the Late Upper Palaeolithic is well-known in Europe and may be linked to high individual and group mobility related to herd following, for example.

In general, the Mesolithic shows evidence of less extensive movement. This is most obviously and commonly seen in the presence of marine shells at inland sites, typically at distances of up to 50 km from the modern coast. In some cases this is best explained as individual or group acquisition for subsistence, but in other cases the distance or quantities involved suggest that other forms of mobility and eventual use are involved. Similar arguments can be made for the common finds of Mediterranean-derived shells in inland sites, carried there as perforated ornaments, or for their production. Such evidence has been found in the Ebro valley, for example, with *Columbella* found high in the Pyrenees at Balma Margineda, about 150 km from the coast, and also much further north (Cava Almuzara 1994: 83–4, Barandiarán and Cava 1989: 580, Pallarés et al. 1997: 125). At the open-air inland settlement of Sota Palou, Gerona, northeast Spain, interpreted as a relatively short-term late-summer–autumn site on the basis of the fruit remains, such shells are sometimes associated with ochre (Carbonell 1985), as are those at the Grotta del Pozzo in central Italy (Mussi et al. 2000: 283). Finds of Mediterranean shells in central Europe (Jochim 1990) show that materials were sometimes moved long distances inland, perhaps passing through several hands. Similarly, although there is ample evidence for the expedient use of local raw materials, fine-grained stone was acquired from more distant sources for the production of geometric microliths and tools needing accurate blade production and retouch, showing preferential material use for certain tools (e.g., Straus et al. [1990: 469] for Vidigal, and Aubry et al. [1997: 185] for Buraca Grande in Portugal; Barandiarán and Cava [1989: 578] for Botiqería and Costalena in the lower Ebro valley, Aragon, Spain; Runnels [1995: 722] citing Sordinas for the site of Sidari on northern Corfu; a similar trend can be seen in the report by Vigliardi [1968] on the Grotta di San Teodoro, northern Sicily). This pattern seems to occur commonly for distances of up to 50–60 km. In some areas such as the Salento (the heel of Italy), it seems that distances of four to five times as far were involved (Milliken and Skeates 1989). A single find of obsidian 350 km from the source island of Lipari, Sicily, in the Grotta Romanelli, southeast Italy (Milliken 1998: 78) suggests that exchange as well as direct procurement was a possible mechanism.

Travel by members of sparsely scattered but relatively mobile communities clearly offers opportunities for contact, though how this was structured is difficult to examine. Mesolithic people also travelled by river and sea. This is most famously demonstrated by the appearance of source-specific obsidian from the island of Melos in the southern Greek cave of Franchthi around ten thousand years ago. From around the same time or a little later, larger islands such as Crete, Cyprus, Sardinia, Corsica and Mallorca – 165 km from the present coast – were visited or permanently occupied (Cherry 1990, Costa et al. 2003, Lanfranchi 1998, Peltenburg et al. 2000, Tykot 1999: 68–9, Vigne and Desse-Berset 1995), but not Malta nor most smaller islands. However, the extent, nature and dating of these island occupations is controversial and they have often been described as 'pre-Neolithic' rather than Mesolithic, although Corsica and Sardinia have recently produced several dated sites which suggest fairly persistent occupation (Costa et al. 2003, Lanfranchi 1998). Part of the reason for the ambiguity is the apparently expedient nature of the use of stone (for example, lacking microliths), which makes it difficult to assimilate the assemblages into traditional typological schemes. It also should be noted that many of these large islands had an impoverished faunal spectrum, and especially lacked larger mammals typical of continental Europe. However, there were compensations in endemic (and perhaps more easily captured) fauna such as the small and now extinct Mallorcan antelope (*Myotragus balearicus*) and the 'rabbit deer' (*Prolagus sardus*), about the size of a large rat, on Sardinia.

At the other end of the period the spread of early Neolithic traits shows that soon after eight thousand years ago people with grain and livestock were able to sail out of sight of land across the Mediterranean. Trips were undertaken from Sicily for up to 140 km to the tiny islands of

Lampedusa and Pantelleria, or to the larger landfall of Malta. Even earlier trips took place from Anatolia in southern Turkey to the island of Crete (Broodbank and Strasser 1990). PPNB farmers from the Levant may have settled Cyprus earlier still (Peltenburg et al. 2000). Similarly, people were perfectly capable of crossing the Adriatic, as evidenced in pottery styles from the early Impressed Wares onwards (Bass 1998). Although difficult to demonstrate directly, it seems likely that at least some of these modes of distribution relate to established patterns of Mesolithic movement and contact.

Knowledge and materials were thus able to circulate in various ways and contexts, along with their stories and culturally specific practices. Access and rights to materials and to sacred, spiritual, and practical knowledge were not necessarily distributed equally among or within communities. The ability to transcend distances, undertake movements, and acquire and use practical and spiritual knowledge (Helms 1988), sometimes embodied in material objects and in the understood nature and use of the land, was a focus of social practices that become increasingly archaeologically visible during the Holocene.

Regional Summaries

Mediterranean Iberia

In contrast to central and southern Portugal (Arnaud 1989, Straus this volume), with middens such as those of the Mira and later of the Tagus and Sado valleys, such sites are rare in southernmost Spain (Tortosa and Ripoll 1995: 121). There has been a tendency for radiocarbon samples to be concentrated in the final Palaeolithic and the early Neolithic. As a consequence, attention has been focussed on developing chronotypologies for the Mesolithic based on typological variability in lithic assemblages such as proportions of tool types (especially geometric microliths) (Tortosa and Ripoll 1995: 124–8), at the expense of considering functional, spatial and settlement variation. Yet many sites have low numbers of retouched tools, and some radiocarbon dates suggest overlap between differently characterised assemblages. In addition, we can note that as for Portugal there are sites with macrolithic tools and debitage. In and around the Ebro basin and the Pyrenees there are also sites and layers within sites, which lack geometric microliths but have retouched tools dominated by denticulates and scrapers (Morales and Arnaud 1990: 454, Pallarés et al. 1997: 133). This has led some to suggest that the Sauveterrian *sensu stricto* is restricted to the French side of the Pyrenees. Nevertheless, there is a general tendency through time for the process of 'microlithisation' noted earlier to accelerate, in conjunction with a marked decline in bone tools such as points and harpoons (Tortosa and Ripoll 1995: 125).

Many of the assemblages that seem later on chronotypological grounds (i.e., the geometric facies) are associated with lakes and lagoons, and in recent years coastal midden sites such as El Collado, which also include sites with 'cemetery' burials, have been reported (Aparicio 1992). We also may note that the vast bulk of known early Holocene sites in Mediterranean Spain occurs within 50 km of the present coast, well within any postulated logistic territories or annual rounds (Bernabeu et al. 1995: 210). This might seem analogous to the later Mesolithic in central and southern Portugal, but it is not yet clear how far the comparative rarity of coastal sites in southern and eastern Spain is a 'real' difference, or a result of greater masking or destruction, or lack of survey and recognition. Certainly some sites (most notably the cave of Nerja) show a high proportion of marine resources – fish, shellfish, crabs, sea urchins, and also seal – from the very late Pleistocene onwards, although, interestingly, at El Collado, for example, 'isotopic data clearly show that marine foods were an important part of the diets of some individuals at this site but not the dominant dietary protein sources despite the site's nature as a shell midden and its coastal location' (Guixé et al. 2006: 553).

Much of the published faunal analysis has concentrated on the larger mammals (but see Aura et al. 2002). Most of the Spanish site assemblages are dominated by one species of ungulate, either red deer (e.g., Cova Matutano, Cova dels Blaus, Botiqería de los Moros and Castaleno) or ibex (Tossal de la Roca, Cueva de Nerja). Perhaps contrary to general expectations, if anything there appears to be an increase in such specialisation during the earlier Holocene, with typically 80–90 percent of the large ungulate remains belonging to one species. However, the variety of resources available is shown by the occurrence of species with different habitat preferences in the same deposits: horse, aurochs, wild boar, and sometimes chamois and roe deer, as well as birds, fish, and wild carnivores (Tortosa and Ripoll 1995: 131). Some of this variation may, of course, reflect different mobility, processing, consumption and discard patterns. We also should bear in mind that although species such as ibex and chamois are now confined to high mountain zones, they are likely to have been much more widespread at lower altitudes in the past, albeit with preferences for particular types of terrain such as rocky or karst landscapes. However, especially in those deposits relating to the final Pleistocene and earliest Holocene, the faunal assemblages are often dominated numerically by the remains of lagomorphs (rabbit and occasional hare).

Many more sites, both in caves and rock shelters and in the open, are known from the areas in and on both sides of the Pyrenees. Here, too, it seems as though, unsurprisingly, we can see the (re-) establishment of sites during the very late Pleistocene and early Holocene (García-Argüelles et al. 1992, Bahn 1989, Geddes et al. 1989, Barandiarán and Cava 1989) in areas opened up by warmer conditions and changes in the distribution of flora and fauna, and often based on exploitation of ibex. Sites with particularly good preservation and excavation show the richness of resource availability and use. At Balma Margineda in Andorra, trout and eel bones (probably from autumn capture) have been found, together with remains of hazel shells, seeds from salad plants and fruits such as blackberry, hawthorn, and wild pear (Geddes et al. 1989: 568–9). At Cingle Vermell, there are remains of freshwater fish, acorns, walnuts, pine nuts, cherries, plums, and other plant remains, again probably from autumn collection (Bahn 1989: 558). At the Font del Ros, residue analysis is said to show evidence for the processing of acorns and hazelnuts (Pallarés et al. 1997: 125), and beechnuts also would have been a source of carbohydrate. Charcoal evidence shows that other resources such as wild cherry and almonds were also available, for example, at La Poujade, France (Vernet 1997: 101). Despite the richness of the remains, many of these sites were only seasonally occupied and are sometimes described as specialized ibex-hunting sites of the type identified in northern Spain. Other contemporaneous sites are likely to have been at lower altitudes, in river valleys and nearer to the coast, but have generally been more difficult to identify.

France

Away from the Pyrenees, at sites such as the Balma Abeurador in western Languedoc and now about 50 km away from the coast, the sequence shows the classic growth in microlithic and hyper-microlithic tools throughout the earlier Mesolithic (Philibert 2002). After the earliest Holocene layers, remains of large mammals become rare, although ibex is replaced by red and roe deer and wild boar (Vaquer et al. 1986). Charcoal analysis shows the expected change from open to more wooded temperate and then Mediterranean conditions. However, the importance of this site lies more in the careful recovery procedures for macrofaunal, microfaunal, and botanical remains.

Evidence of extensive use of wild plants has been found, especially legumes (lentils, peas, and chickpeas), together with fruiting trees (*Prunus* sp.). Bones of salmon and of birds, which probably would not have occurred in the immediate vicinity of the cave, show that this upland site (570 m) was a base for trips to lakes, rivers, marshes, woodlands, and upland areas up to at least 10 km away (Vaquer et al. 1986: 6). Although consumption and discard practices may have been different for large mammals, there is the suggestion that the use of microliths is related here to the exploitation of birds, fish, and plants as much as large game.

The area of the eastern Pyrenees and western Languedoc is also interesting for demonstrating many of the chronological and typological problems in defining a Mesolithic: in some areas the shift from herd animals towards ibex, red deer, and boar occurs well before the beginning of the Holocene. Although there are regional groupings in lithic technology such as the late Mesolithic points, many of the assemblages are made on locally available poor-quality materials, which thus appear atypical in classic typological terms. Although there is change as well as continuity of tradition, many of the known sites, mainly rock shelters, seem to show the expedient use of raw materials encountered during fairly specialized activities (Geddes et al. 1986: 70–5).

In general, there is a contrast between inland parts of southwest France and northeast Spain, where specialised dependence on single species is the norm, and areas of southern Iberia, especially coastal areas, where greater variety in resources from the late Glacial onwards encouraged a variety of subsistence practices and associated technologies. It is perhaps for this reason that the changes from Magdalenian-type assemblages to microlaminar or geometric Epipalaeolithic facies seem both typologically and chronologically less marked in southern Iberia (e.g., Aura Tortosa 1992: 174, cf. Straus 1996: 95–6, Straus this volume). Specialisation, while bringing its own rewards, also may necessitate more radical shifts in settlement patterns and technology when it becomes unsustainable, in contrast to already diversified practices in which relatively minor changes may suffice. The practical flexibility of roles within the latter type of communities may also lead to the emphasis of status or identity in other spheres. The marked differentiation of child burials at Moita do Sebastião in Portugal, variation in burial practice at Franchthi, Greece, and apparent increases in perforated shell ornaments may be intimations of these sorts of differences.

In central, southern and southeastern France the same general pattern is observed, although the sequences again derive from caves and rockshelters. Many authors have noted the apparent typological boundary (running northwards from approximately modern-day Toulon), which separates Magdalenian-Azilian-Sauveterrian assemblages of the west (Sacchi 1976) from those to the east and including Italy (Bartolomei et al. 1979, Escalon de Fonton et al. 1979, Onaratini 1979, Graziosi 1983, Martini 1996, Valdeyron this volume), which show continuity with Epigravettian traditions. These are still often defined by regional facies dependent on type-sites and the presence or absence of particular tool types such as Montclus triangles or Istres points. For example, around the lower Rhône at sites such as Abri Cornille and Châteauneuf-les-Martigues, late Glacial 'Valorguien' coastal assemblages are followed by the 'Montadien' and the 'Castelnovien', and demonstrate increasingly smaller points and the introduction of geometric microliths often in the form of trapezes (Escalon de Fonton et al. 1979). There is a contrast between the coastal and interior sequences, with the Mesolithic industries of the latter being seen as variants of the Sauveterrian assemblages typical of the west (Escalon de Fonton 1976c, 1976d). At sites close to the coast such as Châteauneuf-les-Martigues and Gramari, rabbit remains are abundant, and locally horse and aurochs are still important, but generally boar and deer are the dominant game species (Rozoy 1978: 1030). Again evidence of movement is found with seashells (*Columbella*) appearing at inland sites such as the Baume-de-Montclus, 100 km from the modern coastline (Rozoy 1978: 742).

Italy

Many of the sites in southern France show a gap or series of gaps in the archaeological record around the Pleistocene-Holocene boundary (see, e.g., Renault-Miskovsky et al. 1979: fig. 13.3, pp. 64–5), perhaps often because of increased erosion in wetter Holocene environments. A similar pattern emerges for coastal caves on the Tyrrhenian coast of southern Italy, though here later erosion by the sea when at its maximum height also was a factor. In western Liguria, this gap is even more pronounced, with 'Epigravettian' occupation apparently largely coming to an end at the beginning of the Holocene (Biagi et al. 1989, Maggi 1999: 51–3), typified by the famous site of Arene Candide (Maggi 1997). The fact that early (Sauveterrian) and late Mesolithic (Castelnovian) activity is well known from eastern Liguria and Tuscany suggests that there were real regional differences in population and/or settlement pattern and subsistence practices. There are also chronological differences, with the earlier Mesolithic sites generally within 10 km of the coast and at less than 1,000 m altitude, whereas many of the later sites are both higher and further inland (but see Fontana and Guerreschi 2003). This in turn contrasts with the even higher ibex-hunting sites known from northeast Italy, which are dominated by armatures as are some Mesolithic sites in northern Tuscany but not in eastern Liguria (Maggi 1999: 55).

Whatever the terminology, the general pattern in southeast France and much of Italy is for very late Pleistocene and earlier Holocene 'armatures' to be dominated by triangles and crescents, whereas the later Mesolithic Castelnovien assemblages are dominated by trapezes often made by microburin technique on highly standardized blades (Broglio 1980, 1995). With the demise of strictly culture-historical and chronotypological approaches, there has been more emphasis on possible functional explanations of variability (see especially Bietti 1980, Bietti 1990 for Italy). More recently, it has been accepted that in southern Italy, too, a generalized Sauveterrian-Castelnovien sequence can be recognised at certain sites such as the Grotta della Serratura in Campania, the Tuppo dei Sassi and Grotta Latronico 3 in Basilicata, and the Grotta Marisa and Grotta delle Mura in Puglia (Calattini 1996, Martini 1996, Tozzi 1996). These Holocene assemblages sometimes succeed the 'Romanellian', which is similar to the Azilian in that the tool dimensions are reduced, most notably the scrapers, which become small and often circular. Often used as a cultural 'type-fossil', it is more satisfactory to regard these largely as a response to changed socioenvironmental conditions, in which people were prepared to reduce, resharpen, and rehaft scrapers rather than make them from new. This and other practices may sometimes have been a response to absolute or relative scarcity, as in the Salento Peninsula in the heel of Italy (Bietti 1987, Milliken 1998). Besides the morphological changes, there are also general structural changes in the assemblages, with an increase in 'armatures', scrapers, and denticulates and a decline in burins. But there are contemporaneous layers within sites where armatures are rare or absent, for example, the upper layers at Grotta di San Teodoro and Levanzo in Sicily (Segre and Vigliardi 1983), denticulates important and the technology generally much less standardised and expedient – Martini's 'undifferentiated EpiPalaeolithic' (Martini 1996: 39–40, cf. Milliken 1998: 75).

In central and southern Italy, increased evidence of exploitation of birds, fish, and shellfish is seen from the Late Pleistocene as well as the early Holocene. This is true both of inland sites around the Fucino lake basin and at coastal sites such as Grotta Romanelli, Puglia, Grotta della Madonna, Calabria, and Grotta dell' Uzzo, Sicily. The relatively low productivity of the Mediterranean perhaps explains why shellfish exploitation and potentially other activity remain seasonal and often minor activities, albeit with periods of greater residential stability (cf Guixé et al. 2006 for Spain, Mannino et al. 2007, Colonese et al. 2009). Red deer and wild boar became the dominant large game species over much of Italy, although in the north and in some southern sites in or close to mountainous areas (southwest Campania, northwest Calabria, and Basilicata: e.g., Grotta Erica, Grotta La Porta, Grotta della Madonna, Grotta Latronico 3), ibex or chamois were locally important. In the south, the wild ass *Equus hydruntinus* occured in the Holocene, but the main regional contrast is between Puglia, where aurochs and equids remained important, and the deer-boar emphasis in other areas (Mazzetti et al. 1995). The persistence of wild cattle and horse in the Salento peninsula of Puglia probably relates to a much less wooded karst environment (Harding 1992). All this would suggest that much of the interassemblage and regional variation that has been ascribed to cultural or chronological differentiation might be better understood as complex interactions between local conditions, opportunities, practices, and techniques.

Greece

The nature and extent of the Mesolithic in Greece has been the subject of much recent debate. Two factors have been important in this discussion: the small number of known sites (a maximum of twelve according to Runnels 1995: 706, but see Perlès 2001: 20–37, Galanidou and Perlès 2003), of which very few are the subject of detailed or recent excavation and publication; and the marked contrast this makes with the preceding and succeeding periods. A similar picture also may be noted for Turkey, where apart from a few cave sites in the southwest of the country and finds among Black Sea dunes (Gatsov and Özdogan 1994) the Mesolithic *sensu stricto* is virtually unknown. Because this position has persisted despite numerous focused prehistoric surveys, this has sometimes led to Mesolithic Greece being characterised as an almost deserted landscape before extensive Neolithic settlement (Runnels 1995).

The picture is almost certainly more complicated. Evidence from elsewhere in Europe suggests that recognisable and maybe more permanent Mesolithic sites are most commonly found on coasts and in the bottoms of river valleys. If this is so, then in addition to destruction by erosion, many Mesolithic sites will be buried either under the sea, because of the rise in postglacial sea levels, with the loss of perhaps more than half of the maximum extent of land exposed during the Last Glacial Maximum (Runnels 1995: 727), or under deep Holocene alluviation in river valleys. These factors may have been exacerbated by the mountainous topography of Greece in conjunction with a violent Mediterranean climate. At present, however, the reasonably secure Mesolithic sites appear to cluster in two zones: the north-west coast and the south-east of mainland Greece, typified respectively by Sidari on the north coast of Corfu (Sordinas 2003), and the best-known site, the cave of Franchthi in the Argolid (Runnels et al. 1999: 125–9). To these must be added the important cave sites of Theopetra, with Mesolithic as well as Late Upper Palaeolithic levels (Kyparissi-Apostolika 1999, 2003), and Youra in the northern Sporades (Sampson 1998, Sampson et al. 2003, Galanidou and Perlés 2003), together with the important settlement at Maroulas on Kythnos, with circular structures and burials (Sampson et al. 2002).

A strong argument against this 'empty landscape' scenario is the fact that the successful long-term reproduction of any society demands a pool of potential mates numbering several hundred. It is therefore certain, given the size estimates of the small groups who may have used the known sites, that, however sparse, there must have been much more extensive Mesolithic occupation than is currently evident. However, recent predictive survey and reexamination of previously collected materials suggest that even if site sizes are small, there are indeed many more 'hidden' in the landscape and among collections that point to Mesolithic presence (Runnels et al. 2005; Runnels 2009). What does seem to have happened, and perhaps more markedly so than in many other areas of the western Mediterranean, is a major change in occupation strategies immediately preceding the Holocene. Runnels (1995: 706) notes the apparent abandonment of Upper Palaeolithic sites 'producing a significant hiatus between about 13,000 and 10,000 bp'.

However, we do have one or two sites (Franchthi, Theopetra) with apparently more or less continuous sequences, of which so far the most famous and best published is Franchthi in southern Argolid, with a sequence from c. 25,000 BP to the Neolithic and beyond (Jacobsen 1976, Jacobsen and Farrand 1987: fig. 13.9). Even here, however, occupational hiatuses, covering several hundred years, occur between the final Upper Palaeolithic and the early Mesolithic, and again between the early and later Mesolithic (Farrand 2000). The Late Upper Palaeolithic-Mesolithic sequence as a whole demonstrates changes of emphasis in subsistence, from equids, aurochs, and caprines towards red deer and pig, but in subsistence terms the Pleistocene-Holocene boundary is not well marked, with evidence for plant, fish, and shellfish exploitation before the Holocene (Payne 1982, 1988, 1992). Perhaps the most significant change is the presence of a small amount of obsidian from Melos, an island about 100 km southeast of Franchthi, which would definitely have involved a considerable sea voyage. In the later Mesolithic layers, there is an increase in the amount of obsidian (though still a tiny proportion of the total lithic material) and further evidence of orientation towards the sea with the appearance of bones from blue-fin tuna. Bone fishhooks and increased amounts of shellfish, both for consumption and production of decorative ornaments, confirm this change of strategy. The diversity of resource use in the Mesolithic is also shown in terms of the plant material, with much increased use of plants including wild lentils, oats, and barley (Hansen 1992), together with grinding stones, which may have been used for processing. In the upper/final Mesolithic, the evidence of occupation seems to become much sparser, and may be discontinuous. This pattern is also seen in burials, which seem more common in the earlier Mesolithic (Cullen 1995).

Perlés (1990, 1992, 1995, 2003) has concentrated as much on styles of technique, raw material procurement and the behavioural implications as on the typology of the finished product, as well as integrating interpretations with other forms of evidence. At Franchthi, she points out that during the last few millennia of the Pleistocene the assemblages are dominated by microlithic points and backed blades, with the introduction of classic 'Mesolithic' geometric microliths made by the microburin technique towards the end of this sequence. The number of tool types also increases, and there is evidence for foraging for plants, shellfish, and fish. After a gap in the record, the assemblages of the early Mesolithic (lithic stage 7) show radical changes. In the first half of the tenth millennium BP, the tools relate to 'domestic' uses for the working of wood, reeds, and other materials, with pieces with lateral retouch, notches, denticulates, and scrapers comprising 7 percent of the assemblage. Microliths virtually disappear. In the later Mesolithic (stage 8), in conjunction with the dominance of tuna bones in the deposits, microliths of various types, now including trapezes, reappear and are the largest group of tools, but often expediently made on flakes rather than blades. Perlés suggests these relate to fish exploitation (1995: 199). Evidence for occupation in the final Mesolithic (stage 9) is sparse and perhaps discontinuous, but the lithics again resemble those of the earlier Mesolithic (Perlès 1999). Perlés argues convincingly that at Franchthi the changes relate to site use, hunting, processing and residential patterns, and proposes complex and dynamic relations between techniques and traditions, functional requirements, raw materials, and activities at any particular site. Her studies at Franchthi have implications far beyond the Greek Mesolithic. For example, the appearance of tools prefiguring 'Sauveterrian points' and the earliest trapezes in Europe (1995: 187, 193) underlines the poverty of culture historical chronotypologies as the sole basis for explanation, and the need for explanations that consider technical and functional constraints, and requirements and solutions in relation to subsistence activities, as well as cultural traditions. Many of the points made by Perlès have relevance to other Mediterranean sites, where the presence of Holocene assemblages without geometric microliths has been interpreted in purely chronological terms (e.g., in Sicily at the Grotta dell' Uzzo and Grotta di San Teodoro, cf. Perlès 2003: 83, Sordinas 2003).

Despite regional variability, then, in general the hiatus noted by Runnels in final Late Upper Palaeolithic occupation sites may be correlated with changes in the landscape, including floral and faunal communities, and movement within it. At one extreme, for Runnels, the change from steppe and open forest and the loss of large herd animals was so drastic that it led to depopulation of Greece in the final millennia of the Palaeolithic: 'I consider the presently available evidence to point to the introduction of the Mesolithic by sea-faring people who are unrelated to the Pleistocene inhabitants of Greece' (1995: 725). There is nothing inherently implausible in this scenario: we can envisage many if not most final Palaeolithic and Mesolithic communities (in whole or in part) as capable of extreme mobility. Perlès (1995: 205–7, 2001: 20–30) suggests that the coastal strategies seen in the Greek Mesolithic were a necessity, with the forested but still open environments of southern Greece supporting insufficient densities of red deer and pig, or appropriate plant foods, to replace the earlier larger ungulates in dietary terms. Perhaps the Late Upper Palaeolithic hiatus shows a change from extreme movements between (unknown) coastal plain sites and upland exploitation to an emphasis on more restricted occupational mobility centred on the coastal plain (Bailey 1999), and with marked regional variability. On this view, the known Mesolithic in Greece at places such as Franchthi represents the more intensive reoccupation of coastal zones linked in part to continued rises in sea level. The presence of Melian obsidian is the expression of partly sea-oriented logistical mobility developed at the very end of the Pleistocene.

Art

Despite the difficulties of dating parietal art, it is now clear that Mesolithic people continued to produce what seem to us to be nonfunctional representations and other markings in caves and on rock faces, stones, slabs, and pebbles. Clearly, the rarity of organic preservation in the Mediterranean means that huge biases may have developed in the survival of such material, and decoration – of whatever meaning – may have been common on other objects such as wood as well as on human bodies. If there is a contrast to be drawn with the Late Upper Palaeolithic, it is the preponderance of much more schematic rather than naturalistic figures, along with other abstract markings, and in the painted Spanish Levantine art in particular, the appearance of hunting scenes and human figures (Figure 13.9). Numerous attempts have been made to produce chronological schemes based on style (for discussion, see, e.g., Beltrán 1992, Hernandez Perez 1992, Viñas Vallverdú 1992), but with hundreds of sites known from Iberia with potential continuity of parietal and mobiliary 'art' from the Upper Palaeolithic to perhaps the Iron Age in date, isolating Mesolithic representations as a meaningful entity is fraught with difficulty. However, it seems likely that engraved realistic representations, largely of animals, are confined mainly to the period around the Pleistocene-Holocene boundary. Subsequent figures and signs seem to be mainly painted, with a tendency towards smaller size, more schematism, and numerous human figures (Beltrán 1992, Hernandez Perez 1992), although see, for example, the black figures and signs at Nerja near Malaga in southern Spain (Dams 1987). Of the three main types of post-glacial art recognized, it is that called Levantine that has most often been ascribed to the Mesolithic (e.g., Beltran 1992, Hernandez Perez 1992). But the current consensus is that all three should rather be ascribed to the Neolithic or later periods, and that the preponderance of hunting scenes should be given a more ideological rather than realist

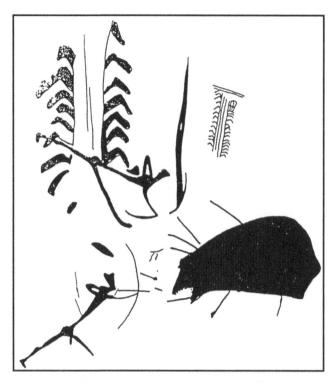

Figure 13.9. Two archers in a 'Levantine' hunting scene with earlier 'geometric' images, at Las Chaparros, Spain (after Beltrán 1993). Height of original panel approximately 60 cm.

interpretation and associated rather with the transition to agriculture (e.g., McClure et al. 2008). In Italy, too, there are engraved naturalistic animals and humans, notably in the cave at Addaura, near Palermo in northern Sicily, and on Levanzo, now a small island off western Sicily (Pluciennik 1994), which may date to the very late Pleistocene or perhaps the early Holocene (Figure 13.10). Rare painted figures and signs elsewhere (e.g., Riparo Ranaldi, Basilicata), and some of the much more prolific material at Grotta dei Cervi, Porto Badisco, Puglia, although largely considered Neolithic, also may be partly ascribed to earlier periods (Whitehouse 1992).

As with all art of whatever period, this material is extremely difficult to interpret, and we should be aware of potentially highly variable contexts of production and meaning in space and time. Criado Boado and Penedo Romero (1993) have tried to suggest that Spanish post-Palaeolithic Levantine art reflects increasing concern for humans and human practices perceived as interacting with nature, whereas the rarity of human representation in the Upper Palaeolithic suggests a passive vision of the natural world. However, this contrast seems an overly simple and homogenized rewriting of the culture-nature divide in the modern West. What is notable in all this figurative art is that by far the greatest number of representations are of large game animals (e.g., ibex, cattle, and deer in Spain), rather than rabbits, fish, shellfish, or plants, which in many cases would have been major components of the diet. One general argument therefore is that much of the material relates to particular and perhaps strongly gendered activities by restricted groups. These associations may therefore have taken on added and changed significance in forms of gender ideology precisely as

Figure 13.10. Incised images at the Grotta dell'Addaura, northern Sicily. The famous 'acrobat' scene is in the top right. Height of original panel approximately 1 m.

other types of subsistence became more widespread, whether fishing, gathering, trapping, cultivation, or herding (cf. Bradley 1997, Whitehouse 1992).

A second widespread category of apparently nonfunctional objects is that of Azilian pebbles, naturally rounded stones, 4–5 cm in length, generally painted with spots and lines (Martini 1992). These seem to be largely confined to the Mesolithic, although they appear slightly earlier, and their use may also extend into the Neolithic (Couraud 1985: 130–1). Some of the pebbles are engraved with abstract designs, and painted bone fragments are also known. By far the largest concentration is at the eponymous Mas d'Azil in SW France, where more than a thousand such pebbles were found, but they are also known in large numbers from elsewhere in southern France and northern Spain (Straus this volume). In Italy, they only occur in small numbers (a maximum of twelve from Arene Candide in Liguria, closest to the 'core' of southwest France) in indeterminate contexts in caves. They may even represent loss rather than intentional placing, though at the Grotta della Madonna in Calabria one pebble was associated with a juvenile burial (Cardini 1970), and at the Baume-de-Montclus in France another was found above the stones filling a grave (Duday 1976: 736). Couraud (1985: 148–9) has tentatively proposed that the decorative syntax may have been a form of calendrical lunar notation. They also have been seen as cult objects, whether for an individual or a larger community, perhaps representing ancestors (Whitehouse 1992), but whatever explanation we prefer, the contrast between the vast numbers found at Mas d'Azil and elsewhere suggests that depositional and other contexts varied along with potential meanings.

A third widespread category overlapping in form and style with the Azilian pebbles is that of the inscribed stone slabs and pieces of bone. These are engraved with animals or animal heads or geometric lattices, ladders, meanders or grid-like markings, at least some of which would appear to date to the early Holocene, for example, Tossal de la Roca, Alicante, and Cova Matutano in Valencia (Beltrán 1992: 406–7), and Levanzo, Sicily (Graziosi 1962). Scratched superimposed lines on animals may perhaps represent 'ritual killing'. In Italy and Sicily, however, this sort of material is absent from the Mesolithic, and cave walls associated with this period are marked only by indeterminate vertical linear markings, followed by the appearance of painted material in the later Neolithic (Pluciennik 1994, 2002). This apparent decline in parietal art contrasts with the situation in Spain and also elsewhere in Europe, for example, the extensive engravings known from the Paris Basin (Hinout 1998). However, there are sites with hundreds of largely geometrically engraved mobiliary pieces, for example, Grotta delle Veneri, Puglia. Dating of these pieces is often uncertain but production would appear to continue from the Late Upper Palaeolithic into the Mesolithic (Martini 1998). So far no categories of 'art' are known from Greece, although very late Pleistocene inscribed parietal and mobiliary art similar to that described earlier for the central and western Mediterranean is known from southern Turkey (Otte et al. 1995). The contrast between the trajectories in these different areas is unlikely to mean that some societies "abandoned'" symbolic practices, but, rather, that such expression was occurring in organic media, via nonmaterial practices, or at other locations.

Demography, Death, and Social Organisation

The rarity of large samples makes it difficult to investigate demography for the Mediterranean Mesolithic. Work on southern Portuguese groups suggests stable populations with a relatively low death rate, despite evidence of seasonal food shortages coupled with 'reliance on tainted stored food' (Lubell et al. 1994: 208). The topographic and ecological variety available to coastal Mesolithic groups may have reduced nutritional and seasonal stress, and it has been argued that Mesolithic populations were in some respects 'healthier' than their Neolithic counterparts. Nevertheless, we must remember that infant and child mortality would have been high and 'should' perhaps represent 50–60 percent of our death populations. In relatively small and flexible groups endemic diseases may have been less prevalent, but clearly injury and infectious disease would have been more life threatening. Physical anthropological evidence and modern studies of hunter-gatherer demography (but clearly in very different conditions) suggest life expectancy would perhaps have been somewhere between thirty and forty years (for discussion, see Kelly 1995: 251–9, Meiklejohn and Zvelebil 1991). Rozoy (1978: 1192) famously characterised Mesolithic hunter-gatherers as 'free and careless [sic] families of bowmen', but the palaeopathological evidence of periodic food shortages, injuries and other stresses (e.g., child-bearing), coupled with high infant and child mortality suggest that this is a highly romanticised view.

However, it is difficult for us to imagine contemporary Mesolithic perceptions and expectations of life. There were individuals who reached ages of fifty or sixty, and it is likely that such elders would have had considerable status for their accumulated knowledge and experience; however, other roles, identities and life-stages were also probably valued, for example, in association with fertility. Certainly we have evidence that all sectors of the population, female and male adults and children, were at times carefully buried, and there is little evidence of overall systematic discrimination, at least in this sphere. Typically, extended Mesolithic inhumations (cremation has rarely been recognised, but see later) contain few grave goods, although antlers, perforated shells that may have been personal ornaments, the presence of ochre, and less certainly intentionally deposited stone tools are often found within grave deposits. Sometimes the grave cuts are surrounded by stones or have slabs placed on top as at the Grotta dell'Uzzo and Franchthi, and evidence of burning above some graves may be evidence of associated hearths for offerings, feasting or other practices. However, given the extreme bias of the record, it is difficult to suggest either broad-scale or localised evidence of systematic treatments that might give us insight into differential meanings (for catalogues of many of the known Mesolithic burials in Europe, see Newell et al. 1979, Grünberg 2000).

The formal cemeteries of northern and eastern Europe and the midden sites of Portugal, often taken to be good pointers to territorial stability, group-boundedness, and even the importance of lineages, are so far largely unknown in the Mediterranean, though the example of El Collado in southern Spain with 15 individuals buried at a midden site (Aparicio 1992) hints at a range of practices and poor survival: otherwise only two separate examples of single Mesolithic remains are known from Mediterranean Spain. Instead, other factors are highlighted at the best known sites. In several coastal or near-coastal sites in northern Sicily (Grotta dell' Uzzo, Grotta di San Teodoro, Grotta Molara), we can consider these burials as founding statements or claims, as the majority are placed in graves dug into archaeologically sterile layers at the beginning of lengthy sequences of cultural deposition. In many cases, the burials are paired, and apparently often contain an adult male and adult female. At the Grotta di San Teodoro, the earliest burials were all aligned relative to the central axis and wholly or partly covered by a thick layer of red ochre (Graziosi 1947: fig. 13). At Uzzo, a layer of ochre was found on the bottom of some graves, and some were 'closed' by rock slabs with evidence of hearths immediately above (Borgognini Tarli and Repetto 1985, Borgognini Tarli et al. 1993). The ten burials from this site of both sexes and all ages and covering a time span of perhaps two thousand years were found towards the walls of the cave, but there may originally have been many more in the central portion, which was removed by later activities.

It is estimated that perhaps around thirty Mesolithic individuals are represented in the excavation materials from Franchthi. These range from more or less *in situ* burials towards the mouth of the cave to numerous fragments distributed throughout the excavated deposits and often only recognised by sorting residues after sieving (Cullen 1995). The remains of at least seven buried individuals have been found at Maroulas on Kythnos (Poulianos and Sampson 2008). Bone scatters are also known from other Mesolithic sites (Meiklejohn and Denston 1987), and may have gone unrecognised at others. At Franchthi, there appears to be a correlation between the frequency of human bone and occupation intensity, with most of the material deriving from the lower Mesolithic strata. Franchthi is also interesting for providing evidence of intentionally cremated and probably subsequently buried human bone. Together with probable associations of perforated shells and burning, and small rocks placed over at least the central area of the most intact skeleton (the lower Mesolithic Franchthi 1), there is evidence of both carefully executed procedures of treatment of the dead and considerable variation within those procedures. This may relate to social status but could equally refer to different circumstances of death (Cullen 1995).

Although most age groups are represented, few patterns emerge from analysis of any (probable) associated grave goods on either the regional or broader scale. However, the bias of our sample is extreme: most burials are known from partially excavated remnants of subsequently disturbed deposits in caves. In southern Italy and Sicily, for example, there are dozens of sites with human bone and lithics of possible Mesolithic age but often deriving from surface collection or within disturbed deposits (e.g., Vaufrey 1928). Similarly, in southern France small numbers of contracted burials are known from cave sites, for example, Abri Cornille, Gramari (Newell et al. 1979, Rozoy 1978: 1117–20) along with isolated fragments of human bone. Although it is tempting to link the apparently greater numbers of individual and collective burials in the Mesolithic with greater or more prolonged attachment to place, burials are well evidenced in the preceding Upper Palaeolithic, for which we may be missing other types of sites on the drowned coastal plains. We are unsure, too, in what manner our sample may have been biased, for example, where other members of the communities may have been buried or otherwise treated. Nevertheless, many authors have commented on the close association between Mesolithic burials and occupation debris (e.g., Cullen 1995, Roche 1989), which suggests a marked difference to the common attitude of physically separating the living and the remains of the dead. There are also hints of regional variations. For example, at Franchthi there is evidence of cremation and the possible reopening of burial sites and subsequent scatters, whereas the burials in northern Sicily show no evidence of near-contemporaneous disturbance. This suggests specific memory of burial place and the meaning of individual burials (if not necessarily *qua* individuals). In their turn, practices at both these sites contrast with the very clear spatial differentiation and arrangement of groups at the Moita do Sebastião midden in Portugal, for example. These may represent in part different attitudes towards the mode of incorporation of the dead into memory and society – as generalised ancestors, as differentiated groups of ancestors or kin, and as burial groups defined primarily by status in life, respectively.

Considering the burial and other evidence, both Skeates (1999) and Robb (1999) have recently plausibly argued that there is little evidence of social differentiation visible in the archaeological record for the Mesolithic of southern and eastern Italy, and this seems to hold for much of the Mediterranean when contrasted with other parts of Europe. However, variability among recent hunter-gatherers in kinship systems and other traditional categories of ethnographic analysis, as well as their apparent lack of correlation with focuses of archaeological interest such as the subsistence base (Kelly 1995, Sanger 1995) warn us that much variation may be masked. Circumscribed seasonally attractive places may have gained some importance as aggregation sites, such as the zone around Lake Fucino in central Italy (Skeates 1999). But the very ubiquity of most resources, coupled with microregional diversity, may have meant that it was difficult to achieve or maintain any materially-based form of social differentiation. With the exception of *Columbella* shells, there is little sign of movement in exotic items or raw materials that we might characterise as 'exchange'. However, the rapid rise in evidence for long-distance movement of materials during the subsequent Neolithic, for example in obsidian (Tykot 1996), greenstone (Leighton and Dixon 1992) and in the procurement and emulation of ceramics, suggests that there were established sociocultural networks which became transformed and/or intensified with the emphasis on new resources. Nevertheless, despite the presence of regional idiosyncrasies of practice best known to archaeologists through styles of stone-working, the impression is of fluctuating 'boundaries', best interpreted in terms of regional traditions rather than closely-defined groups, and facilitating the rapid cultural diffusion of new ideas. Mobility was encouraged by the existence of water-transport, though the labour-investment in boats and related technologies may be considerable and socially circumscribed (Arnold 1995). In these circumstances, producing a social geography of the Mesolithic is a considerable challenge, although new techniques such as bone isotope chemistry may have a significant role to play.

The End of the Mesolithic

The differences apparent in the mode and rate of spread of Neolithic traits throughout the Mediterranean are perhaps also in part a hint about the variation in the preceding Mesolithic. Although the Neolithic has previously often been seen as a stadial leap and single process, in fact we now know that in many areas it was mediated through Mesolithic communities, either through the process of adoption, or by the nature of relations between hunter-gatherer and (sometimes incoming) farming communities (Price 2000). For example, we have continuity in the burial practices associated with the southern French 'cardial' tradition (Beyneix 1998), and good evidence of technological and site continuity, especially in southwest France, northeast Spain, and in the Pyrenees. In much of northern Italy, in western Sicily and southern Puglia, one can also make a case for adoption (but see Biagi and Spataro 2000, Biagi and Spataro 2002), as in northwest Greece, whereas for northern and eastern Greece it is currently easier to argue for the Neolithic as at least partly an intrusive phenomenon (Halstead 1996, Runnels et al. 1999: 129). In western Iberia (as in Greece) there has tended to be polarisation between those arguing for indigenous adoption and those favouring discrete zones of colonisation. Evidence often better fits a model of the acquisition of Neolithic traits to varying degrees, but may also be taken as evidence of 'infill' colonisation and chronological overlap between 'Mesolithic' and 'Neolithic' communities (Zilhão 1993, 2000; but see Straus 1991b, Straus this volume, Jackes et al. 1997; Bamforth et al. 2003). Although there are still blank areas, reevaluation of the radiocarbon dates elsewhere, such as in the central Mediterranean (Pluciennik 1997, Forenbaher and Miracle 2005), generally supports a complex of processes throughout the Mediterranean rather than any single explanation, as for Europe more generally (Bocquet-Appel et al. 2009). We also should note that for any time period up to the mid Holocene at least, an east–west cross-section of Mediterranean societies would have revealed communities that cross-cut conventional archaeological understandings – mobile and settled farmers, herder-hunters, herder-fishers, partly-sedentary gatherer-hunter-fishers, and so on. Under these circumstances, we need to consider the Mesolithic in its own terms as part of a historical continuum, with its own identities and contingencies, not as an intermediate staging post on the way from or to somewhere else.

Conclusion

Despite the continual call (and need) for more data, it is perhaps time to move towards a type of social geography that seeks to understand similarities and differences among and between these societies in terms of social and cultural processes. To do this, geomorphologically informed surveys are needed to identify the less obvious components of landscape occupation, but as experience in Greece and elsewhere has shown, finding the 'windows' onto surviving early Holocene land surfaces in highly dynamic Mediterranean environments can be extremely difficult. Nevertheless, where possible, a landscape-based rather than site-based approach may be helpful, not just environmentally and in terms of resource exploitation, but in order to consider cosmologies, cultural expressions and differences, and the potential of 'place' (cf. Conkey 1997, Zvelebil 1995).

Although it is important not to overemphasize functional determinants, there has often been insufficient attention to possible functional variability in assemblages because of the dominance of culture-historical and typological approaches (cf. Pallares et al. 1997, Perlès 1995). Because of the partial nature of the archaeological record, with large spatial and chronological gaps, there is always a temptation to try and incorporate assemblages from various sites within larger categories in order to try and make sense of them beyond local description. Although there are large-scale similarities in technologies and subsistence practices, for example, which may partly reflect the technical and ecological constraints within which these societies reproduced, it is more difficult to understand the meaning of the differences, especially as we often have poor contextual information and less variation in surviving material culture compared with later societies. It is certainly possible to see within some of the general trends, developing and persistent areal or regional traditions, which generally seem to cover smaller areas than in the preceding Palaeolithic. Some typological approaches have thus assumed an essential 'proto-ethnic' territorially based identity to explain similarities in regional material cultures and practices. Some, notably Rozoy (1978, 1998) and Newell et al. (1990), have used these to identify 'bands' and 'tribes', either though lithic typologies or 'ornaments' from burials, but both social structure and the nature of sociocultural boundaries are likely to have been variable across both time and space. The nature of social organisation in terms of kinship or other entities, and its relationship to material culture, is unlikely to have been either clear-cut or stable, and a more porous notion of groups and social networks may be more appropriate for much of the Mesolithic.

Is there any unity to a Mediterranean Mesolithic? Many coastal or partly coastal communities may have developed similarities of outlook towards notions of travel, cardinal points, distance, or islands, for example, reinforced or stimulated by a related repertoire of cosmological understandings (Barth 1987). But axes of cultural contact, 'borrowing' and variation (which may have been gradual rather than bounded) surely ran in many directions both inland as well as seawards and along the coast. A suitable metaphor for the Mesolithic of the Mediterranean may be that of a mosaic or constellation, in which different communities or societies are seen less as variations on an underlying theme such as environment or adaptation, but, rather, as kaleidoscopes of cultural contingency, interrelatedness and historical depth – a challenge to our archaeological imaginations and methods.

Chapter 14

Mesolithic Europe: Overview
and New Problems

Geoff Bailey*

In drawing together the many rich and diverse strands of new evidence presented in the preceding chapters, we comment briefly on two themes. First, we outline a sketch of the main trends in the Mesolithic, with emphasis on those features that appear from a comparative overview to represent the most striking or novel features associated with the period. Second, we comment on what appear to us to be emerging as unresolved problems or promising avenues for future research.

Comparative Overview

The contributors to this volume are essentially unanimous in their view that the Mesolithic is best treated, at minimum, as a unit of time, whose upper and lower boundaries are arbitrary, disguising technological, social, and cultural continuities across the boundaries, and changes and innovations that occurred between them. The date of 9500 cal BC, traditionally taken as the end of the Ice Age in Europe, is now clearly seen as an arbitrary boundary across a continuum of environmental and cultural changes that extend well back into the Last Glacial period. From an archaeological point of view, there are good reasons to extend the narrative of postglacial developments back to about 13,500 cal BC with the onset of the warming trend initiated by the Late Glacial interstadials, and perhaps back to about 17,000 cal BC, when sea level first began its sustained rise from a low still stand of approximately −130 m at the Glacial Maximum. Already in southern Europe in this earlier period, human groups were beginning to move into new territory at higher altitude with climatic amelioration in pursuit of mountain resources such as ibex and chamois (Bailey 1997, Straus this volume, Pluciennik this volume), and perhaps on the evidence of coastal cave sequences in Spain (Straus this volume) to take a more serious interest in marine resources. Both these trends become more marked with time and are defining characteristics of Mesolithic exploitation patterns in many regions.

* Department of Archaeology, University of York, UK.

Sea-level rise would have exerted a wide range of effects from at least 16,500 cal BC through until the time when the sea reached its present position at about 5000 cal BC. Rising sea levels would have led to progressive inundation of the continental shelf, removed extensive areas of lowland territory, breached land connections, notably that between Britain and mainland Europe, brought existing hinterlands within reach of milder 'oceanic' climates and culminated in the creation of entirely new coastal landscapes. The palaeoecological and palaeogeographical impact of sea-level rise, and its effects on the preservation or visibility of earlier coastal archaeological evidence, would have differed in different regions but would have been far-reaching everywhere, especially where the continental shelf is shallow and extensive as in the Northwest. Here, large areas of hunting territory were lost, but in compensation were replaced by the creation of shallow inshore waters, indented coastlines, and offshore islands and archipelagos offering more productive and more easily accessible supplies of fish, sea mammals and intertidal molluscs, and of course they also were replaced by more productive hinterlands as well. Although most of these effects of sea-level rise have long been recognized, their impact on patterns of human settlement, both direct and indirect, is perhaps even wider than is generally allowed for in archaeological interpretation — and more complicated to measure.

As the ice retreated, new territory became available, and faunal and floral habitats changed, creating a complex mosaic of variable patterns that changed in different ways and at different rates in different regions. Many of the animal species of former significance moved their ranges northwards, as with reindeer and horse, or became extinct, as with mammoth and bison, and were replaced by forest or forest-edge species such as elk, red deer, roe deer, cattle, and wild boar, or chamois, ibex, and saiga antelope in more open or mountainous terrain, according to regional and local circumstances. From about 13,500 cal BC onwards, settlements associated with hunting of reindeer and, later, horse, cattle and elk, became established across newly occupied territory in the North European plain in a broad swathe from the British lowlands in the west to the steppes of Ukraine and Russia in the east (Dolukhanov this volume, Tolan-Smith this volume, Zvelebil this volume), including the now submerged bed of the North Sea on the evidence of an antler harpoon dredged up from the Leman and Ower Bank and dated to 11,600 cal BC (Tolan-Smith and Bonsall 1999). This also was the period that saw decisive occupation of the polar regions of East Siberia (Pitul'ko 1995) and the first unequivocal evidence for the expansion of human populations into the Americas (Dillehay 2000). Another notable innovation of this period, albeit one that first developed beyond European borders, is the use of pottery, with early dates in the 13,500–12,000 cal BC range now recorded from China, the Russian Far East, and Japan (Habu 2004, Kuzmin et al. 2004).

Stone industries were characterized by tanged points for hafting on the ends of spear or arrow shafts, and by 'knife' blades with curved and blunted edges. Variations in the proportion of these artefacts and minor differences in morphology of the key artefact types have given rise to a variety of cultural labels, Kukrekian, Butovian and Kudlevian in Russia and the Ukraine, Swiderian in Poland, Hamburgian, Bromme, and Ahrensburgian in northern Germany and Denmark, and Federmesser and Creswellian in the Low Countries and Britain, respectively. Whether these represent different cultural traditions associated with different founding populations, stylistic markers of distinct social groupings, functional adaptations to different types of weapons and prey species, or simply local names for similar entities, remains poorly understood. The smaller and lighter tanged points of the Ahrensburgian, associated with the final cold phase of the Younger Dryas period between about 11,000 and 9600 cal BC could well have been used as arrow points, since actual wooden bows have been recovered from this period. At any rate, the similarities across this vast territory are as impressive as any differences, with relatively small settlements, specialised toolkits of stone and antler and a considerable degree of mobility. Importation of raw materials for making artefacts from favoured sources over long distances reflects both the extended lines of communication in small mobile populations engaged in the early stages of colonizing new territory and perhaps also the fact that there was neither time nor necessity to devise ways of working with less suitable materials available nearer to hand.

As we move across the chronological boundary of 9500 cal BC, into a period characterised in many regional sequences as Early Mesolithic, there is little obvious break in technological terms with the preceding period, although there is greater diversity of raw materials, techniques of stone working, and tool types. The manufacture of microlithic stone tools made from bladelet segments, with removal of the bulbar end by the microburin technique or by truncation, was already widely established in the Late Glacial, and continued into this period. What is new is the proliferation of new geometric forms, particularly triangles and crescents. Many of these were most probably used to provide replacements for arrow tips, and the bow and arrow was widely in use throughout Europe during this period. Some also may have been used as replaceable components in other multipart tools such as knives with antler, bone, or wooden handles. There also was a general diversification of artefact-types made from stone, bone, antler, and wood, including macrolithic tools, many of the organic materials made visible for the first time by occupation of wetland locations with waterlogged deposits and excellent conditions of preservation. Picks, axes, or mattocks of worked antler, and axes and adzes made of flaked flint or other stone are widely in evidence. Many were presumably used for working timber in those regions where the expansion of forest made available a new or more abundant source of raw material. Others may have been used for digging the ground (Zvelebil this volume, Straus this volume) or processing sea-mammal carcasses (Bjerck this volume). Harpoons of bone or antler and bone fishhooks attest to new techniques for exploiting marine and aquatic resources. Wooden artefacts include dugout canoes, paddles, fish weirs, spear and arrow shafts, sledge-runners, skis, and timber-framed houses. Artificial dwelling structures are more widely in evidence and range from lightly built tent-like structures to substantial stone or timber-built constructions, depending on available raw materials, climatic conditions, and permanence of settlement. Early examples are Mount Sandel and Howick in northern Britain (Tolan-Smith this volume), Ulkestrup and Holmegård in Denmark (Blankholm this volume) and Vega in Norway (Bjerck this volume).

On those areas of the North European plain first occupied in the preceding Late Glacial, there was a consolidation of settlement across this extensive lowland region, with more sites, greater use of local raw materials, a wider range of game animals and a marked preference in site locations for lake-edge settings (or greater visibility of evidence in such locations), represented by the Maglemosian sites of Denmark and England (Blankholm this volume, Tolan-Smith this volume), and by similar material further east, as before characterised by a multiplicity of local culture-names – Komornice and Neman in Poland, Narva and Kunda in the Eastern Baltic, Sandarna in southern Sweden, Suomusjärvi in Finland, and Ienevian in Russia (Zvelebil this volume, Dolukhanov this volume). Riverine settings on the large river systems also attracted settlement, notably on the Danube (Jochim this volume, Bonsall this volume), the Dniestr and the Dniepr (Dolukhanov this volume), with evidence of freshwater fishing from an early date. Further north, there was renewed expansion of settlement along the Norwegian coastline and into the more northerly regions of Britain, in both cases with a marked maritime character.

In south-central and southern Europe, the microlithic and geometric character of the stone tool industries is a more prominent feature, perhaps reflecting in these regions, or at any rate in the sites that are best represented, smaller and more mobile settlements and continuing emphasis on hunting. There is, of course, some variation in primary characteristics and local culture labels, including Beuronian in the Danube basin (Jochim this volume, Svoboda this volume), and Azilian and Sauveterrian in France, with the locally named variants, Montadian and Montclusian, in the south (Valdeyron this volume, Pluciennik this volume). In Spain and the Mediterranean more widely the picture is more variable, with microlithic industries often described as Epigravettian (Pluciennik this volume), and a macrolithic component of simply flaked stone picks around the Spanish and Portuguese littoral including the Asturian 'pic', often associated with limpet-gathering, and the Mirian cobble axes of Portugal, which may have been used for shellgathering, plant food collection or woodworking (Straus this volume). Other amorphous flake assemblages that do not fit any of the classic cultural labels also occur, for example in Franchthi Cave, where they may have been used for the preparation of fishing equipment or the processing of fish. Much of the variability in these southern European regions may relate to local variations in site function or activities.

Coastal sites remain rare in this Early Mesolithic period, with the notable exception of Norway in the north, where isostatic uplift has preserved early-dated shorelines (Bjerck this volume) and, to a lesser extent, Scotland (Tolan-Smith this volume). Other early coastal sites are the Asturian middens of Northern Spain, where marine shells are present in abundance from about 8200 cal BC, apparently representing a culmination of a trend to increased shellgathering that extends back into earlier millennia, and some early-dated open-air coastal sites with marine shells in Portugal (Straus this volume). Fish remains and marine molluscs are represented from an early date at the Franchthi Cave (Pluciennik this volume). Also dated to this period is the coastal site of Laspi 7 on the Black Sea, where however, the shell remains are predominantly of land snails (Dolukhanov this volume). Deposits of terrestrial snail shells are a characteristic feature of many other sites across Europe, particularly in the south.

From about 7000 cal BC onwards, there were further changes, which for the most part represent an elaboration of themes and trends already under way. This period saw the onset of the Climatic Optimum, which lasted for some three thousand years, with average temperatures and rainfall higher than the present, representing the full extent of deciduous forests of oak, lime, and elm, and was probably also the period in which many larger lakes reached their maximum conditions of productivity and eutrophication. This is also the period during which sea levels stabilised at about their present level, shorelines and river estuaries adopted broadly their present configuration, and influx of terrestrial organic material and sediments began to accumulate productive mudflats for marine bivalves and nursery grounds for inshore fish. This environmental context is clearly a significant if not a sufficient factor in the development of substantial settlements on coastlines, lakes, and rivers, often with dwellings and other structures, such as Tågerup in Sweden, Sarnate on the Latvian coast, Kierikki on the Li estuary in northern Finland (Zvelebil this volume), Mirnoe I on the Black Sea and Nizhnee Veret'e I on Lake Lacha in northern Russia (Dolukhanov this volume), Lepenski Vir and Schela Cladovei in the Iron Gates region of the Danube (Bonsall this volume), and Vedbaek and Ertebølle on the Danish coastline (Blankholm this volume). Sometimes, settlements are associated with large numbers of burials, and often in the coastal context with substantial shell mounds.

Shell mounds of varying size and number are apparent in various regions, the largest and best-known grouping being the Ertebølle in Denmark, dated between about 5500 and 3800 cal BC. Over four hundred shell mounds have been recorded, the largest, as at the type-site of Ertebølle itself, several hundred metres long and several metres thick. These sites were built up slowly over many centuries of repeated use and discard of oyster shells and other refuse. The larger sites were residential bases used in all seasons of the year with a full range of artefacts including microlithic arrow barbs and flaked axes, an antler and bone industry, and pottery jars and bowls. Food remains include sea and land mammals, fish, and fowl (Blankholm this volume). Marine resources appear to have been a major source of protein, amongst which fish rather than shellfish were the main food item, a conclusion reinforced by stable-isotope analyses of human bones recovered from coastal locations. Coastal sites without mollusc shells are just as common and probably played the same role in the settlement system, occurring on shorelines lacking local concentrations of oysters or other molluscs, with some sites representing residential bases and other sites used by specialist task groups for the extraction of particular resources.

Some of the Danish coastal settlements of this period have been submerged in shallow water because of isostatic movement, resulting in spectacular conditions of organic preservation, notably at the underwater settlement of Tybrind Vig, which produced a dugout canoe, a richly decorated wooden paddle, and large numbers of wooden stakes associated with a landing stage and a fish weir. Many other submerged sites have been discovered in Danish waters, including other examples of fish weirs, suggesting a major investment in communal facilities.

Inland sites and exploitation patterns also continued to be of importance during the Ertebølle as in the earlier Maglemosian, but their significance has been overshadowed by the more substantial evidence available on the coast, and by problems of poor preservation, stratigraphic resolution and dating of surface material in inland locations (Blankholm this volume).

Other well-studied concentrations of shell mounds are those on the small island of Oronsay in the Western Islands of Scotland, used between about 5000 and 4300 cal BC for seal hunting, fishing, and the collection of limpets – the latter perhaps for fish bait (Tolan-Smith this volume), the Breton sites (Valdeyron this volume) and the Portuguese shell mounds on the Muge and Sado tributaries of the Tagus estuary (Straus this volume). Shell mounds of comparable size are unknown in the Mediterranean region, reflecting less productive conditions for intertidal molluscs, but fishing and shellgathering are clearly in evidence, notably at the Franchthi Cave in Greece and the Uzzo Cave in Sicily, often in combination with gathering of plant foods and hunting of mammals and supporting year-round or multiseason occupations (Pluciennik this volume).

Changes less obviously or directly linked to environmental factors, but most probably linked to regional population growth, were the development or intensification of new economic niches, such as the lowland forest regions of eastern Norway and Sweden (Bjerck this volume), continued penetration of upland regions, and greater regionalisation as indicated by regional variations in stylistic or decorative features of artefacts or distribution of raw materials, notably in Denmark (Blankhom this volume) and Norway (Bjerck this volume).

Amongst the technological innovations of this period are the introduction of trapeze-shaped geometric microliths, associated in France and some other areas with the 'Tardenoisian' (Valdeyron this volume), but widely present throughout much of the wider European region from about 7000 cal BC, the use of polishing techniques for shaping axes, especially in Norway, the distribution of favoured raw materials over considerable distances from quarries such as the Hespriholmen greenstone quarry in Norway, and the production of very regular-shaped blades, also present in Norway (Bjerck this volume), which may hint at specialist craft production. Pottery also came into regular use in some areas in later Mesolithic contexts, notably in the steppe regions of Russia and the Ukraine, perhaps as early as 8300 cal BC (Dolukhanov this volume), and in the Baltic and Denmark from 5500 cal BC (Blankholm this volume, Zvelebil this volume), apparently without any accompanying evidence of introduced crops or livestock.

With regard to subsistence, plant foods have long been recognised as of considerable potential significance during the Mesolithic, but this has often proved difficult to demonstrate. Nuts, greens, roots, seeds, and fruits would undoubtedly have become more widely available with the expansion of woodlands associated with food-bearing trees, shrubs and grasses. Charred hazelnut shells are widely recorded in many Mesolithic sites, but new excavation procedures using flotation and new techniques such as residue analysis of tool edges have produced a growing body of new information. In the Mediterranean, wild olives and pulses have been recovered from the Uzzo Cave, and dental caries on human teeth suggests greater intake of sugar from fruits. Wild lentils, oats, and barley are present at Franchthi (Pluciennik this volume). In the middle Danube, in contrast, few plants were found at the Iron Gates sites in spite of extensive flotation, and the lack of dental caries and the presence of heavy calculus on the teeth at Schela Cladovei suggest that there was little plant carbohydrate in the diet (Bonsall this volume). Residue analysis on stone tools from the Pod Zubem rockshelter in North Bohemia identified the presence of starch indicating contact with plant material, while seeds of a range of plants, nuts, and fruits were recovered at the Jezevčí rockshelter (Svoboda this volume). Pollen evidence in the Jägerhaus Cave in the Schwabian Alb suggests the collection of round-leafed sorrel (Jochim this volume). In the Pyrenees, seeds of leafy greens and fruits such as blackberry, hawthorn, and wild pear have been recovered from Balma Margineda, and acorns, walnuts, pine nuts, cherries, and plums at Cingle Vermell (Pluciennik this volume). Residue analysis at Font del Ros suggests the processing of acorns and hazelnuts, and charcoal evidence at La Poujade the use of wild cherries and almonds, while extensive flotation at Balma Abeurador in the south of France has produced thousands of carbonised seeds of lentils, peas, chickpeas, and fruits (Pluciennik this volume, Valdeyron this volume). Abora in East Latvia, dated between 3800 and 2500 cal BC has produced evidence of water chestnuts, hazelnuts, and hemp and pollen indicators of clearance (Zvelebil this volume), and studies of the carbon isotope composition and barium and strontium content of human bones from the Dniepr burial sites show an increase in plants foods in the later Mesolithic. At the site of Mirnoe I on the Black Sea, dated at about 5900 cal BC, blades with reaping polish were recovered, along with seeds of sorrel, vetch, *Chenopodium*, and *Polygonum* (Dolukhanov this volume), and reaping, grinding, and digging equipment is present in some Baltic sites (Zvelebil this volume).

Apart from the domestic dog, present early on, the question of indigenous domestication remains unclear. For sheep and goat and the main cereal crops, the case for an exotic origin remains difficult to dispute, although this leaves open the question of whether they were introduced by incoming farmers, or adopted by indigenous hunters and gatherers through exchange, theft, or possibly even by spontaneous dispersal northwards without human intervention. Many other animal species had been present in Europe since glacial times, such as reindeer, horse, cattle, and pig, and could in principle have been locally domesticated early on, in the sense of genetic isolation from the wild stock and selective breeding, without external influence. But whether this happened independently without the diffusion of domestic stock or the idea of domestication from the Near East remains obscure. Some earlier claims for local domestication have been rejected as the result of inaccurate observations or of stratigraphic intrusion of later material, notably with the pigs of Tash-Air in the Crimea (Dolukhanov this volume) and domesticates in the western Mediterranean (Pluciennik this volume). In other cases, DNA analyses may throw further light on the question of indigenous versus exotic origins and seem to reinforce the notion of independent European centres of local domestication for pig (Zvelebil this volume) and exotic origins for cattle but involving hybridisation with local aurochs (Götherstrom et al. 2005).

The question of local versus exotic origins may be poorly posed, resting on the assumption that there is a Mesolithic way of life without domestication, and a Neolithic way of life with domestication, and that the transition from one to the other can only have occurred on one occasion and in one restricted region. Such an assumption, along with its requirement to identify the specific ingredient that sharply differentiates the one normative mode of production from the other, would seem increasingly to belong to a discredited theory of social evolution. The broader concept of husbandry may be a more useful way of thinking about the problem and of capturing the subtler gradations of variability apparent in the much richer range of evidence now available. In this respect, there are many indications in Mesolithic contexts of environmental modification for human benefit, including evidence of investment in facilities on a scale that might justifiably presuppose restrictive rights of access. These include communal fish weirs in Danish waters associated with tree pollarding (Blankholm this volume), seagoing boats on Atlantic and Mediterranean coastlines, and pollen evidence of woodland clearance in southern Sweden, southern Finland, and eastern Latvia (Zvelebil this volume), in the Alpine foreland (Jochim this volume) and in upland regions of Britain (Tolan-Smith this volume), presumably for the improvement of plant or animal productivity, or at any rate having that outcome if not that motivation (cf. Davies et al. 2005). Morphological evidence for tamed or captive animals has been claimed, notably for bear in France (Valdeyron this volume) and pigs in Scandinavia (Zvelebil this volume). In the latter case, the predominance of pig bones in large settlements, increased numbers of juvenile pigs in archaeofaunal assemblages, and the presence of pigs on offshore islands all point to some degree of human intervention, even if it fell short of biological domestication. If a contemporary observer at about 7000 cal BC had followed a transect across Europe from the Near East to northern Scandinavia, it is questionable whether they would have identified noticeable differences in modes of subsistence, other than different combinations of animals and plants suited to different environmental conditions, with the combination of pigs, nuts, and fish in the north forming an economic package as capable of supporting permanent and populous settlements as the combination of goats, cereals, and fish in the Levant.

Throughout this period, beginning earlier in the Southeast and progressively later in the west and north, we see evidence for greater or lesser adoption of crops and livestock, whether of resources introduced from outside Europe or locally domesticated, involving complex and regionally variable patterns of interaction between indigenous Mesolithic communities and incoming farmers, or the selective adoption by preexisting Mesolithic populations of innovations associated with farming. The extent to which the introduction of these new elements was brought about by the expansion of new people into Europe from the Near East remains unclear. The case for 'demic diffusion' remains strongest in parts of the Mediterranean and the Southeast corner of the Balkans, with mutually exclusive distributions of Mesolithic and Neolithic sites, and no evidence of interaction between them, at least initially, suggesting 'enclave' colonisation (Price 2000). Elsewhere different elements of the 'Neolithic package' were introduced or adopted selectively and separately, for example, pottery in the absence of domestic resources in much of the Baltic, and cereals in the absence of other indicators in parts of Britain, where, additionally, the scarcity of relevant direct evidence has resulted in a correspondingly high level of theoretical contestation (cf. Rowley-Conwy 2004). Extrapolations from historical linguistics and modern DNA distributions are notoriously unreliable guides to past patterns, especially when studies of modern and ancient DNA produce contradictory results (Zvelebil this volume), but there is at any rate considerable evidence for genetic and perhaps linguistic continuity across the Mesolithic-Neolithic boundary within many areas of Europe. At the same time, morphological evidence from large samples of human burials suggests considerable movement and migration of people long before the advent of agriculture (Dolukhanov this volume), to say nothing of the movement involved in the colonisation of newly available territory opened up by deglaciation.

Whether agricultural communities newly formed on European soil by indigenous people expanded into new territory, encroaching on the resources of their hunter-gatherer neighbours, is a different matter. In several areas of Europe, notably in the Netherlands (Verhart this volume), parts of the Baltic (Zvelebil this volume), and Greece (Pluciennik this volume), evidence of archaeological materials and human activities decreases or disappears in the final period of the Mesolithic just before the arrival of farming communities. That may indicate the abandonment of territory by hunters and gatherers in the face of expanding farmers, the reconfiguration of settlement patterning with the adoption of new patterns of economy and settlement, or the changed visibility of archaeological evidence unrelated to actual patterns of behaviour (Jochim this volume, and later). In the Baltic, the rich evidence of symbolism and ideology suggests both considerable long-term continuity of ritual and belief systems from early in the Mesolithic right through to the historical period, but also the manipulation of symbols and ritual landscapes to create a heightened sense of identity and 'difference' between neighbouring hunter-gatherer and farmer regions (Zvelebil this volume). The continuity between an ethnographic present and a prehistoric past, and the ethnographic insights into archaeological interpretation that flow from such continuity, may of course be peculiar to these northerly regions where agriculture and domestication penetrated only late or in much attenuated form. Whether this pattern is typical of other areas of Europe, and whether the methodology used to identify it can be applied elsewhere, remains to be explored.

Most authors in this volume who address the issue of the Mesolithic-Neolithic transition argue for a degree of involvement of Mesolithic communities in the new economic and social configurations associated with agriculture, and for a range of interactions between agricultural and hunter-gatherer communities in which both types of partners may sometimes have modified their behaviour, including limited use of domesticates by hunter-gatherers, perhaps as status items, continued hunting, gathering or fishing by farmers, exchange of exotic items, patron-client relationships, ideological resistance marked by elaboration of ritual and symbol, and the development of new patterns of hunting to supply new items for exchange (Zvelebil this volume, Dolukhanov this volume, Bonsall this volume, Blankholm this volume, Verhart this volume, Jochim this volume). Whether these interactions ever took the form of violent conflict is also unclear, and a case can be made that there was just as much or greater conflict in earlier periods on the basis of the number of skeletons that indicate death by violence in earlier Mesolithic burials (Jochim this volume, Dolukhanov this volume). Whether it will continue to be useful to continue to draw a major fault-line between Mesolithic and Neolithic modes of existence, or better to regard the changes associated with the Neolithic as part of an ongoing process of social and demographic readjustment and cultural innovation extending back to the Late Glacial, remains to be seen.

New Problems

What of specific highlights and possibilities for new research? Here there is a wide range of possibilities. We have alluded to some of these earlier, particularly in the social sphere (Spikins this volume), and here we elaborate just a few that seem to us to be of particular interest.

Maritime Adaptations and Differential Site Visibility

One of the persistent themes in Mesolithic narratives – and narratives of the Postglacial more widely – is the apparent explosion of evidence for marine and aquatic resources as indicated by the increase in large settlements associated with shell mounds and lake edges. In the European case, this is especially difficult to evaluate, as the most productive coastlines and lakes occur in northerly regions – the shallow basins and associated estuaries of the North Sea and the Baltic, and the lakes created by glacial retreat on the North European plain and in Scandinavia. The difficulty here is that these regions were not available for human settlement until the Holocene and the aquatic resources associated with them did not exist before that period. To cite their exploitation as evidence of some major shift in human attitudes to the environment is to make an unequal comparison with environmental conditions in earlier periods. Even for earlier periods and more southerly regions, the earliest use of marine resources is obscured by the lowered sea levels that persisted throughout the glacial period, and hence by the removal or submergence of relevant evidence before sea level approximated its present position about 6000 to 5000 cal BC.

This problem of differential visibility of evidence is especially acute on the shallower and broader stretches of continental shelf around the coastlines of the North Sea basin and northern and western France, but even on the steeply shelving coastlines of southern Europe the shorelines of the glacial maximum would have been at least 5 km distant, far enough away to take most marine resources out of reach of sites located on the present-day coastline. Underwater survey and excavation is beginning to reveal new evidence, and various authors have argued that late Palaeolithic hunters were hunting sea mammals and fishing and shellgathering along these now submerged coastlines from an early period (Fischer 1985, 1986, Erlandson 2001, Flemming 2004).

Quantities of marine mollusc shells appear in the coastal cave deposits of northern Spain, such as La Riera and El Juyo, from as far back as the Glacial Maximum, with evidence for increased quantities in the Late Glacial period (Straus, this volume). Cueva de la Nerja in Southeast Spain contains evidence of marine molluscs, fish, seal, and birds, associated with an early stage of the Late Glacial dating between about 15,000 and 12,000 cal BC (Morales et al. 1998). Because shorelines were still at some distance from the present coastline, this is a significant indication of interest in marine resources and most probably only the visible tip of a more extensive pattern of marine exploitation, given that the Asturian shell middens with their vastly greater number of discarded mollusc shells only began to form as shorelines approached their present position (Bailey and Craighead 2003).

A notable exception to this general picture of submergence and loss of coastal archaeology is the Norwegian coast, which has undergone substantial isostatic uplift following the removal of the Scandinavian ice sheet, so that fourteen-thousand- to thirteen-thousand-year-old shorelines formed when the eustatic level of the sea was still about 50 m below the present are now elevated above present sea level along much of the Norwegian coastline.

Despite the opportunities for preservation of early coastal sites and the fact that the Norwegian coastline was ice-free from at least as early as 13,000 cal BC, there is no convincing evidence of human occupation, apart from stray and ambiguous finds, until about 9500 cal BC, when numerous sites appear all along the Norwegian coastline in association with the Komsa and Fosna cultures characterized by large numbers of flake adzes, and tanged points of Ahrensburgian type. Preservation of organic materials is almost nonexistent, so that there are few indications of the animals exploited, but the location of the sites, some of them on offshore islands, the nature of the resources available, and the need for substantial intake of animal fats for human survival in these northerly regions, indicates that marine resources and especially sea mammals must have been a major source of subsistence, whereas the flake adzes would have been well suited for scraping blubber from seal carcasses (Bjerck this volume). Substantial weatherproof dwellings were built to provide shelter during winter as at Åsgarden on the Vega Islands with foundations partially excavated into the subsoil ('pit-dwellings') and stone or turf walls (Bjerck this volume).

The absence of sites on the Norwegian coast before about 9500 cal BC may be for a variety of reasons. Successful exploitation of this coastal region would have been impossible without seaworthy boats. It is possible that the technology for boat construction was not known about earlier, resulting in a considerable time lag before it was invented, or that suitable materials were lacking in a largely tree-less environment. But hide-covered boats made on a framework of antler are conceivable and appear to have been already in use on Late Glacial shorelines further south. Both antler and animal hides were abundantly available and the technology of working antler and preparing animal skins was well known from far back in the Upper Palaeolithic period. Alternatively, the high practical and social costs of investing in boat building and maintenance and in the construction of weatherproof dwellings, together with the harsh and extreme environmental conditions, was sufficient disincentive to delay the colonisation of this new territory. Climate change may also be a significant factor. At about 9500 cal BC, or soon after, the Scandinavian ice sheet, which had persisted in close proximity to the coastline, finally disappeared, opening up the hinterland to populations of reindeer. Reindeer-hunting sites appear in the hinterland at about the same time or soon after the earliest coastal sites, and the coastal regions with the largest concentrations of sites are those in closest proximity to an accessible hinterland (Bjerck this volume). In addition, the polar front shifted northwards to the latitude of Iceland, and in its wake the warmer waters of the Gulf Stream reached the Norwegian coastline, creating a more diverse and productive marine and coastal environment. Before this period, then, the resource options available for human survival may have been too narrow and too risky to encourage settlement, regardless of boat-building skills.

At about the same time, during the Preboreal period, the British Isles also witnessed a new phase of expansion northwards and westwards beyond the lowland regions of England, with a number of new settlements appearing around the coastlines of Scotland and in the Western Isles, dating from about 8800 cal BC (Tolan-Smith this volume). Ireland, which appears never to have had a traversable land connection to mainland Britain, also was occupied for the first time. As in Norway, the appearance of the Gulf Stream would have been a significant factor in improving resource productivity and attracting new settlement. Seaworthy boats would have been essential for navigating the Western Isles and especially for the crossing to Ireland, regarded as one of the most treacherous sea crossings in the British Isles. Sturdy dwelling structures also would have been essential in the harsher winter climates of the north. Faunal preservation on many of these sites is poor, but Mount Sandel in Northern Ireland has preserved evidence of salmon fishing and boar hunting, postholes indicating substantial dwelling structures and pits that could have been used for food storage. The coastal site of Howick on the North Sea coast of Northumberland in northern England belongs to this phase of expansion, and has yielded traces of a substantial timber-framed dwelling and evidence of sealing and boar hunting.

In the eastern Mediterranean, the occupants of the Franchthi Cave on the Argolid Peninsula of southern Greece were importing obsidian from the island of Melos eleven thousand years ago, which would have required a sea journey of 100 km by the direct route, or a series of sea crossings of at least 20 km by a more circuitous route. However, apart from a few limpet shells, evidence for the exploitation of marine resources does not appear in the Franchthi deposits until somewhat later in the sequence, most probably because the coastline was still too far away (Pluciennik this volume). The offshore islands of Cyprus Corsica, Sardinia and Mallorca, the latter requiring a sea crossing of 165 km, were occupied or visited from an early period, but not Crete or Malta, indicating the construction of seaworthy vessels, although no consideration has so far been given to the manner of their construction. The Cyclope Cave on the island of Youra in the northern Sporades of the Aegean was occupied between 8300 and 7000 cal BC and has provided evidence of hunting of goats and pigs, and fishing and fowling (Powell 2003, Sampson et al. 2003, Trantalidou 2003). The site could have been reached by island hopping with sea crossings of no more than about 10 km, and it appears that the goats and pigs must have been imported. At any rate, it is clear that there was a wide network of maritime contacts and movements in the millennia preceding the arrival of domestic livestock and cereal crops from the Near East, a network that may well have facilitated the later dispersal of exotic resources.

The significance of these developments in maritime exploration, and in particular the significance of the apparent explosion in coastal settlements and marine exploitation, will remain difficult to assess in the absence of comparable evidence from earlier periods of lower sea level. And this problem will persist until systematic exploration of submerged landscapes and palaeoshorelines is undertaken using the wide range of techniques now available, including sonar surveys, subbottom profiling, coring, remotely operated cameras, and deep diving (Flemming 2004).

It might be thought that inland rivers would provide a more geologically stable environment in which to judge changes in human use of aquatic resources, but here too erosion of earlier evidence or submergence beneath subsequent layers of alluvial sediment introduce comparable distortions in the visibility or preservation of evidence (Bonsall this volume). Moreover, this issue of differential visibility or differential preservation is a more general problem, which has tended to exaggerate the significance of coastal evidence at the expense of the hinterland in a number of regions (Blankholm this volume, Verhart this volume, Straus this volume, Pluciennik this volume). Indeed, the apparent absence of evidence in many hinterlands was one factor that once gave rise to a view of Mesolithic depopulation and impoverishment, reinforcing the notion of a population driven back by the encroachment of thick or unproductive forest. In fact, the inland sites have always been there in some regions but have been difficult to identify as such because of lack of chronologically diagnostic artefacts on surface sites that cannot be dated by other means (Blankhom this volume, Verhart this volume, Jochim this volume). In other cases, as in northern Spain (Straus this volume) or Greece (Pluciennik this volume), the apparent lack of hinterland evidence reflects lack of intensive survey, or geological factors of erosion and sedimentation that have obscured or removed evidence. In both regions, there is now sufficient and well-dated evidence in inland cave and rockshelter sequences to suggest a human presence in the hinterland and the likelihood that further evidence will in due course be forthcoming.

Stable isotope analyses of human bone collagen, with their capacity to discriminate between foods from marine, terrestrial and freshwater ecosystems and from different trophic levels, will continue to make an important contribution to debates about subsistence variation. However, the results will need to take account of vagaries in the availability of human bone, questions about the degree to which particular human individuals are representative of wider populations, and unresolved discrepancies between isotope analyses and other sources of palaeodietary information (Milner et al. 2004, 2006, Hedges 2004, Liden et al. 2004, Richards and Schulting 2006).

Art, Burials, and Symbolism

Rock art was once commonly regarded as absent in the Mesolithic period, an absence taken as evidence of cultural impoverishment compared with the Upper Palaeolithic. However, rock art is notoriously difficult to date with any precision, and the prominence of Upper Palaeolithic rock art in France and northern Spain and the ability to assign it to that period owes much to the fact that it includes representations of animals of the glacial period that are now extinct, or no longer present in that region. In fact, rock art is probably a prominent feature of the Mesolithic period, but concentrated in new centres of population growth or population aggregation, reflecting the major changes in social and ritual geography that followed climate change and the opening up of new territory and the creation of new resources. Portable art is also common, including engraved bone and antler, painted pebbles, and anthropomorphic and animal figures. Some of the portable art is on wooden materials that by their very nature are only found in exceptional conditions of preservation, and these may represent only the visible fragment of a much more widespread medium of symbolic representation.

In Norway, the succession of raised beaches created by rapid isostatic uplift provides a basis for dating by association and demonstrates that rock art was present in northern Norway by at least as early as 8300 cal BC, with naturalistic representations of elk, reindeer, bear, whale, and seal (Bjerck this volume). Many hundreds of sites have been recorded more widely in Norway and Sweden with images of anthropomorphs, deer, boats, sea mammals, bear, water birds, fish, reptiles, tracks, hunting and fishing implements, and abstract designs (Bjerck this volume, Zvelebil this volume). One of the largest such concentrations is the site of Nämforsen (4400–1800 cal BC) in Swedish Norland, which was a major focus of ritual and seasonal aggregation for settlements in the surrounding region. In southern Europe, there is the Levantine rock art of eastern Spain, with schematic and naturalistic representations including hunting scenes and humans, and the Addaura Cave in Sicily (Pluciennik this volume). Of course, many of these representations cannot be dated with any certainty and the Levantine art could have been produced in any period from the Upper Palaeolithic to the Iron Age (Pluciennik this volume) and perhaps in all periods of this broad time range. Whether the techniques of directly dating rock art that have been pioneered in Australia and South Africa (Mazel and Watchman 2003, Cole and Watchman 2005) can be applied in Europe remains to be seen. But there is no doubt that properly dated rock art sequences would add immeasurably to the interpretation of the wider cultural context and symbolic associations of Mesolithic life.

Burials are common, either in intimate association with domestic dwellings or as separately demarcated 'cemetery' areas, and comprise a wide range of evidence and types of burials including males, females and children, corpses in flexed, supine or prone positions, cremation, and evidence of ritual defleshing or cannibalism, notably the evidence of decapitation, defleshing, and separate burial of heads at the Grosse Ofnet cave in Bavaria and other caves in the region (Jochim this volume). The scatter of isolated bones in many other sites may indicate excarnation or removal of the corpse after a temporary period of lying in one place. Cemeteries, or at any rate locations used repeatedly for burial, are present early in the sequence, as at the cave of Aveline's Hole in the Cheddar Gorge of southwest England, dated at approximately 8300 cal BC, with more than seventy human burials (Tolan-Smith this volume) or the cemetery of Vasilyevka on the Dniepr at 9500 cal BC (Dolukhanov this volume), and later as at Zvejnieki in Latvia, where 315 burials have been excavated indicating repeated use between 7200 and 2800 cal BC (Zvelebil this volume), or Lepenski Vir (Bonsall this volume). Olenii Ostrov on an island in Lake Onega in Karelia, dated at about 6400 cal BC, had over three hundred burials, and the grave goods and the position of the skeletons indicate a variety of burial rites and evidence of social ranking based on age, gender, personal wealth, clan membership, and the presence of shamans (Zvelebil this volume). The Portuguese shell mounds of the Muge River are also estimated to have contained at least three hundred burials (Straus this volume), and it is tempting to suppose that the mounds themselves may have been the result of ritual feasting on molluscs and accumulation of the shells over the corpse as part of the burial rite in the manner suggested for the some of the North American shell mounds (Luby and Gruber 1999), with the mounds themselves becoming visible symbols in the landscape of the burial place. In Denmark, human remains are rare in the Ertebølle shell mounds and burials are found at coastal sites lacking shell middens, notably the eighteen burials at Vedbaek in eastern Zealand and the Skateholm sites in southern Sweden, with a total of eighty-five burials including evidence of a wooden mortuary structure (Blankholm this volume).

Amongst the great variety of funerary rituals now in evidence in Mesolithic contexts, social differentiation in grave goods remains largely limited to differences of age, gender, and personal achievement. Clear evidence of institutionalised differences in social rank that persisted independently of kin relations remains elusive, so, too, evidence of organised warfare, both commonly regarded as hallmarks of socially complex societies (Yoffee 1985, Fitzhugh 2003). Evidence of violent death is commonly reported in Mesolithic burial remains, but it is not clear that this marks a general trend over time rather than a situational response to local and regional circumstances, suggesting conflict associated with increased competition or territoriality. Nor is it clear that the Mesolithic evidence marks a significant break with earlier periods. Evidence of status differentiation in burial goods can be found in the Upper Palaeolithic, notably in the case of the adult and child burials at Upper Palaeolithic Sunghir (Dolukhanov this volume), while cemeteries with evidence of violent death, are present early on in the Nile Valley (Close 1996). It is difficult to discern any general pattern in the evidence or trends through time, but the totality of the burial evidence available across Mesolithic Europe represents a rich and varied corpus of information that would repay further comparative investigation.

Technological Innovation and the Adoption of Pottery

Given the rapidity with which people were capable of moving into new territory – 2000 km within a few generations along the Norwegian coastline (Bjerck) – and the evidence for the widespread movement of exotic materials through exchange or trade networks over hundreds of kilometres or more in the Mesolithic – Mediterranean shells in central Europe, for example, or the exchange of flint, obsidian, greenstone, and amber over equivalent distances (Pluciennik this volume, Jochim this volume, Zvelebil this volume) – it seems unlikely that knowledge of an advantageous innovation invented in one location in Europe would not have spread rapidly to the far corners of the continent on an archaeological time scale measured in hundreds of years. From this point of view, the question arises as to why some innovations were adopted swiftly and widely and others more patchily and slowly. The microlithic trapeze, for example, appears across a very wide territory at about 7000 cal BC. Pottery, by contrast, makes a patchy appearance at different dates in different areas. Such differences can hardly be explained as a matter of differential knowledge or skill, or of cultural conservatism. The interesting studies of ideology and exchange of materials made possible by the detailed evidence available in Scandinavia and the Baltic (Blankhom this volume, Zvelebil this volume), suggest that novel items may have been much sought after because of their rarity, offering high prestige value and serving as a powerful weapon in the struggle between individual agency and social convention (cf. Spikins this volume).

Pottery is of particular interest against the background of an apparently early and widespread use in China and the Far East as early as 13,500 cal BC, many millennia before its adoption in western Asia or Europe. In that light, it may be significant that the earliest use of pottery in Europe seems to occur at the far eastern margin, in the steppe zone between the Volga and Ural rivers, between 8300 and 7000 cal BC, in the Yelshanian culture in association with hunting of aurochs, horse, deer, fishing, and collection of freshwater molluscs (Dolukhanov this volume). Pottery has usually been treated as an indicator of Neolithic acculturation or a proxy measure of a Neolithic economy without further comment. The terminological confusion created by this approach is indicated by the description of essentially the same phenomenon as Mesolithic in relation to the Danish Ertebølle, Combed-Ware Neolithic in Finland, and Forest Neolithic in the Baltic (Zvelebil this volume), and by the label of 'aceramic' or 'prepottery' Neolithic in the Aegean and the Near East. The widespread appearance of pottery in southern Scandinavia and the Baltic at about 5500 cal BC in hunter-gatherer-fisher contexts, its apparent absence in the earliest farming settlements in the

Aegean and the Near East, and the appearance of 'hybrid' Mesolithic cultures with pottery that may have been inspired by contact with neighbouring Linearbandkeramik (LBK) farmers, as with La Hoguette in France and Germany and Hardinxveld-Giessendam in the Netherlands (Verhart this volume, Valdeyron this volume, Jochim this volume), suggests a complex picture of variability that raises questions about why ceramic containers were attractive in some contexts but not others.

Pottery can be used for a variety of purposes, for storage of food or liquids, for cooking, for lighting (as in the case of the ceramic bowls used as blubber lamps in the Ertebølle), and in more elaborately shaped and decorated forms for display and the enhancement of individual or group identity (cf. Pearson 2005). The use of pottery for any of these purposes presumably also depended on the availability or easy accessibility of suitable raw materials such as clay and temper, and the suitability of alternatives made from stone, wood, or skin. The V-based pots of the Ertebølle suggest stationary facilities for storage, or perhaps cooking vessels designed to sit in some sort of framework over a fire. Some of the large pottery vessels in the Baltic were evidently used for storage of seal grease (Zvelebil this volume). A new generation of biomolecular techniques involving analysis of lipid and protein residues and isotope and trace element analysis of food crusts is beginning to identify the contents of pots, including milk, plant foods, and marine products (Craig and Collins 2000, Copley et al. 2005, Craig et al. 2005). One wonders, for example, whether the early-dated Yelshanian pots, supposedly associated with 'wild' horse, might have been used for horse milk. At any rate, a new generation of techniques and ideas is opening up the possibility of a comparative contextual and functional analysis of Mesolithic pottery that should be able to move beyond a purely culture-historical approach, and the same may well be applicable to other innovations in material culture.

Conclusion

A major driving force in the developments of the Mesolithic period was the changing environmental conditions associated with the melting of the ice sheets and climatic amelioration, which created new territories for human settlement, new supplies of food and raw materials for subsistence, a rapidly changing mosaic of new faunal and floral communities, new technological demands for tools, shelter, and transport, and new opportunities for population growth, resulting in major reconfigurations of social geography and social interaction. These changes were not merely responses to environmental forces but the exploitation of new opportunities made possible by diverse, large-scale, and all-pervasive environmental change. The growth of archaeological knowledge now makes it possible to view these 'Mesolithic' millennia as representing a period of radical change and innovation, which witnessed the emergence and synthesis of the technological, economic and social capabilities on which the later developments of agriculture, urban civilization, and long-distance trade were founded.

There will undoubtedly be different problems that appear significant to others, and new directions in which future research will develop. Some of these are indicated in the other contributions to this volume, and we have alluded to others in the social sphere in our introductory chapter (Spikins this volume). Continued survey and discovery of new sites, the more widespread application of dating methods to produce more, and more accurate dates, and new techniques of analysis and new questions that we can hardly anticipate or imagine are all likely to produce surprises in the future. What does seem clear is that the detail and range of information now available for the Mesolithic offers the prospect both of opening out to large-scale comparative studies across the whole extent of European territory, and indeed beyond, and of focusing down to smaller-scale questions about local areas, particular sites and individual lives (cf. Warren 2005b).

In this sense, the period does retain a transitional quality, but not so much a transition associated with the demise of one dominant mode of existence and its replacement by another, but rather a transition from a world that is largely alien to us, to one that is increasingly familiar, and a transition in scale of observation from the vast perspectives of the Palaeolithic era dominated by major environmental and biological changes to the smaller-scale rhythms of everyday life and ritual that come more sharply into focus in the Mesolithic and later periods. At any rate, it should no longer be necessary to fight for the coexistence of a Mesolithic perspective alongside those from other periods and regions, or to justify the existence of Mesolithic studies as a coherent field of study in its own right. It is, moreover, one that is now full of new and varied opportunities for research.

Appendix

Approximate Correspondence between Uncalibrated Radiocarbon Dates and Calendar Years BC in the Time Range from 2500 to 13,000 Radiocarbon Years BP

BP	Cal BC	BP	Cal BC	BP	Cal BC
2500	660	4600	3365	6700	5625
2600	795	4700	3455	6800	5690
2700	850	4800	3545	6900	5760
2800	945	4900	3670	7000	5910
2900	1085	5000	3780	7100	5995
3000	1250	5100	3890	7200	6050
3100	1400	5200	4005	7300	6160
3200	1470	5300	4140	7400	6285
3300	1570	5400	4290	7500	6400
3400	1710	5500	4345	7600	6450
3500	1825	5600	4415	7700	6530
3600	1970	5700	4525	7800	6625
3700	2085	5800	4655	7900	6720
3800	2240	5900	4760	8000	6940
3900	2400	6000	4890	8100	7065
4000	2520	6100	5015	8200	7220
4100	2710	6200	5145	8300	7395
4200	2830	6300	5270	8400	7505
4300	2905	6400	5400	8500	7560
4400	3015	6500	5475	8600	7595
4500	3220	6600	5540	8700	7690

(continued)

(*continued*)

BP	Cal BC	BP	Cal BC	BP	Cal BC
8800	7880	10,300	10130	11,700	11595
8900	8101	10,400	10325	11,800	11735
9000	8250	10,500	10555	11,900	11815
9100	8290	10,600	10745	12,000	11895
9200	8390	10,700	10840	12,100	12005
9300	8575	10,800	10880	12,200	12110
9400	8670	10,900	10920	12,300	12205
9500	8785	11,000	10965	12,400	12395
9600	8995	11,100	11060	12,500	12690
9700	9225	11,200	11160	12,600	12905
9800	9270	11,300	11240	12,700	13055
9900	9325	11,400	11310	12,800	13155
10,000	9530	11,500	11385	12,900	13265
10,100	9750	11,600	11470	13,000	13390
10,200	9960				

Courtesy of Robert Hedges, Oxford Radiocarbon Accelerator Unit. See also Table 10.3 for a similar correspondence table using a different calibration.

References

Adam, E. 1999. Preliminary presentation of the Upper Palaeolithic and Mesolithic stone industries of Theopetra Cave, western Thessaly. In G. Bailey, E. Adam, C. Perlès, E. Panagopoulou, and K. Zachos (eds.), *The Palaeolithic archaeology of Greece and adjacent areas: Proceedings of the First International Conference on the Palaeolithic of Greece and the Balkans*. London: British School at Athens, pp. 266–70.

Adan, E., García, E., and J. Quebrada. 1999. El Aziliense de Cueva Oscura de Ania (Las Regueras, Asturias): Primera aproximación y su contexto en la cuenca del Nalón. *Espacio, Tiempo y Forma*. Series I, 12: 215–67.

Ahlbäck, H. 2003. Art: context and tradition in the Palaeolithic-Mesolithic transition in Northern Europe. In L. Larsson, H. Kindgren, K. Knutsson, D. Loeffler, and A. Åkerlund (eds.), *Mesolithic on the move*. Oxford: Oxbow Books, pp. 467–77.

Aikio, P. 1989. The changing role of reindeer in the life of the Sámi. In J. Clutton-Brock (ed.), *The Walking Larder*. London: Unwin Hyman, pp. 169–84.

Aimé, G. 1993. *Les abris sous roche de Bavans, Doubs*. Mémoire de la société d'agriculture, lettres, sciences et arts de la Haute-Saône, archéologie no. 3, 1993.

Aksu, A. E., Hiscott R. N., and D. A. Yasar 1999. Oscillating Quaternary water level of the Marmora sea and vigorous outflow into the Aegean Sea from the Marmora Sea-Black Sea drainage corridor. *Marine Geology* 153: 275–302.

Aksu, A. E., Hiscott, R. N., Yasar, D., Icler, F. I., and S. Marsh. 2002. Seismic stratigraphy of Late Quaternary deposits from the southwestern Black Sea shelf: Evidence for non-catastrophic variations in sea-level during the last ~10000 years. *Marine Geology* 190: 61–94.

Albrecht, G. 1983. Das Spätpaläolithikum. In H. Müller–Beck (ed.), *Urgeschichte in Baden-Württemberg*. Stuttgart: Konrad Theiss Verlag, pp. 354–62.

Albarella, U., Davis, S., Detry, S., and P. Rowley-Conwy. 2005. Pigs of the "Far West": The biometry of *Sus* from archaeological sites in Portugal. *Anthropozoologica* 40 (2): 27–54.

Albarella, U., Dobney, K., and P. Rowley-Conwy. 2006. The domestication of the pig (*Sus scrofa*). In M. A. Zeder, D. G. Bradley, E. Emshwiller, and B. Smith (eds.), *Documenting domestication. New genetic and archaeological paradigms*. Berkeley: University of California Press, pp. 209–27.

Albrethsen, S. E., and E. Brinch Petersen. 1976. Excavation of a Mesolithic cemetery at Vedbæk, Denmark. *Acta Archaeologica* 47: 1–28.

Alday, A. 1998. *Kanpanoste Goikoa*. Memorias de Yacimientos Alaveses 5, Vitoria.

Alday, A. 2005. The transition between the last hunter-gatherers and the first farmers in southwestern Europe: The Basque perspective. *Journal of Anthropological Research* 61: 469–94.

Aldenderfer, M. 1993. Ritual, hierarchy and change in foraging societies. *Journal of Anthropological Archaeology* 12 (1): 1–40.

Aleksandrovsky, A. L., Belanovskaya, T. D., Dolukhanov, P. M., Ya. Kiyashko, V., Kovalyukh, N. N., Kremenetsky, K. V., Lavrentiev, N. V., Shukurov, A. M., Tsybriy, A. V., Tsybriy, V. V., Skripkin, V. V., and G. I. Zaitseva. 2009. The Lower Don Neolithic. In P. Dolukhanov, G. Sarson, and A. Shukurov (eds.), *The East European Plain on the eve of agriculture*. British Archaeological Reports International Series 1964. Oxford: Archaeopress, pp. 99–108.

References

Aleksenko, E. A. 1967. *Kety*. Moskva: Nauka.

Alexander, J. 1978. Frontier studies and the earliest farmers in Europe. In D. Green, C. Haselgrove, and M. Spriggs (eds.), *Social organisation and settlement*. Oxford: British Archaeological Reports International Series 47, pp. 13–29.

Alexandersen, V. 1993. Teeth. In S. Hvass and B. Storgaard (eds.), *Digging into the past: 25 years of archaeology in Denmark*. Århus: Aarhus University Press, p. 81.

Alonso, F., and J. M. Bello. 1997. Cronología y periodización del fenómeno megalítico en Galicia a la luz de las dataciones por C14. In A. Rodríguez (ed.), *O Neolítico Atlántico e as orixes do megalitismo*. Santiago de Compostela: Universidad de Santiago, pp. 507–20.

Alsaker, S. 1987. *Bømlo – steinalderens råstoffsentrum på Sørvestlandet*. Bergen: Historisk museum, University of Bergen.

Alterskjær, K. 1985. Eldre steinalder. In K. Pettersen and B. Wik (eds.), *Helgeland historie* Bd. 1: 20–60. Mosjøen.

Altuna, J. 1972. Fauna de mamíferos de los yacimientos prehistóricos de Guipúzcoa. *Munibe* 24: 1–464.

Altuna, J. 1980. Historia de la domesticación animal en el País Vasco desde sus orígenes hasta la romanización. *Munibe* 32: 3–163.

Altuna, J. 1990. La caza de herbívoros durante el Paleolítico y Mesolítico del País Vasco. *Munibe* 42: 229–40.

Altuna, J. 1995. Faunas de mamíferos y cambios ambientales durante el Tardiglacial cantábrico. In A. Moure and C. González Sainz (eds.), *El Final del Paleolítico Cantábrico*. Santander: Universidad de Cantabria, pp. 77–117.

Ambrose, S. H. 1993. Isotopic analysis of paleodiets: Methodological and interpretive considerations. In M. K. Sandford (ed.), *Investigations of ancient human tissues: Chemical analyses in anthropology*. Langhorne, PA: Gordon and Breach, pp. 59–130.

Ames, K. M. 2004. Supposing hunter-gatherer variability. *American Antiquity* 69(2): 364–74.

Ames, K. M., and H. D. G. Maschner. 1999. *Peoples of the Northwest Coast: Their archaeology and prehistory*. London: Thames and Hudson.

Amiel, C., and L.-A. Lelouvier. 2002. *Gisements post-glaciaires en Bas-Quercy. Variabilité des espaces et des statuts de deux occupations mésolithiques sauveterriennes de plein air*. Toulouse: Archives d'Écologie Préhistorique, Centre d'Anthropologie, Institut National de Recherches Archéologiques Préventives.

Ammermann, A. J., and L. L. Cavalli-Sforza. 1984. *The Neolithic transition and the genetics of population in Europe*. Princeton, NJ: Princeton University Press.

Andersen, B. G. 2000. *Istider i Norge*. Universitetsforlaget. Oslo.

Andersen B. G., and H. Borns. 1997. *The Ice Age world*. Oslo: Scandinavian University Press.

Andersen, B. G., Mangerud, J., Sørensen, R., Reite, A., Sveian, H., Thoresen, M., and B. Bergstrøm. 1995. Younger Dryas ice marginal deposits in Norway. *Quaternary International* 28: 147–69.

Andersen, K. 1983. *Stenalderbebyggelsen i den Vestsjællandske Åmose*. Copenhagen: Fredningsstyrelsen.

Andersen, S. 2009. Ronæs Skov. Marinarkæologiske undersøgelser af kystboplads fra Ertebølletid. National-museet, Moesgård.

Andersen, S. H. 1970. Brovst, en kystboplads fra ældre stenalder. *Kuml* 1969: 67–90.

Andersen, S. H. 1973a. Overgangen fra ældre til yngre stenalder i sydskandinavien set fra en mesolitisk synsvinkel. In P. Simonsen and G. S. Munch (eds.), *Bonde-Veidemann. Bofast-ikke bofast i Nordisk Forhistorie*. Tromsø: Tromsø Museums Skrifter 14, pp. 26–44.

Andersen, S. H. 1973b. Bro, en senglacial boplads på Fyn. *Kuml* 1972: 7–60.

Andersen, S. H. 1975. Ringkloster: En jysk indlandsboplads med Ertebøllekultur. *Kuml* 1973–4: 11–108.

Andersen, S. H. 1976. Et østjysk fjordsystems bebyggelse i stenalderen. In H. Thrane (ed.), *Skrifter fra Institut for Historie og Samfundsvidenskab, Odense Universitet* 17, pp. 18–61.

Andersen, S. H. 1979. Aggersund: En Ertebølleboplads ved Limfjorden. *Kuml* 1978: 7–56.

Andersen, S. H. 1980. Nye østjyske fund av mønstrede Ertebølleoldsager. *Kuml* 1980: 7–59.

Andersen, S. H. 1981. *Stenalderen. Jægerstenalderen*. Copenhagen: Sesam.

Andersen, S. H. 1983. The introduction of trapezes in the south Scandinavian Mesolithic: A brief survey. In J. K. Kozłowski and S. K. Kozłowski (eds.), *Les changements, leurs mécanismes, leurs causes dans la culture du 7ᵉ au 6ᵉ millénaire av. J.-C. en Europe. Archaeologia Interregionalis.*Warsaw: Warsaw University, pp. 257–62.

Andersen, S. H. 1985. Tybrind Vig: A preliminary report on a submerged Ertebølle settlement on the west coast of Fyn. *Journal of Danish Archaeology* 4: 52–69.

Andersen, S. H. 1987. Tybrind Vig: A submerged Ertebølle settlement in Denmark. In J. M. Coles and A. J. Lawson (eds.), *European wetlands in prehistory*. Oxford: Clarendon Press, pp. 253–80.

Andersen, S. H. 1991a. Norsminde: A kjøkkenmødding with Late Mesolithic and Early Neolithic occupation. *Journal of Danish Archaeology* 8: 13–40.

Andersen, S. H. 1991b. Bjørnsholm: A stratified *kjøkkenmødding* on the central Limfjord, north Jutland. *Journal of Danish Archaeology* 10: 13–40.

Andersen, S. H. 1993. Mesolithic coastal settlement. In S. Hvass and B. Storgaard (eds.), *Digging into the past: 25 years of archaeology in Denmark*. Århus: Aarhus University Press, pp. 65–8.

Andersen, S. H. 1995. Coastal adaptation and marine exploitation in late Mesolithic Denmark – with special emphasis on the Limfjord region. In A. Fischer (ed.), *Man and sea in the Mesolithic*. Oxford: Oxbow Monograph 53, pp. 41–66.

Andersen, S. H. 1998. Ringkloster: Ertebølle trappers and wild boar hunters in eastern Jutland: a survey. *Journal of Danish Archaeology* 12: 13–64.

Andersen, S. H. 2000. Undersøisk stenalder – en oversikt. *Arkæologi for alle* 2000 (1): 4–7.

Andersen, S. H., and E. Johansen. 1987. Ertebølle revisited. *Journal of Danish Archaeology* 5: 31–61.

Anderson, J. 1895 Notice on a cave recently discovered at Oban, containing human remains, and a refuse-heap of shells and bones of animals, and stone and bone implements. *Proceedings of the Society of Antiquaries of Scotland* 29: 211–30.

Andersson, M., Karsten, D., Knarrström, B., and M. Svensson. 2004. *Stone Age Scania*. Lund: National Heritage Board, Archaeological Excavations Department.

Andersson, S., and J. Wigforss. 2004. The Late Mesolithic in the Gothenburg and Alingsås area: The project and its aims. In H. Knutsson (ed.), *Coast to coast – arrival: Results and reflections*. Proceedings of the Final Coast to Coast Conference 1–5 October 2002 in Falköping, Sweden. Sweden, Uppsala, pp. 85–104.

Anisimov, A. 1963. Cosmological concepts of the people of the north. In H. Michael (ed.), *Studies in Siberian shamanism*. Toronto: University of Toronto Press.

Antanaitis, I., and N. Ogrinc. 2000. Chemical analysis of bone: Stable isotope evidence of the diet of Neolithic and Bronze Age people in Lithuania. *Istorija. Lietuvos aukštųjų mokyklų mokslo darbai*. Vilnius: VDU leidykla 45: 3–15.

Antanaitis, I. 1998. Interpreting the meaning of East Baltic Neolithic symbols. *Cambridge Archaeological Journal* 8 (1): 55–68.

Antanaitis, I. 1999. Concerning the transition to farming in the East Baltic. *Documenta Praehistorica* 26: 89–100.

Antanaitis, I. 2001. *East Baltic economic and social organization in the Late Stone and Early Bronze Ages*. Unpublished Ph.D. dissertation summary Humanities, History (05 H). Vilnius.

Antanaitis, I., Riehl, S., and K. Kisieliené. 2000. The evolution of the subsistence economy and archaeobotanical research in Lithuania. *Lietuvos archeologija*. Vilnius: Diemedžio leidykla 19: 47–67.

Anthony, D. W. 1994. On subsistence change at the Mesolithic-Neolithic transition. *Current Anthropology* 35: 49–53.

Antl-Wieser, W. 1993. Spätpaläolithikum und Mesolithikum. In *Altsteinzeit im Osten Österreichs, Wiss.* St. Pölten, Wien: Schriftenreihe Niederösterreichs 95–97, pp. 81–90.

Antonović, D. 2006. *Stone tools from Lepenski Vir*. Belgrade: Institute of Archaeology.

Anundsen, K. 1985. Changes in shore-line and ice-front position in Late Weichsel and Holocene, Southern Norway. *Norsk Geografisk Tidsskrift* 39: 205–25.

Anundsen, K. 1996. The physical conditions for earliest settlement during the last deglaciation in Norway. In L. Larsson (ed.), *The Earliest Settlement of Scandinavia and its Relationship with Neighbouring Areas*. Acta Archaeologica Lundensia, Series In 8, 24. Stockholm: Almquist and Wiksell International, pp. 207–17.

References

Aparicio, J. 1992. Los orígenes de Oliva. *Real Academia de Cultura Valenciana, Aula de Humanidades y Ciencias, Serie Histórica* 9: 75–143.

Apelláñiz, J. M. 1971. El Mesolítico de la Cueva de Tarrerón y su datación por el C14. *Munibe* 23: 91–104.

Araújo, A. 1993. A estaçao mesolítica do Forno da Telha. *Trabalhos de Antropología e Etnología* 33:15–44.

Araújo, A. 2003. Long term change in Portuguese Early Holocene settlement and subsistence. In L. Larsson, H. Kindgren, K. Knutsson, D. Loeffler, and A. Åkerlund (eds.), *Mesolithic on the move: Papers presented at the Sixth International Conference on the Mesolithic in Europe, Stockholm 2000.* Oxford: Oxbow Books, pp. 569–80.

Araújo, A. C., and F. Almeida. 2007. Inland insights into the Macrolithic puzzle: The case of Barca do Xerez de Baixo. In N. Bicho (ed.), *From the Mediterranean Basin to the Portuguese Atlantic shore: Papers in honor of Anthony Marks.* Faro: Promontoria Monográfica 7, pp. 185–207.

Araújo, A. C., and F. Almeida. 2008. L'apport de la méthode des remontages dans l'évaluation des processus de formation et d'altération des dépôts archéologiques: le cas de Barca do Xerez de Baixo (Portugal). In T. Aubry, F. Almeida, A. C. Araújo, and M. Tiffagom (eds.), *Space and time.* British Archaeological Reports International Series 1831. Oxford: Archaeopress, pp. 91–9.

Araújo, A. C., Almeida, F., and M. J. Valente. 2009. Macrolithic industries of the Portuguese Mesolithic: A human adaptive response. In S. McCartan, R. Schulting, G. Warren, and P. Woodman (eds.), *Mesolithic horizons. Papers presented at the Seventh International Conference on the Mesolithic in Europe, Belfast 2005.* Oxford: Oxbow Books, pp. 779–87.

Arias, P. 1991. *De cazadores a campesinos.* Santander: Universidad de Cantabria.

Arias, P. 1999. The origins of the Neolithic along the Atlantic coast of continental Europe: a survey. *Journal of World Prehistory* 13: 403–64.

Arias, P. 2004. Comments. In P. Rowley-Conwy, How the West was lost: A reconsideration of agricultural origins in Britain, Ireland, and Southern Scandinavia. *Current Anthropology* 45: 83–113.

Arias, P. 2005–06. Determinaciones de isótopos estables en restos humanos de la región cantábrica. Aportación al estudio de la dieta de las poblaciones del Mesolítico y el Neolítico. *Munibe* 57: 359–74.

Arias, P., Altuna, J., Armendariz, A., González, J. E., Ibáñez, J. J., Ontañón R., and L. Zapata. 1999. Nuevas aportaciones al conocimiento de las primeras sociedades productores en la región Cantábrica. *Saguntum-PLAV* Extra 2: 549–57.

Arias, P., Armendariz, A., et al. 2009. Burials in the cave: New evidence on mortuary practices during the Mesolithic of Cantabrian Spain. In S. McCartan, R. Schulting, G. Warren, and P. Woodman (eds.), *Mesolithic horizons. Papers presented at the Seventh International Conference on the Mesolithic in Europe, Belfast 2005.* Oxford: Oxbow Books, pp. 650–6.

Arias, P., Cerrillo-Cuenca, E., et al. 2009. A view from the edges: The Mesolithic settlement of the interior areas of the Iberian Peninsula reconsidered. In S. McCartan, R. Schulting, G. Warren, and P. Woodman (eds.), *Mesolithic horizons. Papers presented at the Seventh International Conference on the Mesolithic in Europe, Belfast 2005.* Oxford: Oxbow Books, pp. 303–11.

Arias, P., Fano, M., et al. 2007. Programa de sondeos en concheros holocenos del Oriente de Asturias. *Excavaciones Arqueológicas en Asturias, 1999–2002.* Oviedo: Principado de Asturias, pp. 107–16.

Arias, P., Fernández, P., Marcos, C., and I. Rodríguez. 2009. The elusive flint: Raw materials and lithic technology in the Mesolithic of eastern Asturias, Spain. In S. McCartan, R. Schulting, G. Warren, and P. Woodman (eds.), *Mesolithic horizons. Papers presented at the Seventh International Conference on the Mesolithic in Europe, Belfast 2005.* Oxford: Oxbow Books, pp. 860–6.

Arias, P., Fernández-Tresguerres, J., et al. 2007. Excavación arqueológica de urgencia en la Cueva de la Poza l'Egua (Lledias, Llanes). *Excavaciones Arqueológicas en Asturias, 1999–2002.* Oviedo: Principado de Asturias, pp. 227–39.

Arias, P., and C. Pérez. 1990. Las excavaciones en la Cueva de los Canes y otros trabajos en la depresión prelitoral del oriente de Asturias. *Excavaciones Arqueológicas en Asturias, 1983–86.* Oviedo: Principado de Asturias, pp. 135–41.

Armendáriz, A. 1997. Antón Koba. In R. de Balbín and P. Bueno (eds.), *Actas, II Congreso de Arqueología Peninsular*, vol. 1. Zamora: Fundación Rei Afonso Henriques, pp. 297–310.

Arnaud, J. 1989. The Mesolithic communities of the Sado valley, Portugal, in their ecological setting. In C. Bonsall (ed.), *The Mesolithic in Europe: Proceedings of the third international symposium*. Edinburgh: John Donald, pp. 614–31.

Arnaud, J. M. 1993. O Mesolítico e a Neolitizaçao. In G. Carvalho et al. (eds.), *O Quaternario em Portugal*. Lisboa: Colibri, pp. 173–84.

Arnold, J. 1995. Transportation innovation and social complexity among maritime hunter-gatherer societies. *American Anthropologist* 97: 733–47.

Arora, S. 1978. Mesolithikum. In S. Veil (ed.), *Alt- und Mittelsteinzeitliche Fundplätze des Rheinlandes*. Köln: Rheinland Verlag, pp. 31–5.

Arora, S. K. 1976. Die Mittelsteinzeit im westlichen Deutschland und in den Nachbargebieten. *Rheinische Ausgrabungen* 17: 1–65.

Arora, S. K. 1979. Mesolithische Rohstoffversorgung im westlichen Deutschland. *Rheinische Ausgrabungen* 19: 1–51.

Arora, S. K. 1981. Mittelsteinzeit am Niederrhein. *Kölner Jahrbuch* 15: 191–211.

Arts, N. 1987. Mesolithische jagers, vissers en voedselverzamelaars in noordoost België en zuidoost Nederland. *Het Oude Land van Loon* 42: 27–85.

Arts, N. 1989. Archaeology, environment and the social evolution of later band societies in a lowland area. In C. Bonsall (ed.), *The Mesolithic in Europe: Proceedings of the third international symposium*. Edinburgh: John Donald, pp. 291–312.

Arts, N., and J. Deeben. 1981. *Prehistorische jagers en verzamelaars te Vessem, een model*. Bijdrage tot de studie van het Brabants Heem deel 20. Eindhoven: Stichting Brabants Heem.

Arts, N., and M. Hoogland. 1987. A Mesolithic settlement area with a human cremation grave at Oirschot V, municipality of Best, the Netherlands. *Helinium* 27: 172–89.

Aubry, T., Fontugne, M., and M.-H. Moura. 1997. Les occupations de la Grotte de Buraca Grande depuis le Paléolithique supérieur et les apports de la séquence Holocène a l'étude de la transition Mésolithique/Néolithique au Portugal. *Bulletin de la Société Préhistorique Française* 94: 182–90.

Auffermann, B. 1996. Zur Frage der Tauschbeziehungen im Süddeutschen Magdalenien: Das Beispiel Plattenhornstein. In I. Campen, J. Hahn, and M. Uerpmann (eds.), *Spuren der Jagd – Die Jagd Nach Spuren*. Tübinger Monographien zur Urgeschichte 11. Tübingen: Mo Vince Verlag, pp. 273–8.

Aura Tortosa, J. 1992. El Magdaleniense Superior Mediterráneo y su modelo evolutivo. In P. Utrilla Miranda (ed.), *Aragón/Litoral Mediterráneo: Intercambios culturales durante la prehistoria*. Zaragoza: Institución Fernando Il Catolico, pp. 167–77.

Aura, J., Villaverde, V., Pérez, M., Martinez, R., and P. Guillem. 2002. Big game and small prey: Palaeolithic and Epipalaeolithic economy from Valencia (Spain). *Journal of Archaeological Method and Theory* 9: 215–68.

Aura, J. E., Villaverde, V., González Morales, M., González Sainz, C., Zilhao J., and L. Straus. 1998. The Pleistocene-Holocene transition in the Iberian Peninsula. In B. Eriksen and L. Straus (eds.), *As the world warmed*. *Quaternary International* 49/50: 87–104.

Auset, H. n.d. Rapport fra utgravning av steinalderboplass ifm. Rv 680 Foldfjorden, Myrset av Straumsvik gnr. 91/13, Aure, Møre og Romsdal. Unpubl. Report, NTNU Vitenskapsmuseet, Trondheim.

Autio, E. 1995. Horned anthropomorphic figures in Finnish rock-paintings: Shamans or something else? *Fennoscandia archaeologica* 12: 12–18.

Ågotnes, A. 1981. Bosetningsmønster og livbergingsform i steinalderen i Vindenesområdet. *Fra Fjon til Fusa* 1981: 7–64.

Åkerlund, A. 1996. *Human responses to shore displacement*. Riksantikvarieämbetet, Arkeologiska undersökningar.

Aaris-Sørensen, K. 1988. *Danmarks forhistoriske dyreverden*. Copenhagen: Gyldendal.

Åstveit, L. I. 2005. *Arkeologisk registrering på Stavneset, Averøy kommune, Møre og Romsdal. Ormen Lange prosjektet*. Kulturhistoriske skrifter og rapporter 2. Molde: Møre og Romsdal fylke.

References

Åstveit, L. I. 2008a. Senmesolittisk tid (SM) 6500–4000 BC. In H. B. Bjerck (ed.), L. I. Åstveit, T. Meling, J. Gundersen, G. Jørgensen, and S. Normann. *NTNU Vitenskapsmuseets arkeologiske undersøkelser Ormen Lange Nyhamna*. Trondheim: Tapir Akademisk Forlag, pp. 576–87.

Åstveit, L. I. 2008b. Lokalitet 30 Fredly – Boplass med mesolittiske tufter og dyrkningsaktivitet i neolitikum/bonsealder. In H. B. Bjerck (ed.), L. I. Åstveit, T. Meling, J. Gundersen, G. Jørgensen, and S. Normann. *NTNU Vitenskapsmuseets arkeologiske undersøkelser Ormen Lange Nyhamna*. Trondheim: Tapir Akademisk Forlag, pp. 119–68.

Åstveit, L. I. 2009. Different ways of building, different ways of living: Mesolithic house structures in western Norway. In S. McCartan, R. Schulting, G. Warren, and P. C. Woodman (eds.), *Mesolithic horizons. Papers presented at the Seventh International Conference on the Mesolithic in Europe, Belfast 2005*. Oxford: Oxbow Books, pp. 414–21.

Baales, M., and M. Street. 1996. Hunter-gatherer behavior in a changing Late Glacial landscape: Alleröd archaeology in the Central Rhineland, Germany. *Journal of Anthropological Research* 52: 281–316.

Baales, M., Bittmann, F., and B. Kromer. 1999. Verkohlte Bäume im Trass der Laacher See-Tephra bei Kruft (Neuwieder Becken). *Archäologisches Korrespondenzblatt* 28: 191–204.

Bagnienvski, Z. 1986. Remarks on Mesolithic settlement in the southern part of the Kashubian Lakeland. In T. Malinowski (ed.), *Problems of the Stone Age in Pomerania*. Warsaw: Warsaw University, pp. 127–54.

Bagolini, B., Broglio, A., and R. Lunz. 1983. Le Mésolithique des Dolomites. *Preistoria Alpina* 19: 15–36.

Bahn, P. 1989. The early postglacial period in the Pyrenees: Some recent work. In C. Bonsall (ed.), *The Mesolithic in Europe: Proceedings of the third international symposium*. Edinburgh: John Donald, pp. 556–60.

Bailey, G. 1973. Los concheros del norte de España: Una hipótesis preliminar. *Congréso Nacional de Arqueología*, 1971, Jaén, 12: 73–84.

Bailey, G. 1999. The Palaeolithic archaeology and palaeogeography of Epirus with particular reference to the investigations of the Klithi rockshelter. In G. Bailey, E. Adam, C. Perlès, E. Panagopoulou, and K. Zachos (eds.), *The Palaeolithic archaeology of Greece and adjacent areas: Proceedings of the First International Conference on the Palaeolithic of Greece and the Balkans*. London: British School at Athens, pp. 159–69.

Bailey, G. 2004. The wider significance of submerged archaeological sites and their relevance to world prehistory. In N. C. Flemming (ed.), *Submarine prehistoric archaeology of the North Sea: Research priorities and collaboration with industry*. London: CBA Research Report 141, pp. 3–10.

Bailey, G., and A. Craighead. 2003. Late Pleistocene and early Holocene coastal palaeoeconomies: a reconsideration of the molluscan evidence from Northern Spain. *Geoarchaeology: an International Journal* 18 (2): 175–204.

Bailey, G. N., and N. J. Milner. 2002. Coastal hunters and gatherers and social evolution: Marginal or central? *Before Farming: The Archaeology of Old World Hunter-Gatherers* 3–4 (1): 1–15.

Bailloud, G. 1967. Informations archéologiques. *Gallia Préhistoire*, 301–16.

Bakka, E. 1973. Om alderen på veideristningene. *Viking* 36: 151–87.

Bakka, E. 1975. Geologically dated Arctic rock carvings at Hammer near Steinkjer in Nord-Trøndelag. *Arkeologiske Skrifter fra Historisk Museum vid Universitetet i Bergen* 2.

Bakkevig, S. 1980. Phosphate analysis in archaeology – problems and recent progress. *Norwegian Archaeological Review* 13 (2): 73–100.

Balabanov, I. P. 2007. Holocene sea-level changes of the Black Sea. In V. Yanko-Hombach, A. Gilbert, N. Panin, and P. Dolukhanov (eds.), *The Black Sea flood question: Changes in coastline, climate, and human settlement*. Dordrecht: Springer, pp. 711–30.

Balanovsky, O. P. 2009. Human genetics and Neolithic dispersals. In P. Dolukhanov, G. R. Sarson, and A. M. Shukurov (eds.), *The East European Plain on the eve of agriculture*. British Archaeological Reports International Series 1964. Oxford: Archaeopress, pp. 235–46.

Baldeón, A., and E. Berganza. 1997. *Kukuma*. Vitoria: Memorias de Yacimientos Alaveses 3.

Ballin, T. B. 1995. Teknologiske profiler: Datering av steinalderboplasser ved atributanalyse. *Universitetets Oldsaksamlings årbok 1993/1994*: 25–46.

Ballin, T. B. 1998. *Oslofjordsforbindelsen: Arkæologiske undersøgelser ved Drøbaksundet*. Varia 48. Oslo: Universitetets Oldsaksamling.

Ballin, T. B. 1999. The middle mesolithic in Southern Norway. In J. Boaz (ed.), *The Mesolithic of Central Scandinavia*. Universitetets Oldsaksamlings Skrifter Ny Rekke 22. Oslo: Universitetets Oldsaksamling, pp. 203–15.

Ballin, T. B., and O. L. Jensen. 1995. *Farsundprosjektet – steinalderbopladser på Lista*. Varia 29. Oslo: Universitetets Oldsaksamling.

Balzer, M. M. 1981. Rituals of gender identity: Markers of Siberian Khanty ethnicity, status, and belief. *American Anthropologist* 83: 50–67.

Balzer, M. M. 1990. *Shamanism: Soviet studies of traditional religion in Siberia and Central Asia*. New York: Sharpe.

Bamforth, F., Jackes, M., and D. Lubell. 2003. Mesolithic-Neolithic population relationships in Portugal: The evidence from ancient mitochondrial DNA. In L. Larsson, H. Kindgren, K. Knutsson, D. Loeffler, and A. Åkerlund (eds.), *Mesolithic on the move: Papers presented at the Sixth International Conference on the Mesolithic in Europe, Stockholm 2000*. Oxford: Oxbow Books, pp. 581–87.

Bandi, H. 1963. *Birsmatten-Basisgrotte*. Acta Bernensia I. Bern: Verlag Stämpfli and Cie.

Bang-Andersen, S. 2003a. Southwest-Norway at the Pleistocene/Holocene transition: Landscape development, colonization progress, site types, settlement patterns. *Norwegian Archaeological Review* 36 (1): 5–27.

Bang-Andersen, S. 2003b. Encircling the living space of Early Postglacial reindeer hunters in the interior of southern Norway. In L. Larsson, H. Kindgren, K. Knutsson, D. Loeffler, and A. Åkerlund (eds.), *Mesolithic on the move: Papers presented at the Sixth International Conference on the Mesolithic in Europe, Stockholm 2000*. Oxford: Oxbow, pp. 193–205.

Barandiarán, I., and A. Cava. 1989a. *El yacimiento prehistórico de Zatoya*. Pamplona: Trabajos de Arqueología Navarra 8.

Barandiarán, I., and A. Cava. 1989b. The evolution of the Mesolithic in the north east of the Iberian peninsula. In C. Bonsall (ed.), *The Mesolithic in Europe: Proceedings of the third international symposium*. Edinburgh: John Donald, pp. 572–81.

Barbaza, M. 1993. Technologie et cultures du Mésolithique moyen au Néolithique ancien dans les Pyrénées de l'Est. In J. Guilaine (ed.), *Dourgne. Derniers chasseurs-cueilleurs et premiers éleveurs de la haute vallée de l'Aude*. Toulouse: Edition du CASR, EHESS/CNRS, pp. 425–41.

Barbaza, M. 1999. *Les civilisations postglaciaires. La vie dans la grande forêt tempérée*. Paris: Edition la Maison des Roches, Histoire de la France Préhistorique.

Barbaza, M., Valdeyron, N., André J., Briois, F., Martin, H., Philibert, S., Allios, D., and E. Lignon. 1991. *Fontfaurès en Quercy. Contribution à l'étude du Sauveterrien*. Toulouse: Archives d'Ecologie Préhistorique 11.

Barker, G. 1981. *Landscape and society: Prehistoric Central Italy*. London: Academic Press.

Barker, G. 1985. *Prehistoric farming in Europe*. Cambridge, UK: Cambridge University Press.

Barker, G. 2006. *The agricultural revolution in prehistory*. Oxford: Oxford University Press.

Barlindhaug, S. 1996. Hvor skal vi bygge og hvor skal vi bo? En analyse av lokaliseringsfaktorer i tidlig eldre steinalder i Troms. Unpublished thesis, University of Tromsø.

Barnard, A. (ed.) 2004. *Hunter-gatherers in history, archaeology and anthropology*. Oxford: Berg.

Barrett, J. 1994. *Fragments from antiquity*. Oxford: Blackwell.

Barrière, C. 1973–1974. Rouffignac. L'archéologie. *Travaux de l'Institut d'Art Préhistorique*. 15: 65–160; 16: 3–47; 17: 3–83. Université de Toulouse-Le Mirail.

Bárta, J. 1981. Das Mesolithikum im nordwestlichen Teil des Karpatenbeckens. In B. Gramsch (ed.), *Mesolithikum in Europa*. Berlin: Veröffentlichungen des Museums für Ur- und Frühgeschichte Potsdam 14/15, pp. 295–300.

Bárta, J. 1990. Mezolitickí lovci v Medvedej jaskyni pri Ružíne. *Slovenská archeológia* 38: 5–30.

Barth, F. 1956. Ecological relationships and ethnic groups in Swat, North Pakistan. *American Anthrolopogist* 58: 1079–89.

References

Barth, F. 1987. *Cosmologies in the making: A generative approach to cultural variation in Inner New Guinea*. Cambridge, UK: Cambridge University Press.

Bartolomei, G., Broglio, A., and A. Palma di Cesnola. 1979. Chronostratigraphie et écologie de l'Epigravettien en Italie. In D. de Sonneville Bordes (ed.), *La fin des temps glaciaires en Europe: Chronostratigraphie et écologie des cultures du Paléolithique Final*. Paris: CNRS, pp. 297–324.

Barton, N., Roberts, A. J., and D. A. Roe (eds.). 1991. *The Late Glacial in north-west Europe: Human adaptation and environmental change at the end of the Pleistocene*. London: CBA Research Report 77.

Barton, R. N. E., and S. Dumont. 2000. Recolonisation and settlement of Britain at the end of the Last Glaciation. In B. Valentin, P. Bodu, and M. Christensen (eds.), *L'Europe septentrionale au Tardiglaciaire*. Table-ronde de Nemours, 13–16 mai 1997. Memoires du Musée de Préhistoire d'Ile de France, 7, 2000, pp. 151–62.

Bartosiewicz, L. 2005. Plain talk: Animals, environment and culture in the Neolithic of the Carpathian Basin and adjacent areas. In D. Bailey, A. Whittle, and V. Cummings (eds.), *(Un)settling the Neolithic*. Oxford: Oxbow Books, pp. 51–63.

Bartosiewicz, L., and C. Bonsall. 2004. Prehistoric fishing along the Danube. *Antaeus* 27: 253–72.

Bartosiewicz, L., Bonsall, C., Boroneanţ, V., and S. Stallibrass. 1995. Schela Cladovei: a preliminary review of the prehistoric fauna. *Mesolithic Miscellany* 16 (2): 2–19.

Bartosiewicz, L., Boroneanţ, V., Bonsall, C. and S. Stallibrass. 2001. New data on the prehistoric fauna of the Iron Gates: a case study from Schela Cladovei, Romania. In R. Kertész and J. Makkay (eds.), *From the Mesolithic to the Neolithic*. Budapest: Archaeolingua, pp. 15–22.

Bartosiewicz, L., Bonsall, C., and V. Şişu. 2008. Sturgeon fishing in the Middle and Lower Danube region. In C. Bonsall, V. Boroneanţ, and I. Radovanović (eds.), *The Iron Gates in prehistory: New perspectives*. Oxford: Archaeopress, pp. 39–54.

Bar-Yosef, O., Vandermeersch, B., Arensburg, B., Belfer-Cohen, A., Goldberg, P., Laville, H., Meignen, L., Rak, Y., Speth, J. D., Tchernov, E., Tillier, A.-M., and S. Weiner. 1992. The excavations in Kebara Cave, Mt. Carmel. *Current Anthropology* 33 (5): 497–550.

Bass, B. 1998. Early Neolithic offshore accounts: Remote islands, maritime exploitations, and the trans-Adriatic cultural network. *Journal of Mediterranean Archaeology* 11: 165–90.

Baudou, E. 1977. Den Förhistoriska fångstkulturen I Västernorrland. *Västernorrlands förhistoria*. Härnösand, pp. 11–152.

Baudou, E. 1992 Boplatsen vid Nämforsen. *Arkeologi i nor* 3: 71–82.

Baudou, E. 1993. Hällristningarna vid Nämforsen – datering och kulturmiljö: Ekonomi och näringsformer i nordisk bronsålder. *Studia archaeologica universitatis Umensis* 3: 247–61.

Baudou, E. 2003. Stenåldern i Mellannorrland. En forskningsoversikt. In A. Beverfjord (ed.), *Midtnordisk arkeologisymposium 1999*. Vitark 3, 9–26. Trondheim: Vitenskapsmuseet, NTNU.

Baum, N. 1991. Sammler/Jäger oder Ackerbauern? Eine Paläodontologische Untersuchung zur Kulturhistorischen Stellung der Kopfbestattungen aus der Grossen Ofnet-Höhle in Schwaben. *Archäologisches Korrespondenzblatt* 21: 469–74.

Bay-Petersen, J. L. 1978. Animal exploitation in Mesolithic Denmark. In P. Mellars (ed.), *The early postglacial settlement of northern Europe*. London: Duckworth, pp. 115–45.

Bazile, F., and C. Monnet-Bazile. 1998. Le gisement épipaléolithique de la Grange des Merveilles II, Rochefort du Gard, Gard. Note préliminaire. *Bulletin de la Societé Préhistorique Française* 95: 467–74.

Becker, B., Kromer, B., and P. Trimborn. 1991. A stable-isotope tree-ring timescale of the late glacial/Holocene boundary. *Nature* 353: 647–9.

Becker, C. J. 1947. Mosefundne lerkar fra Yngre Stenalder. Studier over Tragtbægerkulturen i Danmark. *Årbøger for Nordisk Oldkyndighed og Historie 1947*. København: Nordisk.

Belanovskaya, T. D. 1995. *Iz drevneishego proshlogo Nizhnego Podonya. Poselenie vremeni neolita i eneolota Rakushechnyi Yar [The most distant past of the Lower Don. Rakushechnyi Yar Neolithic and Chalcolithic settlement]*. St Petersburg: St Petersburg University Press.

Bell, T., and P. Renouf. 2004. Prehistoric cultures, reconstructed coasts: Maritime Archaic Indian site distribution in Newfoundland. *World Archaeology* 35 (3): 350–70.

Beltrán, A. 1992. El arte prehistórico en la zona del Valle del Ebro y del litoral Mediterráneo: Estado de la cuestión y bases para un debate. In P. Utrilla Miranda (ed.), *Aragón/Litoral Mediterráneo: Intercambios culturales durante la prehistoria*. Zaragoza: Institución Fernando Il Catolico, pp. 401–14.

Beltrán, A. 1993. *Arte rupestre preistorica*. Milano: Editoriale Jaca.

Bender, B. 1978. Gatherer-hunter to farmer: A social perspective. *World Archaeology* 10: 204–23.

Bender, B. 1985. Emergent tribal formations in the American midcontinent. *American Antiquity* 50: 52–62.

Benecke, N., and S. Hanik. 2002. Dogs for the living and the dead – on the exploitation of dogs in Mesolithic Europe. Abstract of a paper presented at the 9th ICAZ Conference, University of Durham, 23–28 August 2002.

Bengtsson, L. 2003. Knowledge and interaction in the Stone Age: Raw materials for adzes and axes, their sources and distributional patterns. In L. Larsson, H. Kindgren, K. Knutsson, D. Loeffler, and A. Åkerlund (eds.), *Mesolithic on the move: Papers presented at the Sixth International Conference on the Mesolithic in Europe, Stockholm 2000*. Oxford: Oxbow, pp. 388–94.

Bennett, K., Tzedakis, P., and K. Willis. 1991. Quaternary refugia of north European trees. *Journal of Biogeography* 18: 103–15.

Bennike, P. 1985. *Palaeopathology of Danish skeletons: a comparative study of demography disease and injury*. Copenhagen: Akademisk Forlag.

Bennike, P. 1993. The People. In S. Hvass, and B. Storgaard (eds.), *Digging into the past: 25 years of archaeology in Denmark*. Århus: Aarhus University Press, pp. 34–39.

Bentley, R. A., Price, T. D., Lüning, J., Gronenborn, D., Wahl, J., and P. D. Fullager. 2002. Prehistoric Mmigration in Europe: Strontium isotope analysis of Early Neolithic skeletons. *Current Anthropology* 43 (5): 799–804.

Bentley, R. A., Chikhi, L., and T. D. Price. 2003. The Neolithic transition in Europe: Comparing broad scale genetic and local scale isotopic evidence, *Antiquity* 77 (295): 63–50.

Berg Hansen, I. M. 1999. The availability of flint at Lista and Jæderen, Southwest Norway. In J. Boaz (ed.), *The Mesolithic of Central Scandinavia*. Universitetets Oldsaksamlings Skrifter Ny Rekke 22. Oslo: Universitetets Oldsaksamling, pp. 255–66.

Berg, E. 1995. *Dobbeltspor/E6-prosjektet. Steinalderlokaliteter fra senmesolittisk tid i Vestby, Akershus*. Varia 32. Oslo: Universitetets Oldsaksamling.

Berg, E. 1997. *Mesolittiske boplasser ved Årungen i Ås og Frogn, Akershus*. Varia 44. Oslo: Universitetets Oldsaksamling.

Berg, E. 1999. Raw material use and axe production in the mesolithic of southeastern Norway. In J. Boaz (ed.), *The Mesolithic of Central Scandinavia*. Universitetets Oldsaksamlings Skrifter. Ny Rekke 22. Oslo: Universitetets Oldsaksamling, pp. 267–82.

Berg, E. 2003. The spatial and chronological development of the Late Mesolithic Nøstvet period in coastal southeastern Norway from a lithic raw material perspective. In L. Larsson, H. Kindgren, K. Knutsson, D. Loeffler, and A. Åkerlund (eds.), *Mesolithic on the move: Papers presented at the Sixth International Conference on the Mesolithic in Europe, Stockholm 2000*. Oxford: Oxbow, pp. 283–90.

Berganza, E. 1990. El Epipaleolítico en el País Vasco. *Munibe* 42: 81–9.

Berglund, B. E. 1969. Vegetation and human influence in south Scandinavia during prehistoric time. *Oikos* (supplement) 12: 9–28.

Berglund, B. E. (ed.). 1991. The cultural landscape during 6000 years in southern Sweden *The Ystad project*. Ecological Bulletins 41. Copenhagen: Munksgaard.

Berglund, B. E. (ed.). 2001. *'Gassprosjektet' – Arkeologiske undersøkelser på Tjeldbergodden, Aure k., Møre og Romsdal, i forbindelse med bygging av metanolanlegg*. Rapport – Arkeologisk serie, 2001/1. Trondheim: NTNU.

Bergman, C. 1993. The development of the bow in western Europe: a technological and functional perspective. In G. Peterkin, H. Bricker, and P. Mellars (eds.), *Hunting and animal exploitation in the Later Palaeolithic and Mesolithic of Eurasia*. Archeological Papers of the American Anthropological Association 4. Washington, DC: American Anthropological Association, pp. 95–105.

References

Bergman, I. 1995. *Från Döudden til Varghalsen: En studie av kontinuitet och förändring inom ett fångstsamhälle i Övre Norrlands inland, 5200 f Kr–400 e Kr*. Umeå: Arkeologiska institutionen, Umeå Universiet, Studia Archaeologica Universitatis Umensis.

Bergman, I., A. Olofson, G. Hörnberg, O. Zackrisson, and E. Hellberg. 2004. Deglaciation and colonization: Pioneer settlements in Northern Fennoscandia. *Journal of World Prehistory* 18 (2): 155–77.

Bergsvik, K. A. 1991. Ervervs- og bosetningsmønstre på kysten av Nordhordland i steinalder, belyst ved funn fra Fosenstraumen. Unpublished thesis, University of Bergen.

Bergsvik, K. A. 1994. Lokaliseringsanalyse av stein- og bronsealderbosetningen på Kollsnes i Øygarden, Hordaland. In A. J. Nærøy (ed.), *Troll-prosjektet. Arkeologiske undersøkelser på Kollsnes, Øygarden k. Hordaland, 1989–1993*. Bergen: Universitetet i Bergen, pp. 239–62.

Bergsvik, K. A. 1995: Bosetningsmønstre på kysten av Nordhordland i steinalder. En geografisk innfallsvinkel. *Steinalderkonferansen i Bergen 1993*. Arkeologiske skrifter, Arkeologisk Inst., Bergen Museum 8: 111–30.

Bergsvik, K. A. 1999. A new reference system for classification of lithic raw materials: a case study from Skatestraumen, Western Norway. In J. Boaz (ed.), *The Mesolithic of Central Scandinavia*. Universitetets Oldsaksamlings Skrifter. Ny Rekke 22, Oslo: Universitetets Oldsaksamling, pp. 283–99.

Bergsvik, K. A. 2001a. Strømmer og steder i vestnorsk steinalder. *Viking* 64: 11–34.

Bergsvik, K. A. 2001b. Sedentary and mobile hunter-fishers in Stone Age Western Norway. *Arctic Anthropology* 38 (1): 2–26.

Bergsvik, K. A. 2002. *Arkeologiske undersøkelser ved Skatestraumen. Bind 1*. Arkeologiske thesiser og rapporter fra Univ. i Bergen 7. Bergen.

Bergsvik, K. A. 2003a. Ethnic boundaries in Neolithic Norway. Unpublished Ph.D. thesis, University of Bergen.

Bergsvik, K. A. 2003b. Mesolithic ethnicity – too hard to handle? In L. Larsson, H. Kindgren, K. Knutsson, D. Loeffler, and A. Åkerlund (eds.), *Mesolithic on the move: Papers presented at the Sixth International Conference on the Mesolithic in Europe, Stockholm 2000*. Oxford: Oxbow, pp. 290–302.

Bergsvik, K. A. 2004. En etnisk grense ved Stad i steinalderen. *Primitive tider* 7: 7–29. Oslo.

Bergsvick, K. A. 2009. Caught in the middle: Functional and ideological aspects of Mesolithic shores in Norway. In S. B. McCartan, R. Schulting, G. Warren, and P. Woodman (eds.), *Mesolithic horizons. Papers presented at the Seventh International Conference on the Mesolithic in Europe, Belfast 2005*. Oxford: Oxbow Books, pp. 602–9.

Bergsvik, K. A., and A. B. Olsen. 2003. Traffic in stone adzes in Mesolithic Western Norway. In L. Larsson, H. Kindgren, K. Knutsson, D. Loeffler, and A. Åkerlund (eds.), *Mesolithic on the move: Papers presented at the Sixth International Conference on the Mesolithic in Europe, Stockholm 2000*. Oxford: Oxbow, pp. 395–404.

Bernabeu, J., Emili Aura, J., and E. Badal. 1995. *Al Oeste del Eden*. Madrid: Editorial Sintesis.

Bernaldo de Quirós, F., and A. Neira. 1996. Occupations de haute montagne dans la région cantabrique espagnole. In H. Delporte and J. Clottes (eds.), *Pyrénées Préhistoriques*. Comité des Paris: Travaux Historiques et Scientifiques, pp. 193–205.

Beuker, J. R., and M. J. L. T. Niekus. 1997. De kano van Pesse-de bijl erin. *Nieuwe Drentse Volksalmanak* 114: 122–5.

Bevan, L, and J. Moore. 2003. *Peopling the Mesolithic in a northern environment*. Oxford: British Archaeological Reports, Archaeopress.

Beyneix, A. 1998. Rubanés et cardiaux à travers les pratiques funéraires: état des recherches en France. *Bulletin de la Societé Préhistorique Française* 95: 547–53.

Biagi, P., and M. Spataro. 2000. Plotting the evidence: Some aspects of the radiocarbon chronology of the Mesolithic-Neolithic transition in the Mediterranean basin. *Atti della Societa di Preistoria e Protostoria della regione Friuli-Venezia Giulia* 12: 15–54.

Biagi, P., and M. Spataro. 2002. The Mesolithic/Neolithic transition in north eastern Italy and in the Adriatic Basin. In E. Badall, J. Bernabeu, and B. Martí (eds.), *Saguntum. Supp. 5 El Paisaje en el Neolítico Mediterráneo*, pp. 167–78.

Biagi, P., Maggi, R., and R. Nisbet. 1989. Liguria: 11,000–7000 BP. In C. Bonsall (ed.), *The Mesolithic in Europe: Proceedings of the third international symposium*. Edinburgh: John Donald, pp. 533–40.

Biagi, P., Shennan, S., and M. Spataro. 2005. Rapid rivers and slow seas? New data for the radiocarbon chronology of the Balkan Peninsula. In L. Nikolova and J. Higgins (eds.), *Prehistoric archaeology and anthropological theory and education (Reports of Prehistoric Research Projects 6–7, 2005)*. Salt Lake City: International Institute of Anthropology, pp. 43–51.

Bibikov, S. N. 1950. Pozdndeishii paleolit Kryma [Late Palaeolithic of the Crimea]. *Materialy po chetverticnomu periodu SSSR [Materials on the Quaternary of the USSR]* 2: 118–26.

Bibikov, S. N., and V. G. Zbenovich. 1985. Rannii etap tripol'skoi *kul'tury [The early stage of Tripolye Culture]*. In D. Y. Telegin (ed.), *Arheologiya Ukrainskoi SSR [Archaeology of the Ukrainian SSR]*, vol. 1. Kiev: Naukova Dumka, pp. 189–206

Bibikov, S. N., Stanko V. N., and V. N. Koen. 1994. *Final'nyi paleolit i mezolit Kryma [The Final Palaeolithic of the Crimea]*. Vest: Odessa.

Bicho, N. 1993. Late Glacial prehistory of central and southern Portugal. *Antiquity* 67: 761–75.

Bicho, N. 1994. The end of the Paleolithic and the Mesolithic in Portugal. *Current Anthropology* 35: 664–74.

Bicho, N. 1998. The Pleistocene-Holocene transition in Portuguese prehistory. In S. Milliken (ed.), *The organization of lithic technology in late glacial and early postglacial Europe*. Oxford: British Archaeological Reports International Series 700, pp. 39–62.

Bicho, N. 2009. On the edge: Early Holocene adaptations in southwestern Iberia. *Journal of Anthropological Research* 65: 185–206.

Bietti, A. 1980. The Mesolithic cultures in Italy: New activities in connection with Upper Paleolithic cultural traditions. *Veroffentlichungen des Museums für Ur- und Frühgeschichte, Potsdam* 14: 33–50.

Bietti, A. 1987. Considerazioni sul significato e sull'utilizzazione delle liste tipologiche delle industrie Paleolitiche. *Atti della XXVII Riunione Scientifica del Istituto Italiano di Preistoria e Protostoria* 1: 147–63.

Bietti, A. 1990. The Late Upper Palaeolithic in Italy: An overview. *Journal of World Prehistory* 4: 95–155.

Binder, D. 1987. *Le Néolithique ancien provençal, typologie et technologie des outillages lithiques*. XXIVème supplément à Gallia-Préhistoire, Edition du CNRS.

Binder, D. 2000. Mesolithic and Neolithic interaction in southern France and northern Italy: New data and current hypotheses. In T. D. Price (ed.), *Europe's First Farmers*. Cambridge, UK: Cambridge University Press, pp. 117–43.

Binford, L. R. 1980. Willow smoke and dog's tails: Hunter-gatherer settlement systems and archaeological site formation. *American Antiquity* 45: 4–20.

Binford, L. R. 1982. The archaeology of place. *Journal of Anthropological Archaeology* 1: 5–31.

Binford, L. R. 1983. *In pursuit of the past: Decoding the archaeological record*. London: Thames and Hudson.

Bintz, P. 1991. *Paléoenvironnement holocène et archéologie dans les Alpes du Nord et leur piédmont*. Sous la direction de Robert Vivian. Paris: Editions du CTHS.

Bintz, P., Ginestet, J. P., and G. Pion. 1988. Le Mésolithique et la néolithisation dans les Alpes françaises du nord. In *Mésolithique et néolithisation en France et dans les régions limitrophes*. Actes du 113e Congrès National des Sociétés Savantes (Strasbourg, 1988), 1991. Paris: Editions du CTHS, pp. 245–67.

Bintz, P., Argant, J., André, G., Picavet, R., and J.-M. Roche. 1999. Occupations territoriales du Mésolithique au Néolithique ancien en Vercors et en Chartreuse (Isère, Drôme): Programme de prospection thématique, de sondages palynologiques et premiers résultats. In *Préhistoire de l'espace habité en France du sud et actualité de la recherche*. Actes des premières rencontres méridionales de préhistoire récente, Valence, 3 et 4 juin 1994, Beeching A., Vital J. (Dir.), Valence: Centre d'Archéologie préhistorique, pp. 143–50.

Bird-David, N. 1990. The giving environment: Another perspective on the economic system of gatherer-hunters. *Current Anthropology* 31 (2): 189–96.

Bird-David, N. 1992a. Beyond 'The Original Affluent Society': A culturalist reformation. *Current Anthropology* 33(1): 25–47.

Bird-David, N. H. 1992b. Beyond 'the hunting and gathering mode of subsistence': Culture-sensitive observations on the Nayaka and other modern hunter-gatherers. *Man (N. S.)* 27: 19–44.

References

Bird-David, N., Viveiros de Castro, E., Hornberg, A., Ingold, T., Morris, B., Palsson, G., Rival, L. M., and A. R. Sandstrom. 1999. 'Animism Revisited': Personhood, environment and relational epistemology. *Current Anthropology* 40: 67–91.

Bjerck, H. B. 1982. Archaeological and radiocarbon dating of the transgression maximum (Tapes) at Skuløy, Sunnmøre, western Norway. *Norsk geologisk Tidsskrift* 62: 87–93.

Bjerck, H. B. 1983. Kronologisk og geografisk fordeling av mesolitiske element i Vest- og Midt-Norge. Unpublished thesis, University of Bergen.

Bjerck, H. B. 1985. De kulturhistoriske undersøkelsene på Tjernagel, Sveio. Del I. Boplassundersøkelsene. *Arkeologiske rapporter* 9: 7–97. Bergen: Historisk museum, University of Bergen.

Bjerck, H. B. 1986. The Fosna–Nøstvet problem. A consideration of archaeological units and chronozones in the south Norwegian Mesolithic Period. *Norwegian Archaeological Review* 19 (2): 103–22.

Bjerck, H. B. 1989. *Forskningsstyrt forvaltning på Vega, Nordland. En studie av steinaldermenneskenes boplassmønstre og arkeologiske letemetoder.* Gunneria 61. Trondheim.

Bjerck, H. B. 1990. Mesolithic site types and settlement patterns at Vega, Northern Norway. *Acta Archaeologica* 60 (1989): 1–32.

Bjerck, H. B. 1991. Spor etter de første nordlendinger i Steigen. Om funn av en 9600 år gammel boplass på Fure. *Årbok for Steigen* 1991: 32–40. Bodø.

Bjerck, H. B. 1994. Nordsjøfastlandet og pionerbosetningen i Norge. *Viking* 57: 25–57.

Bjerck, H. B. 1995. The North Sea continent and the pioneer settlement of Norway. In A. Fischer (ed.), *Man and sea in the Mesolithic.* Oxbow Monograph 53. Oxford: Oxbow, pp. 131–44.

Bjerck, H. B. 2000. Stone Age settlement on Svalbard? A re-evaluation of previous finds and results of a recent field survey. *Polar Record* 36 (197): 97–122.

Bjerck, H. B. 2007. Mesolithic coastal settlements and shell middens (?) in Norway. In N. Milner, O. Craig, and G. N. Bailey (eds.), *Shell middens in Atlantic Europe.* Oxford: Oxbow Books, pp. 5–31.

Bjerck, H. B. 2009. Colonizing seascapes: comparative perspectives on the development of maritime relations in the Pleistocene–Holocene transition in north-west Europe. In S. McCartan, R. Schulting, G. Warren, and P. C. Woodman (eds.), *Mesolithic horizons. Papers presented at the Seventh International Conference on the Mesolithic in Europe, Belfast 2005.* Oxford: Oxbow Books, pp. 16–24.

Bjerck, H. B. (ed.), Åstveit, L. I., Meling, T., Gundersen, J., Jørgensen, G., and S. Normann. 2008. *NTNU Vitenskapsmuseets arkeologiske undersøkelser Ormen Lange Nyhamna.* Trondheim: Tapir Akademisk Forlag.

Bjerck, H. B., and M. Callanan. 2005. Rapport fra utgravning av tidligmesolittisk lokalitet på Brannhaugen, Storli, Oppdal, Sør-Trøndelag. Unpublished Report, Vitenskapsmuseet, NTNU, Trondheim.

Bjerck, H. B., Østmo, E. Mikkelsen, E. Skar, B. Engelstad, E., and P. Woodman. 1987. Comments/Reply to Comments on "The Fosna–Nøstvet problem". *Norwegian Archaeological Review* 20 (1): 31–45.

Björck, S. 1995. Late Weichselian to early Holocene development of the Baltic Sea – with implications for coastal settlements in the southern Baltic region. In A. Fischer (ed.), *Man and sea in the Mesolithic.* Oxford: Oxbow Monograph 53, pp. 23–34.

Bjørgo, T. 1981. Flatøy:et eksempel på steinalderens kronologi og levemåte i Nordhordland. Unpublished thesis, University of Bergen.

Bjørgo, T., Kristoffersen, S., and C. Prescott. 1992. *Arkeologiske undersøkelser i Nyset-Steggevassdragene 1981–1987.* Arkeologiske rapporter 16. Bergen: Historisk museum, University of Bergen.

Bjørn, A. 1928. Noen norske stenaldersproblemer. *Norsk geologisk tidsskrift* 1928: 53–75.

Bjørn, A. 1930. Studier over Fosnakulturen. *Bergen Museums Årbok 1929. Historisk-antikvarisk rekke* 2: 1–33. Bergen.

Bjørn, A. 1931. Hovedlinjer i den norske nasjonens tilblivelseshistorie. *Naturen* 55: 224–45. Bergen.

Bjørn, A. 1934. Hedemarks seinalder. *Universitetets Oldsaksamlings Årbok 1931–1932:* 1–30. Oslo.

Blanchet, J. C., and B. Lambot. 1977. Les dragages de l'Oise de 1973 à 1976. Première partie. *Cahiers Archéologique de Picardie* 4: 61–88.

Blankholm, H. P. 1984. Maglemosekulturens hyttegrundrids. *Årbøger for Nordisk Oldkyndighed og Historie* 1984: 61–77.

Blankholm, H. P. 1987a. Maglemosian hut floors: An analysis of the dwelling unit, social unit, and intra-site behaviour patterns in early Mesolithic Southern Scandinavia. In P. Rowley-Conwy, M. Zvelebil, and H. P. Blankholm (eds.), *Mesolithic Northwest Europe: Recent trends*. Sheffield: Department of Archaeology and Prehistory, pp. 109–20.

Blankholm, H. P. 1987b. Late Mesolithic hunter-gatherers and the transition to farming in southern Scandinavia. In P. Rowley-Conwy, M. Zvelebil, and H. P. Blankholm (eds.), *Mesolithic Northwest Europe: Recent Trends*. Sheffield: Department of Archaeology and Prehistory, pp. 155–62.

Blankholm, H. P. 1990. Stylistic analysis of Maglemosian microlithic armatures in southern Scandinavia: An essay. In P. M. Vermeersch and P. van Peer (eds.), *Contributions to the Mesolithic in Europe*. Leuven: Leuven University Press, pp. 239–58.

Blankholm, H. P. 1991. *Intrasite spatial analysis in theory and practice*. Århus: Aarhus University Press.

Blankholm, H. P. 1996. *On the track of a prehistoric economy: Maglemosian subsistence patterns in early Postglacial southern Scandinavia*. Århus: Aarhus University Press.

Blankholm, H. P. 2004. Earliest Mesolithic site in Northern Norway? A reassessment of Sarnes B4 *Arctic Anthropology* 41(1): 41–57.

Blankholm, H. P. 2008. *Målsnes 1. An Early Mesolithic coastal site in Northern Norway*. Oxford: Oxbow Books.

Bleed, P. 1986. The optimal design of hunting weapons: Maintainability or reliability. *American Antiquity* 51: 737–47.

Blockley, S. P. E., Donahue, R. E., and A. M. Pollard. 2000. Radiocarbon calibration and Late Glacial occupation in northwest Europe. *Antiquity* 74 (283): 112–21.

Blystad, P., Thomsen, H., Simonsen, A., and R. W. Lie 1983. Find of a nearly complete late Weichselian polar bear skeleton, *Ursus Maritimus* Phipps, at Finnøy, Southwestern Norway. a preliminary report. *Norsk Geologisk Tidsskrift* 63: 193–7. Oslo.

Boas, F. 1940. The decorative art of the North American Indians. In F. Boas (ed.), *Race, language and culture*. New York: Macmillan.

Boas, N. A. 1987. Rude Mark: A Maglemosian Settlement in East Jutland. *Journal of Danish Archaeology* 5: 14–30.

Boaz, J. 1997. *Steinalderundersøkelsene på Rødsmoen*. Varia 41. Oslo: Universitetets Oldsaksamling.

Boaz, J. 1998. *Hunter-Gatherer Site Variability. Changing patterns of site utilization in the interior of eastern Norway, between 8000 and 2500 B.P.* Universitetets Oldsaksamlings Skrifter, Ny rekke 20. Oslo: Universitetets Oldsaksamling.

Boaz, J. 1999a. The Mesolithic of Central Scandinavia. Status and perspectives. In J. Boaz, (ed.), *The Mesolithic of Central Scandinavia*. Oslo: Universitetets Oldsaksamlings Skrifter Ny Rekke 22. Oslo: Universitetets Oldsaksamling, pp. 11–25.

Boaz, J. 1999b. Pioneers in the Mesolithic. The Initial Occupation of the Interior of Eastern Norway. In J. Boaz (ed.), *The Mesolithic of Central Scandinavia*. Universitetets Oldsaksamlings Skrifter Ny Rekke 22, Oslo: Universitetets Oldsaksamling, pp. 125–52.

Bocherens, H., Grupe, G., Mariotti, A., and S. Turban-Just. 1997. Molecular preservation and isotopy of Mesolithic human finds from the Ofnet Cave (Bavaria, Germany). *Anthropologischer Anzeiger* 55: 121–9.

Bocquet-Appel, J.-P., Naji, S., Vander Linden, M., and J. Kozłowski. 2009. Detection of diffusion and contact zones of early farming in Europe from the space-time distribution of 14C dates. *Journal of Archaeological Science* 36: 807–20.

Bogucki, P. I. 1988. *Forest farmers and stockherders: Early agriculture and its consequences in North-Central Europe*. Cambridge, UK: Cambridge University Press.

Bogucki, P. 1995. The Linear Pottery culture of central Europe: Conservative colonists? In W. K. Barnett, and J. W. Hoopes (eds.), *The emergence of pottery: Technology and innovation in ancient societies*. Washington, DC: Smithsonian Institution Press, pp. 89–97.

Bogucki, P. 1996. Sustainable and unsustainable adaptations by early farming communities of northern Poland. *Journal of Anthropological Archaeology* 15: 289–311.

References

Bogucki, P. 1998. Holocene climatic variability and early agriculture in temperate Europe: The case of northern Poland. In M. Zvelebil, R. Dennell, and L. Domańska (eds.), *Harvesting the sea, farming the forest*. Sheffield: Sheffield University Press, pp. 77–86.

Bogucki, P. 2000. How agriculture came to north-central Europe. In T. Douglas Price (ed.), *Europe's first farmers*. Cambridge, UK: Cambridge University Press, pp. 197–218.

Bogucki, P., and R. Grygiel. 1993. Neolithic sites in the Polish lowlands: Research at Brześć Kujawski, 1933 to 1984. In P. Bogucki (ed.), *Case studies in European prehistory*. Boca Raton: CRC Press, pp. 147–80.

Bohmers, A., and A. M. Wouters. 1956. Statistics and graphs in the study of flint assemblages III. A preliminary report on the statistical analysis of the Mesolithic in northwestern Europe. *Palaeohistoria* 5: 27–38.

Bohmers, A., and A. M. Wouters. 1962. Belangrijke vondsten van de Ahrensburgcultuur in de gemeente Geldrop. *Brabants Heem* 14: 3–28.

Bokelmann, K. 1971. Duvensee, ein Wohnplatz des Mesolithikums in Schleswig-Holstein, und die Duvensee-gruppe. *Offa* 28: 5–26.

Bokelmann, K. 1991. Duvensee, Wohnplatz 9. Ein präborealzeitliche Lagerplatz in Schleswig-Holstein. *Offa* 48: 75–114.

Bokelmann, K. 1995. 'Faint flint fall-out', Duvensee, Wohmplatz 19. *Offa* 52: 45–56.

Bokelmann, K. 1999. Zum Beginn des Spätmesolithikums in Südskandinavien. Geweihaxt, Dreieck und Trapez, 6100 cal BC. *Offa* 56: 183–97.

Bokelmann, K., Averdieck, F.-R., and H. Willkomm. 1981. Duvensee, Wohnplatz 8. Neue Aspekte zur Sammelwirtschaft im frühen Mesolithikum. *Offa* 38: 21–40.

Bokelmann, K., Averdieck, F.-R., and H. Willkomm. 1985. Duvensee, Wohnplatz 13. *Offa* 42: 13–33.

Bökönyi, S. 1972. The vertebrate fauna. In D. Srejović (ed.), *Europe's first monumental sculpture. new discoveries at Lepenski Vir*. London: Thames and Hudson, pp. 186–9.

Bökönyi, S. 1975. Vlasac: An early site of dog domestication. In A. T. Clason (ed.), *Archaeozoological Studies. Papers at the Archaeozoological Conference 1974, held at the Biologisch-Archaeologisch Instituut of the State University of Groningen*. Amsterdam: North Holland Publishing Company, pp. 167–78.

Bökönyi, S. 1978. The vertebrate fauna of Vlasac. In D. Srejović and Z. Letica (eds.), *Vlasac, vol. II*. Belgrade: Serbian Academy of Sciences and Arts, pp. 34–6.

Bolomey, A. 1970. Cîteva observatii asupra faunei de mamifere din straturile Romanello-Aziliene de la Cuina Turcului. *Studii şi Cercetări de Istorie Veche* 21(1): 37–39.

Bolomey, A. 1973. An outline of the late Epipalaeolithic economy of the 'Iron Gates': The evidence on bones. *Dacia* N. S. 17: 41–52.

Bolus, M. 1992. *Die Siedlungsbefunde des Späteiszeitlichen Fundplatzes Niederbieber (Stadt Neuwied)*. Mainz, Bonn: Monographien des RGZM 22.

Bondevik, S. 2003. Storegga tsunami sand in peat below the Tapes beach ridge at Harøy, western Norway, and its possible relation to an early Stone Age settlement. *Boreas* 32: 476–83.

Bondevik, S., Svendsen, J. I., Johnsen, G., Mangerud, J., and P. E. Kaland. 1997. The Storegga tsunami along the Norwegian coast, its age and runup. *Boreas* 26 29–53.

Bonsall, C. 1981. The coastal factor in the Mesolithic settlement of north-west England. In B. Gramsch (ed.), *Mesolithikum in Europa*. Internationales Symposium Potsdam, 3. bis 8. April 1978. Veröffentlichungen des Museums für Ur- und Frühgeschichte Potsdam, 14/15 (Berlin 1981). Berlin: Deutscher Verlag, pp. 451–72.

Bonsall, C. (ed.). 1989. *The Mesolithic in Europe: Proceedings of the third international symposium*. Edinburgh: John Donald.

Bonsall, C. 2003. The Iron Gates Mesolithic., In P. Bogucki and P. Crabtree (eds.), *Ancient Europe 8000 B.C. to A.D. 1000: Encyclopedia of the Barbarian World*. New York: Scribner, pp. 175–8.

Bonsall, C. 2007. When was the Neolithic transition in the Iron Gates? In M. Spataro and P. Biagi (eds.), *A Short Walk Through the Balkans: the First Farmers of the Carpathian Basin and Adjacent Regions*. Società per la Preistoria e Protostoria della Regione Friuli-Venezia Giulia. Trieste, pp. 53–65.

Bonsall, C., Boroneanţ, V., Macklin, M., McSweeney, K., and S. Stallibrass. 1992. *Schela Cladovei (Romania) Project. First Interim Report*. Edinburgh: University of Edinburgh Department of Archaeology.

Bonsall, C., Lennon, R., McSweeney, K., Stewart, C., Harkness, D., Boroneanţ, V., Payton, R., Bartosiewicz, L., and J. C. Chapman 1997. Mesolithic and Early Neolithic in the Iron Gates: A palaeodietary perspective. *Journal of European Archaeology* 5 (1): 50–92.

Bonsall, C., Cook, G., Lennon, R., Harkness, D., Scott, M., Bartosiewicz, L., and K. McSweeney. 2000. Stable isotopes, radiocarbon and the Mesolithic–Neolithic transition in the Iron Gates. *Documenta Praehistorica* 27: 119–32.

Bonsall, C., Macklin, M. G., Payton, R. W., and A. Boroneanţ. 2002. Climate, floods and river gods: Environmental change and the Meso-Neolithic transition in south-east Europe. *Before Farming: The archaeology of Old World hunter-gatherers* 3–4 (2): 1–15.

Bonsall, C., Cook, G. T., Hedges, R. E. M., Higham, T. F. G., Pickard, C., and I. Radovanović. 2004. Radiocarbon and stable isotope evidence of dietary change from the Mesolithic to the Middle Ages in the Iron Gates: New results from Lepenski Vir. In R. J. Sparks and N. Beavan-Athfield (eds.), Proceedings of the 18th International Radiocarbon Conference. *Radiocarbon* 46 (1): 293–300.

Bonsall, C., Radovanović, I., Roksandić, M., Cook, G. T., Higham, T. F. G., and C. Pickard. 2008. Dating burials and architecture at Lepenski Vir. In C. Bonsall, V. Boroneanţ, and I. Radovanović (eds.), *The Iron Gates in prehistory: new perspectives*. Oxford: Archaeopress, pp. 175–204.

Borgognini Tarli, S., and E. Repetto. 1985. Dietary patterns in the Mesolithic samples from Uzzo and Molara caves (Sicily): The evidence of teeth. *Journal of Human Evolution* 14: 241–54.

Borgognini Tarli, S., Canci, E., Piperno, M., and E. Repetto. 1993. Dati archeologici e antropologici sulle sepolture mesolitiche della Grotta dell'Uzzo (Trapani). *Bullettino di Paletnologia Italiana* 84: 85–179.

Borić, D. 1999. Places that created time in the Danube Gorges and beyond, c. 9000–5500 BC. *Documenta Praehistorica* 26: 41–70.

Borić, D. 2002. The Lepenski Vir conundrum: Reinterpretation of the Mesolithic and Neolithic sequences in the Danube Gorges. *Antiquity* 76: 1026–39.

Borić, D., and V. Dimitrijević. 2007. When did the 'Neolithic package' reach Lepenski Vir? Radiometric and faunal evidence. *Documenta Praehistorica* 34: 53–72.

Borić, D., French, C., and V. Dimitrijević. 2008. Vlasac revisited: Formation processes, stratigraphy and dating. *Documenta Praehistorica* 35: 261–87.

Borić, D., and Miracle, P. 2004. Mesolithic and Neolithic (dis)continuities in the Danube gorges: New AMS dates from Padina and Hajdučka Vodenica (Serbia). *Oxford Journal of Archaeology* 23 (4): 341–71.

Borić, D., and S. Stefanović. 2004. Birth and death: Infant burials from Vlasac and Lepenski Vir. *Antiquity* 78: 526–46.

Boroneanţ, V. 1973. La période épipaléolithique sur la rive roumaine des Portes de Fer du Danube. *Praehistorische Zeitschrift* 45 (1): 1–24.

Boroneanţ, V. 1989. Thoughts on the chronological relations between the Epi-Palaeolithic and the Neolithic of the Low Danube. In C. Bonsall (ed.), *The Mesolithic in Europe: Proceedings of the third international symposium*. Edinburgh: John Donald, pp. 475–80.

Boroneanţ, V. 2000. *Paléolithique Supérieur et Épipaléolithique dans la zone des Portes de Fer*. Bucureşti: Silex.

Boroneanţ, V., and D. Nicolaescu-Plopşor. 1990. Lésions traumatiques violentes datant de l'Epipaléolithique tardif du sud-ouest de la Roumanie. *L'Anthropologie* 28 (1): 55–65.

Boroneanţ, V., Bonsall, C., McSweeney, K., Payton, R., and M. Macklin. 1999. A Mesolithic burial area at Schela Cladovei, Romania. In A. Thévenin *L'Europe des derniers chasseurs: Épipaléolithique et Mésolithique*, Actes du 5ᵉ colloque international UISPP, commission XII, Grenoble, 18–23 septembre 1995. Paris: Éditions du Comité des Travaux Historiques et Scientifiques, pp. 385–90.

Borrero, L. A., and C. McEwan. 1997. The peopling of Patagonia: The first human occupation. In C. McEwan, L. A. Borrero, and A. Prieto (eds.), *Patagonia. natural history, prehistory and ethnography at the uttermost end of the earth*. Princetown: Princetown University Press, pp. 32–46.

Bostwick Bjerck, L. G., and A. B. Olsen. 1983. *Kulturhistoriske undersøkelser på Botnaneset, Flora 1981–82*. Arkeologiske Rapporter 5. Bergen: Historisk museum, Universitetet i Bergen.

Bottema, S. 2003. The vegetation history of the Greek Mesolithic. In N. Galanidou and C. Perlès (eds.), *The Greek Mesolithic: Problems and perspectives*. London: British School at Athens, pp. 33–49.

References

Boulestin, B. 1999. *Approche taphonomique des restes humains. Le cas des Mésolithiques de la grotte des Perrats et le problème du cannibalisme en préhistoire récente européenne.* Oxford: British Archaeological Reports International Series 776.

Bourdieu, P. 1977. *Outline of a theory of practice.* Cambridge, UK: Cambridge University Press.

Bowie, F. 2000. *The anthropology of religion.* Oxford: Blackwell.

Bradley, R. 1984. *The Social foundations of prehistoric Britain.* London: Longman.

Bradley, R. 1997. *Rock art and the prehistory of Atlantic Europe: Signing the land.* London: Routledge.

Bradley, R. 1998. *The significance of monuments: On the shaping of human experience in Neolithic and Bronze Age Europe.* London: Routledge.

Bradley, R. 2000. *An archaeology of natural places.* London: Routledge.

Bramanti, B., et al. 2009. Genetic discontinuity between local hunter-gatherers and Central Europe's first farmers. *Science* 326 (5949): 137–40.

Bratlund, B. 1996. Archaeozoological comments on final Palaeolithic frontiers in south Scandinavia. In L. Larsson (ed.), *The earliest settlement of Scandinavia and its relationship with neighbouring areas.* Acta Archaeologica Lundensia, Series In 8, 24. Stockholm: Almquist and Wiksell International, pp. 23–34.

Braudel, F. 1958. Histoire et sciences sociales, la longue durée. *Annales ESC* 13 (4): 725–53.

Breuil, H., and H. Obermaier. 1912. Les premiers travaux de l'Institut de Paléontologie Humaine. *L'Anthropologie* 23:1–27.

Bridault, A., and L. Chaix. 1999. Contribution de l'archéozoologie à la caractérisation des modalités d'occupations des sites alpins et jurassiens, de l'Epipaléolithique au Néolithique. In A. Thévenin (ed.), *L'Europe des derniers chasseurs. Épipaléolithique et Mésolithique, Actes du 5ᵉ colloque international UISPP, commission XII, Grenoble, 18–23 septembre 1995.* Paris: Éditions du Comité des Travaux Historiques et Scientifiques, pp. 547–68.

Bridges, E. L. 1948. *Uttermost part of the Earth.* London: Hodder and Stoughton.

Broglio, A. 1980. Culture e ambienti della fine del Paleolitico e del Mesolitico nell'Italia nord-orientale. *Preistoria Alpina* 16: 7–29.

Broglio, A. 1995. The end of the Glacial Period in the Alpine-Po valley area and in the Italian peninsula. In V. Bonilla (ed.), *Los ultimos cazadores: Transformaciones culturales y económicas durante el tardiglaciar y el inicio del holoceno en el ambito Mediterráneo.* Alicante: Istituto de Cultura Juan Gil Albert, pp. 147–63.

Bronk Ramsey, C. R. 1995. Radiocarbon calibration and analysis of stratigraphy. The OxCal Program. *Radiocarbon* 37 (2): 425–30.

Bronk Ramsey, C. R. 2001. Development of the radiocarbon program OxCal. *Radiocarbon* 43 (2A): 355–63.

Bronk Ramsey, C. R., Pettitt, P. B., Hedges, R. E. M., Hodgkins, G. W. L., and D. C. Owen. 2000a. Radiocarbon dates from the Oxford AMS system. Archaeometry datelist 29. *Archaeometry* 42 (1): 243–54.

Bronk Ramsey, C. R., Pettitt, P. B., Hedges, R. E. M., Hodgkins, G. W. L., and D. C. Owen. 2000b. Radiocarbon dates from the Oxford AMS system. Archaeometry datelist 30. *Archaeometry* 42 (2): 459–79.

Bronk Ramsey, C. R., Higham, T. F. G., Owen, D. C., Pike, A. W. G., and R. E. M. Hedges. 2002. Radiocarbon dates from the Oxford AMS system. Archaeometry datelist 31. *Archaeometry* 44 (3), Supplement 1: 1–150.

Brown, J. A., and T. D. Price. 1985. Complex hunter-gatherers: Retrospect and prospect. In T. D. Price and J. A. Brown (eds.), *Prehistoric hunter-gatherers: The emergence of cultural complexity.* New York: Academic Press, pp. 435–42.

Brugal, J. P., and J. Desse (eds.). 2004. *Petits animaux et sociétés humaines. Du complément alimentaire aux ressources utilitaires.* Actes des XXIVe rencontres internationales d'Archéologie et d'Histoire d'Antibes, 2004, Ed. APDCA.

Brøgger, A. W. 1905. Øxer af Nøstvettypen. Bidrag til kundskaben om ældre norsk stenalder. *Norges Geologiske Undersøgelse* 42. Kristiania.

Brøgger A. W. 1908. *Vistefundet, en ældre stenalders kjøkkenmødding fra Jæderen.* Stavanger: Stavanger Museum.

Brøgger, A. W. 1909. *Den arktiske steinalder i Norge.* Videnselskabets Skrifter. II. Hist. -Filos. Klasse 1: 1–278.

Brøgger, A. W. 1925. *Det norske folk i oldtiden.* Instituttet for sammenlignende kulturforskning. Serie A: Forelesninger VIa.

Brøndsted, J. 1957. *Danmarks oldtid i stenalderen*. Copenhagen: Gyldendal.

Braathen, H. 1985. *Sunde 34: Deskriptiv analyse av en sørvestnorsk boplass fra atlantisk tid*. AmS Varia 14. Stavanger: Arkeologisk museum i Stavanger.

Budil, I. T. 2001. *Za obzor Západu*. Czech Republic: Academia Prague.

Buisson, D. 1988. Les occupations mésolithiques en Haute-Corrèze. Bilan des prospections de surface sur l'arrondissement d'Ussel. In *Mésolithique et néolithisation en France et dans les régions limitrophes*. Actes du 113ᵉ Congrès National des Sociétés Savantes (Strasbourg, 1988), 1991. Paris: Editions du CTHS, pp. 147–71.

Burdkiewicz, J. M. 1986. *The Late Pleistocene shouldered point assemblages in western Europe*. Leiden: Brill Academic.

Burdkiewicz, J. M. 1996. Spatio-temporal zonality of the Palaeolithic settlement of northern Europe. In L. Larsson (ed.), *The earliest settlement of Scandinavia and its relationship with neighbouring areas*. Acta Archaeologica Lundensia, Series In 8, 24. Stockholm: Almquist and Wiksell International, pp. 35–42.

Burleigh, R., and S. Zivanović. 1980. Radiocarbon dating of a Cro-Magnon population from Padina, Yugoslavia, with some general recommendations for dating human skeletons. *Zeitschrift für Morphologie und Anthropologie* 70: 269–74.

Burov, G. M. 1989. Some Mesolithic wooden artefacts from the site of Vis I in the European North-East of the USSR. In C. Bonsall (ed.), *The Mesolithic in Europe: Papers presented at the Third International Symposium, Edinburgh 1985*. Edinburgh: John Donald, pp. 391–401.

Butrimas, A., Kazakevicius, V., Cesnys, G., Balciuniene, I., and R. Jankauskas. 1985. Ankstyvieji virvelines keramikos kulturos Kapai. *Lietuvos Archeologija* 4: 14–24.

Buus Eriksen, L. 1992. Ornehus på Stevns – en tidligneolitisk hustomt. *Årbøger for Nordisk Oldkyndighed og Historie* 1991: 7–19.

Bøe, J. 1932. *Felszeichnungen im Westlichen Norwegen I. Die Zeichnungsgebiete in Vingen und Hennøya*. Bergens Museums Skrifter nr. 15. Bergen: A. S. John Griegs boktrykkeri.

Bøe, J. 1934. Boplassen i Skipshelleren på Straume i Nordhordland. *Bergen Museums Skrifter* Nr 17. Bergen: A. S. John Griegs Boktrykkeri,

Bøe, J. 1942. *Til høgfjellets forhistorie. Boplassen på Sumtangen ved Finsevatn på Hardangervidda*. Bergen: A. S. John Griegs Boktrykkeri.

Bøe, J., and A. Nummedal. 1936. *Le Finmarkien. Les origines de la civilisation dans l'extreme-nord de l'Europe*. Instituttet for sammenlignende kulturforskning. Serie B: Skrifter 32: 1–263.

Calattini, M. 1996. Il mesolitico di Grotta delle Mura nella problematica della neolitizzazione dell'Italia meridionale. In V. Tiné (ed.), *Forme e tempi della neolitizzazione in Italia Meridionale e in Sicilia* 1. Rossano: Istituto Regionale per le Antichità Calabresi e Bizantine, pp. 48–52.

Callahan, E. 1987. *An evaluation of the lithic technology in middle Sweden during the Mesolithic and Neolithic*. AUN 9. Uppsala: Societas Archaeologica Upsaliensis.

Callanan, M. 2007. On the edge – a survey of Early Mesolithic tools from Central Norway. Unpublished MA thesis, NTNU, Trondheim.

Campen, I., Kind, C.-J., and C. Lauxmann. 1983. Ein Rotgefärbter Kalkstein aus dem Mesolithischen Horizont vom 'Felsställe', Ehingen-Mühlen, Alb-Donau Kreis. *Archäologisches Korrespondenzblatt* 13: 299–303.

Carbonell, E. (ed.). 1985. *Sota Palou – Campdevànol: Un Centre d'Intervenció Prehistòrica Postglaciar a l'Aire Lliure.* Centre d'Investigacions Arqueològiques Sèrie monogràfica 5. Girona: Diputació de Girona.

Cardini, L. 1970. Praia a Mare: Relazione degli scavi 1957–1970 dell'Istituto Italiano di Paletnologia Umana. *Bullettino di Paletnologia Italiana* 79: 31–59.

Cardoso, F., and J. Rolão. 2003. Prospecção e escavação nos concheiros mesoliticos de Muge e Magos. *Estudos Arqueológicos de Muge* 1: 7–169.

Carlsson, T. 2003. Expressing identities. Contact as a social strategy during the Mesolithic. In C. Samuelsson and N. Ytterberg (eds.), *Uniting sea. Stone Age societies in the Baltic Sea region*. Uppsala: Department of Archaeology and Ancient History, pp. 43–50.

Carpelan, C. 1975. Alg-och björnhuvudföremål från Europas nordliga delar. *Finskt Museum* 82: 5–67.

Carpelan, C. 1979. Om asbestkeramikens historia I Fennoskandien. *Finskt Museum* 85: 5–25.

References

Carrión, J., Andrade, A., Bennett, K., Navarro, C., and M. Munuera. 2001. Crossing forest thresholds: Inertia and collapse in a Holocene sequence from south-central Spain. *The Holocene* 11: 635–53.

Carvalho, E., Straus, L., Vierra, B., Zilhao J., and A. Araújo. 1989. More data for an archaeological map of the county of Torres Vedras. *Arqueología* 19: 16–33.

Casparie, W. A., and J. H. A. Bosch. 1995. Bergumermeer-De Leijen (Friesland, the Netherlands), a Mesolithic wetland in a dry setting. *Mededelingen Rijks Geologische Dienst* 52: 271–82.

Cassoli, P., Segre, A., and E. Segre. 1979. Evolution morphologique et écologique de la côte de Castro (Pouilles) dans le Pléistocène final. In D. de Sonneville Bordes (ed.), *La fin des temps glaciaires en Europe: Chronostratigraphie et écologie des cultures du Paléolithique Final.* Paris: CNRS, pp. 325–32.

Cauwe, N. 1988. La sépulture collective de la grotte Margeaux à Freyer (province de Namur), rapport préliminaire. *Notae Praehistoricae* 8: 103–8.

Cauwe, N. 1995. Chronologie des sépultures de l'abri des Autours à Anseremme-Dinant. *Notae Praehistoricae* 15: 51–60.

Cauwe, N. 1998. La grotte Margaux à Anseremme-Dinant. Étude d'une sépulture collective du Mésolithique ancien. Liège: *Études et Recherches Archéologiques de l'Université de Liège 59.*

Cauwe, N., Steenhoudt, F., and D. Bosquet. 1993. Deux sépultures collectives dans un abri-sous-roche de Freyr, pérennité d'un site funéraire du mésolithique au néolithique moyen-récent. *Notae Praehistoricae* 12: 162–5.

Cava Almuzara, A. 1994. El Mesolítico en la cuenca del Ebro: Un estado de la cuestion. *Zephyrus* 47: 65–91.

Cava, A. 1978. El depósito arqueológico de la Cueva de Marizulo. *Munibe* 30: 155–72.

Chaix, L., Bridault, A., and R. Picavet. 1997. A tamed brown bear (*Ursus arctos* L.) of the late Mesolithic from la Grande Rivoire (Isère, France)? *Journal of Archaeological Science* 24:1067–74.

Champagne, F., Champagne, C., Jauzon, P., and P. Novel. 1990. La grotte des Fieux à Miers (Lot). Etat actuel des recherches. *Gallia Préhistoire* 32: 1–28.

Chapman, A. 1982. *Drama and power in a hunting society: The Selk'nam of Tierra del Fuego*, Cambridge, UK: Cambridge University Press.

Chapman, A. 1987. The Great Ceremonies of the Selk'nam and the Yamana: A comparative analysis. In C. McEwan, L. A. Borrero, and A. Prieto (eds.), *Patagonia: Natural history, prehistory and ethnography at the uttermost end of the Earth.* London: British Museum Press.

Chapman, J. C. 1989. Demographic trends in Neothermal south-east Europe. In C. Bonsall (ed.), *The Mesolithic in Europe. Papers presented at the Third International Symposium, Edinburgh 1985.* Edinburgh: John Donald, pp. 500–15.

Chapman, J. C. 1993. Social power in the Iron Gates Mesolithic. In J. Chapman, and P. Dolukhanov (eds.), *Cultural transformations and interactions in Eastern Europe.* Aldershot: Avebury, pp. 71–121.

Chapman, R. W., and K. Randsborg. 1981. Approaches to the archaeology of death. In R. Chapman, I. Kinnes, and K. Randsborg (eds.), *The archaeology of death.* Cambridge, UK: Cambridge University Press, pp. 1–24.

Chatterton, R. 2006. Ritual. In C. Conneller and G. Warren (eds.), *Mesolithic Britain and Ireland: New approaches.* Stroud: Tempus, pp. 101–20.

Chepalyga, A. L. 2002. Chernoe more [The Black Sea]. In A. A. Velichko (ed.), *Dinamika landshaftnyh komponentov i vnutrennih basseinov Vostochnoi Evropy za poslednie 130000 let [Dynamics of landscape components and internal basins of Eastern Europe in the course of the last 130,000 years].* Geos: Moscow.

Chernetsov, V. N. 1963. Ideas of the soul amongst Ob-Ugrians. In H. M. Michael (ed.), *Studies in Siberian shamanism.* Anthropology of the North 4. Toronto: University of Toronto.

Cherry, J. 1990. The first colonization of the Mediterranean islands: A review of recent research. *Journal of Mediterranean Archaeology* 3: 145–221.

Childe, V. G. 1925. *The Dawn of European civilization.* London: Kegan Paul.

Chmielewska, M. 1954. Grób kultury tardenoaskiej w Janisławicach pow. Skierniewice. *Wiadomości Archeologiczne* 30 (1): 23–48.

Christensen, C. 1993. Land and sea. In S. Hvass and B. Storgaard (eds.), *Digging into the past: 25 years of archaeology in Denmark.* Århus: Aarhus University Press, pp. 20–3.

Clark, G. A. 1976. *El Asturiense Cantábrico*. Madrid: Bibliotheca Praehistorica Hispana 13.

Clark, G. A. 1983. *The Asturian of Cantabria*. Tucson: Anthropological Papers of the University of Arizona 41.

Clark, G. A. 1989. Site functional complementarity in the Mesolithic of northern Spain. In C. Bonsall (ed.), *The Mesolithic in Europe: Papers presented at the Third International Symposium, Edinburgh 1985*. Edinburgh: John Donald, pp. 589–603.

Clark, G. A. 2004. The Iberian Mesolithic in the European context. In M. González Morales and G. Clark (eds.), *The Mesolithic of the Atlantic Façade*. Anthropological Research Papers 55. Tempe: Arizona State University, pp. 205–23.

Clark, G. A., and M. Neeley. 1987. Social differentiation in European Mesolithic burial data. In P. Rowley-Conwy, M. Zvelebil, and H. P. Blankholm (eds.), *Mesolithic Northwest Europe: Recent trends*. Sheffield: University of Sheffield, pp. 121–30.

Clark, G. 1975. *The earlier Stone Age settlement of Scandinavia*. Cambridge, UK: Cambridge University Press.

Clark, G. 1980. *Mesolithic prelude*. Edinburgh: Edinburgh University Press.

Clark, J. G. D. 1932. *The Mesolithic Age in Britain*. Cambridge, UK: Cambridge University Press.

Clark, J. G. D. 1934. A late Mesolithic settlement at Selmeston, Sussex. *Antiquaries Journal* 14: 134–58.

Clark, J. G. D. 1936. *The Mesolithic settlement of northern Europe*. Cambridge, UK: Cambridge University Press.

Clark, J. G. D. 1952. *Prehistoric Europe: The economic basis*. London: Methuen.

Clark, J. G. D. 1954. *Excavations at Star Carr*. Cambridge, UK: Cambridge University Press.

Clark, J. G. D. 1958. Blade and trapeze industries of the European Stone Age. *Proceedings of the Prehistoric Society* 24: 24–42.

Clark, J. G. D., and W. F. Rankine. 1939. Excavations at Farnham, Surrey, (1937–38). *Proceedings of the Prehistoric Society* 5: 61–118.

Clarke, A., and D. Griffiths. 1990. The use of bloodstone as a raw material for flaked stone tools in the west of Scotland. In C. R. Wickham-Jones, *Rhum. Mesolithic and Later Sites at Kinloch: Excavations 1984–86*. Society of Antiquaries of Scotland Monograph 7. Edinburgh: Society of Antiquaries of Scotland, pp. 149–56.

Clarke, D. 1976. Mesolithic Europe: The economic basis. In G. de G. Sieveking, I. H. Longworth, and K. E. Wilson (eds.), *Problems in economic and social archaeology*. London: Duckworth, pp. 449–81.

Clason, A. T., 1980. Padina and Starčevo: Game, fish and cattle. *Palaeohistoria* 22: 142–73.

Cleyet-Merle, J.-J., and S. Madelaine. 1995. Inland evidence of human sea coast exploitation in Palaeolithic France. In A. Fischer (ed.), *Man and Sea in the Mesolithic*. Oxbow Monograph 53. Oxford: Oxbow, pp. 303–8.

Close, A. E. 1996. Plus ça change: The Pleistocene-Holocene transition in northeast Africa. In L. G. Straus, B. V. Eriksen, J. M. Erlandson, and D. R. Yesner (eds.), *Humans at the end of the Ice Age*. New York: Plenum, pp. 43–60.

Coe, A. L., Bocene, D. W. J., Church, K. D., Flint, S. S., Howell J. A., and R. C. L. Wilson. 2003. *The sedimentary record of sea-level change*. Cambridge, UK: Cambridge University Press.

COHMAP 1988. Climatic changes of the last 18,000 years: Observations and model simulations. *Science* 241: 1043–52.

Cole, N., and A. Watchman. 2005. AMS dating of rock art in the Laura region, Cape York Peninsula, Australia – protocols and results of recent research. *Antiquity* 79: 661–78.

Coles, B. J. 1998. Doggerland: A speculative survey. *Proceedings of the Prehistoric Society* 64: 45–82.

Coles, J. M. 1971. The early settlement of Scotland: Excavations at Morton, Fife. *Proceedings of the Prehistoric Society* 37: 28–366.

Coles, J. M. 1983. Morton revisited. In A. O'Connor, and D. V. Clarke (eds.), *From the Stone Age to the 'Forty-Five'*. Edinburgh: John Donald, pp. 9–18.

Coles, J. M. 1991. Elk and Ogopogo: Belief systems in the hunter-gatherer rock art of northern lands. *Proceedings of the Prehistoric Society* 57 (1): 129–48.

Colonese, A., Troelstra, S., Ziveri, P., Martini, F., Lo Vetro, D., and S. Tommasini. 2009. Mesolithic shellfish exploitation in SW Italy: Seasonal evidence from the oxygen isotopic composition of *Osilinus turbinatus* shells. *Journal of Archaeological Science* 36: 1935–44.

References

Conkey, M. 1997. Beyond art and between the caves: Thinking about context in the interpretive process. In M. Conkey, O. Soffer, D. Stratmann, and N. Jablonski (eds.), *Beyond art: Pleistocene image and symbol.* Memoirs of the California Academy of Sciences 23. San Francisco: California Academy of Sciences, pp. 343–67.

Conneller C., and G. Warren (eds.). 2006. *Mesolithic Britain and Ireland.* Stroud: Tempus.

Constandse-Westermann, T. S., and R. R. Newell. 1989. Limb lateralization and social stratification in western Mesolithic societies. In I. Herkovitz (ed.), *People and culture change.* Oxford: British Archaeological Reports International Series 508, pp. 405–34.

Cook, G. T., Bonsall, C., Hedges, R. E. M., McSweeney, K., Boroneanţ, V., and P. B. Pettitt. 2001. A freshwater diet-derived ^{14}C reservoir effect at the Stone Age sites in the Iron Gates gorge. In I. Carmi and E. Boaretto (eds.), Proceedings of the 17th International Radiocarbon Conference, Judean Hills, Israel, June 18–23, 2000. *Radiocarbon* 43 (2A): 453–60.

Cook, G. T., Bonsall C., Hedges R. E. M., McSweeney K., Boroneanţ V., Bartosiewicz L., and P. B. Pettitt. 2002. Problems of dating human bones from the Iron Gates. *Antiquity* 76: 77–85.

Cook, J., and R. Jacobi. 1994. A reindeer antler or 'Lyngby' axe from Northamptonshire and its context in the British Late Glacial. *Proceedings of the Prehistoric Society* 60: 75–84.

Copley, M. S., Berstan, R., Dudd, S. N., Aillaud, S., Mukherjee, A. J., Straker, V., Payne, S., and R. P. Evershed. 2005. Processing of milk products in pottery vessels through British prehistory. *Antiquity* 79: 895–908.

Costa, L., Vigne, J. -D., Bocherens, H., Desse-Berset, N., Heinz, C., de Lanfranchi, F., Magdeleine, J., Ruas, M.-P., Thiebault, S., and C. Tozzi. 2003. Early settlement on Tyrrhenian islands (8th millennium cal BC): Mesolithic adaption to local resources in Corsica and northern Sardinia. In L. Larsson, H. Kindgren, K. Knutsson, D. Loeffler, and A. Åkerlund (eds) *Mesolithic on the move: Papers presented at the Sixth International Conference on the Mesolithic in Europe, Stockholm 2000.* Oxford: Oxbow Books, pp. 3–10.

Costantini, L. 1981. Semi e carboni del Mesolitico e Neolitico della Grotta dell'Uzzo, Trapani. *Quaternaria* 23: 233–47.

Costantini, L. 1989. Plant exploitation at Grotta dell'Uzzo, Sicily: New evidence for the transition from Mesolithic to Neolithic subsistence in southern Europe. In D. Harris and G. Hillman (eds.), *Foraging and farming: The evolution of plant exploitation.* London: Unwin Hyman, pp. 197–206.

Coulonges, L. 1928. Le gisement préhistorique du Martinet à Sauveterre-la-Lémance (Lot-et-Garonne). *L'Anthropologie* 38: 495–503.

Coulonges, L. 1935. *Les gisements préhistoriques de Sauveterre-la-Lémance (Lot-et-Garonne).* Archives de l'Institut de Paléontologie Humaine. Mémoire no. 14.

Couraud, C. 1985. *L'art Azilien: Origine, survivance.* Supplément 20 à Gallia Prehistoire. Paris: CNRS.

Craig O. E., and M. J. Collins. 2000. An improved method for the immunological detection of mineral bound protein using hydrofluoric acid and direct capture. *Journal of Immunological Methods* 236: 89–97.

Craig, O. E., Chapman, J., Heron, C., Willis, L. H., Bartosiewicz, L., Taylor, G., Whittle, A., and M. Collins. 2005. Did the first farmers of central and eastern Europe produce dairy foods? *Antiquity* 79: 882–94.

Crombé, P. 1998. *The Mesolithic in northwestern Belgium, recent excavations and surveys.* Oxford: British Archaeological Reports International Series 716.

Crombé, P. 2002. Quelques réflexions sur la signification de la variabilité des industries lithiques Mésolithiques de Belgique. *ERAUL* 99: 99–114.

Crombé, P., and N. Cauwe. 2001. The Mesolithic. In N. Cauwe, A. Hauzeur, and P.-L. van Berg (eds.), *Prehistory in Belgium.* Special issue on the occasion of the XIVth Congress of the International Union for Prehistoric and Protohistoric Sciences. *Anthropologica et Praehistorica* 112: 49–62.

Crombé, P., and M. Van Strydonck. 2004. The Neolithic transition and European population history. *Antiquity* 78: 708–10.

Crombé, P., Groenendijk, H. A., and M. Van Stydonck. 1998. Dating the Mesolithic of the Low Countries, some practical considerations. *Proceedings of the third International Symposium 14C and Archaeology.* Lyon, pp. 57–63.

Crombé, P., Perdaen, Y., and J. Sergant. 1998. The Early Mesolithic site of Verrebroek 'Dok', preliminary results of the 1998 excavation campaign. *Notae Praehistoricae* 18: 101–5.

Crombé, P., Perdaen, Y., and J. Sergant. 2003. The site of Verrebroek 'Dok' (Flanders, Belgium): Spatial organisation of an extensive Early Mesolithic settlement. In L. Larsson, H. Kindgren, K. Knutsson, D. Loeffler, and A. Åkerlund (eds.), *Mesolithic on the move: Papers presented at the Sixth International Conference on the Mesolithic in Europe, Stockholm 2000*. Oxford: Oxbow, pp. 205–15.

Crombé, P., Perdaen, Y., and J. Sergant. 2008. Le Mésolithique ancien dans l'ouest de la Belgique: Quelques réflections concernant l'occupation du territoire. In T. Ducrocq, J.-P. Fagnart, B. Souffi, and A. Thévenin (eds.), *Actes de la table ronde – Le Mésolithique ancien et moyen de la France septentrionale et des pays limitrophes, Amiens 9–11/10/2004*. Paris: Mémoires de la Société Préhistorique Française, pp. 193–204.

Crombé, P., Van Strydonck, M., and V. Hendrix. 1999. AMS-dating of antler mattocks from the Schelde river in northern Belgium. *Notae Praehistoricae* 19: 111–19.

Crombé, P., Van Roeyen, J.-P., Sergant, J., Perdaen, Y., Cordemans, K., and M. Van Strydonck. 2000. Doel "Deurganckdok" (Flanders, Belgium), settlement traces from the Final Palaeolithic and the Early to Middle Neolithic. *Notae Praehistoricae* 20: 111–19.

Cullen, T. 1995. Mesolithic mortuary ritual at Franchthi Cave, Greece. *Antiquity* 69: 270–89.

Cunha, E., and F. Cardoso. 2003. New data on Muge shell middens: A contribution to more accurate numbers and dates. *Estudos Arqueológicos de Muge* 1:171–83.

Cupillard, C., and A. Richard (eds.). 1998. *Les derniers chasseurs-cueilleurs du massif jurassien et de ses marges (13000–5500 avant Jésus-Christ)*. Lons-le-Saunier: Centre Jurassien du Patrimoine.

Cupillard, C., Chaix, L., and J. F. Piningre. 2000. Les occupations mésolithiques de la grotte de la Baume de Montandon à Saint-Hippolyte (Doubs, France). In *Les derniers chasseurs-cueilleurs d'Europe occidentale*. Actes du colloque international de Besançon (Doubs, France), 1998, pp. 219–52.

Cyrek, K. 1995. On the distribution of chocolate flint in the Late Mesolithic of the Vistula basin. *Archaeologia Polona* 33: 99–109.

Cyrek, K., Grygiel, R., and K. Nowak. 1986. The basis for distinguishing the ceramic Mesolithic in the Polish lowland. In T. Malinowski (ed.), *Problems of the Stone Age in Pomerania*. Warsaw: Warsaw University, pp. 95–126.

Czaplicka, M. A. 1914. *Aboriginal Siberia: A study in social anthropology*. Oxford: Clarendon Press.

Cziesla, E. 1992. *Jäger und Sammler: Die Mittlere Steinzeit im Landkreis Permasens*. Brühl: Lindersoft.

Cziesla, E. 1997. The Weidental Cave: Changing use in changing times. In C. Bonsall and C. Tolan-Smith (eds.), *The Human use of caves*. Oxford: British Archaeological Reports International Series 667, pp. 52–62.

Cziesla, E. 1998. Die Mittlere Steinzeit im Südlichen Rheinland–Pfalz. In N. Conard (ed.), *Aktuelle Forschungen zum Mesolithikum/Current Mesolithic Research*. Tübingen: Mo Vince Verlag, pp. 111–20.

Cziesla, E., and A. Tillman. 1984. Mesolithische Funde der Freinlandfundstelle "Auf'm Benneberg" in Burgalben/Waldfischbach, Kreis Pirmasens. *Mitteilungen des Historischen Vereins der Pfalz* 82: 69–110.

d'Acy, E. 1893. Marteaux casse-têtes et gaines de hache Néolithiques en bois de cerf ornementées. *L'Anthropologie* 4: 385–401.

Dalton, G. 1981. Anthropological models in archaeological perspective. In I. Hodder, G. Isaac, and N. Hammond (eds.), *Pattern of the past: Studies in honour of David Clarke*. Cambridge, UK: Cambridge University Press, pp. 17–48.

Dams, L. 1987. *L'art paléolithique de la Grotte de Nerja (Malaga, Espagne)*. Oxford: British Archaeological Reports International Series 385.

Danilenko, V. N. 1969. *Neolit Ukrainy [The Neolithic of the Ukraine]*. Kiev: Naukova Dumka.

Darvill, T. 1987. *Prehistoric Britain*. London: Batsford.

Daugnora, L., and A. Girinkias. 1995. Neolithic and Bronze Age mixed farming and stock breeding in the traditional Baltic culture-area. In V. Kazakevičius and R. Sidrys (eds.), *Archaeologia Baltica*. Vilnius: Institute of Lithuanian History, pp. 43–51.

References

David, A. 1989. Some aspects of the human presence in West Wales during the Mesolithic. In C. Bonsall (ed.), *The Mesolithic in Europe: Papers presented at the Third International Symposium, Edinburgh 1985*. Edinburgh: John Donald.

David, H. 2005. Les premiers peuplements de insulaires de Méditerranée occidentale. In *Territoires, déplacements, mobilité, échanges durant la Préhistoire*. Actes du 126ᵉ Congrès National des Sociétés Historiques et Scientifiques, Toulouse, 2001; dir. Jacques Jaubert et M. Barbaza. Paris: Editions du CTHS, pp. 463–70.

Davies, P., Robb, J. G., and D. Ladbrook. 2005. Woodland clearance in the Mesolithic: The social aspects. *Antiquity* 79: 280–8.

Davis, S. J. M., and F. R. Valla. 1978. Evidence for domestication of the dog 12,000 years ago in the Natufian of Israel. *Nature* 276: 608–10.

Dawson, A. G., Long, D., and D. E. Smith. 1988. The Storegga Slides: Evidence from eastern Scotland for a possible tsunami. *Marine Geology* 82: 271–6.

Dawson, S., and D. E. Smith. 2000. Sedimentology of middle Holocene tsunami facies in northern Sutherland, Scotland. *Marine Geology* 170: 69–79.

De Bie, M., and J.-P. Caspar. 2000. *Rekem, a Federmesser Camp on the Meuse River Bank*. Leuven: Leuven University Press.

Deeben, J. 1988. The Geldrop sites and the Federmesser occupation of the southern Netherlands. In M. Otte (ed.), *De la Loire à l'Oder. Les civilisations du Paléolithique final dans le nord-ouest Européen. Actes du Colloque Liège 1985*. Oxford: British Archaeological Reports International Series 444, pp. 357–98.

Deith, M. 1983a. Seasonality of shell collecting, determined by oxygen isotope analysis of marine shells from Asturian sites. In C. Grigson and J. Clutton-Brock (eds.), *Animals and Archaeology*, vol. 2. Oxford: British Archaeological Reports International Series 183, pp. 67–76.

Deith, M. R. 1983b. Molluscan calendars: The use of growth line analysis to establish seasonality of shellfish collection at the Mesolithic site of Morton, Fife. *Journal of Archaeological Science* 10: 423–40.

Deith, M. R. 1986. Subsistence strategies at a Mesolithic camp site: Evidence from stable isotope analysis of shells. *Journal of Archaeological Science* 13: 61–78.

Deith, M. R. 1989. Clams and salmonberries: Interpreting seasonality data from shells. In C. Bonsall (ed.), *The Mesolithic in Europe: Papers presented at the Third International Symposium, Edinburgh 1985*. Edinburgh: John Donald, pp. 73–9.

Dennell, R. 1983. *European economic prehistory: A new approach*. London: Academic Press.

Dennell, R. 1992. The origins of crop agriculture in Europe. In C. W. Cowan and P. J. Watson (eds.), *The origins of agriculture*. Washington, DC: Smithsonian Institute.

Dentan, K. 1979. *The Semai*. New York: Holt, Reinhart, and Winston.

De Puydt, M. 1885. Découverte de silex taillé à Maffe, Huccorgne. *Bulletin de l'Institut Archéologique Liègeois* 18: 500–1.

Desse, J. 1987. La pêche: Son rôle dans l'économie des premières sociétés néolithiques en Méditerranée occidentale. In J. Guilaine, J. Courtin, J.-L. Roudil, and J.-L. Vernet (eds.), *Premières communautés paysannes en Méditerranée Occidentale*. Paris: CNRS, pp. 281–5.

Devlet, E. 2001. Rock art and the material culture of Siberian and central Asian shamanism. In N. Price (ed.), *The archaeology of shamanism*. London: Routledge, pp. 43–55.

Diamond, J. 1997. *Guns, germs and steel: A short history of everybody for the last 13,000 Years*. London: Vintage.

Dillehay, T. D. 2000. *The settlement of the Americas: A new prehistory*. New York: Basic Books.

Dimitrijević, V. 2000. The Lepenski Vir fauna: Bones in houses and between houses. *Documenta Praehistorica* 27: 101–17.

Dimitrijević, V. 2008. Lepenski Vir animal bones: What was left in the houses? In C. Bonsall, V. Boroneanţ, and I. Radovanović (eds.). *The Iron Gates in prehistory: New perspectives*. Oxford: Archaeopress, pp. 117–30.

Dinu, A., Soficaru, A., and D. Miriţoiu. 2007. The Mesolithic at the Danube's Iron Gates: New radiocarbon dates and old stratigraphies. *Documenta Praehistorica* 34: 31–52.

Diószegi, V., and M. Hóppal (eds.), 1996. *Shamanism in Siberia*. Budapest: Akadémiai Kiadó.

Divale, W. 1972. Systematic population control in the Middle and Upper Palaeolithic: Inferences based on contemporary hunters and gatherers. *World Archaeology* 4: 221–43.

Dobney, K., Ervynck, A., Albarella, U., and P. Rowley-Conwy. 2004. The chronology and frequency of a stress marker (linear enamel hypoplasia) in recent and archaeological populations of *Sus Scrofa* in North-West Europe. And the effects on early domestication. *Journal of Zoology* 264 (2):197–208.

Dobosi, V. 1972. Mesolithische Fundorte in Ungarn. *Alba Regia* 12: 39–60.

Dolukhanov, P., Lavento, M., and K. German. 2009. Mesolithic and Neolithic in North Eastern Europe. In P. Dolukhanov, G. R. Sarson, and A. M. Shukurov (eds.), *The East European Plain on the eve of agriculture.* British Archaeological Reports International Series 1964. Oxford: Archaeopress, pp. 189–96.

Dolukhanov, P., Sarson, G. R., and A. M. Shukurov (eds.). 2009. *The East European Plain on the eve of agriculture.* British Archaeological Reports International Series 1964. Oxford: Archaeopress.

Dolukhanov, P., Shukurov, A., Gronenborn, D., Sokoloff, D., Timofeev, V., and G. Zaitseva. 2005. The chronology of Neolithic dispersal in Central and Eastern Europe. *Journal of Archaeological Science* 32 (10): 1441–58.

Dolukhanov, P. M. 1979. *Ecology and economy in Neolithic Eastern Europe.* London: Duckworth.

Dolukhanov, P. M. 1986. Natural environment and the holocene settlement pattern in the north-western Part of the USSR. *Fennoscandia archaeologica* 3: 3–16.

Dolukhanov, P. M. 1996. *The Early Slavs: Eastern Europe from the initial settlement to the Kievan Rus.* London and New York: Longman.

Dolukhanov, P. M. 1998a. The Neolithic with a human face or dividing lines in Neolithic Europe. *Baltic-Pontic Studies* 5: 13–23.

Dolukhanov, P. M. 1998b. The most ancient north Europeans: Consensus in sight? In K. Julku and K. Wiik (eds.), *The roots of peoples and languages of Northern Eurasia I.* Turku: Societas Historiae Fenno-Ugricae, pp. 9–27.

Dolukhanov, P. M. 2000. Archaeology and languages in prehistoric Europe. In A. Künnap (ed.), *The roots of peoples and languages of Northern Eurasia II and III.* Turku: Societas Historiae Fenno-Ugricae, pp. 11–22.

Dolukhanov, P. M. 2002. Plants and subsistence of hunter-gatherers in the prehistoric East European Plain (Upper Palaeolithic, Mesolithic and Sub-Nelithic). In S. L. R. Mason and J. G. H. Hather (eds.), *Hunter-gatherer archaeobotany: Perspectives from the northern temperate zone.* London: Institute of Archaeology, University College London, pp. 180–7.

Dolukhanov, P. M., Kovalyukh, N. N., Skripkin, V. V., and G. I. Zaitseva. 2009. Early Neolithic in the south of East European Plain. In P. Dolukhanov, G. Sarson, and A. Shukurov (eds.), *The East European Plain on the eve of agriculture.* British Archaeological Reports International Series 1964. Oxford: Archaeopress, pp. 109–23.

Dolukhanov, P. M., and A. N. Miklyaev. 1986. Prehistoric lacustrine pile dwellings in the northwestern part of the USSR. *Fennoscandia Archaeologica* 3: 81–90.

Dolukhanov, P. M., Shukurov, A. M., and D. D. Sokoloff. 2001. Improved radiocarbon chronology and the colonization of East European Plain by Modern Humans. *Journal of Archaeological Science*, 28 (7): 699–712.

Dolukhanov, P. M., Arslanov, K. A., Shukurov, A. M., Mazurkevich, A. N., Savelieva, L. A., Dzinroridze, E. N., Kulkova, M. A., and G. I. Zaitseva. 2004. The Holocene environment and transition to agriculture in Boreal Russia (Serteya Valley Case Study). *Internet Archaeology Journal* 17. http://intarch.ac.uk/journal/issue17/dolukhanov_index.html.

Donner, J., Eronen M., and H. Junger. 1977. The dating of Holocene relative sea-level changes in Finnmark, North Norway. *Norsk geografisk Tidsskrift* 31: 103–28.

Driver, H. E. 1961. *Indians of North America, 2nd Edition.* Chicago: University of Chicago Press.

Ducrocq, T. 1990. Le Mésolithique ancien et moyen du bassin de la Somme (Nord de la France). *Bulletin de la Société Préhistorique Luxembourgeoise* 12: 21–37.

Ducrocq, T. 1992. Une nouvelle occupation mésolithique datée dans le Nord de la France. *Bulletin de la Société Préhistorique Française* 90: 72–3.

Ducrocq, T. 1999. Le Mésolithique de la vallée de la Somme (Nord de la France). In A. Thévenin (ed.), *L'Europe des derniers chasseurs: Épipaléolithique et Mésolithique. Actes du 5ᵉ Colloque International UISPP, Commission XII, Grenoble, 18–23 septembre 1995.* Paris: Éditions du Comité des Travaux Historiques et Scientifiques, pp. 247–61.

References

Ducrocq, T. 2001. *Le Mésolithique du bassin de la Somme: Insertion dans un cadre morpho-stratigraphique, environnemental et chronoculturel.* Villeneuve-d'Ascq: Centre d'Etudes et de Recherches Préhistoriques, Université des Sciences et Technologies de Lille.

Ducrocq, T., and I. Ketterer. 1994. Le gisement mésolithique du 'Petit-Marais', La chaussée-Tirancourt, Somme. *Bulletin de la Société Préhistorique Française*, 92 (2): 249–59.

Ducrocq, T., Bridault, A., and A. V. Munaut. 1991. Un gisement mésolithique exceptionnel dans le Nord de la France: Le Petit-Marais de la Chaussée-Tirancourt (Somme). *Bulletin de la Société Préhistorique Française* 88: 272–6.

Ducrocq, T., Le Goff, I., and F. Valentin. 1996. La sépulture secondaire mésolithique de La Chaussée-Tirancourt (Somme). *Bulletin de la Société Préhistorique Française* 93: 211–16.

Duday, H. 1976. Les sépultures des hommes du Mésolithique. In H. de Lumley (ed.), *La préhistoire Française 1: Les civilisations Paléolithiques et Mésolithiques de la France.* Paris: CNRS, pp. 734–7.

Dugstad, S. A. 2007. Hushold og teknologi. En studie av tidlig preboerale lokaliteter i Rogaland. Unpuplished MA thesis, University of Bergen.

Dumitrescu, V., Bartolomey A., and F. Mogosanu. 1983. *Esquisse d'une préhistoire de la Roumanie, jusq'à la fin de l'Âge du Bronze.* Bucarest: Editura Štiinfica si Enciclopedica.

Duplessy, J., Delibrias, G., Turon, J., Pujol C., and J. Duprat. 1981. Deglacial warming of the north-eastern Atlantic Ocean. *Palaeogeography, Palaeoclimatology, Palaeoecology* 35: 121–44.

Dupré, M. 1988. *Palinología paleoambiente.* Trabajos Varios 84. Valencia: Servicio de Investigación Prehistórica.

Durkheim, E. 1995. *The elementary forms of religious life.* Translation and introduction by K. E. Fields. First published in 1912. New York: Free Press.

Ebbesen, K. 1992. Simple, tidligneolitiske grave. *Årbøger for Nordisk Oldkyndighed og Historie*: 45–102.

Eberhardt, H., Keefer, E., Kind, C.-J., Rensch, H., and H. Ziegler. 1987. Jungpaläolithische und Mesolithische Fundstellen aus der Aichbühler Bucht. *Fundberichte aus Baden-Württemberg* 12: 1–51.

Edgren, T. 1966. *Die Jäkärlä Gruppen.* Finska Fornminnesföreningens Tidskrift 68.

Edgren, T. 1982. Formgivning och function, en kamkeeramisk studie. *Iskos 3.*

Edmonds, M. 1999. *Ancestral geographies of the Neolithic: Landscape, monuments, and memory.* London: Routledge.

Edsman, C.-M. 1965. The hunter, the games and the unseen powers: Lappish and Finnish bear rites. In H. Hvarfner (ed.), *Hunting and fishing.* Sweden: Norrbottens Museum, pp. 159–88.

Edwards, K. J. 1996. A Mesolithic of the Western and Northern Isles of Scotland? Evidence from pollen and charcoal. In A. Pollard and A. Morrison (eds.), *The early prehistory of Scotland.* Edinburgh: Edinburgh University Press, pp. 23–38.

Eidlitz, K. 1969. Food and emergency food in the circumpolar area. *Studia Ethnographica Uppsaliensis 32.*

Eigeland, L. 2006. Blod fra Stein. En eksperimentell tilnærming til råstoffstrategier og teknologiske tradisjoner i sørøst-norsk senmesolitikum. Unpublished MA thesis, University of Oslo.

Eliade, M. 1989. *Shamanism: Archaic techniques of ecstasy.* Translated from French by W. R. Trask. London: Penguin Books.

Engelstad, E. S. 1934. *Østnorske ristninger og malninger av den arktiske gruppe.* Oslo.

Engelstad, E. 1984. Diversity in Arctic maritime adaptations. *Acta Borealia* 2: 3–25.

Engelstad, E. 1989. Mesolithic house sites in Arctic Norway. In C. Bonsall (ed.), *The Mesolithic in Europe: Proceedings of the third international symposium.* Edinburgh: John Donald, pp. 331–7.

Engelstad, E. 1990. The meaning of sedentism and mobility in an archaeological and historic context. *Acta Borealia* 7 (2): 21–35. Tromsø.

Enghoff, I. B. 1995. Fishing in Denmark during the Mesolithic period. In A. Fischer (ed.), *Man and sea in the Mesolithic.* Oxford: Oxbow Monograph 53, pp. 67–75.

Erdal, D., and A. Whiten. 1996. Egalitarianism and Machiavellian intelligence in human evolution. In P. Mellars, and K. Gibson (eds.), *Modelling the early human mind.* Cambridge, UK: MacDonald Institute for Archaeology, pp. 139–150.

Eriksen, B. 1991. *Change and continuity in a prehistoric hunter-gatherer society.* Archaeologica Venatoria 12. Tübingen: Archaeologica Venatoria.

Eriksen, B. V. 1996. Regional variations in Late Pleistocene subsistence strategies: Southern Scandinavian reindeer hunters in a European context. In L. Larsson (ed.), *The earliest settlement of Scandinavia and its relationship with neighbouring areas*. Acta Archaeologica Lundensia, Series In 8, 24. Stockholm: Almquist and Wiksell International, pp. 7–22.

Eriksen, B. V. 2002. Reconsidering the geochronological framework of Lateglacial hunter-gatherer colonization of Southern Scandinavia. In B. V. Eriksen and B. Bratlund (eds.), *Recent studies in the Final Palaeolithic of the European plain*. Højbjerg: Jutland Archaeological Society, pp. 25–41.

Eriksen, B. V., and B. Bratlund (eds.). 2002. *Recent studies in the Final Palaeolithic of the European plain: Proceedings of a Union Internationale des Sciences Préhistoriques et Protohistoriques symposium, Stockholm, 14–17 October 1999*. Højbjerg, Denmark: Jutland Archaeological Society (distributed by Århus University Press).

Eriksen, E. 1996. Arkeologers søken etter de første menneskene i Norge. Et forskningshistorisk tilbakeblikk. Unpublished thesis, University of Tromsø.

Eriksson, G. (ed.). 2003. *Norm and difference. Stone Age dietary practice in the Baltic Region*. Stockholm: Archaeological Research Laboratory.

Eriksson, G., Lõugas, L., and I. Zagorska. 2003. Stone Age hunter-fisher-gatherers at Zvejnieki, northern Latvia: Radiocarbon, stable isotope and archaeozoology data. *Before Farming* 2003/1 (2).

Erlandson, J. M. 1994. *Early Holocene hunter-gatherers of the California Coast*. New York: Plenum Press.

Erny-Rodman, C., Gross-Klee, E., Haas, J., Jacomet, S., and H. Zoller. 1997. Früher 'Human Impact' und Ackerbau im Übergangsbereich Spätmesolithikum-Frühneolithikum im Schweizerischen Mittelland. *Jahrbuch der Schweizerischen Gesellschaft für Ur- und Frühgeschichte* 80: 27–56.

Eronen, M. 1974. The history of the Litorina Sea and associated Holocene events. *Societas Scientiarum Fennica, Commentationes Physico-Mathematicae* 44 (4): 79–195.

Escalon de Fonton, M. 1976a. La Baume de Montclus. *Livret-Guide de l'excursion C2. Provence et Languedoc méditerranéen. Sites paléolithiques et néolithiques*. Congrès UISPP, Nice, pp. 135–45.

Escalon de Fonton, M. 1976b. Abri de Châteauneuf-les-Martigues. *Livret-Guide de l'excursion C2. Provence et Languedoc méditerranéen. Sites paléolithiques et néolithiques*. Congrès UISPP, Nice, pp, 59–69.

Escalon de Fonton, M. 1976c. Les civilisations de l'Epipaléolithique et du Mésolithique en Languedoc oriental. In H. de Lumley (ed.), *La préhistoire Française 1: Les civilisations Paléolithiques et Mésolithiques de la France*. Paris: CNRS, pp. 1382–9.

Escalon de Fonton, M. 1976d. Les civilisations de l'Epipaléolithique et du Mésolithique en Provence littorale. In H. de Lumley (ed.), *La préhistoire Française 1: Les civilisations Paléolithiques et Mésolithiques de la France*. Paris: CNRS, pp. 1367–78.

Escalon de Fonton, M., Bonifay, M., and G. Onoratini. 1979. Les industries de filiation magdalénienne dans le sud-est de la France, leurs positions géo-chronologiques et les faunes. In D. de Sonneville Bordes (ed.), *La fin des temps glaciaires en Europe: Chronostratigraphie et écologie des cultures du Paléolithique Final*. Paris: CNRS, pp. 269–86.

Fábregas, R., Fernández, C., and P. Ramil. 1997. La adopción de la economía productora en el Noroeste ibérico. In A. Rodríguez (ed.), *O Neolítico Atlántico e as orixes do megalitismo*, Santiago de Compostela: Universidad de Santiago, pp. 463–84.

Facorellis, Y. 2003. Radiocarbon dating the Greek Mesolithic. In N. Galanidou and C. Perlès (eds.), *The Greek Mesolithic: Problems and perspectives*. London: British School at Athens, pp. 51–67.

Fagnart, J. P. 1991. La fin du mésolithique dans le nord de la France. In A. Thévenin (ed.), *Mésolithique et Néolithisation en France et dans les régions limitrophes*. Paris: Éditions du Comité des Travaux Historiques et Scientifiques, pp. 437–52.

Fairbanks, R. G. 1989. A 17,000-year glacio-eustatic sea level record. influence of glacial melting rates on the Younger Dryas event and deep-ocean circulation. *Nature* 342: 637–42.

Fano, M. A. 1998. *El hábitat Mesolítico en el Cantábrico occidental*. Oxford: British Archaeological Reports International Series 732.

Fano, M. A., and M. González Morales: 2004. Nine decades of research on the "Asturian" of Cantabria. In M. González Morales and G. Clark (eds.), *The Mesolithic of the Atlantic Façade*. Anthropological Research Papers 55. Tempe: Arizona State University, pp. 167–79.

References

Farrand, W. 2000. *Depositional history of Franchthi cave – sediments, stratigraphy, and chronology.* Excavations at Franchthi Cave, Fascicle 12. Bloomington: Indiana University Press.

Faught, M. K. 2004. The underwater archaeology of paleolandscapes, Apalache Bay, Florida. *American Antiquity* 69(2): 275–90.

Fedorov, P. V. 1978. *Pleistocen Ponto-Kaspiya* [*The Pontic-Caspian Pleistocene*]. Moscow: Nauka.

Fernández Eraso, J. 1985. *Las culturas del Tardiglaciar en Vizcaya.* Vitoria: Universidad del País Vasco.

Fernández Tresguerres, J. 1980. *El Aziliense en las provincias de Asturias y Santander.* Monografías 2. Santander: Centro de Investigación y Museo de Altamira.

Fernández Tresguerres, J. 1994. El arte aziliense. *Complutum* 5: 81–95.

Fernández Tresguerres, J. 2004. The Azilian in the Cantabrian region. In M. González Morales, and G. Clark (eds.), *The Mesolithic of the Atlantic Façade.* Anthropological Research Papers 55. Tempe: Arizona State University, pp. 149–66.

Fewster, K. J. 1994. Basarwa and Bamangwato interaction in Botswana: Implications for the transition to agriculture in European prehistory. *Archaeological Review from Cambridge* 13 (1): 83–103.

Fewster, K. J. 2001. Petso's field: Ethnoarchaeology and agency. In K. J. Fewster and M. Zvelebil (eds.), *Ethnoachaeology and hunter-gatherers: Pictures at an exhibition.* Oxford: British Archaeological Reports International Series 995, pp. 81–90.

Finlay, N. 2003. Microliths and multiple authorship. In L. Larsson, H. Kindgren, K. Knutsson, D. Loeffler, and A. Åkerlund (eds.), *Mesolithic on the Move: Papers presented at the Sixth International Conference on the Mesolithic in Europe.* Oxford: Oxbow Books, pp. 169–7.

Finlayson, B. 1998. *Wild harvesters: The first people in Scotland.* Canongate books with Historic Scotland.

Fischer, A. 1982. Bonderup-bopladsen. Det manglende led mellem dansk palæolitikum og mesolitikum? *Antikvariske Studier* 5: 87–100.

Fischer, A. 1989. Hunting with flint-tipped arrows: Results and experiences from practical experiments. In C. Bonsall (ed.), *The Mesolithic in Europe: Proceedings of the third international symposium.* Edinburgh: John Donald, pp. 29–39.

Fischer, A. 1991. Pioneers in deglaciated landscapes: The expansion and adaptation of Late Palaeolithic societies in southern Scandinavia. In N. Barton, A. J. Roberts, and D. A. Roe (eds.), *The Late Glacial in north-west Europe: Human adaptation and environmental change at the end of the Pleistocene.* London: CBA Research Report 77, pp. 100–21.

Fischer, A. 1993. Mesolithic inland settlement. In S. Hvass, and B. Storgaard (eds.), *Digging into the Past: 25 years of archaeology in Denmark.* Århus: Aarhus University Press, pp. 58–63.

Fischer, A. 1994. Dating the early trapeze horizon, radiocarbon dates from submerged settlements in Musholm Bay and Kalø Vig, Denmark. *Mesolithic Miscellany* 15: 1–7.

Fischer, A. (ed.), 1995a. *Man and sea in the Mesolithic.* Oxbow Monograph 53. Oxford: Oxbow.

Fischer, A. 1995b. An entrance to the Mesolithic world below the ocean. In A. Fischer (ed.), *Man and Sea in the Mesolithic.* Oxbow Monograph 53. Oxford: Oxbow, pp. 371–84.

Fischer, A. 1996. At the border of human habitat: The Late Palaeolithic and Early Mesolithic in Scandinavia. In L. Larsson (ed.), *The earliest settlement of Scandinavia and its relationship with neighbouring areas.* Acta Archaeologica Lundensia, Series In 8, 24. Stockholm: Almquist and Wiksell International, pp. 157–76.

Fischer, A. 2001. Mesolittiske bopladser på den danske havbund – udfordringer for forskning og forvaltning. In O. Lass Jensen, S. A. Andersen, and K. Møller Hansen (eds.), *Danmarks jægerstenalder: Status og perspektiver.* Hørsholms Egns Museum.

Fischer, A. 2002. Food for feasting? An evaluation of explanations of the neolithisation of Denmark and southern Sweden. In A. Fischer and K. Kristiansen (eds.), *The Neolithisation of Denmark – 150 years of debate.* Sheffield Archaeological Monographs 12. Sheffield: J. R. Collis Publications.

Fischer, A. 2003a. Exchange: Artefacts, people and ideas on the move in Mesolithic Europe. In L. Larsson, H. Kindgren, K. Knutsson, D. Loeffler, and A. Åkerlund (eds.), *Mesolithic on the move: Papers presented at the Sixth International Conference on the Mesolithic in Europe, Stockholm 2000.* Oxford: Oxbow Books, pp. 385–7.

Fischer, A. 2003b. Trapping up the rivers and trading across the sea – steps towards the Neolithisation of Denmark. In L. Larsson, H. Kindgren, K. Knutsson, D. Loeffler, and A. Åkerlund (eds.), *Mesolithic on the move: Papers presented at the Sixth International Conference on the Mesolithic in Europe, Stockholm 2000*. Oxford: Oxbow Books, pp. 405–13.

Fischer, A., and K. Kristiansen (eds.). 2002. *The Neolithisation of Denmark – 150 years of debate*. Sheffield Archaeological Monographs 12. Sheffield: J. R. Collis Publications.

Fischer, A., and J. Schou Hansen. 2005. Mennesket og havet i ældre stenalder. In C. Bunte (ed.), *Arkeologi och Naturvetenskap*. Lund: Gyllenstiernska Krapperupstiftelsen, pp. 276–97.

Fischer, A., and H. Tauber. 1986. New C-14 datings of late Palaeolithic cultures from Northwestern Europe. *Journal of Danish Archaeology* 5: 7–13.

Fisher, L. 1990. *Mobility and technology: Variable core reduction strategies in the southwest German Magdalenian*. Unpublished MA thesis, University of Michigan, Ann Arbor.

Fitzhugh, B. 2003. *The evolution of complex hunter-gatherers. Archaeological evidence from the North Pacific*. New York: Kluwer/Plenum.

Flannery, K. V. 1969. Origins and ecological effects of early Near Eastern domestication, In P. J. Ucko and G. W. Dimbleby (eds.), *The domestication and exploitation of plants and animals* London: Duckworth, pp. 73–100.

Flemming, N. (ed.). 2004. *Submarine prehistoric archaeology of the North Sea: Research priorities and collaboration with industry*. London: CBA Research Report 141.

Flint, R. F. 1971. *Glacial and Quaternary geology*. New York: John Wiley and Sons.

Follieri, M. 1968. Determinazioni xilotomiche dei carboni del Paleolitico Superiore di Grotta Romanelli in Terra d'Otranto. *Quaternaria* 10: 125–35.

Fontana, F., and A. Guerreschi. 2003. Highland occupation in the southern Alps during the Early Holocene. In L. Larsson, H. Kindgren, K. Knutsson, D. Loeffler, and A. Åkerlund (eds.), *Mesolithic on the move: Papers presented at the Sixth International Conference on the Mesolithic in Europe, Stockholm 2000*. Oxford: Oxbow Books, pp. 96–102.

Forenbaher, S., and P. Miracle. 2005. The spread of farming in the Eastern Adriatic. *Antiquity* 79: 514–28.

Formozov, A. A. 1966. Mezoliticheskie plemena na territorii Vostochnoi Evropy [Mesolithic tribes on the territory of Eastern Europe]. In B. N. Ponomarev (ed.), *Istoriya SSSR s drevneishih vremen do nashih dnei* [*History of USSR from the oldest times to present day*]. Moscow: Nauka, pp. 35–42.

Forsberg, L. 1985. *Site variability and settlement patterns: An analysis of the hunter-gatherer settlement system in the Lule River Valley, 1500 BC – BC/AD*. Archaeology and Environment 5. Umeå: Department of Archaeology, Umeå University.

Forsberg, L. 1996. The earliest settlement of northern Sweden – problems and perspectives. In L. Larsson (ed.), *The earliest settlement of Scandinavia and its relationship with neighbouring areas*. Acta Archaeologica Lundensia, Series In 8, 24. Stockholm: Almquist and Wiksell International, pp. 241–50.

Forsberg, L. 2003. Förhistoriska Fångstsamhällen i Indalsälvens avrinningsområde. In A. Beverfjord (ed.), *Midtnordisk arkeologisymposium 1999*. Vitark 3. Trondheim: Vitenskapsmuseet, NTNU, pp. 41–70.

Forstén, A. 1972. The refuse fauna of the Mesolithic Suomusjärvi period in Finland. *Finskt Museum* 79: 74–85.

Forstén, A., and P. Alhonen. 1975. The subfossil seals of Finland and their relations to the history of the Baltic Sea. *Boreas* 4: 143–55.

Forstén, A., and L. Blomquist. 1974. Refuse faunas of the Vantaa Mesolithic and Neolithic periods. *Finskt Museum* 81: 50–6.

Fossum, G. 2009. Å knuse stein? En studie av bipolar teknikk belyst ved arkeologisk materiale fra Ormen Lange Nyhamna. Unpublished MA thesis, NTNU, Trondheim.

Foucher, P., Wattez, J., Gebhardt, A., and J. Musch. 2000. Les structures de combustion de la Pierre Saint-Louis (Geay, Charente-Maritime), *Paléo* 12: 165–200.

Fowler, C. 2004. *The archaeology of personhood: An anthropological approach*. London: Routledge

Franz, L. 1933. Mittelsteinzeitliche Funde bei Drum. *Mitteilungen des Nordböhmischen Vereins für Heimatforschung und Wanderpflege* 56: 33–35.

Frayer, D. 1997. Ofnet: Evidence for a Mesolithic massacre. In D. Martin and D. Frayer (ed.), *Troubled times: Violence and warfare in the past*. New York: Gordon and Breach, pp. 181–215.

Frenzel, B. 1983. Die Vegetationsgeschichte Süddeutschlands im Eiszeitalter. In H. Müller-Beck (ed.), *Urgeschichte in Baden-Württemberg*. Stuttgart: Konrad Theiss Verlag, pp. 91–165.

References

Fretheim, S. E. 2002. Steinalderminner i Alvdal Vestfjell. Utsnitt av livsmønstre gjennom 6500 år. Unpublished thesis, NTNU, Trondheim.

Fretheim, S. E. 2009. Feast in the forest: Creating a common cultural identity in the interior of the Scandinavian Peninsula in the Late Mesolithic. In S. McCartan, R. Schulting, G. Warren, and P. C. Woodman (eds.), *Mesolithic horizons. Papers presented at the Seventh International Conference on the Mesolithic in Europe, Belfast 2005.* Oxford: Oxbow Books, pp. 378–84.

Freundt, E. A. 1949. Komsa-Fosna-Sandarna: Problems of the Scandinavian Mesolithicum. *Acta Archaeologica* 19 (1948): 1–68.

Fuglestvedt, I. 1989. Norges landnåm. *Nicolay* 1989/1. Oslo.

Fuglestvedt, I. 1992. Svevollen – et senmesolittisk boplassområde i det østnorske innland. Unpublished thesis, University of Oslo.

Fuglestvedt, I. 1995. Svevollen – spor av senmesolittisk bosetning i lavlandets indre skogssone. *Arkeologiske skrifter, Arkeologisk inst., Bergen Museum*, Nr. 8. Steinalderkonferansen i Bergen 1993, pp. 95–110.

Fuglestvedt, I. 1999a. The early mesolithic site at Stunner, southeast Norway. In J. Boaz (ed.), *The Mesolithic of Central Scandinavia.* Universitetets Oldsaksamlings Skrifter Ny Rekke 22, Oslo: Universitetets Oldsaksamling, pp. 189–202.

Fuglestvedt, I. 1999b. Inter-Regional Contact in the Late Mesolithic: The productive Gift Extended. In J. Boaz (ed.), *The Mesolithic of Central Scandinavia.* Universitetets Oldsaksamlings Skrifter Ny Rekke 22, Oslo: Universitetets Oldsaksamling, pp. 27–38.

Fuglestvedt, I. 2001. Pionerbosetningens fenomenologi. Sørvest-Norge og Nord-Europa 12200/10000–9500 BP. Unpublished Ph.D. thesis, University of Bergen.

Fuglestvedt, I. 2003. Enculturating the landscape beyond Doggerland. In L. Larsson, H. Kindgren, K. Knutsson, D. Loeffler, and A. Åkerlund (eds.), *Mesolithic on the move: Papers presented at the Sixth International Conference on the Mesolithic in Europe, Stockholm 2000.* Oxford: Oxbow Books, pp. 103–7.

Fuglestvedt, I. 2007. The Ahrensburgian Galta 3 site in SW Norway. Dating, technology and cultural affinity. *Acta Archaeologica* 78 (2): 87–110.

Galanidou, N., and C. Perlès (eds.). 2003. *The Greek Mesolithic: Problems and perspectives.* London: British School at Athens.

Gamble, C. 1986. *The Palaeolithic settlement of Europe.* Cambridge, UK: Cambridge University Press.

Gamble, C. 1993. *Timewalkers: The prehistory of global colonization.* Stroud: Sutton.

Gamble, C. 1999. *The Palaeolithic societies of Europe.* Cambridge, UK: Cambridge University Press.

Gamble, G., Davies, W., Pettitt, P., Hazelwood, L., and M. Richards. 2005. The archaeological and genetic foundations of the European population during the late glacial: Implications for 'agricultural thinking'. *Cambridge Archaeological Journal* 15 (2): 193–223.

Gamble, C., Davies, W., Pettit, P., Hazelwood, L., and M. Richards. 2006. The late glacial ancestry of Europeans: Combining genetic and archaeological evidence. *Documenta Praehistorica* 33: 1–10.

Garašanin, M., and I. Radovanović. 2001. A pot in house 54 at Lepenski Vir I. *Antiquity* 75: 118–25.

Garcia Guinea, M. A. 1985. Las cuevas azilienses de El Piélago. *Sautuola* 4: 11–154.

García-Argüelles, P., Adserías, M., Bartrolí, R., Bergadà, M., Cebrià, A., Doce, R., Fullola, J., Nadal, J., Ribé, G., Rodón, T., and R. Viñas. 1992. Síntesis de los primeros resultados del programa sobre Epipaleolítico en la Cataluña central y meridional. In P. Utrilla Miranda (ed.), *Aragón/Litoral Mediterráneo: Intercambios culturales durante la Prehistoria.* Zaragoza: Institución Fernando Il Catolico, pp. 269–84.

Garnes, K., and O. F. Bergersen. 1980. Wastage features of the inland ice sheet in central south Norway. *Boreas* 9: 251–69.

Gatsov, I., and M. Özdogan. 1994. Some Epi-Paleolithic sites from NW Turkey. Ağaçli, Domali and Gümüsdere. *Anatolica* 20: 97–120.

Gaustad, F. 1969. Stone age investigations in Northern Norway. *Norwegian Archaeological Review* 2: 86–93.

Geddes, D., Barbaza, M., Vaquer, J., and J. Guilaine. 1986. Tardiglacial and postglacial in the eastern Pyrenees and western Languedoc (France). In L. Straus (ed.), *The end of the Paleolithic in the Old World.* Oxford: British Archaeological Reports International Series 284, pp. 63–80.

Geddes, D., Guilaine, J., Coularou, J., Le Gall, O., and M. Martzluff. 1989. Postglacial environments, settlement and subsistence in the Pyrenees: The Balma Margineda, Andorra. In C. Bonsall (ed.), *The Mesolithic in Europe: Proceedings of the third international symposium*. Edinburgh: John Donald, pp. 561–71.

Gehlen, B. 1988. Steinzeitliche Funde im Östlichen Allgäu. In H. Küster (ed.), *Vom Werden einer Kulturlandschaft*. Munich: Acta Humaniora, pp. 195–209.

Gendel, P. A. 1984. *Mesolithic social territories in Northwestern Europe*. Oxford: British Archaeological Reports International Series 218.

Gendel, P. A. 1987. Socio-stylistic analysis of lithic artefacts from the Mesolithic of Northwestern Europe. In P. Rowley-Conwy, M. Zvelebil, and H. P. Blankholm (eds.), *Mesolithic Northwest Europe: Recent trends.* Sheffield: Department of Archaeology and Prehistory, University of Sheffield, pp. 65–73.

Gendel, P. A. 1989. The analysis of lithic styles through distributional profiles of variation, examples from the western European Mesolithic. In C. Bonsall (ed.), *The Mesolithic in Europe: Proceedings of the third international symposium.* Edinburgh: John Donald, pp. 40–7.

Gendel, P. A., Van de Heyning, H., and G. Gijselings. 1985. Helchteren-Sonnisse Heide 2, a Mesolithic site in the Limburg Kempen (Belgium). *Helinium* 25: 2–22.

Geppert, P. 1992. Hundeschlachtungen in Deutschland im 19. und 20. Jahrhundert under besonderer Berücksichtigung der Verhältnisse in München. *Berliner und Münchener Tierarztliche Wochenschrift* 105 (10): 335–42.

Gersbach, E. 1951. Das Mittelbadische Mesolithikum. *Badische Fundberichte* 19: 1–17.

Gersbach, E. 1968. Urgeschichte des Hochrheins. *Badische Fundberichte,* Sonderheft 11.

Giddens, A. 1984. *The constitution of society*. Berkeley and Los Angeles: University of California Press.

Gietz, F.-J. 1998. Das Mesolithikum in der Burghöhle Dietfurt an der Oberen Donau. In N. Conard (ed.), *Aktuelle Forschungen zum Mesolithikum/Current Mesolithic Research*. Tübingen: Mo Vince Verlag, pp. 237–50.

Gillespie, R., Gowlett, J. A. J., Hall, E. T., Hedges, R. E. M., and C. Perry. 1985. Radiocarbon dates from the Oxford AMS system. Archaeometry datelist 2. *Archaeometry* 27 (2): 237–46.

Gimbutas, M. 1991. *The civilization of the goddess*. San Francisco: Harper.

Girininkas, A. 1990. *Kretuonas: Middle and Late Neolithic*. Vilnius (in Russian).

Girininkas, A. 1998. The influence of the natural environment on the inhabitants of the shores around lake Kretuonas during the Holocene. In M. Kabailiene, D. Moe, U. Miller, and T. Hackens (eds.), *Environmental history and Quaternary stratigraphy of Lithuania*. Pact 54.

Gjerland, B. 1988. Stildrag ved vest-norske bergartsøkser. *Arkeologiske Skrifter, Historisk museum* 4: 214–24.

Gjerland, B. 1990a. Raw materials used in the production of stone adzes in western Norway. *Universitetets Oldsaksamlings Årbok* 1989/1990: 73–85.

Gjerland, B. 1990b. *Arkeologiske undersøkingar på Haugsneset og Ognøy i Tysvær og Bokn kommunar, Rogaland.* AmS-Rapport 5. Stavanger.

Gjessing, G. 1932. *Arktiske helleristninger i Nord-Norge*. Institutet for Sammenlignende Kulturforskning B, Oslo.

Gjessing, G. 1936. *Nordenfjeldske ristninger og malninger av den arktiske gruppe*. Institutet for Sammenlignende Kulturforskning B, 30. Oslo.

Gjessing, G. 1937. Mellem Komsa og Fosna. Noen eldre stenaldersfunn fra Nordland. *Från stenålder til rokoko. Studier tilägnade Otto Rydbäck,* Lund: Gleerup. pp. 1–16.

Gjessing, G. 1943. *Træn-funnene*. Institutet for Sammenlignende Kulturforskning B, 41. Oslo.

Gjessing, G. 1944. *Circumpolar Stone Age*. Acta Arctica 2.

Gjessing, G. 1945. *Norges steinalder*. Norsk arkeologisk selskap. Oslo.

Gjessing, G. 1975. Maritime adaptations in northern Norway's prehistory. In W. Fitzhugh (ed.), *Prehistoric maritime adaptations of the circumpolar zone*. Paris: Mouton, pp. 87–100.

Gjessing, H. 1920. *Rogalands stenalder*. Stavanger: Stavanger Museum.

Gjærevoll, O. 1992. *Plantegeografi*. Trondheim: Tapir.

References

Gkiasta, M., Russell, T., Shennan, S., and J. Steele. 2003 Neolithic transition in Europe: The radiocarbon record re-visited. *Antiquity* 77 (295): 45–62

Glørstad, H. 1998a. Senmesolitikum i Østfold – et kronologisk perspektiv. In E. Østmo (ed.), Fra Østfolds oldtid. Foredrag ved 25-årsjubileet for universitetets arkeologiske stasjon Isegran. Universitetets Oldsaksamlings Skrifter Ny Rekke. 21. Oslo: Universitetets Oldsaksamling, pp. 69–82.

Glørstad, H. 1998b. En senmesolittisk boplass på Skavli i Borre kommune, Vestfold og dens plass i forhistorien. *Universitetets Oldsaksamlings Årbok 1997–1998*. pp. 63–82.

Glørstad, H. 1999. Lokaliteten Botne II – et nøkkelhull til det sosiale livet i mesolittikum i Sør-Norge. *Viking* 62: 31–68.

Glørstad, H. 2002. Østnorske skafthullhakker fra mesolitikum. Arkeologisk og forhistoriskt betydning – illustrert med et eksempelstudium fra vestsiden av Oslofjorden. *Viking* 65: 7–48.

Glørstad, H. (ed.). 2004. *Oppsummering av svinesundprosjektet.* Varia 57. Oslo: Universitetets kulturhistoriske museer.

Gob, A. 1981. *Le Mésolithique dans le Bassin de l'Ourthe.* Liège: Societé Walonne de Palethnologie Memoire No. 3.

Gob, A. 1985. Extension géographique et chronologique de la Culture Rhein-Meuse-Schelde (RMS). *Helinium* 25: 23–36.

Gokhman, I. I. 1966. *Naselenie Ukrainy v epohi mezolita i neolita [The population of the Ukraine of the Mesolithic and Neolithic epochs].* Moscow: Nauka.

Gokhman, I. I. 1986. Antropologicheskie osobennosti drevnego naselenija severa evropeiskoi chasti SSSR [Anthropological peculiarities of the ancient populations of the USSR's northern part]. In I. I. Gokhman and A. G. Kozinysev (eds.), *Antropologija sovremennogo i drevnego naselenija evropeiskoi chasti SSSR i puti ih formirovanija [Anthropology of contemporary and ancient populations of the USSR's European part].* Moscow: Nauka, pp. 216–22.

Goldhahn, J. 2002. Roaring rocks: An audio-visual perspective on hunter-gatherer engravings in northern Sweden and Scandinavia. *Norwegian Archaeological Review* 35 (1): 29–61.

Goldstein, L. 1981. One-dimensional archaeology and multi-dimensional people: Spatial organisation and mortuary analysis. In R. W. Chapman, I. A. Kinnes, and K. Randsborg (eds.), *The archaeology of death.* Cambridge, UK: Cambridge University Press, pp. 53–67.

Golovnev, A. V. 1984. From one to seven: Numerical symbolism in Khanty culture. *Arctic Anthropology* 31 (1): 6–271.

González Morales, M. 1982. *El Asturiense y otras culturas locales.* Monografías 7. Santander: Centro de Investigación y Museo de Altamira.

González Morales, M. 1989. Asturian resource exploitation. In C. Bonsall (ed.), *The Mesolithic of Europe: Proceedings of the third international symposium.* Edinburgh: John Donald, pp. 604–6.

González Morales, M. 1990. La prehistoria de las Marismas. *Cuadernos de Trasmiera* 2: 13–28.

González Morales, M. 1992. Mesolíticos y megalíticos. In A. Moure (ed.), *Elefantes, ciervos y ovicaprinos.* Santander: Universidad de Cantabria, pp. 185–202.

González Morales, M. 1995. La transición al Holoceno en la región Cantábrica. In V. Villaverde (ed.), *Los ultimos cazadores.* Alicante: Instituto de Cultura Juan Gil-Albert, pp. 63–78.

González Morales, M. 1996. Obermaier y el Asturiense. In A. Moure (ed.), *'El Hombre Fósil' 80 años después.* Santander: Universidad de Cantabria, pp. 371–89.

González Morales, M., and J. Arnaud. 1990. Recent research on the Mesolithic in the Iberian Peninsula. In P. Vermeersch and P. Van Peer (eds.), *Contributions to the Mesolithic in Europe.* Leuven: Leuven University Press, pp. 451–61.

González Morales, M., and L. Straus. 2000. La prehistoria del Valle del Asón: La Cueva del Mirón. In R. Ontañón (ed.), *Actuaciones Arqueológicas en Cantabria 1984–1999.* Santander: Gobierno de Cantabria, pp. 331–6.

González Morales, M., Straus, L., Diez, A., and J. Ruiz. 2004. Postglacial coast and inland: The Epipaleolithic-Mesolithic-Neolithic transitions in Vasco-Cantabrian Spain. *Munibe* 56: 61–78.

González Sainz, C. 1989. *El Magdaleniense Superior-Final en la región Cantábrica.* Santander: Tantín.

Goodenough, W. H. 1965. Rethinking 'status' and 'role': Toward a general model of the cultural organisation of social relationships. In M. Banton (ed.), *The relevance of models for social anthropology*. London: Tavistock, pp. 1–24.

Göransson, H. 1986. Man and the forests of nemoral broad-leaved trees during the Stone Age. In L.-K. Königsson (ed.), Nordic Late Quaternary biology and ecology. *Striae* 24: 143–52.

Gosden, C. 2004. Aesthetics, intelligence and emotions, implications for archaeology. In E. DeMarrais, C. Gosden, and C. Renfrew (eds.), *Rethinking materiality, the engagement of mind with the material world*. Cambridge, UK: McDonald Institute Monographs.

Götherstrom, A., Anderung, C., Hellborg, L., Elburg, R., Smith, C., Bradley, D. G., and H. Ellegren. 2005. Cattle domestication in the Near East was followed by hybridization with aurochs bulls in Europe. *Proceedings of the Royal Society: Biological Sciences* 272 (1579): 2345–50.

Gouraud, G. 1992. Le campement mésolithique des étangs de la Brenière à Montbert (Loire-Atlantique). *Revue Archéologique de l'Ouest* 9: 39–55.

Gouraud, G. 1996. *Le microlithisme de la Pierre Saint-Louis à Geay (Charente-Maritime) dans le cadre du mésolithique régional*. Mémoire de diplôme de DEA, Université Toulouse-Le Mirail/EHESS, dactylographiées.

Gourdin, W. H., and W. D. Kingery. 1975. The beginnings of pyrotechnology: Neolithic and Egyptian lime plaster. *Journal of Field Archaeology* 2: 133–50.

Gowlett, J. A. J., Hedges, R. E. M., Law, I. A., and C. Perry. 1986. Radiocarbon dates from the Oxford AMS system. Archaeometry datelist 4. *Archaeometry* 29 (1): 125–55.

Gowlett, J. A. J., Hedges, R. E. M., Law, I. A., and C. Perry. 1987. Radiocarbon dates from the Oxford AMS system. Archaeometry datelist 5. *Archaeometry* 28 (2): 206–21.

Gramsch, B. (ed.). 1981. *Mesolithikum in Europa*. 2. Internationales Symposium Potsdam, 3. bis 8. April 1978. Veröffentlichungen des Museums für Ur- und Frühgeschichte Potsdam, 14/15 (Berlin 1981). Berlin: Deutscher Verlag.

Gramsch, B., and K. Kloss. 1989. Excavations near Friesack: An early Mesolithic marshland site in the northern plain of central Europe. In C. Bonsall (ed.), *The Mesolithic in Europe: Proceedings of the third international symposium*. Edinburgh: John Donald, pp. 313–24.

Graziosi, P. 1947. Gli uomini paleolitici della Grotta di San Teodoro (Messina). *Rivista di Scienze Preistoriche* 2: 123–223.

Graziosi, P. 1962. *Levanzo: Pitture e incisioni*. Firenze: Sansoni.

Graziosi, P. (ed.). 1983. Actes du Colloque International 'La position taxonomique et chronologique des industries à pointes à dos autour de la Méditerranée Européenne'. *Rivista di Scienze Preistoriche* 28.

Green, S., and S. Perlman. 1985. *The archaeology of frontiers and boundaries*. New York: Academic Press.

Greenfield, H. 2008. Reanalysis of the vertebrate fauna from Hajdučka Vodenica in the Danubian Iron Gates of Yugoslavia: Subsistence and taphonomy from the Early Neolithic and Mesolithic. In C. Bonsall, V. Boroneanţ, and I. Radovanović (eds.), *The Iron Gates in prehistory: New perspectives*. Oxford: Archaeopress, pp. 205–26.

Grichuk, V. P. 1992. Main types of vegetation (ecosystems) during the maximum cooling of the Last Glaciation. In B. Frenzel, M. Pesci, and A. A. Velichko (eds.), *Atlas of paleoclimates and paleoenvironments of the Northern Hemisphere*. Stuttgart: Gustav Fischer, pp. 123–4.

Groenendijk, H. 1997. *Op zoek naar de horizon het landschap van Oost-Groningen en zijn bewoners tussen 8000 voor Chr. en 1000 na Chr.* Groningen: Regio-Project Uitgevers.

Groenewoudt, B. J., Deeben, J., Van Geel, B., and R. C. G. M. Lauwerier. 2001. An early Mesolithic assemblage with faunal remains in a stream valley near Zutphen, the Netherlands. *Archäologisches Korrespondenzblatt* 31: 1–20.

Gronenborn, D. 1990. Mesolithic-Neolithic interactions: The lithic industry of the earliest Bandkeramik culture site at Friedberg-Bruchenbrücken. In P. Vermeersch and P. Van Peer (eds.), *Contributions to the Mesolithic in Europe*. Leuven: Leuven University Press, pp. 173–82.

Gronenborn, D. 1994. Überlegungen zur Ausbreitung der Bäuerlichen Wirtschaft in Mitteleuropa: Versuch einer Kulturhistorischen Interpretation Ältestbandkeramischer Silexinventare. *Praehistorische Zeitschrift* 69: 135–51.

409

References

Gronenborn, D. 1997. Sarching 4 und der Übergang vom Früh- zum Spätmesolithikum im Südlichen Mitteleuropa. *Archäologisches Korrespondenzblatt* 27: 387–402.

Groupe d'Etude de l'Epipaléolithique-Mésolithique. 1969. Epipaléolithique-mésolithique, les microlithes géométriques. *Bulletin de la Société Préhistorique Française* 66: 355–66.

Groupe d'Etude de l'Epipaléolithique-Mésolithique. 1972. Epipaléolithique-mésolithique, les armatures non géométriques. *Bulletin de la Société Préhistorique Française* 69: 364–75.

Grünberg, J. 2000. *Mesolitische bestattungen in Europa: Ein beitrag zur vergleichenden gräberkunde. Auswertung und Katalog.* Rahden: Verlag Marie Leidorf.

Grupe, G., Mikić, Ž., Peters, J., and H. Manhart. 2003. Vertebrate food webs and subsistence strategies of Meso- and Neolithic populations of central Europe. In G. Grupe and J. Peters (eds.), *Decyphering ancient bones: The research potential of bioarchaeological collections.* Rahden: Leidorf, pp. 193–214.

Grydeland, S. E. 2005. The pioneer of Finnmark – from the earliest coastal settlement to the encounter with the inland people of Northern Finland. In H. Knutsson (ed.), *Pioneer settlements and colonization processes in the Barents region.* Vuollerim Papers on Hunter-Gatherer Archaeology, vol. 1, pp. 27–49.

Grøn, O., and O. Kuznetsov. 2003. Ethnoarchaeology among Evenkian forest hunters. Preliminary results and a different approach to reality. In L. Larsson, H. Kindgren, K. Knutsson, D. Loeffler, and A. Åkerlund (eds.), *Mesolithic on the Move: Papers presented at the Sixth International Conference on the Mesolithic in Europe, Stockholm 2000.* Oxford: Oxbow, pp. 216–22.

Grønnesby, G. 1998. Skandinaviske helleristninger og rituell bruk av transe. *Arkeologiske skrifter Universitetet i Bergen* 9: 59–82.

Guixé, E., Richards, M., and M. Subirá. 2006. Palaeodiets of humans and fauna at the Spanish Mesolithic site of El Collado. *Current Anthropology* 47 (3): 549–56.

Gumiński, W. 1998 The peat-bog site Dudka, Masurian Lakeland: An example of conservation economy. In M. Zvelebil, R. Dennell, and L. Domańska (eds.), *Harvesting the Sea, Farming the Forest.* Sheffield: Sheffield University Press, pp. 103–10.

Gumiński, W., and M. Michniewicz. 2003. forest and mobility. a case from the fishing camp site Dudka, Masuria, north-eastern Poland. In L. Larsson, H. Kindgren, K. Knutsson, D. Loeffler, and A. Åkerlund (eds.), *Mesolithic on the Move: Papers presented at the Sixth International Conference on the Mesolithic in Europe, Stockholm 2000.* Oxford: Oxbow, pp. 119–127.

Gundersen, S. M. 2009. Settlement patterns, landscape and society in western Norway during the Late Mesolithic. In S. McCartan, R. Schulting, G. Warren, and P. C. Woodman (eds.), *Mesolithic horizons. Papers presented at the Seventh International Conference on the Mesolithic in Europe, Belfast 2005.* Oxford: Oxbow Books, pp. 235–42.

Gurina, N. N. 1956. *Oleneostrovskii mogil'nik [The Olenii Ostrov cemetery]. Materialy i Issledovaniya po arheologii SSSR [Materials and investigations on archaeology of the USSR]*, 47. Moscow-Leningrad: Nauka.

Gurina, N. N. (ed.). 1966. *Sources of ancient culture (Mesolithic epoch).* Materialy i Issledovaniya po Arkheologii SSSR 126 (in Russian).

Gurina, N. N. 1989. Mezolit Litvy I Belorussii [The Mesolithic of Lithuania and Byelorussia]. In L. V. Kol'tsov (ed.), *Mezolit SSSR – Arheologiya SSSR [Mesolithic of the USSR – Archaeology of the USSR]* Moscow: Nauka, pp. 55–62.

Gusinde, M. 1986. *The Yámana: The life and thought of the Water Nomads of Cape Horn*, 5 vols. Buenos Aires: Argentina. Centro Argentino de Etnologia Americana.

Gustafson, L. 1986. Norges eldste treskrud, fra Oppdal. *Spor* 1986(2): 34. Trondheim.

Gustafson, L. 1987. Innerdalen gjennom 8000 år. Oversikt over de arkeologiske undersøkelsene. In Aa. Paus, O. E. Jevne, and L. Gustafson. *Kulturhistoriske undersøkelser i Innerdalen, Kvikne, Hedemark.* Rapport Arkeologiske serie 1987 (1). Vitenskapsmuseet, Universitetet i Trondheim, pp. 91–151.

Gustafson, L. 1988. Fjellpionerene. *Arkeologiske Skrifter, Historisk museum* 4. Bergen.

Gustafson, L. 1990. Bukkhammeren, en beverfangstplass i Innerdalen, Kvikne. *Viking* 53: 21–50.

Gustafson, L. 1999. Stunner – the first early mesolithic site in Eastern Norway. In J. Boaz (ed.), *The Mesolithic of Central Scandinavia.* Universitetets Oldsaksamlings Skrifter. Ny Rekke 22. Oslo: Universitetets Oldsaksamling, pp. 181–8.

410

Gustavsson, K. 1997. *Otterböte: New light on a Bronze Age site in the Baltic*. Stockholm: Ekenäs Tryckeri AB.

Gutierrez Zugasti, F. I. 2009. La Explotación de Moluscos y otros Recursos Litorales en la Región Cantábrica durante el Pleistoceno Final y Holoceno Inicial. Doctoral dissertation, Universidad de Cantabria, Santander.

Haak, W., Forster, P., Bramanti, B., Matsumura, S., Brandt, G., Tänzer, M., Villems, R., Renfrew, C., Gronenborn, D., Werner Alt, K., and J. Burger. 2005. *Ancient DNA from the First European Farmers in 7500-year old Neolithic Sites*. *Science* 310 (November 2005): 1016–18.

Haak, W., et al. 2005. Ancient DNA from the first European farmers in 7500-year-old Neolithic sites. *Science* 310: 1016–18.

Haak, W., et al. 2008. Ancient DNA, Strontium isotopes, and osteological analyses shed light on social and kinship organisation of the Later Stone Age. *Proceedings of the National Academy of Sciences* 105 (47): 18226–31.

Haas, J. 1996. Pollen and plant macrofossil evidence of vegetation change of Wallisellen-Langachermoos (Switzerland) during the Mesolithic-Neolithic transition 8500 to 6500 years ago. *Dissertationes Botanicae* 267: 1–67. Stuttgart.

Habu, J. 2004. *Ancient Jomon Japan*. Cambridge, UK: Cambridge University Press.

Hafsten, U. 1983. Shore-level changes in South Norway during the last 13 000 years, traced by biostratigraphical methods and radiometric datings. *Norsk geografisk Tidsskrift* 37: 63–79.

Hagen, A. 1946. Fra innlandets steinalder: Hedemark fylke. *Viking* 10: 1–93.

Hagen, A. 1963a. Mesolittiske jegergrupper i norske høyfjell. Synsmåter om Fosna-kulturens innvandring til Vest-Norge. *Universitetets Oldsaksamlings Årbok 1960–61*. Oslo. Høyfjellsundersøkelsene.

Hagen, A. 1963b. Problemkompleks Fosna. Opphav – kontakt med kontinentale grupper – forholdet til Komsa. Boplatsproblem vid Kattagatt och Skagerack. *Studier i Nordisk Arkeologi* 5: 53–9.

Hagen, A. 1969. *Studier i vestnorsk bergkunst. Ausevik i Flora*. Årbok for Universitetet i Bergen Humanistisk Serie 3. Bergen.

Hagen, A. 1976. *Bergkunst*. Oslo: Cappelen.

Hagen, A. 1979. Arkeologene og 14C metoden. In R. Nydal, S. Westin, U. Hafsten, and S. Gulliksen (eds.), *Fortiden i søkelyset. Datering med 14C metoden gjennom 25 år*. Trondheim: Laboratoriet for Radiologisk Datering, pp. 93–101.

Hagen, A., and I. Martens. 1961. *Arkeologiske undersøkelser langs elv og vann*. Oslo: Norske Oldfunn X, Universitetets Oldsaksamling.

Hahn, J. 1983. Die Frühe Mittelsteinzeit. In H. Müller-Beck (ed.), *Urgeschichte in Baden–Württemberg*. Stuttgart: Konrad Theiss Verlag, pp. 363–92.

Hahn, J. 1984. *Die Steinzeitliche Besiedlung des Eselburger Tales bei Heidenheim*. Stuttgart: Konrad Theiss Verlag.

Hahn, J. 1998. Opportunistic patterns of lithic reduction at the Mesolithic site of Rottenburg-Siebenlinden I. In N. Conard (ed.), *Aktuelle Forschungen zum Mesolithikum/Current Mesolithic Research*. Tübingen: Mo Vince Verlag, pp. 251–6.

Hahn, J., and A. Scheer. 1983. Das Helga-Abri am Hohlenfelsen bei Schelklingen: Eine Mesolithische und Jungpaläolithische Schichtenfolge. *Archäologische Korrespondenzblatt* 13: 19–28.

Hahn, J., and C.-J. Kind. 1991. Neue Mesolithische Fundstellen in Rottenburg a. N., Kreis Tübingen. *Archaeologische Ausgrabungen in Baden-Württemberg* 1990: 26–9.

Hahn, J., and C.-J. Kind. 1992. Sondierungen im Bereich der Fundstelle Rottenburg-Siebenlinden III, Kreis Tübingen. *Archäologische Ausgrabungen in Baden-Württemberg* 1991: 38–40.

Hahn, J., Kind, C.-J., and K. Steppan. 1993. Mesolithische Rentierjäger in Südwestdeutschland? Der Mittelsteinzeitliche Freilandfundplatz Rottenburg 'Siebenlinden I' (Vorbericht). *Fundberichte aus Baden-Württemberg* 18: 29–52.

Hald, M., and R. Aspeli. 1997. Rapid climatic shifts in the northern Norwegian Sea during the last deglaciation and the Holocene. *Boreas* 26: 15–28.

Halén, O. 1994. *Sedentariness during the Stone Age of northern Sweden*. Stockholm: Gotab.

Hallström, G. 1938. *Monumental art of Northern Europe from the Stone Age. I. The Norwegian localities*. Stockholm: Bokförlaget Aktiebolaget Thule.

Hällström, G. 1960. *Monumental art of northern Sweden from the Stone Age*. Stockholm: Almquist and Wiksell.

References

Halstead, P. 1996. The development of agriculture and pastoralism in Greece: When, how, who and what? In D. Harris (ed.), *The origins and spread of agriculture and pastoralism in Eurasia*. London: UCL Press, pp. 296–309.

Hansen, A. M. 1904. *Landnåm i Norge. En udsigt over bosætningens historie*. Kristiania: Fabritius.

Hansen, J. 1992. Franchthi cave and the beginnings of agriculture in Greece and the Aegean. In P. Anderson (ed.), *Préhistoire de l'agriculture: Nouvelles approches experimentales et ethnographiques*. Paris: CNRS, pp. 231–47.

Harbitz, C. B. 1992. Model simulation of tsumanis generated by the Storegga Slides. *Marine Geology* 105: 1–21.

Hardy, B. 1999. Preliminary results of residue analysis of stone tools from the Mesolithic sites, Northern Bohemia, Czech Republic. *Archeologické rozhledy* 51: 274–9.

Hardy, K., and C. Wickham-Jones. 2002. Scotland's first settlers: The Mesolithic seascape of the Inner Sound, Skye and its contribution to the early prehistory of Scotland. *Antiquity* 76: 825–33

Harris, D. R. (ed.). 1996. *The origins and spread of agriculture and pastoralism in Eurasia*. London: UCL Press.

Hartz, S. 1991. Hochatlantische Besiedlung in Schleswig-Holstein ein Beispiel. *Offa* 48: 115–32.

Haswell-Smith, H. 2000. *An island Odyssey: Among the Scottish Isles in the wake of Martin Martin*. Edinburgh: Canongate.

Hauglid, M. 1993. Mellom Fosna og Komsa. En preboreal "avslagsredskapskultur" i Salten, Nordland. Unpublished thesis, University of Tromsø.

Haukalid, S. 1999. Menneskets bilde. En studie av 10 veideristinger i Øst-Norge. Unpublished thesis, University of Oslo.

Havas, H. 1999. Innland uten grenser. Bosetningsmodeller i det nordligste Finland og Norge i perioden 9000–6000 BP. Unpublished thesis, University of Tromsø.

Hayden, B. 1990. Nimrods, piscators, pluckers, and planters: The emergence of food production. *Journal of Anthropological Archaeology* 9: 31–69.

Hayden, B. 2003. *Shamans, sorcerers and saints*. Washington, DC: Smithsonian Books.

Healey, F., Heaton, M., and S. J. Lobb. 1992. Excavations at the Mesolithic site at Thatcham, Berkshire. *Proceedings of the Prehistoric Society* 58: 41–76.

Hedges, R. E. M. 2004. Isotopes and red herrings: Comments on Milner et al. and Lidén et al. *Antiquity* 78: 34–7.

Hedges, R. E. M., Housley, R. A., Law, I. A., Perry, C., and J. A. J. Gowlett. 1987. Radiocarbon dates from the Oxford AMS system. Archaeometry datelist 6. *Archaeometry* 29 (2): 289–306.

Hedges, R. E. M., Housley, R. A., Law, I. A., and C. R. Bronk Ramsey. 1989. Radiocarbon dates from the Oxford AMS system. Archaeometry datelist 9. *Archaeometry* 31: 207–34.

Hedges, R. E. M., Housley, R. A. Bronk Ramsey C. R., and C. J. van Klinken. 1990. Radiocarbon dates from the Oxford AMS System. Archaeometry datelist 11. *Archaeometry* 32 (2): 211–37.

Hedges, R. E. M., Housley, R. A., Bronk Ramsey, C. R., and G. J. van Klinken. 1994. Radiocarbon dates from the Oxford AMS system. Archaeometry datelist 18. *Archaeometry* 36 (2): 337–74.

Hedges, R. E. M., Housley, R. A., Bronk Ramsey, C. R., and C. J. van Klinken. 1995. Radiocarbon dates from the Oxford AMS System. Archaeometry datelist 19. *Archaeometry* 37(1): 195–214.

Hedges, R. E. M., Housley, R. A., Bronk Ramsey, C. R., and G. J. van Klinken. 1996. Radiocarbon dates from the Oxford AMS system. Archaeometry datelist 21. *Archaeometry* 38 (1): 181–207.

Hedges, R. E. M., Pettitt, R. B., Bronk Ramsey, C. R., and G. J. van Klinken. 1996. Archaeometry datelist 22. *Archaeometry* 38 (2): 391–415.

Heinrich, J, and F. J. Gil-White. 2001. The evolution of prestige. Freely conferred deference as a mechanism for enhancing the benefits of cultural transmission. *Evolution and Human Behaviour* 22: 165–96.

Heinrich, J., Boyd, B., Bowles, S., Camerer, C., Fehr, E., Gintis, H., and R. McElreath. 2001. In search of *Homo economicus*: Behavioural experiments in 15 small scale societies. *American Economic Review* 91 (2): 73–8.

Heizer, R. F. (ed.). 1978. *Handbook of North American Indians. Vol. 8, California*. Washington, DC: Smithsonian Institution.

Helms, M. 1988. *Ulysses sail*. Princeton, NJ: Princeton University Press.

Helskog, K. 1980a. Subsistence-economic adaptations to the mountain region of interior North Norway. Unpublished thesis, University of Wisconsin-Madison, USA.

Helskog, K. 1980b. The Chronology of the younger stone age in Varanger, North Norway, revisited. *Norwegian Archaeological Review* 13 (1): 47–60.

Helskog, K. 1984. Younger Stone Age Settlements in Varanger. *Acta Borealia* 1984(1): 39–69.

Helskog, K. 1985. Boats and meaning: A study of change and continuity in the Alta fjord, Arctic Norway, from 4200 to 500 years B.C. *Journal of Anthropological Archaeology* 4: 177–205.

Helskog, K. 1987. Selective depictions: Study of 3,500 years of rock carvings from Arctic Norway and their relationship to the Sami drums. In I. Hodder (ed.), *Archaeology as long term history*. Cambridge, UK: Cambridge University Press, pp. 17–30.

Helskog, K. 1995. Maleness and femaleness in the sky and the underworld – and in between. In K. Helskog and B. Olsen (eds.), *Perceiving rock-art: Social and political perspectives*. Olso: Novus Forlag, pp. 247–62.

Helskog, K. 1999. The shore connection: Cognitive landscape and communication with rock carvings in Northernmost Europe. *Norwegian Archaeological Review* 32 (2): 73–94.

Helskog, K., and B. Olsen (eds.). 1995. *Perceiving rock art: Social and political perspectives*. Oslo: Novus.

Helskog, K., Indrelid, S., and E. Mikkelsen. 1976. Morfologisk klassifisering av slåtte steinartefakter. *Universitetets Oldsaksamlings Årbok 1972/1974*: 9–52.

Hemdorff, O. 2001. De første fangstfolk på Hundvåg – 10. 500 år gamle boplasser. *Fra Haug ok Heidni* 4: 10–22.

Hernández Pérez, M. 1992. Arte rupestre en la región central del Mediterráneo peninsula. In P. Utrilla Miranda (ed.), *Aragón/Litoral Mediterráneo: Intercambios culturales durante la Prehistoria*. Zaragoza: Institución Fernando Il Catolico, pp. 435–46.

Hernek, R. 2009. Soul-trips to the underworld? Interpretations of a decorated slate pickaxe from western Sweden. In S. B. McCartan, R. Schulting, G. Warren, and P. Woodman (eds.), *Mesolithic horizons. Papers presented at the Seventh International Conference on the Mesolithic in Europe, Belfast 2005*. Oxford: Oxbow Books, pp. 621–6.

Hesjedal, A. 1994. The hunters' rock art in northern Norway: Problems of chronology and interpretation. *Norwegian Archaeology Review* 27 (1): 1–14.

Hesjedal, A., and A. R. Niemi (eds.). 2003. *Melkøya: Dokumentasjon av mennesker og miljø gjennom 10 000 år*. Ottar 248. Tromsø: Tromsø Museum.

Hesjedal, A., Damm, C., Olsen, B., and B. Storli. 1996. *Arkeologi på Slettnes. Dokumentasjon av 11.000 års bosetning*. Tromsø museums Skrifter 26. Tromsø 1996.

Hinout, B. 1998. Essai de synthèse à propos de l'art schématique mésolithique dans les massifs gréseux du Bassin parisien. *Bulletin de la Société Préhistorique Française* 95: 505–23.

Hiscott R. N., Aksu, A. E., Mudie, P. J. et al. 2005. High resolution records show continuous sedimentation at 69 m water depth on SW Black Sea shelf. In *Black Sea – Mediterranean Corridor during the last 30 ky, sea level change and human adaptations*. Abstracts of the 1st Plenary Meeting. Istanbul, pp. 67–70.

Hjelle, K. L., Hufthammer, A. K., Kaland, P. E., Olsen, A. B., and E. C. Soltvedt. 1992 (eds.). *Kotedalen – en boplass gjennom 5000 år. Bind 2: Naturvitenskapelige undersøkelser*. Bergen: Historisk museum, Universitetet i Bergen.

Hodder, I. 1980. Social structure and cemeteries: A critical appraisal. In P. Rahtz, T. Dickinson, and L. Watts (eds.), *Anglo-Saxon cemeteries, 1979: The fourth Anglo-Saxon symposium at Oxford*. Oxford: British Archaeological Reports 82: 161–9.

Hodder, I. 1990. *The domestication of Europe*. Oxford: Blackwell.

Holliman, S. E. 2001. The gendered peopling of North America: Addressing the antiquity of systems of multiple genders. In N. Price (ed.), *The archaeology of shamanism*. London: Routledge, pp. 123–34.

Holm, J., and F. Rieck. 1983. Jels I – the First Danish Site of the Hamburgian Culture: A Preliminary Report. *Journal of Danish Archaeology* 2: 7–11.

Holm, L. 1985. Variations in flake material: Different utilization of stone material. *Archaeology and Environment* 4: 303–11.

413

References

Holm, L. 1991. *The use of stone and hunting of reindeer: A study of stone tool manufacture and hunting of large mammals in the central Scandes c. 6000–1BC.* University of Umeå.

Holm, L. 1992. *The use of stone and hunting of reindeer.* Umeå: University of Umeå, Department of Archaeology.

Holm, L. 1994. Stone artefacts as transmitters of social information: Towards a wider interpretation with a north Swedish example. *Current Swedish Archaeology* 1994: 151–8.

Hood, B. 1988. Sacred pictures, sacred rocks: Ideological and social space in the North Norwegian Stone Age. *Norwegian Archaeological Revew* 21 (2): 65–84.

Hood, B. C. 1992. *Prehistoric foragers of the North Atlantic: Perspectives on lithic procurement and social complexity in the north Norwegian Stone Age and the Labrador maritime archaic.* Unpublished Ph.D. dissertation. Michigan: University of Ann Arbor.

Hóppal, M. (ed.). 1984. *Shamanism in Eurasia.* Göttingham: Herodot.

Hóppal, M. 1996. Shamanism in a postmodern age. Folklore: An electronic journal of folklore. Available online at: <http://haldjas. folklore.ee/folklore/vol2/hoppal. htm> [Accessed 3 January, 2004].

Horáček, I. 1999. Fauna obratlovců z převisu Pod zubem (k. o. Česká Lípa). *Archeologické rozhledy* 51: 268.

Horáček, I., Ložek, V., Svoboda, J., and A. Šajnerová. 2002. Přírodní prostředí a osídlení krasu v pozdním paleolitu a mezolitu. In J. Svoboda (ed.), *Prehistorické jeskyně.* Brno: The Dolní Věstonice Studies 7, pp. 313–43.

Horden, P., and N. Purcell. 2000. *The corrupting sea.* Oxford: Blackwell.

Horváth, F., and E. Hertelendi. 1994. Contribution to the C14 based absolute chronology of the Early and Middle Neolithic Tisza region. *Jósa András Múzeum Évkönyve* 36: 111–33.

Housley, R. 1991. AMS dates from the Late Glacial and early Postglacial in north-west Europe: A review. In N. Barton, A. J. Roberts, and D. A. Roe (eds.), *The Late Glacial in north-west Europe: Human adaptation and environmental change at the end of the Pleistocene.* London: CBA Research Report 77, pp. 25–39.

Housley, R. A., Gamble, C. S., Street, M., and P. Pettitt. 1997. Radiocarbon evidence for the Lateglacial human recolonisation of northern Europe. *Proceedings of the Prehistoric Society,* 63: 25–54.

Hufthammer, A. K. 1992. De osteologiske undersøkelsene fra Kotedalen. In K. L. Hjelle, A. K. Hufthammer, P. E. Kaland, A. B. Olsen, and E. C. Soltvedt (eds.), *Kotedalen − en boplass gjennom 5000 år. Bind 2. Naturvitenskapelige undersøkelser, 9–64.* Bergen: Historisk Museum, University of Bergen.

Huiskes, B. 1988. Tietjerk-Lutse Geast I, a reconstruction of a Mesolithic site from an anthropological perspective. *Palaeohistoria* 30: 29–62.

Hulst, R. S., and A. D. Verlinde.1976. Geröllkeulen aus Overijssel und Gelderland. *Berichten van de Rijksdienst voor het Oudheidkundig Bodemonderzoek* 26: 93–126.

Hultkrantz, Å. 1965. Types of religion in the arctic hunting cultures: A religio-ecological approach. In H. Hvarfner (ed.), *Hunting and fishing.* Luleå: Norrbottens Museum, pp. 265–318.

Hultkrantz, Å. 1984. Shamanism and soul ideology. In M. Hoppál (ed.), *Shamanism in Eurasia.* Part I. Göttingen: Herodot.

Hultkrantz, Å. 1985. Reindeer nomadism and the religion of the Saamis. In L. Bäckman and A. Hulktkrantz (eds.), *Saami pre-Christian religion.* Studies in Comparative Religion 25. Stockholm, pp 11–28.

Hultkrantz, Å. 1986. Rock drawings as evidence of religion: Some principal points of view. In G. Steinsland (ed.), *Words and objects, towards a dialogue between archaeology and history of religion.* Oslo.

Hultkrantz, Å. 1989. The place of shamanism in the history of religions. In M. Hoppál and O. von Sadovsky (eds.), *Shamanism past and present.* Budapest and Los Angeles, pp. 43–52.

Hultkrantz, Å. 1990. The drum in shamanism: Some reflections. In N. G. Holm (ed.), *Scripta Instituti Donneriani Aboensis XIV.* Åbo.

Hultkrantz, Å. 1996. Ecological and phenomenological aspects of shamanism. In V. Diószegi and M. Hoppál (eds.), *Shamanism in Siberia.* Budapest: Akadémiai Kiadó, pp. 25–58.

Huntley, B. 1990. European vegetation history: Palaeovegetation maps from pollen data − 13000 yr BP to present. *Journal of Quaternary Science* 5 (2): 103–22.

Huntley, B., and H. Birks.1983. *An atlas of past and present pollen maps for Europe: 0–13000 years ago.* Cambridge, UK: Cambridge University Press.

Hvarfner, H. (ed.). 1965. *Hunting and fishing*. Luleå: Norrbottens Museum.

Hyvärinen, H. 2000. The history of the Baltic Sea. In P. Sandgren (ed.), *Environmental changes in Fennoscandia during the Late Quaternary*. LUNDQUA Report 37. Lund: Lund University, Department of Quaternary Geology, pp. 45–54.

Igegren, E. 1985. Osteological evaluation of reindeer bone finds from the territory of the southern Saamis. In L. Bäckman, and Å. Hultkrantz (eds.), *Saami pre-Christian religion*. Studies in Comparative Religion 25. Stockholm, pp. 101–13.

Indrelid, S. 1973a. *Hein 33. En steinalders boplass på Hardangervidda; forsøk på kronologisk og kulturell analyse*. Årbok for Universitetet i Bergen. Humanistisk serie 1972:1, Bergen.

Indrelid, S. 1973b. Mesolitiske tilpasningsformer i høyfjellet. *Stavanger Mus. Årbok* 1972: 5–27.

Indrelid, S. 1973c. En mesolittisk boplass i Dysvikja på Fjørtoft. *Arkeo* 1: 7–11.

Indrelid, S. 1975. Problems relating to the early Mesolithic settlement of southern Norway. *Norwegian Archaeological Review*, vol 8 (1): 1–18.

Indrelid, S. 1977. Eldre steinalder i sørnorske høyfjell. Boplasser, bosetningsmønstre og kulturformer. *Viking* 40 (1976): 129–46.

Indrelid, S. 1978. Mesolithic economy and settlement patterns in Norway. In P. A. Mellars (ed.), *The early postglacial settlement of northern Europe*. London: Duckworth, pp. 147–77.

Indrelid, S. 1989. Dei fyrste menneskja på Vestlandet. *Naturen* 1989(1): 26–35.

Indrelid, S. 1994. *Fangstfolk og bønder i fjellet – bidrag til Hardangerviddas førhistorie 8500–2500 år før nåtid*. Oslo: Universitetets Oldsaksamlings Skrifter. Ny Rekke 17. Oslo: Universitetets Oldsaksamling.

Ingold, T. 1986. *The appropriation of nature*. Manchester: Manchester University Press.

Ingold, T. 1988. Notes on the foraging mode of production. In T. Ingold, D. Riches, and J. Woodburn (eds.), *Hunters and gatherers*. Oxford: Berg, pp. 269–85.

Ingold, T. 1996. Hunting and gathering as ways of perceiving the environment. In R. Ellen, and K. Fukni (eds.), *Redefining nature: Ecology, culture and domestication*. Oxford: Berg.

Innostrantsev, A. A. 1882. *Doistoricheskii Chelovek Kamennogo Veka Proberezhia Ladozhskogo Ozera*. St Petersburg.

Iriarte, M. J., Arrizabalaga, A., Etxeberria, F., and L. Herrasti. 2005. La inhumación humana en conchero de J3 (Hondarribia, Guipuzkoa). In P. Arias, R. Ontañón, and C. García-Muncó (eds.), *Actas del III Congreso del Neolítico en la Península Ibérica*. Santander: Universidad de Cantabria, pp. 607–13.

Isarin, R. F. B., and S. J. P. Bohnke. 1999. Mean July temperatures during the Younger Dryas in North-western and Central Europe as inferred from climate indicator plant species. *Quaternary Research* 51: 158–73.

Ivaniščev, A. M. 1992. Jantarnie ukrašenija mogilnika *Tudozero* VI v Obonežje. Novgorod: Novgorod I novgorodskaja zemlja, pp. 86–89.

Ivaniščev, A. M. 1996. Poselenije I mogilnik na *Tudozere* II. Vologda: Drevnosti russkogo severa 1: 75–84.

Ives, J. W. 1990. *A theory of northern Athapaskan prehistory*. Calgary: University of Calgary Press.

Izagirre, N., and C. de la Rua. 1999. A mtDNA analysis in ancient Basque populations: Implications for haplogroup V as a marker for a major Palaeolithic expansion from Southwestern Europe. *American Journal of Human Genetics* 65: 199–207.

Jaanits, K. 1995. Two Late Mesolithic/Early Neolithic coastal sites of seal hunters in Estonia. In A. Fischer (ed.), *Man and sea in the Mesolithic*. Oxford: Oxbow Monograph 53, pp. 247–9.

Jaanits, L. 1957. Neue gauf dem spätneolithischen wohnplatz Tamula in Estland. *Suomen muinaismuistoyhdistyksen aikakauskirja*. Helsinki. *Finska Fornminnes för eningens tidskrift* 58: 80–100.

Jaanits, L. 1959. *Poselenie Epokhi Neolita I Rannego Metala v Priustye Reky Emaigi*. Tallinn, Estonskoi, SSSR: Akademiya Nauk.

Jaanits, L. 1966. Novye danye po mesolitu Estonii. *MIA* 126.

Jaanits, L. 1971. Über die estnischen bootaxte von Karlova typus. *Finskt Museum* 78: 46–76.

Jaanits, L. 1975. Frühmesolitische siedlung in Pulli. In IAN-ESSR. *Ob. Nauki* 24 (2) 64–70.

Jaanits, L. 1984. Die kennzeichende züge der siedlung Tamula. *Iskos* 4: 183–93.

Jackes, M., and D. Lubell. 1999. Human skeletal biology and the Mesolithic-Neolithic transition in Portugal. In A. Thévenin and P. Bintz (eds.), *L'Europe des derniers chasseurs: Épipaléolithique et Mésolithique, Actes du*

References

5e *colloque international UISPP, commission XII, Grenoble, 18–23 septembre 1995.* Paris: Comité des Travaux Historiques et Scientifiques, pp. 59–64.

Jackes, M., D. Lubell, and C. Meiklejohn. 1997. On physical anthropological aspects of the Mesolithic-Neolithic transition in the Iberian peninsula. *Current Anthropology* 38: 839–46.

Jacobi, R. M. 1976. Britain inside and outside Mesolithic Europe. *Proceedings of the Prehistoric Society* 42: 67–84.

Jacobs, K. 1994. Human dento-gnathic metric variation in Mesolithic/Neolithic Ukraine: Possible evidence of demic diffusion in the Dnieper Rapids region. *American Journal of Physical Anthropology* 95: 1–26.

Jacobs, K. 1995. Return to Olenii Ostrov: Social, economic and skeletal dimensions of a boreal forest Mesolithic cemetery. *Journal of Anthropological Archaeology* 14: 359–403.

Jacobsen, T. 1976. 17,000 years of Greek prehistory. *Scientific American* 234: 76–87.

Jacobsen, T., and W. Farrand. 1987. *Franchthi cave and Paralia: Maps, plans, and sections.* Excavations at Franchthi Cave, Greece, Fascicle 1. Bloomington: Indiana University Press.

Jaksland, L. 2001a. *Vinterbrolokalitetene – en kronologisk sekvens fra mellom- og senmesolitikum i Ås, Akershus.* Varia 52. Oslo: Universitetets kulturhistoriske museer.

Jaksland, L. 2001b. Kjøkkenmøddingen på Skoklefald. *Nicolay* 84: 4–23.

Jaksland, L. 2002. Berget 1 – En senmesolittisk boplass med hyttetuft. In H. Glørstad (ed.), Svinesundprosjektet. Bind 1. *Varia* 54: 35–72. Oslo: Universitetets kulturhistoriske museer.

Jaksland, L. 2003. Torpum 13 – en senmesolittisk lokalitet med hyttetuft. In H. Glørstad (ed.), Svinesundprosjektet. Bind 2. *Varia* 55: 239–76. Oslo: Universitetets kulturhistoriske museer.

Janik, L. 1998. The appearance of food procuring societies in the southeastern Baltic sea region. In M. Zvelebil, R. Dennell, and L. Domańska (eds.), *Harvesting the sea, farming the forest.* Sheffield: Sheffield University Press, pp. 237–44.

Janik, L. 2005. Redefining social relations – tradition, complementarity and internal tension. In N. Milner and P. Woodman (eds.), *Mesolithic studies at the beginning of the 21st century.* Oxford: Oxbow Books, 176–93.

Jankovská, V. 1992. Vegetationsverhältnisse und Naturumwelt des Beckens Jestřebská kotlina am Ende des Spätglazials und im Holozän (Doksy-Gebiet). *Folia Geobotanica et Phytotaxonomica* 27: 137–48.

Jankovská, V. 2000. Komořanské jezero lake (CZ, NW Bohemia) – A unique natural archive. In *Upper Pleistocene and Holocene climatic variations. Proceedings of the International Conference on Past Global Changes.* Prague: Institute of Geology AS CR. GeoLines 11, pp. 115–7.

Jelgersma, S. 1979. Sea-level changes in the North Sea basin. In E. Oele, R. T. E. Schüttenhelm, and A. J. Wiggers (eds.), *The Quaternary History of the North Sea.* Uppsala: Acta Univeritatis Upsaliensis Annum Quingentesimum Celebrantis 2, pp. 233–48.

Jelsma, J. 2000. *A bed of ochre: Mortuary practices and social structure of a maritime archaic Indian society at Port Au Choix, Newfoundland.* Groningen: Rijksuniversiteit Groningen.

Jennbert, K. 1984. *Den produktive gåvan: Tradition och innovation i sydskandinavien för omkring 5300 år sedan.* Acta Archaeologica Lundensia, Series 4, 16.

Jensen, J. 1982. *The Prehistory of Denmark.* London: Methuen.

Jeunesse, C. 1997. *Pratiques funéraires au Néolithique ancien. Sépultures et nécropoles danubiennes 5500–4900 av. J.-C.* Paris: Editions Errance.

Jochim, M. A. 1976. *Hunter-gatherer subsistence and settlement, a predictive model.* New York: Academic Press.

Jochim, M. 1990. The late Mesolithic in Southwest Germany: Culture change or population decline? In P. Vermeersch and P. Van Peer (eds.), *Contributions to the Mesolithic in Europe.* Leuven: Leuven University Press, pp. 183–92.

Jochim, M. 1991. Archaeology as long-term ethnography. *American Anthropologist* 93: 308–21.

Jochim, M. 1993. *Henauhof NW: Ein Mittelsteinzeitlicher Lagerplatz am Federsee.* Materialhefte zur Vor- und Frühgeschichte 19, Landesdenkmalamt Baden–Württemberg. Stuttgart: Konrad Theiss Verlag.

Jochim, M. 1995. Two late Palaeolithic sites on the Federsee, South Germany. *Journal of Field Archaeology* 22: 263–73.

Jochim, M. 1998. *A hunter-gatherer landscape: Southwest Germany in the Late Paleolithic and Mesolithic.* New York: Plenum Publishing Corporation.

Jochim, M. 2000. The origins of agriculture in south-central Europe. In T. D. Price (ed.), *Europe's First Farmers*. Cambridge, UK: Cambridge University Press, pp. 183–96.

Jochim, M., Glass, M., Fisher, L., and P. McCartney. 1998. Mapping the Stone Age: An interim report on the South German Survey Project. In N. Conard (ed.), *Aktuelle Forschungen zum Mesolithikum/Current Mesolithic Research*. Urgeschichtliche Materialhefte 12. Tübingen: Mo Vince Verlag, pp. 121–32.

Johansen, A. B. 1970. *Høyfjellsfunn i Lærdalsfjella I*. Oslo: Universitetsforlaget.

Johansen, A. B. 1971. Prehistoric sites in the Lærdal basin: A theoretical and practical approach to the archaeological analysis of non-tool lithic material. Comments by C. Cullberg, S. Indrelid, K. Odner, P. Simonsen, and S. Welinder. *Norwegian Archaeological Review* 4 (2): 36–64.

Johansen, A. B. 1973. The Hardangervidda project for interdisciplinary research: A presentation. *Norwegian Archaeological Review* 6 (2): 60–6.

Johansen, A. B. 1975. *Forholdet mellom teori og data i arkeologi og andre erfaringsvitenskaper*. Arkeologiske skrifter No 1 – 1974. Bergen: Historisk museum, Universitetet i Bergen.

Johansen, A. B. 1978. *Høyfjellsfunn i Lærdalsfjella II*. Oslo: Universitetsforlaget.

Johansen, A. B., and I. Undås. 1992. Er Blomvågmaterialet et boplassfunn. *Viking* 55: 9–26.

Johansen, E. 1964. Høgnipenfunnene. Et nytt blad av norges eldste innvandringshistorie. *Viking* 27: 177–9.

Johansen, K. 1990. En teknologisk og kronologisk analyse av tidligmesolittiske steinartefakter. Unpublished thesis, University of Oslo.

Johansen, O. S. 1972. Nordiske petroglyfer, terminiologi, kronologi, kontaktpunkter utenfor Norden. *Universitetets Oldsaksamlings Årbok* 1969: 220–34. Oslo.

Johansson, A. D. 2006. Maglemosekulturens fiskepladser i Køng Mose og Barmose, Sydsjælland. In B. V. Eriksen (ed.), *Stenalderstudier. Tidlig mesolitiske jægere og samlere i Sydskandinavien*. Århus: Aarhus University Press, pp. 119–34.

Johnson, G. 1982. Organisational structure and scalar stress. In C. Renfrew, M. Rowlands, and B. Seagraves (eds.), *Theory and explanation in Archaeology*. New York: Academic Press, pp. 389–421.

Jonsson, L. 1986. From wild boar to domestic pig – a reassessment of Neolithic swine of northwestern Europe. In L.-K. Königsson (ed.), *Nordic Late Quaternary Biology and Ecology, Striae* 24: 125–9.

Jonsson, L. 1995. Vertebrate fauna during the Mesolithic on the Swedish west coast. In A. Fischer (ed.), *Man and sea in the Mesolithic*. Oxford: Oxbow Monograph 53, pp. 147–60.

Jordan, P., and M. Zvelebil (eds.). 2009. *Ceramics before farming. The dispersal of pottery among prehistoric Eurasian hunter-gatherers*. Walnut Creek, CA: Left Coast Press.

Jordan, P. D. 2001. The materiality of shamanism as a 'world-view': Praxis, artefacts and landscape. In N. Price (ed.), *The archaeology of shamanism*. London: Routledge, pp. 87–104.

Jordan, P. D. 2003a. Investigating postglacial hunter-gatherer landscape enculturation: Ethnographic analogy and interpretative methodologies. In L. Larsson, H. Kindgren, K. Knutsson, D. Loeffler, and A. Åkerlund (eds.), *Mesolithic on the Move: Papers presented at the Sixth International Conference on the Mesolithic in Europe, Stockholm 2000*. Oxford: Oxbow, pp. 128–38.

Jordan, P. D. 2003b. *Material culture and sacred landscape: The anthropology of the Siberian Khanty*. Walnut Creek, CA: AltaMira Press.

Jordan, P. D. 2006. Analogy. In C. Conneller and G. Warren (eds.), *Mesolithic Britain and Ireland*. Stroud: Tempus, pp. 83–100.

Jovanović, B. 1967. Nekropola starijeg gvozdenog doba u Hajdučkoj Vodenici. *Starinar* 18: 181–92.

Jovanović, B. 1969a. Chronological frames of the Iron Gate Group of the Early Neolithic Period. *Archaeologica Iugoslavica* 10: 23–38.

Jovanović, B. 1969b. Hajdučka Vodenica – naselje i nekropola starijeg gvozdenog doba. *Arheološki pregled* 11: 92–7.

Jovanović, B. 1984. Hajdučka Vodenica, praistorijska nekropola. *Starinar* 33–4 (1982–1983): 305–13.

Joyce, R. A, Preucel, R. W., Lopiparo, J., Guyer, C., and M. Joyce. 2002. *The languages of archaeology: Dialogue, narrative and writing*. Oxford and Malden, MA: Blackwell.

Juel Jensen, H. 1988. Functional analysis of prehistoric flint tools by high-power microscopy: A review of west European research. *Journal of World Prehistory* 2(1): 53–88.

References

Juel Jensen, H. J. 1994. *Flint tools and plant working: Hidden traces of stone age technology*. Århus: Aarhus University Press.

Juhl, K. 2001: *Austbø på Hundvåg gennem 10 000 år. Arkæologiske undersøgelser i Stavanger kommune 1987–1990, Rogaland, Syd-Vest Norge*. AmS-Varia 38. Stavanger: Arkeologisk museum i Stavanger.

Julien, M. 1988. Organisation de l'espace et fonction des habitats du Magdalénien du Bassin-Parisien. In M. Otte (ed.), *De la Loire à l'Oder: Les civilisations du Paléolithique final dans le nord-ouest européen*. Actes du colloque de Liège, 1985. British Archaeological Reports International Series 444 (i), vol. 1, pp. 84–124.

Julku, K. 1997. Eurooppa – suomalais-ugrilaisten ja Indoeurooppalaisten pelikentta (Europe – an arena for Finno-Ugric and Indoeuropean interaction). In K. Julku (ed.), *Itamerensuomi-eurooppalainen Maa*. Oulu, Studia Historica Fenno-Ugrica 2, Societas Historiae Fenno-Ugricae, pp. 249–75.

Julku, K. (ed.). 2002. *The roots of peoples and languages of northern Eurasia IV*. Oulu, Societas Historiae Fenno-Ugricae.

Julku, K., and K. Wiik. 1998. *The roots of peoples and languages of northern Eurasia I*. Societas Historiae Fenno-Ugricae.

Jussila, T., and H. Matiskainen. 2003. Mesolithic settlement during the Preboreal in Finland. In L. Larsson, H. Kindgren, K. Knutsson, D. Loeffler, and A. Åkerlund (eds.), *Mesolithic on the move: Papers presented at the Sixth International Conference on the Mesolithic in Europe, Stockholm 2000*. Oxford: Oxbow Books, pp. 664–70.

Kaland, P. E. 1984. Holocene shore displacement and shorelines in Hordaland, Western Norway. *Boreas* 13 (2): 202–42.

Kaland, P. E., and K. Krzywinski. 1978. Hasselens innvandring. *Arkeo* 1978. Historisk museum, Universitetet i Bergen.

Karjalainen, K. F. 1921, 1922, 1927. *Die religion der Jugra-völker*. Vols. 1–3. Helsinki and Porvoo: Suomalainen tiedeakatemia, Finnish Academy of Sciences, Folklore Fellows Communications.

Karjalainen, T. 1996. Pithouse in Outokumpu Sätös excavated in 1992–1994. In T. Kirkinen (ed.), Pithouses and potmakers in eastern Finland. Reports of the Ancient Lake Saimaa project. *Helsinki Papers in Archaeology* 9: 71–88.

Karjalainen, T. 1999. Sedentariness and dating Stone Age Houses and sites. In M. Huurrei (ed.), *Dig it all. Papers dedicated to Ari Siiriäinen*. Helsinki: The Finnish Antiquarian Society and The Archaeological Society of Finland, pp. 185–190.

Karle, I. 1998. Bochingen I – Eine Freilandfundstelle aus dem Frühmesolithikum Süddeutschlands. In N. Conard (ed.), *Aktuelle Forschungen zum Mesolithikum/Current Mesolithic Research*. Tübingen: Mo Vince Verlag, pp. 229–36.

Karsten, K., and B. Knarrström. 1999. Tågerup: Tvåtusen år av mesolitisk bosätning I sydvästra Skåne. In G. Burenhult (ed.), *Arkeologi i norden. natur og kultur 1*. Stockholm: Natur og Kultur, pp. 202–5.

Karsten, P., and B. Knarrström. 2001. Tågerup – fifteen hundred years of Mesolithic occupation in western Scania, Sweden: A preliminary view. *European Journal of Archaeology* 4 (2): 165–74.

Kayser, O. 1988. Le Mésolithique breton: Un état des connaissances en 1988. In *Mésolithique et Néolithisation en France et dans les régions limitrophes*. Actes du 113e Congrès National des Sociétés Savantes (Strasbourg, 1988), 1991. Paris: Editions du CTHS, pp. 197–211.

Kellogg, T. B. 1976. Late Quaternary climate changes: Evidence from deep sea cores of Norwegian Greenland Seas. *Geological Society of America Memoir* 145: 77–110.

Kelly, R. 1995. *The foraging spectrum: Diversity in hunter-gatherer lifeways*. Washington, DC: Smithsonian Institution Press.

Kelly, R. L., and L. C. Todd. 1988. Coming into the country: Early Paleoindian hunting and mobility. *American Antiquity* 53 (2): 231–44.

Kempisty, E. 1986. Neolithic cultures of the forest zone in northern Poland. In T. Malinowski (ed.), *Problems of the Stone Age in Pomerania*. Warsaw: Warsaw University, pp. 187–214.

Kent, S. 1990. A cross-cultural study of segmentation, architecture, and the use of space. In S. Kent (ed.), *Domestic architecture and the use of space: An interdisciplinary cross-cultural study*. Cambridge, UK: Cambridge University Press, pp. 127–52.

Kértész, R., Sümegi, P., Kozák, M., Braun, M., Félegyházi, E., and E. Hertelendi. 1994. Mesolithikum im nördlichen Teil der Grossen Ungarischen Tiefebene. *Józa András Múzeum Évkönyve* 36: 15–61.

Kieselbach, P., and D. Richter. 1992. Die Mesolithische Freilandstation Rottenburg-Siebenlinden II, Kreis Tübingen. *Archäologische Ausgrabungen in Baden-Württemberg* 1991: 35–7.

Kijas, J. M. H., and L. Andersson. 2001. A phylogenetic study of the origin of the domestic pig estimated from the near-complete mtDNA genome. *Journal of Molecular Evolution* 52 (3): 302–8.

Kind, C.-J. 1992. Der Freilandfundplatz Henauhof Nord II am Federsee und die' Buchauer Gruppe' des Endmesolithikums. *Archäologisches Korrespondenzblatt* 22: 341–53.

Kind, C.-J. 1995. Eine Weitere Frühmesolithische Feuerstelle in Rottenburg Siebenlinden III. *Archäologische Ausgrabungen in Baden-Württemberg* 1994: 30–4.

Kind, C.-J. 1996. Bemerkungen zur Diversität des Südwestdeutschen Frühmesolithikums. In I. Campen, J. Hahn, and M. Uerpmann (eds.), *Spuren der Jagd–Die Jagd Nach Spuren*. Tübinger Monographien zur Urgeschichte 11. Tübingen: Mo Vince Verlag, pp 325–30.

Kind, C.-J. 1997. *Die Letzten Wildbeuter*. Materialhefte zur Vor- und Frühgeschichte 39, Landesdenkmalamt Baden–Württemberg. Stuttgart: Konrad Theiss Verlag.

Kind, C.-J. 1998. Operationskette und Räumliche Verteilung der Steinartefakte im Spätmesolithischen Horizont II von Rottenburg-Siebenlinden 3. In N. Conard (ed.), *Aktuelle Forschungen zum Mesolithikum/Current Mesolithic Research*. Tübingen: Mo Vince Verlag, pp. 293–301.

Kindgren, H. 1995. Hensbacka – Horgen – Hornborgasjön: Early Mesolithic coastal and inland settlement in western Sweden. In A. Fischer (ed.), *Man and Sea in the Mesolithic*. Oxbow Monograph 53. Oxford: Oxbow, pp. 171–84.

Kindgren, H. 1996. Reindeer or seals? Some Late Palaeolithic sites in central Bohuslän. In L. Larsson (ed.), *The earliest settlement of Scandinavia and its relationship with neighbouring areas*. Acta Archaeologica Lundensia, Series In 8, 24. Stockholm: Almquist and Wiksell International, pp. 193–203.

Kindgren, H. 1999. Torskärr. Stenkyrka 94 revisited. In B. V. Eriksen and B. Bratlund (eds.), *Recent studies in the Final Palaeolithic of the European plain*. Højbjerg: Jutland Archaeological Society.

Kingery, W. D. Vandiver, P. B., and M. Prickett. 1988. The beginnings of pyrotechnology, Part II: Production and use of lime and gypsum plaster in the Pre-Pottery Neolithic Near East. *Journal of Field Archaeology* 15: 219–40.

Kjemperud, A. 1986. Late Weichselian and Holocene shoreline displacement in the Trondheimsfjord area, Central Norway. *Boreas* 15: 61–82.

Klassen, L. 2002. The Ertebølle culture and Neolithic continental Europe: Traces of contact and interaction. In A. Fischer, and K. Kristiansen (eds.), *The Neolithisation of Denmark – 150 years of debate*. Sheffield Archaeological Monographs 12. Sheffield: J. R. Collis Publications.

Kleivan, H. 1962. Økologisk endring i Labrador. *Naturen* 4.

Klemsdal, T. 1982. Coastal classification and the coast of Norway. *Norsk geogr. Tidsskrift* 3/1982: 129–52.

Kleppe, E. J. 1985. *Archaeological data on shore displacement in Norway*. Norges geografiske oppmåling 1/1985. Hønefoss.

Klíma, B. 1953. Nové mesolitické nálezy na jižní Moravě. *Archeologické rozhledy* 5: 297–302.

Knutsson, H. (ed.), 2004. *Coast to coast – arrival: Results and reflections*. Proceedings of the Final Coast to Coast Conference 1–5 October 2002 in Falköping, Sweden. Sweden, Uppsala.

Knutsson, K. 1993. Garaselet-Lappviken-Rastklippan. Introduktion till en discussion om Norrlands äldsta bebyggelse. *Tor* 25.

Knutsson, K., Lindgren, C., Hallgren, F., and N. Björck. 1999. The Mesolithic in Eastern Central Sweden. In J. Boaz (ed.), *The Mesolithic of Central Scandinavia*. Universitetets Oldsaksamlings Skrifter Ny Rekke 22. Oslo: Universitetets Oldsaksamling, pp. 87–124.

Knutsson, K., Falkenström, P., and K. F. Lindberg. 2003. Appropriation of the past: Neolithisation in the northern Scandinavian perspective. In L. Larsson, H. Kindgren, K. Knutsson, D. Loeffler, and A. Åkerlund (eds.), *Mesolithic on the move. Papers presented at the Sixth International Conference on the Mesolithic in Europe, Stockholm 2000*. Oxford: Oxbow, pp. 414–30.

References

Kobusiewicz, M., and I. Kabaciński. 1998. Some aspects of the Mesolithic-Neolithic transition in the western part of the Polish lowlands. In M. Zvelebil, R. Dennell, and L. Domańska (eds.), *Harvesting the sea, farming the forest*. Sheffield: Sheffield University Press, pp. 95–102.

Kol'tsov, L. V. 1984. Mezoliticheskie poseleniya Verhnego Povolzh'ya [Mesolithic settlements of the Upper Volga]. In I. P. Gerasimov (ed.), *Arheologiya i paleogeografiya mezolita i neolita Russkoi ravniny* [*Archaeology and palaeogeography of the Mesolithic and Neolithic of the Russian Plain*]. Moscow: Nauka, pp. 82–91.

Kol'tsov, L. V. 1989a. Vvedenie [Introduction]. In L. V. Kol'tsov (ed.), *Mezolit SSSR – Arheologiya SSSR* [*Mesolithic of the USSR – Archaeology of the USSR*]. Moscow: Nauka, pp. 5–10.

Kol'tsov, L. V. 1989b. Mezolit Volgo-Okskogo mezhdurech'ya [The Mesolithic of the Volga-Oka interfluve]. In L. V. Kol'tsov (ed.), *Mezolit SSSR – Arheologiya SSSR* [*Mesolithic of the USSR – Archaeology of the USSR*]. Moscow: Nauka, pp. 68–86.

Konikov, E. 2007. Sea-level fluctuations and coastline migration in the northwestern Black Sea area over the last 18 ky based on high-resolution lithological-genetic analysis of sediment architecture. In V. Yanko-Hombach, A. Gilbert, N. Panin, and P. Dolukhanov (eds.), *The Black Sea flood question: Changes in coastline, climate, and human settlement*. NATO Science Series IV – Earth and Environmental Sciences. Dordrecht: Springer, pp. 405–36.

Kooijmans, L. P. 1993. The Mesolithic/Neolithic transition in the Lower Rhine Basin. In P. Bogucki (ed.), *Case studies in European prehistory*. Boca Raton: CRC Press, pp. 95–145.

Kooijmans, L. P. (ed.). 2001. *Hardinxveld-Giessendam de Bruin*. Netherlands: Rapportage Archeologische Monumentenzorg 88.

Korobkova, G. F. 1993. The technology and function of tools and the context of regional adaptations: A case study of the Upper Paleolithic and Mesolithic of the North-western Black Sea area. In O. Soffer and N. D. Praslov (eds.), *From Kostenki to Clovis: Upper Palaeolithic – Palaeoindian adaptations*. New York, and London: Plenum Press, pp. 159–73.

Kossach, G., and H. Schmeidl. 1975. Vorneolithischer Getreideanbau im Bayerischen Alpenvorland. *Jahresbericht Bayerischer Denkmalpflege* 16: 7–22.

Kozłowski, J. K. 1981. Die Frage des Ursprungs der Steinindustrie der bandkeramischen Kultur. In B. Gramsch (ed.), *Mesolithikum in Europa*. Berlin: Veröffentlichungen des Museums für Ur- und Frühgeschichte Potsdam 14/15, pp. 83–90.

Kozłowski, J. K. 2006. Balkan et Mediterranée. In N. Cauwe, P. Dolukhanov, J. Kozłowski, and P.-L. van Berg (eds.), *Le Néolithique en Europe*. Paris: Armand Colin.

Kozłowski, J. K., and S. K. Kozłowski. 1983. Chipped stone industries from Lepenski Vir, Yugoslavia. *Preistoria Alpina* 19: 259–94.

Kozłowski, S. K. 1965. Z problematyki polskiego mezolitu. *Archeologia Polski* 10 (1).

Kozłowski, S. K. (ed.). 1973. *The Mesolithic in Europe*. Warsaw: Warsaw University.

Kozłowki, S. K. 1976. Les courants interculturels dans le Mésolithique de l'Europe occidentale. *Les civilisations du 8e au 5e millénaire avant notre ère en Europe*. Colloque 19, UISPP, Nice-Prétirage, pp. 135–160.

Kozłowski, S. K. 1981. Bemerkungen zum Mesolithikum in der Tschechoslowakei und in Österreich. In B. Gramsch (ed.), *Mesolithikum in Europa*. Berlin: Veröffentlichungen des Museums für Ur- und Frühgeschichte Potsdam 14/15, pp. 301–8.

Kozłowski, S. K. 1989. A survey of early Holocene cultures of the western part of the Russian Plain. In C. Bonsall (ed.), *The Mesolithic in Europe: Proceedings of the third international symposium*. Edinburgh: John Donald, pp. 391–401.

Kozłowski, S. K. 2003. The Mesolithic: What do we know and what do we believe? In L. Larsson, H. Kindgren, K. Knutsson, D. Loeffler, and A. Åkerlund (eds.), *Mesolithic on the move: Papers presented at the Sixth International Conference on the Mesolithic in Europe, Stockholm 2000*. Oxford: Oxbow, pp. xvii–xxi.

Kracmarova, A., Bruchova, H., Cerny, V., and R. Brdicka. 2006. Podil "paleotickych" versus "neolitickych" haploskupin Y chromozomu u ceske populace. *Archeologicke Rozhledy* 58: 237–49.

Krainov, D. A. 1960. *Peschernaya stoyanka Tash-Air 1 kak osnova dlya periodizacii poznepaleoliticheskih kul'tur Kryma* (*The Tash-Air 1 cave site as a basis for subdivision of the Crimea's Late Palaeolithic cultures*) – *Materialy i Issledovanija po Arheologii SSSR* (*Materials and Investigatins on Archaeology of te USR*), 91. Moscow: Nauka.

Krainov, D. Ya., and N. A. Khotinsky. 1984. Ivanovskie stoyanki, kompleks mezo-neoliticheskih stojanok Volgo-Okskogo mezhdurech'ya [The Ivanovskioe sites, and the assemblage of Mesolithic-Neolithic sites in the Volga-Oka Interfluve]. In I. P. Gerasimov (ed.), *Arheologiya i paleogeografiya mezolita i neolita Russkoi ravniny [Archaeology and palaeogeogaphy of the Mesolithic and Neolithic of the Russian Plain]*. Moscow: Nauka, pp. 92–108.

Kremenetsky, K. V. 1991. *Paleoekologiya drevneishih zemledel'cev I skotovodov Russkoi ravnin [Palaeoecology of the earliest farmers and stockbreeders of the Russian Plain]*. Moscow: Institute of Geography.

Kriiska, A. 2003. Colonisation of the west Estonian archipelago. In L. Larsson, H. Kindgren, K. Knutsson, D. Loeffler, and A. Åkerlund (eds.), *Mesolithic on the move. Papers presented at the Sixth International Conference on the Mesolithic in Europe, Stockholm 2000*. Oxford: Oxbow, pp. 20–8.

Kriiska, A. 2009. The beginning of farming in the Eastern Baltic. In P. Dolukhanov, G. R. Sarson, and A. M. Shukurov (eds.), *The East European Plain on the eve of agriculture*. British Archaeological Reports International Series 1964. Oxford: Archaeopress, pp. 159–79.

Kriiska, A., and A. Tvauri. 2007. *Viron Esihistoria*. Helsonmi: Suomalaisen Kirjallisuuden Seura.

Kristiansen, K. 1984. Ideology and material culture: An archaeological perspective. In M. Spriggs (ed.), *Marxist perspectives in archaeology*. Cambridge, UK: Cambridge University Press, pp. 72–100.

Kristofferen, S. 1990. *FV 018 Austvik – Brandasund 1988–1990*. Arkeologiske rapporter 13. Universitet i Bergen.

Kuijt, I. 2000. Keeping the peace: Ritual, skull caching and community integration in the Levantine Neolithic. In I. Kuijt (ed.), *Life in Neolithic farming communities: Social organization, identity, and differentiation*. New York: Kluwer, pp. 137–62.

Kuijt, I. 2001. Place, death, and the transmission of social memory in early agricultural communities of the Near Eastern Pre-Pottery Neolithic, *Archeological Papers of the American Anthropological Association* 10(1): 80–99.

Kulemzin, V. M. 1984. *Chelovek I priroda v religiosnych vossreniyach Khantov*. Tomsk: Isdatelstvo TGU.

Kulemzin, V. M., and N. V. Lukina. 1977. *Vasiugansko-Vakhovskie Khanty v kontse XIX– nachale XX vv*. Tomsk: Izdatel'stvo Tomskogo Universiteta.

Kulemzin, V. M., and N. V. Lukina. 1992. *Znakom 'tec: Khanty*. Novosibirsk: Nauka.

Künnap, A. (ed.). 2000. *The roots of peoples and languages of northern Eurasia II and III*. Tartu: Societas Historiae Finno-Ugricae.

Küster, H. 1995. *Geschichte der Landschaft in Mitteleuropa: Von der Eiszeit bis zur Gegenwart*. München: Beck.

Kulturhistoriske undersøkelser langs en gassrørtrase i Karmøy og Tysvær, Roganland. AmS-Rapport 14: 61–98. Stavanger.

Kutchera, M. 1999. Vestnorsk tidligmesolitikum i et nordvest-europeisk perspektiv. In I. Fuglestvedt, T. Gansum, and A. Opedal (eds.), *Vennebok til Bjørn Myhre på 60-årsdagen*. AmS-Rapport 11a: 43–52. Arkeologisk museum i Stavanger.

Kutchera, M., and T. A. Waraas. 2000. Steinalderlokaliteten på 'Breivikklubben', Bratt-Helgaland i Karmøy kommune. In T. Løken (ed.), *Åsgard – Natur og Kulturhistoriske undersøkelser langs en gassrørtrase i Karmøy og Tysvær, Roganland*. AmS-Rapport 14: 61–98. Stavanger.

Kuzmin, Y. V., Jull, A. J. T., Burr, G. S., and J. M. O'Malley. 2004. The timing of pottery origins in the Russian Far East: 14C chronology of the earliest Neolithic complexes. In T. Higham, C. Bronk Ramsey, and C. Owen (eds.), *Radiocarbon and archaeology: Proceedings of the 4th symposium, Oxford 2002*. Oxford: Oxford University School of Archaeology, Monograph 62, pp. 153–9.

Kvamme, K., and M. Jochim. 1990. The environmental basis of Mesolithic settlement. In C. Bonsall (ed.), *The Mesolithic in Europe: Proceedings of the third international symposium*. Edinburgh: John Donald, pp. 1–12.

Kyparissi-Apostolika, N. 1999. The Palaeolithic deposits of Theopetra Cave in Thessaly (Greece). In G. Bailey, E. Adam, C. Perlès, E. Panagopoulou, and K. Zachos (eds.), *The Palaeolithic archaeology of Greece and adjacent areas: Proceedings of the First International Conference on the Palaeolithic of Greece and the Balkans*. London: British School at Athens, pp. 232–9.

Kyparissi-Apostolika, N. 2003. The Mesolithic in Theopetra Cave: New data on a debated period of Greek prehistory. In N. Galanidou, and C. Perlès (eds.), *The Greek Mesolithic: Problems and perspectives*. London: British School at Athens, pp. 189–98.

References

Lacaille, A. D. 1954. *The Stone Age in Scotland*. Oxford: Oxford University Press.

Lacam, R., Niederlender, A., and H. V. Vallois. 1944. *Le gisement mésolithique du Cuzoul de Gramat*. Archives de l'Institut de Paléontologie Humaine. Mémoire 21.

Lanfranchi, F. 1998. Prénéolithique ou Mésolithique insulaire? *Bulletin de la Société Préhistorique Française* 95: 537–45.

Lang, V. 2007. *The Bronze and Early Iron Ages in Estonia*. Tartu: Tartu University Press Humaniora: Archaeologica.

Lanting, J. N., and J. Van der Plicht. 1996. De 14C-Chronologie van de Nederlandse pre- en protohistorie I, Laat-Paleolithicum. *Palaeohistoria* 37/38: 71–125.

Lanting, J. N., and J. Van der Plicht. 2000. De 14C-Chronologie van de Nederlandse pre- en protohistorie II, Mesolithicum. *Palaeohistoria* 41: 99–162.

Lanzinger, M. 1991. Popolamento e strategie di caccia nella preistoria delle Dolomiti Ladine. *Mondo Ladino* 15: 273–307.

Larsen, E., Gulliksen, S., Lauritzen, S.-E., Lie, R., Løvlie, R., and J. Mangerud. 1987. Cave stratigraphy in western Norway: Multiple Weichselian glaciations and interstadial vertebrate fauna. *Boreas* 16: 267–92.

Larson, G., Dobney, K., Albarella, U., Fang, M., Matisoo-Smith, E., Robins, J., Lowden, S., Finlayson, H., Brand, T., Willerslev, E., Rowley-Conwy, P., Andersson, L., and A. Cooper. 2005. Worldwide phylogeography of wild boar reveals multiple centres of pig domestication. *Science* 307: 1618–21.

Larsson, G., et al. 2005. Worldwide phylogeography of wild boar reveals multiple centers of pig domestication. *Science* 307: 1618–21.

Larsson, L. 1975. A contribution of the knowledge of Mesolithic huts in southern Scandinavia. In *Meddelanden från Lunds Universitets historiska museum 1973–1974*: 5–28.

Larsson, L. 1978a. Mesolithic antler and bone artefacts from central Scania. In *Meddelanden från Lunds Universitets historiska museum 1977–1978*.

Larsson, L. 1978b. *Ageröd I:B – Ageröd I:D: A study of early Atlantic settlement in Scania*. Lund: Acta Archaeologica Lundensia.

Larsson, L. 1982. *Segebro: En tidigatlantisk boplats vid Sege Ås mynning*. Malmøfynd 4. Malmø: Malmø Museum.

Larsson, L. 1983. *Ageröd V: An Atlantic bog site in central Scania*. Lund: Acta Archaeologica Lundensia.

Larsson, L. 1984. The Skateholm Project: A late Mesolithic settlement and cemetery complex at a southern Swedish bay. *Meddelanden från Lunds Universitets Historiska Museum* 1983–84: 5–46.

Larsson, L. 1988. *The Skateholm Project. I. Man and the environment*. Societatis Humaniorum Litterarum Lundensis 79. Lund: Almqvist and Wiksell.

Larsson, L. 1989a. Ethnicity and traditions in Mesolithic mortuary practices of southern Scandinavia. In S. J. Shennan (ed.), *Archaeological approaches to cultural Identity*. London: Unwin Hyman, pp. 210–18.

Larsson, L. 1989b. Big dog and poor man: Mortuary practices in Mesolithic societies in Southern Sweden. In T. Larsson, and H. Lundmark (eds.), *Approaches to Swedish prehistory*. Oxford: British Archaeological Reports International Series 500, pp. 211–23.

Larsson, L. 1989c. Late Mesolithic settlements and cemeteries at Skateholm, southern Sweden. In C. Bonsall (ed.), *The Mesolithic in Europe. Papers presented at the Third International Symposium, Edinburgh 1985*. Edinburgh: John Donald, pp. 367–78.

Larsson, L. 1990a. Dogs in fraction – symbols in action. In P. Vermeersch and P. Van Peer (eds.), *Contributions to the Mesolithic in Europe*. Leuven: Leuven University Press, pp. 153–60.

Larsson, L. 1990b. The Mesolithic of southern Scandinavia. *Journal of World Prehistory* 4: 257–309.

Larsson, L. 1993. The Skateholm Project: Late Mesolithic coastal settlement in southern Sweden. In P. Bogucki (ed.), *Case studies in European prehistory*. Boca Raton: CRC Press, pp. 31–62.

Larsson, L. 1995. Man and sea in southern Scandinavia during the Late Mesolithic: The role of cemeteries in the view of society. In A. Fischer (ed.), *Man and sea in the Mesolithic*. Oxbow Monograph 53. Oxford: Oxbow Books, pp. 95–104.

Larsson, L. 1996. The colonization of south Sweden during the deglaciation. In L. Larsson (ed.), *The earliest settlement of Scandinavia and its relationship with neighbouring areas*. Acta Archaeologica Lundensia, Series In 8, 24. Stockholm: Almquist and Wiksell International, pp. 141–56.

Larsson, L. 2001. Society and nature – forests, trees and lures. *Archaeologia Polona* 39: 37–54.

Larsson, L. 2003. The Mesolithic of Sweden in retrospective and progressive perspectives. In L. Larsson, H. Kindgren, K. Knutsson, D. Loeffler, and A. Åkerlund (eds.), *Mesolithic on the move: Papers presented at the Sixth International Conference on the Mesolithic in Europe, Stockholm 2000*. Oxford: Oxbow Books, pp. xxii–xxxiii.

Larsson, L. 2004. The Mesolithic period in southern Scandinavia with special reference to burials and cemeteries. In A. Savile (ed.), *Mesolithic Scotland: The early Holocene prehistory of Scotland in its European context*. Edinburgh: Society of Antiquaries of Scotland, pp. 371–92.

Larsson, L. 2004. The Mesolithic period in southern Scandinavia: With special reference to burials and cemeteries. In A. Saville (ed.), *Mesolithic Scotland and its neighbours*. Edinburgh: Society of Antiquaries of Scotland, pp. 371–92.

Larsson, L. 2009. Zvejnieki – past, present and future. A Mesolithic-Neolithic settlement and cemetery site in northern Latvia. In N. Finlay, S. McCartan, N. Milner, and C. Wickham-Jones (eds.), *From Bann Flakes to Bushmills*. Oxford: Oxbow Books, pp. 124–32.

Larsson, L., and M. Larsson. 1986. Stenåldersbebyggelse i Ystadområdet. *Ystadania* 31: 9–78.

Larsson, L., Callmer, J., and B. Stjernquist (eds.). 1992. *The archaeology of the cultural landscape, field work and research in a south Swedish rural region*. Lund: Acta Archaeologica Lundensia 4 (19).

Larsson, L., Kindgren, H., Knutsson, K., Loeffler, D., and A. Åkerlund (eds.). 2003. *Mesolithic on the move: Papers presented at the sixth international conference on the Mesolithic in Europe, Stockholm 2000*. Oxford: Oxbow Books.

Larsson, L., and I. Zagorska (eds.). 2006. *Back to the origin. New research in the Mesolithic-Neolithic Zvejnieki cemetery and environment, northern Latvia*. Acta Archaeologica Lundensia Series in 8°, 52. Stockholm: Almqvist and Wiksell International.

Larsson, M. 1987. Neolithization in Scania – a Funnel Beaker perspective. *Journal of Danish Archaeology* 5: 244–7.

Larsson, M. 1992. The early and middle Neolithic funnel beaker culture in the Ystad area (southern Scania). In L. Larsson, J. Callmer, and B. Stjernquist (eds.), *The archaeology of the cultural Landscape: Fieldwork and research in a south Swedish rural region*. Acta Archaeologica Lundensia, Series 4, 19.

Larsson, M., and F. Molin. 2000. A new world: Cultural links and spatial disposition – the Early Mesolithic landscape in Östergötland on the basis of the Storlyckan investigations. *Lund Archaeological Review* 6: 7–22.

Larsson, R. M., and E. Olsson. 1997. *Regionalt och interregionalt stenåldersundersökningar I Syd- och Mellansverige*. Riksantikvarieämbetet, Arkeologiska Undeersökningar.

Lauritzen S. E. 1993. Natural environmental change in karst. *The Quaternary record, CATENA Supplement* 25: 21–40.

Layton, R. 1985. The cultural context of hunter-gatherer rock art. *Man* 20: 434–53.

Layton, R. 1991. Figure, motif and symbol in the hunter-gatherer rock art of Europe and Australia. In P. Bahn and A. Rosenfeld (eds.), *Rock art and prehistory*. Oxbow Monograph 10. Oxford: Oxbow Books, pp. 23–39.

Lazarovici, G. 1993. Les Carpates méridionales et la Transylvanie. In J. Kozłowski (ed.), *Atlas du Néolithique Européen. Vol. I, L'Europe Orientale*. (ERAUL 45). Liège: Université de Liège, pp. 243–84.

Leacock, E. B. 1980. Montagnais women and the Jesuit program for colonisation. In M. Etienne, and E. B. Leacock (eds.), *Women and colonisation*. New York: Praeger, pp. 25–42.

Leakey, L. S. B. 1951. Preliminary excavations of a Mesolithic site at Abinger Common, Surrey. *Surrey Archaeological Society Research Paper No. 3.*

Lee, R. B. 1969.!Kung Bushmen subsistence: An input/output analysis. In D. Damas (ed.), *Contributions to anthropology: Ecological essays*. National Museum of Canada Bulletin 230. Ottawa: National Museum of Canada, pp. 73–94.

Lee, R. B. 1979. *The !Kung San: Men, women and work in a foraging society*. Cambridge, UK: Cambridge University Press.

Lee, R. B., and I. DeVore (eds.). *Man the Hunter*. Chicago: Aldine.

References

LeGall, O., Altuna, J., and L. Straus. 1994. Les faunes mésolithique et néolithique de Vidigal. *Archaeologia* 7 (1): 59–72.

Legge, A. J., and P. A. Rowley-Conwy. 1988. *Star Carr revisited: A re-analysis of the large mammals.* London: University of London, Centre for Extra-Mural Studies.

Leighton, R., and J. Dixon. 1992. Jade and greenstone in the prehistory of Sicily and southern Italy. *Oxford Journal of Archaeology* 11: 179–200.

Lejeune, M. 1984. Témoins esthétiques du paléolithique supérieur et du mésolithique de Belgique. In D. Cahen, and P. Haesaerts (eds.), *Peuples chasseurs de la Belgique préhistorique dans leur cadre naturel.* Bruxelles: Institut royal des sciences naturelles de Belgique, pp. 211–31.

Lentacker, A. 1986. Preliminary results of the fauna of Cabeço de Amoreira and Cabeço de Arruda. *Trabalhos de Antropologia e Etnologia* 26: 9–26.

Lentacker, A. 1994. Fish remains from Portugal. In W. Van Neer (ed.), *Fish exploitation in the past.* Tervuren; Annales du Musée Royal de l'Afrique Centrale, Sciences Zoologiques 274, pp. 263–71.

Lepiksaar, J. 1986. The Holocene history of theriofauna in Fennoscandia and Baltic countries. *Striae* 24: 51–70.

Levi-Strauss, C. 1968 (1958). *Structural anthropology.* London: Allen Lane.

Li Lui 2004. *The Chinese Neolithic: Trajectories to early states,* New Studies in Archaeology, Cambridge University Press.

Lidén, K., Eriksson, G., Nordquist, B., Götherström, A., and E. Bendixen. 2004. "The wet and the wild followed by the dry and the tame" – or did they occur at the same time? Diet in Mesolithic-Neolithic southern Sweden. *Antiquity* 78 (299): 23–33.

Lie, R. W. 1986. Animal bones from the Late Weichselian in Norway. *Fauna Norvegica Ser. A* 7: 41–6. Oslo.

Lie, R. W. 1988. En oversikt over Norges faunahistorie. *Naturen* 1988 (6): 225–32. Bergen.

Lie, R. W. 1989. Animal remains from the post-glacial warm period in Norway. *Fauna norv. Ser. A* 10: 45–56.

Lie, R. W. 1990. Blomvågfunnet, de eldste spor etter mennesker i Norge? *Viking* 53: 7–21.

Lie, S. E., Stabel, B., and J. Mangerud. 1983. Diatom stratigraphy related to late Weichselian sea-level changes in Sunnmøre, western Norway. *Norges Geologiske Undersøkelse* 380: 203–19.

Lillie, M. C. 1996. Mesolithic and Neolithic populations of Ukraine: Indications of diet from dental pathology. *Current Anthropology* 37: 135–42.

Lillie, M. C. 1997. Women and children in prehistory: Resource sharing and social stratification at the Mesolithic-Neolithic transition in Ukraine. In J. Moore and E. Scott (eds.), *Invisible people and processes: Writing gender and childhood into European archaeology.* Leicester: Leicester University Press, pp. 213–28.

Lillie, M. C. 1998. The Mesolithic-Neolithic transition in Ukraine: New radiocarbon determinations for the cemeteries of the Dniepr Rapids Region. *Antiquity* 72: 184–8.

Lillie, M. C., and M. Richards. 2000. Stable isotope analysis and dental evidence of diet at the Mesolithic-Neolithic transition in Ukraine. *Journal of Archaeological Science* 27: 965–72.

Lindblom, I. 1982. Former for økologisk tilpasning i Mesolitikum, Østfold. *Universitetets Oldsaksamlings Årbok* 1982/83: 46–86.

Linderholm, J. 2003. Miljøarkeologi i nordligste Skandinavia. *Ottar* 248: 47–50.

Lindgren, C. 2003. My way or your way? On the social dimensions of technology as seen in the lithic strategies. In L. Larsson, H. Kindgren, K. Knutsson, D. Loeffler, and A. Åkerlund (eds.), *Mesolithic on the move: Papers presented at the Sixth International Conference on the Mesolithic in Europe, Stockholm 2000.* Oxford: Oxbow Books, pp. 177–84.

Lindgren, C. 2004. *Människor och kvarts: Sociale och teknologiske strategier under mesolittikum i Östre mellansverige.* Stockholm Studies in Archaeology 29.

Lindgren, C. 2009. Between the rock and the sea: Site location and ritual practice in the Mesolithic in eastern central Sweden. In S. B. McCartan, R. Schulting, G. Warren, and P. Woodman (eds.), *Mesolithic horizons. Papers presented at the Seventh International Conference on the Mesolithic in Europe, Belfast 2005.* Oxford: Oxbow Books, pp. 610–13.

Lindqvist, C., and G. Possnert. 1994. *Gotlands faunal history from the Boreal to the Subatlantic chronozone, based on analysed faunal remains from prehistoric dwelling sites.* Materials of the meeting of Faunahistorists in Blekinge, Sweden.

Lindqvist, C., and G. Possnert. 1999. The first seal hunter families on Gotland. On the Mesolithic occupation in the Stora Förvar Cave. *Current Swedish Archaeology* 7: 65–87.

Liversage, D. 1992. *Barkær: Long barrows and settlements.* Arkæologiske Studier IX. Copenhagen: Akademisk Forlag.

Llana, C., Martínez A., and P. Ramil. 1992. Algunas consideraciones acerca de la estratigrafía y del marco temporal para los yacimientos al aire libre del Paleolítico final-Epipaleolítico de Galicia. *Zephyrus* 44/45: 155–66.

Longva, O., and M. K. Thoresen. 1991. Iceberg scours, iceberg gravity craters and current erosion marks from gigantic Preboreal flood in southeastern Norway. *Boreas* 20: 47–62.

Lönnrot, E. 1963. *The Kalevala or poems of the Kaleva District.* Cambridge, MA: Harvard University Press.

López, J., and M. Aguirre. 1997. Patrones de asentamiento en el Neolítico del litoral Vizcaino. In A. Rodríguez (ed.), *O Neolítico Atlántico e as orixes do megalitismo.* Santiago de Compostela: Universidad de Santiago, pp. 335–52.

López, P. 1992. Análisis polínicos de cuatro yacimentos arqueológicos situasos en el Bajo Aragon. In P. Utrilla Miranda (ed.), *Aragón/Litoral Mediterráneo: Intercambios culturales durante la Prehistoria.* Zaragoza: Institución Fernando Il Catolico, pp. 235–42.

Lõugas, L. 1997. Subfossil seal finds from archaeological coastal sites in Estonia, east part of the Baltic sea. *Anthropozoologica* 25–26: 699–706.

Lõugas, L., Lidén, K., and D. E. Nelson. 1996. Resource utilization along the Estonian coast during the Stone Age. In T. Hackens, S. Hicks, V. Lang, U. Miller, and L. Saarse (eds.), *Coastal Estonia: Recent advances in environmental and cultural history,* PACT 51. Rixensart, pp. 399–420.

Louwe Kooijmans, L. P. 1971–1972. Mesolithic bone and antler implements from the North Sea and the Netherlands. *Berichten van de Rijksdienst voor het Oudheidkundig Bodemonderzoek* 20–21: 27–73.

Louwe Kooijmans, L. P. 1993a. Wetland exploitation and upland relations of prehistoric communities in the Netherlands. In J. Gardiner (ed.), *Flatlands and wetlands, current themes in East Anglian archaeology.* East Anglian Archaeology Report 50, pp. 71–116.

Louwe Kooijmans, L. P. 1993b. The Mesolithic/Neolithic transformation in the Lower Rhine Basin. In P. Bogucki (ed.), *Case Studies in European Prehistory.* Boca Raton: CRC Press, pp. 95–145.

Louwe Kooijmans, L. P. 2001a. Hardinxveld-Giessendam Polderweg, een mesolithisch jachtkamp in het rivierengebied (5500–5000 v. Chr.). *Rapportage Archeologische Monumentenzorg* 83.

Louwe Kooijmans, L. P. 2001b. Hardinxveld-Giessendam De Bruin, een kampplaats uit het Laat-Mesolithicum en het begin van de Swifterbant-cultuur (5500–4450 v. Chr.). *Rapportage Archeologische Monumentenzorg* 88.

Louwe Kooijmans, L. P. 2003. The Hardinxveld sites in the Rhine/Meuse Delta, the Netherlands, 5500–4500 cal BC. In L. Larsson, H. Kindgren, K. Knutsson, D. Loeffler, and A. Åkerlund (eds.), *Mesolithic on the move: Papers presented at the Sixth International Conference on the Mesolithic in Europe, Stockholm 2000.* Oxford: Oxbow, pp. 608–24.

Lovis, W. A., Whallon, R., and R. E. Donahue. 2006. Social and spatial dimensions of Mesolithic mobility. *Journal of Anthropological Archaeology* 25: 271–4.

Loze, I. A. 1979. *Pozdnii Neolit i Rannaya Bronza Lubanskoi Ravniny.* Riga: Zinatne.

Loze, I. A. 1980. Voprosy kartografirovaniya nakhodok yantarya epokhi neolita na Evropejskoj chasti SSSR. *Izvestiya Akademii nauk Latvijskoj SSR* 9 (398): 73–86.

Loze, I. A. 1988. Stone Age wooden tools and devices from the multi-layer habitation site of Zvidze (Latvia). *AR* 11: 361–377, 473–6.

Loze, I. 1995. Late Neolithic burial practices and beliefs in Latvia. In V. Kazakevičius and R. Sidrys (eds.), *Archaeologia Baltica.* Vilnius: Institute of Lithuanian History, pp. 33–42.

Loze, I. 1998. The adoption of agriculture in the area of present-day Latvia (the Lake Lubana Basin). *Baltic-Pontic Studies* 5: 59–84.

References

Loze, I. A., and T. V. Yakubovskaya. 1984. Flora pamyatnikov kamennogo veka Lubanskoi niziny. *Izvestiya Akademii nauk Latvijskoj SSR* 5: 85–94.

Loze, I. A., Liiva, A. A., Stelle, V. Y., Eberbards, G. Y., and I. Yakubovskaya. 1984. Zvidze – mnogosloynoe poseleniye epokh mezolita i neolita na Lubanskoy nizine (Latviyskaya SSR). In *Arheologiya i paleogeografiya mesolita i neolita Russkoy ravniny*, pp. 40–55.

Ložek, V., and V. Cílek. 1995. Late Weichselian-Holocene sediments and soils in mid-European calcareous areas. *Anthropozoikum* 22: 87–112.

Lubbock, J. 1865. *Pre-historic times, as illustrated by ancient remains, and the manners and customs of modern savages*. London: Williams and Norgate.

Lubell, D. 2004a. Prehistoric edible land snails in the circum-Mediterranean: The archaeological evidence. In J.-J. Brugal and J. Desse (eds.), *Petit Animaux et Sociétés Humaines. Du Complément Alimentaire aux Ressources Utilitaire. XXIV Recontres Internationales d'Archéologie et d'histoire d'Antibes*. Antibes: Éditions APDCA, pp. 41–62.

Lubell, D. 2004b. Are land snails a signature for the Mesolithic-Neolithic transition? *Documenta Praehistorica* 31: 1–24.

Lubell, D., and M. Jackes. 1988. Portuguese Mesolithic-Neolithic subsistence and settlement. *Supplemento della Rivista di Antropologia (Roma)* 66: 231–48.

Lubell, D. Jackes M., and C. Meiklejohn. 1989. Archaeology and human biology of the Mesolithic-Neolithic transition in southern Portugal. In C. Bonsall (ed.), *The Mesolithic in Europe: Proceedings of the third international symposium*. Edinburgh: John Donald, pp. 632–40.

Lubell, D., Jackes, M., Schwarcz, H., Knyf, M., and C. Meiklejohn. 1994. The Mesolithic-Neolithic transition in Portugal: Isotopic and dental evidence of diet. *Journal of Archaeological Science* 21: 201–16.

Lubell, D., Jackes, M., Schwarcz, H., and C. Meiklejohn. 1986. New radiocarbon dates for Moita do Sebastiao. *Arqueologia* 14: 34–6.

Lubell, D., Jackes, M., Sheppard, P., and P. Rowley-Conwy. 2007. The Mesolithic-Neolithic in the Alentejo: Archaeological investigations, 1984–1986. In N. Bicho (ed.), *From the Mediterranean Basin to the Portuguese Atlantic Shore: Papers in honor of Anthony Marks. Actas do IV Congresso de Arqueologia Peninsular*. Algarve: Universidade do Faro, pp. 209–29.

Lübke, H. 2005. Spät- und endmesolithische Küstensiedlungsplätze in der Wismarbucht. Neue Ausgrabungsergebnisse zur Chronologie und Siedlungsweise. *Bodendenkmalplege in Mecklenburg-Vorpommeren* 52: 83–110.

Luby, E. M., and M. F. Gruber. 1999. The dead must be fed: Symbolic meanings of the shellmounds of the San Francisco Bay area. *Cambridge Archaeological Journal* 9: 95–108.

Luho, V. 1976. The population and prehistory of Finland. In P. Hajdu (ed.), *Ancient cultures of the Uralian peoples*. Budapest: Corvina, pp. 115–35.

Lund, H. E. 1951. *Fangst-boplassen i Vistehulen*. Stavanger Museum.

Lundberg, Å. 1997. *Vinterbyar – ett bandsamhällets territorier i Norrlands inland 4500–2500 f. Kr*. Studia Archaeologica Universitatis Umensis 8. Umeå: Umeå University.

Lüning, J. 1982a. Siedlung und Siedlungslandschaft in bandkeramischer und Rössener Zeit. *Offa* 39: 9–33.

Lüning, J. 1982b. Research into the Bandkeramik settlement of the Aldenhover Platte in the Rhineland. *Analecta Praehistorica Leidensia* 15: 1–29.

Lüning, J., Kloss, U., and S. Albert. 1989. Westliche Nachbarn der Bandkeramischen Kultur: Die Keramikgruppen 'La Hoguette' und 'Limburg'. *Germania* 67: 355–420.

Lødøen, T. K. 1995. Landskapet som rituell sfære i steinalder: En kontekstuell studie av bergartsøkser fra Sogn. Unpublished thesis, University of Bergen.

Lødøen, T. K. 1998. Interpreting Mesolithic axe deposits from a region in western Norway. In V. Kazakevicius, A. B. Olsen, and D. N. Simpson (eds.), *Archaeologica Baltica 3. The Archaeology of Lithuania and Western Norway: Status and Perspectives*. Vilnius: Lithuanian Institute of History, pp. 195–204.

Lødøen, T. K. 2003. Late Mesolithic Rock Art and Expressions of Ideology. In L. Larsson, H. Kindgren, K. Knutsson, D. Loeffler, and A. Åkerlund (eds.), *Mesolithic on the move: Papers presented at the Sixth International Conference on the Mesolithic in Europe, Stockholm 2000*. Oxford: Oxbow Books, pp. 511–20.

426

Lødøen, T. K. 2009. Confronting important animals. In S. McCartan, R. Schulting, G. Warren, and P. C. Woodman (eds.), *Mesolithic horizons. Papers presented at the Seventh International Conference on the Mesolithic in Europe, Belfast 2005.* Oxford: Oxbow Books, pp. 576–82.

MacDonald, G. M., Velichko, A. A., Kremenetski, C. V., Borisova, O. K., Goleva, A. A., Andreev, A. A., Cwynar, L. C., Riding, R. T., Forman, S. T., Edwards, T. W. D., Aravena, R., Hammarlund, D., Szeicz, J. M., and V. N. Gattaulin. 2001. Holocene treeline history and climate change across Eurasia. *Quaternary Research* 53: 302–11.

Madsen, T. 1987. Where did all the hunters go? – an assessment of an epoch-making episode in Danish prehistory. *Journal of Danish Archaeology* 5: 229–39.

Maggi, R. 1997. The radiocarbon chronology. In R. Maggi (ed.), *Arene Candide: A functional and environmental assessment of the Holocene sequence (excavations Bernabó Brea – Cardini 1940–50), Memorie dell' Istituto Italiano di Paleontologia Umana N. S.* 5: 31–52.

Maggi, R. 1999. Coasts and uplands in Liguria and northern Tuscany from the Mesolithic to the Bronze Age. In R. Tykot, J. Morter, and J. Robb (eds.), *Social dynamics of the prehistoric Central Mediterranean.* London: University of London Accordia Research Centre, pp. 47–65.

Magny, M. 1999. *Une histoire du climat. Des derniers mammouths au siècle de l'automobile.* Paris: Errance,

Magny, M., Bégeota, C., Guiot, J., and O. Peyrona. 2003. Contrasting patterns of hydrological changes in Europe in response to Holocene climate cooling phases. *Quaternary Science Reviews* 22: 1589–96.

Magri, D. 1995. Some questions on the late-Holocene vegetation of Europe. *The Holocene* 5: 354–60.

Magri, D. 1999. Late Quaternary vegetation at Lagaccione near Lago di Bolsena (central Italy). *Review of Palaeobotany and Palynology* 106: 171–208.

Mahler, D. L., Paludan-Müller, C., and S. Stumann Hansen. 1983. *Om arkæologi. Forskning, formidling, forvaltning – for hvem?* Copenhagen: Reitzel.

Malinowski, T. (ed.). 1986. *Problems of the Stone Age in Pomerania.* Warsaw: Warsaw University.

Malmer, M. 1975. The rock carvings at Nämforsen, Ångermanland, Sweden, as a problem of maritime adaptation and circumpolar interrelations. In W. Fitzhugh (ed.), *Prehistoric maritime adaptations of the circumpolar zone.* Paris: Mouton, pp. 41–46.

Malmer, M. P. 1981. *A chronological study of north European rock art.* Stockholm: Almqvist and Wicksell.

Mamonov, E. A. 2000. Hronologicheskii aspekt izucheniya yelshanskoi kul'tury, [Chronological aspect in the study of Yelshanian Culture] in E. N. Nosov (ed.), *Hronologiya neolita Vostochnoi Evrop [Chronology of East European Neolithic].* St Petersburg: Institute for History of Material Culture, pp. 50–2.

Mandt, G. 1998. Vingen revisited: A gendered perspective on 'hunter' rock-art. The world-view of prehistoric man. In L. Larsson and B. Stjernquist (eds.), *KVHAA Konferenser* 40: 201–24. Stockholm.

Mandt, G., and T. Lødøen. 2005. *Bergkunst. Helleristningar i Noreg.* Oslo: Det norske samlaget.

Manen, C. 1997. *L'axe rhodano-jurassien dans le problème des relations sud-nord au Néolithique ancien.* Oxford: British Archaeological Reports International Series 665.

Mangerud, J., Andersen, S. T., Berglund, B. E., and J. J. Donner. 1974. Quaternary stratigraphy of Norden, a proposal for terminology and classification. *Boreas* 3(3): 109–28.

Manker, E. 1963. *The nomadism of the Swedish mountain Lapps: The Siidas and their migratory routes in 1945.* Stockholm: Acta Lapponica.

Manker, E. 1968. Seite cult and drum magic of the Lapps. In V. Diószegi (ed.), *Popular beliefs and folklore tradition in Siberia.* The Hague.

Mannino, M., Thomas, K., Leng, M., Piperno, M., Tusa, S., and A. Tagliacozzo. 2007. Marine resources in the Mesolithic and Neolithic at the Grotta dell'Uzzo (Sicily): Evidence from isotope analyses of marine shells. *Archaeometry* 49: 117–33.

Mansrud, A. 2009. Animal bone studies and the perception of animals in Mesolithic society. In S. B. McCartan, R. Schulting, G. Warren, and P. Woodman (eds.), *Mesolithic horizons. Papers presented at the Seventh International Conference on the Mesolithic in Europe, Belfast 2005.* Oxford: Oxbow Books, pp. 198–202.

Marchand, G. 1999. *La néolithisation de l'ouest de la France: Caractérisation des industries lithiques.* Oxford: British Archeological Reports International Series 748.

References

Marchand, G., Laporte, L., Bridault, A., Giraud, C., Giraud, T., and F. Sellami. 2000. L'habitat mésolithique et néolithique de la Grange, à Surgères (Charente-Maritime). In C. Cupillard and A. Richard (eds.), *Les derniers chasseurs-cueilleurs d'Europe occidentale (13 000 – 5 500 avant J.-C.)*. Actes du Colloque International de Besançon, Octobre 1998. Presses Universitaires Franc-Comtoises, pp. 253–64.

Mariezkurrena, K. 1997. Restos de mamíferos del yacimiento epipaleolítico de Kukuma. In A. Baldeón and E. Berganza (eds.), *Kukuma*. Vitoria: Memorias de Yacimientos Alaveses 3, pp. 61–3.

Mariezkurrena, K., and J. Altuna. 1989. Análisis arqueozoológico de los macromamíferos. In I. Barandiarán and A. Cava (eds.), *El yacimiento prehistórico de Zatoya*. Pamplona: Trabajos de Arqueología Navarra 8, pp. 237–66.

Mariezkurrena, K., and J. Altuna. 1995. Fauna de mamíferos del yacimiento costero de Herriko Barra. *Munibe* 47: 23–32.

Marín, A. B. 2004. Análisis arqueozoológico, tafonómico y de distribución espacial de la fauna de mamíferos de la Cueva de La Fragua (Santoña, Cantabria). *Munibe* 56: 19–44.

Marín, A. B., and M. González Morales. 2009. Comportamiento económico de los últimos cazadores-recolectores y primeras evidencias de domesticación en el occidente (sic) de Asturias. La Cueva de Mazaculos II. *Trabajos de Prehistoria* 66: 47–74.

Markevich, V. I. 1974. *Bugo-Dnestrovskaya kul'tura na territorii Moldavii (The Bug-Dniester Culture on the Territory of Moldavia)*. Chişineu: Ştiinca.

Marks, A., Bicho, N., Zilhao J., and R. Ferring. 1994. Upper Pleistocene prehistory in Portuguese Estremadura. *Journal of Field Archaeology* 21: 53–68.

Martin, E. 1995. Early inhabitants and the changing shoreline of Estonia. In A. Fischer (ed.), *Man and sea in the Mesolithic*. Oxbow Monograph 53. Oxford: Oxbow, pp. 243–46.

Martini, F. 1992. I ciottoli dipinti di Grotta della Serratura (Salerno): Osservazioni sulla cronologia e sui contesti industriali dell'arte "Aziliana" in Italia. *Atti della XXVIII Riunione Scientifica del Istituto Italiano di Preistoria e Protostoria*, pp. 261–75.

Martini, F. 1996. I complessi preneolitici in Italia meridionale: Processi di differenziazione delle industrie litiche. In V. Tiné (ed.), *Forme e tempi della Neolitizzazione in Italia Meridionale e in Sicilia* 1. Rossano: Istituto Regionale per le Antichità Calabresi e Bizantine, pp. 35–47.

Martini, F. 1998. Signes et figurations du Mésolithiques en Italie, *L'Anthropologie (Paris)* 102: 167–76.

Martynova, E. P. 1995. Obshchchectvennoe ustroistvo v XVII–XIX vv. In N. V. Lukina (ed.), *Istoriia i kul'tura Khantov*. Tomsk: Izdatel'stvo TGU.

Maschner, H. 1991. The emergence of cultural complexity on the northern Northwest Coast. *Antiquity* 65: 924–34.

Maška, K. 1886. *Der diluviale Mensch in Mähren. Ein Beitrag zur Urgeschichte für das Schuljahr 1885/86*. Neutitschen.

Mason, S., Boroneanţ, V., and C. Bonsall. 1996. Plant remains from Schela Cladovei, Romania. *Mesolithic Miscellany* 17 (2): 11–14.

Mateus, J. E. 1985. The coastal lagoon region near Carvalhal during the Holocene. *Actas da I Reunião do Quaternario Ibérico*, vol. 2. Lisboa, pp. 337–49.

Mateus, J. 1989. Lagoa Travessa: A Holocene pollen diagram from the south-west coast of Portugal. *Revista de Biologia* 14: 17–94.

Mateus, J. E., and P. F. Queiroz. 1993. Os estudos da vegetação quaternária em Portugal. In G. Carvalho, A. Ferreira, and J. C. Senna-Martinez (eds.), *O Quaternário em Portugal: Balanço e perspectivas* Lisboa: Colibri, pp. 105–31.

Mathiassen, T. 1943. *Stenalderbopladser i Åmosen*. Nordiske Fortidsminder III. Bind 3. Hefte. Copenhagen: Konglige Nordiske Oldskriftselskab.

Mathiassen, T. 1948. *Studier over Vestjyllands Oldtidsbebyggelse*. Nationalmuseets Skrifter, Arkæologisk-Historisk Række II. Copenhagen: Konglige Nordiske Oldskriftselskab.

Mathiassen, T. 1959. *Nordvestsjællands Oldtidsbebyggelse*. Nationalmuseets Skrifter, Arkæologisk-Historisk Række VII. Copenhagen: Konglige Nordiske Oldskriftselskab.

Matiskainen, H. 1989. Studies on the chronology, material culture and subsistence economy of the Finnish Mesolithic, 10000–6000 BP. *Iskos* 8.

Matiskainen, H. 1996. Discrepancies in deglaciation chronology and the appearance of man in Finland. In L. Larsson (ed.), *The earliest settlement of Scandinavia and its relationship with neighbouring areas*. Acta Archaeologica Lundensia, Series In 8, 24. Stockholm: Almquist and Wiksell International, pp. 252–62.

Matiskainen, H., and T. Jussila. 1984. Naarajärven kampakeraaminen asumus. *Suomen Museo* 89: 17–52.

Matland, S. 1990. Bone implements: A re-evaluation of Stone Age finds from caves and rockshelters in Western Norway. Unpublished thesis, University of Bergen.

Matoušek, V. 2002. Bacín. Místo pravěkého pohřebního kultu v Českém krasu. In J. Svoboda (ed.), *Prehistorické jeskyně*. Brno: The Dolní Věstonice Studies 7, pp. 355–93.

Matskevoi, L. G. 1991. *Mezolit zapada Ukrainy* [*The Mesolithic of Western Ukraine*]. Kiev: Naukova Dumka.

Maula, E. (ed.), 1990. *Swansongs: Rock art from Lake Onega 4000 – 2000 B. C*. Tartu: Society of Prehistoric Art.

Maury, J. 1977. *The Asturian in Portugal*. Oxford: British Archaeological Reports International Series 21.

Mazálek, M. 1953. Třetí rok výzkumů paleo-mesolitické oblasti u Ražic. *Archeologické rozhledy* 5: 577–89.

Mazálek, M. 1954. Otázka vztahů mesolitu a neolitu. *Anthropozoikum* 3 (1953): 203–34.

Mazel, A. D., and A. L. Watchman. 2003. Dating rock paintings in the uKhalamba-Drakensberg and the Biggarsberg, KwaZulu-Natal, South Africa. Southern African Humanities 15: 59–73.

Mazzetti, M., Mazza, P., Rustioni, M., and B. Sala. 1995. Large-sized Italian ungulates at the Late Pleistocene-Holocene transition: An overview. In *Atti del Primo Convegno Nazionale di Archeozoologia (Rovigo 1993)*. Rovigo: Padusa Quaderni, pp. 89–96.

McCartan, S. B., Schulting, R., Warren, G., and P. Woodman (eds.). 2009. *Mesolithic horizons. Papers presented at the Seventh International Conference on the Mesolithic in Europe, Belfast 2005*. Oxford: Oxbow Books.

McClure, S., Molina, L., and J. Bernabeu. 2008. Neolithic rock art in context: Landscape history and the transition to agriculture in Mediterranean Spain. *Journal of Anthropological Archaeology* 27: 326–37.

McEwan, C., Borrero, L. A., and A. Prieto. 1997. *Patagonia, natural history, prehistory and ethnogaphy at the uttermost end of the Earth*. London: British Museum Press.

McSweeney, K., Bonsall, C., Boroneanţ, V., and A. Boroneanţ. In prep. Evidence of inter-personal violence in the Late Mesolithic. In C. Bonsall and V. Boroneanţ (eds.), *From foraging to farming in the Iron Gates: Excavations at Schela Cladovei, Romania*.

Meehan, B. 1982. *Shell bed to shell midden*. Canberra: Australian Institute for Aboriginal Studies.

Meiklejohn, C., and B. Denston. 1987. The human skeletal material: Inventory and initial interpretation. In P. Mellars (ed.), *Excavations on Oronsay*. Edinburgh: Edinburgh University Press, pp. 290–300.

Meiklejohn, C., and M. Zvelebil. 1991. Health status of European populations at the agricultural transition and the implications for the adoption of farming. In H. Bush and M. Zvelebil (eds.), *Health in past societies: Biocultural interpretations of human skeletal remains in archaeological contexts*. British Archaeological Reports International Series 567: 129–45.

Meiklejohn, C., Brinch Petersen, E., and V. Alexandersen. 1998. The Later Mesolithic population of Sjælland, Denmark and the Neolithic transition. In M. Zvelebil, R. Dennell, and L. Domańska (eds.), *Harvesting the sea, farming the forest*. Sheffield: Sheffield University Press, pp. 203–12.

Meiklejohn, C., Brinch Petersen, E., and V. Alexandersen. 2000. The anthropology and archaeology of Mesolithic gender in the western Baltic. In M. Donald and L. Hurcombe (eds.), *Gender and material culture in archaeological perspective*. Basingstoke: Macmillan, pp. 222–37.

Meiklejohn, C., Roksandic, M., Jackes, M., and D. Lubell. 2009. Radiocarbon dating of Mesolithic human remains in Portugal. *Mesolithic Miscellany* 20 (1): 4–16.

Meinander, C. F. 1984. Om introduktioonen av sädesodling I Finland. *Finskt Museum* 1984: 5–20.

Mellars, P. A. 1976. Fire ecology, animal populations and man: A study of some ecological relationships in prehistory. *Proceedings of the Prehistoric Society* 42: 15–46.

Mellars, P. (ed.). 1978. *The Early postglacial settlement of northern Europe*. London: Duckworth.

Mellars, P. A. 1987. *Excavations on Oronsay*. Edinburgh: Edinburgh University Press.

Mellars, P., and P. Dark. 1998. *Star Carr in context*. Cambridge, UK: McDonald Institute for Archaeological Research.

References

Melton, N. D., and R. A. Nicholson. 2004. The Mesolithic in the Northern Isles: The preliminary evaluation of an oyster midden at West Voe, Sumburgh, Shetland, U. K. *Antiquity*: 78 (299). http://antiquity.ac.uk/ProjGall/nicholson/index.html.

Merezhkovskii, K. S. 1880. Otchet o pervonachalnyh isssledovaniyah kamennogo veka v Krymu [Report on the initial investigations of the Crimean Stone Age]. *Izvestiya Russkogo Geograficheskogo Obschestva*, vol. 16/2.

Merkel, M. 1999. Überlegungen zur Typologie Frühneolithischer Felssteingeräte, ein Beitrag zur Neolithisierung Norddeutschlands Südskandinaviens. *Offa* 56: 223–38.

Midgley, M. 1992. *TRB Culture*. Edinburgh: Edinburgh University Press.

Miettinen, T. 1990. Possibilities of interpreting rock art. *Suomen Antropologisen Seuran Julkaisuja* 1.

Miettinen, M. 1992. The Stone Age cemetery of Hartikka in Laukaa, central Finland. In *Cultural heritage of the Finno-Ugrians and Slavs*. Tallinn, pp. 24–40.

Mikkelsen, E. 1971. Vistefunnets kronologiske stilling. Trekk av Rogalands eldre steinalder. *Stavanger Museums årbok* 1970: 5–38. Stavanger.

Mikkelsen, E. 1975a. Mesolithic in South-eastern Norway. *Norwegian Archaeological Review* 8 (1): 19–35.

Mikkelsen, E. 1975b. *Frebergsvik. Et mesolittisk boplassområde ved Oslofjorden*. Oslo: Universitetets Oldsaksamlings Skrifter Ny Rekke 1.

Mikkelsen, E. 1976. Østnorske veideristninger – kronologi och øko-kulturelt miljø. *Viking* 40: 147–201.

Mikkelsen, E. 1978. Seasonality and Mesolithic adaptation in Norway. In K. Kristiansen and C. Paludan-Muller (eds.), *New directions in Scandinavian Archaeology*. Copenhagen: National Museum of Denmark, pp. 79–119.

Mikkelsen, E. 1986. Religion and ecology: Motifs and location of hunters' rock carvings in eastern Norway. In G. Steinsland (ed.), *Words and objects*. Oslo: Universitetsforlaget, pp. 127–41.

Mikkelsen, E. Ballin, T., and A. K. Hufthammer. 1999. Tørkop: A boreal settlement in South-Eastern Norway. *Acta Archaeologica* 70 (1999): 25–57.

Milliken, S. 1998a. The role of raw material availability in technological organization: A case study from the south-east Italian Late Palaeolithic. In S. Milliken (ed.), *the organization of lithic technology in late glacial and early postglacial Europe*. Oxford: British Archaeological Reports International Series 700, pp. 63–82.

Milliken, S. 1998b. Hunter-gatherer land use in Late Glacial south-east Italy. *Oxford Journal of Archaeology* 17: 269–86.

Milliken, S., and R. Skeates 1989. The Alimini Survey: The Mesolithic-Neolithic transition in the Salento Peninsula (SE Italy). *Institute of Archaeology Bulletin* 26: 77–98.

Milner, N. 2006. Subsistence. In C. Conneller and G. Warren (eds.), *Mesolithic Britain and Ireland: New Approaches*. Stroud: Tempus, pp. 61–82.

Milner, N, and P. Woodman (eds.). 2005. *Mesolithic studies at the beginning of the 21st Century*. Oxford: Oxbow.

Milner, N., Craig, O. C., Bailey, G. N., Pedersen, K., and S. H. Andersen. 2004. Something fishy in the Neolithic? A re-evaluation of stable isotope analysis of Mesolithic and Neolithic coastal populations. *Antiquity* 78 (299): 9–22.

Milner, N., Craig, O. E., Bailey, G. N., and S. H. Andersen. 2006. A response to Richards and Schulting. *Antiquity* 308: 456–7.

Mišić, V., Colić, D., and Dinić, A. 1972. Ecological–phytocenological investigation. In D. Srejović (ed.), *Europe's first monumental sculpture. new discoveries at Lepenski Vir*. London: Thames and Hudson, pp. 171–81.

Mithen, S. J. 1987. Prehistoric red deer hunting strategies: A cost-risk benefit analysis with reference to Upper Palaeolithic northern Spain and Mesolithic Denmark. In P. Rowley-Conwy, M. Zvelebil, and H. P. Blankholm (eds.), *Mesolithic Northwest Europe: Recent trends*. Sheffield: University of Sheffield, pp. 93–108.

Mithen, S. J. 1990. *Thoughtful foragers: A study of prehistoric decision making*. Cambridge: Cambridge University Press.

Mithen, S. J. 1994. The Mesolithic Age. In B. Cunliffe (ed.), *The Oxford illustrated prehistory of Europe*. Oxford: Oxford University Press, pp. 79–135.

Mithen, S. (ed.). 2000. *Hunter-gatherer landscape archaeology: The Southern Hebrides Mesolithic Project (1988–98)* Vols 1 and 2. Cambridge, UK: MacDonald Institute for Archaeological Research.

Mithen, S. 2003. *After the ice: A global human history 20,000–5000 BC.* London: Weidenfeld, and Nicolson.

Moore, J. A. 1985. Forager/farmer interactions: Information, social organization, and the frontier. In S. Green, and S. Perlman (eds.), *The archaeology of frontiers and boundaries.* New York: Academic Press, pp. 93–112.

Morales, A., Roselló, E., and F. Hernández. 1998. Late Upper Palaeolithic subsistence strategies in southern Iberia: Tardiglacial faunas from Cueva de Nerja (Málaga, Spain). *European Journal of Archaeology* 1 (1): 9–50.

Mordant, C., and D. Mordant. 1989. Noyen-sur-Seine, site mésolithique en milieu humide fluviatile. In *L'homme et l'eau au temps de la préhistoire*, Actes 112e Congrès National des Sociétés Savantes. Paris: Editions du CTHS, 1989, pp. 33–52.

Mordant, D., and C. Mordant. 1992. Noyen-sur-Seine, a Mesolithic waterside settlement. In J. M. Coles and A. J. Lawson (eds.), *European wetlands in prehistory.* Oxford: Clarendon Press, pp. 5–64.

Morel, P. 1993. Une chasse à l'ours brun il y a 12000 ans: Nouvelle découverte à la grotte du Bichon (La Chaux-de-Fonds)', in *ArS*, 16: 110–17.

Mortillet, A. De, 1885. Petits silex taillés d'Hédouville. *L'Homme*: 506–7.

Mortillet, G. De, 1874. Intervention à la Société d'Anthropologie de Paris le 16. 4. 1874. *Bulletin de la Société d'Anthropologie de Paris*: 317.

Mortillet, G. De, 1894. Communication à la Société d'Anthropologie de Paris. *Bulletin de la Société d'Anthropologie de Paris*, 4è série, 5: 616–21.

Moss, M. L. 1993. Shellfish, gender and status on the northwest coast: Reconciling archaeological, ethnographic and ethnohistorical records of the Tlingit. *American Anthropologist* 95 (4): 860–74.

Moure, A., González Sainz, C., Bernaldo de Quirós, F., and V. Cabrera. 1996. Dataciones absolutas de pigmentos en cuevas cantábricas. In A. Moure (ed.), *El Hombre Fósil' 80 años después.* Santander: Universidad de Cantabria, pp. 295–324.

Mulk, I.-M., and T. Bayliss Smith. 1999. The representation of Sámi cultural identity in the cultural landscapes of northern Sweden: The use and misuse of archaeological knowledge. In P. J. Ucko and R. Layton (eds.), *The archaeology and anthropology of landscape.* London: Routledge, pp. 358–96.

Müller-Beck, H.-J. 1983. Die Späte Mittelsteinzeit. In H. Müller-Beck (ed.), *Urgeschichte in Baden-Württemberg.* Stuttgart: Konrad Theiss Verlag, pp. 393–404.

Muñoz, M., and E. Berganza. 1997. *El yacimiento de la Cueva de Urratxa III.* Bilbao: Universidad de Deusto.

Mussi, M., Coubray, S., Giraudi, C., Mazzella, G., Toniutti, P., Wilkens, B., and D. Zampetti. 2000. L'exploitation des territoires de montagne dans les Abruzzes (Italie centrale) entre le Tardiglaciaire et l'Holocène ancien. In P. Crotti (ed.), *Meso '97: Epipalèolithique et Mésolithique.* Cahiers d'Archeologie Romande 81. Lausanne: CAR, pp. 277–84.

Myklevoll, L. B. 1998. *Bergartsøkser i Nord-Norge. Forslag til klassifisering, kronologi og tolkning.* Stensilserie/ Universitetet i Tromsø. Institutt for samfunnsvitenskap B 50. University of Tromsø.

Møhl, U. 1971. Fangstdyrene ved de danske strande. *Kuml* 1970: 297–330.

Møllenhus, K. 1977. *Mesolittiske boplasser på Møre- og Trøndelagskysten.* Gunneria 27. Trondheim.

Møller, J. 1984. Holocene shore displacement at Nappstraumen, Lofoten, North Norway. *Norsk geografisk Tidsskrift* 64 (1): 1–5.

Møller, J. 1987. Shoreline relation and prehistoric settlement in northern Norway. *Norsk Geografisk Tidsskrift* 41: 45–60.

Møller, J. 1989. Geometrical simulation and mapping of Holocene relative sea-level changes in Northern Norway. *Journal of Coastal Research* 5 (3): 403–17.

Møller, J. 2003. Late Quaternary sea level and coastal settlement in the European North. *Journal of Coastal Research* 19 (3): 731–7.

Naber, F. 1968. Die 'Schräge Wand' im Bärental, Eine Altholozäne Abrifundstelle im Nördlichen Frankenjura. *Quartär* 19: 289–313.

Naber, F. 1970. Untersuchungen an Industrien Postglazialer Jägerkulturen. *Bayerische Vorgeschichtsblätter* 35: 1–68.

431

References

Naber, F. 1977. Schellnecker Wänd – Abri II, Gemeinde Essing, LKr. Kelheim, Niederbayern. *Archäologisches Korrespondenzblatt* 7: 185–94.

Nalbant, T. T. 1970. Cîteva observatii aspura resturil or de Peşti. Descoperite in locuirile Romanello-Aziliene (I–II) de la Cuina Turcului–Dubova. *Studii şi Cercetari de Istorie Veche* 21 (1): 41–3.

Nansen, F. 1922. *The strandflat and isostasy.* Vitenskapsselskapets Skrifter/I Mathematisk-naturvidenskapelig klasse 1921: 11. Kristiania.

Nansen, F. 1928. *The earth's crust, its surface-forms and isostatic adjustment.* Avhandlinger/I Mathematisk-naturvidenskapelig klasse 1927: 12. Oslo: Det norske Videnskaps-Akademi.

Nash, G. 2002. The landscape brought within: A re-evaluation of the rock-painting site at Tumlehed, Torslada, Göteborg, west Sweden. In G. Nash and C. Chippindale (eds.), *European landscapes of rock-art.* London: Routledge, pp. 176–94.

Nash, G., and C. Chippindale (eds.). 2002. *European landscapes of rock-art.* London: Routledge.

Nash, G. H. 1998. *Exchange, status and mobility: Portable art of southern Scandinavia.* British Archaeological Reports International Series 710, Oxford: Archaeopress.

Nash, G. H. 2001. The subversive male: Homosexual and bestial images on European Mesolithic rock art. In L. Bevan (ed.), *Indecent exposure: Sexuality, society and the archaeological record.* Glasgow: Cruithne Press, pp. 43–55.

Neeley, M. P., and G. A. Clark. 1990. Measuring social complexity in the European Mesolithic. In P. M. Vermeersch and P. van Peer (eds.), *Contributions to the Mesolithic in Europe.* Leuven: Leuven University Press, pp. 127–38.

Newell, R. R. 1973. The post-glacial adaptations of the indigenous population of the Northwest European Plain. In S. Kozłowski (ed.), *The Mesolithic in Europe.* Warsaw: Warsaw University Press, pp. 399–441.

Newell, R. R. 1981. Mesolithic dwelling structures: Fact and fantasy. In B. Gramsch (ed.), *Mesolithikum in Europa. 2. Internationales Symposium Potsdam, 3. bis 8. April 1978.* Veröffentlichungen des Museums für Ur- und Frühgeschichte Potsdam. 14/15 (Berlin 1981), pp. 235–84.

Newell, R. R. 1984. On the Mesolithic contribution to the social evolution of western European society. In J. Bintliff (ed.), *European social evolution: Archaeological perspectives.* Bradford: University of Bradford, pp. 69–82.

Newell, R. R., Constandse-Westerman, T. S., and C. Meiklejohn. 1979. The skeletal remains of Mesolithic man in western Europe: An evaluative catalogue. *Journal of Human Evolution* 8 (1): 1–228.

Newell, R., Kielman, D., Constandse-Westermann, T., Van der Sanden, W., and A. Van Gijn. 1990. *An Inquiry into the ethnic resolution of Mesolithic regional-groups: The study of their decorative ornaments in time and space.* Leiden: E. J. Brill.

Niekus, M. J. L. Th., and H. R. Reinders. 2002. Vuursteenvindplaatsen: Sporen van jager-verzamelaars en vroege landbouwers in het Noord-Nederlandse landschap. *PaleoAktueel* 13: 37–40.

Nielsen, E. 1992. Paläolithische und Mesolithische Fundstellen im Zentralschweizerischen Wauwilermoos. *Archäologisches Korrespondenzblatt* 22: 27–40.

Nielsen, E. 1994. Bemerkungen zum Schweizerischen Spätmesolithikum. *Archäologisches Korrespondenzblatt* 24: 145–55.

Nielsen, E. 1996. Untersuchung einer Alt- und Mittelsteinzeiten Fundstelle in Wauwil-Obermoos. *Heimatkunde des Wiggertals* 54: 47–65.

Nielsen, E. 1997. Die Späteiszeitliche Fundstelle Schötz-Fischerhäusern (Station 1). *Heimatkunde des Wiggertals* 55: 161–83.

Nielsen, E. K., and E. Brinch Petersen. 1993. Burials, people and dogs. In S. Hvass and B. Storgaard (eds.). *Digging into the past: 25 years of archaeology in Denmark.* Århus: Aarhus University Press, pp. 76–80.

Nielsen, F. 1989. Bornholms bebyggelse i yngre stenalder. *Fra Bornholms Museum,* pp. 63–72.

Nilsson Stutz, L. 2003. *Embodied rituals, and ritualized bodies. Tracing ritual practices in Late Mesolithic burials.* Acta Archaeological Lundensia Series in 8 minore, 46; Lund. Stockholm: Almqvist and Wiksell International.

Nilsson Stutz, L. 2009. Coping with cadavers: Ritual practices in Mesolithic cemeteries. In S. B. McCartan, R. Schulting, G. Warren, and P. Woodman (eds.), *Mesolithic horizons. Papers presented at the Seventh International Conference on the Mesolithic in Europe, Belfast 2005.* Oxford: Oxbow Books, pp. 657–63.

Niskanen, M. 1998. The genetic relationships of northern and central Europeans in light of craniometric measurements and gene frequencies. In K. Julku and K. Wiik (eds.), *The roots of peoples and languages of northern eurasia I*. Turku: Societas Historiae Fenno-Ugricae, pp. 134–50.

Noe-Nygaard, N. 1971. Spur dog spines from prehistoric and early historic Denmark. *Meddelelser fra Dansk Geologisk Forening* 21.

Noe-Nygaard, N. 1988. δ13C-values of dog bones reveal the nature of changes in man's food resources at the Mesolithic-Neolithic transition, Denmark. *Chemical Geology* 73: 87–96.

Noe-Nygaard, N. 1995. *Ecological, sedimentary, and geochemical evolution of the late-glacial to postglacial Åmose lacustrine basin, Denmark*. Fossils and Strata 37: 1–436.

Nordqvist, B. 1995. The Mesolithic settlements of the west coast of Sweden – with special emphasis on chronology and topography of coastal settlements. In A. Fischer (ed.), *Man and sea in the Mesolithic*. Oxbow Monograph 53. Oxford: Oxbow, pp. 185–96.

Nordqvist, B. 1999. The chronology of the western Swedish Mesolithic and Late Paleolithic: Old answers in spite of new methods. In J. Boaz (ed.), *The Mesolithic of Central Scandinavia*. Universitetets Oldsaksamlings Skrifter Ny Rekke 22. Oslo: Universitetets Oldsaksamling, pp. 235–54.

Nordqvist, B. 2003. To touch the mind. In L. Larsson, H. Kindgren, K. Knutsson, D. Loeffler, and A. Åkerlund (eds.), *Mesolithic on the Move: Papers presented at the Sixth International Conference on the Mesolithic in Europe, Stockholm 2000*. Oxford: Oxbow, pp. 536–41.

Nowak, M. 2001. The second phase of Neolithization in east-central Europe. *Antiquity* 75 (289): 582–92.

Nummedal, A. 1912. Stenaldersfundene paa kysten af Romsdals amt. *Aftenposten* 14 april 1912.

Nummedal, A. 1922. Nogen primitive stenaldersformer i Norge. *Oldtiden* 9: 145–58.

Nummedal, A. 1924. Om Flintpladsene. *Norsk Geologisk Tidsskrift* 7, 1923: 89–141.

Nummedal, A. 1927. Steinaldersfundene i Alta. *Norsk Geologisk Tidsskrift* 9 (1) 1926: 43–7.

Nummedal, A. 1933. Kan det finnes flintplasser på kyststrekningen mellem Kristiansand og Ålesund? *Naturen* 1933: 227–44. Bergen museum.

Nummedal, A. 1937. En stenaldersboplass ved Molde. *Viking* 1: 29–49.

Nuñez, M. 1987. A model for the early settlement of Finland. *Fennoscandia archaeologica* 4: 3–18.

Nuñez, M. 1990. On subneolithic pottery and its adoption in late Mesolithic Finland. *Fennoscandia archaeologica* 7: 27–50.

Nuñez, M. 1995. Reflections on Finnish rock art and ethnohistorical data. *Fennoscandia archaeologica* 12: 123–34.

Nuñez, M. 1997. Finland's settling model revisited. *Helsinki Papers in Archaeology* 10: 93–102.

Nuñez, M., and K. Liden. 1997. Taking the 5,000 year old 'Jettböle skeletons' out of the closet: A palaeo-medical examination of human remains from the Åland (Ahvenanmaa) Islands. *International Journal of Circumpolar Health* 56: 30–9.

Nuñez, M., and P. Uino. 1998. Dwellings and related structures in prehistoric mainland Finland. *Bebyggelse-historisk Tidskrift* 33: 133–52.

Nuñez, M., and J. Okkonen. 1999. Environmental background for the rise and fall of villages and megas-tructures in north Ostrobothnia 4000–2000 cal BC. In M. Huurrei (ed.), *Dig it all. Papers dedicated to Ari Siiriänen*. Helsinki: The Finnish Antiquarian Society and The Archaeological Society of Finland, pp. 105–15.

Nydal, R., and S. Westin. 1979. Dateringslaboratoriets oppbygging og utvikling. In R. Nydal, S. Westin, U. Hafsten, and S. Gulliksen (eds.), *Fortiden i søkelyset. Datering med 14C metoden gjennom 25 år*. Trondheim: Laboratoriet for Radiologisk Datering, pp. 13–47.

Nygaard, S. 1974. Håvikboplassene på Karmøy: En forsøksvis analyse av Nøstvetkulturen på Vestlandet. *Stavanger museums årbok* 1973: 5–36. Stavanger.

Nygaard, S. E. 1989. The stone age of Northern Scandinavia: A review. *Journal of World Prehistory* 3 (1): 72–116.

Nygaard, S. 1990. Mesolithic western Norway. In P. M. Vermeersch and P. Van Peer (eds.), *Contributions to the Mesolithic in Europe*. Leuven: Leuven University Press, pp. 227–37.

Nyland, A. 2002. Å finne noe kjent ved det ukjente. Unpublished thesis, University of Bergen.

References

Nærøy, A. J. 1988. Teknologiske endringer ved overgangen fra eldre til yngre steinalder på Vestlandet. In S. Indrelid, S. Kaland, and B. Solberg (eds.), *Festskrift til Anders Hagen*. Arkeologiske Skrifter 4. Bergen: University of Bergen, pp. 205–13.

Nærøy, A. J. 1994. *Trollprosjektet. Arkeologiske undersøkelser på Kollsnes, Øygarden k., Hordagland, 1989–1992*. Arkeologiske Rapporter 19. Bergen: Bergen Museum, University of Bergen.

Nærøy, A. J. 1995. Early Mesolithic site structure in western Norway – a case study. *Universitetets Oldsaksamlings årbok* 1993/1994: 59–77.

Nærøy, A. J. 1999. The Norwegian Stone Age in south Scandinavian and northwest European context. *AmS rapport* 12B: 463–88.

Nærøy, A. J. 2000. *Stone Age living spaces in Western Norway*. Oxford: British Archaeological Reports International Series 857.

O'Shea, J. 1984. *Mortuary variability: An archaeological investigation*. New York: Academic Press.

O'Shea, J. 1996. *Villages of Maros: A portrait of an Early Bronze Age society*. New York: Plenum Press.

O'Shea, J. 1998. Reply to review of Villages of Maros. *Cambridge Archaeological Journal* 8 (1): 109–11.

O'Shea, J. M., and M. Zvelebil. 1984. Oleneostrovskii Mogilnik: Reconstructing the social and economic organisation of prehistoric foragers in northern Russia. *Journal of Anthropological Archaeology* 3: 1–40.

Odner, K. 1964. Erverv og bosetning i Komsakulturen. *Viking* 28: 117–28.

Odner, K. 1966. *Komsakulturen i Nesseby og Sør-Varanger*. Oslo: Universitetsforlaget.

Ohnuki-Tierney, E. 1974. *The Ainu of the north-west coast of southern Sakhalin*. New York: Holt, Rinehart, and Winston.

Okladnikov, A. P. 1970. *Yakutia*. Montreal: McGill-Queen's University Press.

Okladnikov, A. P. 1974. *Petroglyphi Baikala – pamiatniki drevney kultury narodov Sibiri*. Novosibirsk: Nauka.

Okladnikov, A. P. 1977. *Petroglyphi verkhnei Leny*. Leningrad: Nauka.

Oliva, M. 2005. *Palaeolithic and Mesolithic Moravia*. Brno: Moravian Museum.

Olsen, A. B. 1981. Bruk av diabas i vestnorsk steinalder. Unpublished thesis, University of Bergen.

Olsen, A. B. 1992. *Kotedalen – en boplass gjennom 5000 år. Bind I. Fangstbosetning og tidlig jordbruk i vestnorsk steinalder: Nye funn og nye perspektiver*. University of Bergen.

Olsen, A. B., and S. Alsaker. 1984. Greenstone and diabase utilization in the Stone Age of Western Norway: Technological and socio-cultural aspects of axe and adze production and distribution. *Norwegian Archaeological Review* 17 (2): 71–103.

Olsen, B. 1994. *Bosetning og samfunn i Finnmarks forhistorie*. Oslo: Universitetsforlaget.

Olsen, B. 1997. Forhistoriske hus i Nord-Norge. *Bebyggelseshistorisk tidsskrift* 3: 185–94.

Olsen, S. F., and N. J. Secher. 2002. Low consumption of seafood in early pregnancy as a risk factor for preterm delivery: Prospective cohort study. *British Medical Journal*, 324: 447–50.

Onoratini, G. 1979. Les industries de la tradition Gravettienne dans le sud-est de la France et en Ligurie. In D. de Sonneville Bordes (ed.), *La fin des temps glaciaires en Europe: Chronostratigraphie et écologie des cultures du Paléolithique Final*, pp. 287–95. Paris: CNRS.

Orquera, L. A., and E. L. Piana. 1987. Human littoral adaptation in the Beagle Channel region: The maximum possible age. *Quaternary of South America and Arctic Peninsula* 5: 133–62.

Orschiedt, J. 1998. Ergebnisse einer Neuen Untersuchung der Spätmesolithischen Kopfbestattungen aus Süddeutschland. In N. Conard (ed.), *Aktuelle Forschungen zum Mesolithikum/Current Mesolithic Research*. Tübingen: Mo Vince Verlag, pp. 147–60.

Ortea, J. 1986. The malacology of La Riera Cave. In L. G. Straus and G. A. Clark (eds.), *La Riera Cave*. Anthropological Research Papers 36. Tempe: Arizona State University, pp. 289–98.

Oshibkina, S. V. 1982. Mezoliticheskii mogilnik Popovo na reke Kineme. *Sovetskaya Arkhaeologiya* 1982: 123–31.

Oshibkina, S. V. 1989a. Mezolit central'nyh i severo-vostochnyh raionov Severa Evropeiskoi chasti SSSR [The Mesolithic of the central and north-eastern parts of the Russian North]. In L. V. Kol'tsov (ed.), *Mezolit SSSR – Arheologiya SSSR [Mesolithic of the USSR – Archaeology of the USSR]*. Moscow: Nauka, pp. 32–45.

Oshibkina, S. V. 1989b. The material culture of the Veretye-type sites in the region to the east of the Lake Onega. In C. Bonsall *The Mesolithic in Europe: Proceedings of the third international symposium*. Edinburgh: John Donald, pp. 412–3.

Oshibkina S. V. 1997. Veret'e I. *Poselemie epohi mezolita na Severe Vostochnoi Evropt [Veret'e I. A Mesolithic settlement in the north of Eastern Europe]*. Moscow: Nauka.

Otte, M. 1990. The Northwestern European Plain around 18 000 BP. In O. Soffer and C. Gamble (eds.), *The World at 18000 BP. Volume 1 High Latitudes*. London: Unwin Hyman, pp. 54–68.

Otte, M., Yalcinkaya, I., Leotard, J.-M., Kartal, M., Bar-Yosef, O., Koslowski, J., Lopez Bayón, I., and A. Marshack. 1995. The Epi-Palaeolithic of Öküzini cave (SW Anatolia) and its mobiliary art. *Antiquity* 69: 931–44.

Owen, L., and A. Pawlik. 1993. Funktionsinterpretationen Durch Merkmals- und Gebrauchsspurenanalysen an Steinartefakten der Spätmesolithischen Fundstelle Henauhof-Nord II. *Archäologisches Korrespondenzblatt* 23: 413–26.

Østmo, E. 1976. Torsrød: En senmesolittisk kystboplass i Vestfold. *Universitetets Oldsaksamlings årbok* 1972–74: 41–52.

Paaver, K. C. 1965. *Formirovaniye Teriofauny i Izmenchivost Mlekopytayushchikh Pribaltiki v Goltsene*. Tartu: Akademiya Nauk Estonskoii SSR.

Paavola, P., and A. Hartikainen. 1973. *Tampereen Seutukaava-Alueen Esi-Historialliset Kohteet Ja Alueet*. Pohjakartat: Tampere Seutukaavaliito.

Paccard, M., Livache, M., Dumas, C., Poulain, T., and J. C. Miskowsky. 1971. Le camp mésolithique de Gramari à Méthamis (Vaucluse). *Gallia-Préhistoire* 14 (1): 47–137.

Pallares, M., Bordas, A., and R. Mora. 1997. El proceso de neolitización en los Pirineos orientales. Un modelo de continuidad entre los cazadores-recolectores neolíticos y los primeros grupos agropastoriles. *Trabajos de Prehistoria* 54: 121–41.

Palma di Cesnola, A. 1963. Prima campagna di scavi nella Grotta del Cavallo presso Santa Caterina (Lecce). *Rivista di Scienze Preistoriche* 18: 41–74.

Paludan-Müller, C. 1978. High-Atlantic food gathering in northwestern Zealand: Ecological conditions and spatial representation. In K. Kristiansen and C. Paludan-Müller (eds.), *New Directions in Scandinavian Archaeology*. Copenhagen: National Museum of Denmark, pp. 120–57.

Pantaléon-Cano, J., Yll, E.-I., Pérez-Obiol, R., and J. M. Roure. 2003. Palynological evidence for vegetational history in semi-arid areas of the western Mediterranean (Almería, Spain). *The Holocene* 13: 109–19.

Paret, O. 1961. *Württemberg in Vor- und Grühgeschichtlicher Zeit*. Stuttgart: Müller und Gräff.

Pashkevich, G. A. 1982. Paleobotanicheskaya harakteristika poseleniya Mirnoe [Palaeobotanical features of the Mirnoe site]. In V. A. Stanko (ed.), *Mirnoe: Problema mezolita stepei Severnogo Prichernomor'ya [Mirnoe: The problems of the Mesolithic of the North Pontic Steppe]*. Kiev: Naukova Dumka, pp. 132–8.

Paul, I. 1995. Aspekte des Karpatisch-Balkanisch-Donauländischen Neolithikums (die Präcriş Kultur). In *Vorgeschichtliche Untersuchungen in Siebenbürgen*. Biblioteca Universitatis Apuliensis 1: 28–68. Alba Iulia.

Păunescu, A. 1970. Epipaleoliticul de la Cuina Turcului-Dubova. *Studii şi Cercetări de Istorie Veche* 21 (1): 3–47.

Păunescu, A. 2000. *Paleoliticul şi Mesoliticul din spaţial cuprins între Carpaţi şi Dunăre*. Bucureşti: Agir.

Payne, S. 1982. Faunal evidence for environmental/climatic change at Franchthi Cave (Southern Argold, Greece), 25,000 BP to 5,000 BP – preliminary results. In J. Bintliff and W. Van Zeist (eds.), *Palaeoclimates, Palaeoenvironments and Human Communities in the Eastern Mediterranean Region in Later Prehistory*. Oxford: British Archaeological Reports International Series 133, vol. 1, pp. 133–8.

Pearson, R. 2005. The social context of early pottery in the Lingnan region of south China. *Antiquity* 79: 819–28.

Pedersen, L. 1995. 7000 years of fishing: Stationary fishing structures in the Mesolithic and afterwards. In A. Fischer (ed.), *Man and sea in the Mesolithic*. Oxbow Monograph 53. Oxford: Oxbow, pp. 75–86.

Pedersen, L., Fischer, A., and B. Aaby (eds.). 1997. *The Danish Storebælt since the Ice Age – man, sea and forest*. Copenhagen: A/S Storebælt Fixed Link.

References

Pedersen, L., Fischer, A., and N. Hald. 1997. Danubian shafthole axes – long-distance transport and the introduction of agriculture. In L. Pedersen, A. Fischer, and B. Aaby (eds.), *The Danish Storebælt since the Ice Age – man, sea and forest*. Copenhagen: A/S Storebælt Fixed Link, pp. 201–5.

Pedersen, V. L. 2006. Fusager. En mindre lokalitet fra Maglemosekulturen. In B. V. Eriksen (ed.), *Stenalder-studier. Tidlig mesolitiske jægere og samlere i Sydskandinavien*. Århus: Aarhus University Press, pp. 175–96.

Pelegrin, J. 2000. Les techniques de débitage laminaire au Tardiglaciaire: Critères de diagnose et quelques réflexions. In *L'Europe centrale et septentrionale au Tardiglaciaire*, table-ronde de Nemours, 13–16 mai 1997. Mémoires du Musée de Préhistoire d'Ile de France 7, pp. 73–86.

Peltenburg, E., Colledge, S., Croft, P., Jackson, A., McCartney, C., and M. A. Murray. 2000. Agro-pastoralist colonization of Cyprus in the 10th millennium BP: Initial assessments. *Antiquity* 74: 844–53.

Penalva, C., and L. Raposo. 1985. Palheiroes do Alegra. *Informação Arqueológica* 7: 16–19.

Penalva, C., and L. Raposo. 1987. A propósito do machado mirense. In J. Serrão, A. H. de Oliveira Marques, M. C. Monteiro Rodrigues (eds.), *Da Pré-História à História*. Lisboa: Delta, pp. 183–215.

Pentikäinen, J. (ed.). 1996. *Shamanism and northern Ecology*. Berlin: Mouton de Gruyer.

Pentikäinen, J. 1998. *Shamanism and culture*. Helsinki: Ernika Co.

Pentikäinen, J., Jaatinen, T., Lehtinen, I., and M.-R. Salonoiemi (eds.). 1998. *Shamans*. Tampere: Tampere Museum.

Péquart, M., and St-J. Péquart. 1929. La nécropole mésolithique de Téviec (Morbihan). *L'Anthropologie* 39: 373–400.

Péquart, M., and St-J. Péquart. 1934. La nécropole mésolithique de l'île de Hoédic, Morbihan. *L'Anthropologie*: 44 (1–2): 1–20.

Péquart, M., Péquart, St-J., Boule, M., and H. V. Vallois. 1937. *Téviec, station-nécropole mésolithique du Morbihan*. Archives de l'Institut de Paléontologie Humaine, 18. Paris: Masson.

Perlès, C. 1988. New ways with an old problem. Chipped stone assemblages as an index of cultural discontinuity in early Greek prehistory. In E. French and K. Wardle (eds.), *Problems in Greek prehistory*. Bristol: Bristol Classical Press, pp. 477–88.

Perlès, C. 1990. L'outillage de pierre taillée Néolithique en Grèce: Approvisionnement et exploitation des matières premières. *Bulletin de Correspondance Hellénique* 114: 1–42.

Perlès, C. 1992. In search of lithic strategies: A cognitive approach to prehistoric chipped stone assemblages. In J.-C. Gardin and C. Peebles (eds) *Representations in archaeology*. Bloomington: Indiana University Press, pp. 223–47.

Perlès, C. 1995. La transition Pléistocène/Holocène et le problème du Mésolithique en Grèce. In V. Bonilla (ed.), *Los ultimos cazadores: Transformaciones culturales y económicas durante el tardiglaciar y el inicio del Holoceno en el ambito Mediterráneo*. Alicante: Istituto de Cultura Juan Gil Albert, pp. 179–209.

Perlès, C. 1999. Long-term perspectives on the occupation of the Franchthi Cave: Continuity and disconti-nuity. In G. Bailey, E. Adam, C. Perlès, E. Panagopoulou, and K. Zachos (eds.), *The Palaeolithic archaeology of Greece and adjacent areas: Proceedings of the First International Conference on the Palaeolithic of Greece and the Balkans*. London: British School at Athens, pp. 311–18.

Perlès, C. 2001. *The Early Neolithic in Greece*. Cambridge, UK: Cambridge University Press.

Perlès, C. 2003. The Mesolithic at Franchthi: An overview of the data and problems. In N. Galanidou, and C. Perlès (eds.). *The Greek Mesolithic: Problems and perspectives*. London: British School at Athens, pp. 79–87.

Perrin, T. 2003. Mesolthic and Neolithic cultures co-existing in the upper Rhone valley, *Antiquity* 77, 298, 732–9

Pesonen, P. 1995. Hut floor areas and ceramics – analysis of the excavation area in the Rääkkylä Pörrinmökki settlement site, eastern Finland. *Fennoscandia Archaeologica* 12: 139–49.

Peters, E. 1935. Die Falkensteinhöhle bei Tiergarten. *Fundberichte aus Hohenzollern* 3: 2–12.

Peters, E. 1941. *Die Stuttgarter Gruppe der Mittelsteinzeitlichen Kulturen*. Stuttgart: Veröffentlichungen der Archiv der Stadt Stuttgart 7

Peters, E. 1946. *Meine Tätigkeit im Dienst der Vorgeschichte Südwestdeutschlands*. Veringenstadt: Privatdruck.

Petersen, E. B. 1973. A survey of the late Palaeolithic and Mesolithic of Denmark. In S. K. Kozłowski (ed.), *The Mesolithic in Europe*. Warsaw: Warsaw University Press, pp. 77–128.

Petersen, E. B. 1986. Maglemosekultur. *Arkæologiske udgravninger i Danmark 1985*. Copenhagen, pp. 34–5.

Petersen, E. B. 1987. Eight people in one grave – the Mesolithic record? *Mesolithic Miscellany* 14: 14–5.

Petersen, E. B. 1990. Nye grave fra Jægerstenalderen. *Nationalmuseets Arbejdsmark*, pp. 19–33.

Petersen, E. B., Juel-Jensen, H., Aaris-Sørensen, K., and P. V. Petersen. 1982. Vedbækprojektet: Under mosen og byen. *Søllerødbogen 1982*.

Petersen, K. S. 1985. The late Quaternary history of Denmark. *Journal of Danish Archaeology* 4: 7–22.

Petersen, P. V. 1984. Chronological and regional variation in the Late Mesolithic of eastern Denmark. *Journal of Danish Archaeology* 3: 7–18.

Petersen, P. V., and L. Johansen. 1993. Sølbjerg I – an Ahrensburgian Site on a reindeer migration route through eastern Denmark. *Journal of Danish Archaeology* 10: 20–37.

Petersen, P. V., and L. Johansen. 1996. Tracking Late Glacial reindeer hunters in eastern Denmark. In L. Larsson (ed.), *The earliest settlement of Scandinavia and its relationship with neighbouring areas*. Acta Archaeologica Lundensia, Series In 8, 24. Stockholm: Almquist and Wiksell International, pp. 75–84.

Peterson, J. T. 1993. Demand sharing: Reciprocity and the pressure for generosity among foragers. *American Anthropologist* 95: 860–74.

Pettersen, K. 1999. The Mesolithic in Southern Trøndelag. In J. Boaz (ed.), *The Mesolithic of Central Scandinavia*. Universitetets Oldsaksamlings Skrifter. Ny Rekke 22. Oslo: Universitetets Oldsaksamling, pp. 153–66.

Philibert, D. 1988. Mésolithique et Néolithisation: Une même réalité?. *Mésolithique et Néolithisation en France et dans les régions limitrophes*. Actes du 113e Congrès National des Sociétés Savantes (Strasbourg, 1988), Paris, 1991. Editions du CTHS, pp. 113–25.

Philibert, S. 2002. *Les dernier "sauvages": Territoires économique et systèmes techno-fontionnels Mésolithique*. Oxford: British Archaeological Reports International Series 1069.

Pickard, C., and C. Bonsall. In prep. The molluscan remains. In C. Bonsall and V. Boroneanţ (eds.), *From foraging to farming in the Iron Gates: Excavations at Schela Cladovei, Romania*.

Piette, E. 1889. Un groupe d'assises représentant l'époque de transition entre les temps quaternaires et les temps modernes. *Compte rendu de l'Académie des Sciences* 108: 422–4.

Piette, E. 1895. Hiatus et lacune. Vestiges de la période de la transistion dans la grotte du Mas d'Azil. *Bulletin de la Société d'Anthropologie de Paris* 6: 235–67.

Pirazzoli, P. 1987. Sea-level changes in the Mediterranean. In M. Tooley and I. Shennan (eds.), *Sea-level changes*. Oxford: Blackwell, pp. 152–81

Pitts, M. W., and R. M. Jacobi. 1979. Some aspects of change in flaked stone of the Mesolithic and Neolithic in southern England. *Journal of Archaeological Science* 6: 163–77.

Pitul'ko, V. V. 1998. *Zhokhovskaya stiyanka* [*The Zhokhov Site*]. St. Petersburg: Vulinin.

Pluciennik, M. 1994. Space, time and caves: Art in the Palaeolithic, Mesolithic and Neolithic of southern Italy. *Accordia Research Papers* 5: 39–71.

Pluciennik, M. 1997. Radiocarbon determinations and the Mesolithic-Neolithic transition in southern Italy. *Journal of Mediterranean Archaeology* 10 (2): 115–50.

Pluciennik, M. 2002. Art, artefact, metaphor. In Y. Hamilakis, M. Pluciennik, and S. Tarlow (eds.), *Thinking through the body*. New York: Kluwer Academic/Plenum, pp. 217–32.

Pollard, A. 2000. Risga and the Mesolithic occupation of a Scottish island. In R. Young (ed.), *Mesolithic lifeways: Current research in Britain and Ireland*. Leicester Archaeology Monographs 7. Leicester: University Department of Archaeology, pp. 143–52.

Poltowicz, M. 2006. The eastern borders of the Magdalenian culture range. *Analecta Archaeological Ressoviensia* 1: 11–28.

Pons, A., and M. Reille. 1988. The Holocene and Upper Pleistocene pollen record from Padul (Granada, Spain): A new study. *Palaeogeography, Palaeoclimatology, Palaeoecology* 66: 243–63.

Pop, E., Boşcaiu, N., and V. Lupşa. 1970. Analiza sporo-polinica a sedimentelore de la Cuina Turcului-Dubova. *Studii şi Cercetări de Istorie Veche* 21 (1): 31–4.

Poplin, F., Poulain, T., Meniel, P., Vigne, J. D., Geddes, D., and D. Helmer. 1986. Les débuts de l'élevage en France. In J. P. Demoule, and J. Guilaine (eds.), *Le Néolithique de la France. Hommage à Gérard Bailloud*. Paris: Picard, pp. 37–51.

References

Potemkina, I. D. 1999. *Naselenie Ukrainy v epohu neolita i rannego eneolita po antropologicheskim dannym* [*The Ukrainian populations during the Neolithic and Early Chalcolithic Ages according to anthropological evidence*]. Kiev: Institute of Archaeology.

Poulianos, A., and A. Sampson. 2008. Mesolithic human remains from Kythnos Island, Greece. *Human Evolution* 23: 187–203.

Powell, J. 2003. Fishing in the Mesolithic and Neolithic – the Cave of Cyclops, Youra. In E. Kotjabopoulou, Y. Hamilakis, P. Halstead, C. Gamble, and P. Elefanti (eds.), *Zooarchaeology in Greece: Recent advances*. British School at Athens Studies 9. London: British School at Athens, pp. 75–84.

Powers, S. 1877. *Tribes of California*. Contributions to North American Ethnology 3. Washington, DC: U.S. Geographical and Geological Survey of the Rocky Mountain Region.

Prescott, C. 1995. *From Stone Age to Iron Age: A study from Sogn, western Norway*. Oxford: British Archaeological Reports International Series 603.

Prescott, C. 1996. Was there *really* a Neolithic in Norway? *Antiquity* 70 (267): 77–87.

Price, N. S. 2001. An archaeology of altered states: Shamanism and material culture studies. In N. Price (ed.), *The Archaeology of Shamanism*. London: Routledge, pp. 3–16.

Price, T. D. 1978. Mesolithic settlement systems in the Netherlands. In P. Mellars (ed.), *The early postglacial settlement of Northern Europe*. London: Duckworth, pp. 81–113.

Price, T. D. 1980. The Mesolithic of the Drents Plateau. *Berichten van de Rijksdienst voor het Oudheidkundig Bodemonderzoek* 30: 11–63.

Price, T. D. 1981a. Regional approaches to human adaptation in the Mesolithic of the north European plain. In B. Gramsch (ed.), *Mesolithikum in Europa. 2. Internationales Symposium Potsdam, 3. bis 8. April 1978. Veröffentlichungen des Museums für Ur- und Frühgeschichte, Potsdam, 14/15*. Berlin: Deutscher Verlag, pp. 217–34.

Price, T. D. 1981b. Complexity in 'non-complex' societies. In S. E. van der Leeuw (ed.), *Archaeological approaches to the study of complexity*. Amsterdam: Albert Egges van Giffen Instituut voor Prae en Protohistorie, pp. 55–99.

Price, T. D. 1985. Affluent foragers of Mesolithic southern Scandinavia. In T. D. Price, and J. A. Brown (eds.), *Prehistoric hunter-gatherers, the emergence of cultural complexity*. Orlando: Academic Press, pp. 341–63.

Price, T. D. 1987. The Mesolithic of Western Europe. *Journal of World Prehistory* 1: 225–332.

Price, T. D. 1989. The reconstruction of Mesolithic diets. In C. Bonsall (ed.), *The Mesolithic in Europe: Proceedings of the third international symposium*. Edinburgh: John Donald, pp. 48–59.

Price, T. D. 1995. Some perspectives on prehistoric coastal adaptations and those who study them. In A. Fischer (ed.), *Man and sea in the Mesolithic*. Oxbow Monograph 53. Oxford: Oxbow Books, pp. 423–4.

Price, T. D. (ed.). 2000. *Europe's first farmers*. Cambridge, UK: Cambridge University Press.

Price, T. D., and J. A. Brown. 1985. Aspects of hunter-gatherer complexity. In T. D. Price and J. A. Brown (eds.), *Prehistoric hunter-gatherers: The emergence of cultural complexity*. Orlando. Academic Press, pp. 3–20.

Price, T. D., and A. B. Gebauer (eds.). 1992. The final frontier: Foragers to farmers in southern Scandinavia. In A. B. Gebauer and T. D. Price (eds.), *Transition to agriculture in prehistory*. Madison, WI: Prehistory Press, pp. 97–115.

Price, T. D., and K. Jacobs. 1990. Olenii Ostrov: First radiocarbon dates from a major Mesolithic cemetery in Karelia, USSR. *Antiquity* 64: 849–53.

Price, T. D., Bentley, A., Lüning, J., Gronenborn, D., and J. Wahl. 2001. Prehistoric human migration in the *Linearbandkeramik* of central Europe. *Antiquity* 75 (289): 593–603.

Prinz, B. 1987. *Mesolithic adaptations on the Lower Danube: Vlasac and the Iron Gates Gorge*. Oxford: British Archaeological Reports International Series 330.

Probst, E. 1991. *Deutschland in der Steinzeit*. München: Bertelsmann.

Prošek, F. 1951. Mesolitická chata v Tašovicích. *Archeologické rozhledy* 3: 12–15.

Prošek, F. 1959. Mesolitická obsidiánová industrie ze stanice Barca I. Archeologické rozhledy 11: 145–8.

Prostředník, J., and Šída, P. 2006: Mesolithic settlement in the pseudo-karst rock caves in the Bohemian Paradise. Z Českého ráje a Podkrkonoší – Supplementum 11: 83–106.

Prošek, F., and V. Ložek. 1952. Mesolitické sídliště v Zátyní u Dubé. *Anthropozoikum* 2: 93–115.

Prostředník, J., and P. Šída. 2006. Mesolithic settlement in the pseudo-karst rock caves in the Bohemian Paradise. *Českého ráje a Podkrkonoší – Supplementum* 11: 83–106.

Prummel, W., Niekus, M. J. L. T., and A. L. Van Gijn. 1999. Een laatmesolithische jacht- en slachtplaats aan de Tjonger bij Jardinga (Fr.) *Paleo-Aktueel* 10: 16–20.

Prøsch-Danielsen, L., and M. Høgestøl. 1995. A coastal Ahrensburgian site found at Galta, Rennesøy, Southwest Norway. In A. Fischer (ed.), *Man and sea in the Mesolithic.* Oxbow Monograph 53. Oxford: Oxbow, pp. 123–30.

Puertas, O. 1999. Premiers indices polliniques de néolithisation dans la plaine littorale de Montpellier (Hérault, France). *Bulletin de la Societé Préhistorique Française* 96: 15–20.

Pugsley, L. B. 2005. Sex, gender and sexuality in the Mesolithic. In N. Milner and P. Woodman (eds.), *Mesolithic studies at the beginning of the 21st century.* Oxford: Oxbow Books, pp. 164–75.

Quitta, H. 1972. The dating of radiocarbon samples. In D. Srejović (ed.), *Europe's first monumental sculpture: new discoveries at Lepenski Vir.* London: Thames and Hudson, pp. 205–10.

Quitta, H. 1975. Die Radiocarbondaten und ihre historische Interpretation. In D. Srejović (ed.), *Lepenski Vir: Eine vorgeschichtliche Geburtsstätte europäischer Kultur.* Bergisch Gladbach, pp. 272–85.

Radley, J. 1970. The Mesolithic period in north-east Yorkshire. *Yorkshire Archaeological Journal* 42: 314–27.

Radley, J., and P. A. Mellars. 1964. A Mesolithic structure at Deepcar, Yorkshire, England and the affinities of its associated flint industries. *Proceedings of the Prehistoric Society* 30: 1–24.

Radley, J., J. H. Tallis, and V. R. Switsur. 1974. The excavation of three 'narrow blade' Mesolithic sites in the Southern Pennines, England. *Proceedings of the Prehistoric Society* 40: 1–19.

Radovanović, I. 1996. *The Iron Gates Mesolithic.* Ann Arbor, Michigan: International Monographs in Prehistory, Archaeological Series 11.

Radovanović, I. 1999. 'Neither person nor beast' – dogs in the burial practice of the Iron Gates Mesolithic. *Documenta Praehistorica* 26: 71–88.

Radovanović, I. 2000. Houses and burials at Lepenski Vir. *European Journal of Archaeology* 3 (3): 330–49.

Radovanović, I., and B. V. Voytek. 1997. Hunters, fishers or farmers: Sedentism, subsistence and social complexity in the Djerdap Mesolithic. *Analecta Praehistorica Leidensia* 29: 19–31.

Raemaekers, D. C. M. 1999. *The articulation of a 'new Neolithic': The meaning of the Swifterbant culture for the process of neolithisation in the western part of the North European Plain (4900–3400 BC).* Leiden: Leiden University Archaeological Studies 3.

Rähle, W. 1978. Schmuckschnecken aus Mesolithischen Kulturschichten Süddeutschlands und Ihre Herkunft. In W. Taute (ed.), *Das Mesolithikum in Süddeutschland, Teil 2: Naturwissenschaftliche Untersuchungen.* Tübinger Monographien zur Urgeschichte 5/2, pp. 163–8.

Räihälä, O. 1996. A comb ware house in Outokumpu Sätös. In T. Kirkinen (ed.), Pithouses and potmakers in eastern Finland. Reports of the Ancient Lake Saimaa project. *Helsinki Papers in Archaeology* 9: 89–117.

Ramil, E. 1997. La transición del Paleolítico Superior al Neolítico en las sierras septentrionales de Galicia. In R. de Balbín and P. Bueno (eds.), *Actas, II Congreso de Arqueología Peninsular* vol. 1. Zamora: Fundación Rei Afonso Henriques, pp. 273–86.

Ramqvist, P. 2002. Rock-art and settlement: Issues of spatial order in the prehistoric rock-art of Fenno-Scandinavia. In G. Nash, and C. Chippindale (eds.), *European landscapes of Rock-Art.* London: Routledge, pp. 144–57.

Ramqvist, P. H., Forsberg, L., and M. Backe. 1985. . . . And here was an elk too . . . a preliminary report of new petroglyphs at Stornorrfors, Ume River. In *Honorem Evert Baudou: Archaeology and environment* 4. Umeå: Department of Archaeology, Umeå University, pp. 313–37.

Ramstad, M. 2000a. Veideristningene på Møre. Teori, kronologi og dateringsmetoder. *Viking* 63: 51–86.

Ramstad, M. 2000b. Brytninga mellom nord og sør. *Primitive tider* 2000: 54–80. Oslo.

Ramstad, M. 2003. Som man graver, finner man! *Ottar* 248: 15–25.

Ramstad, M., Hesjedal, A., and A. Niemi. 2005. The Melkøya project: Maritime hunter-fisher island settlements and the use of space through 11 000 years on Melkøya, Arctic Norway. *Antiquity* 79 (304), http://antiquity.ac.uk/ProjGall/304.html.

References

Randers, K. 1986. *Breheimundersøkelsene 1982–1984. I: Høyfjellet.* Arkeologiske Rapporter 10. Bergen: Historisk Museum, Universitetet i Bergen.

Randsborg, K. 1975. Social dimensions of early Neolithic Denmark. *Proceedings of the Prehistoric Society* 41:105–18.

Rankama, T. 2003. The colonisation of northernmost Finnish Lapland and the inland areas of Finnmark. In L. Larsson, H. Kindgren, K. Knutsson, D. Loeffler, and A. Åkerlund (eds.), *Mesolithic on the move: Papers presented at the Sixth International Conference on the Mesolithic in Europe, Stockholm 2000.* Oxford: Oxbow Books, pp. 37–46.

Rankamaa, T., and J. Kankaanpää. 2004. First preboreal inland site in North Scandinavia discovered in Finnish Lapland. *Antiquity* 78 (301) http://antiquity.ac.uk/ProjGall/rankama/index.html.

Raposo, L., and A. Silva. 1984. O Languedocense: Ensaio de caracterização morfotécnica e tipológica. *O Arqueólogo Português*, series IV, vol. 2, pp. 87–166.

Raposo, L., Penalva, C., and J. Pereira. 1989. Notícia da descoberta da estaçao mirense de Palheiroes do Alegra, Cabo Sardao. *Actas, II Reunión del Cuaternario Ibérico*, vol. 1. Madrid: Associación Española para el Estudio del Cuaternario, pp. 481–91.

Rasmussen, P. 1991. Leaf-foddering of livestock in the Neolithic: Archaeobotanical evidence from Weier, Switzerland. *Journal of Danish Archaeology* 8: 51–71.

Ravdonikas, W. 1936. Les gravures rupestres des bords du lac Onega. *Travaux de l'Institute d'Ethnographie de l' U. R. S. S. 9.*

Reimer, P. J. Baillie, M. G. L., Bard, E., Bayliss, A., Beck, J. W., Bertrand, C. J. H., Blackwell, P. G., Buck, C. E., Burr, G. S., Cutler, K. B., Damon, P. E., Edwards, R. L., Fairbanks, R. G., Friedrich, M., Guilderson, T. P., Hogg, A. G., Hughen, K. A., Kromer, B., McCormac, G., Manning, S., Ramsey, C. B., Reimer, R. W., Remmele, S., Southon, J. R., Stuiver, M., Talamo, S., Taylor, F. W., van der Plicht, J., and C. E. Weyhenmeyer. 2004. IntCal04 Terrestrial Radiocarbon Age Calibration, 0–26 Cal Kyr BP. *Radiocarbon* 46 (3): 1029–58.

Reinerth, H. 1929. *Das Federseemoor als Siedlungsland des Vorzeitmenschen.* Augsburg: Führer zur Urgeschichte 9.

Reinerth, H. 1953. Die Mittler Steinzeit am Bodensee. *Vorzeit am Bodensee, Heft* 1: 1–32.

Reinerth, H. 1956. Die Älteste Besiedlung des Allgäues. *Vorzeit am Bodensee, Heft* 1–4: 1–35.

Renault-Miskovsky, J., Miskovsky, J. -C., Brochier J. E. and J. L. Brochier. 1979. Lévolution sédimento-climatique at la reconstitution du paysage végétal, à la fin des temps glaciaires dans le sud-est de la France. In D. de Sonneville Bordes (ed.), *La fin des temps glaciaires en Europe: Chronostratigraphie et écologie des cultures du Paléolithique Final.* Paris: CNRS, pp. 61–71.

Renfrew, C. 1987. *Archaeology and language: The puzzle of Indo-European origins.* London: Penguin.

Renfrew, A. C. 1988. Archaeology and language: The puzzle of Indo-European origins. *Current Anthropology* 29 (3): 437–41.

Renfrew, C., and K. Boyle. 2000 (eds.). *Archaeogenetics: DNA and the population prehistory of Europe.* Cambridge: McDonald Institute for Archaeological Research.

Renouf, P. 1984. Northern coastal-fishers: An archaeological model. *World Archaeology* 16 (1): 18–27.

Renouf, M. A. P. 1988. Sedentary coastal hunter-fishers: An example from the Younger Stone Age of northern Norway. In G. Bailey and J. Parkington (eds.), *The Archaeology of Prehistoric Coastlines.* Cambridge, UK: Cambridge University Press, pp. 102–15.

Renouf, P. 1989. Sedentary coastal hunter-fishers: An example from the Younger Stone Age of northern Norway. In G. Bailey and J. Parkington (eds.), *The archaeology of prehistoric coastlines.* Cambridge, UK: Cambridge University Press, pp. 102–15.

Renouf, M. A. P. n.d. Paper presented at the "From the Jomon to Star Carr" symposium organized by P. Rowley-Conwy and S. Kaner, Cambridge and Durham 1995.

Resketov, A. 1972. *Okhotniki, Sobirateli, Rybolovy.* Moskva: Nauka.

Rettenbacher, C., and G. Tichy. 1994. Ein frühmesolithisches Kindergrab aus der Zigeunerhöhle in Elsbethen bei Salzburg. *Mitteilungen der Gesellschaft für Salzburger Landeskunde* 134: 625–42.

Reynier, M. J. 1994. Radiocarbon dating of early Mesolithic stone technologies from Great Britain. *Actes du 119e Congrès National des Sociétés Historiques et Scientifiques, Amiens, 1994, Préhistoire et Protohistoire*. Paris: Comité des Travaux Historiques et Scientifiques, pp. 529–42.

Reynier, M. J. 2000. Thatcham revisited: Spatial and stratigraphic analyses of two sub-assemblages from Site III and its implications for Early Mesolithic typo-chronology in Britain. In R. Young (ed.), *Mesolithic lifeways: Current research in Britain and Ireland*. Leicester Archaeology Monographs 7. Leicester: University Department of Archaeology, pp. 33–46.

Richard, A., Cupillard, C., Richard, H., and A. Thévenin (eds.). 2000. *Les derniers chasseurs-cueilleurs d'Europe occidentale. Actes du colloque de Besançon (Doubs, France)*, octobre 1998, Presses Universitaires Franc-Comtoises, Besançon, 2000.

Richards, M. P., and R. E. M. Hedges. 1999a. Stable isotope evidence for similarities in the types of marine foods used by late Mesolithic humans at sites along the Atlantic coast of Europe. *Journal of Archaeological Science* 26: 717–22.

Richards, M. P., and R. E. M. Hedges. 1999b. A Neolithic revolution? New evidence of diet in the British Neolithic. *Antiquity* 73: 891–7.

Richards, M., and R. Schulting. 2006. Touch not the Fish: A response to Milner et al. *Antiquity* 80 (308): 444–56.

Richards, M., Côrte-Real, H., Forster, P., Macaulay, V., Demaine, A., Papiha, S., Hedges, R., Bandelt, H.-J., and B. Sykes. 1996. Palaeolithic and Neolithic Lineages in the European Mitochondrial Gene Pool. *American Journal of Human Genetics* 59: 185–203.

Richards, M. B., Macaulay, V. A., Bandelt, H. J., and B. C. Sykes. 1998. Phylogeography of mitochondrial DNA in western Europe. *Annals of Human Genetics* 62: 241–60.

Richards, M. P., Hedges R. E. M., Jacobi R., Current A., and C. Stringer. 2000. Gough's Cave and Sun Hole Cave human stable isotope values indicate a high animal protein diet in the British Upper Palaeolithic. *Journal of Archaeological Science* 27: 1–3.

Richards, M. P., Price, T. D., and E. Koch. 2003. The Mesolithic/Neolithic transition in Denmark: New stable isotope data. *Current Anthropology* 44: 288–94.

Riches, D. 1982. *Northern nomadic hunter-gatherers: A humanistic approach*. London: Academic Press.

Richmond, A. 1999. *Preferred economies: The nature of subsistence base throughout mainland Britain during prehistory*. Oxford: British Archaeological Reports British Series 290.

Riede, F. 2009. Climate change, demography and social relations: An alternative view of the Late Palaeolithic pioneer colonisation of southern Scandinavia. In S. B. McCartan, R. Schulting, G. Warren, and P. Woodman (eds.), *Mesolithic horizons. Papers presented at the Seventh International Conference on the Mesolithic in Europe, Belfast 2005*. Oxford: Oxbow Books, pp. 3–10.

Rieder, K., and A. Tillman. 1989. Ein Beitrag zu den spätpaläolithisch-mesolithischen Fundstellen im Donaumoos. In K. Rieder (ed.), *Steinzeitliche Kulturen an Donau und Altmühl*. Ingolstadt: Courier Druckhaus, pp. 125–7.

Riera i Mora, S. 1993. Changements de la composition forestière dans la plaine de Barcelone pendant l'Holocene (littoral Méditerraneen de la peninsule Iberique). *Palynosciences* 2: 133–46.

Rimantiené, R. K. 1971. *Paleolit I mesolit Litvy*. Vilnius.

Rimantiené, R. K. 1979. *Šventoji*. Vilnius: Mosklas.

Rimantiené, R. K. 1980. The east Baltic area in the fourth and the third millennia BC. *Journal of Indo-European Studies* 8 (3 and 4): 407–15.

Rimantiené, R. K. 1992a. Neolithic hunter-gatherers at Šventoji in Lithuania. *Antiquity* 66 (251): 367–76.

Rimantiené, R. K. 1992b. The Neolithic in the eastern Baltic. *Journal of World Prehistory* 6: 97–143.

Rimantiené, R. K. 1996. *Akmens amzius Lietuvoe*. Vilnius.

Rimantiené, R. K. 1998. The first Narva culture farmers in Lithuania. In M. Zvelebil, R. Dennell, and L. Domańska (eds.), *Harvesting the sea, farming the forest*. Sheffield: Sheffield University Press, pp. 213–18.

Robb, J. 1999. Great persons and big men in the Italian Neolithic. In R. Tykot, J. Morter, and J. Robb (eds.), *Social dynamics of the prehistoric central Mediterranean*. London: University of London Accordia Research Centre, pp. 111–21.

References

Roberts, N., Meadows, M., and J. Dodson. 2001. The history of Mediterranean-type environments: Climate, culture and landscape. *The Holocene* 11: 631–4.

Robinson, D. E., and J. A. Harild. 2002. Archaeobotany of an early Ertebølle (Late Mesolithic) site at Halsskov, Zealand, Denmark. In S. L. R. Mason and J. G. Hather (eds.), *Hunter-Gatherer archaeobotany*. London: Institute of Archaeology, pp. 84–95.

Robinson, M. A. 2000. Further consideration of Neolithic charred cereals, fruit and nuts. In A. S. Fairbain (ed.), *Plants in Neolithic Britain and beyond*. Oxford: Oxbow, pp. 85–90.

Roche, J. 1972a. Les amas coquilliers (*concheiros*) mésolithiques de Muge. In J. Lüning (ed.), *Die Anfänge des Neolitikums vom Orient bis Nordeuropa, vol. 7. Fundamenta* (Series A, Fascicle 3, H. Schwabedissen, general ed.) Köln: Böhlau, pp. 72–107.

Roche, J. 1972b. *Le Gisement Mésolithique de Moita do Sebastiao*, vol. 1. Lisboa: Instituto de Alta Cultura.

Roche, J. 1989. Spatial organization in the mesolithic sites of Muge, Portugal. In C. Bonsall (ed.), *The Mesolithic in Europe: Proceedings of the third international symposium*. Edinburgh: John Donald, pp. 607–13.

Rohling, E. R., and S. de Rijk. 1999. Holocene climate optimum and Last Glacial Maximum in the Mediterranean: The marine oxygen isotope record. *Marine Geology* 153: 57–75.

Roksandić, M. 2000. Between foragers and farmers in the Iron Gates gorge: Physical anthropology perspective. *Documenta Praehistorica* 27: 1–100.

Rolão, J., Jocquinito, A., Gonzaga, M. 2006. O complexo mesolítico de Muge: novos resultados sobre a occupação do Cabeço da Armoreira. In N. Bicho and A. F. Carvalho (eds.), Actas do IV Congresso Arqueológico Ibérico. Promontoria Monográfica 4. Faro, pp. 27–41

Rolfsen, P. 1972. Kvartærgeologiske og botaniske betingelser for mennesker i Sør-Norge i seinglasial og tidlig postglasial tid. *Viking* 36: 131–53.

Roussot-Larroque, J. 1985. Sauveterre, et après ... In M. Otte (ed.), *La signification culturelle des industries lithiques*. Oxford: British Archaeological Reports International Series 239, pp. 170–202.

Rowley-Conwy, P. 1981. Mesolithic Danish bacon: Permanent and temporary sites in the Danish Mesolithic. In A. Sheridan and G. N. Bailey (eds.), *Economic archaeology: Towards an integration of ecological and social approaches*. Oxford: British Archaeological Reports International Series 96, pp. 51–5.

Rowley-Conwy, P. 1983. Sedentary hunters, the Ertebølle Example. In G. N. Bailey (ed.), *Hunter-gatherer economy: A European perspective*. Cambridge, UK: Cambridge University Press, pp. 111–26.

Rowley-Conwy, P. 1984a. Postglacial foraging and early farming economies in Japan and Korea: A west European perspective. *World Archaeology* 16 (1): 28–42.

Rowley-Conwy, P. 1984b. The laziness of the short-distance hunter: The origins of agriculture in Western Denmark. *Journal of Anthropological Archaeology* 3 (4): 300–24.

Rowley-Conwy, P. 1986. Between cave painters and crop planters: Aspects of the temperate European Mesolithic. In M. Zvelebil (ed.), *Hunters in transition: Mesolithic societies of temperate Eurasia and their transition to farming*, pp. 17–32.

Rowley-Conwy, P. 1993. Mesolithic animal bones from Forno da Talha, Portugal. *Trabalhos de Antropologia e Etnologia* 33: 45–50.

Rowley-Conwy, P. 1995. Wild or domestic? On the evidence for the earliest domestic cattle and pigs in South Scandinavia and Iberia. *International Journal of Osteoarchaeology* 5:115–26.

Rowley-Conwy, P. 1996. Why didn't Westropp's 'Mesolithic' catch on in 1872? *Antiquity* 70 (270): 940–4.

Rowley-Conwy, P. 1998a. Cemeteries, seasonality and complexity in the Ertebølle of southern Scandinavia. In M. Zvelebil, R. Dennell, and L. Domanska (eds.), *Harvesting the sea, farming the forest*. Sheffield: Sheffield Academic Press, pp. 193–202.

Rowley-Conwy, P. 1998b. Meat, furs and skins: Mesolithic animal bones from Ringkloster, a seasonal hunting camp in Jutland. *Journal of Danish Archaeology* 12: 87–98.

Rowley-Conwy, P. 1999. Economic prehistory in southern Scandinavia. *Proceedings of the British Academy* 99: 125–59.

Rowley-Conwy, P. 2001. Time, change and the archaeology of hunter-gatherers: How original is the 'Original Affluent Society'? In C. Panter-Brick, R. H. Layton, and P. Rowley-Conwy (eds.), *Hunter-gatherers: An interdisciplinary perspective*. Cambridge, UK: Cambridge University Press, pp 39–72.

Rowley-Conwy, P. 2004. How the West was lost: A reconsideration of agricultural origins in Britain, Ireland, and Southern Scandinavia. *Current Anthropology* 45: 83–113.

Rowley-Conwy, P., and M. Zvelebil. 1989. Saving it for later: Storage by prehistoric hunter-gatherers in Europe. In P. Halstead and J. O'Shea (eds.), *Bad year economics*. Cambridge, UK: Cambridge University Press, pp. 40–56.

Rowley-Conwy, P., Zvelebil, M., and H. P. Blankholm (eds.). 1987. *Mesolithic northwest Europe: Recent trends.* Sheffield: University of Sheffield.

Rozoy, J.-G. 1978. *Les derniers chasseurs, l'Epipaléolithique en France et en Belgique*. Bulletin de la Société Archéologique Champenoise, no. spécial, juin 1978, 3 tomes. Charleville.

Rozoy, J.-G. 1989. The revolution of the bowmen in Europe. In C. Bonsall (ed.), *The Mesolithic in Europe: Proceedings of the third international symposium*. Edinburgh: John Donald, pp. 13–28.

Rozoy, J.-G. 1994. Les sites éponymes du Mésolithique. *Bulletin de la Société Préhistorique Française* 91 (1).

Rozoy, J.-G. 1998. Stratégies de chasse et territoires tribaux au Mésolithique. *Bulletin de la Société Préhistorique Française* 95: 525–36.

Ruddiman, W., and A. McIntyre. 1981. The North Atlantic Ocean during the last deglaciation. *Palaeogeography, Palaeoclimatology, Palaeoecology* 35: 145–214.

Rudinskii, M. Ya. 1928. Do pitannya pro kul'turi 'mezolitichnoi dobi' na Vkraini (The problems of the culture of Mesolithic age in the Ukraine]. *Antropologiya* 1: 73–84.

Ruiz Cobo, J., and P. Smith. 2001. El yacimiento del Cubio Redondo (Matienzo, Ruesga). *Munibe* 53: 31–55.

Runnels, C. 1995. Review of Aegean prehistory IV: The Stone Age of Greece from the Palaeolithic to the advent of the Neolithic. *American Journal of Archaeology* 99: 699–728.

Runnels, C. 2009. Mesolithic sites and surveys in Greece: A case study from the Southern Argolid. *Journal of Mediterranean Archaeology* 22 (1): 57–73.

Runnels, C., Panagopoulou, E., Murray, P., Tsartsidou, G., Allen, S., Mullen, K., and E. Tourloukis. 2005. A Mesolithic landscape in Greece: Testing a site-location model in the Argolid at Kandia. *Journal of Mediterranean Archaeology* 18 (2): 259–85.

Runnels, C., T. van Andel, K. Zachos, and P. Paschos. 1999. Human settlement and landscape in the Preveza region (Epirus) in the Pleistocene and early Holocene. In G. Bailey, E. Adam, C. Perlès, E. Panagopoulou, and K. Zachos (eds.), *The Palaeolithic archaeology of Greece and adjacent areas: Proceedings of the First International Conference on the Palaeolithic of Greece and the Balkans*. London: British School at Athens, pp. 120–9.

Russell, N. J., Bonsall C., and D. G. Sutherland. 1995. The evidence of marine molluscs in the Mesolithic of western Scotland: Evidence from Ulva Cave, Inner Hebrides. In A. Fischer (ed.), *Man and sea in the Mesolithic*. Oxbow Monographs 53. Oxford: Oxbow, pp. 273–88.

Ryan, W. B. F., Pittman III, W. C., Major, C. O., Shimkus, K., Moskalenko, V., Jones, G. A., Dimitrov, P., Gornur, N., Sakinc, M., and H. Yuce. 1997. An abrupt drowning of the Black Sea shelf. *Marine Geology* 138: 115–26.

Ryan, W. B. F., Major, C. O., Lericolais, G., and S. L. Goldstein. 2003. Catastrophic flooding of the Black Sea. *Annual Review of Earth and Planetary Sciences* 31: 525–54.

Rybníček, K., and E. Rybníčková. 2001. Vegetation and environment as a background of archaeological cultures in the Czech Republic, 28 000 – 1000 B.P. In V. Podborský (ed.), *50 let archeologických výzkumů Masarykovy univerzity na Znojemsku*. Brno: Masarykova univerzita, pp. 301–10.

Rygh, K. 1911. Stenaldersfund i Ytre Nordmøre. *Det Kongelig Norske Vitenskabs Selskabs Skrifter* 10/1910: 36–63. Trondheim.

Rygh, K. 1913. Flintpladsene på Trøndelagens kyst. *Oldtiden* II 1912: 1–9. Stavanger.

Rønne, O. 2004. Fosfatanalyser. In H. Glørstad (ed.), 2004. *Oppsummering av Svinesundprosjektet, Bind 4*. Varia 57. Oslo: Universitetets kulturhistoriske museer.

Sacchi, D. 1976. Les civilisations de l'Epipaléolithique et du Mésolithique en Languedoc occidental (Bassin de lAude) et en Roussillon. In H. de Lumley (ed.), *La préhistoire Française 1: Les civilisations Paléolithiques et Mésolithiques de la France*. Paris: CNRS, pp. 1390–7.

Salo, U. 1972. *Satakunnan Kiinteät Muinaisjäännökset*. Pori: Satakunnan seutukaavaliitto.

References

Sampson, A. 1998. The Neolithic and Mesolithic occupation of the cave of Cyclope, Youra Alenessos, Greece. *Annual of the British School at Athens* 93: 1–22.

Sampson, A., Koslowski, K., Kaszanowska, M., and B. Giannouli. 2002. The Mesolithic settlement at Maroulas, Kythnos. *Mediterranean Archaeology and Archaeometry* 2: 45–67.

Sampson, A., Kozlowski, J., and M. Kaczanowska. 2003. Mesolithic chipped stone industries from the Cave of Cyclope on the island of Youra (northern Sporades). In N. Galanidou and C. Perlès (eds.), *The Greek Mesolithic: Problems and perspectives*. British School at Athens Studies 10. London: British School at Athens, pp. 123–30.

Samuelsson, C., and N. Ytterberg (eds.). 2003. *Uniting sea. Stone Age societies in the Baltic Sea region*. Uppsala: Department of Archaeology and Ancient History.

Sandgren, P. 2000. Environmental changes in Fennoscandia during the late Quaternary. *Lundqua report* 37. Lund: Department of Quaternary Geology.

Sandmo, A. K. 1986. Råstoff og redskap – mer enn tekniske hjelpemiddel. Om symbolfunksjonen som et aspekt ved materiell kultur. Skisse av etableringsforløpet i en nordeuropeisk kystsone 10.000-9.000 BP. Unpublished thesis, University of Tromsø.

Sanger, D. 1981. An alternative approach to Norwegian Mesolithic chronology. *Norwegian Archaeological Review* 14 (1): 39–43.

Sanger, D. 1995. Mesolithic maritime adaptations: The view from North America. In A. Fischer (ed.), *Man and Sea in the Mesolithic*. Oxbow Monograph 53. Oxford: Oxbow, pp. 335–49.

Santos, L., and M.-F. Sánchez Goñi. 2003. Lateglacial and Holocene environmental changes in Portuguese coastal lagoons 3: Vegetation history of the Santo André coastal area. *The Holocene* 13: 459–54.

Sarvas, P., and J.-P. Taavitsainen. 1976. Kaalliomaalauksia Lemiltä ja Ristiinasta. *Suomen Museo*.

Savatteyev, Y. A. 1973. *Petroglify Karelii*. Voprosy Istorii 6.

Saville, A. 1996. Lacaille, microliths and the Mesolithic of Orkney. In A. Pollard and A. Morrison (eds.), *The early prehistory of Scotland*. Edinburgh: Edinburgh University Press, pp. 213–14.

Schaller E. 1984. Organisasjonsmønstre i steinalderen i sørnorske fjellstrøk. Unpublished thesis, University of Oslo.

Schanche, K. 1988. Mortensnes – en boplass i Varanger. En studie av samfunn og materiell kultur gjennom 10.000 år. Unpublished thesis, University of Tromsø.

Schild, R, Tobolski, K., Kubiak-Martens, L., Bratlund, B., Eicher, U., Calderoni, G., Makowiecki, D., and S. Żurek. 2003. Harvesting pike at Tłokowo, In L. Larsson, H. Kindgren, K. Knutsson, D. Loeffler, and A. Åkerlund (eds.), *Mesolithic on the Move: Papers presented at the Sixth International Conference on the Mesolithic in Europe, Stockholm 2000*. Oxford: Oxbow, pp. 149–58.

Schild, R. 1996. Radiochronology of the early Mesolithic in Poland. In L. Larsson (ed.), *The earliest settlement of Scandinavia and its relationship with neighbouring areas*. Acta Archaeologica Lundensia, Series In 8, 24. Stockholm: Almquist and Wiksell International, pp. 285–96.

Schild, R. 1998. The North European Plain and eastern Sub-Balticum between 12,700 and 8,000 BP. In L. G. Straus, B. V. Eriksen, J. M. Erlandson, and D. R. Yesner (eds.), *Humans at the End of the Ice Age*. London, and New York: Plenum, pp. 129–58.

Schmidt, R. A. 2000. Shamans and northern cosmology: The direct historical approach to Mesolithic sexuality. In R. A. Schmidt and B. L. Voss (eds.), *Archaeologies of sexuality*. London: Routledge, pp. 220–35.

Schmitt, L. 1995. The west Swedish Hensbacka: A maritime adaptation and a seasonal expression of the North-Central European Ahrensburgian? In A. Fischer (ed.), *Man and the sea in the Mesolithic*. Oxbow Monograph 53. Oxford: Oxbow, pp. 161–170.

Schmitt, L. 1999. Comparative points and relative thoughts: The relationship between the Ahrensburgian and Hensbacka assemblages. *Oxford Journal of Archaeology* 18 (4): 327–37.

Schmitt, L., Larsson, S., Burdukiewicz, J., Ziker, J., Svedhage, K., Zamon, J., and H. Steffen. 2009. Chronological insights, cultural change, and resource exploitation on the west coast of Sweden during the Late Palaeolithic/Early Mesolithic Transition. *Oxford Journal of Archaeology* 28 (1): 1–27.

Schmitt, L., Larsson, S., Schrum, C., Alekseeva, I., Tomczak, M., and K. Svedhage. 2006. 'Why They Came'. The colonization of the coast of western Sweden and its environmental context at the end of the last glaciation. *Oxford Journal of Archaeology* 25 (1): 1–28.

Schönweiss, W., and H. Werner. 1977. Mesolithische Wohngrundrisse von Friesheim (Donau): *75 Jahre Anthropologische Staatsammlung München 1902–1977.* München: Bertelsmann, pp. 57–66.

Schulting, R. J. 1996. Antlers, bone pins and flint blades: The Mesolithic cemeteries of Téviec and Hoëdic, Brittany. *Antiquity* 70: 335–50.

Schulting, R. J. 1998. Creativity's coffin: Innovation in the burial record of Mesolithic Europe. In S. Mithen (ed.), *Creativity in human evolution and prehistory*. London. Routledge, pp. 203–26.

Schulting, R. J. 1999. Nouvelles dates AMS à Téviec et Hoëdic (Quiberon, Morbihan). Rapport préliminaire. *Bulletin de la Société Préhistorique Française* 96 (2): 203–7.

Schulting, R. J. 2003. The marrying kind: Evidence for an exogamous residence pattern in the Mesolithic of coastal Brittany. In L. Larsson, H. Kindgren, K. Knutsson, D. Loeffler, and A. Åkerlund (eds.), *Mesolithic on the Move: Papers presented at the Sixth International Conference on the Mesolithic in Europe, Stockholm 2000*. Oxford: Oxbow books, pp. 431–41.

Schulting, R., and M. P. Richards. 2000. The use of stable isotopes in studies of subsistence and seasonality in the British Mesolithic. In R. Young (ed.), *Mesolithic lifeways: Current research in Britain and Ireland*. Leicester Archaeology Monographs 7. Leicester: Leicester University Department of Archaeology, pp. 55–65.

Schulting, R. J., and M. P. Richards. 2001. Dating women and becoming farmers: New palaeodietary and AMS data from the Breton Mesolithic cemeteries of Téviec and Hoëdic. *Journal of Anthropological Archaeology* 20: 314–44.

Schwabedissen, H. 1981. Ertebølle/Ellerbek – Mesolithikum oder Neolithikum? In B. Gramsch (ed.), *Mesolithikum in Europa*. Berlin: Veröffentlichungen des Museums für Ur- und Frühgeschichte Potsdam 14/15, pp. 129–42.

Séara, F., Rotillon, S., and C. Cupillard (eds.). 2002. *Campements mésolithiques en Bresse jurasienne, Choisey et Ruffey-sur-Seille*. Paris: Documents d'Archéologie Française.

Séfériadès M. 1993. The European Neolithisation process. *Porocilo o raziskovanju paleolita, neolita in eneolita v Sloveniji, Ljubljana. Neolithic studies 1*.

Segre, A., and A. Vigliardi. 1983. L'Épigravettien évolué et final en Sicile. *Rivista di Scienze Preistoriche* 38: 351–69.

Sellevold, B., and B. Skar. 1999. The first lady of Norway. In G. Gundhus, E. Seip, and E. Ulriksen (eds.), *NIKU 1994–1999. Kulturminneforsknings mangfold*. Oslo: Norsk Institutt for Kulturminneforskning (NIKU), pp. 6–11.

Semenova, V. I. 1998. Kvoprosu o vremeni proiskhozhdeniia olenevodstva u vostochnykh Khantov (po arkheologicheckim istochnikam). Sisteema zhizneobespecheniia traditsionnykh obschchest v drevnosti I sovremennosti. *Teoria, metodologiia, praktika, Materialy IX Zapadno-Sibiriskoi arkheolo-etnograficheskoi konferentsii*. Tomsk: Izdatel'stvo tomskogo universiteta, pp. 136–9.

Semmel, A. 1995. Bodenkundliche Hinweise auf Ackernutzung und Intensive Bodenerosion um 8000 B.P. im Rhein-Main-Gebiet. *Archäologisches Korrespondenzblatt* 25: 157–63.

Senna-Martinez, J., López, M. S., and M. Hoskin. 1997. Territorio, ideología y cultura material en el megalitismo de la plataforma de Mondego. In A. Rodríguez (ed.), *O Neolítico Atlántico e as orixes do megalitismo*. Santiago de Compostela: Universidad de Santiago, pp. 657–76.

Serna, M. 1997. Ocupación megalítica y proceso de neolitización en la Cornisa Cantábrica. In A. Rodríguez (ed.), *O Neolítico Atlántico e as orixes do megalitismo*. Santiago de Compostela: Universidad de Santiago, pp. 353–68.

Shackleton, J., and T. van Andel. 1985. Late Palaeolithic and Mesolithic coastlines of the western Mediterranean, *Cahiers Ligures de Préhistoire et de Protohistoire (Nouvelle Serie)* 2: 7–20.

Shackleton, N., and M. Deith. 1986. Seasonal exploitation of marine molluscs. In L. Straus and G. Clark (eds.), *La Riera Cave*. Anthropological Research Papers 36. Tempe: Arizona State University, pp. 299–313.

Shefferus, J. 1673. *Lapponia*. Rome.

References

Sherratt, A. G. 1982. Mobile resources: Settlement and exchange in early agricultural Europe. In C. Renfrew and S. Shennan (eds.), *Ranking, resources and exchange: Aspects of the archaeology of early European society*. Cambridge, UK: Cambridge University Press, pp. 13–26.

Shetelig, H. 1922. *Primitive tider. En oversigt over stenalderen*. Bergen: J. Griegs

Shilik, K. K. 1997. Oscillations of the Black Sea and ancient landscapes. In J. C. Chapman and P. M. Dolukhanov (eds.), *Landscape in Flux: Central and Eastern Europe in Antiquity* Oxford: Oxbow, pp. 115–30.

Shostak, M. 1981. *Nisa: The life and words of a!Kung woman*. Cambridge, MA: Harvard University Press.

Šída, P., Pokorný, P., and P. Kuneš. 2007. Early Holocene wooden artifacts from the Lake Švarcenberk. *Přehled výzkumů* 48.

Šída, P., and J. Prostředník. 2007. Mezolit a pozdní paleolit Českého ráje: perspektivy poznání regionu. *Archeologické rozhledy* 59: 443–60.

Siiriäinen, A. 1974. Über die chronologie der steinzeitlichen Küstenwohnplätze Finnlands im Lichte der Uferverschreibung. *Suomen Museo* 76: 40–73.

Siiriäinen, A. 1981. On the cultural ecology of the Finnish Stone Age. *Suomen Museo* 87: 5–40.

Siiriäinen, A. 1982. Recent studies on the Stone Age economy in Finland. *Fennoscandia Antiqua* 1: 17–26.

Silva, C. 1997. O Neolítico antigo e a origem do megalitismo no sul de Portugal. In A. Rodríguez (ed.), *O Neolítico Atlántico e as orixes do megalitismo.* Santiago de Compostela: Universidad de Santiago, pp. 575–85.

Simmons, I. G. 1996. *The environmental impact of later Mesolithic cultures*. Edinburgh: Edinburgh University Press.

Simonsen, P. 1958. *Arktiske helleristninger i Nord-Norge 2*. Instituttet for Sammenlignende Kulturforskning Serie B 40.

Simonsen, P. 1961. *Varangerfunnene II*. Tromsø museums skrifter VII:2. Tromsø.

Simonsen, P. 1963. *Varangerfunnene III.* Tromsø museums skrifter, VII:3. Tromsø.

Simonsen, P. 1975a. *Veidemenn på Nordkalotten, hefte 1: Innledning – Eldre steinalder*. Stenilserie B. Institutt for samfunnsvitenskap (ISV), University of Tromsø.

Simonsen, P. 1975b. When and why did occupational specialisation begin at the Scandinavian north coast? In W. Fitzhugh (ed.), *Prehistoric maritime adaptations of the circumpolar zone*. The Hague: Mouton, pp. 75–86.

Simonsen, P. 1979. *Veidemenn på Nordkalotten, hefte 3*. Stensilserie B. Institutt for samfunnsvitenskap (ISV), University of Tromsø.

Simonsen, P. 1986. Fortsatte undersøkelser ved Virdnejavri, Kautokeino kommune, Finnmark. *Tromura, Kulturhistorie* 8: 1–12. Tromsø.

Simpson, D. 1992. Archaeological investigations at Krossnes, Flatøy 1988–1991. Bergen: Historisk museum, Universitetet i Bergen.

Simpson, D. 1999. Lithic raw material frequencies and the construction of site chronology. In J. Boaz (ed.), *The Mesolithic of Central Scandinavia*. Universitetets Oldsaksamlings Skrifter. Ny Rekke 22, Oslo: Universitetets Oldsaksamling, pp. 299–316.

Sjurseike, R. 1994. Jaspisbruddet i Flendalen. En kilde til forståelse av sosiale relasjoner i eldre steinalder. Unpublished thesis, University of Oslo.

Skaarup, J. 1973. *Hesselø-Sølager: Jagdstationen der südskandinavischen Trichterbecker-kultur*. Copenhagen: Arkæologiske Studier I.

Skaarup, J. 1993. Submerged settlements. In S. Hvass and B. Storgaard (eds.), *Digging into the past: 25 years of archaeology in Denmark*. Århus: Aarhus University Press 1993, pp. 70–5.

Skaarup, J., and O. Grøn. 2004. *Møllegebaet: A submerged Mesolithic settlement in southern Denmark*. British Archaeological Reports International Series 1328. Oxford: Archaeopress.

Skar, B. 1989. Foldsjøen 4a, en stenalderboplass i zonen mellem kyst og fjeld. *Viking* 52: 7–21.

Skar, B., and S. Coulson. 1986. Evidence of behaviour from refitting- a case study. *Norwegian Archaeological Review* 19 (2): 90–102.

Skeates, R. 1994. A radiocarbon date-list for prehistoric Italy (c. 46,400 BP – 2450/400 cal BC). In R. Skeates, and R. Whitehouse (eds.), *Radiocarbon dating and Italian prehistory*. London: British School at Rome/University of London Accordia Research Centre, pp. 147–288.

Skeates, R. 1999. Unveiling inequality. Social life and social change in the Mesolithic and Early Neolithic of east-central Italy. In R. Tykot, J. Morter, and J. Robb (eds.), *Social dynamics of the prehistoric central Mediterranean*. London: University of London Accordia Research Centre, pp. 15–45.

Skeates, R., and R. Whitehouse. 1994. New radiocarbon dates for prehistoric Italy I. *The Accordia Research Papers* 5: 137–50.

Skeates, R., and R. Whitehouse. 1995–6. New radiocarbon dates for prehistoric Italy 2. *The Accordia Research Papers* 6: 179–91.

Skeates, R., and R. Whitehouse. 1997–8. New radiocarbon dates for prehistoric Italy 3. *The Accordia Research Papers* 7: 149–62.

Skjelstad, G. 2003. Regionalitet i vestnorsk mesolitikum. Råstoffbruk og sosiale grenser på Vestlandskysten i mellom- og senmesolitikum. Unpublished Thesis, University of Bergen.

Sklenář, K. 2000. Hořín III. Mesolithische und hallstattzeitliche Siedlung. *Fontes Archaeologici Pragenses* 24. Praha.

Škrdla, P., Mateiciucová, I., and A. Přichystal. 1997. Mesolithikum. In L. Poláček (ed.), *Studien zum Burgwall von Mikulčice II*. Brno, pp. 45–91.

Skutil, J. 1940. Paleolitikum v bývalém Československu. *Obzor prehistorický* 12, 5–99.

Skår, Ø. 2003. Rituell kommunikasjon i seinmesolitikum. En analyse av hakker og køllers symbolske betydning. Unpublished thesis, University of Bergen.

Smart, D. 2000. Design and function in fishing gear: Shell mounds, bait and fishing practices. In R. Young (ed.), *Mesolithic lifeways: Current research in Britain and Ireland*. Leicester Archaeology Monographs 7. Leicester: Leicester University Department of Archaeology, pp. 15–22.

Smith, C. 1992. The population of Late Upper Palaeolithic Britain. *Proceedings of the Prehistoric Society* 58: 37–40.

Smith, C. 1997. *Late Stone Age hunters of the British Isles*. London: Routledge.

Smith, C., and S. Openshaw. 1990. Mapping the Mesolithic. In P. M. Vermeersch, and P. van Peer (eds.), *Contributions to the Mesolithic in Europe*. Leuven: Leuven University Press, pp. 17–22.

Smits, E., and L. P. Louwe Kooijmans. 2001a. De menselijke skeletresten. In L. P. Louwe Kooijmans (ed.), Hardinxveld-Giessendam Polderweg, een mesolithisch jachtkamp in het rivierengebied (5500–5000 v. Chr.). *Rapportage Archeologische Monumentenzorg* 83: 419–40.

Smits, E., and L. P. Louwe Kooijmans. 2001b. Menselijke skeletresten. In L. P. Louwe Kooijmans (ed.), Hardinxveld-Giessendam De Bruin, een kampplaats uit het Laat-Mesolithicum en het begin van de Swifterbant-cultuur (5500–4450 v. Chr.). *Rapportage Archeologische Monumentenzorg* 88: 479–98.

Soares, J. 1997. A transiçao para as formaçoes sociais neolíticas na costa sudoeste portuguesa. In A. Rodríguez (ed.), *O Neolítico Atlántico e as orixes do megalitismo*. Santiago de Compostela: Universidad de Santiago, pp. 587–608.

Soares, P., Ermini, L., Thomson, N., Mormina, M., Rito, T., Rohl, A., Salas, A., Oppenheimer, S., Macaulay, V., and M. B. Richards. 2009. Correcting for purifying selection: An improved human mitochondrial molecular clock. *American Journal of Human Genetics* 84: 740–59.

Soffer, O. 1985. *The Upper Palaeolithic of the Central Russian Plain*. Orlando: Academic Press.

Sognnes, K. 1994. Ritual landscapes: Toward a reinterpretation of Stone Age rock art in Trøndelag, Norway. *Norwegian Archaeological Review* 27 (1): 29–50.

Sognnes, K. 1995. The social context of rock-art in Trøndelag, Norway: Rock-art at a frontier. In K. Helskog and B. Olsen. (eds.), *Perceiving rock-art: Social and political perspectives*, 130–45. Oslo: Novus, pp. 130–45.

Sognnes, K. 1998. Symbols in a changing world: Rock-art and the transition from hunting to farming in mid Norway. In C. Chippindale and P. S. C. Taçon (eds.), *The archaeology of rock-art*. Cambridge, UK: Cambridge University Press, pp. 146–62.

Sognnes, K. 2001. Verdens største skiløper (?). *Spor* 2001 (2): 47–8. Trondheim: Vitenskapsmuseet.

Sognnes, K. 2002. Land of elks – sea of whales: Landscapes of Stone Age rock-art in central Scandinavia. In G. Nash and C. Chippindale (eds.), *European landscapes of rock-art*. London: Routledge, pp. 195–212.

Sognnes, K. 2003. On shoreline dating of rock art. *Acta Archaeologica* 74: 189–209.

447

References

Sognnes, K. 2005. Netter ved Bøla. *Spor* 2003 (1): 39–42. Trondheim: Vitenskapsmuseet.

Sokolova, Z. P. 1989. A survey of the Ob-Ugrian shamanism. In M. Hoppál, and O. J. von Sadovsky (eds.), *Shaminism: Past and present*. Budapest/Los Angeles: Fullerton.

Solberg, B. 1989. The Neolithic transition in southern Scandinavia: Internal development or migration? *Oxford Journal of Archaeology* 8: 261–96.

Somme, A. (ed.), 1968. *A Geography of Norden*. London: Heinemann.

Sordinas, A. 2003. The 'Sidarian': Maritime Mesolithic non-geometric microliths in western Greece. In N. Galanidou and C. Perlès (eds.), *The Greek Mesolithic: Problems and perspectives*. London: British School at Athens, pp. 89–97.

Speth, J. D. 1990. Seasonality, resource stress and food sharing in so called egalitarian foraging societies. *Journal of Anthropological Archaeology* 9 (2): 148–88.

Spikins, P. A. 1999. *Mesolithic northern England: Environment, population and settlement*. Oxford: British Archaeological Reports British Series 283.

Spikins, P. A. 2000. GIS models of past vegetation: An example from northern England, 10,000–5,000 BP. *Journal of Archaeological Science* 27, 219–34

Spikins, P. A. 2000. Ethno-facts or ethno-fiction? searching for the structure of settlement patterns. In R. Young (ed). *Mesolithic lifeways: Current research from Britain and Ireland*. Leicester Archaeology Monographs 7. Leicester: University of Leicester, pp. 105–18.

Spikins, P. A. 2008. The bashful and the boastful: Prestigious leaders and social change in Mesolithic societies. *Journal of World Prehistory* 2008 (3–4): 173–93.

Srejović, D. 1969. The roots of the Lepenski Vir culture. *Archaeologia Iugoslavica*. 10: 13–21.

Srejović, D. 1972. *Europe's first monumental sculpture. new discoveries at Lepenski Vir*. London: Thames and Hudson.

Srejović, D. 1989. The Mesolithic of Serbia and Montenegro. In C. Bonsall (ed.), *The Mesolithic in Europe: Proceedings of the third international symposium*. Edinburgh: John Donald, pp. 481–91.

Srejović, D., and Z. Letica. 1978. *Vlasac. A Mesolithic settlement in the Iron Gates*. Beograd: Serbian Academy of Sciences and Arts Monograph DXII.

Stadler, H. 1991. Eine mesolithische Freilandstation auf dem Hirschbichl im Defereggental, Gem. St. Jakob, Osttirol. *Archäologie Österreichs* 2/1: 23–6.

Stanko, V. N. 1982. *Mirnoe: Problema mezolita stepei Severnogo Prichernomor'ya (Mirnoe: The problems of the Mesolithic of the North Pontic Steppe)*. Kiev: Naukova Dumka.

Stanko, V. N. (ed.). 1997. *Davnja istorija Ukraini [Early history of the Ukraine]*, vol. 1, *Pervisne Suspil'stvo [Prehistoric Society]*. Kiev: Naukova Dumka.

Steele, J, Gkiasta, M, and S. Shennan. 2004. The Neolithic Transition and European population history, a response. *Antiquity* 78 (301): 711–3

Stehli, P. 1989. Merzbachtal, Umwelt und Geschichte einer bandkeramischen Siedlungskammer. *Germania* 67: 51–76.

Stewart, A., and M. Jochim. 1986. Changing economic organization in Late Glacial southwest Germany. In L. Straus (ed.), *The End of the Paleolithic in the Old World*. Oxford: British Archaeological Reports International Series 284, pp. 47–62.

Stillborg, O., and I. Bergenstrahle. 2000. Traditions in transition: A comparative study of the patterns of Ertebølle lithic and pottery changes in the Late Mesolithic ceramic phase at Skateholm I, III and Sodattorpet in Scania, Sweden. *Lund Archaeological Review* 6: 23–42.

Stiner, M. C., Bicho N., Lindly, J., and R. Ferring. 2003. Mesolithic to Neolithic transitions: New results from shell-middens in the western Algarve, Portugal. *Antiquity* 77: 75–86.

Stoczkowski, W. 2002. *Explaining human origins: Myth, imagination and conjecture*. Cambridge, UK: Cambridge University Press.

Stoll, H. 1932. Mesolithikum aus dem Ostschwarzwald. *Germania* 16: 91–7.

Stoll, H. 1933. *Urgeschichte des Oberen Gäues*. Stuttgart: Veröffentlichungen des Württembergischen Landesamts für Denkmalpflege.

Stolyar, A. D. 1959. Pervyi Vasil'evskii mezoliticheskii mogil'nik [The First Vasil'evsky cemetery]. *Arheologich-eskii Sbornik Gosudarstvennogo Ermitazha* [*State Hermitage Archaeological Reports*] 1: 78–165.

Strassburg, J. 2000. *Shamanic shadows: One hundred generations of undead subversion in southern Scandinavia, 7000–4000 BC.* Stockholm Studies in Archaeology 20.

Strassburg, J. 2003. Rituals at the Meso 2000 conference and the Mesolithic-Neolithic terminological breakdown. In L. Larsson, H. Kindgren, K. Knutsson, D. Loeffler, and A. Åkerlund (eds.), *Mesolithic on the move: Papers presented at the sixth international conference on the Mesolithic in Europe, Stockholm 2000.* Oxford: Oxbow, pp. 542–6.

Strathern, M. 1988. *The gender of the gift. Problems with women and problems with society in Melanesia.* Berkeley: University of California Press.

Straus, L. G. 1979. Mesolithic adaptations along the northern coast of Spain. *Quaternaria* 21: 305–27.

Straus, L. G. 1985. Chronostratigraphy of the Pleistocene-Holocene transition: The Azilian problem in the Franco-Cantabrian region. *Palaeohistoria* 27: 89–122.

Straus, L. G. 1991a. Epipaleolithic, and Mesolithic adaptations in Cantabrian Spain, and Pyrenean France. *Journal of World Prehistory* 5: 83–104.

Straus, L. 1991b. The 'Mesolithic-Neolithic transition' in Portugal: A view from Vidigal. *Antiquity* 65: 899–903.

Straus, L. G. 1992. To change or not to change: The Late and Postglacial in SW Europe. *Quaternaria Nova* 2: 161–85.

Straus, L. 1993. Upper Paleolithic hunting tactics and weapons in western Europe. In G. Peterkin, H. Bricker, and P. Mellars (eds.), *Hunting and animal exploitation in the Later Palaeolithic and Mesolithic of Eurasia.* Archeological Papers of the American Anthropological Association 4. Washington, DC: American Anthropological Association, pp. 83–93.

Straus, L. 1995. Diversity in the face of adversity: Human adaptations to the environmental changes of the Pleistocene-Holocene transition in the Atlantic regions of Aquitaine, Vasco-Cantabria and Portugal. In V. Villaverde (ed.), *Los ultimos cazadores: Transformaciones culturales y económicas durante el Tardiglaciar y el inicio del Holoceno en el ambito Mediterráneo.* Alicante: Istituto de Cultura Juan Gil Albert, pp. 9–22.

Straus, L. 1996. The archaeology of the Pleistocene-Holocene transition in southwest Europe. In L. Straus, B. Eriksen, J. Erlandson, and D. Yesner (eds.), *Humans at the end of the Ice Age: The archaeology of the Pleistocene-Holocene transition.* New York: Plenum Press, pp. 83–99.

Straus, L. G., and G. Clark. 1986. *La Riera Cave.* Anthropological Research Papers 36. Tempe: Arizona State University.

Straus, L. G., and M. González Morales. 1998. 1998 excavation campaign in El Mirón Cave. *Old World Archaeology Newsletter* 21 (3): 1–9.

Straus, L. G., and M. González Morales. 2003. The Mesolithic in the Cantabiran interior: Fact or fantasy? In L. Larsson, H. Kindgren, K. Knutsson, D. Loeffler, and A. Åkerlund (eds.), *Mesolithic on the move: Papers presented at the sixth international conference on the Mesolithic in Europe, Stockholm 2000.* Oxford: Oxbow, pp. 359–68.

Straus, L. G. Altuna, J., Jackes, M., and M. Kunst. 1988. New excavations in Casa da Moura and at Bocas, Portugal. *Arqueologia* 18: 65–95.

Straus, L., Altuna, J., and B. Vierra. 1990. The concheiro at Vidigal: A contribution to the Late Mesolithic of southern Portugal. In P. Vermeersch and P. Van Peer (eds.), *Contributions to the Mesolithic in Europe.* Leuven: Leuven University Press, pp. 463–74.

Strauss, L. G., Eriksen, B. V., Erlandson, J. M., and D. Yesner (eds.). 1996. *Humans at the end of the Ice Age. The archaeology of the Pleistocene-Holocene transition.* New York: Plenum Press.

Street, M. 1989. *Jäger und Schamanen, Bedburg-Königshoven ein Wohnplatz am Niederrhein vor 10000 Jahren.* Mainz: Verlag des Römisch-Germanische Zentralmuseums.

Street, M. 1991. Bedburg-Königshoven, a Pre-Boreal Mesolithic site in the Lower Rhineland, Germany. In N. Barton, A. J. Roberts, and D. A. Roe (eds.), *The Late Glacial in North-West Europe: Human adaptation and environmental change at the end of the Pleistocene.* London: CBA Research Report No 77, pp. 256–70.

449

References

Street, M. 1999. Remains of Aurochs Bos primigenius from the Early Mesolithic site Bedburg-Königshoven Rhineland, Germany. In G.-C. Weniger (ed.), *Archäologie und Biologie des Aurochsen*. Wissenschaftliche Schriften des Neanderthal Museums 1. Mettmann: Neanderthal Museum, pp. 173–94.

Street, M. 2003. Ein Wiedersehen mit dem Hund von Bonn-Oberkassel. In R. Hutterer (ed.), *Animals in History: Archaeozoological Papers in Honour of Günter Nobis (1921–2002)*. Bonner Zoologische Beiträge 50 (3), (2002). Bonn: Zoologisches Forschungsinstitut und Museum Alexander Koenig, pp. 269–90.

Street, M., Baales, M., and B. Weniger. 1994. Absolute Chronologie des späten Paläolithikums und Frühmesolithikums im nördlichen Rheinland. *Archäologisches Korrespondenzblatt* 24: 1–28.

Ströbel, R. 1959. Tardenoisspitze in einem Bovidenknochen von Schwenningen am Neckar. *Fundberichte aus Schwaben* 15: 13–16.

Stuiver, M., and P. J. Reimer. 1993. Extended ^{14}C data base and revised CALIB 3. 0 ^{14}C age calibration program. *Radiocarbon* 35 (1): 215–30.

Stuiver, M., Reimer, P. J., and R. Reimer. 2005. *CALIB Radiocarbon Calibration (rev. 5. 0. 2): On-line Manual*. http://radiocarbon.pa.qub.ac.uk/calib/manual/.

Stutz, L. N. 2003. *Embodied rituals and ritualised bodies*. Acta Archaeologica Lundensia Series in 8°, 46. Lund: Wallin, and Dahlholm.

Sulgustowska, Z. 1990. Occurrence and utilization of local ochre resources during the early Holocene in the Oder and Vistula River Basins. In P. M. Vermeersch and P. van Peer (eds.), *Contributions to the Mesolithic in Europe*. Leuven: Leuven University Press, pp. 317–21.

Sulgustowska, Z. 1996. The earliest Mesolithic settlement of north-eastern Poland. In L. Larsson (ed.), *The earliest settlement of Scandinavia and its relationship with neighbouring areas*. Acta Archaeologica Lundensia, Series In 8, 24. Stockholm: Almquist and Wiksell International, pp. 297–304.

Sulgustowska, Z. 1998. Continuity, change and transitions. In M. Zvelebil, R. Dennell, and L. Domańska *Harvesting the sea, farming the forests*. Sheffield: Sheffield Academic Press, pp. 87–94.

Sulgustowska, Z. 2003. Mesolithic colonisation of South-Eastern Subbalticum. In L. Larsson, H. Kindgren, K. Knutsson, D. Loeffler, and A. Åkerlund (eds.), *Mesolithic on the move: Papers presented at the Sixth International Conference on the Mesolithic in Europe, Stockholm 2000*. Oxford: Oxbow, pp. 47–51.

Sulgustowska, Z. 2005. *Kontakty Spolecznosci*. Warszawa: Institut Archeologii I Etnologii Polskei Akademii Nauk.

Sulgustowska, Z. 2006. Mesolithic mobility and contacts on areas of the Baltic Sea watershed, the Sudety and Carpathian mountains. *Journal of Anthropological Archaeology* 25 (2): 193–203.

Surmely, F. (ed.). 2003. *Le site mésolithique des Baraquettes (Velzic, Cantal) et le peuplement de la moyenne montagne cantalienne, des origines à la fin du Mésolithique*. Société Préhistorique Française, mémoire 32.

Surovell, T. A. 2000. Early Paleoindian women, children, mobility and fertility. *American Antiquity* 65: 493–508.

Suttles, W. (ed.). 1990. *Handbook of North American Indians. Vol. 7, Northwest Coast*. Washington, DC: Smithsonian Institution.

Suttles, W. 1968. Coping with abundance: Subsistence on the Northwest Coast. In R. B. Lee, and I. DeVore (eds.), *Man the hunter*. Chicago: Aldine, pp. 56–68.

Suzman, J. 2004. Hunting for histories: Rethinking historicity in the Western Kalahari. In A. Barnard (ed.), *Hunter-gatherers in history, archaeology and anthropology* Oxford: Berg, pp. 201–16.

Svendsen, F. 2007. Lokaliteter og landskap i tidlig mesolittisk tid. En geografisk analyse fra Nordvest-Norge. Unpublished MA thesis, NTNU. Trondheim.

Svendsen, J. I., and J. Mangerud. 1987. Late Weichselian and Holocene sea-level history for a cross-section of Western Norway. *Journal of Quarternary Science* 2: 113–32.

Svoboda, J. 1977. The Mesolithic settlement in the region of Polomené Mts. (North Bohemia). *Anthropologie* 15: 123–36.

Svoboda, J. 1992. A Mesolithic feature from Dolní Věstonice. *Archeologické rozhledy* 44: 111–12.

Svoboda, J., (ed). 2003. *Mezolit severních Čech – Mesolithic of Northern Bohemia*. Brno: The Dolní Věstonice Studies 9.

Svoboda, J., Cílek, V., and L. Jarošová. 1998. Zum Mesolithikum in den Sandsteingebieten Nordböhmens. *Archäologisches Korrespondenzblatt* 28: 357–72.

Svoboda, J., Hajnalová, M., Horáček, I., Novák, M., Přichystal, A., Šajnerová, A., and A. Yaroshevich. 2007. Mesolithic settlement and activities in rockshelters of the Kamenice river canyon, Czech Republic. *Eurasian Prehistory* 5: 95–127.

Svoboda, J., Jarošová, L., and E. Drozdová. 2000. The North Bohemian Mesolithic revisited: The excavation seasons 1998–1999. *Anthropologie* 38: 291–305.

Svoboda, J., and V. Ložek. 1993. Nález mezolitu a sled malakofauny v Průchodnicích. *Bulletin České geologické společnosti* 1: 39–40.

Svoboda, J., Ložek, V., and E. Vlček. 1996. *Hunters between East and West. The Paleolithic of Moravia*. New York and London: Plenum.

Svoboda, J., van der Plicht, J., and V. Kuželka. 2002. Upper Palaeolithic and Mesolithic human fossils from Moravia and Bohemia (Czech Republic): Some new C14 dates. *Antiquity* 76: 957–62.

Svobodová, H. 1997. *Die Entwicklung der Vegetation in Südmähren (Tschechien) während des Spätglazials und Holozäns – eine palynologische Studie*. Wien: Verhandlungen der Zoologisch-Botanischen Gesellschaft in Österreich 134, pp. 317–56.

Søborg, H. C. 1988. Knivskarpe grenser for skiferbruk i steinalderen. *Arkeologiske Skrifter* 4: 225–41. Historisk Museum, Bergen.

Sørensen, R. 1979. Late Weichselian deglaciation in the Oslo fjord area, south Norway. *Boreas* 8: 241–6.

Sørensen, S. A. 1988. A Maglemosian hut at Lavringe Mose, Zealand. *Journal of Danish Archaeology* 6: 53–62.

Sørensen, S. A. 1996. *Kongemose-Kulturen i Sydskandinavien*. Jægerpris: Egnsmuseet Færgegården.

Taavitsainen, J.-P. 1978. Hällmlningarna – en ny syn p Finlands förhistoria. *Antropologi i Finland* 4: 179–95.

Taavitsainen, J.-P., and K. Kinnunen. 1979. Puumalan syrjäsalmen kalliomaalauksista ja kalliomaalausten säilymisestä. *Geologi* 31: 37–42.

Taavitsainen, J.-P., Simola, H., and E. Grönlund 1998. Cultivation history beyond the periphery: Early agriculture in the north European boreal forest. *Journal of World Prehistory* 12 (2): 199–253.

Taborin, Y. 1974. La parure en coquillage. *Gallia Préhistoire* 17: 101–79.

Tagliacozzo, A. 1993. *Archeozoologia della Grotta dell' Uzzo, Sicilia. da un economia di caccia ad un economia di pesca ed allevamento*. Supplemento al Bullettino di Paletnologia Italiana 84. Roma: Poligrafico e Zecca dello Stato.

Tainter, J. A. 1976. Spatial organization and social patterning in the Kaloko cemetery, northern Kona, Hawaii. *Archaeology and Physical Anthropology in Oceania* 11: 91–105.

Takala, H. 2005 *The Ristola Site in Lahiti and the earliest postglacial settlement of South Finland*. Lahti: Lahti City Museum.

Tambets, K., Kivisild, T., Metspalu, E., Parik, J., Kaldma, K., Laos, S., Tolk, H.-V., Gölge, M., Demirtas, H., Gebeerhiwot, T., Papiha, S. S., de Stefano, G. F., and R. Villems. 2000. The topology of the maternal lineages of the Anatolian and trans-Caucasus populations and the peopling of Europe: Some preliminary considerations. In C. Renfrew and K. Boyle (eds.), *Archaeogenetics: DNA and the population prehistory of Europe*. Cambridge: McDonald Institute for Archaeological Research, pp. 219–36.

Tansem, K. 1998. *Fra Komsakulturen til eldre steinalder i Finnmark*. Stensilserie/Universitetet i Tromsø. Institutt for Samfunnsvitenskap. B 54. Tromsø.

Tarlow, S. 2000. Emotion in Archaeology. *Current Anthropology* 41 (5): 713–46.

Tauber, H. 1981. 13C evidence for dietary habits of prehistoric man in Denmark. *Nature* Vol. 292 (5821): 332–3.

Tauber, H. 1993. Dating methods. In S. Hvass and B. Storgaard (eds.), *Digging into the past: 25 years of archaeology in Denmark*. Århus: Aarhus University Press, pp. 40–3.

Taussig, M. 1987. *Shamanism, colonialism and the wild man: A study in terror and healing*. Chicago: The University of Chicago Press.

Taute, W. 1967. Das Felsdach Lautereck, eine Mesolithisch-Neolithisch-Bronzezeitliche Stratigraphie an der Oberen Donau. *Palaeohistoria* 12: 483–504.

References

Taute, W. 1972. Die spätpaläolithisch-frühmesolithische Schichtenfolge im Zigeunerfels bei Sigmaringen (Vorbericht). *Archäologische Informationen* 1: 29–40.

Taute, W. 1974a. Neolithische Mikrolithen und andere Neolithische Silexartefakte aus Süddeutschland und Österreich. *Archäologische Informationen* 2/3: 71–125.

Taute, W. 1974b. Neue Forschungen zur Chronologie von Spätpaläolithikum und Mesolithikum in Süddeutschland. *Archäologische Informationen* 2/3: 59–66.

Telegin, D. Y. 1982. *Mezolitichni pam'yatki Ukrainy* [*Mesolithic sites of the Ukraine*]. Kiev: Naukova Dumka.

Telegin, D. Y. 1989. Mezolit Yugo-Zapada SSSR (Ukraina i Moldaviya) [The Mesolithic of the South-western USSR (Ukraine and Moldavia)]. In L. V. Kol'tsov (ed.), *Mezolit SSSR – Arheologiya SSSR.* [*Mesolithic of the USSR – Archaeology of the USS*]. Moscow: Nauka, pp. 106–24.

Terberger, T. 2003. Decorated objects of the older Mesolithic from the northern lowlands. In L. Larsson, H. Kindgren, K. Knutsson, D. Loeffler, and A. Åkerlund (eds.), *Mesolithic on the move.* Oxford: Oxbow Books, pp. 547–57.

Theisen, F., and W. Brude. 1998. Evaluering av omrdevernet p Svalbard. Representativitet og behov for ytterligere vern. *Norsk Polarinstitutt, Meddelelser* 153. Oslo.

Thévenin, A. 1990–91. Du Dryas III au début de l'Atlantique. *Revue Archéologique de l'Est* 41:177–212, and 42: 3–62.

Thévenin, A. (ed.). 1999a. *L'Europe des derniers chasseurs: Épipaléolithique et Mésolithique, Actes du 5ᵉ colloque international UISPP, commission XII, Grenoble, 18–23 septembre 1995.* Paris: Éditions du Comité des Travaux Historiques et Scientifiques.

Thévenin, A. 1999b. L'Épipaléolithique et le Mésolithique en France et régions voisines. In A. Thévenin (ed.), *L'Europe des Derniers Chasseurs:Épipaléolithique et Mésolithique. Actes du 5ᵉ Colloque International UISPP, Commission XII, Grenoble, 18–23 septembre 1995.* Paris: Éditions du Comité des Travaux Historiques et Scientifiques, pp. 17–24.

Thévenin, A., and J. Santy. 1977. Géochronologie de l'Epipaléolithique de l'Est de la France, *XXe Congrès Préhistorique de France*, Martigues 1974, pp. 605–15.

Thomas, G. D. 2005. Early lime plaster technology in the Near East: Experimental work at the Lemba Experimental Village, Cyprus. In *Experimentelle Archäologie in Europa, Bilanz 2004.* Vienna: European Association for the Advancement of Archaeology by Experiment, pp. 91–100.

Thomas, J. 1988. Neolithic explanations revisited: The Mesolithic-Neolithic transition in south Scandinavia. *Proceedings of the Prehistoric Society* 54: 59–66.

Thomas, J. 1991. *Rethinking the Neolithic.* Cambridge, UK: Cambridge University Press.

Thomas, J. 2003. Thoughts on the 'repacked' Neolithic revolution. *Antiquity* 77: 75–86.

Thommesen, T. 1996. The early settlement of Northern Norway. In L. Larsson (ed.), *The earliest settlement of Scandinavia and its relationship with neighbouring areas.* Acta Archaeologica Lundensia, Series In 8, 24. Stockholm: Almquist and Wiksell International, pp. 235–40.

Thorpe, I. J. 1996. *The origins of agriculture in Europe.* London: Routledge.

Thorpe, I. J. N. 2000. Origins of violence: Mesolithic conflict in Europe. *British Archaeology* 52: 8–13.

Thuestad, A. E. 2005. En romlig analyse av tidlig eldre steinalderlokaliteter i Vest-Finnmark og Troms. Upublished MA thesis, University of Tromsø.

Tilley, C. Y. 1991. *Material culture and text: The art of ambiguity.* London and New York: Routledge.

Tilley, C. Y. 1994. *A phenomenology of landscape: Places, paths and monuments.* Oxford: Berg.

Tilley, C., 1996. *An ethnography of the Neolithic: Early prehistoric societies in southern Scandinavia.* Cambridge, UK: Cambridge University Press.

Tillman, A. 1993. Kontinuität oder Diskontinuität? Zur Frage einer Bandkeramischen Landnahme im Südlichen Mitteleuropa. *Archäologische Informationen* 16: 157–87.

Timofeev, V. I. 1987. On the problem of the early Neolithic of the East Baltic area. *Acta Archaeologica* 58: 207–12.

Timofeev, V. I. 1990. On the links of the East Baltic Neolithic and the Funnel Beaker culture. In D. Jankowska (ed.), *Die Trichterbeckerkultur.* Poznan, pp. 135–49.

Timofeev, V. I. 1998a. The beginning of the Neolithic in the Eastern Baltic. In M. Zvelebil, R. Dennell, and L. Domańska (eds.), *harvesting the sea, farming the forest*. Sheffield: Sheffield Academic Press, pp. 225–36.

Timofeev, V. I. 1998b. The east-west relations in the Late Mesolithic and Neolithic in the Baltic region. In L. Domańska, and K. Jacobs (eds.), *Beyond balkanization*. Baltic-Pontic Studies 5: 44–58.

Timofeev, V. I., and G. I. Zaitseva. 1998. Compendium of radiocarbon dates for Mesolithic sites on East European Plain. In G. I. Zaitseva (ed.), *C^{14} and Archaeology*. St. Petersburg: Institute for History of Material Culture, pp. 200–10.

Tipping, R. 1996. Microscopic charcoal records, inferred human activity and climate change in the Mesolithic of northernmost Scotland. In A. Pollard and A. Morrison (eds.), *The early prehistory of Scotland*. Edinburgh: Edinburgh University Press, pp. 39–61.

Tolan-Smith, C. 1998. Radiocarbon chronology and the Lateglacial and early Postglacial resettlement of the British isles. In B. V. Eriksen and L. G. Straus (eds.), As the World Warmed: Human Adaptations across The Pleistocene/Holocene Boundary. *Quaternary International* 49/50: 21–7.

Tolan-Smith, C. 2001. *The caves of Mid Argyll: An archaeology of human use* Society of Antiquaries of Scotland Monograph 20. Edinburgh: Society of Antiquaries of Scotland.

Tolan-Smith, C. 2003a. Colonization – event or process. In L. Larsson, H. Kindgren, K. Knutsson, D. Loeffler, and A. Åkerlund (eds.), *Mesolithic on the move: Papers presented at the Sixth International Conference on the Mesolithic in Europe, Stockholm 2000*. Oxford: Oxbow, pp. 52–6.

Tolan-Smith, C. 2003b. The social context of landscape learning and the Lateglacial-Early Postglacial recolonization of the British Isles. In J. Steele and M. Rockman (eds.), *The colonization of unfamiliar landscapes: The archaeology of adaptation*. London: Routledge, pp. 116–29.

Tolan-Smith, C., and C. Bonsall 1997. The human use of caves. In C. Bonsall and C. Tolan-Smith (eds.), *The human use of caves*. BAR International Series 667. Oxford: Archaeopress, pp. 217–8.

Tolan-Smith, C., and C. Bonsall. 1999. Stone Age studies in the British Isles: The impact of accelerator dating. In J. Evin, C. Oberlin, J.-P. Daugas, and J.-F. Salles (eds.), *14C et Archéologie. Actes du 3ème congrès international (Lyon, 6–10 avril 1998)*. Paris: Mémoires de la Société Préhistorique Française 26, 1999 et Supplément 1999 de la Revue d'Archéometrie, pp. 249–57.

Tomaszewski, A. J. 1988. Foragers, farmers and archaeologists. *Archaeologia Polski* 33: 434–40.

Torke, W. 1993. Die Fischerei am Prähistorischen Federsee. *Archäologisches Korrespondenzblatt* 23: 49–66.

Torrence, R. 1983. Time budgeting and hunter-gatherer technology. In G. Bailey (ed.), *Hunter-gatherer economy in prehistory: A European perspective*. Cambridge, UK: Cambridge University Press, pp. 11–22.

Torroni, A., Bandelt, H. -J., D'Urbano, L., Laherno, P., Moral, P., Sellito, D., Rengo, C., Forster, P. Savontaus, M. -L., Bonne-Tamir, B., and R. Scozzari. 1998. mtDNA analysis reveals a major Late Palaeolithic population expansion from southwestern to northeastern Europe. *American Journal of Human Genetics* 62: 1137–52.

Tortosa, J., and M. Ripoll. 1995. El Holoceno inicial en el Mediterráneo español (11000–7000 BP): Características culturales y económicas. In V. Bonilla (ed.), *Los ultimos cazadores: Transformaciones culturales y económicas durante el tardiglaciar y el inicio del Holoceno en el ambito Mediterráneo*. Alicante: Istituto de Cultura Juan Gil Albert, pp. 119–46.

Tozzi, C. 1996. Grotta Marisa, Grotta Continenza e Latronico 3. In V. Tiné (ed.), *Forme e tempi della Neolitizzazione in Italia Meridionale e in Sicilia* 1. Rossano: Istituto Regionale per le Antichità Calabresi e Bizantine, pp. 53–9.

Trantalidou, K. 2003. Faunal remains from the earliest strata of the Cave of Cyclope, Youra. In N. Galanidou and C. Perlès (eds.), *The Greek Mesolithic: Problems and perspectives*. British School at Athens Studies 10. London: British School at Athens, pp. 143–72.

Tringham, R. 2000. Southeastern Europe in the transition to agriculture in Europe: Bridge, buffer, or mosaic. In T. D. Price (ed.), *Europe's First Farmers*. Cambridge: Cambridge University Press, pp. 19–56.

Troels-Smith, J. 1953. Ertebøllekultur-bondekultur. *Årbøger for Nordisk Oldkyndighed og Historie* 1953: 5–62.

Tsalkin, V. I. 1970. *Drevneishie domashnie zhivotnye Vostochnoi Evropy [The earliest domesticated animals in Eastern Europe]*. Moscow: Nauka.

References

Turnbull, C. 1965. *Wayward servants*. London: Eyre, and Spottiswoode.

Tykot, R. 1996. Obsidian procurement and distribution in the central and western Mediterranean. *Journal of Mediterranean Archaeology* 9: 39–82.

Tykot, R. 1999. Islands in the stream: Stone Age cultural dynamics in Sardinia and Corsica. In R. Tykot, J. Morter, and J. Robb (eds.), *Social dynamics of the prehistoric central Mediterranean*. London: University of London Accordia Research Centre, pp. 67–82.

Ucko, P. J. 1969. Ethnography and archaeological interpretation of funerary remains. *World Archaeology* 1: 262–80.

Umbelino, C., Pérez-Pérez, E., Cunha, E., Hipólito, C., Freitas, M., and J. Cabral. 2007. Outros sabores do passado: um novo olhar sobre as comunidades humanas mesolíticas de Muge e do Sado através de análises químicas dos ossos. *Promontoria* 5: 45–90.

Valdeyron, N. 1994. *Le Sauveterrien. Culture et sociétés mésolithiques dans la France du Sud durant les X et IX millénaires B.P.* Toulouse, Thèse de doctorat nouveau régime, Université Toulouse-Le Mirail, 2 tomes.

Valdeyron, N. 2000a, Géographie culturelle du Mésolithique récent/final dans le Sud-Ouest de la France. In M. Leduc, N. Valdeyron, and J. Vaquer (eds.), *Sociétés et Espaces*. Toulouse: Actes des IIIèmes Rencontres Méridionales de Préhistoire Récente, 1998, pp. 23–34.

Valdeyron, N., 2000b. La grotte de Leherreko-Ziloa (Larrau, Pyrénées Atlantiques). *Bilan scientifique du Service de Recherche Archéologique d'Aquitaine*. Direction Régionale des Affaires Culturelles, p. 117.

Valdeyron, N., Bosc-Zanardo, B., and T. Briand. 2009. The evolution of stone weapon elements and cultural dynamics during the Mesolithic in southwestern France: The case of the Haut Quercy (Lot, France). In J.-M. Pétillon, M.-H. Dias-Meirinho, P. Cattelain, M. Honegger, C. Normand, and N. Valdeyron (eds.), *Projectile weapon elements from the Upper Palaeolithic to the Neolithic. Proceedings of the XVth World Congress UISPP, Lisbon, September 4–9, 2006*. British Archaeological Reports International Series, Oxford: Archaeopress, pp. 269–86.

Valen, V., Larsen, E., Mangerud, J., and A. K. Hufthammer. 1996. Sedimentology and stratigraphy in the cave Hamnsundhelleren, western Norway. *Journal of Quaternary Science* 11: 185–201.

Valente, M. J., and A. F. Carvalho. 2009. Recent developments in Early Holocene hunter-gatherer subsistence and settlement: A view from south-western Iberia. In S. McCartan, R. Schulting, G. Warren, and P. Woodman (eds.), *Mesolithic horizons. Papers presented at the Seventh International Conference on the Mesolithic in Europe, Belfast 2005*. Oxford: Oxbow Books, pp. 312–17.

Valoch, K. 1977. Felssteinartefakte aus dem Endpaläolithikum von Smolín (Mähren). *Anthropologie* 15: 107–9.

Valoch, K. 1978. *Die endpaläolithische Siedlung in Smolín*. Praha: Academia.

Valoch, K. 1981. Spätglaziale und frühholozäne Entwicklung des Paläolithikums in der Tschechoslowakei. In B. Gramsch (ed.), *Mesolithikum in Europa*. Berlin: Veröffentlichungen des Museums für Ur- und Frühgeschichte Potsdam 14/15, pp. 51–62.

Valoch, K. 1985. The Mesolithic site of Smolín, South Moravia. In C. Bonsall (ed.), *The Mesolithic in Europe: Proceedings of the third international symposium*. Edinburgh: John Donald, pp. 461–70.

Van der Plicht, L. 2004. Calibration at all ages. In T. Higham, C. Bronk Ramsey, and C. Owen (eds.). *Radiocarbon and archaeology: Proceedings of the 4th Symposium, Oxford 2002*. Oxford University School of Archaeology Monograph 62. Oxford: Oxford University School of Archaeology, pp. 1–8.

Van der Sloot, P., Remacle, M., Haesaerts, P., López Bayón, I., and J.-M. Léotard 2000. Nouvelles recherches menées dans le secteur "S. D. T." de la place Saint-Lambert à Liège. *Notae Praehistoricae* 20: 143–9.

Van der Sloot, P., F. Damblon, N. Debenham, K. Fecher, A. Gob, P. Haesaerts, A. Hazeur, I. Jadin, J.-M. Léotard, M. Remacle, and B. Vanmontfort. 2003. Le Mésolithique et le Néolithique du site Saint-Lambert à Liège dans leur contexte chronologique, géologique et environnemental. Synthèse des données et acquis recents. *Notae Praehistoricae* 23: 79–104.

Van Es, W. A., and W. A. Casparie. 1968. Mesolithic wooden statuette from the Volkerak, near Willemstad, North Brabant. *Berichten van de Rijksdienst voor het Oudheidkundig Bodemonderzoek* 18: 111–16.

Van Es, W. A., Sarfatij, H., and P. J. Woltering. 1988. *Archeologie van Nederland, de rijkdom van het bodemarchief*. Amsterdam: Meulenhoff.

Van Leeuwaarden, W. 1982. *Palynological and macropalaeobotanical studies in the development of the vegetation mosaic in eastern Noord-Brabant the Netherlands. during Late Glacial and Early Holocene times.* Unpublished thesis, University of Utrecht.

Van Roeyen, J.-P., Minnaert, C., Van Strydonck, M., and C. Verbruggen. 1991. Melsele-Hoften Damme, prehistorische bewoning, landschappelijke ontwikkeling en kronologisch kader. *Notae Praehistoricae* 11: 41–51.

van Zeist, W., and S. Bottema. 1982. Vegetational history of the eastern Mediterranean and the Near East during the last 20,000 years. In J. Bintliff and W. van Zeist (eds.), *Palaeoclimates, palaeoenvironments and human communities in the eastern Mediterranean.* Oxford: British Archaeological Reports International Series 133, vol. 1, pp. 277–323.

Vankina, L. V. 1970. *Torfyanikovaya Stoyanka Sarnate.* Riga: Zinatne.

Vaquer, J., and M. Barbaza. 1987. Cueillette ou horticulture mésolithique: La Balma de l'Abeurador. *Premières communautés paysannes en Méditerranée occidentale.* Paris: Editions du CNRS, pp. 231–42.

Vaquer, J., Geddes, D., Barbaza, M., and J. Erroux. 1986. Mesolithic plant exploitation at the Balma Abeurador (France). *Oxford Journal of Archaeology* 5: 1–18.

Vasić, R. 2008. Velesnica and the Lepenski Vir culture. In C. Bonsall, V. Boroneanţ, and I. Radovanović (eds.), *The Iron Gates in prehistory: New perspectives.* Oxford: Archaeopress, pp. 227–41.

Vasil'ev, I. B. 1981. *Eneolit Povolzh'ya* [*The Chalcolithic of the Volga Basin*]. Kuibyshev: Kuibyshev State Paedagogical Institute.

Vasil'ev, I. B., and A. T. Sinyuk. 1985. *Eneolit Vostochno-evropeiskoi lesostepi* [*The Chalcolithic of the Volga Forest-Steppe*]. Kuibyshev: Kuibyshev State Paedagogical Institute.

Vaufrey, R. 1928. *Le Paléolithique Italien.* Archives de L'Institut de Paleontologie Humaine, Memoire 3. Paris: Masson.

Vázquez Varela, J. 1988. El Neolítico en Galicia. In P. López (ed.), *El Neolítico en España.* Madrid, pp. 329–35.

Vázquez Varela, J. 2004. The Mesolithic on the northwest coast of the Iberian Peninsula. In M. González Morales, and G. Clark (eds.), *The Mesolithic of the Atlantic Façade.* Anthropological Research Papers 55. Tempe: Arizona State University, pp. 103–10.

Vega del Sella, Conde de la 1930. *Las Cuevas de la Riera y Balmori,* Comisión de Investigaciones Paleolontógicas y Prehistóricas, Memoria 38. Madrid.

Vekilova, E. A. 1971. Prirodnye usloviya i chelovek v paleolite Kryma [Natural environment and humans of the Crimean Palaeolithic]. In A. A. Velichko (ed.), *Pervobytnyi chelovek i prirodnaya sreda* [*Prehistoric man and natural environment*]. Moscow: Nauka, pp. 160–5.

Vencl, S. 1960. *Kamenné nástroje prvních zemědělců ve střední Evropě.* Praha: Sborník Národního muzea A, 14, volumes 1–2.

Vencl, S. 1970. Das Spätpaläolithikum in Böhmen. *Anthropologie* 8: 3–68.

Vencl, S. 1971. Topografická poloha mesolitických sídlišt v Čechách. *Archeologické rozhledy* 23: 169–87.

Vencl, S. 1986. The role of hunting-gathering populations in the transition to farming: A Central European perspective. In M. Zvelebil (ed.), *Hunters in transition.* Cambridge, UK: Cambridge University Press, pp. 43–51.

Vencl, S. 1989. Mezolitické osídlení na Šumavě. *Archeologické rozhledy* 41: 481–501.

Vencl, S. 1990. K současnému stavu poznávání kamenných surovin mezolitu. *Archeologické rozhledy* 42: 233–43.

Vencl, S. 1996. Archeologický výzkum jeskyně Martina. In L. Pecka and R. Živor (eds.), *Tetín historický a speleologický.* Praha: ČSS, pp. 63–7.

Vencl, S. 1999 *Stone Age warfare.* In J. Carman and A. Harding (eds.), *Ancient warfare.* Stroud: Sutton, pp. 101–42.

Vencl, S. 2001. Prvý doklad mezolitické výtvarné aktivity z Čech? *Archeologické rozhledy* 53: 675–81.

Vencl, S., Fröhlich, J., Horáček, I., Michálek, J., Pokorný, P., and A. Přichystal. 2006. *Nejstarší osídlení jižních Čech. Paleolit a mezolit.* Praha: Institute of Archaeology.

Verhart, L. B. M. 1988. Mesolithic barbed points and other implements from Europoort, the Netherlands. *Oudheidkundige Mededelingen uit het Rijksmuseum van Oudheden Leiden* 68, 145–94.

References

Verhart, L. B. M. 1995. Fishing for the Mesolithic. The North Sea, a submerged Mesolithic landscape. In A. Fischer (ed.), *Man and Sea in the Mesolithic*. Oxbow Monograph 53. Oxford: Oxbow Books, pp. 291–302.

Verhart, L. B. M. 2000. *Times fade away, the Neolithization of the southern Netherlands in an anthropological and geographical perspective*. Leiden: Archaeological Studies Leiden University 6.

Verhart, L. B. M. 2002. Mesolithic economic and social changes in the southern Netherlands, in Mesolithic Conference Sweden. In L. Larsson, H. Kindgren, K. Knutsson, D. Loeffler, and A. Åkerlund (eds.), *Mesolithic on the move: Papers presented at the Sixth International Conference on the Mesolithic in Europe, Stockholm 2000*. Oxford: Oxbow, pp. 442–50.

Verhart, L. B. M. 2009. Interaction, exchange and imitation. Some short and preliminary notes on the distribution of Breitkeile in Belgium and the Netherlands and its implications for the transition from Mesolithic to Neolithic. In S. McCartan, R. Schulting, G. Warren, and P. Woodman (eds.), *Mesolithic horizons. Papers presented at the Seventh International Conference on the Mesolithic in Europe, Belfast 2005*. Oxford: Oxbow Books, pp. 570–5.

Verhart, L. B. M., and M. Wansleeben. 1990. Tussen America en Siberië, enkele aspecten van het Maasdalproject. In A. T. L. Niklewicz-Hokse and C. A. G. Lagerwerf (eds.), *Bundel van de Steentijddag 1 april 1989*. Groningen: Biologisch-Archaeologisch Instituut, pp. 45–54.

Verjux, C. 1999. Chronologie des rites funéraires mésolithiques à Auneau (Eure-et-Loir, France). In P. Bintz and A. Thévenin (eds.), *L'Europe des derniers chasseurs. Epipaléolithique et Mésolithique, Actes du 5ᵉ colloque international UISPP, commission XII, Grenoble, 18–23 septembre 1995*. Paris: Comité des Travaux Historiques et Scientifiques, pp. 293–302.

Verjux, C. 2003. The function of Mesolithic sites in the Paris basin (France): New data. In L. Larsson, H. Kindgren, K. Knutsson, D. Loeffler, and A. Åkerlund (eds.), *Mesolithic on the move: Papers presented at the Sixth International Conference on the Mesolithic in Europe, Stockholm 2000*. Oxford: Oxbow, pp. 262–8.

Verlinde, A. D. 1982. Archeologische kroniek van Overijssel over 1980/181 Mariënberg, gemeente Hardenberg. *Overijsselse Historische Bijdragen* 97: 171–5.

Vermeersch, P. M. 1982. Contributions to the study of the Mesolithic of the Belgian lowland. *Studia Praehistorica Belgica* 1.

Vermeersch, P. M. 1984. Du paléolithique final au mésolithique dans le nord de la Belgique. In D. Cahen and P. Haesaerts (eds.), *Peuples chasseurs de la Belgique préhistorique dans leur cadre naturel*. Bruxelles: Institut royal des scienes naturelles de Belgique, pp. 181–93.

Vermeersch, P. M. 1989. Ten years' research on the Mesolithic of the Belgian Lowland, results and prospects. In C. Bonsall (ed.), *The Mesolithic in Europe: Proceedings of the third international symposium*. Edinburgh: John Donald, pp. 284–90.

Vermeersch, P. M. 1996. Mesolithic in the Benelux, south of the Rhine. In S. K. Kozlowski and C. Tozzi (eds.), *XIII International Congress of Prehistoric and Protohistoric Sciences. Forli, Italia, 8/14 september 1996, 7, The Mesolithic*, pp. 33–9.

Vermeersch, P., and P. Van Peer (eds.). 1990. *Contributions to the Mesolithic in Europe*. Leuven: Leuven University Press.

Vernet, J.-L. 1997. *L'Homme et la forêt Méditerranéenne de la préhistoire à nos jours*. Paris: Errance.

Vierra, B. D. 1992. *Subsistence diversification and the evolution of microlithic technologies: A study of the Portuguese Mesolithic*. Unpublished Ph.D. thesis, Department of Anthropology, University of New Mexico.

Vierra, B. 1995. *Subsistence diversification and the evolution of microlithic technologies: A study of the Portuguese Mesolithic*. Anthropological Research Papers 47. Tempe: Arizona State University.

Vierra, B., and J. Arnaud. 1996. Raw material availability and stone tool technology: An example from the Portuguese Mesolithic. In N. Moloney, L. Raposo, and M. Santonja (eds.), *Non-Flint stone tools, and the Palaeolithic occupation of the Iberian Peninsula*. Oxford: British Archaeological Reports International Series 649, pp. 183–8.

Vigliardi, A. 1968. L'industria litica della Grotta di San Teodoro, in Provincia di Messina. *Rivista di Scienze Preistoriche* 23: 33–144.

Vigne, J. D., and N. Desse-Berset. 1995. The exploitation of animal resources in the Mediterranean islands during the pre-neolithic: The example of Corsica. In A. Fischer (ed.), *Man and Sea in the Mesolithic*. Oxbow Monograph 53. Oxford: Oxbow, pp. 309–18.

Vilette, P. 1999. Bilan provisoire sur la chasse aux oiseaux pendant le leptolithique dans le sud de la France. In *Les faciès leptolithiques du nord-ouest méditerranéen: Milieux naturels et culturels*. Actes du XXIVè Congrès Préhistorique de France, Septembre 1994, Carcassonne. Paris: Edition de la Société Préhistorique Française, pp. 267–76.

Villems, R., Adojaan, M., and T. Kivisild.1998. Reconstruction of maternal lineages Finno-Ugric speaking people and some remarks on their paternal inheritance. In K. Julku, and K. Wiik (eds.), *The roots of peoples and languages of northern Eurasia I*. Turku: Societas Historiae Finno-Ugricae, pp. 180–200.

Villems, R., Rootsi, S., Tambets, K., Adojaan, M., Orekhov, V., Khusnutdinova, E., and N. Yankovsky. 2002. Archaeogenetics of Finno-Ugric speaking populations. In K. Julku (ed.), *The roots of peoples and languages of northern Eurasia*. Oulu: Societas Historiae Finno-Ugricae, pp. 271–84.

Viñas Vallverdú, R. 1992. El arte rupestre en Catalunya: Estado de la cuestión sobre las manifestaciones pictográficas. In P. Utrilla Miranda (ed.), *Aragón / Litoral Mediterráneo: Intercambios culturales durante la prehistoria,*. Zaragoza: Institución Fernando Il Catolico pp. 415–34.

Voytek, B., and R. Tringham. 1989. Rethinking the Mesolithic: The case of south-east Europe. In C. Bonsall (ed.), *The Mesolithic in Europe: Proceedings of the third international symposium*. Edinburgh: John Donald, pp. 492–9.

Vuorela, I. 1972. Human influence on the vegetation of the Katinhanta bog, Vihiti, S. Finland. *Acta Botanica Fennica* 98: 1–21.

Vuorela, I. 1976. An instance of slash and burn cultivation in S. Finland investigated by pollen analysis of a mineral soil. *Memoranda Societatis pro Fauna et Flora Fennica* 52: 29–45.

Vuorela, I. 1998. The transition to farming in southern Finland. In M. Zvelebil, R. Dennell, and L. Domańska (eds.), *Harvesting the sea, farming the forest*. Sheffield: Sheffield University Press, pp. 175–80.

Vuorela, I., and T. Lempiäinen. 1988. Archaeobotany of the oldest cereal grain find in Finland. *Annales Botanici Fennici* 25 (1): 33–45.

Vybornov, A. 2008. *Neolit Volgo-Kamya [The Volga-Kama Neolithic]*. Samara: Samara University Press.

Vybornov, A., Dolukhanov, P., Aleksandrovsky, A., Kovalyukh, N. N., Skripkin, V. V., Sapelko, T. V., Zaitseva, G. I., and A. Shukurov. 2009. The Middle Volga Neolithic. In P. Dolukhanov, G. Sarson, and A. Shukurov (eds.), *The East European Plain on the eve of agriculture*, British Archaeological Reports International Series 1964. Oxford: Archaeopress, pp. 71–80.

Vybornov, A., Kovalyukh, N. N., Skripkin, V. V., Zaitseva, G. I., Dolukhanov, P., and A. Shukurov. 2009. Mesolithic and Neolithic of North Caspian Lowland. In P. Dolukhanov, G. Sarson, and A. Shukurov (eds.), *The East European Plain on the eve of agriculture*. British Archaeological Reports International Series 1964. Oxford: Archaeopress, pp. 89–98.

Waddington, C. (ed.). 2007. *Mesolithic settlement in the North Sea Basin: A case study from Howick, north-east England*. Oxford: Oxbow Books.

Waddington, C., Bailey, G., Bayliss, A., Boomer, I., Milner, N., Shiel R., and T. Stevenson. 2003. A Mesolithic settlement site at Howick, Northumberland: A preliminary report. *Archaeologia Aeliana* 32: 1–12.

Wall, E. 1961. Der Federsee von der Eiszeit bis zur Gegenwart. In W. Zimmermann (ed.), *Der Federsee*. Stuttgart: Schwäbischer Albverein, pp. 228–315.

Wallis, R. J. 2001. Waking ancestor spirits: Neo-shamanic engagements with archaeology. In N. Price (ed.), *The archaeology of shamanism*. London: Routledge, pp. 213–30.

Wansleeben, M., and L. B. M. Verhart. 1990. Meuse Valley project, the transition from the Mesolithic to the Neolithic in the Dutch Meuse valley. In P. M. Vermeersch and P. Van Peer (eds.), *Contributions to the Mesolithic in Europe*. Leuven: Leuven University Press, pp. 389–402.

Wansleeben, M., and L. B. M. Verhart. 1995. GIS on different spatial levels and the Neolithization Process in the south-eastern Netherlands. In G. Lock and Z. Stancic (eds.), *Archaeology and geographical information systems, a European perspective*. London: Taylor and Francis, pp. 153–69.

References

Wansleeben, M., and L. B. M. Verhart. 1998. Geographical analysis of regional data, the use of site typology to explore the Dutch Neolithization process. *Internet Archaeology* 4. http://intarch.ac.uk/journal/issue4. [Accessed 7 January, 2004].

Warren, E. J. 1994. Coastal sedentism during the Atlantic period in Nordhordland, Western Norway? The middle and late Mesolithic component at Kotedalen. Unpublished MA thesis, Memorial University of Newfoundland.

Warren, G. 2005a. Complex arguments. In N. Milner and P. Woodman (eds.), *Mesolithic studies at the beginning of the 21st century*. Oxford, Oxbow, pp. 69–80.

Warren, G. 2005b. *Mesolithic lives in Scotland*. Oxford: Tempus.

Warren, G. 2006. Technology. In C. Conneller and G. Warren (eds.), *Mesolithic Britain and Ireland*. Stroud: Tempus, pp. 13–34.

Waraas, T. A. 2001. Vestlandet i tidleg Preboeral tid. Fosna, Ahrensburg eller vestnorsk tidlegmesolitikum? Unpublished thesis, University of Bergen.

Waraas, T. A. 2005. *Arkeologisk registrering på Baraldsnes, Haram kommune, Møre og Romsdal. Ormen Lange prosjektet*. Kulturhistoriske skrifter og rapporter 1. Molde: Møre og Romsdal fylke.

Waterbolk, H. T. 1962. Hauptzüge der eisenzeitliche Besiedlung der nördliche Niederlande. *Offa* 19: 9–46.

Welinder, S. 1975. Agriculture, inland hunting and sea hunting in the western and northern region of the Baltic, 6000-2000 BC. In W. Fitzhugh (ed.), *Prehistoric maritime adaptations of the circumpolar zone*. Paris: Mouton, pp. 21–55.

Welinder, S. 1977. *The Mesolithic Stone Age of Eastern Middle Sweden*. Antikvariskt Arkiv 65.

Welinder, S. 1981. Den kontinentaleuropeiska bakgrunden till Norges äldsta stenlder. *Universitetets Oldsaksamlings Årbok* 1980/81: 21–34.

Welinder, S. 1981a. The disappearance of a hunting-gathering economy. In B. Gramsch (ed.), *Mesolithikum in Europa*. Berlin: Veröffentlichungen des Museums für Ur- und Frühgeschichte Potsdam 14/15, pp. 151–63.

Welinder, S. 1989. Mesolithic forest clearance in Scandinavia. In C. Bonsall (ed.), *The Mesolithic in Europe: Proceedings of the third international symposium*. Edinburgh: John Donald, pp. 362–6.

Welinder, S., Pedersen, E. A., and M. Widgren. 1998. *Jordbrukets första femtusen r. 4000 f. Kr. –1000e. Kr.* Natur och kultur/Lts Förlag I samarbete med Nordiska museet och Stiftelsen Lagersberg. Bors: Centraltryckeriet AB.

Westropp, H. M. 1872. *Pre-historic phases; or, introductory essays on pre-historic archæology*. London: Bell and Daldy.

Wheeler, R. E. M. 1954. *Archaeology from the earth*. Harmondsworth: Penguin.

Whitehouse, R. 1992. *Underground religion: Cult and culture in prehistoric Italy*. London: University of London Accordia Research Centre.

Whittle, A. 1985. *Neolithic Europe: A survey*. Cambridge, UK: Cambridge University Press.

Whittle, A. 1996. *Europe in the Neolithic*. Cambridge, UK: Cambridge University Press.

Whittle, A. 1999. The Neolithic period, c. 4000–2500/2200 BC. In J. Hunter and I. Ralston (eds.), *The archaeology of Britain*. London: Routledge, pp. 58–76.

Whittle, A., L. Bartosiewicz, D. Borić, P. Pettitt, & M. Richards 2002. In the beginning: New radiocarbon dates for the Early Neolithic in northern Serbia and south-east Hungary. *Antaeus* 25, 63–117.

Wick, L., Lencke, G., and M. Sturm. 2003. Evidence of Lateglacial and Holocene climatic change and human impact in eastern Anatolia: High resolution pollen, charcoal, isotopic and geochemical records from the laminated sediments of Lake Van, Turkey. *The Holocene* 13: 665–75.

Wickham-Jones, C. R. 1990. *Rhum, Mesolithic and later sites at Kinloch: Excavations 1984–86*. Society of Antiquaries of Scotland Monograph 7. Edinburgh: Society of Antiquaries of Scotland.

Wickham-Jones, C. 1997. *Scotland's first settlers*. Edinburgh: Historic Scotland and Batsford.

Wickham-Jones, C. R., and C. R. Firth. 2000. Mesolithic settlement of northern Scotland: First results of fieldwork in Caithness and Orkney. In R. Young (ed.), *Mesolithic lifeways: Current research in Britain and Ireland*. Leicester Archaeology Monographs 7. Leicester: Leicester University Department of Archaeology, pp. 119–132.

Wikell, R., and M. Pettersson. 2009. Entering new shores. Colonization processes in early archipelagos in eastern central Sweden. In S. McCartan, R. Schulting, G. Warren, and P. C. Woodman (eds.), *Mesolithic horizons. Papers presented at the Seventh International Conference on the Mesolithic in Europe, Belfast 2005*, Oxford: Oxbow Books, pp. 24–30.

Wiget, A., and O. Balalaeva. 1997. Black snow, oil and the Khanty of West Siberia. *Cultural Survival Quarterly* 20: 13–15.

Wigforss, J. 1995. West Swedish Mesolithic settlements containing faunal remains – aspects of the topography and economy. In A. Fischer (ed.), *Man and sea in the Mesolithic*. Oxbow Monograph 53. Oxford: Oxbow, pp. 197–206.

Wiik, K. 1997. Suomalaistyyppistä ääntämistä germaanisissa kielissä. In K. Julku (ed.), *Itämerensuomi eurooppalainen maa*. Oulu: Societas Historiae Fenno-Ugricae, pp. 75–103.

Wiik, K. 1999. Some ancient and modern linguistic processes in northern Europe. In C. Renfrew, A McMahon, and L. Trask (eds.), *Time depth in historical linguistics*. Cambridge, UK: McDonald Institute for Archaeological Research, pp. 463–79.

Wiik, K. 2000. European Lingua Francas. In A. Künnap (ed.), *The Roots of Peoples and Languages of Northern Eurasia II–III*. Tartu: Societas Historiae Fenno-Ugricae. 202–36.

Wiik, K. 2002a. On the emergence of the main Indo-European language groups of Europe through adstratal influence. In K. Julku (ed.), *The Roots of Peoples and Languages of Northern Eurasia IV*. Oulu: Societas Historiae Fenno-Ugricae. 285–92.

Wiik, K. 2002b. *Eurooppalaisten juuret*. Jyväkylä: Atena Kustannus Oy.

Willis, K. 1994. Altitudinal variation in the late Quaternary vegetational history of northwest Greece. *Historical Biology* 9: 103–16.

Willis, K., Rudner, E. and P. Sümegi. 2000. The Full-Glacial forests of central and southeastern Europe. *Quaternary Research* 53: 203–13.

Wobst, H. M. 1978. The archaeo-ethnology of hunter-gatherers or the tyranny of the ethnographic record in archaeology. *American Antiquity* 43: 303–9.

Woodburn, J. 1980. Hunters and gatherers today and reconstruction of the past. In E. Gellner (ed.), *Soviet and Western Anthropology*. London: Duckworth, pp. 95–117.

Woodburn, J. 1982. Egalitarian societies. *Man* 17: 431–51.

Woodburn, J. 1988. African hunter-gatherer social organisation: Is it best understood as a product of encapsulation? In T. Ingold, D. Riches, and J. Woodburn (eds.), *Hunters and gatherers 1*. Oxford: Berg, pp. 31–64.

Woodman, P. C. 1977. Recent excavations at Newferry, Co. Antrim. *Proceedings of the Prehistoric Society* 43: 155–99.

Woodman, P. C. 1978. *The Mesolithic in Ireland: Hunter-gatherers in an insular environment.* Oxford: British Archaeological Reports British Series 58.

Woodman, P. C. 1985. Excavations at Mount Sandel 1973–77. *Northern Ireland Archaeological Monographs 2.* Belfast: Her Majesty's Stationery Office.

Woodman, P. 1993. The Komsa Culture: A re-examination of its position in the Stone Age of Finmark. *Acta Archaeologica* 63 (1992): 57–76.

Woodman, P. 2003. Colonising the edge of Europe: Ireland as a case study. In L. Larsson, H. Kindgren, K. Knutsson, D. Loeffler, and A. Åkerlund (eds.), *Mesolithic on the move: Papers presented at the Sixth International Conference on the Mesolithic in Europe, Stockholm 2000.* Oxford: Oxbow Books, pp. 57–61.

Woodman, P. C., Anderson, E., and N. Finlay. 1999. *Excavations at Ferriter's Cove 1983–95: Last foragers, first farmers in the Dingle Peninsula.* Bray: Wordwell.

Wymer, J. J. 1962. Excavations at the Maglemosian sites at Thatcham, Berkshire, England. *Proceedings of the Prehistoric Society* 28: 329–61.

Wyss, A. 1968. Das Mesolithikum. In H.-G. Bandi (ed.), *Ur- und Frühgeschichtliche Archäologie der Schweiz, Band I*. Basel: Verlag Schweizerische Gesellschaft für Ur- und Frühgeschichte, pp. 123–44.

Yanko-Hombach, V. 2007. Controversy over Noah's Flood in the Black Sea: Geological and foraminiferal evidence from the shelf. In V. Yanko-Hombach, A. Gilbert, N. Panin, and P. Dolukhanov (eds.), *The*

References

Black Sea flood question: Changes in coastline, climate, and human settlement. Dordrecht: Springer, pp. 149–204.

Yellen, J. E. 1977. *Archaeological approaches to the past: Models for reconstructing the past*. New York: Academic Press.

Yoffee, N. 1985. Perspectives on 'trends toward social complexity in prehistoric Australia and Papua New Guinea'. *Archaeology in Oceania* 20 (2): 41–8.

Young, R. (ed.), 2000a. *Mesolithic lifeways: Current research in the Mesolithic in Britain and Ireland*. Leicester Archaeology Monographs 7. Leicester: Leicester University Press.

Young, R. (ed.), 2000b. Waiting for the great leap forwards: Some current trends in Mesolithic research. In R. Young (ed.), *Mesolithic lifeways: Current research in the Mesolithic in Britain and Ireland*. Leicester Archaeology Monographs 7. Leicester: Leicester University Press, pp. 1–12.

Zachrisson, I. 1994. Archaeology and politics: Saami prehistory and history in central Scandinavia. *Journal of European Archaeology* 2: 361–8.

Zachrisson, I., and E. Igegren. 1974. Lappish bear graves in northern Sweden: An archaeological and osteo-logical study. *Early Norrland* 5. Stockholm: KungligaVitterhets Historie och Antikvitets Akademien.

Zagorska, I. 1999. The earliest settlement of Latvia. *Pact* 57 (1. 6): 131–56.

Zagorska, I. 2000. The art from Zvejnieki burial ground, Latvia. *Acta Academiae Artium Vilnensis* 20: 79–92.

Zagorska, I. 2001. Amber graves of Zvejnieki burial ground. *Acta Academiae Artium Vilnensis* 22: 109–24.

Zagorska, I. 2009. People and places in the Latvian Mesolithic: A case study from the Zvejnieki archaeological complex. In S. B. McCartan, R. Schulting, G. Warren, and P. Woodman (eds.), *Mesolithic horizons. Papers presented at the Seventh International Conference on the Mesolithic in Europe, Belfast 2005*. Oxford: Oxbow Books, pp. 255–60.

Zagorska, I., and L. Lõugas. 2000. The tooth-pendant head-dresses of Zvejnieki cemetery. *De temporibus antiquissimis ad honorem Lembit J*. Tallinn: Muinasaja Teadus 8, pp. 223–44.

Zagorska, I., and F. Zagorskis. 1989. The bone and antler inventory from Zvejnieki II, Latvian SSR. In C. Bonsall (ed.), *The Mesolithic in Europe: Proceedings of the third international symposium*. Edinburgh: John Donald, pp. 414–23.

Zagorskis, F. 1987. *Zvejnieku Akumens Laikmeta Kapulauks*. Riga: Zinatne.

Zagorskis, F. 2004 (1987). Zvejnnieki, Northern Latvia – Stone Age cemetery. British Archaeological Reports International Series S1292. Oxford: Archaeopress.

Žák, K., and J. Melková. 1999. *C14 dating of charcoal from Martina Cave near Tetín*. Český kras 25.

Zalizniak, L. L. 1989. *Okhotniky na Severnogo Olenya Ukrainskogo Polesya v Epokhu Finalnogo Paleolita*. Kiev: Naukova Dumka.

Zalizniak, L. L. 1991. *Naselenie Polessya v mezolite* [*The Mesolithic populations of the Polissie*]. Kiev: Naukova Dumka.

Zalizniak, L. L. 1997. *Mesolithic forest hunters in Ukrainian Polessye*. Oxford: British Archaeological Reports International Series 659.

Zapata, L. 1995. El yacimiento arqueológico de la cueva de Pico Ramos. *Eusko Ikaskuntza. Cuadernos de Sección Prehistoria-Arqueología* 6: 251–8.

Zhao, C., and X. Wu. 2000. The dating of Chinese early pottery and a discussion of some related problems. *Documenta Praehistorica* 27: 233–40.

Zhilin, M. G. 1996. The western part of Russia in the Late Palaeolithic-early Mesolithic. In L. Larsson (ed.), *The earliest settlement of Scandinavia and its relationship with neighbouring areas*. Acta Archaeologica Lundensia, Series In 8, 24. Stockholm: Almquist and Wiksell International, pp. 273–84.

Zhilin, M. G. 2001. *Kostyanaya Industriya Mezolita Lesnoi Zony Vosidchnoi Evropy*. Moskva: Editoria YURSS.

Zhilin, M. 2003. Early Mesolithic communication networks in the East European forest zone. In L. Larsson, H. Kingdren, K. Knutsson, D. Loeffler, A. Åkerlund (eds.), *Mesolithic on the move*. Oxford: Oxbow Books, pp. 688–93.

Zilhão, J. 1984. *A Gruta da Feteira*. Trabalhos de Arqueologia 1, Lisboa.

Zilhão, J. 1993. The spread of agro-pastoral economies across Mediterranean Europe: A view from the Far West. *Journal of Mediterranean Archaeology* 6: 5–63.

Zilhão, J. 1995. *O Paleolítico Superior da Estremadura Portuguesa*. Unpublished doctoral dissertation, Universidade de Lisboa.

Zilhão, J. 1998. A passagem do Mesolítico ao Neolítico na costa do Alentejo. *Revista Portuguesa de Arqueologia* 1: 27–44.

Zilhão, J. 2000. From the Mesolithic to the Neolithic in the Iberian Peninsula. In T. D. Price, (ed.), *Europe's first farmers*. Cambridge, UK: Cambridge University Press, pp. 144–82.

Zilhão, J. 2004. Mesolithic/Neolithic transition in Portugal. In M. González Morales and G. Clark (eds.), *The Mesolithic of the Atlantic façade*. Anthropological Research Papers 55. Tempe: Arizona State University, pp. 121–32.

Zilhão, J., Carvalho, E., and A. C. Araújo. 1987. A estação epipaleolítico da Ponta da Vigia. *Arqueologia* 16: 8–18.

Zoffmann, Z. 1983. Prehistorical skeletal remains from Lepenski Vir (Iron Gate, Yugoslavia). *Homo* 34: 129–48.

Zvelebil, M. 1978. Subsistence and settlement in the north-eastern Baltic. In P. Mellars (ed.), *The early postglacial settlement of northern Europe*. London: Duckworth, pp. 205–42.

Zvelebil, M. 1981. *From forager to farmer in the Boreal zone*. Oxford: British Archaeological Reports International Series 115.

Zvelebil, M. 1985. Iron age transformations in Northern Russia and the northeast Baltic. In G. Barker and C. Gamble (eds.), *Beyond domestication in prehistoric Europe*. London: Academic Press, pp. 147–80.

Zvelebil, M. 1986a. Mesolithic societies and the transition to farming: Problems of time, scale and organization. In M. Zvelebil (ed.), *Hunters in Transition: Mesolithic societies of temperate Eurasia and their transition to farming*. Cambridge, UK: Cambridge University Press, pp. 167–88.

Zvelebil, M. 1986b. Postglacial foraging in the forests of Europe. *Scientific American* 254 (5): 104–15.

Zvelebil, M. (ed.). 1986c. *Hunters in transition: Mesolithic societies of temperate Eurasia and their transition to farming*. Cambridge, UK: Cambridge University Press.

Zvelebil, M. 1987. Wetland settlements in Eastern Europe. In J. M. Coles and A. J. Lawson (eds.), *European wetlands in prehistory*. Oxford: Clarendon Press, pp. 94–116.

Zvelebil, M. 1989. Economic intensification and postglacial hunter-gatherers in north temperate Europe. In C. Bonsall (ed.), *The Mesolithic in Europe: Proceedings of the third international symposium*. Edinburgh: John Donald, pp. 80–8.

Zvelebil, M. 1992. Hunting in farming societies: The prehistoric perspective. *Anthropozoologica* 16: 7–17.

Zvelebil, M. 1993a. Concepts of time and 'presencing' the Mesolithic. *Archaeological Review from Cambridge* 12 (2): 51–70.

Zvelebil, M. 1993b. Hunters or farmers? the Neolithic and Bronze Age societies of north-east Europe. In J. Chapman, and P. Dolukhanov (eds.), *Cultural transformation and interactions in Eastern Europe*. Aldershot: Avebury, pp. 146–63.

Zvelebil, M. 1994. Plant use in the Mesolithic and the implications for the transition to farming. *Proceedings of Prehistoric Society* 60: 95–134.

Zvelebil, M. 1995a. At the interface of archaeology, linguistics and genetics: Indo-European dispersals and the agricultural transition in Europe. *Journal of European Archaeology* 3 (1): 33–70.

Zvelebil, M. 1995b. Hunting, gathering, or husbandry? Management of food resources by the Late Mesolithic communities of temperate Europe. In D. V. Campana (ed.), *Before Farming*, MASCA Research Papers in Science and Archaeology 12. Philadelphia: University of Pennsylvania Press, pp. 79–104.

Zvelebil, M. 1995c. A final word on 'Man and the Sea in the Mesolithic' – good news for women? in A. Fischer (ed.), *Man and Sea in the Mesolithic*. Oxbow Monograph 53. Oxford: Oxbow, pp. 421–2.

Zvelebil, M. 1996a. Hunter-gatherer ritual landscapes: Spatial organisation, social structure and ideology among hunter-gatherers of Northern Europe and Western Siberia. *Analecta Praehistorica Leidensia* 29: 33–50.

Zvelebil, M. 1996b. The agricultural frontier and the transition to farming in the circum-Baltic region. In D. Harris (ed.), *The Origin and spread of agriculture and pastoralism in Eurasia*. London: UCL Press, pp. 323–45.

References

Zvelebil, M. 1996c. Farmers our ancestors and the identity of Europe, In P. Graves-Brown, S. Jones, and C. Gamble (eds), *Cultural identity and archaeology: The construction of European communities*. London, Routledge, pp. 145–66.

Zvelebil, M. 1997. Neolithization in eastern Europe: A view from the frontier. *Poročilo o raziskovanju paleolitika, neolitika in eneolitika v Sloveniji* 22: 107–51.

Zvelebil, M. 1998. What's in a name: The Mesolithic, the Neolithic and social change at the Mesolithic-Neolithic transition. In M. Edmonds and C. Richards (eds.), *Social life and social change: The Neolithic of North Western Europe*. London: Routledge, pp 1–35.

Zvelebil, M. 2000a. The social context of the agricultural transition in Europe. In C. Renfrew and K. Boyle (eds.), *Archaeogenetics: DNA and the population prehistory of Europe*. Cambridge: McDonald Institute for Archaeological Research, pp. 57–79.

Zvelebil, M. 2000b. Fat is a feminist issue: On ideology, diet and health in hunter-gatherer societies. In M. Donald and L. Hurcombe (eds.), *Gender and material culture in archaeological perspective*. Basingstoke: Macmillan, pp. 209–21.

Zvelebil, M. 2002. Indo-European dispersals and the agricultural transition in northern Europe: Culture, genes and language. In K. Julku (ed.), *The roots of peoples and languages of northern Eurasia IV*. Oulu: Societas Historiae Fenno-Ugricae, pp. 318–43.

Zvelebil, M. 2003a. People behind the lithics: Social life and social conditions of Mesolithic communities in temperate Europe. In L. Bevan and J. Moore (eds.), *Peopling the Mesolithic in a northern environment*. Oxford: British Archaeological Reports International Series 1157, pp. 1–26.

Zvelebil, M. 2003b. Demography and dispersal of early farming populations at the Mesolithic-Neolithic transition: Linguistic and genetic implications. In P. Bellwod and C. Renfrew (eds.), *Examining the farming/language dispersal hypothesis*. Cambridge, UK: McDonald Institute for Archaeological Research, pp. 379–94.

Zvelebil, M. 2003c. Enculturation of Mesolithic landscapes. In L. Larsson, H. Kindgren, K. Knutsson, D. Loeffler, and A. Åkerlund (eds.), *Mesolithic on the move: Papers presented at the Sixth International Conference on the Mesolithic in Europe*. Oxford: Oxbow Books, pp. 65–73.

Zvelebil, M. 2004a. Social structure and ideology of the late Mesolithic communities in north temperate Europe. In G. A. Clark and M. Gonzales-Morales (eds.), *The Mesolithic of the Atlantic façade*. Arizona State University, Anthropological Research Papers 35, pp. 23–37.

Zvelebil, M. 2004b. Who were we 6000 years ago? In search of prehistoric identities. In M. Jones (ed.), *Traces of ancestry: Studies in honour of Colin Renfrew*. Cambridge, UK: McDonald Institute for Archaeological Research, pp. 41–60.

Zvelebil, M. 2005. Homo habitus: Agency, structure and the transformation of tradition in the constitution of the TRB foraging-farming communities in the North European plain (ca 4500–2000 BC). *Documenta Praehistorica* 32: 87–101.

Zvelebil, M. 2006. Mobility, contact, and exchange in the Baltic Sea Basin 6000–2000 B.C. In W. Lovis, R. Donahue, and R. Whallon (eds.), *Mobility, contact and exchange in Mesolithic Europe. Journal of Anthropological Archaeology* 25 (2): 178–92.

Zvelebil, M. 2009. The Mesolithic and the 21st century. In S. B. McCartan, R. Schulting, G. Warren, and P. Woodman (eds.), *Mesolithic horizons. Papers presented at the Seventh International Conference on the Mesolithic in Europe, Belfast 2005*. Oxford: Oxbow Books, pp. xlviii–lviii.

Zvelebil, M. in press. Rite, ritual and materiality of information in Mesolithic Europe. In R. Whallon, W. A. Lovis, and R. K. Hitchcock (eds.), *The role of information in hunter-gatherer band-level societies*.

Zvelebil, M., and P. Dolukhanov. 1991. Transition to farming in Eastern and Northern Europe, *Journal of World Prehistory* 5 (3): 233–78.

Zvelebil, M., and K. J. Fewster. 2001. Pictures at an exhibition: Ethnoarchaeology and hunter-gatherers. In K. J. Fewster and M. Zvelebil (eds.), *Ethnoarchaeology and hunter-gatherers: Pictures at an exhibition*. Oxford: Archaeopress, British Archaeological Reports International Series 955, pp. 153–7.

Zvelebil, M., and P. Jordan. 1999. Hunter fisher gatherer ritual landscapes. In J. Goldhahn (ed.), *Rock art as social representation*. Oxford: British Archaeological Reports International Series 794, pp. 101–27.

462

Zvelebil, M., and M. Lillie. 2000. Transition to agriculture in eastern Europe. In T. D. Price (ed.), *Europe's first farmers*. Cambridge, UK: Cambridge University Press, pp. 57–92.

Zvelebil, M., and P. Pettit. 2006. Contribution of Palaeolithic and Neolithic Y-chromosome lineages to the modern Czech population. *Archeologicke Rozhledy* 58: 250–60.

Zvelebil, M., and P. A. Rowley-Conwy. 1984. Transition to farming in northern Europe: A hunter-gatherer perspective. *Norwegian Archaeological Review* 17: 104–28.

Zvelebil, M., and P. A. Rowley-Conwy. 1986. Foragers and farmers in Atlantic Europe. In M. Zvelebil (ed.), *Hunters in Transition*. Cambridge, UK: Cambridge University Press, pp. 67–93.

Zvelebil, M., Dennell, R., and L. Domanska (eds.). 1998a. *Harvesting the sea, farming the forest*. Sheffield: Sheffield Academic Press.

Zvelebil, M., Dennell, R., and L. Domańska. 1998b. Introduction: The Baltic and the transition to farming. In M. Zvelebil, R. Dennell, and L. Domańska (eds.), *Harvesting the sea, farming the forest*. Sheffield: Sheffield Academic Press, pp. 1–8.

Index

Index

Lightning Source UK Ltd.
Milton Keynes UK
UKOW07n1949080216

267957UK00001B/8/P